Abnormal Psychology

Abnormal

Psychology

DAVID C. RIMM

Southern Illinois University at Carbondale
Now at Old Dominion University

JOHN W. SOMERVILL

Southern Illinois University at Carbondale
Now at University of Northern Iowa

ACADEMIC PRESS   New York   San Francisco   London
A SUBSIDIARY OF HARCOURT BRACE JOVANOVICH, PUBLISHERS

Cover design by Susan Gobel. Cover painting © 1976 by Glen Heller.

ACADEMIC PRESS, INC.
111 Fifth Avenue, New York, New York 10003

United Kingdom Edition published by
ACADEMIC PRESS, INC. (LONDON) LTD.
24/28 Oval Road, London NW1

Library of Congress Cataloging in Publication Data
Main entry under title:

Abnormal psychology.

  Bibliography: p.
  1. Psychology, Pathological.   I. Rimm, David C.
II. Somervill, John. [DNLM: 1. Psychopathology.
WM100 R577a]
RC454.A24   616.8′9   76-13945
ISBN 0-12-588840-6

PRINTED IN THE UNITED STATES OF AMERICA

To our wives, Sandy and Christine

Preface

This book had its origins in our experiences as teachers and researchers in the field of abnormal psychology. As researchers, we had learned how often a neat theoretical model will bend and even collapse under the weight of experimental evidence. As teachers, we felt that the available textbooks tended to start off on the wrong foot, because they relied too heavily on theoretical models, some of which are of questionable validity.

We wanted a textbook that would explore topics and theories in the light of relevant research findings, rather than relying on a theoretical model of abnormal behavior. We sought a broadly based coverage of the traditional subjects, however, and we also looked for topics of lively current research interest. In addition, we wanted a text that would give a full and fair hearing to a variety of treatment approaches. Because no single text seemed to satisfy all of these requirements, we decided to write such a book ourselves.

Abnormal Psychology is the outcome of this decision. An eclectic, empirically based exploration of the subject, it does not simply present the current consensus on a concept such as schizophrenia. Rather, it describes the evolution of the concept and then examines its validity and usefulness in the light of the latest research findings. The text also scrutinizes the findings themselves, so that students may see how research is interpreted—and sometimes misinterpreted. In this way, students may learn how to reach informed judgments about aspects of abnormal behavior that all too often are shrouded in unconfirmed assumptions.

This approach to the subject guided the organization of the chapters. Part I gives the historical background, exploring the changing conceptions of abnormal behavior and the many problems that beset attempts to establish meaningful classification systems. Part II examines the traditional categories of psychopathology in the light of relevant experimental findings, and describes many of the treatment theories and methods that have been devised to cope with these disorders.

Parts I and II comprise the core of the text, but we felt they could not, by themselves, provide a complete introduction to this vast and rapidly changing field. We wanted to show students some of the newer research areas in abnormal psychology, and we wanted to present a broad spectrum of treatment methods and theories. We soon realized that such chapters required a combination of expertise and enthusiasm that we could not always provide, and so we turned to contributors who possessed these necessary qualities in abundance. As a result, Parts III and IV are written by specialists in each field.

Part III explores the latest findings about criminal and dangerous behavior, sexuality, sleep disorders and hypnosis, and drug use and abuse. Each chapter is written by an author with a specialized research interest in that field. As a result, each chapter gives an accurate and knowledgeable account of the most recent discoveries about the subject.

Part IV covers a variety of treatment theories and applications. This area is full of pitfalls for textbook authors, for any good selection of treatment approaches will include some that are antithetical to others, and few authors can give a balanced and fair account of every one. If we had assumed all responsibility for these chapters, our preference for a behavioral approach inevitably would have colored our presentation of other treatment theories and methods. The contributors of the treatment chapters were selected for the precise purpose of avoiding this kind of bias. We wanted each type of therapy to be presented positively and enthusiastically by a person genuinely supportive of the approach. By doing so, of course, we have deliberately left the task of evaluating these approaches to the reader.

With the exception of these chapters by other contributors, however, the book is truly co-authored. We shared all responsibilities equally from beginning to end—including the selection of contributors.

A number of people rendered us valuable assistance during the preparation of this book, and we would like to acknowledge their contributions here. We owe a special debt of gratitude to our contributing authors for the expertise, the writing skills, and the cooperative spirit that each of them brought to this project. We are very grateful to our editor at Academic Press, who performed an important role in helping us achieve stylistic and organizational consistency as well as assisting us in condensing and clarifying each chapter. We are grateful as well to Professors Sol L. Garfield of Washington University and William C. House of Case Western Reserve University, whose constructive and professional comments helped us to strengthen many portions of the text. We wish to thank Dr. Glenn Shean, who provided access to certain case history material, and Ms. Susan Jonas, who did an outstanding job of photo research. We also extend special thanks to

Ms. Trish Ribich, Ms. Beverly Stanley, and Ms. Donna Hackbarth for their tolerance as well as their excellent secretarial assistance. Finally, we are grateful to our families for their support and patience throughout the long years of work that brought this book into being.

David C. Rimm   John W. Somervill

Contents

I

HISTORY AND BASIC CONCEPTS

II

TRADITIONAL CATEGORIES OF PSYCHOPATHOLOGY

III

AREAS OF CURRENT INTEREST

I

HISTORY AND
BASIC CONCEPTS

1

Historical and Cultural Perspectives

For any culture there is a range of acceptable behaviors. The extent of that range and the kinds of behaviors tolerated may vary from culture to culture and from time to time within the same culture. Even within a culture, behavioral standards may vary as a function of social class, ethnic identity, sex, or other social grouping. Behaviors that deviate markedly from a society's allowable range have generated numerous professional and nonprofessional labels, such as *demon-possessed, bewitched, weird, queer, insane, nuts, crazy, unbalanced, emotionally disturbed, mentally ill,* and *sick*. The difficulties involved in developing an adequate classification system for deviant behavior will be explored in Chapter 2.

The complexities of the environmental and physiological variables are such that psychological problems seldom can be traced to a single cause. But regardless of the origin of psychological problems, their classification and treatment have been heavily influenced by historical and cultural trends. Perhaps for this reason, steady scientific advancement in the understanding and treatment of abnormal behavior has not been readily apparent.

This chapter will view psychological problems from a historical as well as a cultural perspective. It will describe how individuals in the past perceived, labeled, and treated persons whose behavior exceeded the range of behavior acceptable in their culture. The prevailing belief systems of a culture determined who was in charge of treatment as well as what behaviors were the object of treatment.

Psychological Problems among the Ancients (2000 B.C.–A.D. 200)

GODS, DEMONS, AND MILIEU THERAPY (2000–450 B.C.)

Early accounts of man's problems are often embellished with supernatural explanations. Around 2000 B.C., the Babylonians attributed psychological problems to a demon named Idta, who served Ishtar, the goddess of witchcraft and darkness. Servants of Idta were sorcerers who relied on the powers of an evil eye and various concoctions. Treatment most likely involved incantations and other magical practices believed to be effective in combatting demons.

Early Egyptians, like the Babylonians, relied on supernatural explanations. However, the Ebers Papyrus, a medical document written in about 1550 B.C., suggests that the Egyptians also emphasized physical explanations of various maladies. Still, the document contains a specific remedy to be used against all kinds of witchcraft: Select a large beetle, cut off its head and wings, boil it, dip it in oil, and apply it to whatever part of the body has been affected by the witchcraft. Following this procedure, the head and wings of the beetle should be warmed in snake fat, and the mixture should be drunk by the afflicted person (Withington, 1964).

In Memphis, Egypt, probably around 525 B.C., the temple of the healing god Imhotep became a hospital and medical school. "Incubation," or sleep therapy, was practiced, and to fill the idle hours, patients were encouraged to pursue artistic endeavors, travel along the Nile, and attend dances and concerts. Although "cures" were attributed to the god of the temple, the treatment procedures were similar to that referred to as *milieu therapy* in many of today's psychiatric settings. Milieu therapy consists of an inpatient environment that fosters a variety of individual and group activities within a social context.

The Egyptians also described behaviors that the Greeks later called *hysteria* (derived from *hysteron*, "uterus"). Hysteria consisted of various physical symptoms, such as fainting, deafness, or partial paralysis.[1] The symptoms of hysteria were believed to be caused by the uterus wandering from its natural position. Treatment was to "fumigate" the vagina in order to lure the uterus back to its proper position.

Early Egyptian conceptions probably influenced early Hebrew conceptions of behavior as well as those of the Hippocratic era in Greece. A few individuals in ancient Hebrew history recommended practices in dealing with psychological problems that resemble contemporary approaches. Rabbi Ami suggested diversion, and Rabbi Asi advocated that one should talk freely about one's worries (Alexander & Selesnick, 1966). Still, the pervasive Mosaic position was simple and straightforward: God makes alive, kills, wounds, and heals. As one form of punishment He had the prerogative to "smite thee with madness." Demons were available as an alternative cause of insanity. If a person's behavior was very

---

[1] Today, the word *hysteria* refers to similar physical symptoms for which there is no anatomical basis. A discussion of hysterical disorders will be presented in Chapter 4.

peculiar, it was possible that he could be labeled a witch. If so, the command of "Thou shalt not suffer a witch to live" was unambiguous (Exodus 22:18). A similar pronouncement is also found in Leviticus: "A man also or woman that hath a familiar spirit, or that is a wizard, shall surely be put to death: they shall stone them with stones: their blood shall be upon them." Centuries later, these statements were taken literally by zealots who vigorously pursued witches during the period of the Inquisition.

In the Far East, too, demonology and witchcraft flourished. The inhabitation of the body by angry demons was readily accepted as an explanation for deviant behavior. In the Brahmanic period in India (800 B.C.–A.D. 1000), medical texts contained a mixture of incantation rites and naturalistic explanations of behavior. The vital elements were presumed to be air, bile, and phlegm. A balance of these ingredients ensured good health. Brahman physiology may have influenced the Greek, Empedocles (490–430 B.C.), who postulated four humors: blood, phlegm, black bile, and yellow bile (Alexander & Selesnick, 1966). The humoral theory attributed bad health and mood changes to imbalance among the four humors. This theory became a standard explanation of man's nature and persisted for centuries.

In ancient Greece, supernatural explanations of psychological problems were also common. If an individual exhibited very unusual behavior, it was simply assumed that the gods had taken his mind away. One case of divinely caused madness presumably occurred around 1300 B.C. The daughters of the king of Argos angered the gods and were punished with "madness." They believed themselves to be cows and ran around the forest mooing. Melampus, who had helped Hercules with his psychological problems, was called in as a consultant. His first prescription was white hellebore, a plant that has a pronounced laxative effect. Next, he had other children chase the girls across the fields until the girls were physically exhausted. Finally, they were bathed in the fountains of Arcadia and were presumably cured of their identification with cows (Zilboorg & Henry, 1941).

During the Homeric period (about 1000 B.C.) a man named Aesculapius gained great fame as a traveling healer. He was later deified as the god of medicine, and hundreds of Aesculapian temples were constructed throughout the Greek countryside (Alexander & Selesnick, 1966). Administrators of the temples were priests who had presumably inherited the healing secrets of Aesculapius. There is some mystery as to what went on behind the temple walls and what kinds of psychological problems and illnesses were treated. Presumably, "incubation," or sleep combined with suggestion and possibly hypnosis, was used both to promote and to influence the content of dreams. Odoriferous herbs, conceivably opium derivatives, were used to enhance suggestibility. The purpose of dream induction may have been to provide the patient with visionary experiences that might show him how to resolve his difficulties.

Another form of treatment was having a harmless snake "lick" the patient's eyelids and wounds. To the Greeks, snakes were a powerful symbol of the underworld, so it is likely that the use of snakes by the temple priests heightened suggestibility. The staff of Aesculapius, a rod with a snake wrapped around it, is still the emblem of medicine today. Other aspects of therapy involved dieting, exercise, baths, and massages (Walker, 1959). Descriptions suggest that treatment in the temple took place under more favorable conditions then those in American hospitals in the early 1900s (Beers, 1953). Still, the ancient Greeks relied heavily on supernatural explanations. Their reactions to psychological problems were inconsistent. An individual exhibiting peculiar behavior might have been taken into a temple to be healed, viewed as having the power to heal others, or chased away from the temple with stones (Zilboorg & Henry, 1941).

HIPPOCRATES: FATHER OF PSYCHIATRIC LABELING AND THE CONCEPT OF MENTAL DISEASE (460–377 B.C.)

There is little evidence of any systematic scientific attempt to understand the nature of man's behavior prior to 450 B.C. The works of Hippocrates (ca. 460–377 B.C.) represent a dramatic departure from earlier, supernatural explanations of man's nature. The basic writings consist of more than 76 treatises on more than 50 subjects. Variations in writing style and inconsistencies in content suggest that the documents were authored by different writers. For this reason, specific quotes or ideas are more properly attributed to the entire school of medicine in the Greek city of Cos, rather than exclusively to Hippocrates.

The conception of man's nature by the Hippocratic school was chiefly physiological. A humoral theory similar to that postulated by Empedocles was espoused in Cos. Health depended on harmony among four humors: blood (heat), phlegm (cold), yellow bile (dryness), and black bile (moisture). The brain was recognized as being of central importance. *Pneuma,* air that circulates and enters the brain, was considered critical for intellectual processes. Hippocrates was probably the first to introduce a system of labels for deviant behavioral patterns (Alexander & Selesnick, 1966). The labels included *epilepsy, mania, melancholia,* and *paranoia.* Epilepsy, or *falling sickness,* referred to the same neurological disorder that is prevalent today.[2] The Hippocratic school refuted the common belief of the time that epilepsy was a sacred disease, and taught that cold phlegm secreted by the brain entered the veins and blocked the passage of air. The afflicted was thus rendered speechless and senseless (Hoch & Knight, 1965).

Melancholy was believed to be caused by an abundance of black bile. Mania was presumed to involve large amounts of blood (heat) and black bile (moisture). It was also thought that epilepsy, mania, and melancholy were seasonal; they were considered diseases of spring. The early Greek meaning of the term *paranoia* is unclear; it probably referred to some form of mental deterioration, rather than the behaviors currently covered by the term. The Hippocratic school

[2] Although there may be psychological factors associated with epilepsy, the disorder itself involves a form of central nervous system (CNS) dysfunction. A complete discussion of epilepsy is presented in Chapter 8. In the great majority of cases, epilepsy is unrelated to disturbances in personality or intellectual functions.

also adopted the belief that a wandering uterus caused hysteria. The suggested treatment was marriage or sexual intercourse.[3]

What proved to be of historical importance was not whether melancholy was due to black bile or hysteria was caused by a vagrant uterus. Hippocrates set the medical precedent of equating patterns of behavioral deviations with disease entities. Once psychological problems were conceptualized as diseases, given a label, and inferred to have an organic cause, then they fell within the domain of medicine. Physicians treat diseases. The Hippocratic conception of madness as a mental disease or illness led to an enduring bias against environmental explanations of deviant behavior. Even today, within the medical specialty of psychiatry, there are individuals who maintain that no person outside the field of medicine should render therapy to individuals with psychological problems. The current dissension between clinical psychology and psychiatry is based upon the fundamental issue of who is and who is not qualified to treat psychological problems. The goal of the Hippocratic writings was not to advocate an organic as opposed to an environmental explanation of psychological problems. Indeed, no environmental causes of problems were recognized at all. The goal was to rid medicine of supernatural beliefs that gods and demons accounted for health and illness (Galdston, 1967). As we will see later, demons are remarkably resistant to extinction and their temporary exile from Cos was not a major setback.

ROME: THE HARSH AND THE HUMANE (150 B.C.–A.D. 150)

In Rome, the teachings of the Hippocratic school in Greece were looked upon with disfavor. A Greek physician named Asclepiades (150 B.C.), though not a follower of Hippocrates, initially was prevented from practicing medicine in Rome. However, while witnessing a Roman funeral procession, he noted signs of life in the corpse. He stopped the procession, manipulated the body, and to the astonishment of onlookers, the "dead" man revived. Following this incident, Asclepiades was exalted as a miraculous physician and granted the privilege of practicing medicine in Rome. His treatment procedures contributed to his fame. They involved baths, massages, wine, and pleasant surroundings, and so had particular appeal to Roman taste. Asclepiades was one of the first to reject the

---

[3] Perhaps the Greeks assumed the link between hysteria and sexual behavior that was to be proposed by Freud 2300 years later. During the first century A.D., Aretaeus of Cappadocia expounded the same concept, declaring that upward migration of the uterus caused hysterial suffocation because it compressed the intestines and produced a choking sensation. One of the first authorities to reject the wandering uterus theory was Galen, a famous Greek physician of the second century A.D. However, he believed that the real cause of hysteria was some form of uterine congestion. Galen's advice for treatment also anticipated Freud; he recommended stimulation of the clitoris and the neck of the uterus (Zilboorg & Henry, 1941). Although the wandering uterus eventually wandered out of history, the belief among professionals that hysteria was strictly a female disorder persisted until at least the seventeenth century. Charles Lepis (1563–1633) was one of the first to suggest that hysteria probably involved the brain and occurred in men as well as in women (Schneck, 1960). The persistence over many centuries of this erroneous "explanation" of behavior typifies the slow progress made in efforts to understand psychological problems.

word *insanity* as a label for psychological problems. He preferred to describe such problems as "passions of sensation." To the early Greeks and Romans, the word *passion* connoted strong, often unacceptable emotionality. Asclepiades' views resemble twentieth-century beliefs that problem behaviors are related to emotional disturbance. His conception of the nature of man assumed an atomistic theory originally proposed by Democritus. He believed that man was composed of attracting and repelling atoms. Between atoms were pores. If the movement of the atoms was out of phase, then spaces or pores between the atoms became too large or too small and illness resulted. Therapy consisted of applying the "principle of contraries" to restore the atoms to proper motility. As Alexander and Selesnick ask (1966), what could be a more pleasant treatment, when the "contraries" meant consuming chilled wine while immersed in a warm tub?

Asclepiades emphasized humaneness. He invented swinging beds to soothe disturbed patients and he devised numerous kinds of baths. Pleasant music and light, airy surroundings were part of therapy. He objected violently to housing people with "emotional disturbance" in dungeons and dark cells and considered bloodletting to be equivalent to strangling. He saw bloodletting as particularly harmful for Romans, who were likely to be exhausted from excessive indulgence. Asclepiades' rejection of harsh treatment techniques did not bring to him the historical status of a Pinel, Tuke, Chiarugi, Dix, or other champions of humane care. Perhaps his general rejection and criticism of the Hippocratic school led medical historians who lauded Hippocrates to downplay the historical prominence of Asclepiades.

Cornelius Celsus (25 B.C.–A.D. 50), unlike Asclepiades, favored harsh treatment techniques. He attributed some forms of illnesses to the wrath of the gods and believed that frightening patients could scare out undesirable spirits. Regarding psychological problems, Celsus stressed that whenever a patient said or did anything wrong, he should be subjected to hunger, chains, and sudden fright. He recommended confinement in total darkness, bloodletting, hellebore, and agents that induce vomiting. The practice of frightening patients was to reappear centuries later. The expression, "scare the devil out of" someone, at some points in history had a quite literal meaning.

Another prominent Roman physician was Aretaeus of Cappadocia (A.D. 50–130). Aretaeus was the first to propose that personality differences among individuals were predictive of later differences in "mental diseases." Aretaeus postulated that those individuals who were irritable, excitable, and became easily joyous were prone to mania. Individuals prone to depressive states were seen as more likely to develop melancholy. Aretaeus may have been the first physician to hypothesize that certain kinds of psychological problems represent an extension of normal personality traits.

A strong supporter of gentle treatment was Soranus. He provided careful descriptions of the "maniacs" of his day. Some had convinced themselves that they were a grain of mustard and were continually afraid of being eaten by a hen. Others refused to urinate because they were afraid they would cause a flood. Soranus felt that "mania" was frequently caused by excessive use of alcohol. He objected strenuously to harsh treatment techniques. Noting that patients were being chained, whipped, intimidated, and locked in dark rooms, he proposed the use of moderately lighted rooms located on the ground floor to prevent injury if patients jumped out of windows. In contrast to Asclepiades, he recommended reduced stimulation—no paintings, music, or visits by strangers. Talking to the patients on topics of their interest was considered therapeutic and complimenting them was used as a form of encouragement. Although he believed the origin of psychological problems was basically physiological, his approach to treatment emphasized environmental conditions.

Caelius Aurelianus (A.D. 98–138), who was responsible for the translation of Soranus' works, was a devoted follower of the principles set forth by Soranus. Aurelianus exemplified the transition from the brief period of "medico-psychological humanism" enjoyed under Soranus to the moralistic, superstitious period that was to follow. The age that preceded Aurelianus was one of rational hedonism; Aurelianus, however, was repulsed and disgusted by excessive eroti-cism. He considered the sensuality of the period as a manifestation of "the most malignant and fetid passion of the mind." He incorporated into his system the ancient belief that a special demon disguised as a man was devoted entirely to the practice of sexual temptation and seduction of women. Aurelianus, however, generally opposed harsh measures for treating the insane. He also objected to a popular belief that castration was the best therapy for epilepsy (Zilboorg & Henry, 1941). Nonetheless, castration continued to be advocated as helpful for epilepsy until 1850. Even in 1880, Lawson Tait recommended removal of the ovaries as a treatment for epilepsy (Hoch & Knight, 1965). In short, neither the opposition of Aurelianus to castration nor the Hippocratic belief that epilepsy was a disturbance of the brain eliminated abusive modes of treatment.

GALENISM AND THE REVIVAL OF HIPPOCRATIC THOUGHT (A.D. 130–200)

Galen was a prolific Greek medical writer who revived and popularized the thinking of the Hippocratic school. He composed nearly 500 treatises on a variety of topics including logic, ethics, grammar, philosophy, anatomy, physiology, and medicine. Galen's treatise "on the passions and errors of the soul" describes a psychotherapeutic approach that vaguely resembles rational–emotive therapy (an approach developed by Albert Ellis in the twentieth century). According to Galen, errors of passion were a result of faulty judgment or mistakes due to irrational emotional behavior such as anger, fear, and envy. Galen's approach to the control of such passions was basically a rational confrontation. He believed that all individuals engage in self-deception because of self-love. Because of self-deception, a person is not capable of judging or evaluating his own errors of passion.

Galen advised that one should select an individual recommended by others as a nonflatterer. Such a "therapist" had to be carefully evaluated for his honesty. If he patronized the wealthy, the powerful, or monarchs, he was likely to be dishonest. After an honest man had been selected, it was important to establish a long association or relationship. When the therapist gained full understanding, he would be able to point out the irrational behavior. Galen suggested that defensiveness against criticism may alter the course of therapy; the client must be able and willing to respond to criticism in a rational way. Galen acknowledged the influence of Plato and Aristotle, but Stoicism was the dominant philosophy in most of his writings. Interestingly, Albert Ellis considers Stoicism to be the philosophical origin of rational–emotive therapy (Ellis, 1962). Galen also stressed the importance of habit, training, and practice in liberating man from the control of passions. Unlike the Hippocratic school, therefore, Galen recognized environmental causes for some forms of psychological problems.

The classical era saw many figures struggling against supernatural explanations of man's psychological problems and his diseases. The alternative to superstitution was an organismic explanation for both diseases and deviant behavior. But the treatment of "mental disease" saw no real medical advancements. The use of purgatives and emetics, vaginal "fumigation," bloodletting, and castration did more to foster misery and sickness than to cure. Individuals who advocated humane care and pleasant surroundings for patients did not advance science; they simply prevented cruelty. Small wonder that treatment in the Aesculapian temples and the approaches used by Asclepiades and Soranus represented brief periods of enlightenment when contrasted with the chainers, flagellators, and intimidators who confined the insane to dark rooms and cells. In short, the classical era was a period of highly varied responses to those whose behavior exceeded the tolerance limits of society.

The Decline of the Classical Era (200–475)

THE TEMPORARY ABANDONMENT OF THE MENTAL DISEASE CONCEPT

After the death of Galen, the waning years of the classical era saw a rejection of both medical and philosophical conceptions of man's nature. Alexander and Selesnick (1966) suggest that a prevailing fear and marked demoralization enhanced the reemergence of supernatural systems. Six plagues killed hundreds of thousands between the first and the fourth centuries A.D. Barbaric tribes were on the march toward Rome and the Roman security system was degenerating. Christianity, with Christ as the healer and comforter, began to achieve immense popularity in a frightened society. Saints replaced physicians as protectors against illness. Initially, psychological problems were regarded with sympathy by Arab physicians and early Christian scholastics. The humanity of the Arabs was probably due to their belief that psychological problems were divinely inspired rather than caused by demons. But the spirit of charity and the humanistic attitudes of early Christianity became less prominent as Christianity was transformed into an organizational hierarchy. A sentiment against the science of medicine was rapidly developing. Explanations for psychological problems and ill health began to stress lack of faith and the work of demons. The activities of Father Origen (185–254) exemplified the rejection of humanistic approaches to treatment. At the age of 18, Origen was converted. Soon after, he demonstrated his religious zeal by castrating himself to kill the carnal part of his body. Care of the sick and the disabled, according to Origen, was best left to an angel. He credited evil spirits with causing food shortages and sterility in women.

Christianity emerged as an institutionalized religion following the Edict of Milan in 313. By this act, Christianity was established as the official religion of the Roman Empire. Consquently, studying the works of Plato and Aristotle was banned (Zilboorg & Henry, 1941). Philosophies about man's nature and the structure of government were viewed as detrimental to the process of establishing Christianity as a state religion. The acceptable limits of man's behavior were to be defined by the Church, not by philosophical systems, which were perceived as pagan in origin. Hence, both medical and philosophical views of man's nature were replaced by theological views. The later effect of this change was to attribute unacceptable behavior to the work of the devil. Early Christianity, however, placed greater emphasis on the responsibility of man for his own behavior.

A major historical figure who helped shape the doctrine of Christianity was Aurelius Augustinus, better known as Augustine (354–430). Augustine has been credited with making the most significant contribution to psychology of all the medieval thinkers. He stressed the importance of introspection—looking within or self-analysis—as a means of discovering knowledge. According to Alexander and Selesnick (1966), he "can be justly considered as the earliest forerunner of psychoanalysis [p. 59]." Like Freud, Augustine engaged in extensive self-analysis, the process of which is evident in his major work, the *Confessions*.

Early Christian attitudes toward sexuality proved to be an important source of conflict for Augustine. As he entered his early forties he rejected his own sexual adventures as a younger man. He endorsed the belief that sexual behavior should be restricted to marriage and even then should be indulged in only for the purpose of procreating. He felt that, ideally, no man should marry. This would result in an earlier date for perfection of the "city of God" and the subsequent ending of the world. In his *Confessions*, Augustine suggested that he might have more happily awaited the embraces of God if, for the sake of the kingdom of heaven, he had been made a eunuch. Indeed, others besides Origen had castrated themselves to "rid themselves of sexual desire as an obstruction to salvation [Mitamura, 1970, p. 23]."

Augustine's attitudes toward sexuality were not original; they were a reflection of both Hebrew and early Christian conceptions. Augustine, however, was a brilliant systematist and his codification of existing views on sexuality had a lasting impact. Perhaps the later emphasis in psychological theory on the role of sexual behavior stemmed from such views.

One aspect of the Augustinian period that was not characteristic of the later Middle Ages was that the devil was relatively passive. Augustine claimed a great deal of the responsibility for his own behavior. His *Confessions* are replete with examples of self-blame. There also appeared to be a relatively strong reliance on the belief that parents were important socializing agents. He acknowledged repeatedly the influence of his parents, particularly his mother, in the shaping of his behavior. He described the negative impact of his early friends as well as the positive and negative influences of later associates. Augustine did, however, assume that the devil was a real force working against the power of God. In the administration of the sacrament of baptism, a form of exorcism was used that involved breathing out the evil spirit possessing the nonbeliever. This form of exorcism, however, was considerably milder and possibly more symbolic in nature than the methods of exorcism that were to appear in the Middle Ages and extend throughout the Renaissance.

The Middle Ages (476–1700)

THE FALL OF WOMAN AND
THE RISE OF THE DEVIL (476–1200)

During the Middle Ages, more direct control of behavior was attributed to demons and relatively less control to man. Rather than weakness in man leading to his succumbing to the devil, the emphasis was on a forceful devil who required man actively to defend himself against the devil's evil powers.

At some point during the early Middle Ages there was a significant transition from the gentle "breathing the devil out" of a person to much harsher practices. The relatively open expression of sexuality became a source of alarm for church officials. Sensual women were blamed for causing the sexual misconduct of men. The motto of the times was that "woman is a temple built over a sewer [Alexander & Selesnick, 1966, p. 67]." Women with psychological problems who publicly expressed their fantasies were particularly vulnerable to the accusation of being in league with the devil. The link between demons and the female sex made it easy to blame degenerate women for threatening the practice of celibacy in monasteries. These ideas probably strengthened the tendency to associate the female sex with witchcraft.

In 1022, King Robert II conducted a trial at Orleans for a group of heretics. The charges brought against the group contain a description of behaviors that were to appear again and again in later witch trials. The group was accused of chanting the names of demons at secret night meetings. When an evil spirit responded to the chant of his name and appeared, torches were immediately extinguished. In the dark, males took the nearest female for a sex partner, whether it was his mother, sister, or a wayward nun. Children born to women impregnated at the orgies were said to be ceremoniously burned to death 8 days after birth. The ashes of the children were made into a substance to be eaten at a mock Communion. The accused heretics were later burned to death; whether they were guilty of any or all of the charges must remain a matter of historical speculation. The basic elements commonly attributed to European witch cults thereafter were sexual orgies, child sacrifice, burning of the children's bodies, and cannibalism (Russell, 1972).

The perception of heretics as indiscriminate sexual animals in league with the devil played an important role during the period of the Inquisition. The Inquisition was an ecclesiastical tribunal charged with the responsibility of investigating and punishing heretics. The Inquisition began in the thirteenth century under Pope Innocent III and remained active until the nineteenth century. Investigative officers of the Inquisition were called *inquisitors*. An obsession with the virtues of chastity by many inquisitors is well depicted by examples in the *Malleus Maleficarum*.[4] Abbot S. Serenus, after praying for relief from his "genital instincts," was rewarded with the vision of an angel who "seemed to open his belly and take from his entrails a burning tumore of flesh [Summers, 1969, p. 93]." The angel joyfully informed the Abbot that he would "never again be pricked with that natural desire which is aroused even in babes and sucklings [p. 93]." Another man was visited by an angel who "seemed to make him a eunuch" thereby making him not only preeminent among men but, finally, "pre-eminent over women [p. 93]." In view of these attitudes, it was not surprising that the sexual activities believed practiced by the heretic and witch became a focal point of interrogation by inquisitors.

Later guidelines for identifying heretics and obtaining their confessions included intimidation and torture, often to the point of death. To suggest that most inquisitors or heretics were persons afflicted with psychological problems would be an oversimplification. Political and economic factors played a prominent role during the Inquisition. A charge of heresy, for example, was often a way of obtaining property from the accused. Still, it is possible that some activities of both inquisitors and accused were uniquely attractive to individuals with psychological problems. This possibility will become more obvious in subsequent sections. The onset of the thirteenth century marked the emergence of a number of heretical sects, many of which were characterized by bizarre, ritualistic behavior.

FLAGELLATORS, HERETICAL CULTS, AND
THE NORMALITY OF EXTREMISM (1200–1400)

The period from 1200 to 1400 saw not only an increase in witchcraft but also mass outbreaks of wild dancing and flagellation rituals (Russell, 1972). Despite opposition by the Church, the flagellation movement became especially strong, and priests who opposed the strange sect were sometimes put to death. One sect

---

[4] The *Malleus Maleficarum* (the "witch hammer") was a book written in either 1485 or 1486 by Heinrich Institoris (Henry Kramer) and Jakob Sprenger (James Sprenger). During the period of the Inquisition, this book served as the guideline for identifying witches and obtaining their confessions. According to Russell (1972), Heinrich Institoris (Kramer) was the principal author and Sprenger's contributions were relatively minor. Parrinder (1963) believes Sprenger to be the major author.

of flagellants, wearing long white robes with red crosses on the front and back, wandered from town to town. Their ritual consisted of going to the center of a town, forming a circle, then stripping to the waist. One person would lie down with his head at the feet of the next person in the circle. The individual behind him then struck him with a whip. Each person took a turn as a victim, then as a whipper, while others in the circle prayed and sang hymns. At the conclusion of the circular whipping ceremony, all individuals flogged themselves with a whip imbedded with iron hooks. When an individual became too weak to continue the self-mutilation, he would fall to the ground. The ceremony was performed twice during the day and once at night. Many of the onlookers became participants.

Although flagellant movements were condemned as heresy by the Church, the fanatical sects appealed to people who were disillusioned with the Church's inability to protect them from plagues and other tragedies. The flagellants preached that the world would soon come to an end, and the promise of immediate spiritual relief was welcomed by many suffering individuals. Self-purification and penitence as achieved by self-mutilation prepared them to welcome the end of the world. By present standards, such behavior would be considered sadomasochistic (pleasure is derived from inflicting pain and having pain inflicted). Given the cultural climate of the thirteenth and fourteenth centuries, however, it is unlikely that either the flagellator or the flagellated were viewed as abnormal.

For those who found no relief in punishing others or themselves, other sects in the thirteenth century offered hedonic reveling that was strictly forbidden by the institutionalized church. In Germany and Italy, the Brethren of the Free Spirit taught a form of pantheism where sinning was impossible because a God who could do no evil was a God who "is all things in all things." Sexual feelings came from God and the only evil was in resisting their expression. Consequently, incest, homosexuality, and heterosexuality were not only accepted as lawful but were an integral part of ceremonies.

A more significant heretical sect was that of the Luciferans who were the most important prototype for witchcraft as defined by the Inquisition. The Luciferans maintained that all things were God and that this included the devil. They believed that casting him out of heaven was an unjust act. Since the devil was now on earth, it was he who should be worshiped by earth's inhabitants. Orgies were an important part of the Luciferans' ceremonies but, unlike the Brethren of the Free Spirit, they considered sexual activity on the face of the earth a sin. Consequently, the orgies were held underground where they were not considered sinful.

Between 1230 and 1300, Christian scholastics enhanced the credibility of witchcraft. An essential element of witchcraft was the notion of a "pact." Albertus Magnus (Russell, 1972) distinguished between two types of pacts, implicit and explicit. An implicit pact could cover a multitude of vague agreements with the devil. An explicit pact indicated a face-to-face meeting with the devil in which specific bargaining took place. Thomas Aquinas accepted the notion of an implicit pact but had reservations as to whether people ever entered into an explicit pact. Although he doubted that witches or demons flew at night, he believed in the existence of *incubi,* male demons, and *succubi,* female demons, who could assume human form and seduce members of the opposite sex. William of Auvergne was much more liberal in what he would accept regarding existing beliefs. Unlike Aquinas, he believed that aerial flights by "ladies of the night" were real. He maintained that people worshiped Lucifer, who took the form of a cat or a toad. Reverence to the devil was evidenced by ritual kissing of the cat's buttocks or the toad's mouth. Acceptance of such beliefs by scholastics ensured that trials involving absurd charges would not be opposed by intellectuals of the institutionalized church. In 1275, for example, 56-year-old Angele de la Barthe confessed to having intercourse with an incubus. She admitted giving birth to a creature, half wolf and half snake, that ate small children for 2 years and then disappeared. Like many others, she was burned to death.

In 1335, the trial of Catherine Delort was typical of many to follow in regard to the tactics of the inquisitors and the nature of the material confessed. Catherine admitted to having sexual intercourse with a shepherd who convinced her to enter into a pact with the devil. They robbed graves and burned the bodies. When Catherine cut her left arm and allowed drops of blood to fall into the fire, a devil appeared as a purple flame and granted her powers to work evil. She admitted to being transported to witch assemblies every Saturday night. She confessed to stealing children from their homes and eating them. This confession represented an extension of killing and eating children born at orgies to eating children stolen from families outside the cult. Catherine also admitted her love for a goat, with whom she had sexual intercourse when not participating in orgies. The inquisitors had her tortured until she named other people she supposedly had met during witch assemblies. Despite her ultimate cooperation, she was later burned to death (Russell, 1972).

PSYCHOLOGICAL PROBLEMS AND
THE SIGNIFICANCE OF THE *WITCH* LABEL (1400–1700)

From 1400 to 1700, the activity of the inquisitors was relentless. Thousands of witches were tried and burned. They were accused of night flights on wolves, cats, sticks, brooms, and even on the manure of mules and horses. Killing and eating their own children and the children of others was a frequent accusation. The children's bodies were said to have been eaten raw, roasted, or fresh from the grave, though the inedible baptized head was often left behind. It was believed that the witches made a salve from the child's insides, which, when rubbed on chairs, sticks, brooms, or other objects, transformed them into means of aerial transportation. The "obscene kiss" was a standard accusation. Witches were accused of kissing the anus of the devil and masters of their assemblies as well as the anus and genitals of demon-possessed cats. Regular attendance at orgies was a consistent charge against witches. The inquisitors took great pains to detail almost every conceivable form of bizarre behavior.

The major guidelines for witch-hunting and obtaining confessions were laid down in the *Malleus Maleficarum,* mentioned earlier. The principal author, Heinrich Institoris, was fanatical in his pursuit and punishment of witches. Even Jakob Sprenger, who contributed to the writing of the *Malleus Maleficarum,* eventually turned against Institoris for his excesses in torturing witches (Russell, 1972). Unrestrained torture was practiced by many inquisitors in their zeal to obtain confessions. Murray (1970) suggests that some cannibalism may have occurred as a result of the witch persecutions. Before a witch could be sentenced, a confession was required. It was believed by some who feared the Inquisition that if they ate the flesh of a preverbal child, it would render them speechless and thereby make confession to inquisitors impossible.

The importance of the belief in witchcraft is underscored by the fact that tens of thousands were tortured and burned in the name of protecting society. As Russell (1972) points out, historians have held varying views, ranging from one extreme, that witchcraft was totally an invention of self-serving inquisitors, to the other, that witchcraft was real and proof of the power and existence of the devil. It is probable that some cult practices, such as secret meetings and orgies, were real and many others, such as aerial flights, were the products of the imagination of a frightened society. There is reason to suspect that some persons accused of witchcraft, but certainly not all, had psychological problems. It is common for delusions and hallucinations accompanying psychotic episodes to include fantasies and concerns unique to a culture. Thus, disturbed individuals were likely to report that they bargained with the devil or flew through the air and such reports could easily lead to persecution and torture. One might also wonder about the psychological stability of inquisitors who vigorously tortured the accused until they confessed to highly unusual activities.

To understand the extreme reactions to witchcraft in the Middle Ages, it is necessary to view the phenomenon in its cultural context. Witches were viewed not only as degenerate beings in league with the devil, but also as causes of sickness, disease, personal tragedies, and the stealing and killing of children. They were perceived as vicious instigators of terror, highly dangerous to a threatened and unstable society. The passion with which they were hated, tortured, and killed can only be understood in this context. Witchcraft was largely the product of the most horrible fantasies prevalent in a society victimized by plagues, famine, and a very real uncertainty of survival. Man's only hope was a stern and militant God who would lead him in the destruction of evil forces and provide the comfort of heaven should he die. In the Middle Ages, failure to accept the existence of witches and demons would have been construed as abnormal.

Although execution and torturing of witches had largely ended by the early eighteenth century, belief in witches and their rituals persisted into the nineteenth century. (The popularity of *The Exorcist* as a book and movie suggests that some people still believe in a link between evil supernatural forces and psychological problems, especially problems with sexual connotations.) Despite this, the beginning of the eighteenth century was characterized by a notable reduction in supernatural conceptions of man's nature and a surge of interest in science and technology. One consequence of this interest was a return to physical explanations for deviant behavior.

Social Change and the Development of Humane Treatment (1700–1885)

THE FALL OF DEMONS AND THE RISE OF MESMERISM

During the eighteenth century, the identification and management of psychological problems slipped out of the hands of the priests and back into the hands of physicians. Demonology was not abandoned, but its central role as an explanation for human difficulties was greatly diminished. Rapid social changes were occurring, and men and women became fascinated with monumental scientific discoveries such as electricity and the use of hot-air balloons to give man his first real aerial experience. There was a pervasive optimism about what people could do with their developing technology. People began to feel more in control of the universe, and it followed that supernatural agents were less in control. Particularly in Paris, the excitement surrounding scientific discoveries was fed by an exaggerated confidence in the swift application of forces such as electricity and magnetism to solve human ailments. Francois de Plantade's drawing of a little man, which he claimed was based upon microscopic examination of human sperm, was no less credible than the real phenomenon of invisible electrical force (Darnton, 1968).

Science had finally obtained its divorce from the stifling theology of the Middle Ages, and almost anything offered under the scientific banner was readily entertained. The climate was ideal for a man like Franz Anton Mesmer (1733–1815) to attain vast popularity. Had the same man been born 100 years earlier, he might well have been burned at the stake. His lilac robe, his wand, his treatment room replete with astrological signs and background music, would have delighted a seventeenth-century witch-hunter. Mesmer cannot be dismissed as a quack or charlatan. He held a doctorate in philosophy and a medical degree from the Vienna medical school. In 1774, an astronomer named Pater Hehl informed Mesmer of a woman who had been "cured" of a stomach problem by a magnetic rod that Hehl had given her husband. Mesmer interviewed the woman and became convinced that the cure was attributable to the magnet. Within a short period of time, Mesmer "cured" several patients by placing magnets over the areas where they complained of pain. In seeking an explanation for the healing power of the magnets, he postulated a universal, invisible, gaslike fluid in which all life forms were immersed. He concluded that this fluid, which he had earlier called *gravitas universalis,* was really magnetic energy. From that point on, until his death in 1815, he maintained adamantly that the key to all health lay in understanding the magnetic forces of the universe.

From the standpoint of psychology, what is impressive about Franz Anton Mesmer has nothing to do with his notions of magnetism. Psychologists are impressed by his mastery of the power of suggestion and the incredible changes he was able to achieve in some of his patients. Perhaps the most dramatic example is that of Maria Theresa Paradies. Maria was an 18-year-old pianist who had been blind since the age of 4. She had seen an eminent eye specialist named Barth as well as other physicians in Vienna. All were convinced that her blindness was incurable and due to permanent "paralysis of the optic nerve." Mesmer agreed to take Maria and two other young women into his household for treatment. Soon she began to respond. As reported by Zweig (1931), a document on her recovery, written by an unknown author, gave a very convincing description of how a person with restored sight gradually adjusts to a world of vision. Maria developed a strong attachment to Mesmer and rumors spread throughout Vienna that they were having an affair. The medical faculty pressured the Empress, the court, and a powerful agency called the Committee to Sustain Morality to act against Mesmer. Finally, the Empress ordered Mesmer to render no further treatment to Maria. Her blindness returned and she was forcibly removed from Mesmer's home by her father (Zweig, 1931). Today, a case such as Maria's would be considered a form of hysteria called a *conversion reaction*.

Shortly after Maria's treatment was forcibly terminated, Mesmer left Vienna for Switzerland and then went on to Paris. The Mesmer who gradually achieved a position of social power in France bore little resemblance to the man who had treated many patients in Vienna without charge.

His treatment center in Paris became quite stylish and held a special attraction for wealthy, upper-class citizens. From Darnton's (1968) description, the treatment setting must have been quite enticing: The curtains were drawn, heavy carpets softened the floor, mirrors reflected lights, and astrological wall decorations provided mystic appeal. Patients gathered in groups around large tubs containing magnetized bottles of water and movable iron rods. While soft music was played in the background, the patients linked their thumbs and index fingers to form a "mesmeric" chain, which linked them to the magnetic forces of the tub. If patients were overcome with emotion or entered a convulsion-like state, they were carried to a mattress-lined room to prevent injury while they writhed themselves into a curative state of exhaustion. This was the ultimate goal of mesmerism, to produce a state of crisis that would restore the normal ebb and flow of the universal fluid. If these procedures failed to induce a crisis, then Mesmer himself, dressed in a lilac robe and carrying a magnetized wand, would approach a patient to force the universal fluid into her body. If the power of his eyes or of his wand still proved insufficient, then he would gently run his fingers along the sides of the "hypochondria" (the upper abdomen) until the sensual procedure induced the patient to tingle as she "felt" the universal fluid pass into her. Most of Mesmer's patients were women and this particular aspect of his treatment gave rise to many rumors about the intentions of the mesmerist.

Although Mesmer undoubtedly treated a number of disorders that today would fall under the label of neuroses, there were other, more severe psychological problems that Mesmer avoided. According to Zweig (1931), the only persons excluded from treatment were those with running sores, epileptics, idiots, and the "insane." For persons declared insane there were no carpeted rooms with background music.

A PERIOD OF REFORM: FROM CHAINS TO HUMANE CARE

In the eighteenth century, insanity was considered an incurable disease. Chains, dungeons, dark cells, and floggings were among the conditions reserved for those whose problems were beyond comprehension and treatment. Strange and sometimes violent behavior was a threat to others and constraints and physical abuse of such individuals was widely accepted.

The most notable French figure in the eighteenth century to challenge these practices was Philippe Pinel (1745–1826). Unlike Mesmer, who enjoyed luxury, friends in high society, and a taste of power and self-importance, Pinel was a small, mild man who began life in poverty and died in poverty. He was interested in the lot of the indigent and the insane. In La Bicêtre and La Salpêtrière, hospitals for the insane in Paris, the inmates were shackled permanently with chains, and given only one ration of bread per day. They shared filthy living conditions with rats; their keepers made fun of them and frequently beat them into submission. Pinel devoted most of his adult life to opposing these atrocities.

As a boy, Pinel was quiet and tended to withdraw from his peers in order to pursue his studies. An early interest in theology shifted to the study of natural history and medicine. After he completed his medical studies at the University of Montpellier, he traveled on foot with an English friend to Paris. Despite his shyness he cultivated a number of friends who were to become influential figures after the French Revolution in 1789. In his early years in Paris he was unsuccessful in securing a medical appointment. During these years, a tragedy occurred that may have spurred his later dedication to the plight of the insane. One of his close friends suddenly "lost his reason" and was locked up in a madhouse. He managed to escape and fled into the forest that surrounded Paris. A week later the body was found, half devoured by wolves (Walker, 1959). Following this incident, Pinel began to read all that he could find on the subject of insanity, even though little information was actually available.

After the French Revolution, two of Pinel's friends were appointed as administrators of the hospitals in Paris. Their influence was such that in 1793, Pinel received a medical appointment as doctor in charge of the insane at La Bicêtre. In this institution he observed at first hand the punitive, often bizarre treatment of the 213 inmates. Pinel persistently sought permission from the authorities to remove chains and other mechanical restraints. After several refusals a ruthless, powerful, but paralyzed Revolutionary figure named Georges Couthon agreed to inspect conditions at La Bicêtre. Carried on a stretcher, he accompanied Pinel on a tour of the hospital. After seeing the naked, agonized inmates and hearing them screaming senselessly, Couthon told Pinel, "You must be mad yourself to think of unchaining such animals [McKown, 1961, p. 31]." Pinel argued that the inmates were deranged, in part, because they had been deprived of freedom and clean air. Couthon, although dismissing Pinel's belief as foolish sentimentality, raised no further objections to freeing some of the inmates from their chains. He left with the prediction that Pinel would die at the hands of the inmates.

Pinel had 12 inmates unshackled immediately. An English captain who had

A priest exorcises the devil from a possessed woman in this painting from the Middle Ages. The exorcist has called upon a saint, seen above his head, and the devil is literally in flight. The woman has fainted, but not from relief; her hand has been held to the purifying flame of the candle. (The Bettmann Archive, from the Horne Museum, Florence)

Pinel unchains the inmates at La Salpêtrière, 1795. The painter, working in 1876, has prettified the scene, but the details are realistic. The women on the right are shackled to their outdoor stalls like cattle in a barn. (National Library of Medicine; painting by Tony Robert-Fleury)

Benjamin Rush's "tranquilizer
chair" was not a success; too
many patients broke their bones
against it in vain attempts to free
themselves from its restraints.
(National Library of Medicine)

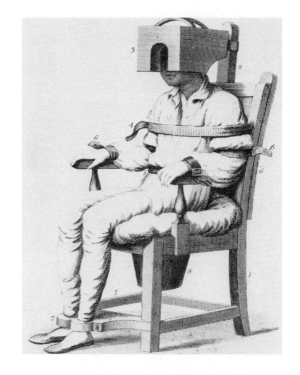

Though often criticized, today's
mental hospitals are a vast
improvement over yesterday's
madhouses. These patients,
doing kneebends along with the
TV exercise class, also have a
piano to play, books to read, and
curtained windows to brighten
their institutional surroundings.
(Inge Morath, Magnum)

lived in chains for 40 years was the first to be released. After the man promised to behave as a gentleman, Pinel ordered the blacksmith to remove the chains. Hardly able to walk, the old man tottered into the courtyard, and seeing the sky for the first time said softly, "How beautiful it is! [McKown, 1961, p. 31]" The second inmate to be freed was a huge man named Chevigne, who, 10 years earlier, in a state of drunkenness, had claimed he was a general. Following his release, he served as Pinel's bodyguard for 3 months. Subsequently, he was pronounced cured and discharged from the institution. A year after Chevigne's discharge, Pinel was seized by a group of dissidents who accused him of releasing lunatics to slay friends of the Revolution. As they prepared to hang Pinel from a lamp post, Chevigne emerged from the darkness and fought off the would-be murderers. Such an act exemplified the devotion that many of the inmates felt toward Pinel for his sympathetic treatment of them.

In the course of his stay at La Bicêtre, Pinel was successful in doubling the bread ration for inmates, promoting cleanliness in previously filthy cells, instituting work and reading as activities to reduce idleness, and halting brutality toward patients by attendants. Some patients who had been considered incurable improved remarkably and were released. Others at least benefited from the more pleasurable surroundings. Restraining devices were still used but less frequently and less inhumanely. Pinel remained at La Bicêtre for 2 years before being transferred to La Salpêtrière, a women's asylum for the indigent, the aged, prostitutes, and the insane. Pinel instituted similar reforms there. After 30 years of service at La Salpêtrière, Pinel refused a pension. He died in poverty in 1826. The most eminent scientific men of France, along with hundreds of former inmates of La Bicêtre and La Salpêtrière, were part of an enormous funeral procession.

Pinel was not the only figure of his time to champion humane treatment for persons committed to asylums. Contemporaries in two other countries made similar efforts to eliminate cruel and abusive treatment. Ten years before Pinel removed chains at La Bicêtre, Vicenzo Chiarugi (1759–1820) had unchained some inmates at the St. Boniface Asylum in Florence, Italy. Like Pinel, Chiarugi sought to eliminate deplorable conditions. In England, a Quaker named William Tuke (1732–1822) condemned abuses at the York Asylum. In 1792, he established the York Retreat as a haven for the insane (Roback, 1961).

Pinel, Chiarugi, and Tuke did not have a sophisticated understanding of the etiology and management of psychological problems. Nor did they make any real scientific discoveries in medicine or psychology. Their place in history is due entirely to the contrast between their sympathetic, humane approach and the prevailing punitive approach of their era.

EARLY AMERICAN TREATMENT OF THE INSANE

Pinel's belief in the effectiveness of "moral remedies" as a cure for the insane and Tuke's humane methods of care at the York Retreat had a definite impact on nineteenth-century attitudes in the United States. In 1817, Pennsylvania Quakers patterned Friends' Asylum after the York Retreat. In Connecticut, an American physician named Eli Todd harbored fears about his own sanity because both his father and sister had died "insane." He studied Pinel's methods and the mode of care administered to patients at the York Retreat. In 1824, he succeeded in persuading the Connecticut Medical Society to sponsor the Hartford Retreat. As its director, Todd emphasized kindness and the moral remedies of Pinel. Within 30 years after the establishment of Friends' Asylum, 18 American hospitals were utilizing what has been referred to as *moral treatment* approaches. Moral treatment approaches stressed humane care, compassion, understanding of the patient's needs, and the importance of activity within the social milieu. Moral treatment was hailed by Bockoven (1963, 1972) as an effective "cure" for mental illness, one that has been only recently rediscovered since its decline following the construction of large state hospitals.

THE BEGINNINGS OF AMERICAN PSYCHIATRY

The American contemporary of Pinel, Tuke, and Chiarugi was Benjamin Rush (1745–1813). Rush has been called the "first American psychiatrist" (Alexander & Selesnick, 1966). He was also active in social and political movements—a signer of the Declaration of Independence, Physician General of the Continental Army, Treasurer of the United States, and a constant supporter of the poor and of minority groups. Among the causes he championed were the abolition of slavery, public schools for the poor, the admission of women to institutions of higher education, the elimination of capital punishment, and an end to poor hygienic conditions in both madhouses and prisons. In 1784 he joined the medical staff at Pennsylvania Hospital and for the next 30 years he made the treatment of the insane his primary goal. He instituted a work program to prevent idleness and build a sense of worth; he hired men who would befriend rather than abuse patients, and he instituted notable improvements in hygienic conditions. Rush may even be credited with a system of therapy in which patients were encouraged to talk about their feelings and the nature of their problems.

Despite his many accomplishments, Rush's specific treatment procedures led to misery and probably to death as well. He was literally obsessed with bloodletting as a mode of treatment. One of his notions about insanity was that it was primarily due to an arterial dysfunction which supplied too much blood to the brain or, less frequently, too little blood to the brain. For the former, bloodletting was his standard remedy. He often removed 20 ounces to 2½ pints at a time. He claimed success in calming one of his more violent patients by removing a total of 29 pints of blood in 47 different bleeding sessions.[5]

If an inmate's problem was "torpid madness," which Rush thought was due to too little blood supplied to the brain, then he was subjected to treatment with a large device called a gyrator. The patient was placed on a large rotating table with his head at the periphery. As the turntable was rotated at increasing speed, blood was forced to the patient's head, thus correcting the undersupply of blood to the

---

[5] Bloodletting was not restricted to treatment of the inmates. During an outbreak of yellow fever, Rush boasted that 6000 Philadelphians owed their lives to his practice of bleeding and purging.

brain. In addition to these treatment devices, Rush designed the "tranquilizer chair," which he considered to be more humane than a straitjacket. Violent inmates were strapped to this armchair and their heads were restrained by pressure applied by means of a hinged wooden block fastened to the back of the chair. Because it led to a large number of fractures and bruises, Rush eventually discontinued use of the device.

Among other remedies, Rush recommended cold baths and starvation diets for rebellious inmates, sudden loud sounds or severe frightening for some cases, and for others, a technique called *ducking* in which the patient's head was periodically forced under water. On rare occasions, whippings were recommended (McKown, 1961). Rush made no real scientific contributions, and some of his notions served to impede rather than advance understanding of human behavior. For example, Rush believed that frequent masturbation was one cause of insanity. Still, Rush was genuinely concerned with the welfare of his patients. Most of his life was spent attempting to help people whom other professionals chose to ignore.

A RELENTLESS AMERICAN CRUSADER FOR THE INSANE POOR

One of the most remarkable women in the nineteenth century was Dorothea Dix (1802–1887). Her father was an unstable Harvard dropout who became a frequently drunk preacher. Dorothea's childhood may be best described as poor and unhappy. At the age of 12 she ran away to live with her grandmother.

When she was 14 she left her grandmother's home and opened her own school. At 17, she returned to live with her grandmother, who reluctantly allowed her to use a part of her home to teach small classes. During this period, a brief engagement with a cousin was broken and Dorothea developed serious lung problems.

Dorothea remained at her grandmother's until she was 34. Then, following an extended illness, she closed her school and sailed to Europe for a rest. She was warmly welcomed by a European family and nursed back to health. In England she met both Samuel and Hack Tuke, grandson and great-grandson of William Tuke. Their discussions may well have included the goals and methods of the York Retreat.

When Dorothea returned to America her mother, father, and grandmother were dead. After several seemingly uneventful years she did a favor for a Harvard divinity student who was nervous about teaching Sunday school to 20 women prisoners. He asked Dorothea if she could recommend someone to teach the class, and she suggested herself. She found out that the insane were also in prison, and her first glimpse of their treatment horrified her. From that moment, she dedicated herself to the lifelong task of investigating conditions to which the poor and insane were subjected.

In her first investigations in Massachusetts, she found "insane" people confined in stalls, closets, cages, and chains. Often there was no heat in the winter because it was believed that the insane were insensitive to heat and cold. Many were beaten with rods or abused in other ways. She met a mistress of an almshouse (house for the destitute) who exemplified the type of indifference shown by persons charged with care of the insane. When Dix pointed out that a female inmate was tearing off her skin, the mistress of the almshouse said, "Oh, we can't help it, half the skin is off sometimes; we can do nothing with her; and it makes no difference what she eats, for she consumes her own filth as readily as the food which is brought her [Rothman, 1971, p. 7]." That such conditions actually prevailed in Massachusetts was confirmed by an investigating committee appointed by the state legislature.

By 1847, Dix had visited and written careful descriptions of conditions at 500 almshouses, 300 county jails and houses of correction, and 18 penitentiaries (McKown, 1961). Despite having frequent lung problems (probably tuberculosis), she traveled over 30,000 miles and was credited with founding or enlarging 32 hospitals. It is important to note that Dix was not merely concerned with adequate hospital space. She knew of the relatively favorable conditions existing in small American hospitals patterned after York Retreat. Humane care and treatment of the insane *poor* was her primary mission. The huge, understaffed, and often poorly run state hospitals that resulted did not, in fact, replace smaller private hospitals in which better care was feasible. Patients who entered the state hospitals found no bed of roses or "moral treatment," but they avoided the far worse conditions that existed in prisons and almshouses. Dix, more than any other figure in the nineteenth century, made people in America and virtually all of Europe aware that the insane were being subjected to incredible abuses. Although Bockoven (1963, 1972) holds Dix responsible for the rise of large hospitals and the decline of "moral therapy," she was not to blame for lack of advancement in psychiatry.

Dix died in 1887, the same year that 31-year-old Sigmund Freud was elected to the Society of Medicine in Vienna (Ellenberger, 1970).

Early Systems of Psychological Treatment (1886–1939)

THE DEVELOPMENT OF PSYCHOANALYSIS

Sigmund Freud (1856–1939) is the most widely cited and the most controversial figure in the history of psychiatry. Indeed, to many in the field of psychiatry and to a lesser number in clinical psychology, constructs such as repression and the unconscious have become well-established truisms. The adulation of Freud by his followers virtually transformed psychoanalytic theory into a religion, first to be accepted on faith and later to be examined empirically. Freud, possibly in jest, referred to early disiciples who ventured systems of their own as "heretics" (McKown, 1961).

Freud was the first of seven children born to Jacob and Amalia Freud. Amalia was Jacob's third wife and, at 20, she was no older than Jacob's two sons by a previous marriage. Amalia, according to Ellenberger (1970), was a beautiful woman with a "boundless" admiration for Sigmund. The Freud family was not wealthy but there was sufficient money for family vacations and other minor luxuries. School records confirmed Freud's assertion that he was consistently "first in his class." Freud began his medical studies at the University of Vienna in 1873 and received his degree in 1881. During the later phase of his medical training, Freud was most impressed with his experiences under Ernst Brucke (1819–1892). Brucke adhered to a mechanistic–organistic approach and believed all processes could be reduced to physical and chemical laws. Freud's deterministic views may have been partly due to Brucke's early influence (Ellenberger, 1970).

At Brucke's institute, Freud became friends with Josef Breuer (1842–1925). Breuer's greatest influence on Freud stemmed from discussions about an unusual patient. Anna O., as she was referred to under a pseudonym, exhibited a variety of hysterical symptoms. As we have noted, hysteria refers to various physical manifestations of psychological origin that involve no actual physical damage. Breuer's treatment approach was mainly the gradual eradication of symptoms through the use of hypnosis. Anna O. referred to the process as the "talking cure." Later, Breuer reluctantly allowed the case of Anna O. to appear in a joint publication by Freud and Breuer called *Studies of Hysteria.* Breuer had confided to Freud that Anna O., during the course of treatment, had caused him great embarrassment by confessing her love for him (McKown, 1961). She even developed a phantom pregnancy followed by a hysterical delivery. According to Jones (1953), Breuer was so shocked that he hypnotized her, terminated therapy, and immediately went on a second honeymoon with his wife.[6] The case of Anna O. and the use of hypnosis as a form of treatment intrigued Freud.

In Paris, Charcot was hypnotizing hysterical patients but not for the purpose of treatment. After studying with Theodor Meynert, a well-known brain anatomist, Freud secured a travel grant to study with Charcot. Although Charcot conceptualized hysteria primarily as an inherited organic disorder, he demonstrated that it was possible to cause the appearance and disappearance of paralysis through the use of hypnosis (Stewart, 1967). Such demonstrations were of intense interest to Freud, particularly those involving male patients who had earlier experienced some form of trauma.

Between 1886 and 1896, Freud gradually drifted away from neurological explanations of psychological problems in favor of psychological interpretations. The shift in his thinking was probably facilitated by his interest in the use of hypnosis and suggestion in the treatment of his patients. He became curious as to why Anna O. was able to talk about her sexual feelings only when rendered uninhibited through hypnosis. During the same period, he placed an increasing emphasis on the role of sexual factors in the development of neuroses.

By 1895, Freud was convinced that sexual conflicts were the only valid ex-

---

[6] Ellenberger (1970) has noted inconsistencies in the various reports about Anna O. that cast some doubt on Jones's account. Reports were also inconsistent as to what kinds of problems Anna O. had after Breuer terminated their relationship.

planation of neuroses. His "seduction theory" resulted in considerable criticism, particularly from his former friend Breuer. The seduction theory was based on the incredible revelations by his patients that they had been sexually accosted early in their development. Seduction of the daughter by her father was an especially prominent theme. Freud was so convinced of the reality of these revelations that when his sister began to seem somewhat neurotic, he suspected that his father had committed an incestuous act (Stewart, 1967). In 1897, however, he indicated in a letter to his close friend, Wilhelm Fleiss, that the seduction stories told by his patients were mere fantasies. The discarding of the seduction theory did not decrease the role of sexuality. In fact, it led Freud to consider the role of sexuality in young children and even infants. If patients were reporting sexual fantasies they had as children, then it was consistent to conclude that they had sexual feelings as children. The concept of infantile sexuality was rejected by a Vienna society in which sexual matters were not discussed and young children were exalted for their innocence. However, the recognition of childhood sexuality proved to be one of Freud's most original insights into behavior.

In the years 1894–1899, Freud undertook his own analysis. Freud's major written work of this 5-year period was the *Interpretation of Dreams.* By 1900, concepts fundamental to psychoanalytic theory such as conflict, repression, and the unconscious had become basic constructs in a system that was to undergo continual organization, revision, and expansion until Freud's death in 1939.

The early 1900s marked the beginning of a worldwide psychoanalytic movement. In 1909, George Stanley Hall invited Freud to America to present an address at Clark University. This invitation marked the beginning of the psychoanalytic movement in the United States.

Freud published *Lay Analysis* in 1926. A major contention was that the practice of psychoanalysis required no medical training, a contention that further emphasized the role of psychological factors over neurological factors in the etiology and treatment of psychoneurosis. The later years of Freud's life were not pleasant. A cancer of the jaw and a total of 33 operations were to plague him from 1923 until his death in 1939 (Ellenberger, 1970). Hitler came to power in 1933; in 1934, Freud's books were burned in Berlin. In 1938, the Gestapo invaded his house in Vienna, burned his books, impounded his money, and confiscated his passport (McKown, 1961). Only through pressures applied by such persons as Princess Marie Bonaparte and President Franklin Roosevelt was Freud released by the Nazis to spend the last year of his life as a refugee in London.

Freudian or neo-Freudian views are still widely held, particularly in the field of psychiatry. The popularity of psychoanalytic theory in the United States grew rapidly between 1930 and 1950. By 1960, however, interest in Freudian theory among clinical psychologists began to decline. A major criticism of psychoanalytic theory has been that empirical support is lacking for many of its major constructs. Despite this criticism, the theory has excited much interest in the field of abnormal psychology. A tremendous amount of research activity has been directed toward testing hypotheses derived from psychoanalytic theory. Thus, even though the scientific value of the theory has been questioned, its heuristic value has been substantial. A major contribution of Freud was the directing of psychiatry away from a strictly organic model of behavior by focusing on the socializing influences of the family. The focus on environmental forces was also characteristic of a significant competing system, American behaviorism.

THE HERESY OF BEHAVIORISM

Behaviorism developed rapidly following its introduction in 1912 by John B. Watson (1878–1958). Widespread clinical applications of behavioristic methods to psychological problems did not begin until the late 1950s or early 1960s. However, the belief that these methods could be applied in the treatment of behavioral problems was strongly argued by Watson in the 1920s.

Watson was an ardent critic of psychoanalytic theory. He stated that "the scientific level of Freud's concept of the unconscious is exactly on a par with the miracles of Jesus [Watson, 1928, p. 95]." He accused psychoanalytically oriented physicians of popularizing the unconscious "because they needed something to help them explain so-called 'mental' diseases [p. 92]." Later behaviorists either ignored psychoanalysis or attempted to reconcile the system with that of behaviorism.[7]

Watson greatly underestimated the impact of Freudian theory. In 1928 he suggested that the layman was tired of discussing his dreams and complexes and that the novelty of psychoanalysis had gone. Disdainfully, he stated that there was "too little science—real science—in Freud's psychology, and hence it held its news value for only a relatively brief span of years [Watson, 1928, p. 5]."

Watson expounded behaviorism with the same dogmatic fervor that Freud had displayed when expounding psychoanalysis. He ruled that both consciousness and unconsciousness were not publicly observable and therefore had no place in a science of behavior. He adopted the conditioned reflex model of Pavlov and made it basic to a learning theory that accounted for *all* differences in behavior, whether deviant or nondeviant. He objected to postulating any nonobservable processes. For example, thinking was defined as subvocal speech that was potentially observable in the form of slight muscular movements of the larynx. "The unverbalized world of emotions" was his substitute for the unconscious. He rejected virtually any explanation for deviant behavior based on an assumption of brain pathology. The role of heredity was ruled out in accounting for individual differences among "healthy" people. Psychoanalysis as a way of treating psychological problems was viewed as inefficient and a waste of time. According to Watson (1928), treatment should be reeducation "along manual, verbal, and visceral lines [p. 106]." He argued that "you can build up a whole string of emotional reactions, then tear them down; . . . you can implant, alter, and wholly change vocational patterns, and all without any psychoanalytic pat-

---

[7] As noted by Ellenberger (1970), John Dollard and Neal Miller attempted to reconcile learning theories and psychoanalysis in 1950.

ter [p. 109]." The tool for this optimistic power over human behavior was *conditioning* or *unconditioning*.

The extreme environmentalism of Watson led to a naive rejection in experimental psychology of genetics and neurophysiology as factors underlying behavior—a mistake equal to the medical rejection of powerful environmental determinants of behavior. The current views of both psychology and psychiatry have been somewhat altered by the recognition of each other's mistakes.

Historical Problems in a Contemporary Context

In our view, it is difficult to construe the history of abnormal psychology as a linear advance from naive primitive views to a scientifically enlightened understanding of psychological problems. Demons have come and gone as explanations for behavior—for all we know, they might come again. In the future, some contemporary approaches to treatment may be viewed as negatively as we now view bloodletting and other undesirable treatment approaches of the past.

However, to say that we have learned no lessons from history would be to ignore significant and positive changes. Mental patients are no longer tortured, chained, whipped, starved, and denied hygienic conditions. The public is more aware and less tolerant of abuses in institutional settings.

Within the past two decades, professionals have recognized that the "moral treatment" approaches employed in small institutions a century and a half ago provided a more favorable milieu than the huge, depersonalized state institutions that replaced them. Efforts to rectify this situation have led to the community mental health movement and the establishment of comprehensive community centers. The primary goal of this movement is to reduce the population of patients in large state hospitals and provide medical care and social services for mental patients in their own communities.[8]

According to Warren (1976), "Thirteen years ago community mental health was hailed as the 'bold approach' needed to dramatically improve the treatment of mental patients and eliminate the 'backward' conditions of most state mental hospitals [p. 1]." Today, the patient populations of large hospitals have declined but community mental health centers have been the target of much criticism. The adequate treatment of mental patients remains the central issue. Severe financial problems, community hostility, and differences among the mental health professions regarding treatment goals have been cited as factors threatening the success and survival of community centers (Warren, 1976).

Historically, the responsibility for care and treatment of mental patients has resided primarily in the hands of either religious officials or physicians. With few exceptions, the causes of psychological problems were attributed to either supernatural forces or organic disorders. Although supernatural explanations have declined, organic explanations inherent in the early Hippocratic conception of

[8] A full discussion of community approaches to mental health will be presented in Chapter 20.

mental disease are still characteristic of contemporary medical approaches. Environmental causes for psychological problems have been implicated at various times in history but have achieved extensive credibility only with the emergence of psychoanalytic and behavioral systems in the twentieth century.

The historical etiological issue of demons versus mental disease has been replaced by the issue of environmental versus organic causation. As will be discussed in subsequent chapters, environmental and organic variables often interact in complex ways. For many disorders, the etiological contribution of both classes of variables has been implicated.

Regardless of the causes of behavior, the prevailing belief system of a culture has an important influence on whether behavior is perceived as normal or abnormal. Thus far, we have focused on cultural differences in the context of history. In the next chapter, we will see how current differences among cultures affect the classification of behavior as normal or abnormal.

Summary

The history of abnormal behavior from ancient times until the beginnings of psychological systems in the twentieth century has been discussed. Reactions to psychological problems at various points in history have been highly variable. Kind and gentle treatment apparently existed in the Aesculapian temples as early as 1000 B.C. The humaneness or harshness with which psychological disorders were treated varied considerably until the Middle Ages, when a threatened society in the turmoil of wars, plagues, and famine attributed human misery to the work of the devil. Seriously disturbed individuals were likely to be perceived as witches and tortured or killed. The end of the Middle Ages in A.D. 1700 was followed by a period of social change marked by an interest in technology and scientific inquiry. Treatment of the insane, however, largely consisted of the use of chains or other mechanical restraints, whippings, semistarvation, and unsanitary cells. In Europe, Pinel, Chiarugi, and Tuke all gained recognition for their opposition to these conditions.

In the United States, Benjamin Rush instituted a number of positive reforms for institutionalized patients, but his reliance on bloodletting and other undesirable treatment approaches contributed to misery. The most outstanding figure of the 1800s was Dorothea Dix. More than any other individual, she was responsible for alleviating severe abuses in the treatment of the poor and insane.

In the early twentieth century, both Freud and Watson were responsible for shifting the focus from organic explanations of psychological problems to the forces of the environment. Preference for a relative emphasis on either organic or environmental causes of psychological problems remains as an important difference between medical and psychological conceptions of abnormal behavior.

2

Some Basic Concepts
and Issues

Conceptions of Abnormal Behavior

What precisely do we mean when we use the term or label *abnormal* in relation to human behavior? Obviously, this question is basic to the subject matter of this text. It is also, unfortunately, a question that does not yield a pat, ready-made answer. As you, the reader, shall soon learn, there are many different conceptions and definitions of abnormality. Let us now explore the various ways in which people have attempted to deal with this fundamental concept.

ABNORMALITY AS DEVIANCE,
IN THE STATISTICAL SENSE

"Deviance from some established norm" is the most literal meaning of the term *abnormal*. Indeed, almost all contemporary writers cite deviation, in the statistical sense, as one possible criterion of abnormality. Such a definition is flawed, however, because it fails to take into account the *direction* of the deviance. To borrow an example from Buss (1966), a person with 20/100 vision would be described as having abnormal eyesight. A person with 20/10 vision would be said to have superior vision. Yet both individuals have vision that deviates from the norm. Clearly, deviation *by itself* does not imply abnormality. The importance of the direction or nature of the deviance is further seen in the following example.

A client in psychotherapy asks his therapist, "Am I psychologically abnormal?" If the therapist were to reply "Yes," on the grounds that his client was "sick" or "mentally ill" or simply "in for a lot of trouble," such a reply would probably make some sense to the client, although it might well be distressing for him to hear. But suppose the therapist said "Yes, you are abnormal because you are so much healthier and better adjusted than the average person." Such a reply would probably do more to confuse than to reassure our client! The confusion would be well founded, because *although psychological abnormality does imply deviance, what makes the deviant behavior abnormal is that it is in some sense troublesome*. The behavior may be troublesome to the individual labeled abnormal, or to the society in which he lives, or to both.

At this point, you may feel somewhat frustrated. After all, when professional people such as psychologists and psychiatrists use the term *abnormal*, do they not have some highly specific and absolute definition in mind? The answer to this question is no, for two reasons. First, since there is not widespread agreement regarding the definition of abnormal behavior, it does not make sense to talk about an absolute definition. Second, and perhaps more important in relation to human behavior, abnormality is as much a layman's term as it is a technical term. This means that, to a considerable degree, abnormality is whatever society says it is! Of course there *are* a large number of technical psychological and psychiatric concepts of abnormal psychology, such as schizophrenia, neurosis, and mental deficiency. We will examine concepts of this nature in subsequent chapters of this text. But we cannot define abnormality simply in terms of these technical concepts.

ABNORMALITY AS A DEPARTURE FROM CULTURAL NORMS

Standards of conduct vary from culture to culture. Behaviors that fail to conform to one culture's standards, and therefore are labeled as abnormal, may be well within the range of normality in another culture (Benedict, 1934; Scheff, 1966), a point made in Chapter 1. The driving habits of individuals in different cultures do not constitute a psychologically exotic class of behaviors, but serve as a highly visible example of cultural relativism and abnormality. For instance, in Caracas, Venezuela, if the concept of right-of-way exists at all, the rules must be very subtle indeed. Driving in such a manner in any major United States city would be grossly deviant and highly dangerous, hence abnormal. For that matter, driving habits in small midwestern towns in the United States would be viewed as dangerously deviant in New York City, and the converse of this is certainly true.

We believe that any valid definition of psychological abnormality must emphasize cultural relativism. You should be aware that other writers disagree with this emphasis. For example, Buss (1966) argues that even though some cultures accept hallucinations as normal, they are still abnormal, "and if a society is too backward technologically to recognize this fact, it does not alter the matter [p. 12]." In short, Buss views hallucinations as abnormal in some absolute sense. We disagree, and we would also hasten to point out that certain so-called primitive

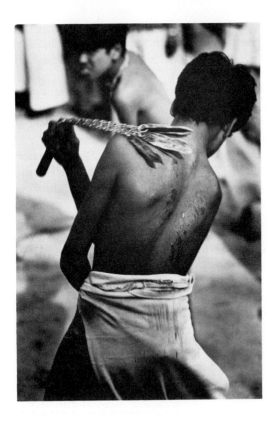

A flagellant lacerates his back with a flail during a religious ceremony in Lucknow, India. In Europe in the Middle Ages, such behavior was widely practiced and admired. In the Western world today, such behavior is considered deviant, threatening, and obviously masochistic—and so public flagellants are likely to be hospitalized for psychiatric care. (Jehangir Gazdar, Woodfin Camp & Associates)

cultures consider hallucinations to be messages from the gods. Thus one may become an influential priest or medicine man for acting as if one is experiencing hallucinations.

In taking a culturally relativistic view of abnormality, we do not assume that behaviors labeled as normal are therefore good, in the sense of being socially constructive, and vice versa. Ullmann and Krasner (1969/1975) correctly note that the actions of Nazis prior to and during World War II were considered normal within their own cultural context, but we also agree that they were most abhorrent. On the opposite side of the coin, at least through the middle 1960s the vast majority of Americans viewed homosexual acts between consenting adults as abnormal. Merely because such behavior was seen as abnormal does not imply that it was necessarily evil, again in the sense of being socially destructive. Moreover, anyone who doubts that cultural and social factors influence the use of the label *abnormal* must explain why the same homosexual acts in 1977 are more normal than they were in 1967!

ABNORMALITY AS TROUBLESOME BEHAVIOR

As we have said, deviant actions, in order to be labeled abnormal, must in some sense be troublesome. The adult American who puts away two fifths of bourbon daily is clearly deviant; so is the adult American who has never tasted an alcoholic beverage. But only the former is likely to be seen as abnormal. The reason is that whereas the abstainer presents no particular problem for society (excluding the liquor industry), our whiskey guzzler will probably require special care. His physical health is almost certainly impaired; he is more likely than most to cause an auto accident; perhaps when drunk he becomes physically abusive; he may not be able to provide economic support for himself or his family. In short, he presents a danger or threat to his community's sense of well-being.

Many writers have defined abnormality in terms of deviance of a threatening nature (e.g., Erikson, 1962; Goffman, 1961). The threat may take many forms: physical, political, or economic. Frequently, the threat posed by deviant individuals is far more imagined than real. In such instances the labelers have erroneous expectations about the behavior of the persons seen as abnormal. For instance, it is not uncommon for laymen to view all homosexuals as potential child molesters. Similarly, in the 1960s many people associated long hair on males with illicit drug use, and some considered long hair the symbol of radical political activism.

THE BREAKING OF RULES. Any threatening action may be thought of as a violation of some rule. Rules may be explicit, as in the case of criminal statutes, statements of public morality, and accepted principles of etiquette. When such rules are broken, people are more likely to invoke the label *abnormal* when no plausible motive is apparent. Duster (1969) illustrates this very well in the following example. One woman is employed as a housemaid. She has three children to support. She steals a piece of jewelry worth $650 and is tried as a criminal, because her criminal intent is clear. A second woman is married to a man who earns $175,000 a year. She steals a piece of jewelry worth $1400. Since no reasonable need is apparent, she is judged to be suffering from a psychological abnormality and is "sentenced" to outpatient psychiatric treatment.

Certain behaviors violate no explicit rules of conduct, but nevertheless are disconcerting to significant elements of society and are viewed as abnormal. For example, there is no explicit rule forbidding a person to claim he is Napoleon Bonaparte, but this will frighten many people who will label this behavior as "crazy" or "sick." This illustrates what certain sociologists (Mechanic, 1962; Scheff, 1966) term a violation of *residual* or nonexplicit rules. When engaging in a conversation, for example, there is a residual rule that you face your partner. At the very least, if you consistently broke this rule you would be labeled as odd.

LACK OF PREDICTABILITY. When a person breaks explicit rules without plausible motivation he is behaving in an unpredictable fashion. The same can be said of a person who violates implicit or residual rules. Thus, it is not uncommon for people to associate lack of predictability with abnormality (London, 1969; Ullmann & Krasner, 1969/1975). One would not predict that a wealthy person would shoplift, nor that a person proclaim himself emperor of America. Both are examples of what society would label as abnormal behavior. Thus, abnormality carries a connotation of lack of predictability; the labels, however, are not synonymous. A political dissident may be labeled abnormal by the Establishment in spite of the fact that he shows a very predictable pattern of behavior, because he threatens the established order. On the other hand, when a person is described as unpredictable the referent behavior may be of a socially inconsequential nature. Situation comedies in the past often characterized female behavior in this way, referring to minor examples of unexpected emotionality. In such instances, the behavior was not threatening and the term *abnormal* would be out of place.

To summarize, abnormal behavior deviates from existing cultural standards and is a threat to some portion of society. It may involve violations of explicit codes of behavior in the absence of plausible motivation, or the violation of implicit rules of conduct. Inability to predict the behavior of another may lead to invoking the label *abnormal,* providing the lack of predictability presents some sort of threat. Let us now consider some other terms often used to characterize or define abnormal behavior.

BIZARRE BEHAVIOR AND ABNORMALITY

Sometimes so-called bizarre behavior is used as a criterion for abnormality (e.g., Buss, 1966). Examples of bizarre behavior include delusions, hallucinations, certain acts of violence, and, for some, so-called sexual perversions. The word *bizarre* is to a considerable degree a layman's term; in meaning it is similar to *abnormal,* although the latter covers a wider latitude of behaviors. Perhaps it is best to reserve the term *bizarre* for the more extreme or striking examples of abnormal behavior.

PERCEPTION OF REALITY AND ABNORMALITY

Some (for example, Jahoda, 1958) suggest that misperception of reality is indicative of abnormality. The concept of perception, and therefore of misperception, is difficult to deal with because we have no direct knowledge of another person's subjective experience. Such a conception of abnormality may lead to the following circular logic: A person behaves in a manner considered abnormal. Others infer misperception of reality solely on the basis of this behavior. Then they proceed to explain his behavior in terms of the assumed misperception.

BEHAVIORAL EFFICIENCY AND ABNORMALITY

Lack of efficiency is sometimes cited as a defining attribute of abnormality. Unfortunately, definitions of inefficiency are not very precise. Even if people could agree that certain activities are marked by inefficiency, we would anticipate that, more often than not, the label *abnormal* would not be invoked.

PERSONAL DISCOMFORT AND ABNORMALITY: SUBJECTIVE STATES

Many writers in the field allude to some manner of personal discomfort as a defining characteristic of abnormality. In talking about personal discomfort, we are dealing with a presumed subjective state, usually inferred from a person's verbal behavior—for example, the person says he is miserable, or anxious, or depressed. Sometimes nonverbal cues, such as facial expressions or postural cues, are also employed in making a judgment regarding another person's subjective state. Psychophysiological measures or indicants, such as changes in skin resistance or elevations in blood pressure, occasionally are used as well. Regardless of the ultimate reality of private experience, in short, external judgments of personal discomfort are *always* based upon or inferred from public behavior, that is, from responses that may be observed in some way.

Would society be inclined to label a person abnormal solely on the basis of indications of personal discomfort? To answer this, reconsider our working definition of abnormality: behavior that is deviant and threatening. Mr. X informs his friends he is quite unhappy and has been for several years. He does not love his wife and finds his work most unrewarding. For our present purposes, the *reasons* for his misery are relevant only if they themselves might constitute a basis for judging this person abnormal. In this instance they do not. Also, let us assume that when he proclaims his unhappiness, he is not at the same time laughing with glee; such a discrepancy between verbal content and affect would be viewed as bizarre, hence abnormal. Now, is his behavior especially deviant and threatening? The answer is no. But what if he states that he is unhappy and plans to do himself in? Most people would probably take him at least somewhat seriously (as well they should, see Chapter 6), and would consider some sort of action to protect him. Now, to the extent that he is viewed as abnormal, is this judgment based on his reported unhappiness? We believe the answer is no. The judgment is based upon a *suicide threat,* which *is* deviant, and which would alarm most people.

Suppose our Mr. X proclaims to everyone he meets, including strangers, that he is unhappy. This is, by our definition, abnormal, not because of the content of his verbal behavior, but because of the conditions of its occurrence. You can imagine one of the "target" strangers telling his wife, "This guy came up to me, I don't even know him, and he says how miserable he is. What a nut!" This is a clear violation of a residual rule. We would not expect the stranger to say to his wife, "I think this man is abnormal *because he is unhappy*." Similarly, if Mr. X cries all the time, he is considered abnormal because of the *crying behavior*. If he is so depressed he fails to tend to his basic physical needs and is therefore incontinent, he is labeled abnormal because of the incontinence. In neither instance is presumed unhappiness the basis for applying the label.

In suggesting that occasional statements of subjective unhappiness (made in a socially appropriate manner) are not sufficient grounds for labeling someone psychologically abnormal, we do not mean to imply that indications of subjective pain are not important. If a friend of yours says he is very unhappy, we hope you will approach the friend with sympathetic understanding and constructive suggestions. If you are unhappy yourself, we hope you will seek help from a sympathetic friend or a professional person. Finding solutions to personal problems should not be predicated on their being viewed as a sign of abnormality. Abnormality, after all, is a culturally defined entity rather than a state of affairs existing somewhere beneath a person's skin.

THE MEDICAL DEFINITION OF ABNORMALITY

According to the medical definition, a person is abnormal if he can be assigned to one of the many psychiatric categories—for example, obsessive–compulsive neurotic, or schizophrenic. This is, of course, the psychological counterpart to the physical approach to abnormality.

This medical definition of psychological abnormality may seem at odds with the definition we have provided, or at least unrelated to our definition. In fact, when a person is assigned a particular diagnostic label, this usually implies that the person is deviant and at least potentially threatening. Often, such implications are inherent in the diagnostic categories themselves. Indeed, the belief that a person's behavior is deviant and threatening may motivate the practitioner to assign that individual to some diagnostic category.

The value of this approach depends entirely upon the validity of the diagnostic categories employed. Chapters 3 through 10 are devoted to examining the scientific validity of each of these categories.

THEORETICAL BIASES AND ABNORMALITY

Whether we care to admit this or not, any conception of abnormality reflects a theoretical bias. Thus behaviorists, in dealing with abnormality, are far more concerned with overt behavior than with any internalized state of pathology. As you may know, other schools of thought place great emphasis on such hypothetical internalized states. For example, Kubie (1954), a psychoanalyst, states that abnormality is marked by a predominance of the unconscious over the conscious. Jahoda's oft-quoted definition of normality (1958) includes a balance of psychic forces, self-actualization, resistance to stress, autonomy, competence, and perception of reality. Concepts such as *psychic forces* and *self-actualization,* as well as the *unconscious,* reflect particular theoretical biases. The desirability of postulating loosely defined internal states in the conceptualization of abnormal behavior is a subject of enduring controversy in psychology. Though the present authors may question the worth of many such concepts, the concepts are very much a part of psychology. In the Treatment Theories section of this text, knowledgeable proponents of schools of thought that depend heavily on such concepts have their day in court; when you read them you will be in a position to form your own conclusions.

The Medical Model and Mental Illness

A model may be defined as a representation or depiction of some segment of reality. Models may be very concrete and literal, like a scale model of an airplane or a globe, or they may be symbolic or conceptual, like a mathematical formula or a collection of verbal axioms. Most scientific models are conceptual. In talking about the medical model, we are referring to a conceptual model consisting of a set of statements about the nature and treatment of illness. The model of physical illness popular in the Western world postulates disease states characterized by biochemical imbalance or tissue damage, frequently caused by an invasion of hostile microorganisms. These states give rise to signs of illness such as elevations in temperature and symptoms such as reports of chills or physical pain. Ideally, treatment removes the underlying causative agents—for instance, with the use of antibiotics. Actual medical practice more often involves direct symptomatic treatment, such as treating cold symptoms with antihistamine drugs while essentially ignoring the presumed viral invaders.

Recall the development of the concept of mental illness presented in Chapter 1. During the Middle Ages and even as late as the eighteenth century, aberrant, threatening behavior was generally considered a result of demoniac possession. With the emergence of science and the coming of the Age of Reason, so-called naturalistic interpretations of such behavior came to be preferred to interpretations that invoked demons and spirits. It is important to realize that any naturalistic explanation is defined according to whatever rules characterize the most successful science of the time. During the eighteenth century, physics had come into its own. During the eighteenth and nineteenth centuries, physical medicine—founded in part on physiology, which in turn is based upon the principles of physics—was beginning to make significant strides. Given the demise of demoniac theories and the acceptance of a physically oriented conception of bodily disorders, many came to view psychological abnormality as a manifestation of a diseased brain. In this way, the concept of mental illness arose.

Actually, this is something of an oversimplification. Some (e.g., Sarbin, 1969) have argued that the term *mental illness* was originally used metaphorically; that is, people showing extreme behavioral abnormality acted "as if" they were ill. Subsequently, as Galen's model of illness became widely accepted, it was applied to matters psychological, and the metaphor was turned into a "real thing." The motives for reifying mental illness were probably diverse. Because the model of physical illness had met with some success and considerable acceptance, it is understandable that people would attempt to apply its assumptions to behavioral disorders. Beyond this, in the opinion of certain writers, powerful social forces operated to foster the belief in mental illness. Szasz (1970) has argued, especially in relation to the involuntary hospitalization of mental patients, that mental illness served as a replacement for witchcraft and that, in a very real sense, mental illness was "manufactured" for precisely that purpose. If the mental patient is the twentieth-century version of the witch, the institutional psychiatrist is seen by Szasz as the modern counterpart to the inquisitor.

Although Szasz's position may be overstated, it is not without plausibility. We have described abnormality as deviance that presents a social threat and usually is not viewed as criminal, either because legal codes have not been violated or because plausible criminal intent cannot be found. If we think of mental illness as a label given to individuals displaying extreme abnormality, people so labeled would probably be seen as troublemakers. In the absence of the category *mental illness*—or perhaps more to the point, in the absence of mental institutions— modern society would have no way of dealing with such people. In Szasz's view, fifteenth-century Europe dealt with this very problem by invoking witchcraft.

On a somewhat less cynical note, Sarbin (1969) has pointed to possible humanistic motives for invoking concepts such as mental illness. He cites the efforts of Teresa of Avila to save some nuns from the physical abuse of their inquisitors by regarding them *comas enfermas* ("as if sick") rather than as evil beings. It should be pointed out, however, that Sarbin is no more friendly to the concept of mental illness than Szasz; both view mental illness as a socially destructive myth.

Regardless of the actual sociological factors responsible for creating and maintaining the mental illness concept, early medical model conceptualizations appear to have assumed some physical brain pathology. In the latter part of the nineteenth century, syphilis was identified as the cause of paresis, a disorder characterized by gross psychological impairment and progressive deterioration of the brain. Syphilis, in turn, was subsequently traced to microorganisms. Paresis then was seen as the prototype of all mental disorders, and if direct evidence for brain pathology underlying most such disorders had not yet been found, it was simply a matter of time. As shall become clear in the forthcoming chapters, this expectation rarely has been fulfilled.

Modern usage of the term *medical model,* as applied to psychological disorders, is a good deal more encompassing. The basic assumption is that "outer symptoms are caused by inner dysfunctions [Buss, 1966, p. 26]." Such dysfunction could be organic in nature or it could be psychological, such as an unresolved sexual conflict or a discrepancy between one's real and ideal selves. When we speak of the medical model as it pertains to psychological disorders, we refer to *any one of a sizable number of approaches, each resting on the assumption that inner causative factors give rise to external signs and symptoms.*

The merits of the medical model approach to psychological disorders are a subject of considerable controversy and will be for many years to come. The most important single question, when evaluating the merits of any approach, is whether it ultimately leads to effective and efficient treatment. The medical model conceptualization of paresis, and of other disorders for which organic pathology has been directly identified, is certainly of value. The focus of the controversy, however, is not on organic disorders, but rather on those that are assumed to have a psychological origin or etiology.

In relation to disturbances of a psychological origin, the value of the medical model approach depends on the disorder in question and on the particular version of the medical model employed. Thus, when we consider the wide latitude of conceptions and practices within the medical model, a single overall evaluation is simply not appropriate.

AN EVALUATION OF THE LABEL *MENTAL ILLNESS*

We have just suggested that sometimes a medical model approach to psychological disorders may be useful. At the same time, we agree with a growing number of writers who are quite uncomfortable with the label *mental illness.* Whereas the medical model, as we have used the term, does not necessarily postulate some mystical and foreboding disease state, the term *mental illness* unfortunately has precisely this connotation. Thus, adherence to the mental illness concept may give rise to a tacit assumption of irreversibility (Albee, 1967) or to the inevitability of progressive deterioration (Scheff, 1966). Neither of these assumptions is generally true; however, pessimism generated by a belief in them might well interfere with treatment. In the extreme, such assumptions may constitute a self-fulfilling prophecy: Neither the practitioner nor the patient believe the patient can improve, so nothing is done to foster improvement. Therefore the patient does not get better.

It has been argued (Zax & Cowen, 1972) that conceptualizing such disorders in terms of disease or illness releases the patient from a sense of responsibility, fostering a "passive receptive" stance. It is as if the person has a virus, and although rest may be of value, one must simply wait until the disease runs its course or until the doctors come up with a cure. We have seen many patients in mental hospitals exhibit this attitude—along with a dismaying number of hospital staff members. This can be a source of nightmarish frustration to a therapist eager to witness improvement. For a patient with this attitude, it is not anything that he *does* or *thinks* or *the behavior of significant others* that gives rise to his difficulties. Rather, his problems emanate from an obscure state of internal pathology, "mental illness," which is not observable and is quite resistant to alteration.

THE LABELING PROCESS.   Thus, a belief in mental illness may give rise to attitudes of pessimism and helplessness. Such attitudes may well interfere with the progress of the person carrying this label: From the point of view of a person's welfare, being labeled mentally ill is often harmful. This will become even more apparent when we discuss society's negative attitudes toward mental illness. For the present, let us consider how a person comes to be labeled mentally ill. We have already intimated that mental illness may be thought of as an extreme form of abnormality, which we have defined in detail. It is not this simple, however, because many people who by definition are quite abnormal do not carry the formal label or diagnosis of mental illness (Goffman, 1961). Surprisingly, one critical element is the *fact of hospitalization* (Cumming & Cumming, 1957; Goffman, 1961). Goffman (1961) points to a kind of backward labeling process when he states that "a man in a political prison must be traitorous; a man in prison must be a lawbreaker; a man in a mental hospital must be sick. If not traitorous, criminal, or sick, why else would he be there?"

How do people end up in mental institutions? Many mental patients are legally committed, often involuntarily. Typically, the signature of one or two physicians is sufficient to initiate a commitment proceeding, which consists of a hearing before a judge and a court-appointed physician. Sometimes the hearings have a decidedly perfunctory appearance (Kutner, 1962; Scheff, 1964). The physicians in the community who are involved are usually acting in response to complaints from nonprofessional members of the community. That is, the initial judgment that someone is in need of psychiatric hospitalization is usually made by a layman who may be frightened or seriously inconvenienced by the behavior of the person in question (Mechanic, 1962). Not surprisingly, factors quite unrelated to the individual's psychological state are often decisive in determining whether he does or does not end up as a committed mental patient. Thus, Goffman (1961) points out that a man who might be labeled psychotic may be tolerated by his wife until she finds a boy friend, or an alcoholic may be sent to a mental institution because the local jail is full.

Just how capricious factors associated with commitment can be is illustrated in the following case history described by Kutner (1962):

■   On October 5, 1960, Mrs. Anna Duzynski, a recent Polish emigrant who lived with her husband on the northwest side of Chicago, discovered that $380 in cash had been stolen from her apartment. Suspecting that the money had been taken by the building janitor, the only other person who had a key to the apartment, Mrs. Duzynski rushed to his flat and demanded that the money be returned. The janitor in turn called the police, and upon their arrival stated that both Mr. and Mrs. Duzynski were insane and should be committed to a mental institution. Without any further examination, the police seized both Anna and Michael Duzynski, neither of whom spoke English, and took them in handcuffs to the Cook County Mental Health Clinic. At the Mental Health Clinic, unable to answer questions in English and thereby defend themselves, the Duzynskis were duly pronounced mentally ill and committed to the Chicago State Hospital. Six weeks later, Michael Duzynski still had less idea why he had been imprisoned than he had when thrown into a Nazi concentration camp in World War II. Finally, in desperation, he hanged himself. The gross injustice of the entire affair thus vividly pointed out to them, hospital officials hurriedly released Anna Duzynski the next day [p. 383].

The Duzynski case is obviously extreme. The point, however, is that factors not at all medical in nature are often involved in assigning the label of mental illness. The problem, in large measure, stems from the fact that mental illness is not easy to define (London, 1969). Certainly, few who see the mental illness concept as valuable would accept a definition of mental illness as any state of affairs that leads to incarceration in a mental institution! And yet this seems to be a kind of working definition. It is true that everyone in an institution carries a psychiatric diagnosis of some sort, but as we have implied, often this diagnosis is made *after* an initial but crucial nonprofessional judgment that the person in question is "crazy." In other words, *mental illness,* like *abnormality,* is as much a layman's term as it is a technical one. Let us now explore the ways in which lay society conceives of or reacts to mental illness.

ATTITUDES TOWARD MENTAL ILLNESS

In recent years, researchers have attempted to measure societal attitudes toward individuals considered to be mentally ill.

As is the case with many issues in psychology, opinions differ about the degree to which people negatively valuate mental illness.[1] The bulk of the literature, however, does indeed suggest that people carrying such a label are not viewed in favorable terms. For example, Lamy (1966) asked male and female college undergraduates to choose between ex-convicts and ex-mental patients in response to 30 items associated with role status. For 23 of the 30 items, a significantly greater number of students chose one category (that is, ex-convicts or ex-mental patients) over the other. Of these 23 items, the majority clearly cast the ex-patients in a negative role relative to the ex-convicts. For example, 121 of 158 students felt that most people would place *more* confidence in the ex-convict in an emergency situation, 129 of 158 felt the ex-patient would be *less* successful in seeing to it that his children did not end up in a similar institution, and 105 of 158 respondents felt that most men would prefer to be ex-convicts than ex-mental patients. Lamy also found that a "solicitous" mother would prefer to have her children in sole care of the ex-convict than the ex-patient on a weekend camping trip, and that an employer would be less likely to hire an ex-patient than an ex-convict to fill an important supervisory job.

Nunnally (1961) had subjects indicate the extent to which they agreed with a large number of statements pertaining to the nature of mental illness. The data were then factor analyzed. Factor analysis is a complex statistical procedure allowing one to determine whether responses tend to "go together" or intercorrelate. Among the 10 factors or general attitudes to emerge in the Nunnally study was one suggesting that mentally ill people could be distinguished from normals, that is, they stood out. A second attitude was that willpower was basic to a person's adjustment, implying that mental illness was indicative of a lack of willpower. A third was that mental illness was hopeless. That is, many of the respondents tended to see mentally ill people as different, weak-willed, and hopeless.

Cumming and Cumming (1957) reported negative, rejecting public attitudes toward the mentally ill. They reported that efforts to change such attitudes generated a good deal of hostility toward the would-be educators among people in the small Canadian community that was the site of the investigation. In the opinion of these authors, their efforts were perceived as a threat to the established method of dealing with deviance.

In an experimental investigation, Farina, Holland, and Ring (1966) had undergraduate males provide what they thought was electric shock whenever the person with whom they were paired erred in a learning task. The learners, in fact, were confederates who received no shock. The essential element in the investigation was what the subject was told about the status and history of the learner. The learner was described either as well adjusted or as having been hospitalized following a nervous breakdown. He was also described either as having had a typical childhood or as having come from a broken home. The subjects could vary the degree of shock. The principal findings were that strongest shock was directed toward people identified as having a history of

---

[1] For a stimulating debate concerning this and related issues, see Sarbin and Mancuso (1970, 1972) versus Crocetti, Spiro, Lemkau, and Siassi (1972).

mental illness but a normal childhood; the mildest shock was directed toward those with a normal childhood and good adult adjustment. Those labeled as mentally ill were also rated as significantly less likable than those perceived as normal. Subjects indicated a preference for working with normals on future such tasks, and those working with the "ex-mental patients" believed their team performance was poorer. In actuality, the confederates' behaviors in each of the conditions did not vary in any systematic way. The obtained differences were purely a function of what the subjects had been told about their partners.

Not surprisingly, mental patients tend to take a negative view of their status (Crumpton, Weinstein, Acker, & Annis, 1967). That is, mental patients appear to be aware of the stigma associated with the mentally ill role. One study by Farina, Gliha, Boudreau, Allen, and Sherman (1971) demonstrated how believing that another person (an observer) knows one is a mental patient can have a disrupting effect on the patient's behavior. Half of a group of male ex-mental patients were told their partner in a maze game knew of their psychiatric status, and half were told the partner had been led to believe they had been medical–surgical patients. The "partners" who were described as personnel trainees were actually confederates of the experimenters. The principal finding was that the ex-patients who thought their partners knew of their true status performed somewhat more poorly on a maze task than those who believed they were perceived as medical–surgical patients. Also, those identified as mental patients described the task as more difficult and were rated as somewhat more tense than those who believed they were identified as medical–surgical patients. (The confederates themselves were not able to identify the condition to which their partner had been assigned.)

The studies we have presented clearly suggest that individuals carrying the label of mental illness are indeed stigmatized in our culture (Sarbin & Mancuso, 1970).

Crocetti *et al.* (1972) summarize findings that suggest the picture is somewhat less bleak than the aforementioned studies indicate. For example, the vast majority of respondents (well over 80%) across several studies indicated they would be willing to work with a former mental patient. In one investigation 57%, and in another 54%, said they would be willing to room with an ex-mental patient. Similarly, in one study 51%, and in another 44%, could imagine falling in love with a former mental patient. A third study reported that only 13% definitely rejected the possibility. Although these findings indicate that a history of mental illness is by no means sufficient for complete social rejection, Sarbin and Mancuso (1972) point out that asking about a *former* mental patient is not equivalent to asking about someone who *presently* carries the label. Also, the data do suggest that as intimacy increases (that is, going from working with a former patient to rooming with him or falling in love with him), rejection increases. Finally, if approximately half the respondents indicated they would be willing to room with an ex-patient, then half apparently would not. An important question is this: If a person were described only as a former surgical patient or as normal, would half the population categorically refuse to room with him?

We are strongly inclined to agree with Sarbin (1969) when he notes that the term *mental illness* is used in a demeaning fashion. Those who carry this label are treated as if they possess some highly generalized trait of incompetence. Often there is the implication, at least, that a person considered mentally ill is dangerous, a view that seems to be perpetuated by the popular media (Nunnally, 1961). In actuality, studies indicate that former mental patients are probably no more prone to violence than anyone else (Gulevich & Bourne, 1970).

In summary, the term *mental illness* implies that psychological disorders are fundamentally analogous to physical illness, which does not seem to be the case. The mental illness concept tends to promote attitudes of passivity and helplessness on the part of patients and pessimism on the part of both patients and helpers, which may interfere with treatment. The term *mental illness* is not well defined; factors of a more or less capricious nature may contribute in a major way to people being labeled as mentally ill. Social attitudes toward those carrying the label tend to be negative. In view of these considerations, the concept of mental illness would seem to be of limited value and may well be detrimental to the welfare of the person so labeled. In truth, it is kinder to label someone as mentally ill than to pronounce him guilty of witchcraft and deserving of torture. But in a culture that no longer believes in witchcraft, branding an already troubled person with an ill-defined label that provides little real information and is socially stigmatizing is hardly a humanitarian act.

INSANITY: A LEGAL TERM

In the layman's parlance, *insanity* is a psychological term, suggesting some manner of bizarre or "crazy" behavior, but in modern technical usage it is a legalism. That is, one is judged insane by a court; one is not diagnosed insane by a psychiatrist or a psychologist—although a court involved in making such judgments usually will seek the advice of psychiatrists and psychologists. When a person is declared legally insane he is then considered to be *legally incompetent,* which means he loses a variety of rights, for example, the right to make major financial decisions, or the right to drive an automobile. Usually, the court appoints a guardian to oversee his affairs; the guardian may be a relative or even a bank. Indeed, the individual declared insane is treated by society as incompetent in a very concrete sense. He is, of course, confined to a mental hospital for an indeterminate period of time—until he is "well," which is primarily a medical decision.

Commitments may be civil or criminal. Laws for *civil commitment* vary from state to state; usually there is some criterion specifying the individual to be a *potential* danger to himself or others, though this potential danger is not always supported by objective evidence. A person is subject to *criminal commitment* when there is clear evidence that he has committed a crime, usually a serious one, but when there is evidence that he is not responsible. A person held responsible for a serious crime is incarcerated in a penal institution rather than a mental hospital. How then does society, or more specifically the court, decide whether the perpetrator of a criminal act is or is not responsible for his behavior? A given court operates under a specific guideline or rules often based upon some prior case.

One such early guideline, the M'Naghten rule (set down in England in 1843) states that a person is not to be held criminally responsible for an act provided that he was "labouring under such a defect of reason, from disease of the mind, as not to know the nature and quality of the act he was doing." In the United States, this rule was supplanted by the so-called Durham rule (1869) wherein "an accused is not criminally responsible if his unlawful act was the product of mental disease or mental defect." The Durham rule itself was supplanted by the ALI (American Law Institute) rule wherein "a person is not responsible for criminal conduct if at the time of such conduct as a result of mental disease or defect he lacks substantial capacity either to appreciate the *criminality* of his conduct or to conform his conduct to the requirement of the law." At this writing the ALI rule is in effect in the majority of states, excluding Maine, which operates under the Durham rule, and South Carolina, which uses the M'Naghten rule (see Pierce & Acker, 1973).

Although there are differences between these rules, each is concerned with whether or not a person should be viewed as *blameworthy* for his misbehavior. When a person is blamed for a particular act, there is the implication that he chose, of his own free will, to engage in that act. Some would argue that people are products of heredity and environment, therefore the concept of free will makes little sense. Those who take this position do not believe that antisocial or criminal behavior should be ignored. Rather, they believe that it should be approached with an attitude of problem solving and should not be dealt with in a moralistic or vindictive fashion.

A Scientific Approach to the Study of Psychological Disorders

Although people have been interested in things psychological since the beginning of recorded history, the formal discipline of psychology is of relatively recent vintage. In part, it grew out of philosophy, which was never intended to be scientific in the modern sense of the word. Throughout the field's some 100 years of existence, many theories put forth in the name of psychology have not been especially scientific in nature. Perhaps for these reasons, undergraduate psychology texts and instructors are inclined to stress, almost self-consciously, that psychology *is* a science. What this means, of course, is that psychology follows the scientific method. In our view, what is often not stressed is *why* psychology should be a scientific discipline.

WHY A SCIENTIFIC APPROACH?

Science facilitates the making of decisions. Everyone is confronted with literally hundreds of decisions every day—for instance, whether or not to wear a raincoat. Decisions really involve or reduce to predictions; taking a raincoat indicates that the individual is predicting rainfall with a fairly high probability. Such predictions are usually based upon a sizable number of personal observations. In a person's previous experience, clouds, thunder, and lightning usually have meant rain. Observations of this nature may be thought of as forerunners of science. The observations constitute empirical data, but they are not *systematic*. A systematic approach would involve carefully recording the degree of cloud cover, the presence or absence of thunder, and the presence and amount of rainfall. To the extent that observations are haphazard rather than systematic, a person's ability to make accurate predictions is impaired. Science, which observes and when possible manipulates events in a very systematic fashion, allows for the best possible predictions to be made given the circumstances, thus enabling the consumer of scientific information (all of us) to engage in relatively wise decision-making.

Consider a more pertinent example. You have a family, including two small children. In order to pick up a little extra money, you rent out several rooms of your house. You learn that one would-be roomer is a former mental patient released several months ago from the state hospital. Should you rent the room to him? The critical question is whether or not he is likely to injure members of your family. Now, most people have had considerable opportunity to observe a relationship between clouds, thunder, and rain, but few have had occasion to rent rooms to a reasonably large sample of former mental patients. Here, if you are wise, you will rely on the scientific observations of others—which, as we have noted, indicate that former mental patients are no more likely to be violent than are normals.

In this example, you are confronted with an important decision involving a high potential cost and a lack of relevant personal experience. You are not, unfortunately, confronted with a lack of informational input, since the media so often portray the mentally ill as violent. This is precisely the kind of situation we are frequently confronted with when making decisions about psychological issues. The decisions are important, and we are inclined to get emotional; we do not have a wealth of personal, even unsystematic, observations. Further, we are bombarded with popular myths, which, indeed, may be contradictory. Clearly, in such situations a scientific approach is not only desirable but imperative. It is not our purpose to deify science. The point is that we make important decisions anyway, and we might just as well make them as intelligently as possible!

EMPIRICAL INFORMATION AND LEVELS OF BELIEVABILITY

We have suggested that the nonsystematic observations that collectively define personal experience may be thought of as the forerunner of science. From a practical point of view, this means that the believability of statements such as "Well, in my experience . . ." from individuals not trained in or committed to systematic observation is limited. As it turns out, scientific believability is best seen as on a kind of continuum. At one extreme are unsystematic observations based upon casual personal experience—not totally without value, but not to be relied on. Somewhat more convincing information might come from case histories, reported by people presumably trained in systematic observation, such as might appear in clinical journals. Correlational reports involving objective and careful measurements would be more convincing or believable, but the most credible source of information is the controlled experiment. We shall now discuss each of these approaches.

THE CASE HISTORY APPROACH.　Consider the following proposition: "Librium (a popular tranquilizer) reduces anxiety." Suppose a psychologist or psychiatrist reports that several of his patients stated they felt less anxious after taking 30 milligrams of this drug. There are several reasons for still questioning the value of the drug, given only this information. (Throughout this discussion, let us assume that all observers reporting data are completely honest. This is a bit naive, but it simplifies things.) First of all, we are assuming that he has perfect recall of what his patients said, which is not likely. Second, he is basing his impression entirely on his patients' *verbal reports*. Would other measures of anxiety—for example, physiological measures—have indicated an anxiety reduction? Third, perhaps his patients would have experienced less anxiety had he given them *any* pill; perhaps they expected such positive effects, in part, because he told them in a very convincing manner that it *would* work. Fourth, perhaps the patients would have gotten better simply as a function of the passage of time in the absence of any formal treatment. Fifth, assuming the drug really did reduce anxiety in these few patients, would the effect have been experienced in a larger, more general population?

Now assume that several practitioners, working independently, each report similar positive results. This will provide a noticeable increase in believability. First, it will be difficult to attribute the effects to personal attributes of the dispenser of the drugs, such as persuasiveness. Second, the sample of patients is larger and presumably more representative. Nevertheless, important sources of error or bias remain, pointing to the serious limitations of the case history method.

THE CORRELATION STUDY APPROACH.　Let us assume that we have an objective measure of anxiety considered to be valid. Let us also assume that we carefully monitor (but not manipulate) the amount of drug taken. We now have two *variables,* and a correlation study would assess the degree to which these two variables covaried or correlated.[2] Now suppose the two variables were negatively related. That is, following Librium ingestion less anxiety was observed. Can we

[2] Correlation is usually measured by some variant of what is called the *product–moment* correlation coefficient (abbreviated r). It is a number that may vary between $+1$ and -1. A plus sign means the relationship between the two variables or measures in question is positive: As one increases, the other increases. For example, a moderately large positive correlation exists between IQ and school grade-point average (r is on the order of $+.50$). A minus sign means the relationship between the variables is negative: As one increases, the other decreases (one would expect a negative correlation between grade-point average and the number of class days missed). Correlations of $+1.00$ or -1.00 are said to be perfect correlations and are very rarely encountered. A zero correlation means no relationship between the two variables has been obtained. When using the product–moment correlation coefficient, relationships between the two variables are assumed to be linear.

now conclude that Librium works? Not really, though such a finding certainly suggests that it does. First, the drug may merely be functioning as a pharmacologically ineffective or inert *placebo;* that is, the observed anxiety reduction reflects the user's positive expectations rather than any effect of the drug itself. Second (and this is a problem with most correlation studies), *correlation does not imply causality.* It is possible that people who decide that their condition warrants taking Librium may engage in other anxiety-reducing activities, such as lying down for an hour, which actually account for the observed results.

THE CONTROLLED EXPERIMENTAL APPROACH.   Again let us assume that we have an objective measure of anxiety. Now, from the population of anxious people we randomly select a fairly large number, say 45. *Random* means that any member of the population has an equal chance of being included in our sample. We then assign them, again randomly, to three groups. We now measure the anxiety level for each subject. One group is given a pill (the drug) and not informed what it is or what its effects are likely to be. This is the *experimental* group or *treatment* group. The second group is given a pill that is indistinguishable from the drug in taste and appearance; again, the subjects are provided with no information about its effects. This is the *placebo control* group. As the name implies, its purpose is to control for, or assess, the effects of expectancy or suggestion. The third group is given no pill of any kind. This is the *nontreated control* group. Its purpose is to assess the effects of the initial anxiety measure and the passage of time. After a specified period of time we measure the anxiety level of each subject again. Our experiment is complete.

Suppose we obtain the following results. In comparison to the anxiety measure given at the beginning of the experiment, our experimental or treatment group has shown an average reduction of 10 anxiety units, the placebo subjects have shown a reduction of 3 units, and the nontreated controls have shown a reduction of zero units. Let us further assume that the reduction of anxiety noted for the experimental group is *significantly* greater than that for either of the two control groups.[3] The greater improvement noted for the experimental (drug) group cannot be attributed to a placebo effect (the placebo subjects improved only slightly), or to the passage of time (the nontreated control group failed to improve), or to experimenter characteristics (both the placebo and drug group were exposed to the same experimenters behaving in the same way), or to other treatment the patients administered to themselves or received elsewhere (again because both control groups were as likely to receive extra-experimental treatments as the drug group), or to the effects of the initial measurement of anxiety, again because of the inclusion of the control groups. That is, we have established a genuine cause-and-effect relationship by using the experimental method. Incidentally, note that the placebo subjects did show some improvement relative to

[3] Throughout this text, whenever the term *significant* is used in connection with an experiment it has a very explicit statistical meaning consistent with a widespread convention in psychological research. A result is said to be significant when the likelihood of obtaining such a finding by *chance* is less than one in 20, or .05. One can say that significant results are *reliable* or real.

the nontreated controls. However, given the small magnitude of the placebo effect, it probably would not differ significantly from the average change obtained for the nontreated control subjects.

We have not yet discussed the issue of generalizability of results, which is very important. Briefly, the foregoing results are applicable or generalizable to individuals who are like those people included in the sample. If the individuals in the sample were college sophomores, one should not automatically assume the drug will also work with hospitalized schizophrenics. It *might* be effective with such a group but this must be demonstrated.

Before leaving our discussion of experiments, we will describe a research strategy or approach that does not involve the use of statistics. In clinical psychology it is used mainly by people who engage in *behavior modification* (see Chapter 15). Instead of having subjects assigned to separate experimental and control groups, each subject serves as his own control. First, you establish a baseline for the behavior you wish to change; that is, you determine how often or to what degree the behavior occurs before any kind of treatment. Then you present the treatment and note the results. Then you *remove* the treatment and observe whether the problem behavior returns to the baseline level. If a treatment effect is observed and if this effect disappears when the treatment is removed, you may conclude the treatment was effective. Both this strategy and the aforementioned statistical strategy have strengths and weaknesses, and a discussion of these is beyond our scope here. But both approaches can provide valuable, reliable information.

THE ROLE OF THEORY IN SCIENTIFIC PSYCHOLOGY

A theory in science is a set of interrelated ideas or propositions that tries to explain relationships between observed events and to predict new relationships. Sometimes the terms *theory* and *model* are used interchangeably, although a model more often illustrates a specific case of the more general theory (Atkinson, Bower, & Crothers, 1965; Levine & Burke, 1972). Theories almost always postulate unseen and therefore hypothetical entities, and such entities are usually referred to as *hypothetical constructs*. The term *hypothetical construct* has an academic or esoteric flavor, but constructs are used at least as much by laymen in day-to-day discourse as by scientists. For instance, if you have ever suggested that a friend's popularity may be attributed to that person's pleasing personality, you are postulating a hypothetical "thing" (pleasing personality) that cannot be directly observed but supposedly accounts for why others react toward that person in a particular way. You are engaging in similar behavior when you say that a soldier's battlefield behavior is explicable in terms of his courage, or that a spouse's philandering is explained by his lack of character.

The problem with such hypothetical constructs is that by themselves, they really explain nothing. Thus, if you infer a pleasing personality from a pattern of popularity and then explain that popularity in terms of a pleasing personality, your so-called explanation is completely circular. You might as well say, "She has a pleasing personality because she has a pleasing personality." In fact, the value of theory in psychology has been a matter of controversy for some years. Those who have taken an antitheory position (most notably the famous behaviorist, B. F. Skinner) have done so mainly on the grounds that the constructs of psychologists tend to be circular (see Skinner, 1950, 1953, 1971). The discipline of abnormal psychology is replete with hypothetical constructs (for example, mental illness, ego, libido), and many of these do seem to suffer from circularity. Unfortunately, many writers and practitioners tend to reify these constructs—to treat them as real things rather than as models of reality that must stand or fall on the basis of their usefulness. *Thus, the question is not whether schizophrenia really exists, but whether it is useful to postulate an entity called schizophrenia to account for the behavior of certain people. Similarly, the question is not whether people really do use defense mechanisms to maintain self-esteem, but whether constructs such as defense mechanisms and self-esteem are of real value.* Throughout this book, we will evaluate many such constructs in terms of their usefulness.

What then are the general guidelines for deciding whether a particular construct is of value? There are two. First, the construct must be *measurable*, which means that numbers may be assigned to it in some orderly fashion. Naturally, the behaviors that form the basis for measurement of a construct should not be the same as those the construct purportedly explains, or the construct will be circular. In principle, any construct can be defined in a manner that makes it measurable. However, a major problem is that theorists, especially in the area of personality theory and abnormal psychology, have not always done this. Freud talked about libido and repression but was not at all explicit about how one could go about measuring these constructs, which are basic to classical psychoanalytic theory. Researchers interested in examining the validity of certain Freudian tenets have been forced to define them in explicit ways—but how can one be sure that a particular explicit definition is what Freud *really* meant? Obviously one cannot, and in this sense, many Freudian propositions can never really be proved or disproved.

The second guideline for establishing the value of a hypothetical construct has to do with whether the construct (or more precisely, theoretical statements that incorporate the construct) *accounts for existing facts and allows for novel predictions*. The first part, accounting for existing facts, is not difficult to accomplish. With a little imagination and a sufficient number of constructs one can account for virtually any observable event. What this means is that you can explain *anything* after the fact if you have enough jargon at your disposal. Partly for this reason, but perhaps more because prediction is what science is all about, the second part, predictability, is the crucial element. We have said that theory ought to make for novel predictions. Suppose someone announced a new theory that unequivocally predicted that the sun would rise once a day. One hardly needs a theory to predict anything as obvious as this! On the other hand, when Einstein predicted that the mass of an object would increase with velocity, he was making a very novel prediction. That is, in the absence of such a theory, it simply would not occur to people to try to find out whether mass increases with velocity. Closer to home, in psychology, certain cognitive theorists have postulated hypothetical constructs dealing with the way in which people organize and remember material, which allows for relatively novel predictions. For example, the studies of Bower and his associates (Bower, Clark, Lesgold, & Winenz, 1969) those of Bower (1967), and those of Paivio and his co-workers (Paivio & Yuille, 1967; Yuille & Paivio, 1968) have demonstrated remarkable increases in memory when subjects were instructed in the use of certain organizational strategies or strategies involving visual imagery. Examples of this nature provide a convincing counterargument for those, such as Skinner, who see little value in psychological theorizing.

You may be familiar with the term *operationalism*. The term pertains to the measurement of constructs, and in its narrowest sense, an operational definition is one that equates a particular construct with a set of measurements (Neale & Liebert, 1973). For instance, a narrow operational definition of intelligence might be the administration and scoring of an IQ test. In this context, *intelligence means nothing more than this*. The value of narrow operationalism is that definitions lose any ambiguity. The problem is that such definitions tend to make for theoretical sterility. Constructs, so defined, are not really hypothetical constructs—there is nothing hypothetical about administering and scoring an IQ test. Theoretical or hypothetical constructs have what is described as *surplus meaning* (Hilgard & Bower, 1966), which means that they are not defined merely by a single set of measuring operations; that is, there is more to the construct that a single operational definition. Throughout this text, when the term *construct* is used, we shall be referring to hypothetical constructs unless otherwise indicated.

CLINICAL DIAGNOSIS

Among the major hypothetical constructs of abnormal psychology are the psychiatric diagnostic categories, for instance, neurosis or schizophrenia. We shall examine each of these in detail throughout the next chapters. For the present, we will discuss the two key issues associated with any classification scheme—reliability and validity.

RELIABILITY OF DIAGNOSIS. Reliability in relation to psychiatric diagnosis often means agreement between observers. The obervers in question are professionals, usually psychologists or psychiatrists, and the data usually are percentages of agreements. For example, two psychologists might observe a number of hospitalized patients; each psychologist provides his own diagnosis of each patient. Suppose that psychologist A rated patients 1, 4, 5, and 9 of a 10-patient sample as schizophrenic, and psychologist B rate patients 1, 2, 4, 8, and 9 as schizophrenic. Three patients were diagnosed as schizophrenic by both observers, and both agreed that four patients were not schizophrenic. Thus, there were a total of 7 agreements out of 10, or 70% agreement.[4] This percentage can

---

[4] A difficulty with this particular procedure is that if you have a very small number of schizophrenics and most of the patients are classified as nonschizophrenic by both raters, the percentage agreement will be high even if it is the case that whenever one rater indicates "schizophrenia," the other disagrees. Zubin (1967) has suggested considering in the calculation only those who have been labeled by at least one diagnostician as having the illness. In the present example, doing this reduces the percentage of agreement to 50%.

vary between zero and 100. We shall discuss reliability findings when we deal with each of the diagnostic categories in Chapters 3 through 10. For our present purpose, it is sufficient to point out that reliability varies considerably with diagnosis, generally being higher for psychosis than for neurosis and for general categories (e.g., schizophrenia) than for specific categories (e.g., paranoid schizophrenia).

Another approach to reliability involves assessment of temporal stability. Here the question is this: What is the likelihood that a patient with a given diagnosis will receive the same diagnosis at a later time (usually during a second hospital admission)? Available data (Zubin, 1967) again suggest somewhat greater reliability for psychosis than for neurosis. One risk in employing temporal stability as a measure of reliability is that the patient's behavior may actually change. That is, inconsistency in diagnosis may not necessarily reflect unreliable judgment on the part of the rater.

VALIDITY OF DIAGNOSIS.   There are many definitions or types of validity (see Chronback, 1960; Horst, 1966; Ley, 1972). The four most commonly used (and they are not intended to compete with each other) are *predictive validity, concurrent validity, content validity,* and *construct validity.* Zubin (1967) has related each of these to the issue of psychological diagnosis. A diagnosis has predictive validity to the extent that it allows for correct predictions regarding the outcome of the disorder, the most effective selection of therapy (what works), and the appearance of other correlated behaviors. Concurrent validity means that other measures (those other than the psychiatric interview) lead to the same diagnosis. Content validity refers to whether or not characteristics typically thought of as belonging to a particular diagnosis are sought in making the diagnosis. For example, since interpersonal withdrawal is often thought of as an important attribute of schizophrenia, seeking information pertaining to this during an interview would add to the content validity of the diagnosis. Construct validity means the degree to which theoretical or defining attributes of a particular diagnosis can be verified objectively. For example, an objective measure of interpersonal withdrawal could provide a degree of construct validity to the diagnosis.

Note that prediction is central to each of the definitions of validity, with the exception of content validity. Content validity in isolation may be quite meaningless. It is only of value in the presence of validity as established by at least one of the other definitions. Thus, it is of no importance to say that a psychologist sampled one of the behaviors that defines a particular diagnosis, if the diagnosis tells nothing additional about the subject's behavior. In short, if a diagnosis provides no new information about the way a person is likely to act, it is clearly of no value.

Therefore, in dealing with psychological classification, as in dealing with any theoretical construct, the critical question is not whether the category exists or is real, but whether it is useful in making predictions. To ask whether modern psychology or psychiatry "believes" in schizophrenia would be silly. On the other hand, it is most productive to ask whether postulating and defining an entity called schizophrenia will lead to better predictions—and ultimately better decisions—about anyone given this label. Much of this book will be devoted to answering just such questions.

THE RELATIONSHIP BETWEEN VALIDITY AND RELIABILITY. It should be obvious by now why it is essential that diagnosis be valid. But what about reliability? The answer, simply stated, is that validity presupposes reliability. In order for a diagnostic category or any other measure to be valid, it must be reliable. The converse of this is not true: It is quite possible for something to be totally reliable and not at all valid.

To illustrate, consider the proposition: Dogs generally bite people. Suppose we wish to establish whether this is true or not. Let us assume that we have a reliable measure of "being bitten." But now let us assume that any two observers, when presented with a large number of common domestic animals, cannot agree as to which ones are dogs; but they can agree that certain of the animals do bite people with great regularity. Can it be possible to establish any real relationship between being-a-dog and biting? Obviously the answer is negative; the answer would also be negative if people could reliably agree on what constituted a dog, but not on being bitten. Thus, making a valid statement about any class of organisms (dogs, corporation presidents, schizophrenics, mosquitoes) assumes they can be identified in a reliable manner.

Standard Psychiatric Classification

There are many systems for classification of psychological disorders in use throughout the world (Zubin, 1967, reports there are at least 50). In the United States, the most influential system was put forth in 1952 by the American Psychiatric Association (APA) and later revised by that body in 1968, in concert with the World Health Organization and incorporating ideas contained in the International Classification of Diseases. The APA classification schemes are founded to a considerable degree on Emil Kraepelin's *Lehrbuch der Psychiatrie* ("Textbook of Psychiatry"), which first appeared in Germany in 1883. Thus, such psychiatric diagnostic schema are sometimes referred to as *Kraepelinian*.

The American Psychiatric Association diagnostic system is contained in *The Diagnostic and Statistical Manual of Mental Disorders—II*; the Roman numeral II merely indicates that it is a revised version (1968) of the 1952 manual. The abbreviations DSM-I and DSM-II will be used in this book. The DSM-II disorders are divided into 10 major groupings; most of these groupings or categories will be dealt with in later chapters.

THE VALIDITY OF THE SYNDROME CONCEPT

A syndrome is a collection, constellation, or set of maladaptive responses assumed to "go together." The primary question about syndromes is whether the defining behaviors regularly are found in the same persons (at least with a high probability). The construct validity of any syndrome is a matter for experimental investigation, and data relevant to this issue will be presented throughout this book.

Summary

In this chapter we have dealt with certain basic issues central to the study of abnormal behavior. One fundamental issue is the definition of abnormality. There are many different conceptions of abnormality; in our view, the most useful conception or definition derives from popular usage, since the term *abnormal* is as much a popular or lay term as it is a technical term. We concluded that, in general, when people describe behavior as abnormal, that behavior is perceived as deviant from social norms and in some sense constitutes a threat; the threat may be physical or economic or even political.

The medical model of psychological abnormality evolved from the medical or disease model of physical illness. The critical assumption in the medical model is that some inner disorder gives rise to abnormal or pathological behavior. Earlier versions of the medical model assumed the inner disorder was physiological or organic in nature. For the most part, modern usage is broader than this: The medical model includes any conception of abnormal behavior that postulates that such behavior arises from internal factors, whether physical or psychological. Thus, there are many versions of the medical model, some having more scientific value than others; therefore, a blanket evaluation is not in order.

The concept of mental illness, which developed concurrently with early versions of the medical model, is of questionable scientific value. It is not well defined, and often leads to an unrealistically pessimistic view on the part of the person given this label as well as society at large. The social factors that lead to labeling a person as mentally ill are often precarious, and in our view the concept does more harm than good.

We discussed the value of a scientific approach to psychological abnormality, pointing to the key role of prediction in science. We examined ways in which information of a scientific nature may be obtained, illustrated the somewhat limited value of the case history approach, and outlined certain critical elements in a controlled experiment. We also discussed the role of theory in scientific psychology, again emphasizing that theory is indeed useful, but only to the extent that it allows for prediction. In abnormal psychology, clinical diagnostic categories are theoretical constructs of major importance. We have pointed to the importance of reliability of diagnosis, which is necessary in order for such a construct to have validity or utility.

II

TRADITIONAL CATEGORIES
OF PSYCHOPATHOLOGY

3

The Neuroses
I: Introduction,
Anxiety Neurosis, and Anxiety

A Brief History of the Label

According to Knoff (1970), the term *neurosis* was introduced by a Scottish physician, William Cullen, in 1769 in his *System of Nosology*. For Cullen, *neurosis* referred to any disease resulting from "disordered motions or sensations of the nervous system [Knoff, 1970, p. 80]." Any disorder that today might be labeled psychotic, neurotic, psychosomatic, or neurological was included. Kraepelin, in the famous fifth edition of his textbook on classification (published in 1896; see Knoff, 1970, p. 83), provided a more restrictive definition of neurosis that is quite consistent with modern usage. He also distinguished between neurosis and psychosis. Freud (see Veith, 1965) complicated matters somewhat by distinguishing between what he termed *actual neuroses* (neurasthenia and anxiety neurosis) and *psychoneuroses* (hysteria and obsessive–compulsive neuroses). Although most modern writers do not make this particular distinction, Freud's theorizing regarding the causes of neurosis had a profound impact on how a sizable portion of the psychiatric and psychological establishments use the term.

MODERN USAGE

Most modern writers define neurosis as a pattern of maladaptive or self-defeating behavior usually marked by high levels of *anxiety*. (Some define it in terms of emotion rather than behavior.) We will have a good deal more to say about anxiety later in this chapter, but for the present we can view it as a state of unpleasant or aversive emotional arousal (what a person experiences when he is afraid or "uptight"). Typically, neurotic reactions are seen as not grossly incapacitating. People labeled as neurotic are not usually viewed as requiring hospitalization, although some neurotics do suffer from severe behavioral debilitation—for instance, an agoraphobic housewife who is so fearful of venturing outside that she is chronically housebound. Not uncommonly it is suggested (e.g., Zax & Cowen, 1972) that neurotics, in contrast to psychotics, maintain good contact with reality. *Reality contact* is a term that is not at all well defined. We have described the problems associated with "perception of reality" as a possible criterion for abnormality in Chapter 2.

Neuroses and the Reliability of Diagnoses

In Chapter 2 we stressed the paramount importance of reliability of diagnoses. We indicated that the goal of any scientific or therapeutic endeavor was ultimately to make predictions. We further stated that validity in making such predictions presupposed reliability of diagnoses. Unfortunately, existing data about the reliability with which the various neuroses are diagnosed are quite disconcerting. Zubin (1967) has summarized several studies dealing with this issue. For example, Kreitman (1961) reported only 27% agreement in relation to the diagnosis *anxiety state,* whereas Beck (1962) reported 55% agreement. For *reactive depression,* Kreitman (1961) reported 18% agreement; Beck (1962) reported 63% agreement.[1]

Related to the issue of reliability of diagnoses is stability over time. Zubin (1967) has also summarized data pertinent to this question. Hunt, Wittson, and Hunt (1953) reported a diagnoses–rediagnoses agreement of 18% for anxiety reactions and only 15% for hysteria, with a corresponding figure of 24% for total neuroses (presumably all neuroses combined). Unfortunately, no test–retest time periods are reported. Kaelbling and Volpe (1963) reported diagnoses–rediagnoses agreement of 42% for depression (with intervals of 1 day to 26 weeks) and a figure of 49% (again, 1-day to 26-week intervals) for total psychoneuroses.

There are several general comments pertinent to these data. First, given the paramount importance of the issue of diagnostic reliability, the amount of available data is scant indeed. Second, when comparisons across studies are possible, the variability is very great. Third, for many of the classic neurotic categories such as phobic reactions and obsessive–compulsive reactions, data appear nonexistent. Fourth, the data, viewed as a whole, are generally unimpressive.

[1] Some of these figures have been derived from the original data by Zubin. Percentage of agreement is based upon the number of patients receiving the same diagnosis by two different diagnosticians, relative to the total number of patients receiving diagnostic labels by the pair.

POSSIBLE SOURCES OF LOW DIAGNOSTIC RELIABILITY

PROBLEMS INHERENT IN THE CLASSIFICATION SYSTEMS. Perhaps the main difficulty stems from inadequacies inherent in the classification systems themselves (that is, systems such as DSM-I, 1952, and DSM-II, 1968). The data of Ward, Beck, Mendelson, Mock, and Erbaugh (1962) support this view. They report that most disagreements in diagnosis reflect problems associated with the nosological (i.e., classification) system. Relatively few disagreements reflect an observable inconsistency in the behavior of the psychiatrists. As Costello (1970) and others have noted, the syndromes or classes tend to be ill defined. Costello's comments appear to be directed at the entire nosological system, not merely the neuroses. However, even a cursory examination of DSM-II (1968) reveals a combination of built-in ambiguity and symptomatic overlap across different types of neuroses, which makes accurate differential diagnosis an onerous task indeed. For instance, with respect to phobic neurosis, according to DSM-II,

> His apprehension may be experienced as faintness, fatigue, palpitations, perspiration, nausea, tremor, and even panic. Phobias are generally attributed to fears displaced to the phobic object or a situation from some other object of which the patient is unaware [p. 40].

Note that for a specific fear reaction to be classified as a phobia, there must be evidence that it is in fact *displaced* from some other object that is the more basic source of anxiety. But how is one to know this, especially since the patient himself is unaware of the "true" source of his anxiety? Suppose, for instance, a therapist is presented with the case of a 12-year-old child who had been attacked and severely injured by a German shepherd dog at age 6 and has been terrified of all dogs ever since. Must the diagnostician look for something other than the traumatic experience with the German shepherd—that is, some more basic fear, which has been displaced to dogs—before he can apply the label *phobia*? It would seem so. As you may know, the concept that displacement is inherent in phobic neuroses comes from classical psychoanalytic theory.

Now, consider the DSM-II definition of anxiety neurosis:

> This neurosis is characterized by anxious overconcern extending to panic and frequently associated with somatic symptoms. Unlike Phobic neurosis, anxiety may occur under any circumstances and is not restricted to specific situations or objects. This disorder must be distinguished from normal apprehension or fear, which occurs in realistically dangerous situations [p. 39].

In terms of anxiety and somatic symptoms, anxiety neurosis has much in common with phobic neurosis. However, we are told that in the former, anxiety *may* occur under any circumstances. Consider for the moment a person who might be described as a *people phobic;* that is, he is afraid of just about everyone. Unless he lives a hermitlike existence or he lives in a very rural area, he will be exposed to the phobic stimuli almost constantly. You can easily see how he might be diagnosed as suffering from anxiety neurosis since his distress appears to be omnipresent. As we examine the other neurotic syndromes, similar problems inherent in the various diagnostic categories will become apparent.

One major difficulty with such classification systems is this: Although any given syndrome is assumed to consist of several coexisting symptoms, the number of symptoms that must be present in order for the diagnostician to impart the particular label is often unspecified (see Lorr, Klett, & McNair, 1963). As Costello (1970) points out, frequently only one or two symptoms are used in making a diagnosis when in fact the particular syndrome or category may be defined by many symptoms. Then there is the question of the degree to which a person must be disturbed before his disturbance is elevated to the status of a neurosis. For example, DSM-II suggests that somnambulism (sleepwalking) is an example of dissociative hysterical neurosis, but nothing is said of frequency. Thus, would an average of one sleepwalking episode a year warrant labeling a person as hysteric? This, it would appear, is an exercise left to the diagnostician! In truth, most writers are inclined to see neurotic behavior on a kind of continuum. That is, all of us may be said to suffer from some neurosis to some degree (Cattell & Scheier, 1961). Perhaps for this reason, proponents of the traditional classification systems are unwilling to go out on a limb to the extent of providing behavioral cutoff points that clearly separate the neurotic from the normal. However, given this state of affairs, statements such as the following are not very meaningful:

> The incidence of neuroses is difficult to determine, *but it has been estimated that there are at least 10 million individuals in the United States who might be classified as neurotic* [Coleman, 1972; italics added].

PROBLEMS ASSOCIATED WITH PEOPLE MAKING DIAGNOSES. If, as Ward *et al.* (1962) suggest, most of the inadequacy associated with nosological systems is inherent in the systems themselves, those doing the diagnoses also contribute to the obvious lack of reliability. Clearly, all diagnosticians (e.g., clinical psychologists, psychiatrists) do not receive identical training. Thus, a behaviorist not trained in traditional nosology will rarely, if ever, use labels like *conversion hysteria* or *neurasthenic neurosis,* whereas a dynamically oriented clinician, unfamiliar with the language of the behavior therapist, would not be expected to assess a patient in terms of the formal language of learning theory.

Those charged with making clinical diagnoses, being human, are not without bias or prejudice. Such bias is often based upon unsubstantiated clinical lore. To illustrate, although there is evidence to the contrary, many consider conversion hysteria (see Chapter 4) to be an exclusively female disorder. A diagnostician imbued with this lore would not be likely to use this particular neurotic typing for a male patient. On the other hand, were the diagnostician free of this bias, he might indeed perceive in his male patient characteristics of conversion hysteria. Thus, different biases may lead to different diagnoses.

For reasons more related to tradition than to logic, there is a strange and rather pervasive insistence on providing each client or patient with a so-called *primary diagnosis*. That is, the person examined is assumed to suffer mainly from only one of the many possible clinical syndromes. At the bottom of a patient's chart one might read the following: *Primary Diagnosis: Neurotic Depressive Reaction* or *Primary Diagnosis: Hysterical Reaction, Conversion Type*. Pigeonholing the patient in this manner has the obvious effect of masking or downplaying other potentially relevant aspects of his behavior, although it no doubt provides many a clinician with a comfortable feeling of certainty or closure. Insisting on a single primary diagnosis can only have the effect of lowering reliability of diagnoses, given the ambiguity present in the classification system. Consider the clinician who is presented with a patient who might be diagnosed as suffering from a *neurotic depressive reaction* or from *neurasthenic neurosis* (all these terms will be defined as subsequent points throughout this text). He is 60% certain that the first diagnosis is correct and labels his client accordingly. A second clinician presented with the same patient perceives the same two alternatives, but he is 60% certain that the *second* diagnosis is correct and so labels his patient neurasthenic. Thus, for the first clinician the client is reported as depressed, and for the second, the same client is described as neurasthenic. The end product is disagreement. If each had ignored the practice of providing a primary diagnosis, both would have described the patient as depressed and neurasthenic—and we would have diagnostic agreement.

The problems we have raised in relation to diagnostic reliability are applicable to the other broad psychiatric categories, such as schizophrenia and organic disorders. However, the traditional approach to the classification of neurotic disorders is particularly vulnerable. On the other hand, the traditional neurotic categories have been with us for nearly a century. Whatever their shortcomings, very probably they will continue in widespread usage for many years to come. Thus, they cannot be ignored simply on the grounds that they are flawed.

The remainder of this chapter deals with anxiety neurosis, one of the eight traditional neurotic classifications, followed by a general discussion of anxiety. In Chapter 4, six of the remaining seven categories are described and evaluated. On empirical and theoretical grounds, but also as a matter of convenience, depressive neurosis is presented in Chapter 6.

Anxiety Neurosis

Let us look again at the DSM-II definition of anxiety neurosis:

> This neurosis is characterized by anxious overconcern extending to panic and frequently associated with somatic symptoms. Unlike Phobic neurosis, anxiety may occur under any circumstances and is not restricted to specific situations or objects. This disorder must be distinguished from normal apprehension or fear, which occurs in realistically dangerous situations   [1968, p. 39].

According to this classic view, the person is anxious most of the time and there are intermittent periods of panic. Since the person is assumed to be unable to pinpoint the source of his discomfort, the anxiety is often labeled *free-floating* (Buss, 1966). Thus, the anxiety neurotic is seen as someone who "doesn't know

Some anxious moments are a part of everyday life. This young Hungarian girl clings to her mother's hands for one last touch of reassurance before beginning her first day of school. (David Seymour, Magnum)

what he fears, hence doesn't know which way to run [Buss, 1966, p. 52]." The anxiety neurotic has been described as a person who is overly sensitive to what others think, who experiences difficulty making decisions and is highly perfectionistic (Zax & Cowen, 1972). In addition, he may be restless, experience insomnia and loss of appetite, and feel inadequate (CRM, 1972).

In terms of common usage, this category covers a lot of ground. Perhaps this is why it is one of the most commonly diagnosed disorders. After reviewing several studies, Coleman (1972) suggests that between 30 and 40% of all neurotics receive this label, though he admits this is a rough estimate. As we have noted, figures of this nature should not be taken too seriously because of problems of reliability of diagnosis.

As we have intimated, the assumption that anxiety cannot be traced to an external source is questionable. This assumption stems from another assumption; namely, that the anxiety arises from some very faint awareness of frightening thoughts or impulses. This is essentially the psychoanalytic view. The impulses typically are thought of as aggressive or sexual in nature, and they conflict with what the individual has been taught is proper or safe. His primary method of coping with such unacceptable thoughts or impulses is *repression,* which means forcing something out of awareness and into the *unconscious* mind. You have no doubt heard the term *defense mechanism;* repression is one of the most fundamental of the many defense mechanisms postulated by psychoanalytic writers. From their point of view, the anxiety neurotic suffers because the repression is not completely effective (if it were, he would not be anxious) and because he does not have other defense mechanisms readily available. If the "successful neurotic" is one who is able to ward off anxiety with defense mechanisms, the poor anxiety neurotic must be viewed as a failure.

Now, before you commit to memory the foregoing formulation, let us stress that (contrary to what many texts imply) *this is merely a point of view*. It is neither a self-evident truth nor a theory founded upon a vast amount of empirical evidence. It rests upon several constructs (defense mechanisms, repression, unacceptable impulses erupting from the inner recesses of one's psyche, the unconscious), which in our judgment are of questionable value. Again, please remember that articulate spokesmen for views differing from ours present their arguments in Part IV, on treatment approaches; psychoanalytic formulations are covered in Chapter 16.

Our main point is that it is quite possible to operate on another set of assumptions. For example, assume that the distress of the so-called anxiety neurotic is not free-floating at all, but is tied to specific external events that happen to occur with a high frequency. The example given earlier in this chapter was of a person afraid of people. Let us assume that this person has learned to be fearful in a relatively straightforward way—for instance, the people in his immediate environment have been consistently cruel to him. A psychologist or psychiatrist operating under this set of assumptions is not likely to use the label *anxiety neurotic;* in characterizing people who seem anxious a good deal of the time, he is likely to use the term *phobic* rather freely. We, as behaviorally oriented psychologists, are partial to this second point of view, which emphasizes the importance of external events in controlling human behavior. In our clinical experience, we have never encountered a patient or client who could be given the label *anxiety neurotic* in a clear-cut manner. It has always been possible to obtain information indicating that the anxiety level did, indeed, vary considerably from situation to situation, and in a fairly predictable way. Obviously, what one "sees" in a clinical situation depends partly on one's theoretical orientation, and behaviorists are no exception.

The following case history, taken from Rimm's files, illustrates the relationship between feelings of distress and external events in a patient diagnosed as an anxiety neurotic.

■ J.R., age 40, had spent most of his adult life in a mental institution in the Southwest. The diagnosis, unchanged throughout his many hospitalizations, was anxiety neurosis. At age 18 he entered college, intending to become a minister. Although above average in intelligence he found college distasteful and after 1 year he dropped out. He soon married and is the father of two children. Interestingly, his wife, who had been diagnosed as schizophrenic, was not hospitalized, while J.R., a neurotic, remained in an institution.

His chief complaint was what he described as ever-present anxiety. Often his halting speech, distraught facial expression, and tremulous bodily movements suggested intense anxiety. He also reported physical complaints, including severe leg cramps, and difficulty passing urine. He often reported severe insomnia.

It was clear that J.R. had accepted the traditional view of anxiety neurosis; he seemed unable or unwilling to see any connection between external events and his level of anxiety. Yet, from all observable indications, his distress was markedly influenced by external events, and in a strikingly predictable manner. He showed much more anxiety after spending time with his wife, who most observers described as a shrew. He became visibly shaken whenever the subject of his children was broached; he believed himself to be inadequate as a father. He evidenced a reaction best described as panic whenever his therapist raised the possibility that he might get better and leave the hospital. He had no history of employment, his family relationships were highly unsatisfactory and his only friends were in the hospital. When interacting with his friends, or engaging in nondemanding routine hospital activities, he appeared to be relatively calm.

It is likely that no two individuals will show the same degree of emotion, given the same set of environmental stimuli. The noted British psychologist Hans Eysenck has stressed such individual differences in his general theory of neurotic behavior (1961).[2] Eysenck has also suggested that people differ with respect to how readily their anxiety can be conditioned to external stimuli. Eysenck assumes that both emotional reactivity and conditionability are, to a large extent, inherited traits.

Let us assume for the moment that Eysenck's views regarding inherited traits of emotional reactivity and conditionability are essentially correct. A person who does show excessive emotional reactivity to a variety of specific situations might meaningfully be seen as suffering from anxiety neurosis, assuming of course that the characteristic emotion is anxiety. A person predisposed to acquire conditioned anxiety responses to a variety of specific situations might also legitimately be labeled as an anxiety neurotic. In both cases the anxiety is not free-floating but is related to external events in a more or less orderly fashion. Such a characterization of anxiety neurosis differs from that found in DSM-II, since external events are assumed to be critical. It also differs from a strict learning or

---

[2] Actually, what Eysenck proposes is a three-dimensional view of personality. The three dimensions or traits are emotional reactivity, conditionability, and psychoticism. An exposition of this provocative and controversial theory is beyond the scope of the present text; the interested reader is referred to Eysenck and Eysenck (1968).

behavioral view, inasmuch as underlying traits or predispositions are presumed to be involved.

Whether hereditary predispositions do play a major role in anxiety neurosis, as well as in other types of neuroses, is a critical question. Studies examining the importance of genetic factors in neuroses have been few (see Rosenthal, 1970); in general, the results have only weakly supported the role of heredity. However, the issue is far from being resolved.

By definition, the construct of anxiety is critically related to anxiety neurosis. However, anxiety is thought to be fundamental to the other neurotic disorders as well. In addition, anxiety plays an important role in theories dealing with other major classes of psychopathology, such as schizophrenia and psychophysiological disorders—as you shall learn. The term *anxiety* is now in common usage. But what precisely is anxiety? We shall now explore this issue at some length.

Anxiety

When we say that anxiety is a useful construct, we are really saying that knowing how anxious a person is in a given situation tells you something about other aspects of his behavior in that situation. For example, suppose that you have an indication (other than the person's overt motor behavior) that he is very anxious around large dogs. One obvious prediction is that, relative to the average person, this individual is more likely to remove himself physically from the presence of such a dog. A second prediction is that if you do something to that person to lower his anxiety level in the presence of dogs, he will be less avoidant (for a discussion of such anxiety-reducing procedures, see Chapter 15).

It turns out, as it almost always does in psychology, that things are not quite this simple. In the last paragraph we mentioned an anxiety measure, and you may have inferred that there is some universally agreed-upon, absolute measure of or definition of anxiety. Would that this were true! The situation in fact is almost the opposite (see Cattell & Scheier, 1961; Maher, 1966; Sarbin, 1964). In the first place, the psychological literature describes many different ways of measuring anxiety—Cattell and Scheier (1961) report 120 different assessment procedures.

By itself, the fact that there are many different assessment procedures is not a bad thing, although obviously it makes for some confusion. The problem is that the various measures are not, in general, highly intercorrelated (Maher, 1966; Martin & Sroufe, 1970). Such considerations have led certain authors, such as Ullmann and Krasner (1969/1975), virtually to exclude the construct of anxiety from their conceptualization of abnormal human behavior. By now you should be well aware of our willingness to abandon any and all constructs of abnormal psychology that are of very limited (or negative) value, no matter how entrenched they happen to be. In our view, anxiety is deserving of a more positive fate. A willingness on the part of researchers to confront rather than evade this construct has led to a variety of theoretically interesting and clinically relevant findings, and this really is all one can ask of a theoretical construct. For example, you may be familiar with the term *systematic desensitization*. It is a method developed by Joseph Wolpe (1958, 1969) for reducing or eliminating phobic responding; we describe it in detail in Chapter 15. Basically, the client is required to imagine whatever it is he fears, while engaging in an activity antithetical to anxiety (usually a state of muscle relaxation). As we make clear in Chapter 15, a good deal of clinical and experimental evidence supports the validity of the technique. The question we would raise is this: What is the likelihood that Wolpe, or anyone else for that matter, would have developed such a technique, while at the same time disavowing anxiety? We think the likelihood is small.[3]

Many experiments have compared measures of anxiety with measures of performance in human subjects taking a variety of tests. These tests have involved memory, simple conditioning, complex learning, and perception (see Martin & Sroufe, 1970). We will summarize some of this work later in this chapter. Many of these findings are intrinsically interesting and some have obvious practical implications. Again, we would like to point out that if the construct of anxiety had been "outlawed" by the research community, these experiments would not have been done, and we would have been deprived of some important and useful findings.

ANXIETY VERSUS FEAR. We use these terms synonymously. Such use is characteristic of behaviorally oriented psychologists—excepting those who are so behaviorally oriented they refuse to consider *any* theoretically based mediating process such as anxiety. More traditional writers often do make a distinction. For example, Kleinmuntz (1974) states that "fear refers to a reality-based response to a frightening stimulus or situation; anxiety is a *vague fear* in the sense that it is not a response to an identifiable object [p. 158]." Our view is that fear (or anxiety) is almost always attached to identifiable objects, and we do not consider this distinction useful. Our approach to anxiety is by no means novel (for example, see Mandler & Sarason, 1952).

The term *anxiety* is in common use today, among laymen as well as psychologists and psychiatrists. Surprisingly, it was rarely found in standard texts until the late 1930s, according to Sarbin (1964). "It was a result of Freud's writings about *Angst*, translated as anxiety, that the term now has wide currency [p. 634]."

COMMON MEASURES OF ANXIETY

PHYSIOLOGICAL RESPONSES. Many researchers who find the concept of anxiety a useful one think of it in terms of a set of physiological or psychophysiological responses. It is not surprising, therefore, that such responses are often measured in research pertaining to anxiety. These measures or responses are not

---

[3] This is not to say that all Wolpe's *theoretical* notions about systematic desensitization, or anxiety in particular, are correct; this is not the case (for example; see Rimm & Masters, 1974).

thought of as *defining* anxiety but rather as a means of *detecting* anxiety. One could, of course, arbitrarily define anxiety as the magnitude of any one of the commonly used responses. This would illustrate what we referred to in Chapter 2 as *narrow operationalism*. The problem with this approach is that such physiological changes are often brought about by stimuli or events that one would not expect to give rise to anxiety (Weinar, 1962), for example, stimuli leading to sexual arousal or novel stimuli. To illustrate, the galvanic skin response (the GSR, also sometimes referred to as the *electrodermal response*) is perhaps the most commonly used single physiological measure. Electrodes are attached to two of the subject's fingers; wires from these electrodes lead to a very sensitive amplification system. For reasons that are not entirely understood, when a person becomes emotional there is typically an increase in the electrical conductivity of the skin, and this is what the GSR reflects. The amplified GSR is transmitted from the amplification system to a pen resting upon a continuously moving supply of graph paper, thereby providing a visual record of the subject's response. This is the general procedure employed when any physiological measure is taken. But although external events that frighten most people do give rise to an increase in skin conductivity, so do many other events, such as novelty, orientation responses (Sokolov, 1963), and events designed to induce anger (Ax, 1953). That is, an increase in GSR does not *necessarily* mean that the individual has just experienced a fear-arousing event.

Nonetheless, a sizable number of studies have demonstrated that when people are exposed to fearsome situations the expected GSR changes indeed occur. For example, Geer (1966) found that people who rated themselves as spider phobics showed a greater GSR to a photo of a spider than did subjects who were not fearful of spiders. McGlynn, Puhr, Gaynor, and Perry (1973) obtained similar results when snake-avoidant subjects were compared with those who were not snake-avoidant. In an imaginative study, Epstein (1962) worked with novice parachutists. His subjects showed a greater GSR before a jump than after. In addition, the parachutists showed a greater GSR to stimuli related to jumping (pictures, words) on the day of a jump than when a jump was 2 weeks away. Among groups of patients, people rated as anxious show greater GSR activity than patients in other diagnostic categories (Lader, 1967; Lader & Wing, 1964). There also is evidence that when efforts are made to reduce the subject's anxiety level, for example, by using deep muscle relaxation (Lehrer, 1972; Rimm, Kennedy, Miller, & Tchida, 1971), a decrease in GSR occurs.

Another frequently employed measure is heart rate. You have no doubt observed your own heart pounding furiously when you are suddenly confronted with a frightening or highly aversive situation, and there is ample experimental evidence that this is a typical response (see Graham & Clifton, 1966). The anticipation of pain may cause an increase in heart rate (Spielberger & Hodges, 1966). As with the GSR, there is evidence suggesting that anxious patients have higher heart rates than less anxious patients (Malmo & Shagass, 1952) or normals (Wishner, 1953), and that effective therapy with fearful subjects reduces heart rate when the subject is confronted with a stressful situation (Lehrer, 1972).

Interestingly, Lacey (1959) found that activities such as mental arithmetic, not usually thought of as anxiety inducing, result in an increase in heart rate.

Two measures used somewhat less frequently are blood pressure and rate or depth of respiration. Actually there are two measures usually associated with blood pressure, the systolic pressure (associated with a heart beat) and diastolic pressure (the pressure between beats). Somewhat elevated systolic pressure has been found in anxious patients (Malmo & Shagass, 1952) or in normals when they were exposed to stress (Ax, 1953).

With respect to respiration, you may well recall experiencing changes of some sort, such as rapid breathing, gasping for breath, or a brief cessation of breathing, when confronted with a frightening situation. Studies by Malmo and Shagass (1949) and Rimm and Litvak (1969) support this. In the experience of the present authors, respiration changes are very often observed when clients discuss issues or areas of particular concern. The pattern appears to involve an initial catching or holding of the breath, followed either by a sigh or relatively rapid breathing.

In addition to the foregoing four measures, others are sometimes employed as indicators of anxiety, including perspiration on the palms—literally, *sweaty palms* (Lore, 1966); activity of the voluntary muscles (e.g., Malmo, 1966); stomach activity (Wolf & Wolff, 1946, in a classic study reported decreases in acid output and stomach movements associated with anxiety); and pupillary reactivity. Among these additional measures, voluntary muscle activity may well be the most promising. We base this statement on research (for example, Malmo, 1966; Sainsbury, 1964) and on our own clinical experience and the clinical experiences of others. Clients who undergo deep muscle relaxation (described in Chapter 15), a series of exercises aimed at relaxing the major voluntary muscles, almost always report marked decreases in felt anxiety. It is interesting that the term *uptight,* which connotes muscle tension, has become so popular over the past decade as a synonym for anxiety.

We mentioned earlier that people who do anxiety research often have some notion of an underlying physiological mechanism that gives rise to anxious behavior. Throughout the history of modern psychology, the underlying psychophysiological mechanism or system most often linked to anxiety has been the *sympathetic* nervous system. Anatomists divide the nervous system into three parts: the central nervous system (CNS), which includes the brain and spinal cord; the somatic nervous system, which serves the senses as well as the voluntary muscles; and the autonomic nervous system, which controls or innervates the heart, glands, blood vessels, and other internal organs. The autonomic nervous system is divided into two parts, the sympathetic nervous system and the parasympathetic nervous system. As we have just suggested, it is heightened activity of the sympathetic nervous system that psychologists (and many laymen) associate with anxiety. There are many bodily changes associated with increased sympathetic nervous activity, including increases in heart rate and blood pressure, increased blood circulation to the large voluntary muscles, dryness of the mouth, and dilation of the pupils of the eyes, to mention but a few. You may be familiar with the term *adrenalin*. One of the effects of increased sympathetic nervous activity is to stimulate the adrenal glands to secret increased amounts of adrenalin—also called *epinephrine*—which has the effect of continuing the various bodily changes brought about by sympathetic nervous stimulation.

Keeping this in mind, pretend for the moment that anxiety (fearfulness, feeling uptight) is a direct result of increased sympathetic nervous activity. You would predict that if you were to inject a person with epinephrine, he would behave in a more anxious manner. This is precisely what Stanley Schacter and his colleagues tested (Schacter & Singer, 1962; Schacter & Wheeler, 1962). In one experiment, they found that subjects given epinephrine were made either more angry or more elated than the controls, depending upon whether the model they were exposed to behaved in a manner that was clearly angry or elated. In another experiment, individuals who received epinephrine prior to observing part of a humorous film laughed more than subjects who had not received epinephrine. Neither of these studies suggests that epinephrine causes people to feel anxious. Rather, they suggest that whatever emotion is called for by external circumstances will be exaggerated by increased amounts of epinephrine. These findings, together with the results of certain animal studies (for example, Wynne & Solomon, 1955) seem to indicate that one cannot define anxiety merely in terms of activity of the sympathetic nervous system. However, when a person says he is anxious or fearful, or acts in such a manner, he will show evidence of increased sympathetic nervous activity. In other words, increased sympathetic activity is part of the anxiety response, but such activity does not necessarily *cause* a person to experience anxiety.

ANXIETY QUESTIONNAIRES. Although the popular Minnesota Multiphasic Personality Inventory (the MMPI) does not have a separate anxiety scale per se, clinical psychologists do use some of its scales, such as the so-called psychasthenia scale (see Dahlstrom & Welsh, 1960; Welsh, 1952), to assess anxiety. The first inventory designed specifically to measure anxiety was published by Taylor in 1953. It is called the Taylor Manifest Anxiety Scale (TMAS); many of the items were taken from the MMPI. The following are three sample items:

I frequently find myself worrying about something.	True	False
I am usually calm and not easily upset.	True	False
I have diarrhea once a month or more.	True	False

Obviously, for the first and third items, a *true* is taken as indicating anxiety, whereas for item 2, a *false* points to anxiety.

Notice that each of the three sample items requires that the person taking this test make some statement about his typical or modal way of responding; the scale is designed to assess the degree to which the individual experiences generalized, chronic anxiety.[4] In other words, anxiety is thought of by Taylor as a trait rather than a specific response to a specific set of stimuli.

The TMAS has been in widespread use as a tool in anxiety research for over two decades and has generated much research. Some of these studies will be discussed in a later section of this chapter.

Another commonly used scale was developed by the Institute for Personality and Ability Testing (and is therefore called the IPAT). Actually, like the MMPI, the test was designed to measure many dimensions of human personality. The IPAT Anxiety scale includes the following items:

I need my friends more than they seem to need me.

Rarely   Sometimes   Often

I sometimes feel compelled to count things for no particular reason.

True   Uncertain   False

As in the case of the TMAS, the IPAT is assumed to measure a pervasive and continuing anxiety trait.

The Affect Adjective Check List (Zuckerman, 1960) is also in relatively common use, at least in research. The scale contains a series of "anxious" adjectives, such as *afraid, desperate,* and *worrying,* and a series of "non-anxious" adjectives, such as *calm, cheerful,* and *steady.* The subject merely indicates whether the various items are applicable to him; obviously, agreement with the non-anxious items lowers the anxiety score. As Levitt (1967) points out, this measure can be used in two ways. As with the TMAS and IPAT, it can be used to assess an enduring anxiety trait or a transient state of anxiety, depending upon whether the subject is asked to indicate the way he *is* or the way he *feels now* with respect to the various items. If a person states that he *is afraid,* that would suggest that he sees himself as a generally fearful person (whether this is true is another matter), whereas if he says he *feels afraid,* this at least suggests a temporary state of affairs.

We have already questioned the validity of the notion of free-floating anxiety, and the concern in recent years with assessing momentary states of anxiety strikes us as a step in the right direction. In fact, the term *anxiety state* has come into widespread use lately. One questionnaire that has done much to popularize the state–trait distinction is the State–Trait Anxiety Inventory (Spielberger, 1966). Sample items are as follows: "I am calm." "I am a steady person." "I am overexcited and 'rattled.'" The same items are used to measure both state and trait anxiety; the distinction, as with the Affect Adjective Check List, is based upon instructions given the subject. To illustrate how this instrument may be used in research, Spielberger, Auerbach, Wadsworth, Dunn, and Taulbee (1973) administered it to patients 18 to 24 hours prior to surgery and 3 to 9 days after surgery (after they were told they were recovering without complications). State

---

[4] Actually, Taylor's primary purpose in developing the TMAS was to assess the subject's "drive" level (see Levitt, 1967) in relation to the learning formulations of Hull and Spence. She was apparently not interested in developing a clinical measure of anxiety.

anxiety showed a decrease of about 25%, whereas essentially no change was noted for trait anxiety.[5]

As we have just indicated, state anxiety refers to momentary levels of arousal. The presumption is, of course, that such arousal is related to the specific situation, but measures such as the State–Trait Anxiety Inventory cannot specify the situation. An example of a measuring instrument that does measure situation-specific or stimulus-specific fears is the Fear Survey Schedule. This measure was apparently originally developed by Wolpe and Lang in 1964, although there have been several modifications since then. It consists of a large number of items—for example, "being alone," "snakes," "driving a car"—and the subject is asked to rate each specific fear. Contrary to what Levitt (1967) has suggested, the measure should not be viewed as assessing a trait of anxiety (unless one wants to construe each of the specific fears as a kind of "mini-trait," which is inconsistent with popular usage of the term *trait*). The measure is in widespread use among behavior therapists, for both research and clinical purposes.

Again with respect to assessing specific fears, self-ratings are in widespread use, especially among behavior therapists. Here the subject or client rates his fear, perhaps on a 10-point scale, while imagining a particular situation or while he is in such a situation. These measures, especially in a clinical setting, are frequently administered verbally by the therapist, in a relatively informal manner.

BEHAVIORAL MEASURES. Strictly speaking, the aforementioned inventories are behavioral measures, since the subject must exhibit some behavior such as writing or talking to complete them. However, when the term *behavioral measure* is used in relation to anxiety, some direct measure of physical avoidance usually is meant. Such measures are necessarily situation- or stimulus-specific. That is, behavioral measures require an external referent. For instance, using a common procedure for assessing behavioral avoidance, Rimm, Saunders, and Westel (1975) studied subjects who were fearful of snakes. These subjects were asked to carry out as many of a series of snake-approach tasks as they were able to complete. The tasks were graduated with respect to fear arousal, beginning with entering a room with a caged harmless snake approximately 8 feet from the entrance and terminating with the subject handling the snake bare-handed for a period of 60 seconds. The subject's approach score was simply the sum of the tasks completed, with higher scores presumably reflecting less anxiety.

In clinical practice, behavioral avoidance is usually assessed indirectly, by way of an interview in which the client is asked about the frequency of avoidance behaviors. For example, suppose a particular client reports anxiety in relation to

[5] Some see this as evidence supporting the validity of the trait concept of anxiety as well as that of state anxiety, since an enduring trait would not be expected to change over a short period of time. However, a person who is fearful of some specific but virtually ever-present stimuli or who has severe specific phobias would probably describe himself in generally fearful terms, erroneously implying that indeed he suffered from free-floating anxiety.

sexual experiences. The therapist might inquire about the frequency of sexual encounters and at what point during any given encounter the client became avoidant. The therapist must trust the validity of the client's report, which may or may not be accurate. The alternative of direct behavioral observation would probably drive away most clients! A more reasonable alternative would be to have the client's partner provide corroboration for the client's report.

There are measures of anxiety other than physical avoidance that might be described as behavioral. Tremor or shakiness would be one example (Buss, Wiener, Durkee, & Baer, 1955; Malmo & Shagass, 1949). Speech difficulties such as stuttering and pauses also are sometimes taken as reflecting anxiety (Brutten & Shoemaker, 1971; Kasl & Mahl, 1965; Paul, 1966; Webster & Brutten, 1972).

SOME EFFECTS OF ANXIETY ON MEMORY, LEARNING, AND PERFORMANCE

Psychologists distinguish between short-term and long-term memory. Short-term memory refers to retention of a relatively small amount of information just presented. To illustrate, read the following series of numbers to yourself. Then immediately close the book and recite them.

2 9 4 1 8 5

You have just taken a *digit span* test. This is a common measure of short-term memory. If 1 hour from now you are unable to recall the numbers in their correct order—which is, of course, perfectly normal—you are evidencing failure of long-term memory. Intuitively speaking, long-term memory may be thought of as memory for things you have learned, such as your address, or your telephone number.

Available evidence suggests that short-term memory is impaired by anxiety, whether the anxiety is merely measured using a questionnaire or whether it is experimentally induced or situationally related. For example, Kaye, Kirschner, and Mandler (1953) found that anxious subjects, as measured by a test anxiety scale, had a shorter memory span (short-term memory) than low-anxious subjects. Moldawsky and Moldawsky (1952) found that criticizing their subjects resulted in poorer digit span performance, and Wright (1954) noted poorer short-term memory in patients presented with the threat of surgery. In the Moldawsky and Moldawsky experiment, subjects were also given a vocabulary test, a measure of long-term memory. Vocabulary was not affected, suggesting that long-term memory may be relatively stable as a function of anxiety level. In practical terms, these findings suggest that when you are feeling especially uptight, you will be more likely to forget information such as new telephone numbers or names but no more likely to forget things you already know.

Let us now discuss the relationship between anxiety and learning, beginning with simple conditioning. There have been many studies dealing with eyelid conditioning. In eyelid conditioning, some neutral stimulus is paired with a puff

The Marine Corps drill instructor is doing his best to induce a state of anxiety in the gasping recruit. For centuries, armies have followed the principle that anxiety enhances learning. (Thomas Hopker, Woodfin Camp & Associates)

of air directed into the subject's eye. The air puff causes the subject to blink, and with sufficient pairings the neutral stimulus will have the same effect. The evidence strongly indicates that higher levels of anxiety, whether simply measured by the TMAS or experimentally induced, facilitate eyelid conditioning (see Spence, 1964). There is some evidence (Beam, 1955; Bitterman & Holtzman, 1952) that conditioning of the galvanic skin response is similarly effected by anxiety. One might make the generalization that in the case of simple conditioning, anxiety enhances learning.

The situation becomes a little more complicated when we examine the effects of anxiety on verbal learning; for example, learning to associate pairs of words or learning a series of words in alphabet-like fashion. These studies have also been numerous. In summary, what these findings show (see Martin & Sroufe, 1970) may be illustrated by the following hypothetical experiment. Suppose you are presented with the following pairs of words (in an actual experiment the list would contain more than four pairs, but this is sufficient to make our point):

```
cat      dog
black    white
hot      cold
fish     swim
```

Following a very brief exposure to these pairs of words, you are presented with a second list showing the words on the left only, and your task is to recall the corresponding right-hand words. For obvious reasons this type of learning is called *paired-associate* learning. Note that the particular pairs go together. That is, given the stimulus word *cat* it is likely that you would have thought of *dog* even before participating in the experiment. Thus, the word *dog* may be thought of as a *dominant* response or association to the word *cat*. Here is where anxiety level comes in. Studies (for example, Spence, Farber, & McFann, 1956; Spence, Taylor, & Ketchel, 1956) using as the measure of anxiety the Taylor Manifest Anxiety Scale have shown that high-anxious individuals do *better* than low-anxious individuals when the correct response is dominant; that is, in tasks such as the one just presented. But what if the correct response is not dominant, as illustrated by the following?

```
cat      cold
black    swim
hot      white
fish     dog
```

Now, it turns out that, for initial learning at least, the situation is reversed (Ramond, 1953; Spence, Farber, & McFann, 1956; Spence, Taylor, & Ketchel, 1956). Low-anxious people do *better* than high-anxious people! If you keep in mind that high levels of anxiety tend to favor dominant behaviors, this makes a good deal of sense. The more anxious you are, the more likely you are to give the dominant response *dog* when presented with *cat*, but the second list has been deliberately constructed so that this will be an error. On the most general level, the following statement may be made: The more anxious a person is, the more likely he is to revert to familiar habits.[6] Whether this gets him into trouble or not depends on whether this familiar habit is appropriate to the situation. Not uncommonly, highly anxious patients are described as *rigid,* and it may well be that this apparent inflexibility reflects their tendency to stay with familiar behaviors when novel reactions are called for by the situation.

Another conclusion that seems to follow from clinical experience as well as from research findings is that the relationship between anxiety level and learning, or more generally, performance, may be represented by an inverted U. This is illustrated in an experiment by Matarazzo and Phillips (1955). These ex-

[6] This was humorously illustrated in a television situation comedy, popular some years ago, starring the husband-and-wife team of Lucille Ball and Desi Arnaz. Arnaz, whenever confronted with a situation that was especially emotionally arousing (for example, ineptitude on the part of his wife), would immediately revert to shouting in his native tongue, which was Spanish. At all other times he spoke English.

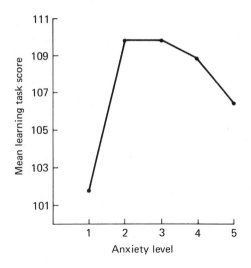

Figure 3-1. Mean learning task score for each of five groups ranging from low anxiety (group 1) to high anxiety (group 5). (From J. D. Matarazzo & J. Phillips, Digit symbol performance as a function of increasing levels of anxiety. *Journal of Consulting Psychology,* 1955, *19,* 131–134. Copyright 1955 by the American Psychological Association. Reprinted by permission.)

perimenters found that male subjects who were moderately anxious (as measured by the Taylor Manifest Anxiety Scale) performed better on a timed learning task than those who were very low on the anxiety measure or very high on the anxiety measure (see Figure 3-1). These and other findings suggest that for a given task, there tends to be a middle range of anxiety that is associated with most efficient performance. Below this range, the individual may be described as too poorly motivated to do well. Much above this range, performance may be said to suffer from debilitatingly high levels of anxiety. In short, the ideal level of anxiety depends on the task as well as on the individual. More complex tasks appear to have a lower optimal level of anxiety.

Put in intuitive terms, it is possible to care *too little* but it is also possible to care *too much.* In our experience, laymen are more likely to be aware of the former possibility than the latter. Rimm recently worked with a college baseball player who was in the midst of a hitting slump. In interviewing him, it became obvious that he was very anxious about his poor performance, and his approach to solving his problem was to castigate himself continually, on the assumption that all that was needed was "more desire"—an assumption frequently made by novice athletes. He was given training in deep muscle relaxation along with the suggestion that although he certainly wanted to do well, he did not *have* to do well, that his worth as a human being was not a function of the number of home runs he hit.[7] His batting average showed an increase of over 100 points following the brief treatment. Rimm obtained similar results with an overanxious pitcher.

[7] Deep muscle relaxation is a standard behavior therapy technique. The notion of personal worth being unrelated to performance is very much part of the philosophy of Albert Ellis. See Chapter 15 for discussions of both aspects of the treatment of the baseball player.

Summary

In this chapter, we traced the modern usage of the term *neuroses* to Kraepelin and to Freud. We noted that neuroses are commonly defined in terms of maladaptive behavior usually accompanied by heightened anxiety. Reliability of diagnoses for the various categories of neuroses is based on limited data, and the reliabilities tend to be low; much of this lack of reliability may be attributed to problems with the classification systems. The tradition that requires a single, primary diagnosis may also contribute to the lack of agreement.

Anxiety neurosis is one of the traditional neurotic disorders. We question the classic view of this disorder as being free-floating; we assume that the anxiety neurotic is fearful of specific situations or events that happen to be very pervasive. It is possible, however, that certain people are constitutionally more disposed to this disorder than are other individuals.

We have devoted considerable attention to the construct of anxiety, which we believe is scientifically useful in spite of the fact that different writers define it in different ways. The most common means for assessing anxiety are physiological measures, anxiety questionnaires, and behavioral avoidance tests. Very high levels of anxiety may give rise to inflexible or inefficient patterns of behavior, especially if the individual is attempting to engage in a complex task. Extremely low levels of anxiety may also interfere with performance. For most tasks, there appears to be some middle range of anxiety associated with maximal efficiency.

4

The Neuroses
II: Other Categories of Neuroses

This chapter deals with six of the remaining traditional categories of neuroses; as we indicated earlier, depressive neurosis is discussed in Chapter 6.

Hysterical Neurosis

As we noted in Chapter 1, the word *hysteria* was coined by the ancient Greeks to describe behaviors such as fainting, deafness, and partial paralysis that had no evident anatomical basis. The Greeks attributed these behaviors to a wandering uterus, and hysteria has been considered a female emotional affliction ever since. This historical perspective is important, especially when we consider its key role in the development of psychoanalysis and related approaches.

The term *hysteria* is commonly used by laymen, perhaps more than any of the other neurotic labels, but lay usage is quite different from the technical meaning of the term. For the layman, hysteria refers to a state wherein the person is overcome by, or controlled by, emotion. As such, it is the antithesis of reason. In our culture, to describe someone as hysterical is to issue a rather strong insult. Thus, it is a preferred way to characterize politicians of the opposing party, or more generally, anyone whose beliefs differ markedly from those of the labeler. These popular conceptions of hysteria have their uses, but they bear little relationship to the concept of *hysterical neurosis* as defined by the psychiatric establishment. At a general level, DSM-II (1968) describes hysterical neurosis as follows:

> This neurosis is characterized by a psychogenic loss or disorder of function. Symptoms characteristically begin and end suddenly in emotionally charged situations and are symbolic of the underlying conflicts. Often they can be modified by suggestion alone [p. 39].

CONVERSION HYSTERIA

Consistent with established usage, hysteria is divided into two major subcategories. We shall deal with conversion hysteria first (again quoting DSM-II):

> *Hysterical Neurosis, Conversion Type:* In the conversion type, the special sense or voluntary nervous system are affected, causing such symptoms as blindness, deafness, anosmia, anaesthesias, and dyskinesias.[1] Often the patient shows an inappropriate lack of concern or *belle indifference* about these symptoms, which may actually provide secondary gains by winning him sympathy or relieving him of unpleasant responsibilities. This type of hysterical neurosis must be distinguished from psychophysiologic disorders. . . . from malingering . . . and from neurological lesions [pp. 39–40].

In *conversion hysteria,* the person shows some sort of apparent malfunction, such as blindness or paralysis, that one might ordinarily associate with physical illness. However, examination by a physician will reveal no physical or organic basis for the complaint. If there is evidence the patient is merely "faking"—that is, engaging in a conscious deception—the label *hysteria* is considered inappropriate and the person is referred to as a *malingerer,* which is another word for faker. People sometimes confuse this category with *hypochondriacal neurosis* (discussed in a later section of this chapter), which refers to an extreme concern with bodily function in the absence of actual serious impairment. It is also confused with a *psychophysiological disorder,* or psychosomatic reaction, which is a condition of real physical impairment brought about by psychological stress.

Without intimating that these three terms or labels are of equally unquestionable validity (they are not), you are advised to take a few minutes and learn the distinctions between them. To illustrate how the terms are used, consider a person who makes an appointment with his physician, complaining of lower-back pain. Suppose that a thorough physical examination, including X rays and neurological tests, reveals no organic basis for the complaint, but the person consistently behaves (at least in the waking state) as if in pain, and there is no evidence he is deliberately faking. He would probably be classified as a conversion hysteric. Now suppose that an examination and a careful interview reveal that the subject only infrequently experiences pain, and also that there is little or no physical basis for pain. This preoccupation with a virtually imaginary physical ailment would probably result in the label *hypochondriacal neurosis;* that is, the

---

[1] Undoubtedly, some of these terms will be unfamiliar to you. It is sufficient to realize they all refer to apparent physical dysfunction.

patient would be characterized as a hypochondriac, a term often used by laymen to mean essentially the same thing. Finally, suppose that the patient complaining of back pain does indeed show physical impairment such as spinal cord damage or strained tendons in the lower back and there is clear evidence that this has been brought about by muscle tension related to chronic psychological stress. His diagnosis might then be psychophysiological disorder.[2]

The term *conversion hysteria* provides an excellent illustration of how a particular theory and a diagnostic label may be inseparable even in the absence of strong corroboration for the theory. The term apparently originated in the writings of Freud, who conceived of the disturbance as a transformation or conversion of a psychosexual conflict into a physical disorder. Thus, according to the orthodox psychoanalyst Otto Fenichel:

> In conversion, symptomatic changes of physical functions occur which, unconsciously and in a distorted form, give expression to instinctual impulses that previously had been repressed [1945, p. 216].

Coleman (1972) has argued that people no longer view conversion hysteria in this way, that the name *conversion* has been retained as a convenience. However, this is not entirely accurate (for example, see Zax & Cowen, 1972). In our view, it is unfortunate that the label *conversion* is still used. First, on a purely behavioral or descriptive level, the label provides nothing in the way of information. On a theoretical level the concept of conversion leaves much to be desired. Precisely how a psychological conflict, or the energy associated with such a conflict, can somehow be transformed into an apparent physical ailment has never been clarified. We are not arguing that people with symptoms typical of this diagnosis do not exist. We do think the label is misleading and would prefer an alternate term—for instance, *somatic hysteria*.

As we noted in Chapter 1, Hippocrates viewed hysteria as an exclusively female ailment. Although Freud revived the assumed relationship between hysteria and sex, he apparently shocked his colleagues (see Kleinmuntz, 1974) when he described a case of male hysteria. Freud's influence notwithstanding, there is still a tendency in some quarters to view hysteria as an exclusively female syndrome. For example, Guze and Perley (1963) argue that when males receive the diagnosis, it is almost always a misdiagnosis. Though this view has some support (see Buss, 1966), it may reflect an unwillingness of certain diagnosticians to describe men as hysterical. In one study, the number of males diagnosed as hysterical exceeded the number of females (Chodoff & Lyons, 1958).

With respect to *la belle indifference,* which traditionally has been associated with hysteria, the evidence is quite conflicting. Buss (1966) believes this attitude is seen in only a minority of conversion hysterics; studies by Ziegler, Imboden, and Meyer (1960) and Stephens and Kamp (1962) revealed an attitude of indiffer-

---

[2] Many physicians might give a purely physical diagnosis in such a case (that is, something relating to lower-back injury). The term *psychophysiological reaction* more often is applied to situations involving autonomic malfunctions such as high blood pressure or ulcers; see Chapter 7. However, technically the example given does illustrate a psychophysiological reaction.

ence in only about a third of the subjects sampled. On the other hand, Mucha and Reinhardt (1970) reported that all 56 of a group of student fliers with conversion hysteria symptoms showed little concern about the long-term debilitating effects of their disorder. Obviously, additional research is needed before a definite statement regarding *la belle indifference* can be made.

It is commonly believed that the incidence of conversion hysteria is lower today than it was in the early part of this century (see Coleman, 1972). This is usually attributed to the fact that people today are more psychologically sophisticated. But Proctor (1958), whose sample included many people from impoverished rural sections of the South, found a surprisingly high percentage of hysterical reactions (13%). There is also evidence (Wittkower & Dubreuil, 1968) suggesting that in developing countries such as India and Egypt, where the level of education is generally low, dramatic instances of conversion hysteria such as blindness, deafness, and convulsions may be higher than in the United States and Western Europe. However, the one study that did compare the frequency of this diagnosis among outpatients over two different periods (1913–1919 versus 1945–1960) found the same frequency, 2%, over both periods (Stephens & Kamp, 1962).

Whether or not conversion hysteria is on the decline, we can testify to the fact that so-called classic cases are rather hard to come by. Perhaps partly for this reason, there is little well-controlled research in the area. Much of what is written about hysteria appears to be based on the clinical experience of a limited number of people. We are not suggesting that the existing clinical lore about conversion hysteria is without validity. We do suggest that "factual" statements, which so often appear in the literature, should be taken with a grain of salt. The following sample of observations concerning this syndrome is presented to give you a taste of how hysteria is seen by the psychiatric and psychological establishments:

1. Conversion symptoms tend to disappear during sleep or hypnosis.
2. The hysteric is suggestible and histrionic. According to Batchelor (1969), hysterical insensitivity to feeling in one side of the body, or hemianesthesia, can actually be transferred to the other side of the body by the use of suggestion.
3. Hysterical symptoms often do not make sense from a neurological point of view. For instance, consider hysterical loss of sensation in the hand. The term *glove anesthesia* was coined to accentuate the observation that the loss of sensation does not usually correspond to those nerve endings that would be affected if the ailment had an actual physical basis.
4. Hysterical dysfunction is highly selective. This is seen in the so-called craft palsies—for example, the violinist who is able to play tennis but is paralyzed when he tried to play his violin (Ullmann & Krasner, 1969/1975).
5. In contrast to the malingerer, when the hysteric is confronted with inconsistencies of the aforementioned sort, he is not likely to behave in a defensive or perturbed manner.

The last observation warrants additional discussion. Unless we arbitrarily define hysteria in terms of an absence of defensiveness when confronted with such inconsistencies, malingering can never be ruled out. As CRM (1972) suggests, perhaps the person who receives the label *hysteric* is merely a good actor. The following cogent point is made in the same book:

> Because the typical definition of a hysteric demands that he *believe* the genuineness of his disorder, a diagnosis of hysteria cannot be certain until someone finds an infallible method of mind reading [p. 158].

This raises an intriguing question. If it is so difficult to distinguish between hysteria and malingering, why should anyone want to make this distinction in the first place? The answer is simple, although perhaps not entirely satisfying. According to long-established rules of the psychiatric establishment, the malingerer, because he is a deliberate faker, is held responsible for his behavior. The hysteric, on the other hand, who is not consciously aware that his symptom is contrived, is "ill" and is therefore not to be held responsible for his behavior.[3] Although the category called hysteria has made for much diagnostic confusion throughout the twentieth century, the motives for its inclusion and continued use in psychiatry are in part humanitarian. The malingerer is, after all, regarded as a villain; in the absence of the alternative characterization, hysteria, anyone with a nonorganic physical impairment would be considered a faker and would be subject to aversive consequences. For example, suppose a soldier behaves as if unable to walk, in the absence of neurological or other organic damage. Were it not permissible to label him hysteric, he might be forced to return to combat, possibly with disastrous consequences, or face a court-martial. As we noted, the traditional Freudian view of conversion hysteria is that it constitutes an unconscious effort to deal with an unconscious psychosexual conflict. Traditional writers readily agree that hysterics experience so-called *secondary gain:* There is some external reward or compensation associated with the symptom. The term *secondary* is used because the primary gain supposedly results from dealing with the unconscious conflict itself. In fact, Ironside and Batchelor's (1945) classic study of World War II airmen revealed that the conversion symptoms were closely related to their duties; the airmen experienced visual problems, such as blurring or night blindness, that made flying impossible.

In our view, it is more plausible to assume that for most conversion hysterics, the so-called secondary gain is actually the *primary reason* for the disorder. Thus, the airmen with visual problems are attempting to avoid an external task that they find frightening. The wife who systematically develops an "incapacitating"

---

[3] The notion that thoughts or behaviors that are "unconsciously" motivated are not within the domain of responsibility of the person is very pervasive. In our experience, patients accept this notion quite readily. A sophisticated patient familiar with the construct *unconscious* may retain his composure even when confronted with the most unflattering interpretations of his actions. The idea is to begin the confrontation with "Mr. X, this is obviously unconscious on your part, but you take pleasure in inflicting pain . . . you desire to have sex with your sister"—and so on.

headache whenever her spouse makes sexual advances is similarly avoiding an external event—intercourse with her husband—that she finds distasteful.

From a practical point of view, the issue of whether a person labeled hysteric is unconscious of his motivation may be largely irrelevant. Obviously, people learn new ways of responding or coping with their environment when they are fully aware of their motives. Moreover, there is evidence that people may learn adaptive responses even when they are not consciously aware of these consequences of their behavior (for example, see Kennedy, 1970, 1971). The important point is that regardless of his level of awareness, the patient has learned to cope with the environment in a manner that is burdensome to himself and to others. In this light, it does not make a great deal of difference whether we use the label *hysteric* or *malingerer*. The paramount task, in our view, is to assist him in learning more satisfying, acceptable strategies for dealing with his environment.[4]

Consider the following summary of a case history, based upon a report by Parry-Jones, Santer-Weststrate, and Crawley (1970):

■   The patient, a married woman of average intelligence, age 47, had experienced difficulty in seeing for approximately 3 years. At least two ophthalmologic examinations failed to reveal any physical impairment, and observations on the hospital ward suggested that at least at certain times she was able to see. Consistent with the traditional view of conversion hysteria, "she tended to be complacent and indifferent when talking about her disability and expressed only mild surprise when the suggestion was made that she might be normally-sighted [p. 80]."

Opinion was divided as to whether she was deliberately feigning blindness or was evidencing true hysterical blindness. Dynamically based psychotherapy was not successful, certainly in part because she failed to delve into details of her personal life, including marital and familial difficulties. At age 41 she had married a man with a history of psychiatric disorder and encounters with the police, mainly for fraud and embezzlement. Her husband deserted her 5 years after they were married.

A behavioristic approach modeled after a treatment devised by Brady and Lind (1961) was successfully employed. Treatment stressed feedback and social reward (praise) for correctly responding to visual cues. Two years following formal treatment her vision remained normal, and she was gainfully employed.

The authors of this case report note that even after treatment there was no real basis for labeling the patient as a hysteric as opposed to a malingerer. Accord-

[4] This assumes that effective alternatives to hysterical or malingering behaviors exist, which is probably a reasonable assumption most of the time. But not always. The airman who is confronted with the real possibility of death if he goes on a combat mission and who develops incapacitating "physical" symptoms may have no reasonable alternative—aside from deliberately damaging the aircraft, which apparently was not uncommon during World War II.

ing to their report, no effect was made to assess, either in behavioral or dynamic terms, the motivation behind the patient's blindness. The question of whether she feigned blindness or was rendered sightless as a result of some unconscious conflict was essentially ignored, but treatment was successful nonetheless.

DISSOCIATIVE HYSTERIA

Let us now consider the second subcategory of hysterical neurosis, *dissociative hysterical reactions.* According to DSM-II, this type of reaction is marked by "alterations which occur in the patient's state of consciousness or in his identity to produce such symptoms as amnesia, somnambulism, fugue, and multiple personality [p. 40]." Considering how often books, movies, and television depict individuals suffering from dissociative reactions, you may surprised to learn that well-documented cases showing clear-cut symptoms are extremely rare. Absee (1966), in reviewing the psychiatric and psychological literature, was able to come up with only 200 such cases (excluding somnambulism or sleepwalking, which is not especially uncommon). In connection with conversion hysteria, we mentioned a tendency on the part of many writers to rely heavily of limited case history data, thus inadvertently perpetuating what might only be lore. This is probably even more the case with dissociative reactions. For example, when the subject of multiple personality is discussed, the case history most often presented is the much publicized "Three Faces of Eve" (Thigpen & Cleckley, 1954, 1957, cited in Coleman, 1972; Kleinmuntz, 1974; Rosen, Fox, & Gregory, 1972; Suinn, 1970). Obviously, there is a danger of poor representation when a diagnostic category is built on minimal case history data, and you are again advised to view what follows as tentative.

HYSTERICAL AMNESIA.   This is characterized by a massive memory loss, which may endure for only a few hours or for months. The classic clinical picture involves a loss of memory of identity (i.e., name and residence), possibly the loss of occupational skills, but not the loss of language. The loss of identity is probably requisite to receiving this label. This is unfortunate, because it is likely that a much larger sample of people experience non-organic memory impairment that is serious, but not so extensive that it involves loss of identity. Having a larger sample of subjects with which to work could do much to help answer questions about the nature of this disorder. The psychoanalytic view is that such forgetting is a result of massive repression of threatening sexual or aggressive impulses. As behaviorists, our inclination is to view amnesia as essentially an escape from or an avoidance of an unpleasant external situation. As with conversion hysteria, whether the avoidance response is conscious or unconscious may be irrelevant, at least from the treatment standpoint; it is usually assumed that the memory loss may be lifted by using drugs or hypnosis.

FUGUE STATES.   Fugue may be thought of as a special case of hysterical amnesia. The classic picture of this rare phenomenon is that of a person who literally flees his present life circumstances, finding a new physical environment. The fugue state may last for a matter of days, or as long as several years. While in the fugue state the individual's behavior appears normal—except, obviously, to those in the environment from which he fled. He may seek different employment and may actually assume a different identity. The literature suggests that while in the fugue state, the individual is at least partially amnesic with respect to his former life. When he comes out of the fugue, he has little or no recall of his behavior while in the state. Most writers conceptualize the fugue as an escape, psychological as well as physical, from an unpleasant situation. Because of its rarity it is difficult to provide a scientific evaluation of this diagnostic category.

MULTIPLE PERSONALITY. Here the person presents two or more personalities. The classic picture requires that the original personality be unaware of the other personalities. Often, the second personality (if there are only two) has essential characteristics opposite to the original identity. Thus, if the original identity is inhibited and restrained, the second identity may be wild and uncontrolled.

Although it is unlikely that you have ever met anyone who fits this description, you may have met people who have been reared in highly restrictive, religious homes and yet show diametrically opposite behaviors. Such people may indulge in drinking and sexual promiscuity when they get their first taste of freedom, and yet periodically revert to their conservative family life style. Whether such a behavior pattern is usefully viewed as a mild version of multiple personality is a matter of conjecture. Certainly, in those persons we have known who exhibited such behavior patterns, there was no hint that they were periodically unaware of prior segments of their own behavior.[5]

The case history that follows was reported by Kohlenberg (1973). At age 35, the male patient received a diagnosis of schizophrenia with multiple personality; after 16 years of continuous confinement, a schizophrenic component to his behavior was still apparent. Our preference would have been to present a "pure" example of multiple personality, but as we have indicated, well-documented cases are quite rare. Interestingly, in this case the schizophrenic component was primarily associated with one of the three personalities.

■ Kohlenberg labeled the three personalities as high, medium, and low, referring to the pitch of the patient's voice during the various states. The high personality was marked by a high voice, and rapid speech that at times was unintelligible. Movements were rapid and abrupt. The patient made frequent references to communications from the dead who, he reported, controlled his behavior at times. Antisocial actions such as breaking glass and windows and

[5] Money and Ehrhardt (1972) have drawn an interesting parallel between male transvestites (males who periodically act out a feminine role, and dress accordingly) and multiple personalities. "A great many . . . who do not desire a permanent sex reassignment, are uncannily expert at metamorphosing from one sex role and mode of dress to the other. Even the voice is changed in pitch and loudness [p. 244]." Transvestism is discussed in Chapter 12. Typically, there is no evidence that either of the two roles is unaware of the other.

physically threatening others were observed only during the high personality. During the high state, he claimed that he was of the Spirtualist religion.

During the middle state, or middle personality, he was relatively relaxed, and acted in a more or less normal manner. The low personality was marked by a very low-pitched voice; he appeared to be depressed, showing little activity of any type. In this state, he often made references to world destruction and to fatalistic beliefs about his own existence. Kohlenberg notes that "during a typical half-hour interview, all three personalities would often alternate in rapid succession. When one personality was asked questions about the other personalities, the patient would either deny the presence of the other personalities or would not answer [p. 138]."

When the patient received rewards following the relatively normal middle-personality behaviors, the frequency of these behaviors sharply increased. That is, the middle personality became more dominant.

You may have encountered the term *split personality*. This is not really a technical term, although it is used more or less synonymously with dual or multiple personality. Confusion arises when the term *schizophrenia* is used, because schizophrenia implies a "split" as well. The difference is that schizophrenia refers to a splitting off from reality and a split between thought and emotions rather than a dividing of personality into two or more component identities.

SOMNAMBULISM (SLEEPWALKING).   We question whether this behavior should even be described as neurotic. Most people would agree that neurotic behavior ought to be a self-defeating problem behavior. We know of no strong evidence that occasional somnambulism qualifies as self-defeating or even as a problem. Sleepwalking is, of course, interesting in its own right. It is discussed in more detail in Chapter 13.

Phobic Neurosis

A phobia may be defined as an intense fear response to a specific class of stimuli that most people would not view as dangerous. Most traditional definitions of phobias include an assumption that is a subject of controversy. Consider the DSM-II definition of phobic neurosis:

> This condition is characterized by intense fear of an object or situation which the patient consciously recognizes as no real danger to him. His apprehension may be experienced as faintness, fatigue, palpitations, perspiration, nausea, tremor, and even panic. Phobias are generally attributed to fears displaced to the phobic object or situation from some other object of which the patient is unaware. A wide range of phobias has been described [p. 40].

The assumption in question is that of displacement, as we noted in Chapter 3. It follows from classical psychoanalytic theory, which assumes that what the phobic "really" fears are unacceptable thoughts or impulses related to sex or aggression. This displacement notion of phobia, which until relatively recently pervaded the fields of psychiatry and clinical psychology, had a most unfortunate effect: Since what the phobic *really* feared (that is, unconsciously feared) was only symbolically related to what he *said* he feared, there was no point in even attempting to deal with the stated fear; after all, that was not his real problem. The common expectation was that if one were able to eliminate the stated or manifest fear, another symptom—perhaps a different fear—would take its place, because the unconscious core phobia had not been ferreted out. This is the famous doctrine of *symptom substitution*: Remove a superficial symptom, without getting at the underlying, unconscious cause of the symptom, and a new substitute symptom will appear.

This doctrine has been applied to disorders other than phobias, but we present it here because it has been contested largely in connection with the treatment of phobias. As it turns out, when clients' fears are treated directly, without attempting to get at any underlying, deep-seated cause, and when the treatment is successful (and it often is), symptom substitution is rarely, if ever, observed (see Bandura, 1969; Lazarus, 1971; Wolpe, 1969). In the judgment of many writers, including the present authors, this is strong evidence against the displacement view of phobic behavior. We are not suggesting that no human being has ever shown a displaced fear response or that symptom substitution never occurs. We are suggesting that it is generally far more productive to treat phobic reactions as problems in and of themselves, rather than as manifestations of other, hidden problems.

There is a paradox associated with phobic disorders. On one hand, everyday experience suggests that they are very common and research tends to corroborate this—for example, Brandon (1960) found that 38% of the girls and 20% of the boys in an urban community in northern England had phobias in some degree, although other studies have found somewhat lower percentages. On the other hand, among patients the clinical diagnosis of phobic neurosis or phobic disorder is relatively rare (3.1% in a study by Ingram, 1961). There are several likely reasons for this. First, most people with phobias are not so incapacitated that they require hospitalization. Second, when they are seen in a clinical setting, other diagnoses are seen as more appropriate. As we suggested earlier, many people we would describe as phobic might be diagnosed as suffering from anxiety neuroses by more traditionally oriented therapists. Third, until relatively recently it was rather widely believed in psychiatric circles that treatment could do little to eliminate phobias. This attitude may explain why movies and novels rarely have depicted psychiatric treatment of phobias. Thus, the layman who saw himself as phobic would have no more reason to anticipate successful treatment by a practitioner than would the practitioner himself. Recent advances in behavior-therapy treatment of phobias have changed this in some degree, although most lay people are not yet familiar with these developments. If they were, we suspect the percentage of phobics in a clinical setting—especially an outpatient setting—would be higher.

RELIABILITY OF DIAGNOSIS

Apparently, no studies have sought to discover whether different diagnosticians agree regarding the diagnosis of phobic neuroses. When phobic reactions are dealt with behaviorally, the phobic person is tested in a behavioral avoidance situation and also rates his fear in relation to the phobic object. Issues such as displacement are ignored. Thus, reliability is built into the measure of fear. For example, if a subject is asked to approach a harmless snake in a series of graduated tasks and he is able to complete 15 of the 19 tasks, most observers would agree that he did, in fact, complete 15 tasks.

THE CLUSTERING OF PHOBIC FEARS

Not surprisingly, in individuals certain phobic fears tend to intercorrelate. As we suggested in Chapter 2, the standard statistical procedure for dealing with this issue is factor analysis. Several studies have factor analyzed the Fear Survey Schedule, a questionnaire commonly used to assess a wide variety of fears (Wolpe & Lang, 1964). One such study (Rubin, Lawlis, Tasto, & Namenek, 1969) found five such clusters of interrelated fears among college students, including fears of small animals, fears of interpersonal hostility, moralistic and sexual fears, fears of isolation, and fears of bodily destruction and pain. Landy and Gaupp (1971), also working with college students, found fear clusters that overlap with those reported by Rubin and associates: animate nonhuman organisms, interpersonal events, the unknown, noise, and medical–surgical procedures. Bates (1971) worked with hospitalized male patients diagnosed as neurotic. Although he described a total of 17 such factors or clusters, the five most important concerned medical–surgical events, interpersonal events, loud noise, birds and worms, and travel. In a study dealing with children's fears, Miller, Barrett, Hampe, and Noble (1972) found three principal categories of fears, one pertaining to physical injury, a second pertaining to natural events, and a third pertaining to psychological stress.

THE ORIGIN OF PHOBIAS

Few therapists or writers presently take the position that phobic reactions in humans are innate. It is generally accepted that phobias come about as a result of experience or interaction with the individual's environment. Controversy comes about when one wishes to specify those classes of environmental events most likely to precipitate phobic behavior. As you may know, orthodox psychoanalytic theory looks to the first years of life in accounting for many types of behavior disorders that appear in adulthood, including phobias. This theory is discussed in some detail in Chapter 16; essentially, it says that phobic fears originate with the child's sexual desires toward the opposite-sexed parent and the child's belief that the same-sexed parent will provide dire punishment (in the case of the male child, perhaps castration, hence the term *castration anxiety*) for such desires.

The most popular alternative to this view has been put forth by behaviorists, dating back to John Watson. Watson and Rayner (1920) were able to condition a fear response in Albert, an 11-month-old infant. Prior to the experiment, Albert had no such response to a white rat. But after the rat was paired with a loud sound several times, the rat came to elicit a fear reaction in Albert. This illustrates *classical conditioning*, a type of conditioning or learning made famous by the Russian Pavlov (1927). Classical conditioning is sometimes referred to as Pavlovian conditioning or respondent conditioning. In classical conditioning terminology, the rat initially is a *neutral stimulus*, but as a result of pairing it with the loud noise, which is the *unconditioned stimulus*, the rat becomes a *conditioned stimulus*, eliciting the *conditioned response*, which is a fear reaction.

This conception of how phobic responses are acquired is beautiful in its simplicity. However, it is unlikely that human phobic reactions are usually acquired in exactly this manner. We base this statement on evidence demonstrating that fears may be learned by other means and on evidence suggesting that cognitions may play a crucial role in phobic behavior. With respect to the acquisition of fear reactions, it has been shown in both adults and children (and in monkeys as well) that merely observing another person experiencing pain or anxiety is sufficient for the conditioning of an emotional reaction in the observer (see Bandura, 1965; Bandura & Rosenthal, 1966; Jones, 1924; Miller, Banks, & Ogawa, 1962, 1963). We shall refer to this type of learning as *vicarious conditioning*, a term popularized by Bandura and his associates. Movies and television probably contribute heavily to human phobic behavior in precisely this manner. As a case in point, a fear of harmless snakes is not uncommon in our culture. Yet in our experience and in the experience of others, it is very rare indeed to find a snake phobic who reports any direct experience with harmless snakes that would account for the fear. In fact, few snake phobics have even touched a harmless snake; they almost universally assume snakes are slimy, which is not true. On the other hand, almost everyone has had numerous opportunities to observe people in the movies or on television evidencing terror in the presence of a snake, while "friendly" interactions between actors and harmless snakes are almost never depicted.

In this example, the actor portraying fear of the snake may be accomplishing this in a variety of ways. He may run away from the snake, present a facial expression suggesting terror, or visibly shake. He may emit another class of behaviors, verbal responses, which in our view may be critical in teaching observers to fear snakes. He might, for example, scream "That snake is deadly!" or "I'm a goner if he strikes me!" The situation is like a parent admonishing her child to avoid snakes because "they are very dangerous." It is a truism to say that people, especially children, are prone to imitate (see Bandura, 1969, for a review of the influence of imitation on human behavior). People learn to imitate verbal as well as motor responses, If parents or actors often give verbal models to the effect that snakes are deadly, in the absence of compelling information to the contrary, the observer will begin to say things of this nature, if not aloud, certainly to himself.

There is ample evidence (for example, Ellis, 1962; Meichenbaum, 1971; Meichenbaum & Goodman, 1969; Rimm & Litvak, 1969; see Chapter 15 for a discussion of some of this material) that what people *say to themselves* does affect the way they feel and behave. There is also evidence that people who are fearful in certain situations can be made less fearful by getting them to say different things to themselves in these situations (Maes & Heimann, 1970; Rimm, 1973; Rimm, Saunders, & Westel, 1975). Our own clinical experience tends to corroborate this strongly, especially with respect to phobics. Almost without exception, the phobics we have interviewed are quickly able to catch themselves engaging in frightening ruminations whenever they are confronted with the phobic situation. To illustrate, Rimm recently worked with a graduate student who for some years had been quite nervous whenever flying in an airplane. On a purely behavioral level, he could be described as a *flying phobic.* However, a little probing soon revealed that under certain specified situations (when the plane was taking off, hitting an air pocket, or beginning its landing approach) he would say to himself things such as "What's that noise . . . we won't make it . . . the plane is going to crash." In other words (and his case, in our experience, is very typical), it is far more correct to say he was afraid of crashing and dying than of flying. This may seem all too obvious to certain readers; the point is that the phobic is often not especially fearful of the situation *as it is* but rather of the situation *as he re-creates it* by engaging in terrifying thoughts (and visual images as well, such as watching his plane go down in flames). In our experience (see Rimm, 1973; Rimm *et al.*, 1975) it is not difficult to modify these patterns of self-verbalization so that the person soon experiences much less anxiety in the target situations. Clinical methods for accomplishing this goal are described briefly in Chapter 15. For our present purpose, realize that this formation, while hardly Freudian in nature, definitely is not consistent with a simple classical conditioning interpretation of the acquisition (and maintenance of) phobic behavior.

PHOBIC BEHAVIOR AND TWO-FACTOR THEORY

Some individuals who suffer from severe phobias manage to overcome their fears without formal treatment.[6] Many others do not show much improvement, which raises an interesting question. Given that phobias are discomforting and self-defeating, why do they persist in so many cases? If phobic responses are learned, and apparently quite readily, why are they not readily unlearned, since they are a source of great personal distress? This question, when applied to neuroses in general, has traditionally been called the *neurotic paradox.*

In relation to phobic behavior, a partial answer to this paradox is that the avoidance response is rewarding in the short run, because it takes the phobic person out of the supposedly dangerous situation. To illustrate, imagine you are afraid of high places. You are at the seaside walking toward the ocean and suddenly realize that you are approaching the edge of a high cliff. Perhaps you

[6] Surveys by Eysenck (1952) and others have suggested that roughly two-thirds of the persons labeled as neurotic improve in the absence of formal psychological treatment. The term *spontaneous remission* is used to describe this phenomenon. However, many writers have raised serious questions about the validity of the two-thirds spontaneous-remissions figure (see Kiesler, 1966). The actual rate of spontaneous improvement among neurotics remains a matter of debate.

say to yourself, "My God, I might fall and be crushed to death on the rocks below, or drown." You turn around and walk away. In a few seconds you experience immense relief—(the reward or reinforcement). This experience will probably further encourage you to avoid high places, thus reinforcing your phobia.

The foregoing example illustrates the second factor in the so-called *two-factor theory* of avoidance behavior (Mowrer, 1947, 1960). Before discussing this theory it is important to note the distinction between classical conditioning and instrumental or operant conditioning. We have already described the former in recounting the experiment involving little Albert. *Instrumental conditioning* involves the presentation of a reward of some sort *after* a response has been made. Rewarding the response of course, has the effect of strengthening it, that is, making it more likely to occur. One class of rewards may be defined as any event that reduces pain or negative emotional arousal, ordinarily characterized as fear or anxiety. In the example, the person avoided a high place and then experienced anxiety reduction, thereby strengthening his tendency to avoid high places in the future. The *first factor* in two-factor theory involves classical conditioning, which is traditionally assumed to be the basis for learning the fear response in the first place. As we have indicated, simple classical conditioning does not adequately explain how human beings typically acquire phobic responses. But we find it very plausible to assume that once the fear reaction is acquired—whether vicariously, through some sort of verbal communication, or *occasionally* through simple classical conditioning—the phobic avoidance behavior is maintained by fear reduction, the second of the two factors.[7]

What keeps the phobic person from unlearning his fear reaction? At least part of the answer is as follows: One way to unlearn a fear, although perhaps not the best way (see Chapter 15), is to remain in the fearsome situation until the fear undergoes extinction—"burns itself out," so to speak. If cognitive factors are as important as we think they are, this would be equivalent to remaining in the phobic situation until the ruminations (for example, "The earth might collapse beneath my feet") cease because the person becomes aware they are simply not valid. In any case, regular avoidance would have the obvious effect of preventing the unlearning or extinction of the fear. This is a plausible answer to the question posed by the neurotic paradox. Although we have presented this within the context of phobic behavior, similar arguments may apply to other neurotic reactions.

We just said that one way to get over a phobia is to remain in the phobic situation until the fear is extinguished. However, there is *some* evidence that extinction may not always occur under these circumstances. Solomon and Wynne (1953) conditioned an avoidance response in dogs, using a very strong electric shock. These dogs became extremely resistant to extinction; that is, they con-

---

[7] No theory is perfect, and two-factor theory is no exception (see Herrnstein, 1969; Rachman, 1976). Fear does not always lead to avoidance, for example, and avoidance may not always be motivated by fear. Nonetheless, we consider two-factor theory to have considerable merit. However, for a more critical view of the theory, see Rachman (1976).

tinued to show strong avoidance responses long after shock was no longer used in the experiment. Therefore, Solomon and Wynne postulated a principle of partial irreversibility: Avoidance conditioning involving traumatic levels of pain is incapable of total extinction. Campbell, Sanderson, and Laverty (1964) worked with volunteer human subjects in an experiment that parallels the Solomon and Wynne study in that it also involved conditioning under traumatic circumstances. The subjects were given a drug, scoline, which has the effect of making breathing impossible. The effect lasted for more than 1 minute. The experiment was arranged so that immediately prior to the cessation of breathing, the subject was exposed to a neutral stimulus. The experiment involved only one conditioning trial, after which the previously neutral stimulus was presented repeatedly by itself. The conditioned emotional response did not extinguish at all!

Before any reader concludes tht he is "stuck" with his phobias for the remainder of his life, several important points must be made. First, aversive experiences of the magnitude described in the Solomon and Wynne and Campbell *et al.* studies are rarely experienced in everyday life. Second, the majority of patients exhibiting phobic behavior are not able to point to any such traumatic precipitating events.[8] That is, the characteristics of the typical human phobia may be quite different from those of Solomon and Wynne's dogs or the human subjects of Campbell *et al.* (we have already postulated the key role of cognitive factors in typical phobias). Third and probably most important, in recent years phobias, some of them quite severe and debilitating, have been dealt with successfully using certain behavior therapy techniques (for examples, see Chapter 15).

The case history that follows is taken from Rimm's files.

■   E.M., a 33-year-old female, married, with a 2-year-old child, reported a very severe fear of flying. She was attractive, well above average in intelligence, with a college degree. In spite of its intensity, the phobia was of relatively recent onset. Her husband, an agricultural expert with the government, was involved in consulting in developing countries in various parts of the world; prior to the acquisition of her phobia, she would regularly accompany him on flights, some of very long duration. Approximately 1 year prior to her seeking professional help, she was returning with her husband and year-old daughter from southeast Africa. While over a range of mountains, the commercial airliner ran into considerable turbulence. Her husband, who had had two drinks, was comfortably asleep. She reported that she suddenly felt quite helpless and was panic-stricken. It is not entirely clear why she so suddenly developed this intense phobic reaction; from her report, the fact that she was traveling with her child for the first time was critical. When asked to verbalize the thoughts she had at the time of the incident, she stated that her concern was with her child's safety, should something happen

[8] Lazarus (1971) examined the records of 100 of his own patients who had specific phobias. In only *two* cases was the patient able to recall a traumatic experience clearly related to the fear. In our experience, traumatic conditioning occurs somewhat more frequently than this, but the majority of our patients have been like those of Lazarus.

to the plane—"my child will be injured if the plane suddenly loses altitude . . . if we crash my child will be killed, and I will be helpless to do anything . . . my husband is asleep . . . he can't help."

For the past several months her husband had been consulting in South America. Repeatedly, he had asked her to join him. Although she stated, with apparent sincerity, that she loved and missed him, she had avoided making the journey; flying was the only practical means of making the trip, and she was terrified at the prospect. Much to her husband's relief, since he had interpreted her continued absence as rejection, she finally admitted her fear to him. He was, she stated, very understanding and at last she made airline reservations. Now, however, she dwelled continually on the prospect of the flight and was chronically anxious. In recent weeks she had lost several pounds, and her friends, who ordinarily saw her as a well-adjusted person, now described her as a "nervous wreck." Since she was to make the trip in 10 days, the treatment was necessarily brief, involving training her to control her thoughts using thought-stopping (described in Chapter 15). Following the single 2-hour session, she reported feeling a great deal more confident.

Obsessive–Compulsive Neurosis

The DSM-II description of obsessive–compulsive neurosis is as follows:

This disorder is characterized by the persistent intrusion of unwanted thoughts, urges, or actions that the patient is unable to stop. The thoughts may consist of single words or ideas, ruminations, or trains of thought often perceived by the patient as nonsensical. The actions vary from simple movements to complex rituals such as repeated hand washing. Anxiety and distress are often present either if the patient is prevented from completing his compulsive ritual or if he is concerned about being able to control it himself [p. 40].

To help make the definition a bit clearer, each of the following would ordinarily be given this diagnostic label:

1. A person who reportedly says to himself, perhaps 100 times a day, "I'm going insane."
2. A person who reportedly cannot resist silently reading license plates.
3. A person who reportedly has persistent thoughts of harming others whenever in contact with sharp objects such as knives.
4. A person who is observed to wash his hands perhaps 50 times a day, until they are raw and bleeding.
5. A person who is observed to spend a good part of each working day symmetrically arranging objects on his desk.

This list is presented merely to provide a flavor of what is meant by obsessive–compulsive neurosis. Obviously, the list is not exhaustive. Moreover, such behaviors do not necessarily result in a primary diagnosis of obsessive–

compulsive neurosis. Sometimes people diagnosed as schizophrenic or psychotically depressed show such behaviors, but the behaviors are viewed as secondary to the psychotic diagnosis.

This diagnostic category is a bit confusing because it lumps together *thoughts* ("I am going insane") and *observable behaviors* (hand washing). In addition, the thoughts may have a passive quality, as when a person goes over the lyrics of a song again and again. Or, they may be described as *urges* if, for instance, a person states that he feels compelled to hurt people or to engage in sexual exposure. As a matter of convenience, when we use the term *obsession* we shall refer to thoughts in the absence of action, even if the thought is described as an urge or impulse. When we use the term *compulsion*, we shall refer to overt behaviors such as repetitive hand-washing.

Of course, *everyone* engages in some degree of obsessional thinking. The reciting of song lyrics is a commonplace example. Perhaps you have had the experience of literally being obsessed with thoughts of a lover's infidelity—though not for long, we hope. Similarly, some degree of compulsive, ritualistic behavior is common in most people, For instance, the person who must ritualistically clear his desk before he commences work is engaging in behavior that is compulsive in nature. The truth is, there may be sizable rewards for moderate amounts of obsessive thinking or compulsive behaviors. The student who stubbornly persists in ruminating over a physics problem until he finds the solution may be expected to do better in the course and perhaps ultimately experience success in the field of physics. A person who compulsively attends to his appearance may indeed present a better image to others—and may well have a higher probability of succeeding in the military. Both obsessional thinking and compulsive behaviors would seem to be on a continuum. Only when such activities begin to jeopardize one's feelings of well-being and productivity are they considered a problem.

You may wonder why obsessive thinking and compulsive behavior are lumped together. Traditionally, people have thought of the two as occurring together, although as Buss (1966) points out, some tend to use the term *obsessional neurosis* whereas others use the term *compulsion neurosis*. The question of whether obsessive thinking and compulsive behavior go together is mainly an empirical one, which has not yet been answered in a satisfactory way. On *logical* grounds, it can be argued that anyone showing compulsive behavior is also at least somewhat obsessive, since prior to engaging in some compulsive act the person probably engaged in some thought tied to the act. For instance, the compulsive hand-washer might say to himself, "My hands are contaminated . . . I must wash them" before every overt act of hand-washing. This, of course, is merely an assumption.

By way of contrast, clinical experience suggests that it is quite possible to engage in obsessional thinking that has no obvious relationship to overt behavior. This presents an interesting problem for the behaviorally oriented psychologist. Unlike almost every other psychological disorder, obsessional thinking (in the absence of compulsive behaviors) has no observable behavioral manifestation.

The conversion hysteric who says he is blind in some situations *behaves* like a blind person. The phobic who says he fears flying, typically *behaviorally avoids* flying. But what does the person who says he is obsessed, let us say, with thoughts of going insane, actually *do* that is different or unusual? Nothing! In other words, since we cannot "read his mind," there is no basis for corroboration. The practitioner must simply take his patient's word for it. Perhaps part of the reason that practitioners are willing to do this is that they themselves have experienced obsessional thinking in a mild form (we suspect *everyone* has), so that for them it is a "real" thing, although they can never really know what goes on inside their client's head.

There is some difference of opinion about how common obsessive–compulsive neuroses are. Coleman (1972) cites estimates of from 4 to 20% of the neurotic population. Buss (1966) suggests that the incidence of obsessive–compulsive neurosis is probably the lowest of all the neuroses.

OBSESSIVE THINKING

Traditionally, writers have held that obsessions, like other so-called neurotic reactions, are defensive in nature. That is, they are carried out in order to reduce anxiety, perhaps by preventing the person from thinking about unpleasant things. Wolpe (1958) has suggested, however, that certain obsessions may increase anxiety. Clinical experience seems to support this. The authors have treated patients who have been plagued with thoughts of going insane or harming others—thoughts which, from their own reports, did increase the anxiety they experienced. If one takes the position (and most psychologists certainly do) that people ordinarily behave in a way to minimize anxiety at least in the short run, this is most perplexing. It is tempting in situations like this to postulate an innate "masochistic drive," but this will add nothing useful in the way of explanation or description.

Guilt is sometimes considered to be a correlate of obsessional disorders (see Mather, 1970), and it is possible that anxiety-elevating thoughts are really aimed at reducing guilt. Perhaps the person has committed some act that he considers to be morally reprehensible. He experiences intense guilt whenever he thinks about it (and we assume that this experience is as uncomfortable as intense anxiety). It is conceivable that by engaging in some obsession that has catastrophic personal consequences ("This plane is going to crash"; "I'm going to jump off the bridge") he does experience momentary relief from guilt. The subsequent *increase* in tension might come about when he contemplates what he has just said to himself ("My God, what if I really *did* jump!"). Note that in this account, the so-called anxiety-elevating obsession has an *immediate* effect of *relieving intense discomfort* but a delayed effect of increasing discomfort. If you have taken a course in the psychology of learning, you know that immediate reinforcers are more effective than delayed reinforcers.

We can analyze anxiety-increasing obsessions involving thoughts of hurting others in a somewhat similar fashion. Consider a socially nonassertive person who is continually thwarted by others. The thought, "I'm going to murder so-and-so," may result in some immediate relief, but as soon as the person begins to contemplate the impact of such an act, he will experience an increase in anxiety. Again, we are assuming that the immediate relief has a positive reinforcing effect which, *because* of its immediacy, is stronger than the delayed punishing effect of an increase in anxiety. Please remember that this analysis, although plausible, is at this point speculative.

RESEARCH ON COMPULSIVE BEHAVIOR

The obsessive–compulsive category traditionally has received less research attention than many other neurotic categories (Buss, 1966), although recently more attention has been focused on research, especially that concerned with treatment (for example, Hodgson, Rachman, & Marks, 1972; Rachman, Hodgson, & Marks, 1971; Rachman, Marks, & Hodgson, 1973). In this chapter, our main concern is with the origins or etiology of this disorder. The bulk of the experimentation has been done with animals rather than humans (see Mather, 1970). Not surprisingly, it has dealt with behaviors presumed to be analogous to human compulsions—that is, no one has attempted to examine obsessional thought patterns in laboratory rats!

Compulsive behavior is, by definition, rigid and stereotyped or fixated. The research has been concerned with what experimental manipulations contribute to behavioral rigidity. For example, the work of Maier (Maier, 1949; Maier, Glaser, & Klee, 1940) involved forcing a rat to attempt to "solve a problem" that was actually impossible to solve. In their typical experiment, the rat is placed on a stand and forced to jump toward one of two stimuli presented in front of him. If he jumps toward the "correct" stimulus, he is reinforced. If his jump is toward the "incorrect" stimulus, he runs into a locked door and falls into a net—a rather punishing event. What makes this discrimination task impossible to solve is that the experimenter decides which response is correct on a totally random basis. This procedure would be expected to frustrate the poor rat, and in fact, this is precisely the purpose. As it turns out, the rats do develop behavioral fixations, most often consistently jumping to the left or to the right. After the "compulsion" has been established, the problem is made soluble—that is, one stimulus is now always associated with reward, and the other always leads to nose bumping and a fall into the net. Nonetheless, about 75% of the "compulsive" rats always go to the right or the left, even though the experiment is arranged so that going consistently to the same side leads to a shock about half the time. Analogous findings with human subjects have been reported, as by Marquart (1948) and Marquart and Arnold (1952), who used flashing lights as a reward and electric shock as a punishment.

If frustration tends to produce compulsive types of behavior, intermittent or partial reinforcement may have a similar effect. Partial reinforcement means that some, but not all, of a particular type of response is rewarded. For example, suppose that a husband makes sexual overtures to his wife every night, but she responds positively on the average of one night in three. He is then said to be on a *partial reinforcement schedule*. The remarkable thing about partial reinforcement, in contrast to situations where *every* response is rewarded, is that behavior that is intermittently reinforced is usually much more resistant to extinction. If this wife suddenly decided that she would *never* make love to her husband again (that is, if she put him in total extinction), she would probably find that his romantic overtures would continue for many nights before he "got the message." On the other hand, had she responded positively to each of his amorous overtures, and then put him in total extinction, in all likelihood he would have ceased to woo her much sooner. Now, let us take this example to what is admittedly an unlikely extreme. Suppose that the wife reinforces every response during the first year of marriage. During the second year she reinforces every third response, and by the tenth year of marriage she is responding affectionately on the average of only one time in 100 overtures. By this time, the husband is probably receiving psychiatric help! The psychiatrist will no doubt be puzzled by the fact that the husband has a "compulsion" to make amorous advances knowing full well they will be rejected. This assumes, of course, that the psychiatrist is unaware of the peculiar reinforcement schedule his client has been experiencing. In fact, one of the characteristics of compulsive behavior is that it does not appear to be followed by any tangible reward. Thus, a person who was observed to receive $5 each time he washed his hands would not be classified as a compulsive hand-washer.

It is known that partial reinforcement can produce considerable behavior fixation in rats (Wilcoxon, 1952), and there is also ample experimental evidence that human beings on a partial reinforcement schedule show considerable resistance to extinction (see Ayllon & Azrin, 1965; Ferster & Skinner, 1957). Does this mean that partial reinforcement contributes to compulsive behavior as seen in the clinic? We think so, but can point to no direct evidence so far.

Compulsive behavior is anxiety reducing. This is, at least among clinical psychologists and psychiatrists, the prevailing view. In fact, Farber (1948) has provided data from the rat laboratory supporting this and Hodgson and Rachman (1972) and Roper, Rachman, and Hodgson (1973) have made some studies with compulsive patients that support this notion. In the Hodgson and Rachman experiment, patients who had washing compulsions touched a "contaminated" object and experienced noticeable subjective discomfort, which was readily decreased by washing themselves. Roper *et al.* (1973) studied compulsive "checkers"—people who are debilitated by the need to check to make sure they have not done something potentially dangerous; for example, repeatedly making sure a door is locked or a stove is not lit. These "checkers" showed an increase in subjective anxiety when provoked to check, and a decrease following the checking response. In the long run, a person who is aware that he is subject to uncontrollable compulsions will probably experience discomfort when contemplating his plight, but in the short run, there is evidence that compulsive behavior does reduce anxiety.

We have already suggested that society rewards some degree of obsessive thinking and compulsive behavior. Ingram (1961) found that obsessive–compulsive neurotics tended to be of a higher social class than other classes of neurotics, and were more intelligent. It may be that such individuals, having achieved a certain level of success for engaging in great amounts of careful thinking and behavior, experience a kind of "spillover" into thought and behavioral patterns that are now self-defeating.

The following case history, reported by Rachman, Hodgson, and Marzillier (1970), illustrates debilitating compulsive behavior. Note that the patient also is troubled by intrusive obsessional thoughts.

■   The patient had developed some obsessional–compulsive behavior patterns during adolescence but did not seek psychological assistance until the age of 20 when he was admitted to a psychiatric hospital suffering from a marked obsessional disorder. His request for treatment had been precipitated by dismissal from his job as a result of excessive washing rituals which interfered with his working capacity. At the time of his admission to the hospital, the washing rituals occupied the greater part of his day. He also complained of persistent and intrusive fears of contamination by dirt and displayed extensive avoidance behavior patterns. After largely unsuccessful treatment by drugs and supportive therapy he was discharged only to be re-admitted later in the same year. On his fourth hospital admission, a modified leucotomy [a form of psychosurgery; see Chapter 21 of the present text] was carried out and the operation was followed by a reduction in tension. The obsessional and compulsive behavior was not improved. Six months later he was transferred to Maudsley Hospital with a request that he be considered for a second leucotomy. This was felt to be inadvisable and instead he was given supportive therapy and a course of desensitization treatment [see Chapter 15 of the present text] in which he was asked to imagine aversive, contaminating stimuli while relaxed. Some slight improvement was observed but he was still considerably disabled and clearly in need of help [p. 386].

A behaviorally oriented treatment involving modeling of appropriate behavior and the prevention of hand-washing was subsequently employed. Over a 17-week period, the total time the patient spent in behaviors associated with his compulsion dropped from an average of 4 hours and 10 minutes per day to about 80 minutes per day.

Hypochondriacal Neurosis

Very probably you have heard the term *hypochondriac*. Hypochondriacal neurosis is nothing more than this everyday occurrence elevated to the status of a formal psychiatric disorder.

According to DSM-II (1968):

This condition is dominated by preoccupation with the body and with fear of presumed diseases of various organs. Though the fears are not of delusional quality as in psychotic depression, they persist despite reassurance. The condition differs from hysterical neurosis in that there are no actual losses or distortions of functions [p. 41].

Coleman (1972) suggests that this condition is relatively rare, afflicting perhaps only 5% of the neurotic population. However, the characteristics of hypochondriasis and neurasthenic neurosis (to be discussed later in this chapter) as well as certain types of depressive disorders (see Chapter 6) show such considerable overlap that a precise statement of relative frequency is very difficult to make. According to Kenyon (1966), hypochondriacal neurosis is more likely to be found among older people and among women.

Note that the DSM-II description states that the fears are not of the delusional quality found in psychotic depression. Although we shall discuss this further in Chapter 6, individuals labeled as psychotic depressives often make bizarre statements regarding physical deterioration ("worms are eating out my insides"). The classical hypochondriac's symptoms are a good deal more plausible, especially as the general public becomes more sophisticated regarding the nature of actual physical ailments (an observation reported by Kleinmuntz, 1974). In general, then, a careful physical examination is needed to rule out a legitimate physical disorder. All of us are worried about the possibility of some serious illness from time to time, and when a competent physician assures us that our fears are groundless, most of us experience tremendous relief. *By definition*, this is not so with the hypochondriac, who may go from physician to physician until he finds one sympathetic to his complaints. This implies that there is absolutely nothing physically wrong with the hypochondriac. However, we suspect that many a hypochondriac has some actual but mild physical disorder that he exaggerates out of all proportion, or perhaps a history of some legitimate severe complaint from which he has in fact recovered, although he is obsessed with the idea that he has not.

ETIOLOGICAL FACTORS

Psychoanalytically oriented writers see displacement in hypochondriasis, just as they see it in phobic disorders. In the case of hypochondria, "anxieties are displaced to bodily functioning instead of other objects and situations [Kleinmuntz, 1974, p. 170]." We hasten to point out that this view is really highly speculative. We do not doubt that there *are* many people in this world who can legitimately be called hypochondriacs. If we view this disorder on a continuum, we would anticipate that almost everyone occasionally is somewhat hypochondriacal—that is, exaggerates the seriousness of physical ailments or simply fabricates them. In our view, the social consequences of such behavior are the critical element. If hypochondria is reinforced with parental nurturance and subsequently reinforced by sympathy from friends, the tendency to use physical complaints as a vehicle for obtaining attention may become very strong indeed, perhaps to the exclusion of other, more satisfying means of coping with one's social environment. We cannot provide "hard" data that indeed most, if not all, hypochondriacs have had such a learning history, but if it is merely speculative, it is also plausible.

The following case history is from our own files. You will note that the patient's primary diagnosis was not hypochondriacal neurosis. In our experience, it is very rare to find an individual with a "pure" diagnosis of hypochondriacal neurosis, at least in a psychiatric setting. Such a person would not be likely to seek psychological assistance, because he would not see his problem as psychological in origin. On the other hand, it is quite common to find patients hospitalized for reasons other than hypochondriacal symptoms, who nevertheless do have such symptoms.

■   The patient was 35 years of age, married, and was hospitalized for about a year. His formal diagnosis was anxiety neurosis, although as is typical of individuals with this label, his anxiety varied considerably, usually reaching a peak whenever his therapist suggested that he might leave the hospital. He was a shy, passive man, showing a woeful lack of self-confidence. Throughout most of his hospitalization he repeatedly complained of a stomach disorder, which he was convinced was an indication of a serious ulcer. He showed no loss of weight, his eating habits were normal, and gastrointestinal examinations revealed no trace of an ulcer. In spite of repeated assurances that he was in good physical health, he steadfastly maintained that his ulcer persisted. When one hospital physician would pronounce him healthy, he would seek out another one, apparently hoping for verification of his symptom, which he never received. While in the hospital he received vocational training as a barber and gradually his confidence increased. With this increasing confidence, his complaints about the ulcer diminished, and by the time he had obtained employment as a barber and was processing out of the hospital, his "ulcer" had disappeared.

Neurasthenic Neurosis

Let us consider the DSM-II (1968) description of neurasthenic neurosis:

> This condition is characterized by complaints of chronic weakness, easy fatigability, and sometimes exhaustion. Unlike hysterical neurosis the patient's complaints are genuinely distressing to him and there is no evidence of secondary gain. It differs from Anxiety neurosis and from the Psychophysiological disorders in the nature of the predominant complaint. It differs from Depressive neurosis in the moderateness of its course [pp. 40-41].

This description is interesting in that it makes no effort to distinguish this category from hypochondriacal neurosis, although they have been linked, historically at least (see Buss, 1966). In fact, the description covers complaints that may be hypochondriacal in character. One major weakness of the DSM-II description is the presumption that the complaints are genuine, without any indication of how one is to know this. Whether neurasthenia can readily be distinguished from psychophysiological disorders (perhaps we should say, other psychophysiological disorders) and depression is questionable at best. In short, without denying that some people do show such behavioral characteristics, in terms of differential diagnosis it is not a very helpful category. We know of no data pertaining to the reliability of diagnosis.

Textbooks typically list a large number of symptoms associated with this category, including concern over body functioning, sensitivity to sudden increases in sensory input (such as loud noises), sexual dysfunctioning, disturbed sleep, feelings of exhaustion, especially in the morning, and lack of self-assertiveness. Consistent with our view of hypochondriacal neurosis, Kolb (1973) believes that many neurasthenics have received parental attention for such symptoms rather than for behaviors that are more socially constructive. According to CRM (1972), the neurasthenic symptoms, especially the chronic fatigue, tend to disappear when the individual's life situation improves. They suggest that the typical neurasthenic is a middle-aged housewife who has little in the way of personal satisfaction.

As we have suggested, there are real problems with this category. In our view, it would be better to treat the specific symptoms separately, rather than viewing this as a unitary syndrome, distinct from other neurotic categories. We have known individuals (indeed, mostly older females) who do manifest some of these symptoms. We have found it far more productive to treat their specific complaints than to attempt to apply to them a primary diagnosis of neurasthenia.

Depersonalization Neurosis

Little has been written about depersonalization neurosis, at least in the United States. It shares an important feature with obsessional disorders (viewing an obsession as separate from a compulsion): Like an obsession, it has no overt manifestations or correlations. Again, one must simply take the patient's word for it. According to DSM-II,

> This syndrome is dominated by a feeling of unreality and estrangement from the self, body, or surroundings. This diagnosis should not be used if the condition is part of some other mental disorder, such as an acute situational reaction. A brief experience of depersonalization is not necessarily a symptom of illness [p. 41].

Schilder (1914) presents an interesting account of depersonalization:

> The individual feels totally different from his previous being; he does not recognize himself as a person. His actions seem automatic, and he behaves as if he were an observer of his own actions. The outside world appears to him strange and new and it has lost the character of reality. The "self" does not behave any longer in its former way [p. 54].

This is a rather dramatic characterization; from our own experience with patients reporting depersonalization-like symptoms, it seems a bit exaggerated. You may wonder why we bother to deal with a category so subjectively defined. The answer is that we have found so many patients who report symptoms of this general nature. Often the patients were not especially sophisticated and there was no reason to assume that they were verbalizing a role they had picked up from a psychology text.

Ackner (1954) studied 50 patients who were diagnosed as suffering from depersonalization. On the basis of his observations, he reported several principal features: (1) a feeling a change, (2) a feeling of unreality, (3) unpleasant sensations, (4) no evidence of delusional thinking, (5) overt responding marked by a lack of affect (that is, a lack of emotion).

The feelings of unreality may apply to the person himself ("It's like I'm not real, Doc, like I'm on the outside, looking at myself . . . sort of like I'm an actor") or to the external world (some use the term *derealization*—see Weckowicz, 1970), which seems flat and colorless and where people have an almost robotlike quality.

Although the data on its incidence as a psychiatric disorder are scarce, Lewis (1934) has argued that it often occurs in psychotic depression, and Mayer-Gross, Slater, and Roth (1954) state that it often is seen in the early stages of schizophrenia, especially hebephrenic schizophrenia. Lest you be so alarmed by this that you contemplate turning yourself in at the nearest mental hospital, consider the data reported by Roberts (1960). He studied a student population and found that nearly half (45%) reported experiencing some symptoms of depersonalization. Dixon (1963) reported similar results, with some evidence of a higher incidence among women than men. In short, certainly in its less dramatic forms, depersonalization seems to be quite a common experience. There is rather consistent evidence (reported in Weckowicz, 1970) that depersonalization and obsessional thoughts tend to go together—but remember that all evidence for these two states must rely on self-reports.

ETIOLOGICAL FACTORS

Both Mayer-Gross (1935) and Shorvon (1946) have suggested that epileptic-like activity (see Chapter 8) may be a causal factor, although Roth (1959) has disputed this. Beyond this organic interpretation, a variety of physiological and psychological theories have attempted to account for this apparently rather pervasive phenomenon in terms of disturbance of sense perception, stress, hyperactivity of memory, a defense against forbidden impulses, and disturbances in self-image, among other things. For a thorough review of this literature see Weckowicz (1970).

Summary

In this chapter we have described and evaluated six major categories of neurotic behavior. Conversion hysteria refers to a behavioral impairment in the absence of real physical or organic malfunctioning. Historically, conversion hysteria was viewed as an exclusively female disorder, but this is highly questionable. Conversion hysterics sometimes show a lack of concern over their symptoms. It is not easy to distinguish between conversion hysteria and malingering—that is, deliberately faking a symptom—and we wonder whether it is fruitful to attempt to make the distinction. Classic cases of conversion hysteria are rare in our culture, and the number may be decreasing. Even less common are cases of dissociative hysteria, which includes hysterical amnesia (severe memory loss without organic basis), fugue state (hysterical amnesia in which the person flees to a new environment), and multiple personality (wherein the person manifests more than one personality or identity).

Phobic neurosis refers to an irrational fear. Traditionally it has been thought the phobic is really fearful of something else, perhaps sexual impulses, but displaces his fear to some external object. We question the usefulness of this assumption; we also believe it makes diagnosing phobic neurosis more difficult. Attempts have been made to account for the origin of fears through classical conditioning, but there is evidence that other factors may be important in learning to be phobic. Some people seem to acquire their fears through imitation, and there is evidence that what people say to themselves may be important in the acquisition and maintenance of phobias. It is commonly believed that one of the reasons phobic behavior is persistent is that when one avoids the phobic situation, the feeling of relief acts as a reward that strengthens the tendency to avoid.

Obsessive–compulsive neurosis refers to either intrusive and disquieting thoughts or ritualistic and uncontrollable behaviors, or both; we think it is useful to treat obsessive thinking and compulsive behavior separately, because they do not always go together. Compulsive behavior can be observed directly, but one must infer obsessive thinking. There is clinical evidence that some obsessions reduce anxiety and other obsessions increase anxiety. It is possible that anxiety-increasing obsessions reduce guilt. Research dealing with obsessional thinking has been sparse. Much of the research pertaining to compulsive behavior has involved animals; the animals, when faced with a problem that is insoluble, show rigid, stereotyped behavior. We have also suggested that a history of intermittent reinforcement may lead to behavioral rigidity, and we have presented evidence that compulsive behavior does appear to reduce anxiety in humans.

Hypochondriacal neurosis refers to an exaggerated concern with presumed diseases. In its severe form it is rare and may be more common in women and older people. Some writers believe that hypochondriasis is a displaced fear, but we conjecture that receiving undue attention for physical complaints is a more plausible origin for this neurosis. Research on hypochondriasis is lacking.

Neurasthenic neurosis is associated with complaints of weakness and easy fatigability and sometimes depression, in the absence of organic malfunction. This category overlaps to a considerable extent with hypochondrical neurosis, neurotic depression, and certain other disorders. As a result, it is difficult to deal with diagnostically. It is sometimes said that this disorder is common to middle-aged housewives whose lives are lacking in personal satisfaction.

In depersonalization neurosis, the subject complains of a feeling of unreality and estrangement from self. Such symptoms are sometimes associated with schizophrenia and severe depression; in such cases the diagnosis depersonalization neurosis is not used. Research on this disorder is severely limited, although available evidence shows that occasional feelings of depersonalization are quite normal.

5

Schizophrenic Disorders

Schizophrenia is a label applied to a broad category of behavior aberrations, most of which are associated with disturbances in thinking. It is considered a psychosis because the thought disturbance is severe and debilitating.

As we have mentioned, Kraepelin (1913/1919) provided the foundation for present-day classification of psychological disorders. Schizophrenia is no exception, although he used the term *dementia praecox*. According to Coleman (1972), Morel, a Belgian psychiatrist, used the term *démence précoce* in 1860; *dementia praecox* is the latinized version. Kraepelin viewed these disorders as forms of *dementia*, by which he meant irreversible, organic brain disorders inevitably leading to a state of severe mental deterioration. He also believed these disorders began relatively early in life, hence the term *praecox*, meaning "early." The Swiss psychiatrist Bleuler (1911) introduced the term *schizophrenia*, implying a schism involving the mental processes; current usage suggests a split between thought and reality. Unlike Kraepelin, Bleuler believed that schizophrenic disorders are not necessarily irreversible and improvement is quite possible. In keeping with Bleuler's view, many individuals labeled schizophrenic do show marked improvement. In addition, as measured by first admission to a mental hospital, onset is maximum between the ages of 20 and 45 (Landis & Page, 1938).

In his portrayal of schizophrenia, Bleuler stressed difficulties in making *associations;* disordered *affect* (today people would use the term *flattening*, or *blunting*, of emotion); *ambivalence,* a tendency toward mixed feelings; and *autism*, highly idiosyncratic ways of thinking and behaving. Associative difficulties and autism may be subsumed under the *thought disorder* label. As we noted, modern usage tends to view schizophrenia mainly as a thought disorder, although some writers (e.g., Henderson & Gillespie, 1962) stress emotional blunting and a discordance between emotion and thought. Current literature gives little attention to the ambivalence that Bleuler viewed as an important feature of schizophrenia.

Of course a disturbance in thinking is necessarily *inferred*, since it is not possible to observe another's thoughts. On a purely descriptive level, what is deviant is the schizophrenic's observable behavior. His speech may lack coherence, or he may talk of hallucinations or delusions as though they are realities. He may giggle for no apparent reason. He may have difficulty with certain intellectual tasks, such as interpreting proverbs or forming concepts. He may show extreme social withdrawal. This by no means exhausts the possible schizophrenic symptoms, nor is it the case that anyone having the schizophrenic label necessarily shows all of these symptoms. The point we wish to make here is that beyond such overt behavioral manifestations, any statements about disordered thinking are of an inferential nature. For some proportion of persons who are labeled schizophrenic, it *is* plausible to assume a deviant and self-defeating thinking pattern—at least at the time the patient is manifesting overt schizophrenic symptoms. However, there are other possibilities. A person may feel overburdened by life's responsibilities and wish, for a time, to be cared for, in the absence of any real deviance in his fundamental thought processes. Some mental institutions are not at all like the asylums of old (see Chapter 1) and may present rather attractive living accommodations. This view of schizophrenia is carried to an extreme by the Braginskys (Braginsky & Braginsky, 1967; Braginsky, Braginsky, & Ring, 1969) who argue that the "hospital is really like a . . . resort where patients can indulge their hedonistic inclinations [Braginsky *et al.*, 1969, p. 161.]." Some hospitalized "schizophrenics" would seem to fit the Braginsky model, but clearly many do not.

One reason for acting schizophrenic—although certainly a rare occurrence—is to find out what it is like to be treated as a psychotic person. We have known graduate students in psychology who have done this; what is instructive is that under such circumstances, it is so easy to be labeled schizophrenic. As an experiment, Rosenhan (1973) and some of his associates presented themselves at various mental hospitals. Their *only* complaint was that they were hearing voices; in all other respects they behaved as they normally would. With but one exception, each was diagnosed as schizophrenic. After admission, their "symptom" ceased, but they were not immediately discharged. When they were discharged, they were still viewed by hospital personnel as schizophrenic, although in remission, that is, improved. Rosenhan's experiment serves to point out two things: First, that it is very easy to receive the label of schizophrenic, and second, that once the diagnosis has been made, the label tends to remain, and is somewhat independent of the patient's behavior.

Diagnostic Issues

DSM-II provides the following general definition of schizophrenia:

> This large category includes a group of disorders manifested by characteristic disturbances of thinking, mood, and behavior. Disturbances in thinking are marked by alterations of concept formation which may lead to misinterpretation of reality and sometimes to delusions and hallucinations, which frequently appear psychologically self-protective. Corollary mood changes include ambivalent, constricted, and inappropriate emotional responsiveness and loss of empathy with others. Behavior may be withdrawn, regressive, and bizarre. The schizophrenias, in which the mental status is attributable primarily to a *thought* disorder, are to be distinguished from the *Major affective illnesses*, which are dominated by a mood disorder. The *Paranoid States* are distinguished from the schizophrenia by narrowness of their distortions of reality and the absence of other psychotic symptoms. [p. 33]

If the reader finds this definition a bit difficult to "pin down," he is by no means alone. The Chapmans (Chapman & Chapman, 1973) make the following observations:

> This is a definition written by a committee. It is sufficiently ambiguous to please clinicians who embrace any one of several competing views concerning criteria for diagnosing schizophrenia. The vagueness of the definition allows clinicians with divergent practices to claim to use it but does not help clinicians who wish to follow a common diagnostic practice to do so [p. 19].

What the Chapmans are saying is that the general definition of schizophrenia is of limited value, both from a practical and scientific point of view.

The data on the reliability of diagnosis of schizophrenia, although more impressive than those noted earlier for neuroses, still leave something to be desired. For example, in one study (Schmidt & Fonda, 1956) among psychiatric residents, the percentage of agreement for schizophrenics was 51%,[1] although in the same study, the agreement between residents and staff was a surprisingly high 91%. The latter figure may be somewhat inflated as a result of the tendency on the part of both residents and staff to label the vast majority of patients as schizophrenic. Beck, Ward, Mendelson, Mock, and Erbaugh (1962) report 53% agreement; Kaelbling and Volpe (1963) report a figure of 60%; and Sandifer, Pettus, and Quade (1964) report an agreement of 74%.

As we have suggested, when relatively specific behavior patterns are rated, in contrast to vaguely defined diagnostic syndromes such as schizophrenia, agreement would be expected to be higher. Yusin, Nihira, and Mortashed (1974)

---

[1] Percentage of agreement refers to the percentage of occasions when two or more diagnosticians provide a given patient with the same label, in this case, schizophrenia. Recently, Feighner, Robins, Guze, Woodruff, Winokur, and Munoz (1972) obtained agreement coefficients ranging from 86% to 92%, but this is based on an analysis among all major diagnostic categories, not merely schizophrenia.

found that when raters were asked to indicate the presence or absence of each of 27 *specific* textbook symptoms asociated with schizophrenia, the average agreement was 93%!

One recent study (Blashfield, 1973) attempted to examine reliabilities associated with the various subcategories of schizophrenia defined by DSM-II. Fifty-five judges, all clinical psychologists having an interest in issues related to classification, rated descriptions of various patients. (These were "artificial patients," whose symptoms were described so as to coincide with classificatory concepts.) Of the 10 subtypes listed in DSM-II, only four revealed significant agreement among the raters. A detailed description of these subtypes appears in the next section of this chapter. Here, we will just give the agreement coefficients:[2]

paranoid	24
schizoaffective	15
hebephrenic	13
catatonic	12

Keep in mind that the clinicians were not rating live patients, but merely verbal descriptions. Presumably, a comparable experiment using actual patients would have resulted in agreement coefficients higher in magnitude; nonetheless, these findings do raise serious questions concerning DSM-II subclassifications in schizophrenia. But despite their limitations, classification systems such as DSM-II are the prevailing systems and cannot be ignored. Three of the four listed— paranoid, hebephrenic, and catatonic—are among the four "classic" schizophrenic subtypes. The fourth is labeled *simple schizophrenia;* for this one Blashfield found essentially zero agreement. However, as Blashfield points out, this diagnosis is based to a large degree on historical data, and the clinicians doing the ratings were presented only with current symptomatology. This clearly biases the results against obtaining agreement in relation to simple schizophrenia. For this reason, and because it is one of the classic subtypes, we shall include this category in our discussion.

An important point is that diagnostic practices vary to a surprisingly large (and reliable) degree from time to time and from locale to locale. This is well illustrated by Chapman and Chapman (1973). Their data, based on U.S. Bureau of Census and U.S. Public Health Service reports, span a period from 1939 through 1963, and pertain to first-admission diagnoses in public mental institutions. As Figure 5-1 shows, there is clearly a trend toward increasing use of the label *schizophrenia* and this trend appears to correspond to a decrease in the use of the label *manic-depressive.*

These trends could reflect an actual change in patient symptomatology. On

[2] Blashfield had separate ratings for the two subclasses of the subcategory catatonic schizophrenia and for the two subclasses of the subcategory schizoaffective schizophrenia. For the sake of simplicity we have averaged the agreement coefficients for each of the subclasses.

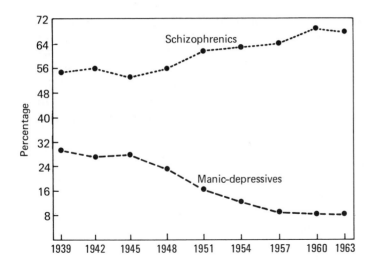

Figure 5-1. The percentage of patients labeled schizophrenic versus manic-depressive. (Adapted from *Disordered thought in schizophrenia* by L. J. Chapman and J. P. Chapman, © 1973. Used with permission of Prentice-Hall, Inc., Englewood Cliffs, N.J.)

the other hand, the data, in concert with results of two additional studies cited by Chapman and Chapman (1973), seem to support hypotheses favoring changes in diagnostic practices. Kramer (1965) noted that the usage of the label *schizophrenia* in England and Wales (1956–1957) was 33% lower than in the United States, but the manic-depressive label was used nine times as often in England and Wales. That these differences, at least in part, have resulted from differences in diagnostic practices is seen in the results of a study by Katz, Cole, and Lowery (1969). A large number of American and British psychiatrists witnessed the same film of a psychiatric interview. One-third of the 42 Americans labeled the patient as schizophrenic; not one of the 32 British psychiatrists used the label. Further evidence that the American conception of schizophrenia is broader than that of the British is seen in a similar study by Kendall, Cooper, Gourlay, and Copeland (1971). Almost without exception, a greater proportion of American than British psychiatrists rated a videotape case as schizophrenic; sometimes the discrepancy between the ratings of the two groups was dramatic. Thus, 69% of the American psychiatrists rated one patient as schizophrenic while only 2% of the British psychiatrists rated him as such. For another patient, the comparable figures were 85% versus 7%!

Chapman and Chapman (1973) further note that there are reliable differences in the United States between hospitals—and even between states—in the relative use of the labels *schizophrenia* and *manic-depression*. Thus the percentage of psychotics labeled manic-depressive varied from 1.1% in North Dakota to 21.8% in Vermont. Again, these differences could be real, but the Chapmans also note an apparent resurgence in the manic-depressive diagnosis following demonstrations of the efficacy of lithium in its treatment. This finding supports the hypothesis that it is the diagnostic practices that vary, rather than the patients sampled.

The Principal Schizophrenic Subcategories

As you read the following discussion, remember that the behaviors of actual schizophrenics do not fall neatly into these five subtypes. In the real world there is a great deal of overlap in symptomatology. Also, persons labeled schizophrenic generally show schizophrenic behaviors only a very small percentage of the time. Most schizophrenic patients on most hospital wards act relatively normal most of the time.

SIMPLE SCHIZOPHRENIA

DSM-II defines this condition as follows:

> This psychosis is characterized chiefly by a slow and insidious reduction of external attachments and interests and by the apathy and indifference leading to impoverishment of interpersonal relations, mental deterioration, and adjustment on a lower level of functioning. In general, the condition is less dramatically psychotic than are the hebephrenic, catatonic, and paranoid types of schizophrenia. Also, it contrasts with schizoid personality, in which there is little or no progression of the disorder [p. 33].

The classic textbook description (for example, see Buss, 1966; Coleman, 1972; Kleinmuntz, 1974), consistent with DSM-II, suggests a gradual onset, perhaps beginning in adolescence or the late teens, of marked interpersonal withdrawal. The jobs such persons seek are typically menial and nondemanding. They show a marked lack of emotionality and their conversion is characteristically sparse and trivial. It is suggested (Rosen, Fox, & Gregory, 1972; CRM, 1972) that they are more likely than normals to be labeled as prostitutes or petty criminals. CRM (1972) notes that they are often drifters or vagrants.

The present authors have seen relatively few patients with this formal diagnosis. In fact, this label is given rather infrequently in mental hospitals; the supposition is that simple schizophrenics are able to function in society, however marginally, and usually do not require institutionalization. For the researcher attempting to study this type of schizophrenia, this presents a real problem, as virtually all schizophrenic research subjects are hospitalized patients.

Since this category is defined rather loosely, it is easy to label certain fringe elements of our society as having a high proportion of simple schizophrenics. Kleinmuntz (1974) illustrates this very well:

> The population of street people, the flower children of the late 1960s, and the more recent commune dwellers have included in their ranks many simple schizophrenics [p. 262].

A layman hostile to flower children or commune dwellers is now in a position to cite an "expert" to the effect that such people are "mostly a bunch of psychos or schizos." Obviously this is as imprecise as it is an overinterpretation of Kleinmuntz's observation. Nevertheless, such unsubstantiated observations play right into the hands of people who wish to stigmatize others whose life styles are markedly different from their own. Whether the observation is based on Kleinmuntz's personal interaction with such individuals or on reports of others is not indicated by that author. As the following case study indicates, many simple schizophrenics appear coherent and well-oriented most of the time:

■   R.S., a 51-year-old black male, was first admitted to a mental hospital at age 26. He had recently been discharged from the military and since his release had been drinking heavily. According to the patient, the drinking was the reason he had sought help. The original diagnosis was depression, but subsequent behavior suggested that a schizophrenic label was more appropriate.

Aside from one arrest for disorderly conduct in 1939 at age 14, his childhood was uneventful. He completed 1 year of high school, which he disliked; he indicated that he had always been uncomfortable in crowds. During his 25 years of hospitalization (as of 1975 he was still hospitalized) he had almost no visits from family or friends, although this did not seem to distress him greatly. He could be described as a social isolate, typical of simple schizophrenics. As with most schizophrenics, but especially simple schizophrenics, his modal ward behavior was marked by cooperativeness (in many hospital settings this translates into passive compliance) and a relatively pleasant, if rather seclusive manner. Occasionally, however, his verbal behavior was bizarre. For example, at times he stated that he had conversations with God, could see nonexistent snakes, believed he had no heart, would occasionally mumble to himself incoherently and laugh for no apparent reason, and on one occasion maintained that he had 10 children by five different girl friends and that he heard trucks and cars all around. It should be stressed that behavior of this nature was exceptional for this patient. Often, when reference was made to such beliefs or experiences, he would volunteer that they were, after all, merely his imagination. Most of the time he was coherent and well oriented with respect to place, time, and his own identity. His emotional tone, or affect, was repeatedly described as "flat" and it was and is difficult to establish a good verbal rapport with this man.

PARANOID SCHIZOPHRENIA

According to DSM-II, paranoid schizophrenia is defined as follows:

This type of schizophrenia is characterized primarily by the presence of persecutory or grandiose delusions, often associated with hallucinations. Excessive religiosity is sometimes seen. The patient's attitude is frequently hostile and aggressive, and his behavior tends to be consistent with his delusions. In general, the disorder does not manifest the gross personality disorganization of the hebephrenic and catatonic types, perhaps because the patient used the mechanism of projection, which ascribes to others characteristics he cannot accept in himself. Three subtypes of the disorder may sometimes be differentiated, depending on the predominant symptoms: hostile, grandiose, and hallucinatory [p. 34].

Before addressing ourselves to the specifics of this category, it will be helpful to clarify some terms. A *delusion* refers to a belief, or at least behavior suggesting a belief, that is lacking in support or corroboration. Clinically, delusions involve beliefs about oneself; for example, the belief that one is being *persecuted*, in the absence of actual persecution, or that one is possessed of unusual or supernatural power or identity, referred to as a *delusion of grandeur*. A third class of delusions, *delusions of reference,* are beliefs that *actual* events occurring in the world are somehow related to or centered around oneself, when this is clearly not the case.

Hallucinations refer to perceptual experiences (we must qualify this by saying *presumed* perceptual experiences) not shared by others, for example, "seeing things" or "hearing voices." Hallucinations must be distinguished from *illusions*—perceptual distortions that *are* shared by others, such as mirages and the pictorial illusions found in the perception chapter of an introductory psychology textbook.

Now to return to paranoid schizophrenia. The DSM-II characterization is similar to that found in most current texts. The idea of projection as an important underlying process in paranoid thinking originated in the writings of Freud (1914/1953), and is still rather pervasive. Projection means attributing to others one's own unconscious thoughts or actions. The view that projection is fundamental to this disorder persists, although convincing scientific evidence is lacking. However, like many other Freudian explanatory constructs, its importance is quite difficult to disprove.

Textbooks tend to stress the importance of *auditory* hallucinations in paranoid schizophrenia (for example, Kleinmuntz, 1974; Rosen *et al.,* 1972) and delusions of persecution. Most texts suggest that delusions of grandeur follow from delusions of persecution (see Coleman, 1972). The latter view is plausible; if a person believes he is being persecuted, there surely must be a reason for it. For instance, he may attribute the plots against him to the "fact" that he is Jesus Christ, and the conspirators are the Jews or the Romans. This is, of course, a conjectural interpretation of these delusions.

This label is very often used in mental institutions—approximately 50% of first admissions are diagnosed as paranoid schizophrenics—so that most experienced clinicians have had considerable contact with patients so labeled. Although Blashfield's agreement coefficient for this category (1973) was not high in an absolute sense, it was considerably greater than for any other category of schizophrenia, and in our view this is one of the more useful diagnostic categories. The classical picture of the paranoid schizophrenic is more or less consistent with what we have observed in psychiatric settings. Persons with this label do frequently state that they are being persecuted, evidence a preoccupation with religion, and are, on the average, more hostile than other individuals with other types of schizophrenic labels. There is evidence that paranoid schizophrenics are more intelligent, or show less intellectual deterioration, on the average, than other schizophrenics (see Kingsley & Struening, 1966; Payne, 1961; Smith, 1964). A case history follows.

■ This 29-year-old black male is diagnosed paranoid schizophrenic. He has spent most of the past 7 years in and out of mental institutions in the Midwest. He was one of 13 siblings. His father, who was described as pleasant and easygoing, died when the patient was 5 years old. His mother, who is described as a gentle, caring person, has been and is presently employed as a maid. Not surprisingly, his main problems early in life related to poverty. As a child he was seen as quiet and well behaved. He spent a good deal of time reading the Bible and planned to become a preacher, although his major in college was engineering.

In 1968 he was a junior in college. Following an antiwar demonstration in Chicago, he was found wandering in the streets in a confused, disoriented state. He was taken to a hospital, at which time he maintained that he had experiences similar to "Christ on the cross" and that indeed he had seen Christ. His main wish, he said, was to "do something to keep peace in the world." In this patient's case there were some relatively clear-cut precipitating factors. He valued academic achievement, but was doing badly in school. Although not an active participant in the demonstration, he had strong objections to serving in the military, and had recently been called for his preinduction physical. His initial hospitalization lasted for 1 month. Upon returning home, he burned the photo of his girl friend for no apparent reason and refused to have any contact with her. However, when he is actively psychotic, she remains a focus of his preoccupation. Since that time he has been hospitalized four times and is in a mental institution at this writing. As is typical of many schizophrenics, his behavior is highly variable. At times he appears relatively normal and lucid. At other times he evidences a delusional system of a religious nature, for example, maintaining that he is "Polaris and the son of God." Although he has no history of violence, at times he shows extreme negativism, for instance refusing to go to meals without orders from "the Man" (God) and frequently he is withdrawn and quite unsociable. His IQ is 113, which, considering his culturally deprived childhood, must be viewed as well above average.

A number of current authors in the field see no need for five subtypes of schizophrenia; they simply divide schizophrenics into two categories, paranoid and nonparanoid. As we shall see in a later section, there is something to be said for such a simplification.

PARANOID SCHIZOPHRENIA VERSUS PARANOIA. DSM-II and some current textbooks (for example, Coleman, 1972) treat paranoid schizophrenia and paranoia as separate psychological entities. Those who make this distinction point to individuals who have well-defined delusional systems but who do not in any other respects appear to be "crazy." They do not experience hallucinations, nor do they show the characteristic looseness of thinking that forms a major part of the definition of schizophrenia. They are said to be "suffering" from paranoia. We put the term *suffering* in quotes deliberately, because experience suggests that the paranoid may not suffer nearly as much as those close to him. For example, one might become hostile because his brilliance is not recognized. Another might become hostile or even physically abusive because of extreme jealousy over an imagined affair between a spouse and lover.

Although it is common to find persons labeled as paranoid schizophrenics in mental hospitals, hospitalized individuals are rarely given the label *paranoia*. This is because persons who behave in this manner to a degree sufficient to warrant a psychotic label are probably quite rare. As we have noted, their delusional system is circumscribed, and in other respects they can be described as normal and are quite able to function outside the confines of an institution. Thus, one is not ordinarily hospitalized because he is obsessed with delusional thoughts of infidelity on the part of his wife, or because he is continually bringing lawsuits against department stores, or because he has professed to the world that he is a brilliant inventor. Indeed, such people may persuade others that their case is justified or their cause just. To illustrate, recently Rimm was walking down an avenue in a Central American capital. A fellow North American approached him and requested $5 to tide him over until his federal pension check arrived. The man declared he was actively campaigning for the "presidency of the world," on a reasonably articulated platform of curbing overpopulation, war, famine, and other miseries. He carried with him a long list of signatories who supported his candidacy, as well as a clipping from a local newspaper, including his photo, describing a press interview he had conducted. He indicated that he had been on several television and radio talk shows, and we suspect that this was the case—perhaps because the producers felt he had a certain comic value.

Since this "candidate" evidenced no looseness of thinking, a schizophrenic label would not seem appropriate. On the other hand, given his lofty, all-consuming goal and notable lack of resources and political sophistication, we would describe him as clearly delusional. Were a psychiatric label required, paranoia might suffice.[3] If individuals showing dramatic or bizarre forms of paranoia are rare, people showing lesser degrees of paranoid-type thinking are not uncommon. In fact, it is likely that all of us behave in a somewhat paranoid manner on occasion. DSM-II has a special category for persons showing relatively mild paranoid behavior; the label is *paranoid personality*.

HEBEPHRENIC SCHIZOPHRENIA

DSM-II defines this condition as follows:

> This psychosis is characterized by disorganized thinking, shallow and inappropriate affect, unpredictable giggling, silly and regressive behavior and mannerisms, and frequent hypochondriacal complaints. Delusions and hallucinations, if present, are transient and not well organized [p. 33].

[3] From this example it should be clear that paranoia does not necessarily imply a hostile, belligerent attitude. What it does imply is that a major belief system is unfounded or unrealistic. Making such a determination is sometimes very difficult. After all, there are inventors who, after years of being labeled "crazy," produce marvelous inventions (after which none dare call them paranoid), and there are people who do have unfaithful spouses. There is even the possibility, admittedly small, that the man in Central America might some day be world president. Rimm's $5 donation was not predicated on that assumption, however.

Literally, *hebephrenic* means "mind of a child." This is one of the more dramatic forms of schizophrenia, although admittedly, it is not very well defined (see Blashfield, 1973, whose agreement coefficient was a meager 13%). The classic picture of the hebephrenic suggests rather gross behavioral deterioration, generally more pervasive than is found in other types of schizophrenia. Although most schizophrenics do not manifest schizophrenic behavior most of the time, this is less true of hebephrenics, according to the clinical experience of the present writers and others.

Case histories suggest that individuals given this label usually exhibit behaviors such as seclusiveness and preoccupation with philosophy or religion at a relatively early age, perhaps during adolescence. The deterioration appears to progress until, by the time of hospitalization, the patient may be manifesting incoherent babbling, impulsiveness, and inexplicable mood shifts such as crying, laughing, or giggling for no apparent reason. The affect has a superficial or shallow quality to it, suggesting that the patient himself does not take it seriously—an inference stemming from the highly changeable and apparently groundless nature of this emotional behavior.

It is frequently said (see CRM, 1972; Coleman, 1972; Rosen *et al.*, 1972) that hebephrenic schizophrenics show regressive behavior; for example, they smear feces. The idea of regression is important in the writings of Freud and other psychoanalysts (see Fenichel, 1945). Most generally, regression includes the manifesting of behaviors appropriate for an age level far below that of the individual; usually the term is used to characterize childlike behavior. In the psychological literature it can mean one of two things: Either the person is manifesting behaviors that he himself perpetrated when he was a small child or he is manifesting behavioral patterns characteristic of small children in general, irrespective of whether he himself ever engaged in such behaviors. The distinction is very important theoretically, especially since psychoanalytic thinking about schizophrenia usually stresses the idea that the patient regresses to his own previously exhibited patterns of behavior. We shall return to a discussion of regression in relation to schizophrenia later in this chapter.

Delusions are not uncommon among hebephrenic schizophrenics, but unlike those of the paranoid schizophrenic, they lack consistency. The classic description of hallucinations involves voices accusing the patient of engaging in immoral acts. For example, Ullmann and Krasner (1969) report asking a patient diagnosed as hebephrenic schizophrenic why he was giggling. He indicated that it was because of voices, which were not disturbing because "they've been there so long they keep me company. They amuse me by the silly things they tell me [p. 360]." The voices accused the patient of engaging in homosexual behavior.

The reported hallucinations are not always accusatory. Rimm recalls one hebephrenic schizophrenic who appeared to engage in silly chatter a good portion of the waking day. He indicated that he was talking with his "pals"—friends he had known some two decades ago—and there was no indication that the conversation was anything but amiable. He seemed to enjoy these conversations and we suspect he would have been lonely without them. Nor are the hallucinations necessarily auditory. For example, a hebephrenic patient once approached Rimm, complaining that he saw Jesus Christ masturbating on his dormitory wall. The following is a representative case history.

■　This 50-year-old white male has spent all his adult life confined to a mental institution. His diagnosis is hebephrenic schizophrenia. He was the youngest of three siblings. His father, a plumber, was, from the patient's records, a kind and understanding parent. His mother became physically ill when the patient was quite young; she never fully recovered and died when the patient was 13 years of age. As a child he was described as likable, but rather nervous; reportedly, he did not especially enjoy the company of others. He did well in high school, until his last year when he became "very nervous." If there were clear-cut precipitating factors, they are not apparent in his record. After leaving high school he worked with his father, but soon requested medical help because his "nerves were gone." At the time of his first hospitalization, age 16, he was crying a great deal of the time and was seen as highly disturbed.

Throughout the late 1940s and 1950s his hospital record is replete with instances of highly inappropriate, bizarre behavior including public masturbation, putting fecal matter in his mouth, tying ribbons around his toes, stuffing toilet paper in his nose, wetting his pants, and talking to himself in an unintelligible manner while evidencing a silly, vacant smile. On one occasion a stick had to be removed from his rectum (which was consistent with his pattern of putting foreign objects in all of his orifices). Once when asked how he liked the hospital, he put a finger in the back of his throat in an apparent attempt to vomit—one may interpret this to mean he did not like the hospital! Over the years his behavior has lost much of its bizarre character. Perhaps significantly, his improvement coincides roughly with the introduction of phenothiazines into his treatment. (This was the first major class of anti-schizophrenic medications; see Chapter 21 of the present text.) Presently he is described as a quiet but cooperative individual in good "reality contact" but very slow in everything he does. He continues to manifest a meaningless grin. One of his main pleasures in life seems to involve playing with water. He washes his face and hands so frequently that they are constantly irritated, which presents something of a medical problem. His eating and sleeping patterns are described as normal.

Before leaving our discussion of hebephrenic schizophrenia, we would like to make an additional observation. In dealing with persons so labeled, most observers are left with the impression that there really is something different about these people, whether this difference is at a perceptual level, a thinking level, or merely a verbal level. As we intimated earlier, it is possible for a person to act "crazy" in order to gain certain advantages associated with custodial care. Certainly a person with sufficient imagination and clinical sophistication could feign hebephrenic schizophrenia. But given that the level of deviation or "craziness" sufficient to continue one's hospitalization is relatively minimal—an occasional "Gee doc, I keep hearing those voices and they really get to me" is usually more than sufficient—it is difficult to see why an "actor" would resort to such symptomatic overkill to accomplish the same goal. After all, hebephrenics are typically not accorded the same status as most other hospitalized schizophrenics; for example, they may not receive canteen and ground privileges or weekend passes.

CATATONIC SCHIZOPHRENIA

This condition is described as follows by DSM-II:

> It is frequently possible and useful to distinguish two subtypes of catatonic schizophrenia. One is marked by excessive and sometimes violent motor activity and excitement and the other by generalized inhibition manifested by stupor, mutism, negativism, or waxy flexibility. In time, some cases deteriorate to a vegetative state [pp. 33-34].

Relative to other DSM-II categorical descriptions, this is uncommonly brief. Perhaps this is in part because the *catatonic* diagnosis is becoming rather rare in psychiatric populations. Whether this reflects a change in presenting complaints at the time of admission, a change in diagnostic habits of clinicians, or the fact that potential catatonics are especially likely to improve if given chemotherapy, remains to be answered.

The term *catatonic* means a disturbance in motor behavior, which is the defining aspect of this disorder. The DSM-II description is a bit misleading, as it

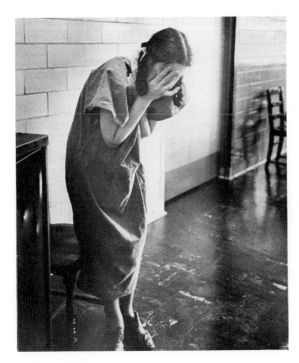

This woman, diagnosed as schizophrenic, is a patient in a state mental hospital. She maintains this grieving posture for hours at a time, which suggests that she is in a state of stuporous catatonic schizophrenia. Presumably, her thoughts are disordered—but there is no way for clinicians to be certain of this. (Esther Bubley)

implies that some catatonics exhibit characteristically excited behavior whereas others typically are in a stuporous state. Case histories suggest that individuals with the *catatonic* label frequently show both types of behavior. At times they may be highly withdrawn and mute, and show a startling lack of motor behavior. While in such a stuporous state, a catatonic may assume an unusual posture for hours at a time. His muscles may be rigid, or they may show waxy flexibility; the latter term means that a limb can be moved into a different position by another person, perhaps with some effort, and the limb will remain in the new position. During the stuporous phase a catatonic may show highly oppositional or negativistic behavior, refusing to comply with requests, sometimes doing the opposite behavior. At other times he may imitate the behavior of others in a seemingly senseless manner.

Coleman (1972) has suggested that while in a stuporous state, the catatonic's behavior is not affected by threats or painful stimulation. The present authors know of individual cases wherein aversive stimulation such as painful electric shock had no apparent effect, although we would hesitate to say that this is true with all stuporous catatonics. When in more lucid states, catatonics frequently indicate that they were very much aware of what was going on while stuporous, suggesting that they are by no means impervious to physical pain. Self-reports suggest that hallucinations and delusional thinking are common during the catatonic stupor.

Somewhat in the manner of a manic-depressive (described in Chapter 6), the catatonic stupor may be replaced by a period of relatively normal behavior, or quite unexpectedly, by a period of extreme agitation or excitement. The patient's speech is typically marked by excitement and incoherence, and his motor behavior shows striking hyperactivity. During such periods he may do violence to himself or others. A case history follows.

■ This 51-year-old white female has been in and out of mental hospitals for the past 22 years. Although her official diagnosis is presently chronic undifferentiated schizophrenia (a category probably overused in the United States), both the referring psychologist and Rimm believe she shows certain characteristics typical of catatonic schizophrenia. She experiences recurrent episodes of withdrawal and mutism. Sometimes she assumes a very rigid posture, including waxy flexibility, lasting perhaps 24 hours. Sometimes she goes into a catatonic stupor lasting several days; during such periods she must literally be dragged to bed and to other essential activities. She does not show the extreme agitation often associated with this label, but does occasionally engage in strange behaviors (taking showers with her clothes on in response to voices telling her to do this; bed wetting). Often she exhibits behavior described as friendly and cooperative.

The patient's mother died when she was 7 years of age. According to a sister (the only sibling), her father was rigid, uncompromising, and highly overprotective. Apparently, she has been shy and seclusive all her life. She has not, in her entire life, had a single date. Her one, unfortunate, sexual experience involved being raped; this occurred while she was at college and had the effect of accelerating her social withdrawal. She failed out of college, has never held gainful employment, and when not hospitalized, lives with her father.

We have suggested that it is difficult or at least implausible to account for hebephrenic behavior entirely in terms of the individual's desire to receive custodial care. These same arguments apply, perhaps even more strongly, to catatonic behavior. If the patient merely wishes to remain in the hospital, there is absolutely no need to exhibit behaviors as extreme, uncomfortable, and sometimes dangerous as those associated with catatonic schizophrenia.

SCHIZOPHRENIA, SCHIZO-AFFECTIVE TYPE

As we have noted, the schizophrenias are primarily viewed as thought disorders. In the next chapter, we will discuss behavior patterns viewed as primarily reflecting disturbances in mood or affect. The schizo-affective label (popularized by DSM-I, 1952) was introduced to deal with persons who showed a mixture of thought and affective symptoms. DSM-I notes that "on prolonged observation, such cases usually prove to be basically schizophrenic in nature [p. 27]." Thus, the authors of the 1952 psychiatric manual viewed this disorder as essentially schizophrenic in nature. However, the revised manual, DSM-II, does not stress the schizophrenic aspect, merely noting that "this category is for patients showing a mixture of schizophrenic symptoms and pronouncd elation or depression. Within this category it may be useful to distinguish excited from depressed types [p. 35]."

Most authors do not deal with this category in any depth, and some popular texts do not even cite it (e.g., CRM, 1972; Kleinmuntz, 1974). Rosen et al., (1972) suggest that schizo-affective schizophrenia is most commonly seen in paranoid schizophrenics with severe depression. Both Coleman (1972) and Buss (1966) cite evidence suggesting that when schizophrenic behavior is mixed with affective symptoms, the prognosis is somewhat better than in cases of "pure" schizophrenia.

Schizo-affective schizophrenia is an especially difficult category with which to deal because it overlaps certain other schizophrenia subtypes as well as certain subtypes of affective disorders, described in the next chapter. This is not to suggest that no patients manifest a mixture of schizophrenic behaviors and severe affective disturbance. Our point is merely that such patients present serious classification problems, given existing diagnostic systems. A case history follows.

■ This 65-year-old white female has had numerous hospitalizations dating back some 30 years. Her case suggests that the schizo-affective category is highly ambiguous. At various times she has had the following diagnoses: schizophrenic reaction, chronic undifferentiated type; schizophrenic reaction, catatonic type; schizophrenic reaction, paranoid type; schizophrenic reaction, schizo-affective type (her present diagnosis); and psychotic depressive reaction.

The patient has shown intermittent episodes of agitation, hostility, and delusional thinking. On one occasion, she punched an admitting physician "squarely on the nose." She has had frequent fights with other patients; once she was bitten and required a tetanus shot. Often she has been loud and demanding on the ward, frequently cursing both patients and staff. Although her delusions are of a paranoid nature, they lack the consistency of paranoid schizophrenia. Once she accused her sister of trying to poison her ice cream; early in her hospitalization, she maintained that people were saying she was a homosexual. Some years later she stated that the hospital was a "communist place" and that she was there because she was a communist.

Her record suggested that her childhood was relatively uneventful and that her home life was generally good. She was one of three siblings; her father, some 20 years older than her mother, was a fire chief. She consistently did well in school and appeared to place considerable value on good manners. She completed college and taught school for several years. She married at age 38 and was divorced 4 years later, shortly after her first hospitalization. Marital difficulties and the divorce may have been precipitating factors, although she had shown paranoid thinking and intense depression some 10 years prior to her marriage.

Presently, her behavior is relatively normal, or at least manageable, and plans are being made to transfer her to a nursing home. Hospital psychiatrists attribute her improvement in part to her current medication, which includes both lithium and phenothiazine. Lithium is useful in the treatment of affective disorders and the phenothiazines are helpful in the treatment of many schizophrenics. (See Chapter 21 of the present text.)

In this section we have described the major "classic" schizophrenic subtypes. We have pointed to problems associated with relatively poor diagnostic reliability. Such problems are by no means trivial. They impede meaningful theorizing about the nature and etiology of schizophrenia—or perhaps it would be better to say "the schizophrenias." If diagnosticians have difficulty in agreeing on how to classify patients, they will obviously have difficulty in relating diagnosis to prognosis and treatment.

Writers, researchers, and practitioners concerned with schizophrenia are keenly aware of these problems, and there have been several attempts to devise alternative diagnostic approaches. In the next section, we shall discuss and evaluate the more popular alternatives to systems such as DSM-II.

Acute Schizophrenia versus Chronic Schizophrenia

The acute versus chronic dimension is defined in two ways. Textbook writers such as Coleman (1972) characterize the acute schizophrenic as an individual who suddenly and dramatically shows schizophrenic behavior, whereas the chronic is seen as evidencing a pattern of gradual behavioral deterioration. When defined in this way, the acute–chronic dichotomy is similar to the process–reactive dichotomy (see Petzel & Johnson, 1973) discussed later.

For the most part, researchers define acute and chronic schizophrenia in terms of *duration* of hospitalization, often using the labels *short term* and *long term* rather than *acute* and *chronic*. This practice has had the effect of diluting or distorting the original acute–chronic distinction, which may be unfortunate. In terms of duration, the length of a hospitalization necessary to qualify a patient as chronic is rather arbitrary. For example, in a study by McInnis and Ullmann (1967), to be labeled *chronic* required a minimum of 3 years of hospitalization; to be labeled *acute*, the patient could not be hospitalized for more than 6 months. This is in sharp contrast to Magaro (1973) who labeled patients with 4 or more years *chronic*, and those hospitalized less than 4 years *acute*. Lack of agreement concerning the length of hospitalization necessary to define a patient as chronic or acute clearly weakens the value of this distinction.

One reason for researching the acute–chronic dimension is to determine what effects prolonged hospitalization has on the patient diagnosed as schizophrenic. Typically the researcher compares a group of acutes and chronics on some psychological measure; for example, learning (McInnis & Ullmann, 1967) or emotional arousal (Magaro, 1973). One difficulty in drawing conclusions from such research is that one cannot be sure that it is simply the amount of hospitalization that accounts for any obtained differences. Later in the chapter, we will explore the value of the paranoid–nonparanoid distinction in studying schizophrenia; there is evidence that paranoid schizophrenics are less likely than nonparanoids to remain hospitalized for protracted periods (Strauss, Sirotkin, & Grisell, 1974). This has the obvious effect of reducing the proportion of paranoids in any sample of chronic patients, relative to the proportion of paranoids in the acute or short-term group of patients. Any differences found between acutes and chronics could conceivably be attributable to the disparity in the proportion of paranoids, rather than duration of hospitalization. This point has been made by Strauss (1973) who has also pointed to the important roles of prehospitalization adjustment, posthospitalization living arrangements, and differential responsiveness to drug therapy as factors associated with the duration of hospitalization. All these factors result in what is usually referred to as sampling bias. Along dimensions *other than chronicity*, patients labeled as acute schizophrenics probably differ from those labeled as chronic schizophrenics. Thus, although there is evidence that chronics, relative to acutes, respond to a narrower range of environmental stimuli (Broen, 1968), there is little justification for attributing this to chronicity per se.

These two considerations—arbitrariness in differentiating acute and chronic patients and the changing character of the patient sample with increasing hospitalization—make interpretation of research findings difficult. Moreover, the experimental results themselves often conflict. For example, certain studies suggest that chronic schizophrenics show higher levels of skin conductance, a measure of presumed emotional arousal, than acutes (Bernstein, 1967; Magaro, 1973) while others (for example, Bernstein, 1970) suggest the opposite. In the same vein, there is some evidence (Braginsky, Grosse, & Ring, 1966) that chronic patients may deliberately respond in a manner that will result in continued hospitalization, whereas acutes respond in a manner which they are led to believe will shorten their hospitalization. However, Ryan and Neale (1973) found that one group of chronic schizophrenics behaved in precisely the opposite manner.

For research purposes, we do not believe that diagnosing schizophrenics as acute or chronic is especially useful.

On the other hand, it is useful to find out what factors or variables relate to or *predict* length of hospitalization, as well as the number of hospitalizations. For example, Lorei and Gurel (1973) found that the best predictor of admission to the hospital is the number of prior hospitalizations. Anthony, Buell, Sharratt, and Althoff (1972) summarize research indicating that aftercare may be important in reducing the likelihood of rehospitalization. As we shall see shortly, whether the patient is labeled as process (versus reactive) or paranoid (verus nonparanoid) has some utility in predicting the future course of hospitalization of schizophrenic patients.

The clinical value of employing the acute–chronic distinction is also questionable. In principle, the distinction is based in part on the suddenness of onset. In practice, duration of hospitalization, whether based on a single hospital stay or several hospitalizations, appears to be paramount. Usually, very early during a first admission to a mental hospital, a schizophrenic is viewed as acute. If his hospitalization is protracted, he becomes a "chronic." In becoming chronic, the patient is not required to undergo some major psychological change. In fact, there is evidence that this is not the case, at least in relation to intellectual functioning (see Chapman & Chapman, 1973).

Process Schizophrenia versus Reactive Schizophrenia

The process–reactive distinction reflects one of the more interesting approaches to the study of schizophrenia. The process schizophrenic is one who shows gradual behavioral deterioration, perhaps beginning in late adolescence. The reactive schizophrenic, on the other hand, has had a relatively normal adjustment prior to undergoing some sort of psychological trauma. Presumably as a consequence of the psychological stress, schizophrenic behaviors suddenly appear.

As is often noted, the term *process* connotes some sort of basic malfunction in the brain, whether it is specified in terms of genetics, biochemistry, or physiology. The term *reactive* places far greater emphasis on environmental precipitating factors.

The chief defining characteristic of the process–reactive distinction is the nature of the onset. If it is gradual and no clear-cut precipitating trauma is apparent, the label *process* is invoked. Because a gradual onset is usually defined in terms of poor social adjustment prior to being identified as schizophrenic, process schizophrenics are often characterized in terms of a "poor premorbid adjustment."[4] Similarly, reactive schizophrenics are viewed as having a "good premorbid adjustment." In the literature, the process–reactive and good–poor premorbid adjustment distinctions overlap to a great extent. In the present text, the terms are used synonymously.

There are reasons for considering the process–reactive distinction as having considerable merit. First, the process–reactive dimension is defined in terms of specific behaviors or events, although admittedly these behaviors or events are usually inferred after the fact (that is, after hospitalization). There are several procedures or scales for assessing where a patient is on the process–reactive dimension; for example, Phillips (1953), Wittman (1941), and Ullmann and Giovannoni (1964). In terms of content the various measures show considerable overlap, and they tend to intercorrelate (see McCreary, 1974). For our purposes it is sufficient to describe one scale, that proposed by Ullmann and Giovannoni (1964): The patient is required to answer yes or no to each of a series of questions. Agreement with any of the following items will elevate the patient's process score:

Has never married.

Has never held one job for as long as 2 years.

Has received no training after high school.

Was not a member of a gang or group in high school.

Was never deeply in love and informed the other party.

Has not held jobs where people expected to stay for long periods of time.

Has never made house payments.

Has experienced no change in life (marriage, birth of a child, death or loss of loved one, loss of a job) prior to hospitalization.

You may find the last item rather puzzling. Keep in mind, however, that a defining characteristic of process schizophrenia is the absence of a potentially stressful precipitating event.

A more basic reason for considering the process–reactive distinction of value is that it has predictive utility. For example, people labeled as good premorbids (that is, reactives) show less psychological deficit at first hospitalization than poor premorbids (Higgins, 1969; Neale & Cromwell, 1970). Good premorbids have a higher probability of discharge and of briefer hospitalizations, and are less likely to be rehospitalized (Strauss, 1973). Interestingly, there is evidence that *poor* premorbids are more likely to benefit from so-called "antipsychotic" drugs (see Chapter 21) than good premorbids (Goldstein, Judd, Rodnick, & La Polla, 1969).

Chapman and Chapman (1973) have reviewed a large number of studies comparing process and reactive schizophrenics on a variety of performance

---

[4] The term *premorbid*, borrowed from physical medicine, means "prior to evidencing clear symptoms of an 'illness.' " In actual practice in relation to schizophrenia, what it usually means is "prehospitalization."

tasks; for example, problem solving, abstract thinking, proverb interpretation, and deviant word-associations. Although they also present some conflicting findings, their general conclusion is that process schizophrenics perform less adequately than reactive schizophrenics. More recent evidence would seem to support the Chapmans (Kilburg & Siegel, 1973, analogy test performance; O'Keefe & DeWolfe, 1973, concept learning; Petzel & Johnson, 1973, concept formation; Watson, 1973, abstract thinking).[5]

We have talked about process and reactive schizophrenics as if they constituted two very distinct types of patients. Actually, many writers (e.g., Buss, 1966; Kleinmuntz, 1974; Ullmann & Krasner, 1969) appear to view process and reactive as two extreme ends of a continuum. Thus, the question is not whether a particular patient *is* a process schizophrenic, but rather, to what degree the patient shows process characteristics. However, Chapman and Chapman (1973) believe that process and reactive schizophrenics *do* constitute two different types. Thus, this issue remains a subject of controversy.

Paranoid Schizophrenia versus Nonparanoid Schizophrenia

As an alternative to the DSM-II classification approach to schizophrenia, a simple paranoid–nonparanoid classification system has received considerable attention. In fact, concern with whether or not paranoids should even be classified as schizophrenic is evident in the writings of Kraepelin (see Chapman & Chapman, 1973). As we have suggested, the diagnostic category *paranoia* may be of some value, but for now we shall concern ourselves with individuals labeled *paranoid schizophrenic*, since it is rare to encounter a patient with the diagnosis of pure paranoia.

At first hospital admission, those labeled as schizophrenic are most commonly diagnosed as paranoid. In terms of clinical practice (see Morrison, 1974), there is a tendency to employ the paranoid–nonparanoid distinction, with the nonparanoids typically labeled as *undifferentiated*. This practice is justified only if paranoids and nonparanoids differ with respect to important behavioral dimensions. There is evidence that this may well be the case. For example, many studies have shown paranoids to be superior to nonparanoids on measures related to intelligence (for example, Kendig & Richmond, 1940; Kingsley & Struening, 1966; Payne, 1961; Watson & Baugh, 1966). There is also evidence that the two groups differ on measures of reaction time (Court & Garwoli, 1968, Shakow &

---

[5] Meichenbaum (1969) has presented evidence that process schizophrenics perform more poorly than reactives on tasks requiring that the patient report essential similarities between objects. Rimm vividly recalls the first time he administered an intelligence test to a hospitalized schizophrenic; the patient had many characteristics of a process schizophrenic. When asked how a fly and a tree were alike, the patient's response was "they both walk on the ground." At the time, Rimm was so preoccupied with administering the test he noticed only that the response was incorrect. Later, a supervisor pointed out that it was also a bit odd.

McCormick, 1965) and that paranoids tend to be less distractible than non-paranoids (McGhie, Chapman, & Lawson, 1965). Research findings do not always yield greater psychological defects in nonparanoids than in paranoids (for example, see Bauman & Murray, 1968; Furth & Youniss, 1968; Goldberg, Schooler, & Mattsson, 1968). However the literature as a whole suggests that paranoid schizophrenics show less behavioral deterioration than nonparanoid schizophrenics.

Silverman (1964a, 1964b) argues that paranoids learn to filter out external stimulation because much of it is aversive, resulting in a narrowing of attention. Although his experimental findings seem to support his view, other findings suggest that Silverman's characterization of paranoids in contrast to nonparanoids is at best an oversimplification (Strauss, Foureman, & Parwatikar, 1974). At present, any relationship between greater "filtering" and superior test performance on the part of paranoids, in contrast to nonparanoids, must be viewed as rather speculative.

As we noted earlier, paranoid schizophrenics tend to show different patterns of hospitalization (Strauss, 1973; Strauss *et al.*, 1974). Specifically, paranoids tend to be hospitalized more briefly than nonparanoids and experience fewer rehospitalizations. Thus, there are relatively fewer paranoids among long-term patients than among short-term patients. We have previously argued that the observed psychological differences between short- and long-term patients might well reflect the relative proportions of paranoids among the two groups. Clearly, the converse of this could also be true. That is, the observed psychological differences between paranoids and nonparanoids could be reflections of the differences between acute and chronic patients. The question is, Which is the more basic distinction—acute–chronic or paranoid–nonparanoid? In our view, the evidence suggests that the paranoid–nonparanoid distinction is the more basic, but the issue is not yet resolved.

Other Attempts at Classification of Schizophrenia

STATISTICAL APPROACHES

The work of Lorr and his associates (Lorr, 1966, 1968; Lorr, Klett, & McNair, 1963) exemplifies the use of complex statistical procedures in a major effort to develop alternatives to systems such as DSM-I and DSM-II. Lorr's approach has the advantage that it is empirical in its basis. It does not rely upon a popular theory, tradition, or convention. However, the data fed into the statistical analysis (factor analysis and cluster analysis) ultimately rest upon diagnosticians rating the behaviors of patients. Behavioral observations are clearly subject to bias, and it is therefore naive to assume that statistical approaches magically eliminate such bias. Such is not the case, and the use of the term *empirical* in characterizing the Lorr approach is subject to obvious qualification. On the other hand, the approach may be described as a good deal more empirical and scientific than the approaches that led to DSM-I and DSM-II.

The specific syndromes to which Lorr's research led (Lorr, 1966; Lorr et al., 1963) are as follows:

1. *Excitement:* The patient's speech is hurried, loud, and difficult to stop. His mood level and self-esteem are elevated, and his emotional expression tends to be unrestrained or histrionic. He is also likely to exhibit controlling or dominant behavior.

2. *Hostile Belligerence:* The patient's attitude toward others is one of disdain and moroseness. He is likely to manifest much hostility, resentment, and a complaining bitterness. His difficulties and failures tend to be blamed on others.

3. *Paranoid Projection:* The patient gives evidence of fixed beliefs that attribute a hostile, persecuting, and controlling intent to others around him.

4. *Grandiose Expansiveness:* The patient's attitude toward others is one of superiority. He exhibits fixed beliefs that he possesses unusual powers. He reports divine missions and may identify himself with well-known or historical personalities.

5. *Perceptual Distortions:* The patient reports hallucinations (voices and visions) that threaten, accuse, or demand.

6. *Anxious Intropunitiveness:* The patient reports vague apprehension as well as specific anxieties. His attitudes toward himself are disparaging. He is also prone to report feelings of guilt and remorse for real and imagined faults. The patient's underlying mood is typically dysphoric.

7. *Retardation and Apathy:* The patient's speech, ideation, and motor activity are delayed, slowed, or blocked. In addition, he is likely to manifest apathy and disinterest in the future.

8. *Disorientation:* The patient's orientation with respect to time, place, and season is defective. He may show failure to recognize others around him.

9. *Motor Disturbances:* The patient assumes and maintains bizarre postures, and he makes repetitive facial and body movements.

10. *Conceptual Disorganization:* Disturbances in the patient's stream of thought are manifested in irrelevant, incoherent, and rambling speech. Repetition of stereotyped phrases and coining of new words are also common [Lorr et al., 1963, pp. 35–36; italics added].[6]

It must be pointed out that these dimensions are derived from interviews with male and female hospitalized acute patients labeled merely as psychotic. That is, the sizable and diverse patient sample (taken from 14 states) was not restricted to schizophrenics. The factors, or dimensions, are for functional psychosis rather than for schizophrenia per se.

Using a related approach, Everitt, Gourlay, and Kendell (1971) performed a cluster analysis on a large number of American and British patients. Their findings suggest that paranoid schizophrenia and mania (described in the next chapter) reflect relatively well-defined subtypes. Manic-depression, also described in the next chapter, was more poorly defined, but not as poorly defined as the type given the label *chronic schizophrenia*.

[6] Reprinted with permission from M. Lorr, C. J. Klett, and D. M. McNair, *Syndromes of psychosis,* © 1963, Pergamon Press Ltd.

Note that both the work of Lorr and his associates and that of Everitt, Gourlay, and Kendell suggest the usefulness of a category of behaviors labeled *paranoid*. In a Lorr (1968) study, the majority of patients diagnosed as paranoid schizophrenic fell into the broad paranoid category. Everitt *et al.* (1971) explicitly use the term *paranoid schizophrenic* for a relatively tightly defined cluster of behaviors. This may be taken as additional support for the validity or meaningfulness of the traditional diagnostic category, paranoid schizophrenia, and perhaps somewhat more indirectly, for the paranoid–nonparanoid distinction. But chronic schizophrenia was so poorly defined in the Everitt *et al.* study that there is less reason to accept a system dividing patients into paranoids and nondifferentiated categories, a system becoming increasingly popular in the United States. The problem does not lie with the paranoid category, but with the undifferentiated group. Describing a patient as a nondifferentiated schizophrenic may lead a naive observer to believe something uniquely descriptive has been said about the patient. In fact, all that is being said is that the patient is evidencing behavior that is somehow associated with the vaguely defined general category of schizophrenia, in the absence of consistent paranoid behaviors.

COMPARISONS OF BEHAVIOR

Throughout most of this chapter, we have attempted to describe and evaluate the popular approaches to categorizing schizophrenic behaviors. From a practical and theoretical point of view there is good reason to attempt to classify different schizophrenics, but efforts thus far have led to schemes that are far from perfect. Of course, it is possible to ignore diagnostic subcategories and simply investigate how people who happen to have the schizophrenic label differ from those who do not. One straightforward attempt to do just this is seen in a report by Freedman and Chapman (1973).

Freedman and Chapman presented a well-standardized interview to 20 newly admitted patients who had been reliably diagnosed as schizophrenic. A positive feature, and one that is not typical of most investigations of schizophrenics, was that none of the patients in the sample had been on antipsychotic medication prior to the interview.

The 20 schizophrenics were compared with 20 nonschizophrenic patients (diagnosed as having neurotic depression or anxiety neurosis) on a variety of descriptive measures derived from the standardized interview. Only those measures that yielded statistically significant differences between the schizophrenics and nonschizophrenics are reported here.

1. *Thought Disorders.* Nineteen schizophrenics compared with 12 nonschizophrenics showed evidence of thought disorder (referred to as blocking) or apparent mental fatigue. For example, one patient reported:

    I try to think and all of a sudden I can't say anything because it's like I turned off my mind [p. 50].

2. *Changes in Concentration.* Eleven schizophrenics compared with only three nonschizophrenics reported inability to focus their attention on relevant

stimuli or thoughts and to screen out irrelevant stimuli or thoughts. One patient reported that he had difficulty reading books because:

. . . probably an external stimulus would take my attention off the book . . . a sound or just . . . a lack of interest at one moment while something like a piece of sunlight is going on over here and that would probably start me thinking [p. 50].

3. *Perceptual Changes.* Eleven schizophrenics and three nonschizophrenics reported changes in visual perception of actual objects (e.g., "Things look blurry"; "People look scarier"). Seven schizophrenics and only one nonschizophrenic reported greater sensitivity to noise. Eleven schizophrenics and four nonschizophrenics reported difficulty understanding the speech of others. To quote one schizophrenic:

I don't understand a word that they're saying . . . like they might be speaking some foreign language [p. 52].

Eleven schizophrenics and two nonschizophrenics reported tending to misidentify people.

4. *Speech Changes.* Six schizophrenics and no nonschizophrenics said that others had told them their speech was difficult to understand. To quote one schizophrenic:

My speech is like a horse. It pulls back on me. I can't make it go where I want it to [p. 52].[7]

Not surprisingly, the schizophrenics tended to report more hallucinations than the nonschizophrenics. Data on this were not presented, however, because reports of hallucinations formed one of the important criteria for labeling a patient as schizophrenic in the first place.

Theories of Schizophrenia

Theories pertaining to schizophrenia have dealt with two fundamental questions: First, what are schizophrenics like? Put in slightly different terms, what do schizophrenics have in common that make them different from nonschizophrenics? Second, what causes schizophrenia? That is, what are the etiological factors that lead to schizophrenic behavior?

The first question deals with attempts to describe schizophrenia in theoretical terms. Since we have just devoted half of this chapter to describing schizophrenia, you may be puzzled to find that we are now posing this as an issue. In fact, what we have done so far is to provide standard descriptions and alternative attempts at classifying schizophrenic behavior. Although existing classification schemes have some merit, many writers, including the present authors, do not believe they provide a consistent and coherent portrayal of schizophrenia. For this reason, scientists, clinicians, and writers continue to grapple with the very basic issue of description.

[7] From B. Freedman and L. J. Chapman, Early subjective experience in schizophrenic episodes. *Journal of Abnormal Psychology*, 1973, *82*, 46–54. Copyright 1973 by the American Psychological Association. Reprinted by permission.

As we noted earlier, schizophrenia is mainly viewed as a thought disorder. Thus, it is reasonable that theoretical conceptualizations have attempted to pinpoint the nature of the disorder in terms of thinking. We will now discuss a few of the major theories.

The Nature of Schizophrenic Thinking

Bleuler, whose early writings (1911) had and continue to have a major impact on clinicians, described schizophrenia as a *loss or breakdown in the associative process,* disrupting the normal flow of ideas or associations. There is ample evidence that individuals labeled as schizophrenics do indeed give more unusual associations or responses in test situations than do normals (Goldstein & Acker, 1967; Kent & Rosanoff, 1910; Moran, Mefferd, & Kimble, 1964; Murphy, 1923). Such findings are not surprising when one considers that labeling a person as schizophrenic is usually based, in part at least, on the existence of unusual or "loose" associations. Like many other early theorizers about schizophrenia, Bleuler was vague about the nature of the hypothesized associative threads or linkages (see Chapman & Chapman, 1973).

Goldstein (1939, 1944/1964), among others, popularized the view that schizophrenics suffered from a *loss in abstract thinking*. Although abstract thinking is not easily defined, Goldstein (Goldstein & Scheerer, 1941) suggested that the so-called abstract attitude was marked by deliberate, reflective thinking as opposed to the almost reflexive responding to stimuli that characterized Goldstein's "concrete attitude." Schizophrenics as a group do tend to perform somewhat more poorly on concept formation tasks, the most popular method for assessing abstract thinking. Goldstein's characterization of schizophrenic thinking is far-reaching and rather vague. More recent investigators have attempted to redefine the abstract–concrete dimension in ways that may be amenable to experimental investigations (for example, Shimkunas, Gynther, & Smith, 1967; Watson, 1973). The term *concrete* implies, among other things, an inability to generalize. Clinical experience and experimental findings (e.g., Cameron, 1939) indicate that schizophrenics as a group are *not* especially lacking in the ability to generalize; rather, their generalizations would seem wrong or strange to most people. But such unusual, autistic, "private" responses or associations are not readily characterized as concrete.

One theory of schizophrenic thought assumes that such thinking is marked by *overinclusion* (Cameron & Magaret, 1951; Payne, Matussek, & George, 1959). Overinclusion can be defined in a variety of ways, but in general it refers to a tendency to assign an excessive number of stimuli to a particular category or concept. For example, suppose you are presented with the following four words:

cow   dog   horse   cat

and you are asked which words from the following list belong with the first four words:

donkey   ox   bird   tree

If you included *donkey* and *ox,* your response would not be scored as overinclusive, since the donkey and the ox are also mammals. If you also included *bird,* that would be relatively overinclusive—a bird is not a mammal, although it is an animal. Including *tree* would illustrate even greater overinclusiveness, since a tree, although it is a living thing, is not an animal.

Although certain investigations (e.g., Craig, 1973; Epstein, 1953; Payne *et al.,* 1959) have tended to support the view that schizophrenics are more overinclusive than nonschizophrenics, other investigations have not (e.g., Eliseo, 1963; Sturm, 1965). For the present, there is no firm basis for believing that overinclusiveness is a unique characteristic of persons labeled schizophrenic (see Payne, 1971).

Perhaps the single most influential hypothesis regarding the nature of schizophrenic thinking is the *regression hypothesis.* Regression, which means reverting to an earlier, perhaps infantile, mode or style of thinking and behavior, was popularized in the writings of Freud (1914/1953). That this view is still prominent reflects the fact that Freudian ideas, whether scientifically based or not, are still very much part of clinical psychology and psychiatry. Moreover, the regression hypothesis does have some empirical support. We have repeatedly noted that schizophrenics as a group tend to perform somewhat more poorly on a wide variety of cognitive tasks than do normal adults. Children also perform poorly, relative to adults, on many of these same tasks. Evidence pointing to similarities in thinking between children and schizophrenics (relative to normal adults) is seen in studies by Blumberg and Giller (1965), Burstein (1959, 1961), and Gottesman (1964) among others. The Gottesman study demonstrated that schizophrenics are far more likely than normals to give childlike associations to stimulus words. In a more recent investigation, Kilburg and Siegel (1973) gave reactive schizophrenics, process schizophrenics, and normals an analogies test (for example: *father* is to *son* as *uncle* is to: *niece, nephew, aunt, sister, father*). The normals' average score was approximately 40 compared with 20 for the reactive schizophrenics and 9 for the process schizophrenics. Kilburg and Siegel note that the reactives performed at a level expected of children ranging in age from 9 to 12, whereas the process schizophrenics performed more poorly than 9-year-old children.

These observations make it clear that in some respects, the thinking of schizophrenics, or at least the behavior from which we infer thinking, may indeed be described as childlike. However, as Chapman and Chapman (1973) have noted, psychoanalytic writers see regression not merely as a description of schizophrenic behavior; they also see it as a fundamental explanation. In the face of stress, the schizophrenic regresses to a childlike state. To quote from Otto Fenichel (1945), a recognized spokesman for classical psychoanalytic theory:

> In schizophrenia the collapse of reality testing, that fundamental function of the ego, and the symptoms of "disintegration of the ego," which amount to a severe disruption of the continuity of the personality, likewise can be interpreted as a return to the

time when the ego was not yet established or had just begun to be established [pp. 416–417].

At the risk of oversimplification, what Fenichel is saying is that in the process of becoming schizophrenic, an individual unconsciously assumes a mode of interaction with the world that is basically similar to his mode of interaction as an infant or very young child.

The regression explanation (as opposed to description) of schizophrenia is difficult to test in a definitive manner, and is incomplete at best. First, it is impossible to know whether an adult schizophrenic is behaving the way *he* responded as a very young child, or whether he is assuming what he perceives as the "standard" childlike role. Second, as Chapman and Chapman (1973) point out, there is some evidence that whereas children may make errors as a result of ignorance of the correct response, schizophrenics may make similar errors even though they are able to demonstrate that they possess the knowledge that could enable them to respond correctly. Perhaps the most compelling reason for questioning the regression theory of schizophrenia is as follows: If schizophrenic behavior were nothing more than a reflection of regression to childlike thinking and/or behavior, reports of hallucinations or delusions would be very rare, because they are rare among children. Recall that in the Kilburg and Siegel study, some of the schizophrenics behaved like 9 to 12-year-old children. In your experience, how many children *in this age range* report such experiences, or even appear to be relating to imaginary playmates? We would suspect, very few. Inasmuch as such experiences appear to be relatively *common* among individuals labeled as schizophrenic, regression as an explanation of schizophrenic behavior is obviously wanting. In some respects the thinking and behavior of schizophrenics is childlike, but in some important respects, it is not.

One currently popular view of the nature of schizophrenic thinking has been put forth by Chapman and his associates (e.g., Chapman & Chapman, 1973; Chapman, Chapman, & Miller, 1964). These writers see schizophrenic thinking as marked by an *excessive yielding to normal biases*. The Chapman theory is illustrated in the following example: If you were asked to say the first word that came to mind when presented with the word *black,* you would probably respond with *white*. The response *white* is a common or normal association to the stimulus word *black* and therefore can be thought of as reflecting a normal bias. The point that Chapman and his colleagues make is that schizophrenics tend to give such responses *even when they are not appropriate to the given situation*. For example, consider the following item taken from a study by Rattan and Chapman (cited in Chapman & Chapman, 1973):

Shoot means the same as

a. rifle
b. rug
c. sprout
d. none of the above

The correct answer is *sprout,* but if one were to free-associate to the stimulus word *shoot,* one would be far more likely to respond with *rifle,* which is precisely what schizophrenics tended to do, in contrast to normal subjects.

This picture of schizophrenic thinking has a moderate amount of experimental support. Chapman and Chapman (1973) review much of this literature. Some additional support for the Chapman position is seen in experiments by Mourer (1973) and Cohen, Nachmani, and Rosenberg (1974). Chapman does not suggest that this theory accounts for all schizophrenic symptomatology; for example, it does not deal with hallucinations. Despite such limitations, the theory would seem to be one of the most promising conceptualizations of schizophrenic behavior.

This discussion is by no means a comprehensive exposition of the many theories put forth to characterize the thinking of people labeled schizophrenic. The issue is highly complex, with many conflicting findings, perhaps in part because people are labeled schizophrenic for many different reasons. The reader wishing a more comprehensive treatment of this subject may wish to refer to Chapman and Chapman (1973), Payne (1970), and Broen (1968).

The Etiology of Schizophrenia

In this section we shall discuss various factors that are considered by different writers and experimenters to be casually related to the development of schizophrenic behavior. Because of problems with diagnostic reliability and the fact that the population of schizophrenics is anything but a homogeneous group, no single factor will ever emerge as *the* cause of schizophrenia. Most current writers in the field are aware of this, and view particular determinants, whether they be biological or environmental, as contributing factors rather than as unitary causes.

BIOLOGICAL CONSIDERATIONS

GENETIC FACTORS. To what extent can schizophrenic modes of responding be thought of as inherited? This is a question that has intrigued writers, scientists, and practitioners from the time of Kraepelin to the present day.

As you may know, monozygotic or so-called identical twins share the same genes, hence the same heredity. Now, if schizophrenia (which for the moment we shall pretend is a well-defined, unitary concept) is genetically determined to an important degree, we would predict that if one monozygotic twin showed schizophrenia, the other twin would also show the disorder, at least with a very high probability. In genetics, the degree to which related pairs of subjects both show a particular disorder is referred to as the *concordance rate* (discordance occurs when one member shows the disorder and the other does not). Thus, if the genetic hypothesis has validity, the concordance rate for identical (monozygotic) twins should be high relative to that for nonidentical twins (dizygotic twins) and to siblings in general. It should be noted that dizygotic twins and siblings who are not twins share the same proportion of genes, approximately 50%, compared with 100% for identical twins.

As it turns out, the concordance rate for identical twins is appreciably higher than for nonidentical twins. This is the case with virtually every major study reported over the past half-century (see Rosenthal, 1970), although there is a noticeable trend for somewhat lower rates to be associated with more recent investigations, as can be seen in Table 5-1.

The result for concordance rates among monozygotic twins is highly variable, but it averages across studies at slightly less than 50%. In contrast, the rate for dizygotic twins averages about 9% and for siblings in general about 8% (the last figure, for siblings, is an average of some 14 studies summarized by Rosenthal, 1970, p. 109). All these figures are well in excess of the overall rate of schizophrenia, which tends to vary between .5 and 1.5%.

Another important comparison is between identical twins reared together versus those reared apart. Were hereditary factors of no consequence, the concordance rate for twins reared together should be far higher than for those reared separately. In fact, if anything, the concordance rate for those reared

TABLE 5–1

Concordance Rates in the Major Twin Studies of Schizophrenia[a]

Study	Source	Monozygotic twins		Dizygotic twins	
		Number of pairs	Percentage concordant	Number of pairs	Percentage concordant
Luxenburger, 1928, 1934	Germany	17–27	33–76.5	48	2.1
Rosanoff, Handy, Plesset, and Brush, 1934–1935	United States and Canada	41	61.0	101	10.0
Essen-Moller, 1941	Sweden	7–11	14–71	24	8.3–17
Kallmann, 1946	New York	174	69–86.2	517	10–14.5
Slater, 1953	England	37	65–74.7	115	11.3–14.4
Inouye, 1961	Japan	55	36–60	17	6–12
Tienari, 1963, 1968	Finland	16	0–6	21	4.8
Gottesman and Shields, 1966	England	24	41.7	33	9.1
Kringlen, 1967	Norway	55	25–38	172	8–10
Fischer, 1968	Denmark	16	19–56	34	6–15
Hoffer, Pollin, Stabenau, Allen, and Hrubeck, in preparation	United States veterans	80	15.5	145	4.4

[a] Adapted from *Genetic theory and abnormal behavior* by D. Rosenthal. Copyright 1970 by McGraw-Hill Book Company. Used with permission of McGraw-Hill Book Company.

separately is higher (Slater, 1968), although it must be pointed out that the number of twins examined in these studies is very small, and for those reared apart, the age of separation varies from birth to 7 years.

From these and similar familial data (see Rosenthal, 1970), it is reasonable to conclude that heredity probably does play a role in the development of schizophrenic disorders. However, several points are in order. First, referring to Table 5-1, note that in no study is the concordance rate 100% for identical twins. If schizophrenia, like eye color, were entirely a matter of heredity, concordance rates should reach 100%. Second, whether schizophrenia is related to heredity or not, diagnosticians historically have viewed it as such. Consequently, *the knowledge* that one identical twin was schizophrenic increased the likelihood that the second twin would be similarly labeled (the converse of this is also true). This particular biasing factor varies from study to study but undoubtedly has tended to elevate concordance rates in general.

Third, behaviorally, schizophrenia is not a unitary entity. Although it is likely that some people do have a biological predisposition toward showing schizophrenic behavior, others may deliberately feign such symptoms in order to avoid certain difficulties in living. Others may be diagnosed schizophrenic largely because idiosyncratic diagnostic practices favor such a label. Recall the data presented early in this chapter showing that American psychiatrists are more likely than British psychiatrists to label the same behavior as schizophrenic. Such differences in labeling practices can hardly be accounted for in terms of genetic differences in patients (and not very plausibly in relation to genetic differences between psychiatrists of different nationalities!).

Finally, congenital factors—complications associated with pregnancy and birth—may account for at least some small portion of the aforementioned results. S. A. Mednick (1970, 1971), in a continuing investigation that has already become classic, defines high-risk subjects as offspring of mothers who showed severe, chronic schizophrenia. Many of these high-risk children subsequently developed schizophrenia. In 70% of these cases, the mothers had had difficulties during pregnancy or the birth of the child. In contrast, such difficulties occurred with only 15% of the high-risk children who have not yet developed schizophrenic symptomatology (and with 33% of a normal control group.[8] B. R. Mednick (1973) reports that the risk of a subsequent schizophrenic "breakdown" among offspring of schizophrenic mothers is higher when the mother has experienced relatively great emotional stress during pregnancy.

One of the main difficulties with attempting to account for concordance data in terms of congenital rather than hereditary factors is that if the congenital factors were more important, one would expect a far higher rate of concordance

[8] Mednick suggests that anoxia associated with birth complications might be an important causative factor. In particular, he implicates a lower brain structure, the *hippocampus*, as being susceptible to damage resulting from lack of oxygen, suggesting that hippocampal damage might mediate certain schizophrenic symptomatology. Kessler and Neale (1974) argue against the anoxia–hippocampal mediation interpretation, although they do not question the possible role between pregnancy and birth complications and subsequent schizophrenia.

among nonidentical twins than is found. In fact, this figure is consistently lower than for identical twins and is almost the same as the concordance rate for siblings in general.

Diathesis–Stress Theory.   Probably the most popular view of the etiology of schizophrenia is the diathesis–stress theory. This theory assumes that certain individuals are genetically prone to schizophrenia. Paul Meehl (1962), one of the more influential proponents of this view, labels the constitutional defect *schizotaxia*. According to Meehl, schizotaxia inevitably leads to *schizotypy*, a condition marked by some degree of thought disturbance and affective disturbance, not obvious to most observers, and not sufficient to warrant the clinical label of schizophrenia. Meehl assumes that most schizotaxic persons do *not* become schizophrenic because their environment is reasonably benign and because they have the ability to resist stress (the latter is also assumed to have a genetic basis). However, a minority of schizotaxic individuals also suffer from other genetic deficits, making these individuals less resistant to stress. Persons in this category whose socialization process is aversive rather than benign develop clinical schizophrenia.

Another relatively popular version of diathesis–stress theory was put forth by S. A. Mednick (1958). This view identified the primary genetic factor in schizophrenics as a tendency toward high levels of anxiety. Although the theory has undergone important revisions (Mednick & Schulsinger, 1968), excessive emotional arousal is still a key element. Individuals genetically predisposed toward high levels of anxiety experience a conditioning of this anxiety to their thoughts. They learn to "escape" from this anxiety by thinking other thoughts, which are characterized or labeled by others as disordered. Mednick (1971) has presented data suggesting unusual patterns of physiological responding in schizophrenic children. Although Mednick's data are interesting, Chapman and Chapman (1973) have observed that Mednick's theory does not specify why all anxious people do not become schizophrenic.

At its most general level, diathesis–stress theory maintains that schizophrenia is caused by an interaction of genetic and environmental factors. The genetic data by themselves strongly support such a view, although there are probably many individuals with a schizophrenic diagnosis who have no particular genetic predisposition toward behaving in a schizophrenic manner.

BIOCHEMICAL FACTORS.   One major impetus for seeking a biochemical basis or substrate for schizophrenia comes from the genetic studies. If there is an important genetic factor in schizophrenia, this factor must surely manifest itself in terms of some sort of biochemical defect or imbalance in the brain. Other considerations that have encouraged researchers to explore the biochemistry of schizophrenia are that certain drugs (e.g., amphetamines; *d*-lysergic acid diethylamide, or LSD) give rise to schizophrenic-like behaviors whereas other drugs (e.g., the phenothiazines) reduce symptomatology in many active schizophrenics.

Many hypotheses and theories have attempted to account for schizophrenic behavior on the basis of different biochemical considerations. One early hypothesis, put forth by Woolley and Shaw (1954), implicated a brain biochemical, *serotonin*. The theory was based in part on the observation that LSD, which gives rise to schizophrenic-like behavior, inhibits the action of serotonin. The serotonin hypothesis was subsequently expanded (Woolley, 1962) when stuporous behavior was related to a possible *excess* of serotonin.

The serotonin hypothesis has received relatively scant attention recently. In part, this is because observers no longer view the behavior induced by LSD as a "model" for schizophrenia. In contrast to typical clinical schizophrenia wherein auditory hallucinations tend to predominate, LSD psychosis is marked by visual hallucinations. Additionally, as Wyatt, Termini, and Davis (1971) note, attempts at treating schizophrenia with serotonin have in general been unsuccessful.

One popular research strategy has involved searching for metabolites (the end products of biochemical reactions) in the blood or urine of schizophrenics that differ from those found in nonschizophrenics. But Levitt and Lonowski (1975) note that agents such as adrenochrome, adrenolutin, ceruloplasm, and taraxein, once implicated as agents possibly responsible for psychotic behavior, are now viewed with much more skepticism. The *taraxein hypothesis* (Heath *et al.*, 1954; Heath, Cohen, Silva, Leach, & Cohen, 1959; Heath, Guschwan, & Coffey, 1970) generated considerable enthusiasm after it was reported that this substance, prepared from the blood of schizophrenics by an extremely complex set of procedures, produced schizophrenic-like behaviors among prison volunteers. Heath and his co-workers have also reported abnormal EEG patterns in monkeys injected with taraxein. However, there is considerable evidence that conflicts with these findings of Heath and his co-workers (see Wyatt *et al.*, 1971).

The so-called *transmethylation hypotheses* (see Kety, 1972) assume that schizophrenia results from an accumulation of certain hallucination-producing metabolites. The label *transmethylation* comes from the assumption that this class of metabolites have undergone an atypical process of methylation (i.e., the combining of a biochemical substance with the important organic chemical radical, methyl).

Neural messages are transmitted via biochemicals; in the human brain, the major transmitters are *dopamine, norepinephrine, serotonin,* and *acetylcholine*. The considerable research related to transmethylation hypotheses has been inspired mainly by the fact that certain methylated "relatives" of some of these transmitters can be highly hallucinogenic substances (for example, mescaline and psilocybin).

Several investigators (e.g., Brune & Himwich, 1962; Park, Baldessarini, & Kety, 1965; Smythies & Antun, 1970) have reported that the administration of methionine in combination with another drug aggravates the symptoms of patients already diagnosed as schizophrenic. These findings support the transmethylation hypothesis, as methionine is a so-called methyl donor and would be expected to produce the transmethylation effect.

On the basis of theory related to the transmethylation hypotheses, Hoffer and his associates (e.g., Hoffer & Osmond, 1962, 1964, 1968) predicted that treatment of schizophrenia with massive doses of nicotinic acid (niacin, vitamin B_3) should result in a reduction in symptomatology, and indeed this is what they have reported. This treatment has generated a great deal of controversy. It has been frequently noted (e.g., Wyatt *et al.*, 1971) that investigations not conducted by Hoffer and his colleagues have generally failed to confirm the value of this treatment.[9]

One transmethylation hypothesis that has generated a great deal of research was originally suggested by Osmond and Smythies (1952). They postulated that abnormal methylation of the important brain biochemical, dopamine, might lead to the symptoms of catatonic schizophrenia. In 1962, Friedhoff and Van Winkle reported finding a substance in the urine of schizophrenics that could conceivably reflect such abnormal dopamine methylation, DMPEA (3,4-dimethoxyphenethylamine). DMPEA is commonly referred to as the "pink spot" because when this substance is treated with certain chemicals it takes on a pink color. There has been a great deal of controversy (see Wyatt *et al.*, 1971) concerning whether DMPEA indeed does exist in schizophrenic urine (in contrast to the urine of nonschizophrenics). Additionally, if schizophrenics are more likely to excrete this substance, this may reflect only their eating habits rather than some biochemical disorder causing schizophrenic behavior. One major methodological problem that has plagued efforts at isolating unique substances in the urine or blood of schizophrenics is that diet (and sometimes drug therapy) are often extremely difficult to control for.

As the noted researcher Kety (1972) has observed, there are two major lines of research that continue to hold promise in relation to the etiology of schizophrenia. The first, the transmethylation hypotheses, has just been discussed. The second class of hypotheses also stresses the importance of brain transmitter substances, in particular *dopamine* and *norepinephrine*. You are probably familiar with a class of drugs known as amphetamines; methamphetamine is a popular and extremely dangerous street drug known as *speed*, dextroamphetamine has been prescribed as a diet medication. The second class of hypotheses stems partly from presumed neurochemical effects of amphetamine on so-called dopamine and norepinephrine brain "systems" (neural tracts, or anatomical structures in the brain associated with unusually large amounts of these substances). Another source of these hypotheses is the fact that certain amphetamines can produce schizophrenic-like behavior, including well-formed paranoid delusions, stereotypical compulsive behavior, and visual and auditory hallucinations (see Kety, 1972; Snyder, 1972). The kind of loose association characteristic of clinical schizophrenia is not usually seen in amphetamine-induced psychosis. On the other hand, several writers (e.g., Kety, 1972; Levitt & Lonowski, 1975; Snyder,

[9] Niacin is readily available in any pharmacy. Lest you be tempted to experiment with "megadoses" of this vitamin, you should be forewarned that ingestion of large doses (for example, in excess of 100 milligrams) of this drug can cause a very distressing histamine reaction, marked by a sensation of flushing, burning skin, dryness of the mouth, and difficulty swallowing. Lest a practical joker be tempted to give large doses of niacin to a friend, keep in mind that there may be harmful, yet undiscovered additional side effects associated with megadoses of niacin.

1972; Snyder, Banerjee, Yamamura, & Greenberg, 1974) note that of the various drugs that produce schizophrenic-like behavior, the amphetamines produce behaviors closest to natural or clinical schizophrenia. Moreover, amphetamines tend to aggravate symptoms in persons already labeled as schizophrenic, and the drugs most effective in alleviating schizophrenic symptoms (the phenothiazines and the butyrophenones) are also excellent remedies for amphetamine-induced psychosis (see Snyder *et al.,* 1974).

Several studies with lower animals suggest that amphetamine psychosis may be produced by the direct effect of amphetamine on brain dopamine, or on receptors in the brain that normally receive dopamine (see Randrup & Munkvad, 1972). Randrup and Munkvad also cite biochemical and anatomical evidence that the antipsychotic medications phenothiazine and butyrophenone block dopamine receptors, thus effectively decreasing dopamine activity in the brain. In their view, schizophrenia is characterized by hyperactivity of an important dopamine system in the brain.

One provocative biochemical theory of schizophrenia has been put forth by Stein and Wise (1971). They argue that schizophrenic behavior stems from a genetic abnormality associated with a brain reward center.[10] Stein and Wise postulate a reward center that is activated by the brain transmitter norepinephrine. Then they theorize that this reward center is damaged in schizophrenics. In normals, the norepinephrine that stimulates this structure is metabolized from brain dopamine; in schizophrenics, because of a deficiency of a certain enzyme (dopamine hydroxylase), much of the dopamine is not converted into norepinephrine, and thus the ability to experience pleasure or reinforcement is diminished.

There is a reasonable amount of evidence supporting the *pharmacological* aspects of the Stein and Wise view; however, it is rather technical and beyond the scope of this book (see Levitt & Lonowski, 1975, for a readable summary of this literature). *Behavioral* support for the reward-deficit hypothesis has come from Bishop, Elder, and Heath, (1964), who found that stimulation of certain brain reward centers in schizophrenics did *not* result in behavior suggesting that the subjects were experiencing reinforcement. Further, when a certain metabolite (6-hydroxydopamine) presumed by Stein and Wise to be important in mediating schizophrenic symptoms was injected into monkeys, the animals showed "blank affectless faces" and a general reduction in social behavior; such characteristics are often noted among clinical schizophrenics.

The Stein–Wise hypothesis has not gone unchallenged (see Levitt & Lonowski, 1975). It is hard to account for schizophrenic thought disorders such as hallucinations on the basis of a reduced ability to experience reward. Further, a great many people labeled as schizophrenic do engage regularly in behaviors that normals find rewarding, such as eating and sexual behavior. Whether or not

---

[10] Physiological psychologists have known for a good many years that in certain lower animals (see Olds, 1956) and perhaps in humans (see Heath, 1964), when certain lower brain structures are stimulated electrically, the subjects behave as if the experience is rewarding.

the specific Stein–Wise view stands the test of time, the available evidence makes it reasonable to suppose that among some schizophrenics, a genetically based deficit involving the dopamine and norepinephrine brain systems does indeed exist.

ENVIRONMENTAL CONSIDERATIONS

Most writers, including the present authors, do not take an either–or position regarding the role of biological versus environmental factors in producing schizophrenic behavior. The most popular view is that many schizophrenics do have a genetically based biological predisposition toward this disorder, but clear-cut symptoms are less likely to develop in a healthy environment. This is the essence of diathesis–stress theory. We shall now consider environmental factors that are thought to be important in the etiology of schizophrenia.

THE ROLE OF LEARNING.   Behaviorists have been strongly inclined to stress learning, especially operant conditioning, in the etiology of schizophrenia. The principles of operant conditioning are reviewed in Chapter 15. For now, it is sufficient to point out that operant conditioning emphasizes the impact of rewards (technically *reinforcers*) on strengthening those behaviors that precede them.

The operant position in relation to schizophrenia, presented in its most extreme version, might be as follows: The various schizophrenic "symptoms," such as loose thinking, reports of hallucinations, and interpersonal withdrawal, all indicate that in the course of growing up, the schizophrenic has been reinforced for such behaviors. Perhaps the reward has been in the form of praise or other forms of attention; perhaps it has been in the form of toys, money, or even food. At the same time, "healthy," nonschizophrenic ways of responding have not been rewarded; typically, they have been ignored, and perhaps sometimes they have been subject to punishment.

As we have indicated, the foregoing is an extreme point of view; most writers would probably allow for at least some hereditary contribution. In addition, any etiological account of schizophrenia that stresses learning would also postulate the importance of *classical* conditioning (Pavlovian conditioning) and *imitation* learning. Thus, perhaps the schizophrenic avoids other people in part because stimuli associated with others have been paired with aversive events, so that other people cause him to experience anxiety. He may report hallucinations or give unusual associations, in part because he has learned such responses from others by a process of imitation.

In essence, a purely operant account of the etiology of schizophrenia is at best an oversimplification. *However, the data indicating that the behavior of schizophrenics may be modified via operant principles are very compelling indeed.* This is illustrated in a classic demonstration reported by Ayllon, Haughton, and Hughes (1965) who positively reinforced the carrying of a broom in a female patient until the broom and patient become virtually inseparable.

In a more therapeutic vein, Meichenbaum (1969) employed token reinforcers in the form of canteen stubs, together with social approval, to effect a dramatic improvement in the frequency of coherent speech in schizophrenics. Tokens, which increased the percentage of "healthy" talk from approximately 55% to about 80%, were somewhat more effective than praise, which increased healthy talk by 10–15%. Other studies demonstrating operant control of schizophrenics' verbal behavior include Ullmann, Krasner, and Edinger (1964), True (1966), and Panek (1967). Token economies (see Chapter 15) also demonstrate that schizophrenic behavior may be modified using operant principles.

We noted earlier that schizophrenics generally show impaired performance on tasks measuring reaction time. Meiselman (1973) provided schizophrenic patients with feedback relating to their response speed as well as token reinforcement for improvement. The results are very impressive indeed. Toward the end of the experiment, the schizophrenics were performing at levels almost approximating that expected for normals, and *every* subject showed improvement.

This evidence strongly suggests that at least certain aspects of schizophrenic behavior can be modified by learning. Can this be taken as proof that schizophrenic behavior is therefore entirely a function of one's past learning? More generally, does the fact that a given maladaptive behavior can be modified by learning prove that it was acquired by learning? The answer is negative (see Davison, 1968). Consider the individual who as a child developed polio, which weakened certain leg muscles. By diligent practice he learns to develop and rely on other muscles, thus compensating for the defect; by the time he is in college, he excels in sports. Certainly, no one would argue that his initial deficit was a function of learning.

Thus far we have stressed the role of learning—in particular, operant conditioning—in the modification of *overt behavior* among schizophrenics. Ullmann and Krasner (1969) have hypothesized that the schizophrenic *thinking process* may also be subject to operant modification. They argue that schizophrenia develops in large measure because other people fail to reward the individual for "attention to social stimuli to which 'normal' people respond [p. 383]." The person thus learns to respond to highly idiosyncratic, autistic stimuli, including internal stimuli, which may give rise to reports of hallucinations. Normals tune out such stimuli because they have been taught that they are irrelevant.

The idea that many schizophrenics appear to be "marching to a different drummer" did not originate with Ullmann and Krasner, and is not very controversial. The view that schizophrenic thinking, in the main, reflects nothing more than an unfortunate operant learning history (i.e., that anyone would be schizophrenic given such a learning history) is highly questionable. First, results of genetic studies contradict any hypothesis that argues that schizophrenia is a totally learned disorder. Second, it is hard to imagine a social environment that consistently fails to reinforce normal attending behavior to a degree consistent with the Ullmann and Krasner hypothesis. Surely *someone*—if not a member of the immediate family, then an aunt or grandparent or schoolteacher—would reward the would-be schizophrenic for appropriate attending behavior. Clinical experience strongly suggests that schizophrenics react to their symptoms with considerable distress. Even occasional rewards for appropriate attending behavior should be associated with a marked degree of relief, strongly counteracting the negative impact of those persons who regularly ignore such behavior. Finally, if the Ullmann and Krasner view were generally correct, a pattern of child-rearing obviously marked by consistent failure of the parents to respond to normal attending behavior should be regularly associated with schizophrenia. There have been numerous studies of the child-rearing patterns of parents of schizophrenics. Some studies have pointed to atypical and potentially unhealthy interaction between schizophrenics and their parents, but the results are ambiguous (they are discussed in the next section). If there is a specific set of child-rearing practices regularly associated with subsequent schizophrenic behavior, it has yet to be discovered.

In questioning the Ullmann and Krasner view of the etiology of schizophrenia, we are in no sense discounting the important role of learning in the etiology and modification of schizophrenic behavior. The patient who told Rimm that he saw Jesus Christ masturbating on the wall of his dormitory was not born with the concept of Christ or masturbation; he learned these concepts. However, any hypothesis concerning the etiology of schizophrenic behavior that is based exclusively on operant principles, or on learning principles in general, is incomplete.

FAMILIAL FACTORS.   It is a truism to say that much of our adult behavior directly reflects parental and familial influences. Not surprisingly, many theorists have offered hypotheses tying schizophrenic behavior to particular patterns of familial interaction. We shall now review some of the more influential hypotheses.

All these hypotheses emphasize a stressful childhood or adolescence in the etiology of schizophrenia, but they differ according to the degree to which the nature of the stressful experience is specified. One hypothesis stresses early *psychological trauma,* perhaps characterized by violence in interpersonal relationships; for example, physical beatings or sexual abuse. Case history data suggest that although the abuse may have been at the hands of family members, sometimes members of the victim's peer group or even strangers may have been responsible for the traumatic experience.

Loss of one or both parents is often stressed as an important event in the etiology of schizophrenia. In fact, Wahl (1956) noted that among a large sample of Navy personnel diagnosed as schizophrenic, over 40% had lost a parent through death, divorce, or separation prior to age 15. This figure is well in excess of that reported for normals.

For obvious reasons, controlled experiments exposing a child to traumatic experiences and ascertaining whether he subsequently becomes schizophrenic have not been carried out. Thus, hypotheses of the sort just presented are almost exclusively based upon case history data, which puts a severe limitation on the degree to which we can determine their validity. For example, consider an adult female schizophrenic who reports having been raped by her father at age 9. First, we cannot be sure the report is accurate. Freud (see Fenichel, 1945) noted that frequently such reports are more related to fantasy than reality. Second, assuming the accuracy of the report, there are females who have been raped by their fathers and yet present little evidence of psychological impairment. Perhaps the major point is this: One can always uncover childhood experiences among adult schizophrenics that could fairly be described as traumatic (especially when the hypothesis fails to specify the nature of the stress), but a skillful interviewer could probably uncover potentially traumatic childhood experiences in *anyone*. We are not discounting the possible impact of childhood trauma in the etiology of schizophrenia, but we are noting that it is very difficult to assess the degree of impact.

Because loss of a parent is more prevalent among male schizophrenics than among normal males, this might be taken as evidence that such a traumatic loss can indeed be important in causing subsequent schizophrenic behavior. However, the child frequently loses the parent as a consequence of parental divorce or separation; most often, in the Wahl study, the father was the lost parent. In such instances, it may not be the parent loss per se, but rather those factors that precipitated the divorce or separation, which are of major etiological importance. Perhaps the father leaves the mother because she behaves in a schizophrenic manner, a behavior pattern that the child acquires from his mother through learning, heredity, or both. Clearly, data of this nature can be used to support more than one hypothesis.

The so-called *schizophrenogenic parent hypothesis* is most often used in attempts to describe the influence of a mother's behavior on her son's schizophrenia. Typically, the schizophrenogenic mother is described as overprotective and interpersonally insensitive, attempting to gratify her needs with her son rather than her husband. She may behave in an apparently warm, even sexually seductive manner toward her son, only to exhibit shock or outrage at any indication of sexuality on his part. The schizophrenogenic father (schizophrenogenic in relation to his daughter) is often described as passive and ineffectual and also interpersonally insensitive. Sometimes he is seen as making seductive overtures toward the daughter.

It is not difficult to obtain case history data in support of the schizophrenogenic parent hypothesis; however it remains nothing more than a hypothesis because of the limitations of the case history method. Mothers of schizophrenics are more likely to show behaviors described as pathological than are mothers of normals (S. A. Mednick, 1970, 1971). However, the pathological behavioral patterns of the mother do not necessarily fit the schizophrenic mold, and many people interpret this data as supporting a genetic view of schizophrenia.

The *double bind hypothesis* (Bateson, 1960) is related to the schizophrenogenic view. It states that as a child, the schizophrenic was exposed to conflicting messages from a parent—usually the mother. The child is placed in a double bind; for instance, the mother may verbalize that she feels warmth and love for her child but act cold and rejecting when the child responds in kind. It is plausible to assume that being placed in such a bind would lead to a kind of behavioral or emotional paralysis, and perhaps withdrawal into oneself, both of which tend to characterize schizophrenia. On the other hand, available evidence (see Schuham, 1967, for a review of this literature) provides little support for the double bind hypothesis.

Certain writers have noted *open disagreement* or discord between parents of schizophrenics (e.g., Gerard & Siegel, 1950; Lidz, Cornelison, Fleck, & Terry, 1957, 1958) whereas others have reported the parents, and indeed the entire family, present a picture of *warmth, love, and understanding,* but beneath the surface there is considerable withdrawal, rigidity, and even hostility (Rosenbaum, 1961; Wynne, Ryckoff, Day, & Hirsch, 1959).

Imura, Kawakubo, Mochizuki, Misu, and Makihara (1974) evaluated 36 families of schizophrenic patients, employing a measure relating to empathy and a second measure relating to the quality of interaction. They noted two familial patterns. One, which was strongly associated with process schizophrenia in the patient, was marked by a lack of cohesiveness and emotional ties, perhaps corresponding to the "open discord" parental pattern noted above. The second pattern reported by Imura *et al.,* associated mainly with reactive schizophrenics, gave the outward appearance of peace and harmony but allowed for little in the way of individuality on the part of family members. This pattern may correspond to that described by Rosenbaum (1961), and Wynne *et al.* (1959). Whether there are in fact two distinct types of familial interactions, one associated with process and the other with reactive schizophrenia, is an intriguing question, clearly in need of additional empirical investigation.

Although the observation by Lidz (1973) that schizophrenics *always* come from severely disturbed families is probably an overstatement, families of schizophrenics certainly tend to show greater psychological disturbances than families of normals. This makes it harder to account for the fact that when one sibling shows schizophrenic behavior, other siblings very often do not. Part of the answer might be found in the heredity of the schizophrenic sibling. Another obvious explanation is that parents do not behave in the same manner toward each of their offspring. Hoover and Franz (1972) observe that sometimes a sibling who was generally rejected by his parents enters adulthood psychologically intact, relative to another sibling who received considerable parental attention of a harmful or pathological nature. This line of thinking leads to the prediction that parents of a schizophrenic child would behave differently toward that child than toward the nonschizophrenic siblings. Specific tests of this hypothesis (Sharan, 1968; Singer, 1965; Waxler & Mishler, 1971) have, somewhat surprisingly, failed to find such differential behavior patterns.

SOCIOCULTURAL FACTORS.   We stated early in this chapter that differences in diagnostic practices account, in part, for different rates of schizophrenia between different cultures. However, the well-substantiated finding that schizophrenia is more often observed among people in lower socioeconomic classes is not likely to be entirely a function of diagnostic practice. In the United States, the majority of black Americans belong to the lower socioeconomic classes, and indeed blacks tend to show a higher incidence of schizophrenia at first admission than Caucasians (e.g., Vitols, 1961). However, available evidence (e.g., J. Fischer, 1969) suggests that socioeconomic rather than ethnic class is the critical variable.

One can argue (see Murphy, 1968) that membership in the lower class exposes one to unusual stresses, which may precipitate schizophrenic patterns of responding. It can also be argued that certain individuals, as a result of schizophrenic-related psychological impairment, drift down to lower socioeconomic levels, or having been reared at such levels, are not upwardly mobile because of such impairment. It is possible, of course, that both factors are in operation. Given the available data, it is not possible to define a cause-and-effect relationship between the incidence of this disorder and social class.

Summary

In the present chapter we have portrayed schizophrenia as a serious disturbance in thinking, pointing out that a thought disorder is necessarily inferred from observable behavior. As with neuroses, diagnostic reliability in relation to schizophrenia leaves much to be desired; we have discussed factors that contribute to such lack of reliability, including observer bias and ambiguities inherent in systems such as DSM-II. The principal subcategories of schizophrenia are as follows: simple schizophrenia, marked by psychological and interpersonal impairment, but usually not of a degree to necessitate hospitalization; paranoid schizophrenia, characterized by relatively well-defined delusions, usually of persecution and grandiosity; hebephrenic schizophrenia, marked by very disorganized thinking and often childlike inappropriate behavior; catatonic schizophrenia, characterized by grossly disturbed motor behavior suggesting extreme inhibition or excitement; and schizophrenia, schizo-affective type, a category created for patients who show a disorder of both thought and affect. Hallucinations may be reported in any of these subcategories of schizophrenia.

Dissatisfaction with these traditional categories of schizophrenia has led writers and researchers to seek other ways of looking at schizophrenia. Sometimes schizophrenics are classified as to whether they are acute or chronic. Unfortunately, researchers have not been able to agree on the duration of illness or hospitalization that differentiates the acute from the chronic schizophrenic, limiting the usefulness of this approach. Another approach examines the premorbid behavior of the schizophrenic: A patient showing a gradual onset and no precipitating stress is given the label *process schizophrenic:* if the onset is sudden and environmental stress is apparent, the patient is referred to as a *reactive schizophrenic*. A third approach involves classifying schizophrenics as either paranoid or nonparanoid. Both the process–reactive and paranoid–nonparanoid classification schemes appear to be of some diagnostic value, as do some more recent statistical approaches.

Many attempts have been made to describe or characterize the nature of schizophrenic thinking, including loss in the associative process, loss in abstract thinking, overinclusion, regression, and excessive yielding to normal biases. Although the last factor has received some promising empirical support, there is not widespread agreement about which if any of the group best describes the schizophrenic thought process.

We have reviewed data that suggest that there may be a genetic factor in schizophrenia. Perhaps the diathesis–stress theory, which attributes schizophrenia to an interaction between heredity and environment, is the most plausible theory about the etiology of schizophrenia. If genetics are an important consideration in schizophrenia, they must be manifest in the form of some biochemical aberration, and there have been several theories put forth regarding a possible biochemical basis. Among these are the serotonin hypothesis, the taraxein hypothesis, the transmethylation hypotheses, and a theory that states that schizophrenics suffer from an inborn malfunction of a reward center in the brain. Current biochemical theorizing stresses the possible key role of dopamine and norepinephrine which, like serotonin, are important brain transmitter substances.

There is evidence that learning plays an important role in the development and maintenance of schizophrenic behavior and that such behavior may be modified using the principles of operant conditioning. However, a complete theory of schizophrenia must take into account biological factors as well as the patient's learning history. Certain familial patterns have been postulated as important in the etiology of schizophrenia including early trauma, parental loss, parental overprotection, conflicting behavioral patterns on the part of one parent, and overt or covert parental discord. Each of these hypotheses has a certain face validity, but empirical evidence is quite conflicting.

Finally, although the frequency of schizophrenia does vary with social class, cause-and-effect relationships between social class and schizophrenia have not been established.

6

Depression and
Related Disorders

Some Preliminary Definitions

In this chapter, we will explore a broad class of psychological disturbances that includes depression, mania, manic-depressive disorder, and so-called involutional melancholia. These disturbances are often lumped together under the label, *affective disorders*. The term *affect*, which itself is not very rigorous, may be loosely translated as "emotion" or "mood." Indeed, individuals assigned to any of these categories often do exhibit peculiarities in mood or emotional state. But the term *affective disorder* clearly implies that the individual's problem is entirely or primarily one of disturbed mood. As several writers have noted, one can make a very strong case for the central role of disordered, irrational, or self-defeating *thoughts* in individuals labeled as depressive, manic-depressive, or melancholic. We are not arguing that such disorders should be labeled *disturbances in thinking*, which would only add to the confusion. Our point is simply that the term *affective disorder* has a built-in theoretical bias, and when possible we shall avoid its use.

We shall describe depression and the related disorders in considerable detail later in this chapter. Essentially, a depressed person appears to derive little satisfaction from life, may appear to be very sad, engages in relatively minimal goal-directed activity, often verbalizes self-contempt, and may engage in suicidal behavior.

Although depression and the other disorders described in this chapter occur in varying degrees, this does not mean that a severely depressed person requiring custodial care is exactly like a mildly depressed person, only more so. In other words, if you are occasionally "down" or "blue" you need not view yourself as seriously disturbed or as a suicide risk. Fluctuations in mood and self-evaluation are part of everyday existence. However, when mood changes and correlated thinking are such that life becomes seriously unpleasant for the affected individual, and this state *persists* for an extended period, psychiatric labels such as *depression* are invoked. At such times, the individual might choose to seek professional help. Of course, depression following a traumatic event, such as the death of a beloved spouse, is not viewed as a psychiatric disorder. Indeed, it would be surprising if an individual were *not* depressed for a period of time following such a personal loss. However, if such a state persists for an inordinate time, the person is likely to receive the diagnosis of depression.

Although some depressed people show marked agitation, most show what might be described as behavioral retardation. Behaviorally, mania may be thought of as the opposite of depression. Manic behavior is marked by high levels of verbal and motor activity, suggesting joy, elation, or euphoria, and occasional grandiosity. Sometimes aggressiveness is observed, usually when efforts are made to contain the behavior of a person showing marked mania.

In this text, we use the term *manic-depressive disorder* to characterize behavior marked by periods of extreme depression and extreme mania. This is close to the layman's conception of manic-depressive, but note our use of the term *extreme,* implying that the states of mania and depression are of a severe, debilitating nature. Many people with a very limited knowledge of manic-depression apply this term to themselves or others, merely to describe mild day-to-day fluctuations in mood. Clearly this is a misuse of the term. In fact, it is relatively common psychiatric practice to label as manic-depressive people who show severe depression but never mania, and others who show severe mania but never severe depression, in *addition* to those who show periods of both depression and mania. Thus, under the label *manic-depressive illness,* DSM-II (1968) lists "Manic-depressive psychosis, *manic* type [italics added]."

> This disorder consists of exclusively manic episodes. These episodes are characterized by excessive elation, irritability, talkativeness, flight of ideas, and accelerated speech and motor activity [p. 36].

DSM-II also includes under the manic-depressive illness label "Manic-depressive psychosis, *depressed* type [italics added]."

> This disorder consists of exclusively depressive episodes. These episodes are characterized by severely depressed mood and by mental and motor retardation progressing occasionally to stupor. Uneasiness, apprehension, perplexity and agitation may also be present. When illusions, hallucinations, and delusions (usually of guilt or of hypochondriacal or paranoid ideas) occur, they are attributable to the dominant mood disorder [pp. 36–37].

The DSM-II description of manic-depressive psychosis, circular type, begins as follows:

> This disorder is distinguished by at least one attack of both a depressive episode *and* a manic episode [p. 37].

Only the last category is consistent with our use of the term *manic-depressive psychosis*. The DSM-II approach may seem illogical, but it does make sense from a historical point of view. Kraepelin, whose work continues to have a profound impact on diagnostic practices, believed that mania, depression, and the so-called cyclic type (i.e., alternating periods of mania and depression) all reflected the same underlying disorder. Therefore he grouped them together under the single label, *manic-depressive psychosis*. Until there is strong evidence that these three behavioral patterns do indeed have some common underlying mechanism, we see little justification for subsuming them under the single label of manic-depression. We shall therefore deal with them separately.

Melancholia was once a common term implying sadness or depression. It can be thought of as an antiquated version of the present-day term *depression. Involutional* refers to the period in life when an individual's biological functioning and vitality are presumably declining; for example, beginning with the menopause in females and reduced sexual potency in males. Thus, *involutional melancholia* refers to depression observed in middle age, in the absence of any prior history of severe depression. DSM-II treats involutional melancholia as a separate syndrome, although the manual notes that "opinion is divided as to whether this psychosis can be distinguished from the other affective disorders [p. 36]."

DEPRESSIVE REACTIONS

DSM-II explicitly states that the foregoing diagnoses can *only* be made when the disordered behavior cannot be attributed to some clear environmental stress. When external stress is a plausible precipitating factor, the term *depressive reaction* is recommended. Relatively mild reactions are labeled as *neurotic depressive reactions,* whereas the more severe, incapacitating states are called *psychotic depressive reactions*. This implies that when the term *reaction* is not used, as is the case with mania, depression, manic-depression, and involutional melancholia, then the disturbance emanates from an internal disorder or imbalance, presumably of a biological nature. Again, this reflects Kraepelin's thinking; he viewed depression and related states as essentially organic or biological in nature, just as he viewed schizophrenia as a biological disease. Perhaps more than anyone else, Freud (1917/1957) contributed to the belief that environmental factors, especially but not exclusively those experienced early in life, are important in the development of depression and related disorders.

As Depue and Evans (1976) point out, the conflicting views of Freud and Kraepelin probably reflect more than a difference in their respective theoretical biases. Kraepelin studied hospitalized patients who were probably a good deal more disturbed than the sample of outpatients that comprised Freud's source of information. In any event, the issue of the importance of environmental versus biological factors is a major one and we will deal with it later in this chapter.

Issues of Reliability of Diagnosis

As we have repeatedly observed, lack of reliability of diagnosis is a major problem associated with traditional classification systems. Unfortunately, the disorders discussed in this chapter represent no exception. For example, Schmidt and Fonda (1956) note a proportion of agreement among psychiatric residents of only .35 for "affective" psychosis. The corresponding figure for involutional melancholia, which they treated as a separate category, was somewhat higher but still only .57. Sandifer, Pettus, and Quade (1964) note proportions of agreements as follows: manic-depression, .36; involutional psychosis,[1] .26; psychotic depressive reaction, .17.

These reliabilities are so low that you may wonder whether the disorders in question have any real meaning. However, experienced clinicians, including the present authors, have interacted with many patients who do present a relatively clear, coherent picture of depression (and sometimes mania; the specifics of these disorders will be discussed in more detail later). How can clinical impressions be at such variance with reliability data? The answer, we believe, lies largely in the nature of the diagnostic system, a conclusion supported by Ward, Beck, Mendelson, Mock, & Erbaugh (1962) cited in an earlier chapter.

Two factors seem to contribute heavily to the lack of agreement about diagnosis: the patient's prior history and the role of external precipitating events. For example, consider involutional melancholia. Recall that this label requires that the patient have no prior history of severe depression. However, these data are usually based upon the patient's verbal report, almost always given when he is severely depressed and not thinking very clearly. It is easy to imagine a patient giving one interviewer an indication that indeed he had been very depressed on prior occasions, then telling a second interviewer that perhaps those prior depressions were relatively mild, after all. The first interviewer might label the patient as suffering from *manic-depressive psychosis, depressive type,* whereas the second might use the label *involutional melancholia.*

But the interviewers must also make a judgment about the importance of external stress. Again, this judgment is often made on the basis of the depressed patient's self-report. Depressed people often "personalize" their suffering; that is, intimate that they themselves are the sole cause for their misery, rather than relating their depressed state to external factors in some legitimate manner. Again, it is easy to envisage a patient stressing that he alone is responsible for his misery, in the presence of one diagnostician, but telling another interviewer who is more skilled at ascertaining relevant external factors that perhaps "things have

[1] Involutional psychosis includes melancholia, but it also includes so-called involutional paranoia, which refers to paranoid thinking occurring for the first time during the involutional period.

been pretty bad lately" (e.g., marital difficulties, loss of employment). Depending on age and history of the patient, the first interviewer would probably label the client as a depressed manic-depressive or an involutional psychotic, whereas the second would probably use the term *psychotic depressive reaction*.

A third factor, of course, relates to biases on the part of the diagnosticians. Those who believe that severe depression is endogenous in nature (that is, biologically based) are less likely to seek out plausible environmental precipitants. Conversely, those with an exogenous (environmental) bias would almost certainly find *something* in the patient's recent history that could be labeled as stressful.

A fourth consideration pertains to a diagnostic category that we dealt with in the previous chapter, namely schizophrenia, schizo-affective type. This category is for people who show a mixture of the loose, disturbed thinking that is characteristic of schizophrenics and relatively severe depression. The rules for ascertaining whether a patient belongs in this category, as opposed to schizophrenia, or depression, are not well specified.

Finally, it has been frequently observed that people experiencing depression and related disorders typically improve, even without any formal treatment. A person admitted to a mental hospital for the first time (and without an apparent history of depression) might on the day of admission be seen as psychotically depressed, whereas a week later the depression may have lifted to such an extent that a second psychiatrist or psychologist might label the patient as experiencing a neurotic depressive reaction. The Ward *et al.* (1962) findings suggest that this factor may not be of paramount importance in psychiatric diagnostic errors in general. They could attribute only 5% of the disagreements to changes in the clinical state of the patient, in contrast to 37% attributable to inconsistencies on the part of the diagnosing psychiatrists, and 58% to the problems inherent in the diagnostic system. However, given the nature of depression, changes in the behavior of the patient may contribute to diagnostic inconsistency in a more substantial way.

In Chapter 3 we discussed problems associated with requiring that a diagnostician pigeonhole a client into a single primary diagnosis. A reasonable alternative is simply to rate a given patient according to the degree of a particular class of responses he evidences, ignoring the issue of primary diagnosis. The results reported by Beck and his associates (Beck, 1967) indicate just how promising such an approach can be. The raters were first trained to agree on 22 signs and symptoms associated with depression. Each rater then rated the intensity of each sign or symptom on a four-point scale. For example, the symptom of social withdrawal was measured with the following four questions:

0 I have not lost interest in other people.
1 I am less interested in other people now than I used to be.
2 I have lost most of my interest in other people and have little feeling for them.
3 I have lost all my interest in other people and don't care about them at all.

The number preceding each question indicates the intensity of the symptom as reflected by that question. The correlation of ratings between pairs of diagnosticians was high, ranging from .78 to .92. This scale, known as the Beck Depression Inventory, has since come into increasing use.

The Incidence of Depression and Related Disorders

As we noted earlier, the incidence of reported schizophrenia varies considerably from nation to nation, and even within a culture, with a median figure of slightly less than 1% (see Rosenthal, 1970). Rosenthal has found even greater variances with respect to the present class of disorders, especially in relation to international differences. The median values given by Rosenthal for schizophrenia and manic-depression respectively (used in the broad, traditional sense) are .8% and .7% of the total population. Given the considerable variability across surveys, the figure of approximately 1% for each class of disorders is certainly a reasonable approximation. As we noted in Chapter 5, there is evidence that diagnostic practices vary from country to country, and in the United States, from state to state. As you will recall, American psychiatrists are far more likely to use the label *schizophrenia* rather than *depression*, in contrast to British psychiatrists rating precisely the same patients.

If roughly 1% of the general population present indications of severe depression or a related disorder, then clearly such disorders are socially important—especially considering the increased likelihood of suicide among depressed people. But this base rate figure, because of variability and bias in diagnosis, is anything but precise. Nevertheless, it is of interest to note the relative distribution of such disorders. The data in Figure 6-1 are from Rosenthal (1970), and are based on a compilation by Landis and Page (1938). This is rather old, and given the trend noted in Chapter 5 to employ the schizophrenic label at the expense of manic-depression, a more recent compilation might reveal a reduction in the *total* number of such diagnoses, although the relative proportion per age group would probably remain similar.

A Description of Depression and Related Disorders

DEPRESSION

Among the disorders presented in this chapter, depression is clearly the most common. If it is mild, the term *neurotic* is most likely to be invoked; when the depth of depression is severe, the term *psychosis* is likely to be used. Whether there is some fundamental qualitative difference between neurotic and psychotic depressions is debatable; we shall discuss this in a subsequent section.

Table 6-1 summarizes a large-scale clinical investigation into signs and symptoms of depression, based upon observations by psychiatrists (Beck, 1967).

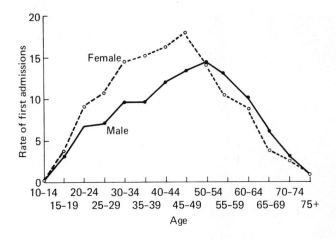

Figure 6-1. First admissions for manics, depressives, and manic-depressives in state hospitals in the United States during 1933. The rates are per 100,000 of the general population. (Based on data from Landis & Page, 1938; adapted from *Genetic theory and abnormal behavior* by D. Rosenthal. Copyright 1970 by McGraw-Hill Book Company. Used with permission of McGraw-Hill Book Company.)

Some of the data are based upon behavioral observations (e.g., crying in the interview, stooped posture), others rely primarily on the patient's verbal reports (e.g., conscious guilt). The percentage of patients having a particular sign or symptom is presented as a function of the severity of the depression as determined by the Beck Depression Inventory.

TABLE 6-1

Frequency of Clinical Features among 486 Patients Varying in Depth of Depression[a]

Clinical feature	Depth of depression			
	None (percentage)	Mild (percentage)	Moderate (percentage)	Severe (percentage)
Sad faces	18	72	94	98
Stooped posture	6	32	70	87
Crying in interview	3	11	29	28
Speech: slow, etc.	25	53	72	75
Low mood	16	72	94	94
Diurnal variation of mood	6	13	37	37
Suicidal wishes	13	47	73	94
Indecisiveness	18	42	68	83
Hopelessness	14	58	85	86
Feeling inadequate	25	56	75	90
Conscious guilt	27	46	64	60
Loss of interest	14	56	83	92
Loss of motivation	23	54	88	88
Fatigability	39	62	89	84
Sleep disturbance	31	55	73	88
Loss of appetite	17	33	61	88
Constipation	19	26	38	52

[a] Adapted from Beck, 1967b.

This woman had been severely depressed for some time when this picture was taken. Her sad face, stooped posture, and social withdrawal are all characteristic signs of depression. Though her ordeal lasted for many months, she eventually recovered without hospitalization. (Larry Fink)

Not surprisingly, as one goes from the "none" category, signifying that the patient was not seen as depressed, to the "severe" category, the percentage of patients showing the various symptoms tends to show a sharp increase. If we assume (and this is a controversial point) that depression is on a continuum, those behaviors or symptoms most characteristic of depression should show a relatively uniform increase in percentage as one goes from the "none" category to the "severe" classification. *Stooped posture,* going from 6% to 32% to 76% to 87%, is one such behavior. Another mark of a useful descriptive sign or symptom would be that it shows a high frequency among severely depressed patients. In this regard, stooped posture also qualifies as a valid predictor. Other symptoms or behaviors meeting these criteria include *sad faces, low mood, suicidal wishes, indecisiveness, hopelessness, feelings of inadequacy, loss of interest, loss of motivation, sleep disturbances,* and *loss of appetite.*

Although most of these behaviors or symptoms are self-explanatory, a few observations are in order. Note that almost all severely depressed patients gave some indication of wanting to commit suicide. We shall have more to say about this later, but you should be aware that actual suicide attempts, including success-ful attempts, are often preceded by statements that the individual is thinking about suicide. Thus, even when they are presented in joking terms, statements of this nature must always be taken seriously. Severely depressed people must be viewed as a high-risk population in relation to suicide.

Almost all the depressed patients viewed themselves as inadequate in some significant respect. As Beck notes, typically such patients do not like themselves because of their *perceived* inadequacies. We have italicized the word *perceived,* because there is little evidence that depressed people would be judged in-adequate by others. Available evidence fails to support their view that they are less able than normals to perform tasks, or function intelligently (Friedman, 1964). Clinical case history literature is replete with patients who seem to view themselves as abject failures in spite of highly successful careers or other ac-complishments most people would describe as praiseworthy. For instance, Rimm treated an "A" student who was seriously depressed (although the label *psychotic* would not have been appropriate). During this depression he "set the curve" on a difficult mathematics examination. Although this apparently elevated his mood slightly, he still insisted that he was stupid, implying that he was lucky or had somehow fooled the instructor.

The majority of depressed people, even those only mildly depressed, report sleep difficulties. They have difficulty falling asleep, sleep fitfully, and often report so-called terminal insomnia; that is, they wake up early, and cannot return to sleep. Perhaps the patterns of irrational thinking so often noted in depression are in part perpetuated by lack of sleep, which may impede clear thinking.

Finally, loss of appetite, which affects so many severely depressed people, can present serious medical problems. In fact, some people have been hos-pitalized more as a function of their self-starvation than for depression per se.

DELUSIONS AND HALLUCINATIONS.   In the chapter on schizophrenia we de-fined a delusion as a belief lacking in corroboration or support. Beck (1967) has compiled some interesting data on the frequency of different types or classes of delusions. The classification pertains *only* to delusions having a depressive content.

Among severely depressed psychotic patients, the most frequent delusions pertained to feelings of *worthlessness, being a sinner,* and *being punished.* As an example of a delusion of worthlessness, consider the following:

> I must weep myself to death. I cannot live. I cannot die. I have failed so. It would be better if I had not been born. My life has always been a burden . . . I am the most inferior person in the world . . . I am subhuman [Beck, 1967, p. 37].

Perceiving oneself as a sinner and either reporting that one is being punished (perhaps by God) or anticipating punishment tend to go together. Although some depressed patients may suggest that the punishment is unfair, there is usually the implication that the punishment is deserved. For instance, 14% of the severely depressed psychotics in the sample apparently believed they were the devil! This is in sharp contrast to the delusions of persecution characteristic of paranoid schizophrenics.

Hallucinations, although a good deal less common than delusions, are sometimes encountered among severely depressed individuals. Typically, the patient reports hearing voices which, not surprisingly, are condemning him. Rennie (1942) presented data suggesting that hallucinations were most apparent among those patients who had recurring episodes of depression.

RETARDATION AND AGITATION IN DEPRESSION.   We have already alluded to retardation and agitation in depression. There is a marked lack of motor movement, a shuffling walk, lack of verbal behavior, and in more extreme cases, the patient may be in a stuporous or semistuporous state. There is a *lack* of waxy flexibility in stuporous depressed patients (recall that in Chapter 5 we noted waxy flexibility of the limbs as a characteristic of certain catatonic schizophrenics).

With nothing more than the information contained in the last paragraph, you might be misled into thinking that a retarded depressed person is in a very relaxed, quiescent state. Keep in mind the other signs and symptoms of depression—suicidal wishes, sleep disturbances, loss of appetite—which are hardly consistent with feelings of well-being. Also, as we shall see, there is physiological evidence that such patients experience considerable stress.

Less is written about agitated depression, and one may infer that it is less prevalent than retarded depression. Certainly, this is consistent with our own experience with depressed patients. The picture is one of an individual showing extreme restlessness, having difficulty sitting in one place, talking a good deal in a clearly depressive way—"My God, how can life be so terrible," and so on.

To help you get a feel for what agitated depression might be like, imagine the following: You have a very strong romantic attachment to someone. The relationship has been going on for a long time and means a great deal to you. A mutual acquaintance has all but convinced you that the one you love so dearly no longer cares for you, and will tell you this directly, in 1 hour. How do you suppose you would feel and behave during that hour? Multiply your distress and agitation by 10 and you have something resembling the clinical picture of agitated depression.

From what we have said, it might seem that retarded and agitated depression are separate clinical entities. A review of statistical investigations (factor analytic studies) by Mendels and Cochrane (1968) and more recent investigations (Depue & Evans, 1976) suggests the following: There exists a subgroup of depressed patients who typically do not show agitation. There exists a second group, somewhat less well delineated in terms of consistency of behavior, who evidence agitation at least some of the time, and some degree of retardation at other times. The work of Lorr and his associates (1968), to which we referred in Chapter 5, gives some support to this view. Among the many categories of patients suggested by this research was one that included many retarded depressives and another that included many who apparently showed both retardation and agitation.

ONSET AND PROGNOSES IN DEPRESSION. Beck (1967), summarizing investigations concerning the onset of depression, notes that in the majority of cases (70–75%), the episode came on rather suddenly. For those patients reporting a *gradual* onset, the most common complaint prior to entering into a relatively clear-cut depressive episode was a vaguely described tension or anxiety.

As we have noted, people usually recover from depression even with no treatment. Kolb (1973) observes that approximately 80% of patients with affective disorders recover. The majority of patients with the *affective disorder* label are depressed, so it is fair to say that the prognosis for depression is positive. Kolb further notes that less than 10% become chronic. For this reason, it is sometimes said that depression and related disorders are *self-limiting*. We are not entirely comfortable with this term because it implies that such patients automatically get better. Clearly, the fact that someone has not received *formal* treatment does not preclude the possibility that the depressed person has engaged in some therapeutic life experience.

Studies by Lundquist (1945) and Paskind (1929) suggest that depressive episodes average 6 or 7 months in duration; there is some indication that the duration tends to be greater, the older the patient.

Sometimes patients showing depression or an associated disorder experience one or more relapses (that is, recurrences of the disorder). Beck (1967) makes the following observation:

> In examining the literature on the intervals between episodes of depression, one is struck by the fact that recurrence may occur after years, or even decades of apparent good health [p. 53].

He goes on to cite Kraepelin to the effect that recurrences may occur after periods as long as 40 years!

These observations may lead to unwarranted pessimism regarding the future of a person in a severe depressive episode. When we examine the *probability* of a recurrence, a brighter picture emerges. Thus, Lundquist (1945) found that the probability of recurrence is on the order of 12% during the 6-year period following the initial depression. For patients under 30 years of age during the initial bout, the probability tends to fall off sharply beyond the 6-year period. For persons over 30, the risk of recurrence also decreases, although not as sharply. Further, Kolb (1973) notes that while 55% of manic-depressive patients at state hospitals are first admissions, only 25% are second admissions and a mere 9% are third admissions.[2] A case history follows.

■ The patient, a 44-year-old black female, is presently hospitalized for psychotic depression. She is married and is the mother of eight children. Her husband has been disabled for the past 3 years, and the family subsists on welfare and

[2] Kolb is using the term *manic-depression* in the traditional sense, including pure mania, pure depression, and some mixture of the two. Certainly, a large proportion of these patients would be viewed as depressed, as we are using the term.

social security. When in a depressive episode, she appears very sad; she cries a great deal, shows marked behavioral retardation, and verbalizes great self-contempt, especially regarding her fitness as a mother. She complains of a loss of interest in sex. Although she spends much time in bed, often weeping, she reports experiencing difficulty sleeping and does give the appearance of being fatigued. In contrast to many depressives, she does not show a marked loss of appetite. Occasionally she hears voices telling her to harm herself or members of her family. Such experiences disturb her very much, although she has never actually attempted to harm herself or others. During depressive episodes she often says that she is ''hopeless'' and will never get better, although her pattern from previous episodes is to show improvement after several months of hospitalization. When not depressed, she behaves in a relatively normal manner, although rarely would anyone describe her as happy.

The patient was one of five children. When she was 7, her father, an alcoholic, was convicted of killing a man and spent 5 years in jail. During this period the family experienced great hardship, virtually facing starvation. She describes her father as very strict, indicating that he beat her frequently. In contrast, her mother is described as a warm person, to whom she felt close. She completed the eighth grade, and characterized herself as a ''loner'' in school. She married a construction worker at age 21. At age 30, when she experienced her first severe depression, she had three children and was employed as a maid. She attributed this initial depression to stress associated with the responsibilities of a job and family at the same time. Whether she would have become depressed in the absence of these responsibilities is a matter of conjecture. On the other hand, her present life circumstances, including five additional children and an invalid husband, must surely contribute to her unhappiness.

MANIA

Among patients suffering from depression and related disorders, the proportion who show only mania is quite low, approximately 9% (Clayton, Pitts, & Winokur, 1965; Rennie, 1942), far less than the percentage showing depression alone, which is probably in excess of 50% (Rennie, 1942, noted 67% of pure depressives). The remainder, roughly 30%, show both mania and depression.

Given the relative rarity of pure mania, much of what is written is based on observing behaviors of manic-depressives during a manic episode. Whether there are important behavioral differences between pure mania and a manic episode in a manic-depressive patient is an interesting question; unfortunately, we cannot provide an answer.

MANIC BEHAVIOR. In many respects, manic behavior may be thought of as virtually the opposite of depression, especially retarded depression. While in a manic episode the individual is expansive, grandiose, and sometimes aggressive—especially when people attempt to constrain him. He appears euphoric and elated, and gives the appearance of having a love affair with himself. He is hyperactive, but unlike the agitated depressed person, there is no indication of discomfort.

Kolb (1973) notes that manic exhilaration may be marked by whistling, singing, dancing, and (in our view an especially cogent observation) "unrestrained playfulness." Rimm, as a novice therapist for a group of female hospitalized patients, had to deal with a middle-aged female going through a typical manic episode. Her antics, which she presumably perceived as humorous and mischievous, totally disrupted the group process and it was not unusual, during a session, for the therapist to ask that she leave. She seemed to take particular delight in referring to the therapist as "Mister-Doctor-Doctor-Mister-Rimm-Brimm-Rimm." She was referring to the supervising psychiatrist's slip in introducing Rimm as "Dr. Brimm," and also to the fact that Rimm had not yet received his Ph.D. and had informed the group of this.

We have mentioned the grandiosity of mania; in our experience it is rather characteristic. It may show up in unrealistic planning, often in relation to proposed business enterprises. Thus, one patient planned to go to a South American republic to buy ocelots, which he planned to sell in the United States. His standard phrase was that he would "get in and get out" (i.e., make the deal quickly). Indeed, he persuaded several naive staff members that the plan had merit, until they were informed that he was persona non grata in several South American countries. This particular patient also had a tendency, not unusual in people going through manic episodes, to spend money in a totally reckless fashion. Thus, although his funds were quite limited, on one occasion he purchased two extremely expensive color television sets.

Table 6-2 describes some of the more prominent features of mania. The data, by Clayton *et al.* (1965), are from Beck's summary (Beck, 1967).

TABLE 6-2

Prominent Symptoms of Mania in a Group of Hospitalized Patients[a]

Symptom	Percentage of manic patients with symptom
Hyperactivity	100
Flight of ideas	100
Push of speech	100
Euphoria	97
Distractibility	97
Circumstantiality (detailed recounting of trivial events)	96
Decreased sleep	94
Grandiosity and/or religiosity	79
Ideas of reference	77
Increased sexuality	74
Delusions	73

[a] Based on data from Clayton, Pitts, and Winokur, 1965; adapted from Beck, 1967b.

Among the various categories of psychotic behavior we have described, mania is obviously highly conspicuous. Thus it is easy to get the impression that of the disorders discussed in this chapter, it is the most prevalent. In fact, depressed behavior is far more prevalent; but since depressed people tend to be withdrawn, depression is less obtrusive. See the following case history.

■ The patient is a 42-year-old white male. This is his second hospitalization in 2 years. When employed, he works as a dishwasher in a restaurant. During a manic episode he is inclined to give all his meager salary to charity; he is very active and shows great reluctance to go to bed at night; his eating habits are poor, and since his episodes typically last for many weeks, he is grossly underweight. His present hospitalization followed an incident at work: he began talking and then singing in a very loud voice, which customers found most disturbing. Lithium carbonate is a drug found to be effective in controlling mania in many patients (see Chapter 21 of the present text), but not infrequently, they refuse to take this medication because they say there is nothing wrong with them. In this patient's case, failure to use his medication was based on his belief that his organic-food diet, which he did not follow in any rigorous manner, was superior.

In addition to the manic diagnosis, he has been labeled as schizo-affective schizophrenic and paranoid schizophrenic. There is little in his present behavior or in his hospital record that would seem to justify a schizophrenic diagnosis. Whether this is a case of "pure" mania is conjectural. There have been no indications of depression in either of his hospitalizations; however, during one brief period while he was receiving outpatient care, his therapist described him as "crying, talkative, depressed, suspicious, and confused."

He has no siblings. His mother died when he was in his teens, and he was reared by his father, a carpenter, with whom he lives when out of the hospital. He completed the eighth grade. According to his father, the patient has had "problems" all his adult life, although the father is vague about the details. The patient has never married, although he has had a girl friend for the past several years. He describes the relationship as good, sexually and in other respects; she generally corroborates this, although she finds him quite unmanageable when in a manic episode, and refuses to see him at such times.

Before leaving our discussion of mania, we should mention a related label, *hypomania*. As the name suggests, the behavior is manic-like in quality, but is less intense or deviant in degree. Most of us, on occasion at least, behave in a manner that might be described as hypomanic, just as most of us are, from time to time, at least mildly depressed (we have never heard the term *hypodepression* used, however).

MANIC-DEPRESSION

Of the so-called affective disorders, manic-depression has received the most attention, in part because traditionalists see pure depression and pure mania as belonging to this broad category. Even the more restricted form we have defined (that is, when both mania and depression occur in the same individual) is a clinical entity of considerable interest. Since we have already described the separate phases of depression and mania, our present discussion will be limited to the relationship between the two types of episodes.

Recall that DSM-II refers to this category as "Manic-depressive illness, circular type." This is potentially misleading, since it implies that the manic-depressive goes through some highly regular pattern of mania–depression–mania–depression, and so on. Although there are reports in the literature (e.g., Bunney & Hartmann, 1956; Richter, 1965) of such cases, they are rare. Although the Bunney and Hartmann cases are of interest (showing regular alterations of mania and depression, each lasting 24 hours), as Beck (1967) and Kolb (1973) note, such fixed cycles are most unusual. More typical are periods of depression lasting for a few weeks to many months, followed by periods of relative normality, followed by a manic episode of a limited but unpredictable length. It is also possible for an individual to show several depressive episodes followed by a period of mania, or vice versa. The striking feature of manic-depressive behavior is not its regular periodicity, so to speak, but rather that, except for the common feature of sleep disorder, mania and depression are virtually mirror images of one another.

INVOLUTIONAL DEPRESSION
(INVOLUTIONAL MELANCHOLIA)

As we said earlier, this is a label given to depression occurring later in life, during the so-called involutional period. Kraepelin was the first to view involutional melancholia as distinct from depression. Subsequently, he was persuaded that it was not a separate clinical entity after all. Nevertheless, in spite of Kraepelin's massive and continuing influence on diagnostic practices, his revised point of view did not prevail. DSM-II and similar publications treat involutional melancholia as separate from the other disorders discussed in this chapter.

There is, or at least was, a certain logic to dealing with depression during middle age as a separate phenomenon. During menopause, women do experience certain well-known endocrinological changes; men do as well, although the changes are considerably more gradual. Thus it made sense to attempt to relate such physiological changes to the increased incidence of depression with advancing years. However, there is no convincing evidence yet that such physiological changes are causally related to severe depression. To illustrate, when a woman completes menopause, a reduction in estrogen (the principal female hormone) is the most prominent endocrinological change. Yet Ripley, Shorr, and Papanicolaou (1940) found little benefit from estrogen therapy in female involutional depressives. Henderson and Gillespie (1963) also found little evidence that physiological changes associated with the involutional period were directly related to depression, either in men or in women.

Behavioral studies (see Beck, 1967) fail to distinguish involutional depressives from younger patients whose diagnosis is depression. Kolb (1973) observes that, prior to the advent of shock therapy (see Chapter 21 of this text), only about 40% of the involutional depressives recovered. Unfortunately, Kolb does not cite the source of his data, nor does he define *recover*. His statement certainly suggests that in terms of prognosis, involutional depression may differ from depression occurring at an earlier age. But as we have noted, depression in older patients (even over 30 years of age) has a somewhat poorer prognosis than in younger patients.

In short, the most reasonable conclusion would seem to be that so-called involutional depression or involutional melancholia is nothing more or less than depression that happens to occur at a certain period in one's life. The relatively higher frequency of depression during the involutional period may simply reflect changes in the patient's life. Children have left home; parents, especially mothers, may feel useless; men at this stage in their lives frequently realize that professional dreams will not come true.

Some Major Classificatory Disputes

Recall from Chapter 5 the issues raised in relation to classifying schizophrenics as chronic versus acute, process versus reactive, and paranoid versus nonparanoid. In relation to depression and related disorders, there are similar controversies. These pertain to whether it is theoretically and practically meaningful to attempt to distinguish between neurotic and psychotic depression, and between endogenous and exogenous depression. These important issues will now be discussed.

NEUROTIC VERSUS PSYCHOTIC DEPRESSION

Most would agree that neurotic and psychotic depressive reactions have at least some features in common, and that psychotic depression is far more serious in nature. The critical question is this: Are neurotic and psychotic depression essentially similar, the difference being merely one of degree of depression, or is there some fundamental *qualitative* difference or differences? DSM-II takes no explicit position on this issue. Thus, depressive neurosis is described as follows:

> This disorder is manifested by an excessive reaction due to an internal conflict or to an identifiable event such as the loss of a love object or cherished possession. It is to be distinguished from Involutional melancholia—and Manic-depressive illness . . . [p. 40].

Thus, although DSM-II suggests a difference, it fails to indicate whether it is anything more than a matter of degree.

The data in Table 6-3 may throw some light on the issue. The tabulated data are based on 50 patients diagnosed as psychotically depressed and 50 patients with a neurotic depressive diagnosis. As would be expected, the percentage of psychotics showing each symptom is greater than the percentage of neurotics. There is also a trend such that the higher the percentage of psychotics showing a particular symptom or sign, the higher the percentage of neurotics exhibiting the

TABLE 6-3

Frequency of Clinical Features in Fifty Patients Diagnosed as Neurotically Depressed (ND) and Fifty Patients Diagnosed as Psychotically Depressed (PD)[a]

Clinical feature	Feature present		Present to severe degree	
	ND (percentage)	PD (percentage)	ND (percentage)	PD (percentage)
Sad faces	86	94	4	24
Stooped posture	58	76	4	20
Speech: slow, etc.	66	70	8	22
Low mood	84	80	8	44
Diurnal variation of mood	22	48	2	10
Hopelessness	78	68	6	34
Conscious guilt	64	44	6	12
Feeling inadequate	68	70	10	42
Somatic preoccupation	58	66	6	24
Suicidal wishes	58	76	14	40
Indecisiveness	56	70	6	28
Loss of motivation	70	82	8	48
Loss of interest	64	78	10	44
Fatigability	80	74	8	48
Loss of appetite	48	76	2	40
Sleep disturbance	66	80	12	52
Constipation	28	56	2	16

[a] Adapted from Beck, 1967b.

same behavior. However, though a correlation exists, it is not very high—.41, according to our calculations. Note that this figure is based on percentages of patients showing a symptom to a *severe* degree (right half of Table 6-3). If one merely asks whether the particular clinical feature is present or absent, independent of degree (refer now to the left half of Table 6-3), the correlation between symptoms of neurotic and psychotic depressives is somewhat higher (.66). Both correlations or relationships are high enough to suggest that, descriptively at least, neurotic and psychotic depression may fall on a continuum. Had the correlations been near zero, this could be taken as rather strong evidence *against* the continuity view. Had the correlations been very strong—for example, on the order of .9—this could be taken as strong evidence that psychotic depression is merely an intense version of neurotic depression. In addition, the poor reliability of diagnosis, which we have pointed to repeatedly throughout this text, would probably tend to minimize any relation between the two types of depression. On the evidence of these data, we might at least tentatively conclude that psychotic and neurotic depression are on a continuum.

There are, however, other data that suggest to some that neurotic and psychotic depression should be viewed as qualitatively separate clinical entities. These findings shall be considered in the next section.

EXOGENOUS VERSUS ENDOGENOUS DEPRESSION

Exogenous depression refers to depression that presumably has come about as a result of changes in the environment (e.g., loss of a loved one, loss of professional status); endogenous depression refers to depression resulting principally from internal physiological or biochemical determinants.

Now, although there is nothing inherent in the definition of exogenous depression to suggest that it is a concept equivalent to neurotic depression, frequently the terms are used synonymously. Likewise, although one can imagine a mild depression emanating from some sort of biochemical imbalance, again it is common practice to equate endogenous depression with psychotic depression. Whether such practices are justifiable is open to question. Ultimately the issue will be decided empirically. For the present, we think that equating the exogenous–endogenous and neurotic–psychotic dimensions merely adds to the confusion.

The fundamental question in relation to neurotic versus psychotic depression is whether the two disorders should best be viewed on a continuum or as two separate entities. This is precisely the same question that clinicians and scientists have raised in relation to the endogenous–exogenous dimension. Are there two fundamentally different disorders, one brought about by external stress (exogenous, sometimes referred to as *reactive*), the other not related to external stress (endogenous)? In spite of considerable investigative effort by many scientists, the issue is not yet settled. As Depue and Evans (1976) note, early work tended to support the view that there was little basis for separating depression into two such categories. Writings that did favor the exogenous–endogenous distinction were largely based on clinical reports rather than controlled investigations (Kendell, 1968).

More recent investigations, relying primarily on complex statistical techniques such as factor analysis, tend to support the view that endogenous and exogenous depression are separate clinical entities (e.g., Kear-Colwell, 1972; Mendels & Cochrane, 1968; Paykel, Prusoff, & Klerman, 1971). These factor analytic investigations point to a relatively well-defined cluster of signs and symptoms that can readily be labeled as endogenous depression. Mendels and Cochrane's review (1968) of such studies found the following attributes associated with endogenous depression:

Behavioral retardation
Deep depression
Low reactivity to environmental changes
Loss of interest in life
Somatic (i.e., physical) complaints
Lack of self-pity
Insomnia in the middle of the night
Lack of precipitating stress

As Depue and Evans (1976) note, the clinical picture of exogenous or reactive depression is not as clearly defined. Exogenous depression tends to be characterized by the following:

High reactivity to the environment
Precipitating stress
Agitation and irritability
What might be described as "personality disturbance"

This clinical picture reveals less consistency and homogeneity than is the case with endogenous depression. In fact, the results of another statistical approach (specifically, examining the nature of the distribution of factor scores, details of which are well beyond the scope of this text) tend to support the view that endogenous and exogenous depression are on a continuum (Depue & Evans, 1976). Thus, the evidence is indeed conflicting.

A possible resolution has been suggested by the noted British researcher, Hans Eysenck (1970). Those who believe the endogenous–exogenous distinction to be valid assume that a depressed person belongs in one of the two categories. Those who hold the continuum view believe that any given depressed patient falls at some point along a single continuum or dimension, one end of which is marked by obvious precipitating stress, and the other by clear evidence for the lack of precipitating stress. However, in Eysenck's view, it would be far more productive to deal with endogenous and exogenous depressions as separate and *independent* clinical entities. What Eysenck is suggesting, in effect, is that a person receive one "score" indicating the degree to which he is evidencing signs or symptoms of reactive depression and a separate, independent score pertaining to endogenous depression. Thus, it would be possible for a person to receive a high score on endogenous depression, suggesting that sometimes his bouts of depression are clearly of an endogenous nature (including lack of precipitating environmental stress). This same person might receive a moderately high score on a test of exogenous depression, indicating that sometimes his depressive episodes are characteristically reactive or exogenous. In our view, there is much to be said for such an approach. As Becker (1974) has observed, it "would more accurately reflect the relative independence of the two syndromes, as well as their tendency to occur together in the same patient in varying degrees [p. 39]."

The Etiology of Depression and Related Disorders

BIOLOGICAL CONSIDERATIONS

GENETIC FACTORS.   As Rosenthal (1970) points out, there is considerably less research on this class of disorders than is available in relation to the schizophrenias.

TABLE 6-4

Concordance Rates for Depression and Related Disorders in Monozygotic and Dizygotic Twins[a]

Study	Monozygotic twins			Dizygotic twins		
	Total pairs	Concordant pairs	Concordance rate	pairs	Concordant pairs	Concordance rate
Luxenburger, 1930	4	3	75.0	13	0	0.0
Rosanoff, Handy, Plesset, and Brush, 1934–1935	23	16	69.6	67	11	16.4
Kallmann, 1952	27	25	92.6; 100.0[b]	55	13	23.6
Slater, 1953: Only manic-depressive psychosis	7	4	57.1; 80.0[b]	17	4	23.5
Other affective disorders	1	0	0.0	13	3	18.8
Da Fonseca, 1959: affective disorders	21	15	71.4	39	15	38.5
Harvald and Hauge, 1965	10	5	50.0	39	1	2.6

[a] Adapted from *Genetic theory and abnormal behavior* by D. Rosenthal. Copyright 1970 by McGraw-Hill Book Company. Used with premission of McGraw-Hill Book Company.
[b] Corrected concordance rate.

As we noted in Chapter 5, data that show a much higher concordance rate for a particular disorder among identical or monozygotic twins than among nonidentical or dizygotic twins may be taken as evidence of a genetic component in that disorder.[3] The data in Table 6-4 (from Rosenthal, 1970) are based upon manic-depression, defined in the broad traditional sense, and other "affective psychoses." It is likely that the majority of these cases showed *monopolar* depression (i.e., an absence of manic symptoms), since this is characteristic of most patients in the affective psychosis category.

As with schizophrenia, the concordance rates are variable, ranging from 50 to 100% depending on the study, excluding the zero concordance rate given by Slater (1953), since it is based on only one pair of monozygotic twins. Comparing the data in Table 6-4 with those in Table 5-1, Chapter 5, we can see that concordance rates for depression and related disorders tend to run somewhat *higher* than those for schizophrenics. The average rate across studies is approximately 74%, in contrast to approximately 45% for schizophrenics. The concordance rate

[3] *Concordance* means that if one member of the pair has the disorder the other also has the disorder, and vice versa. Such data are subject to one obvious source of bias. If the diagnostician believes in the importance of a herediatary component, and *knows* that one monozygotic twin has been diagnosed as psychotically depressed, this may well bias his behavior in favor of providing the same diagnostic label for the other twin.

for nonidentical or dizygotic twins, from Table 6-4, is also variable but is consistently lower than that for identical twins; the average rate across studies is approximately 18%. Other data (see Rosenthal, 1970) examining relationships among relatives of patients suffering from depression and related disorders also support a genetic factor, although clearly the role of environment in such situations is difficult to ascertain. In sum, as was true in relation to schizophrenia, there is some reason to believe that heredity may play an important role in the disorders discussed in this chapter.

BIOCHEMICAL FACTORS.   Data suggesting a possible genetic basis for schizophrenia prompted the search for psychophysiological or biochemical agents. Although more limited in scope, the data from genetic studies dealing with depression are if anything more impressive. For this reason, researchers are actively searching for biological agents for the so-called affective disorders.

In dealing with a possible biochemical basis of schizophrenic disorders, we referred to three fundamental chemical transmitters found in the brains of humans and infrahumans: *norepinephrine, dopamine,* and *serotonin*. These same substances have been assigned important roles in biological explanations of depression and related disorders. The most influential hypothesis, the catecholamine hypothesis (Bunney & Davis, 1965), stresses the importance of norepinephrine in such disorders. Norepinephrine is a neural transmitter belonging to a larger class of biochemicals labeled catecholamines (others being epinephrine and dopamine). Since this hypothesis stresses norepinephrine, we shall refer to it as the *norepinephrine hypothesis*. The hypothesis, most simply stated, assumes that depression is associated with a deficiency of norepinephrine in certain parts of the brain, especially the hypothalamus, a midbrain structure critical to virtually every manifestation of human emotion and motivation. Mania, on the other hand, is assumed to be associated with an excess of this biochemical neural transmitter.

The evidence in support of this hypothesis, although largely indirect and inferential, is nevertheless enticing. Drugs that deplete the brain of norepinephrine and related substances produce sedation or disinterest (see Depue & Evans, 1976). Drugs that increase available norepinephrine include the two principal classes of drugs used to relieve clinical depression in humans (MAO inhibitors and the tricyclics; see Chapter 21). Further, if there is a biochemical basis for depression and related disorders, clearly the hypothalamus is intimately involved, given its key role in human motivational and emotional systems. As Frazer and Stinnett (1973) note, the hypothalamus contains the greatest concentration of norepinephrine-activated nerve cells in the entire brain.[4] In addition, studies that have examined the concentration of certain metabolites (breakdown

[4] Considerable research has led many scientists (see Bolles, 1975) to postulate the existence of reward centers in certain lower brain structures, especially the hypothalamus. In depression, there is a marked loss of apparent reinforcement or reward value associated with a variety of activities; thus it is plausible to raise the possibility of fundamental malfunction of some brain reward system intimately involving the hypothalamus.

products) of norepinephrine in the cerebrospinal fluid of patients, at least indirectly support the norepinephrine hypothesis (Bond, Jenner, & Sampson, 1972; Greenspan, Schildkraut, Gordon, Baer, Aronoff, & Durrell, 1970; Maas, Dekirmenjian, & Fawcett, 1971). Finally, as we will see in Chapter 21, lithium carbonate can be very effective in the treatment of manic patients. In fact, 80–85% of the manic patients in one study (Schou, 1968) responded positively to lithium treatment, and more recent studies have confirmed these initial positive findings (see Prien, Klett, & Caffey, 1974). There is evidence that lithium may have the effect of decreasing the production of norepinephrine (Depue & Evans, 1976). Thus, these lithium studies provide still more evidence in support of the norepinephrine hypothesis.

As we have noted, sleep disturbances are common to depression and mania. Precisely how excesses *and* deficiencies of norepinephrine should lead to sleep disorders has not been made clear. Thus, in spite of considerable supportive evidence, the norepinephrine hypothesis does not readily account for all the major symptoms of the manic-depression syndrome.

The major brain transmitter substances norepinephrine, dopamine, and serotonin are biochemically related. The evidence in support of the norepinephrine hypothesis notwithstanding, this fact alone would suggest that the true biochemical picture is considerably more complex. Bunney, Goodwin, and Murphy (1972) have suggested the importance of dopamine in depressive disorders. In manic-depression, they view depression as the basic symptom, with dopamine somehow involved in a kind of "switching" mechanism that can turn mania on and off. Some supportive evidence for the Bunney *et al.* (1972) hypothesis comes from the observation that the drug L-dopa, which increases brain dopamine, also increases motor activity in retarded depressed patients; further, L-dopa can induce mania in a manic-depressed patient.

Another hypothesis concerning the biochemical process involved in switching in and out of manic episodes has been put forth by Prange, Wilson, Lynn, Alltop, & Stikeleather (1974). They argue that both depression and mania reflect a deficiency in brain serotonin, and switching into and out of mania depends on levels of brain catecholamines (recall that both dopamine and norepinephrine are catecholamines).

Before leaving this section, we will mention two additional physiological characteristics of depression. You probably have heard of the adrenal glands, located on either kidney. One anatomical portion of the gland, the adrenal cortex, produces a variety of important endocrinological substances, among them certain steroids that are released in excessive quantities when an individual is stressed. One indication of an increase in such activity is an increase in the blood level of a substance called *cortisol*. There is considerable evidence (see Beck, 1967) that depressed people show higher levels of cortisol. Because cortisol plays a major role in the metabolism of norepinephrine, the higher levels of cortisol in depression could have some relevance to the norepinephrine hypothesis. However, a normal individual undergoing stress also shows an elevation of blood cortisol, as do anxious mental patients more or less irrespective of formal diagnosis. In other words, elevated cortisol appears to be a general consequence of stress or anxiety and is not specific to depression. That elevated cortisol *is* commonly observed in depression does serve to support a point raised earlier in the chapter: Depressed persons, no matter how apathetic and indifferent they may appear, do not present the biochemical profile of individuals in a calm, relaxed state.

The other characteristic, and one that does seem more specific to depression than to other psychiatric disorders such as schizophrenia, pertains to retention of certain electrolytes. Electrolytes are chemicals important in the transmission of electrical impulses. Since nerve transmission is of an electrical nature, electrolytes are critical to the functioning of the nervous system. The principal electrolytic substances involved in nerve impulse conduction are sodium (common table salt is sodium chloride) and potassium.[5] Although there is evidence for higher retention of both sodium and potassium in depressive patients (see Depue & Evans, 1976), the most consistent finding is of higher sodium retention in depressives. Moreover, sodium retention is reduced when depression improves, either spontaneously or after electroconvulsive shock treatment (see Chapter 21 for a discussion of the latter). But the precise role of sodium retention in the etiology of depression is as yet undiscovered.

PSYCHOLOGICAL CONSIDERATIONS

THE PSYCHOANALYTIC VIEW. Psychoanalytic thinking has had a pervasive influence on writings and theories pertaining to all psychological disorders, including depression. As we have mentioned, a detailed picture of the psychoanalytic position is presented in Chapter 16.

According to classical psychoanalytic thinking, depression is viewed as a regression to an early stage of psychosexual development (Fenichel, 1945). In schizophrenia, the regression is most extreme, carrying the individual back to the earliest stages of development in infancy. In depression, the regression is not as extreme. The clinically depressed person exhibits behaviors reflecting anal and to some degree, oral stages of development. To oversimplify, the schizophrenic has regressed to an infantile stage of development (e.g., 6 months to 1 year); the severely depressed person has regressed to modes of coping with the external world characteristic of a child of 2 to 3 years of age. Dependency is stressed in classical psychoanalytic writing (see Fenichel, 1945) as is a conflict between a strong need to receive gratification (e.g., affection) in a passive, dependent fashion, and a tendency to react violently when such needs are thwarted. Loss of self-esteem is also emphasized. Whatever anger or hostility the depressed person

[5] Lithium is also an electrolyte, rather similar chemically to sodium. A patient undergoing lithium treatment must have his blood concentraton of lithium monitored regularly; the treament is potentially very dangerous, precisely because of the chemical similarity between sodium and lithium. Excess amounts of lithium may interfere with the body's ability to use sodium, which may well be fatal.

experiences toward external factors that thwart his opportunity to experience self-esteem is turned inward; the depressed person hates himself.

Freud (1917/1957) had some interesting although not readily testable views on depression following the death of a loved one. A normal individual initially identifies with the deceased, as if he were still alive. This initial identification is followed by a period of breaking the psychological bonds between the individual and the deceased. In the case of prolonged and incapacitating depression following the death of a loved one, it is assumed that the patient had the predisposing personality structure (tendency to regress to an early stage of development) for depression, and that he deals with whatever hostility he felt toward the deceased by turning this hostility or anger toward himself.

If, for Freud, depression is characterized by self-hate, mania is characterized by self-love. The manic has triumphantly overcome his guilt, and engages in childlike self-adoration.

More recent psychoanalytic theorizing has emphasized *anaclitic depression* (Bowlby, 1960; Spitz, 1946a) which is depression brought about by the loss of one or both parents. There is some supportive evidence in the animal work by Seay, Hansen, and Harlow (1963), who observed that monkeys separated from their mothers for several weeks ultimately showed a generally depressed response, which the experimenters characterized as "despair." Similar findings have been reported by McKinney, Suomi, & Harlow (1971).

Beck (1967) reported that highly depressed patients had a higher incidence of parental loss than people showing mild depression. Recall, however, that Wahl's study (1956) showed a high rate of parental loss prior to age 15 among individuals subsequently diagnosed as schizophrenic. Also, reviews of the literature (see Depue & Evans, 1976) do not show consistent support for a relationship between parental loss and subsequent depression.

Another recent trend in psychoanalytic thinking (e.g., Melges & Bowlby, 1969) associates depression with the belief that one is unable to achieve important life goals. As we shall learn, the view that depressed people have feelings (perhaps it would be more correct to say *thoughts*) of hopelessness tends to overlap with certain cognitive and behavioristic views of depression.

THE REINFORCEMENT SYSTEM AND OBJECT LOSS.   The preceding section refers to theories that loss of a loved object (e.g., a parent) may have some relationship to subsequent depression. In a previous section, we mentioned the possibility that severely depressed individuals have suffered impairment of some general reward system. Akiskal and McKinney (1973) suggest that early separation may contribute to a biochemical malfunction of such a reinforcement system, resulting in increased susceptibility to depression in adulthood. This is highly speculative, of course, and is based to a considerable extent on animal separation studies.

DEPRESSION AND LEARNED HELPLESSNESS.   Virtually all writers in the area of depression (e.g., Beck, 1967; Melges & Bowlby, 1969) have linked helplessness and hopelessness to human depression. Logically, the terms are causally related; helplessness would seem to lead to an attitude of hopelessness. In a classic study of "learned helplessness" in animals (see Seligman, 1975), one group of dogs was exposed to highly painful shock, with escape impossible. A second group of dogs received no such training. Subsequently, both groups were put in a situation involving aversive stimulation, where escape and ultimately avoidance *were* possible. The remarkable finding was that, although almost all of the untrained second group of dogs learned to avoid the shock, approximately two-thirds of the dogs in the first group *failed* to learn either to escape or avoid the shock! Apparently, from the prior "hopeless" situation, the majority of the first group of dogs learned to be helpless in a situation in which escape and avoidance were not only adaptive, but eminently possible. Within 72 hours following a *single* inescapable shock situation, the learned helplessness seems to wear off or dissipate and some (e.g., Depue & Evans, 1976) have taken this as evidence that true learning has not really occurred. However, as Seligman (1975) notes, if the dogs are provided with several sessions of inescapable shock, the pattern of helplessness does not dissipate, suggesting that learning has indeed occurred. Seligman reports that learned helplessness has also been found in other species, including rats, cats, and even fish, and he believes that the only prerequisite for learned helplessness may be that the organism is capable of learning. Hiroto (reported in Seligman, 1975) performed an experiment analogous to the dog study, using college students as subjects. The aversive stimulation was noise instead of shock. Those subjects in the inescapable noise condition showed poor learning in a subsequent finger-maze task (where the correct response resulted in escape from or avoidance of the noise) relative to subjects who had previously experienced escapable noise, or no noise.

Dorwith (1971) provided some indirect support for the learned helplessness hypothesis. Electroconvulsive shock, discussed in Chapter 21, is a rather successful treatment for human depression. Dorwith found that such treatment was effective in reducing learned helplessness in dogs, relative to "helpless" dogs not given the shock treatment. In addition, experiments involving depressed people have shown a reduction in depression when rewards are related to the behavior of the patients in some lawful and predictable manner (Liberman & Raskin, 1971; Loeb, Beck, & Diggory, 1971).

We discussed the reactive–endogenous distinction earlier. Since *learned* helplessness implies a reaction to the environment, the aforementioned findings seem to point to a kind of model for reactive depression. There is evidence that a decrease in brain norepinephrine is found in animals that have just experienced inescapable shock (Weiss, Glazer, & Pohorecky, 1974). Most writers who consider the reactive–endogenous distinction useful assume that endogenous depression is physiologically based. This finding suggests that although reactive depression is triggered by environmental events, those events might lead to depression *because* they decrease brain norepinephrine. This is only a hypothesis, of course, but in view of other evidence relating lowered brain norepinephrine and depression, it is an intriguing one.

DEPRESSION AND LACK OF REINFORCEMENT. The most popular behavioral theory of depression implicates lack of external reinforcement or satisfaction as the critical factor in the etiology of and maintenance of such disorders (e.g., Lazarus, 1974; Lewinsohn & Libet, 1972; Lewinsohn & Shaffer, 1971; Libet & Lewinsohn, 1973). Although a particular patient's environment may dispense reinforcements very infrequently no matter what he does, it is usually argued that the depression-prone person is deficient in those social skills necessary for obtaining many of life's major rewards.

That depressed individuals may indeed experience a deficiency in social reinforcement is suggested by a study by Lewinsohn and Shaffer (1971). Observing interactions in the home between depressed patients and their spouses, they found that the patients tended to receive less positive reinforcement than the spouses, while receiving more negative reinforcement such as criticism. In a similar vein, studies by Lewinsohn and Libet (1972) and Lewinsohn and Graf (1973) indicate a relationship between daily mood ratings and the number of pleasant, reinforcing activities engaged in by the subject. A greater number of pleasant activities was associated with a more positive mood.

These results suggest that depression may be related to a lack of rewards, but they do not deal with the issue of social skill. Lewinsohn and his associates assume that lack of such skill is central to the depressed person's inability to obtain gratification. One investigation (Libet & Lewinsohn, 1973) points to a deficiency in certain critical social skills in persons experiencing depression, compared to nondepressed control subjects. In a group setting, it was found that the depressives initiated considerably fewer social interactions and were less likely to respond positively to the behaviors of others. In addition, when another group member responded positively (i.e., reinforced) a given depressive, the recipient tended to wait longer before responding to the other group member who had provided reinforcement. This finding may require some clarification. Suppose you provide another person with verbal reinforcement—for instance, a compliment. If that person does not respond immediately or ignores your comment altogether, this will probably have the effect of "turning you off." Thus, one clear implication of the Libet and Lewinsohn study is that, indeed, depressed people may effectively discourage others from providing them with praise or other forms of social reinforcement.

The hypothesis put forth by Lewinsohn and his colleagues is plausible; further, research findings are clearly supportive. However, a word of caution is in order. Findings that point to a positive relationship between lack of reinforcement and depression, or a lack of social skills leading to a deficit in external social reinforcement and depression, in no sense *prove* that depression is *caused* by a deficiency in reinforcement. It is quite possible that people become depressed as a result of other factors, such as biochemical imbalances or irrational thinking, and the depression leads to lack of interest in external reinforcers and/or to a deficiency in social skill.

Whatever triggers depression, if the effect is a deficiency in social skills, which leads to a lack of external reward, it is plausible to suppose that lack of reward could perpetuate the state of depression. Naturally, this is merely an assumption. A convincing test of the Lewinsohn hypothesis would require depriving nondepressed individuals of important reinforcements, probably over a prolonged period of time, and observing whether they become seriously depressed. Thankfully, we know of very few researchers who would consider engaging in such an enterprise. An alternative might be to start out with patients who are depressed and provide them with massive reinforcement, on the expectation that this would markedly reduce their depression.

Note that the Lewinsohn formulation and the learned helplessness hypothesis deal specifically with the etiology of depression. Neither hypothesis attempts to explain the origins of manic behavior.

COGNITIVE THEORIES.   Early in this chapter we expressed dissatisfaction with the term *affective* to characterize or describe depression and related disorders. Many writers (Averill, 1973; Beck, 1967; Beck & Lester, 1973; Lazarus, 1974; Minkoff, Bergman, Beck, & Beck, 1973) have stressed the importance of *cognitive factors* in the etiology and maintenance of depression. The role of cognitions, in particular self-defeating self-verbalizations leading to a variety of psychological disorders, including depression, is paramount in the writings of Albert Ellis (Ellis, 1962, 1971).

Writers such as Beck and Ellis agree that depressive disorders are marked by changes in emotion or affect. The critical question may be stated as follows: Which comes first, disordered thinking or disordered affect? Beck's answer is clear. Disordered cognitive processes (i.e., irrational thinking) precede and indeed *cause* the aversive emotional states found in depressives.

According to Beck (1967), three major thought patterns (he uses the term *primary triad*) are critical in predisposing an individual to depression. First, such an individual consistently interprets his experiences in a negative way, viewing his life in terms of defeat, deprivation, or disparagement.

Second, such a person has a negative view of himself. This would seem to follow logically from the first thought pattern, but this is not necessarily the case. Consider the paranoid (see Chapter 5) who, given a similar tendency to interpret experiences negatively, nevertheless maintains a positive view of himself. The paranoid is able to do this because he blames others, such as imagined conspirators, for what he perceives as harsh treatment by the world. In sharp contrast, the depressed or potentially depressed person *blames himself*. In the jargon of clinical psychology, the paranoid would be characterized as *extrapunitive* whereas the depressive would be seen as *intropunitive*. Beck goes on to note that not only does the depressive have a negative view of himself, but he dislikes himself for his perceived inadequacies.

Third, depressed people have *negative expectations* regarding future prospects. Not only do they see themselves as inadequate and dislike this in themselves, but they fully expect that this aversive state of affairs will not change.

Before briefly reviewing some research bearing on this portrayal of depression, we should note that the foregoing characterization of depressed patients is quite consistent with what we and other clinicians have observed, assuming that the patients' verbalizations mirror their thought processes.

The most direct test of Beck's conception of depression would involve an experiment wherein normal people were driven into a state of at least moderate depression as a result of a concerted effort to cause them to construe events negatively, devalue themselves, and experience undue pessimism concerning the future. Because such a cruel experiment has not been done, the research to date can only provide indirect support for Beck's point of view.

There is evidence that depressed patients report more dreams of masochistic character than nondepressed patients do (Beck & Hurvich, 1959; Beck & Ward, 1961). Beck (1961) found that depressed patients evaluated themselves more negatively than nondepressed patients. More recently, Minkoff *et al.* (1973) found a strong relationship between a scale measuring hopelessness and one measuring level of depression. These results support the contention that depressives tend to think in negative terms, especially in regard to how they view themselves and their future prospects. Thus, from the perspective of *describing* depression, the latter two of the three "primary triads" have received research support. Evidence bearing on Beck's assumption that depressives misconstrue external events negatively is conflicting. The general experimental approach has been to provide subjects with some laboratory task and to evaluate their reaction to success and failure. Loeb, Feschbach, Beck, and Wolf (1964), for example, found that depressives who experienced failure subsequently showed a degree of pessimism similar to that associated with nondepressives who underwent the same failure experience. On the other hand, Loeb, Beck, Diggory, and Tuthill (1966) found that failure had a more negative effect on depressives than on nondepressed persons.

Recently LaPointe (1975) examined the effectiveness of a treatment approach derived from Beck (1967). The depressed subjects receiving this treatment showed significantly greater improvement than control subjects, which might be taken as support for Beck's conception of depression. On the other hand, depressed subjects who received *assertive training* (described in Chapter 15 of this text) showed approximately the same degree of improvement as those receiving Beck's cognitive therapy. Although LaPointe's findings do not contradict Beck's position, they could as easily lead to the conclusion that depression results from lack of assertiveness. The fact that a particular treatment is effective in dealing with a given disorder does not *prove* that the assumptions about the etiology of the disorder are therefore valid. After all, aspirin may reduce fever, but it makes little sense to argue that fever is caused by aspirin deficiency.

In summary, the hypotheses of Beck and his associates make a great deal of sense to many of those who have worked with depressives. Additionally, there is some research supporting the view that the thinking of depressives is indeed distorted. However, considerable additional research will be required before it can be said with any certainty that distorted thinking *causes* depression.

Suicide

SUICIDE AND DEPRESSION

Earlier in this chapter we mentioned a relationship between suicide and depression. There are many myths associated with suicide, but the relationship between suicidal thinking and suicidal behavior is clearly not mythical. Beck (1967) reports that 12% of the nondepressed patients in his sample expressed suicidal wishes, but 74% of his severely depressed patients reported such wishes. Beck also reports a relatively high correlation between the intensity of the suicidal thoughts and the intensity or depth of the depression. Studies by Rennie (1942) and Lundquist (1945) state that of patients with the initial diagnosis of affective disorder (remember that the vast majority of individuals in this broad category would exhibit depression), roughly 5% eventually committed suicide. It can be assumed that many among the remaining 95% engaged in suicide gestures or attempts. Shneidman and Mandelkorn (1970) estimate that for every successful suicide, there are between five and eight unsuccessful attempts. Silver, Bohnert, Beck, and Marcus (in press) report that approximately 80% of patients admitted to a nonpsychiatric hospital following a suicide attempt were described as depressed. Barraclough, Nelson, Bunch, and Sainsbury (1969) note that 80% of the successful suicides in their study had been depressed prior to the suicidal act.

In interpreting the results of Silver *et al.* and Barraclough *et al.* a note of caution is in order. After a person has engaged in suicidal behavior, others are prone to *assume* predisposing depression; thus, the figure of 80% may be an overestimate. Indeed, Robins, Gassner, Kayes, Wilkinson, and Murphy (1959) report a figure of 45%.[6]

Although the figures vary from study to study, it is clear that the probability of suicide is far greater among depressives than among normals. For example, Pokorny (1965) reports a figure for depressives in excess of four times that for normals among veterans followed over a 15-year period.

FACTS ABOUT SUICIDE

INCIDENCE.   Although estimates vary, it is likely that at least 25,000 lives are lost in the United States each year as a result of suicide (Shneidman & Mandelkorn, 1970). One can only estimate the number because it is often a matter of judgment whether a particular death should be viewed as a suicide or an accident. There would be little disagreement concerning a depressed person who, after writing a suicide note, shot himself through the head. But what about the person who dies of a self-inflicted overdose of barbiturates, or the driver who misses a turn at high speed, with fatal consequences? Whether either will be

---

[6] Among Robins *et al.*'s sample of successful suicides, 94% were judged to have suffered from some form of psychiatric disorder. Thus, 49% of those judged to have been disturbed were *not* labeled as depressed, implying quite correctly that depressives do not hold a franchise on suicidal behavior.

Precariously balanced between life and death, a young man clings to a ledge on New York's George Washington Bridge while would-be rescuers try to talk him out of suicide. This man chose to live, but in the two decades since this picture was taken, many others have jumped to their deaths from this same bridge. (Ed Clarity, New York Daily News Photo)

labeled as suicide or accidental death will depend upon whether there were prior indications of suicidal thinking; the evidence may be highly ambiguous. The authorities' judgment about whether a particular death is a suicide may be biased by a desire not to add to the pain of those close to the deceased. In such cases, many would favor labeling questionable deaths as accidental. Most authorities agree that because of such considerations, the suicide rate is probably above published figures (Dublin, 1963; Finch, Smith, & Pokorny, 1970).

That suicide rates vary from country to country is clear from the data (Shneidman & Mandelkorn, 1970) presented in Table 6-5. Note that most of the other countries listed report suicide rates higher than that for the United States.

PREDICTORS OF SUICIDE. Davison and Neale (1974) state that research attempting to relate performance on *standard psychological tests* to subsequent suicidal behavior is "either . . . inconclusive or utterly uninterpretable [p. 197]."

TABLE 6-5

Suicide Rates in Twelve Developed Countries[a]

Country	Suicides per 100,000 persons
Hungary	26.8
Austria	21.7
Czechoslovakia	21.3
Finland	19.2
West Germany and Sweden	18.5
Switzerland	16.8
Japan	16.1
France	15.5
United States	11.0
Italy	5.3
Ireland	2.5

[a] Based on data from Shneidman and Mandelkorn, 1970.

But these authors and others point to the potential value of using *demographic variables* as predictors of suicide.

Sex appears to be an important demographic variable. In the United States, for every female suicide, there are three male suicides, although females are far more likely to *attempt* suicide (Shneidman & Mandelkorn, 1970).

The roles of religion and race are as yet somewhat controversial. Davison and Neale (1974) note that in spite of strong antisuicide strictures associated with Catholicism, there is not a lower suicide risk among United States Catholics. On the other hand, if you refer to Table 6-5, you will note a much *lower* rate of suicide in some predominantly Catholic countries (Italy, Ireland) than in some other countries that are not Catholic (Finland, Sweden). This implies that Catholicism may be associated with a lower suicide rate, provided that the population is mostly Catholic. But this tidy correlation is undermined by the fact that the countries with the *highest* suicide rates—Hungary, Austria, and Czechoslovakia—are also predominantly Catholic.

On the subject of race the picture is equally confusing. Kleinmuntz (1974), citing studies by Clark (1965) and Pettigrew (1964), concludes that the overall suicide rates for whites and blacks do not differ, but also notes that suicide occurs twice as frequently among black males as among white males for the age range of 30 to 35 years. Shneidman and Mandelkorn (1970), however, state that the overall rate for whites is twice the rate for blacks. Possibly Shneidman and Mandelkorn are relying on older data; as Litman (personal communication) points out, the suicide rate among blacks is currently on the increase.

Among college students, suicide is the third leading cause of death, with the suicide rate being one and one-half times as great as among comparable persons not attending college (Shneidman & Mandelkorn, 1970). Nationwide, suicide is the tenth leading cause of death. Shneidman and Mandelkorn also note that single people are twice as likely to commit suicide as are married people, and there is evidence that among adults, older people are more likely to commit suicide. Using data collected by Green at the Los Angeles Suicide Prevention Center, CRM (1972) presents some age-related variables. For adult females, the rate is fairly constant from the age of 20 onward. For males, the rate is higher than for females at all ages, but the difference becomes especially marked beyond age 60. Beyond age 70, the male rate is approximately 65 per 100,000 (compare this with the national average of 11 per 100,000 suggested by Shneidman and Mandelkorn).

In examining the demography of suicide, it is important to remember that the suicide *rate* (number of suicides per capita) and the absolute *number* of suicides are very different data. To highlight this point, consider the following statement from Shneidman and Mandelkorn (1970), which we assume to be accurate:

> The most typical American suicide is a white Protestant male in his forties, married with two children. He is a breadwinner and a taxpayer [p. 126].

In view of the facts that married people are lower risks than singles, that religion (at least in the United States) does not appear to be a factor, and that the suicide rate at age 70 or more is about twice as high as in the 40-to-49-year range (Suicide Prevention Center, cited in CRM, 1972), the statement quoted may seem puzzling. However, there are in the United States many more Protestants than members of other religions; men in their forties are far more likely to be married than single; married men on the average have about two children; and there are far more men alive in their mid-forties than in their seventies. In short, the "typical American suicide" comes close to the profile of the typical American male. It is not surprising, then, that a high *number* of American suicides would fit this description. Whether the *rate* of suicide is especially high for males so described is quite a different question.

Other Prognostic Indicators of Suicide.   One predictor of successful suicides is a history of prior suicidal behavior, whether in the form of threats or actual attempts (Farberow & McEvoy, 1970). We have already indicated a relationship between depression and suicide. Suicide also is more common among alcoholics than nonalcoholics (Litman, 1970b).

You would probably have little difficulty identifying a clear-cut suicide attempt, an unambiguous threat of suicide, severe depression, or obvious alcoholism. What can easily be missed are more subtle indications of an impending suicide. Most authorities stress the importance of *any* suicidal statement, no matter how casual or indirect it may appear. Any one of the following statements would give a practitioner cause for concern:

Life doesn't seem worth the effort.
Maybe I'll do myself in [said laughingly].

My life is crummy and I can't do anything about it.

Lately I've been driving my car like I don't give a damn about what happens.

Goodbye [said with an unusual finality].

CAUSES OF SUICIDES. After the fact, one can always rationalize why a particular person chose to end his life. One of the few valid sources of information regarding how the suicide victim was thinking and feeling prior to the act is the suicide note. Although most people who commit suicide do not leave notes, Shneidman and Farberow (1970) were able to analyze the content of over 700 suicide notes. On the basis of their analysis, they describe four categories of suicide. The very nature of the categorization infers some degree of causality. We advise caution, however. The chain of events leading to a suicide is probably long and complex; a suicide note is but one possible indication of what actually led to the act. Also, any inference regarding causality that is based upon suicide notes is biased, because in most cases, notes are not left. With these warnings in mind, here are Shneidman and Faberow's categories:

1. Individuals who are lonely, feel helpless and fearful, and feel pessimistic about making meaningful personal relationships.
2. Individuals who are older, or widowed, or who are in physical pain.
3. Individuals whose beliefs permit them to view suicide as a transition to another life or as a means of saving reputation.
4. Individuals who are delusional and/or hallucinatory.

SUICIDE PREVENTION. To quote Shneidman and Mandelkorn (1970), "Fortunately, no one is 100% suicidal [p. 128]." This short quotation contains two fundamental assumptions: First, it assumes that suicide is bad, because there is something inherently good about a human being continuing to live. Clearly, this is a value judgment, but one shared by most people in most cultures.[7] Second, it assumes that individuals thinking about taking their lives always have at least some desire to live. This view, which is also widely held, is based upon the fact that before attempting suicide, people usually provide some indication of their intentions. Most practitioners, quite plausibly, interpret this as a cry for help.

Suicide prevention centers (and crisis intervention centers, which serve a similar but broader purpose) now exist in many metropolitan areas in the United States. These centers are founded on the assumption that a person contemplating suicide is indeed in a state of ambivalence. The mission of such centers is to help troubled people resolve their conflicts and thereby choose to remain alive. To implement such assistance, centers must provide the community with a well-publicized telephone number. The individual, of course, must choose to call the center, but anyone who calls will speak with a person trained in dealing with potential suicides. Sometimes, trained personnel will then meet with the caller in

[7] It may also be a legal judgment. As of 1964 (according to Litman, 1970a), suicide attempts were considered a crime in nine states. As Litman notes, the laws are seldom enforced.

person. If necessary, a more permanent arrangement can be made. The person can be invited to come to the center for therapy or consultation on a regular basis, or he can be referred to some other therapeutic facility.

Are suicide prevention centers effective? Available data tend to be discouraging; studies suggest, if anything, a slight increase in the suicide rate after the prevention center is established (Nielsen & Videbech, 1973; Lester, 1971). However, a rigorously controlled experiment dealing with the efficacy of such centers is a practical impossibility. It is always possible that in the absence of a center, the number of suicides in the area would have increased at a more rapid rate.

Summary

The incidence of serious cases of depression and related disorders may be on the order of 1%, although problems of diagnostic reliability preclude exact estimates. When one assesses the *degree* of depression independent of traditional diagnosis, reliability of ratings tends to increase markedly. Persons suffering from so-called affective disorders often improve without formal treatment—probably to a greater degree than is the case with most schizophrenics. The four major categories are depression, manic-depression, mania, and involutional melancholia. Depression is the most common, mania the least common; involutional melancholia is best seen as depression that happens to occur during middle age. Whether depression and related disorders are primarily biologically based or are, in the main, reactions to a stressful environment is still a matter of debate. Genetic and biochemical findings do point to the importance of biological factors. At the same time, there is evidence that depression tends to be associated with a lack of external rewards and, further, that depressed people tend to view themselves in a highly negative manner; thus, the roles of environment and learning are implicated as well. Some have suggested an interaction between biological and environmental factors, analogous to the diathesis–stress theory of schizophrenia.

Although most depressed people do not commit suicide, the suicide rate for depression is higher than for other psychiatric disorders. Suicide probably accounts for at least 25,000 deaths each year in the United States. Suicide prevention centers have been set up in many metropolitan areas as one major effort to cope with this serious problem. However, the effectiveness of such centers has yet to be established.

7

Psychophysiological Disorders

The Nature of Psychophysiological Disorders

Disorders that clearly involve both psychological factors and disturbances in specific physiological systems are referred to as *psychophysiological disorders*. The word *psychosomatic* is a more popular label for the group of disorders that will be discussed in this chapter. Unfortunately, the word *psychosomatic*, through popular usage, has come to mean mental *causation* of bodily disturbances. Translated from Greek, the word *psyche* means "mind" or "soul" and the word *soma* means "body." Hence, *psychosomatic* implies a dualistic conception in which mind and body are in some way distinguishable.[1] Traditionally, such a conception is referred to as the *mind–body problem* because of the logical difficulties in reconciling causal relationships between physical (body) and nonphysical (mind) factors. If the word *physical* is broadly defined as anything potentially observable or measurable, and *nonphysical* is defined as the unobservable and unmeasurable, then it is difficult, if not logically impossible, to postulate a nonphysical cause of a physical effect or vice versa.[2] If it is assumed that environmental forces are physical and

[1] Actually, the word *psychophysiological*, which is derived from the Greek words *psyche* ("mind" or "soul") and *physiologia* ("the study of nature or natural functions"), could also imply a mind–body dualism. However, it was coined in an attempt to avoid such dualistic implications.

[2] The mind–body problem is one of the oldest issues in religion, philosophy, and psychology. As presented here, the issue is oversimplified and we do not pretend to offer a solution to the problem.

that they may directly or indirectly affect physiological functions, then it is not necessary to postulate nonphysical constructs to explain psychophysiological disorders.

Sometimes it is difficult to determine whether a construct refers to physical or nonphysical factors. Consider the following statement: "An ulcer may be caused by *worrying too much*." One could define worrying as a form of mental activity that is neither observable nor measurable (nonphysical construct) or one could define worrying as a label for complex physical processes involving both environmental and physiological variables. For example, environmental pressures such as job-related difficulties, money problems, and family disturbances are often associated with loss of sleep, loss of appetite, and excesses of alcohol consumption, smoking, and coffee drinking. If such disturbances continue over a protracted period, physiological changes such as increases in heart rate, blood pressure, and gastric secretions may occur. When the individual is physically run-down, his capacity to cope with continued environmental stress is further diminished. Collectively, the complex interaction between environmental stresses and an individual's pattern of reaction may be referred to as "worrying too much."

Whatever the intended meaning, the statement that "an ulcer may be caused by worrying too much" is too vague and simplistic to serve as a useful scientific explanation for the development of an ulcer. Certainly a more precise, scientifically useful explanation is possible. For example, we may say that environmental factors resulting in frequent or sustained activation of the sympathetic division of the autonomic nervous system may lead to hypersecretion of gastric acid, which, by continual irritation of the mucosa, may cause an ulcer crater. Such an explanation is not vague, and it avoids the use of constructs that might imply a mind–body distinction.

We must emphasize that psychophysiological disorders are *not* imaginary physical disorders, nor are they disorders that an individual deliberately invents for the purpose of manipulation (e.g., "Dear, I have a headache, would you bring me a drink and a cigarette?"). Psychophysiological disorders involve an actual disturbance in a physiological system. For example, in essential hypertension, the individual *has* high blood pressure; he does not merely *think* he has high blood pressure or *say* he has high blood pressure when he really does not. In some cases, severe psychophysiological disorders such as ulcerative colitis may result in serious medical complications or death. Thus, an exclamation such as "Oh, it's *just* psychosomatic" probably reflects a misunderstanding of the nature of disorders traditionally categorized under this label.

Another important point is that psychophysiological disorders are not necessarily *caused* by psychological factors. Although stress has been suspected as a causal agent for a number of the disorders included in this chapter, supporting evidence is often lacking or inconclusive. However, there is ample evidence that stress in some way contributes to nearly all these disorders. In some disorders, such as migraine headaches, there is evidence that the primary cause of the disorder is an inherited or constitutional predisposition. Nonetheless, stress may play a key role in precipitating or in severely aggravating migraine attacks. Thus, stress, although not necessarily a primary causal agent, may be an important contributor to the appearance of symptoms or to the severity of the disorder.

Psychologists have long debated whether specific personality characteristics are unique to particular psychophysiological disorders. For example, is there an *ulcer personality,* which involves certain personality patterns rarely found in the normal population or among people with other kinds of disorders? There is little evidence that particular disorders are associated with specific patterns of personality. However, interest in this issue persists, especially among professionals with a psychoanalytic orientation. For this reason, we will look at past efforts to establish personality correlates for particular psychophysiological disorders.

The present popularity of biofeedback techniques has led to a new emphasis on treatment of psychophysiological disorders. Historically, visceral and emotional responses mediated by the autonomic nervous system have been classified as involuntary—that is, not subject to voluntary control. It was thought that classical conditioning of such responses was possible but that instrumental conditioning was not. For example, it was considered possible to condition a subject to show an increase in blood pressure to a sound that had been repeatedly paired with a painful shock (classical conditioning) but not possible to condition a subject to raise or lower his blood pressure to obtain a reward or avoid punishment (instrumental conditioning). *Skeletal responses,* which are mediated by the CNS have been classified as voluntary and subject to conditioning by both classical and (instrumental conditioning). *Skeletal responses,* which are mediated by the CNS, breathing and an enormous variety of muscle responses involving arm, leg, head, and trunk movements. There has been no question as to whether voluntary control over these types of movements is possible. According to Miller (1969), many psychiatrists have made a distinction between the "hysterical and other symptoms that are mediated by the autonomic nervous system [pp. 434–435]." Basically, the hysterical symptoms were thought to be under a higher type of control whereas psychosomatic symptoms were considered to be physiological consequences of emotions. Both learning theorists and many psychiatrists viewed visceral and emotional responses mediated by the autonomic nervous system as not subject to voluntary control.

A series of studies by Miller and his colleagues have challenged the traditional view that autonomically mediated visceral and emotional responses were not subject to instrumental conditioning. Summarizing these findings, Miller (1969) points out the possible therapeutic implications, particularly for psychophysiological disorders. He concludes that "while it is far too early to promise cures, it certainly will be worth while to investigate thoroughly the therapeutic possibilities of improved instrumental training techniques [p. 445]."

Yates (1975) notes that early studies by Miller and his colleagues, involving instrumental control of heart rate and intestinal contractions in animals, have not been replicated in recent studies either by Miller or by other investigators. Still, Miller's early research inspired a number of studies on the control of autonomically mediated responses in human subjects. The resulting body of literature is best categorized under biofeedback research.

According to Yates (1975), "the essence of biofeedback does, indeed, seem to be in providing the patient with information he can utilize to control his own rate of responding, where under ordinary conditions such information is either not being used or is being used inappropriately [p. 220]." Although the use of reinforcement in addition to informational feedback appears to be more effective than informational feedback alone, informational feedback appears to be the most important variable because it allows the subject to monitor his performance and to make appropriate adjustments. The application of biofeedback to clinical problems has been most successful in three areas: (1) the display of muscular activity, especially in the treatment of tension headaches; (2) feedback on temperature changes in the treatment of migraine headaches; and (3) displays on heart rate and blood pressure—particularly in the treatment of essential hypertension. Preliminary data suggest potential applications to a number of other areas, including improvement of fine motor control in children with cerebral palsy, control of posture, modifying speech disorders, and controlling self-induced seizures (Yates, 1975).

A good example of an application of biofeedback to a clinical problem is a well-controlled study on tension headaches by Budzynski, Stoyva, Adler, and Mullaney (1973). Tension headaches, unlike migraine headaches, are muscular in nature—specifically, they are continuing contractions of the frontalis muscle of the forehead. By using instruments to display electromyographic activity,[3] it was possible to give continuous feedback of frontalis muscle activity. Eighteen patients were randomly assigned to each of three groups: a group that received accurate feedback on frontalis muscle activity, a group that received false feedback information, and no-treatment control group. The two treatment groups received 16 training sessions. The patients given true feedback heard auditory representations of the level of EMG activity of the frontalis muscle recorded by two electrodes taped on their foreheads. The false feedback group heard auditory representations of muscle activity of another patient. Results were that the true feedback group showed a much greater decline in muscle activity than the false feedback group. The true feedback group experienced a substantial reduction in headache activity by the end of the treatment sessions. The headache activity among this group continued to decline during a 3-month follow-up period.

According to Yates (1975), this study represents one of the "most successful applications of biofeedback therapy to date [p. 203]." It is important to point out that activity of the frontalis muscle involves mediation by the cerebrospinal nervous system. Later in this chapter, studies on the application of biofeedback approaches to psychophysiological disorders mediated by the autonomic nervous system will be discussed. As we will see, such studies tend to support Miller's early

[3] Electromyographic activity is muscular activity as measured by a device called the electromyograph (EMG). Increases in muscle activity indicate an increased contractile state of the muscles.

speculations about the therapeutic implications of instrumental control over autonomic functions.

Nine classes of psychophysiological disorders are listed in DSM-II: (1) psychophysiological skin disorders, (2) psychophysiological respiratory disorders, (3) psychophysiological cardiovascular disorders, (4) psychophysiological hemic and lymphatic disorders, (5) psychophysiological gastrointestinal disorders, (6) psychophysiological genitourinary disorders, (7) psychophysiological endocrine disorders, (8) psychophysiological disorders of a sense organ, (9) psychophysiological musculoskeletal disorders. In this chapter, representative disorders will be discussed for four of the nine physiological systems: (1) skin disorders, (2) gastrointestinal disorders, (3) genitourinary disorders, and (4) cardiovascular disorders. The selection of disorders to be covered is based primarily on the extent of research done in the area. One exception to this is asthma, a major psychophysiological respiratory reaction, which will be presented in Chapter 10 and will not be discussed here.

Psychophysiological Skin Reactions

Skin sensations leading to scratching, rubbing, or stroking behaviors are everyday occurrences to which we generally attach little significance. However, if skin sensations such as itching become pronounced and occur frequently, they can be a source of great discomfort. Skin reactions may be precipitated or aggravated by psychological factors. Examples of skin disorders that appear to be related to stress are *neurodermatitis, urticaria* (hives), and *acne*.

NEURODERMATITIS (ATOPIC DERMATITIS)

Neurodermatitis is an inflammatory disease of the skin that is characterized primarily by spells of intense itching. The lesions in the skin may be localized to one or more specific bodily areas or they may be widespread, affecting many different areas of the body (*disseminated form*). The disorder has been distinguished from *eczema* (contact dermatitis), which is usually associated with a specific external irritant that acts directly on the skin. Although allergens such as wool may aggravate neurodermatitis, the role of any particular allergen as a primary causal agent has not been established (Obermayer, 1955).

In neurodermatitis, unlike other forms of dermatitis, itching may precede the appearance of skin lesions. When lesions develop they usually begin in one or a few spots of the skin. Initially these spots are inflamed and scaly; as the disorder progresses they may spread to many areas of the body. The most common locations of these lesions are the inside areas of the elbows and knees and around the neck. Lesions may also appear on the eyelids, the outer portions of the auditory canal, behind the ears, on the upper chest, trunk, arms, forearms, legs, thighs, and around the anus and genitalia. In severe cases, virtually every area of the body may be affected. As the disorder becomes chronic, the skin thickens and cutaneous lines deepen. According to Obermayer (1955), the skin remains thick, dry, and scaly during quiescent periods, but in a matter of minutes or hours, inactive lesions may "change into a roaring inferno with such intense itching that the patient cannot be restrained from scratching [p. 203]."

Although the role of emotional factors has not been clearly established, activation of neurodermatitis may follow stressful situations. For example, Alexander (1950) cited the following case study by Spiegel:

■ The patient, a 22-year-old white, single girl, was referred for treatment because of recurrent bouts of severe neurodermatitis. The lesions, which occurred mostly on the face and upper and lower extremities, were eczematoid in type, consisting of discrete, red, raw, itching areas. The patient scratched the lesions furiously, especially during her sleep, until they wept and bled, so that she was often quite disfigured. She had seen a number of dermatologists and had frequently been told that she could not be helped because the condition was due to emotional factors, a conclusion she herself had drawn on the basis of wide psychological reading.

The skin lesions had been present on and off all the patient's life. She first developed eczema[5] a week after her birth. Her mother had been very disturbed during the pregnancy by the accidental death of her seven-year-old son, and subsequently by desertion and divorce by her husband. The patient's childhood was spent in the homes of various relatives, where she always felt insecure because of her mother's timidity and her depreciated status of almost a servant in the household. The patient was shy and socially backward in school, but bright and alert in her studies. She suffered greatly from feeling "different" and unwanted because of recurrent eczema and the lack of a father and a normal family life. In college, however, with physical maturity, she blossomed out and became popular socially. After graduation she found a good job, and began to form intense attachments to various men. The attachments were always broken off with the appearance of a severe attack of eczema. It was when this recurrent pattern threatened her job and normal interpersonal relations that her dawning insight brought her to treatment [pp. 166–167].[4]

Although stress has been suggested as one causal agent, the etiology of neurodermatitis has not been established. The view that early mother–infant contact is an important etiological factor related to neurodermatitis has been stressed by psychoanalytically oriented writers. Alexander, French, and Pollock (1968) state that "in general, such patients lacked close physical contact in early life and now try to get attention by the means of infantile exhibitionism (the

[4] Reprinted from *Psychosomatic medicine, its principles and applications* by Franz Alexander, M.D. By permission of W. W. Norton & Company, Inc. Copyright 1950 by W. W. Norton & Company, Inc.

[5] As noted by Obermayer (1955), a distinction between neurodermatitis and eczema (contact dermatitis) is often ignored in psychiatric case histories. In the absence of more descriptive detail, it is not possible to determine whether the disorder presented in this case history is clearly neurodermatitis.

attempt to induce adults to cuddle the child) [p. 14]." These writers view scratching as a masturbation substitute, which allows the patient to relieve sexual tension while deriving masochistic pleasure from painful stimulation.

There is some evidence that neurodermatitis may be one of several reactions occurring among individuals who are hypersensitive to allergens. Many patients with neurodermatitis also appear to be susceptible to hay fever and asthmatic attacks. Osborne and Murray (1953) note that neurodermatitis improved in 90% of patients who stayed in allergenfree hospital rooms. The possible etiological significance of allergens, therefore, cannot be dismissed.

Various attempts have been made to designate specific personality attributes for individuals with neurodermatitis. Alexander *et al.* (1968) state that "in cases of neurodermatitis we find a complex configuration between exhibitionism, guilt, and masochism, combined with a·deep-seated desire to receive physical expression of love from others [p. 14]." Obermayer (1955), in a systematic study of personality characteristics of patients with neurodermatitis, was unable to identify any "consistent psychological structure, common to all . . . [p. 227]." He did, however, report that such patients had a propensity to bottle up emotions and that compulsive–obsessive characteristics were present in a preponderance of patients.

As has been noted in previous chapters, alterations of a person's physical appearance may have an adverse effect on social reactions to that person. Many people might be afraid that neurodermatitis is a contagious disease. As a result, some patients may harbor a "leper complex." In other words, patients may view themselves as social outcasts. It is possible, therefore, that psychological problems may be a result rather than a cause of neurodermatitis.

The treatment and prognosis for neurodermatitis depends partly on the age of onset. Osborne and Murray (1953) reported that if the onset of the disorder occurred before age 2, 80% continued to have problems. If the onset occurred between 2 and 10 years, 28% had periodic relief for 1–5 years and 10–20% had spontaneous cures. As previously noted, up to 90% of patients improved when placed in allergenfree rooms. However, the effect of allergenfree rooms was confounded with possible effects of patients being removed from stressful home situations.

Unfortunately, much of the literature on neurodermatitis consists of case histories selected to illustrate speculations derived from psychoanalytic theory. The paucity of empirical research prevents conclusions about the etiological significance of either environmental or organismic variables. Both allergens and stress, however, appear to aggravate or precipitate flare-ups involving intense itching of inflamed, scaly areas.

URTICARIA (HIVES)

Urticaria is derived from the Latin word *urtica,* "the stinging nettle." The disorder is characterized by whitish, slightly elevated bumps in the skin called *wheals* surrounded by halos of reddened skin. The physical appearance of wheals resembles that of insect bites or bee stings. Urticarial lesions are produced when fluid is suddenly forced out of the capillaries and into the tissues. If this process occurs deep under the surface of the skin, wheals do not appear and the disorder is called *angioneurotic edema* (Obermayer, 1955). In this section, however, we will only consider cases in which the process occurs near the surface of the skin and results in prominent wheals.

Urticaria may involve a few or several hundred wheals. Usually itching is severe but in some cases, it may be minimal or absent. The extent and duration of urticaria is highly variable. An acute attack may result in the rapid appearance of wheals, which may subside in a few minutes or persist for hours. In chronic cases, there may be a few wheals present at all times or the eruptions may appear and then disappear for weeks, months, or years. A relationship between stressful situations and the eruption of wheals has been reported frequently (Obermayer, 1955). Graham and Wolf (1951) report that attacks among 30 patients with chronic urticaria were often related to an emotional reaction characterized by intense resentment. Resentment was described as indignation associated with feelings of being unfairly or wrongly treated. Despite these conclusions, there has been some question as to whether attacks of wheals or hives ever result from purely psychological factors. A related disorder called *dermographism* involves the production of skin elevations by rubbing and scratching. In many cases, it is possible that rubbing or scratching may produce the wheals, rather than stress. However, as Obermayer (1955) pointed out, this does not negate the role of psychological factors. In Graham and Wolf's (1951) research, for example, rubbing and scratching the skin only produced wheals when subjects with urticaria were undergoing stressful interviews. There is also evidence that patients with urticaria respond to emotional stimuli with intense vasodilatation (dilation of the blood vessels). It is possible that such vasodilatation may increase the permeability of capillary walls and facilitate the flow of fluid into tissue so that wheals are produced.

It is probable that constitutional factors predispose some individuals to urticarial attacks. It may be that normal individuals show similar but less intense physiological changes under stressful conditions involving intense feelings of resentment. Support for this possibility was provided by Graham, Kabler, and Graham (1962). In an experiment designed to test the specificity-of-attitude hypothesis proposed by Grace and Graham (1952), 20 normal subjects were hypnotized and physiological recordings were taken during the induction of two attitudes—one attitude specific for hives and the other attitude specific for hypertension. The attitude that previously had been postulated as specific for hives involved intense resentment. The induction of this attitude during hypnosis consisted of suggesting to the subject that he was the helpless, innocent victim of unfair treatment. The attitude that had been hypothesized as specific for hypertension involved feelings of impending danger. The suggestion given for this attitude was that the subject must prepare himself to face an attack or a painful injury in the immediate future.

On the basis of previous research it was hypothesized that there would be a greater rise in skin temperature and a smaller rise in diastolic blood pressure during the induction of the hives attitude than during the induction of the hypertensive attitude. Results essentially confirmed the hypothesis. A significantly greater rise in skin temperature occurred during the induction of the hives attitude than during the induction of the hypertensive attitude. Changes in diastolic blood pressure were significantly greater during the induction of the hypertensive attitude than during the induction of the hives attitude. As Grace and Graham point out, these findings are compatible with other findings that suggest that different physiological changes may be associated with particular emotional experiences. In the case of urticaria, it is possible that increases in skin temperature associated with vasodilatation are more likely to occur during emotional arousal characterized by strong feelings of resentment. Intense vasodilatation may be an important factor related to the formation of wheals.

The research by Graham *et al.* (1962) involved normal subjects and the findings cannot be generalized to subjects with urticaria. Further investigation is needed to establish a possible relation between emotional stimulation, vasodilatation, and urticaria. Although both constitutional and psychological variables have been suspected as etiological agents, the causes of urticaria have not been adequately established. Clinical reports, however, suggest that emotional factors appear to precipitate urticarial attacks.

ACNE VULGARIS

Acne is an inflammatory disease involving the sebaceous glands and hair follicles. A hair follicle is a very small depression in the skin that contains a hair. Each hair follicle has two or more sebaceous glands that secrete a fatty matter called *sebum*. If the ducts of the sebaceous gland become plugged up or clogged with sebum, then blackheads develop. If the area becomes inflamed, pustules (acne pimples) form. In severe cases, large abscesses, which may leave extensive scars, may develop.

Acne usually occurs on the face, the back, and the chest. The disorder usually begins at puberty when the sebaceous glands become more active. In many cases, acne subsides after several years. In some cases it may persist into the thirties but rarely occurs after age 40 (Obermayer, 1955). Estimates of the incidence of acne have ranged from 10–20% of all adolescents (Kremer, 1969).

Acne may involve several factors. A notable increase in androgen (a male sex hormone)[6] at puberty is evidently an important factor underlying the increased activity of the sebaceous glands. Other factors that have been implicated include allergies, poor resistance to infection, and a hereditary predisposition. In girls, acne often increases around the time of menstruation (Kremer, 1969).

The onset of puberty brings a notable increase in sexual interest and activity. It is therefore understandable that the concurrent onset of acne has led to speculations regarding a causal relation between sexual activity and acne. According to

[6] Androgen, a male sex hormone, is predominant in males but is secreted by both males and females. In males, androgen is produced by the testes; in females, androgen is produced by the adrenal cortex of the adrenal gland.

Kremer (1969): "The popular mythology which attributes acne to 'bad' thoughts and practices, especially masturbation, is still surprisingly widespread [p. 24]." Although acne may lead to a preoccupation with physical appearance and thus indirectly affect sexual feelings, there is no empirical evidence that acne causes sexual problems or vice versa.

Although there may be multiple causes of acne, the basic disturbance affecting the skin involves excessive discharge of sebum by the sebaceous glands (Obermayer, 1955). One focus of psychological research has been on the relationship between stress and output of facial sebum. Lorenz, Graham, and Wolf (1953) measured sebum output under stress and nonstress interviews. The major finding was that acne patients showed a significant increase in sebum output during stressful interviews when anger was elicited and a decrease in sebum output when remorse was elicited. There were no significant changes in sebum output among a control group of non-acne patients during stressful interviews. These findings suggest that, for some people, certain types of stress may be related to an increased likelihood of acne eruptions.

Similar findings implicating the role of stress in acne formation were obtained by Kraus (1970). A significant increase in free fatty acids (the most irritative component of skin surface lipids) was found among medical students with acne during a stressful period. The stress period consisted of an 8-hour examination covering 10 weeks of study material. In addition, a significant increase in the number of acne pustules was also recorded during the examination period. Although Kraus was careful to note that the research had not demonstrated a causal role of free fatty acids in the production of acne, he suggested that free fatty acids may play a very important role in the pathophysiology of acne. Kraus noted that previous research had demonstrated that even small injections of free fatty acids into the skin produced a marked inflammatory response. An obvious implication of this research is that stress may increase the output of free fatty acids, which in turn may increase acne pustules.

Although stress or emotional factors may precipitate the formation of acne pustules, attempts to establish correlations between specific personality patterns and acne have not yielded clear results (Kremer, 1969). Obermayer (1955) suggests that the great majority of acne patients cannot be considered markedly neurotic. On the basis of clinical observations, he suggests that most acne patients emerge unharmed, both cosmetically and psychologically. Despite this favorable prognosis, it is likely that special difficulties in adjustment are encountered during the time of acne eruptions. For this reason, supportive therapy in addition to medical treatment may be of value. If supportive therapy or counseling is helpful in reducing the stresses encountered during the adolescent and young adult years, then such approaches may aid in reducing the severity of acne eruptions.

In short, although there may be a number of causes of acne, the role of stress as one precipitating factor has been supported by research. As is true of a number of other psychophysiological disorders, no specific personality pattern appears to characterize people with acne.

Stress has been implicated in all the skin reactions discussed in this section. Neither stress nor any other emotional factor has been identified as a primary *cause* of any of these skin reactions; but emotional factors do appear to play an important role in precipitating flare-ups or in aggravating existing conditions. To this extent, the importance of psychological variables should be considered in the treatment of some dermatological disorders.

Psychophysiological Gastrointestinal Reactions

The gastrointestinal system reacts strongly to emotional changes mediated by the autonomic nervous system. Expressions indicating subjective reactions to such changes include "I've got butterflies in my stomach," "He made me sick to my stomach," "My gut feeling is . . . ," and "I've got a nervous stomach." Generally, during daily activities such as eating, digestion, and elimination, the parasympathetic division of the autonomic nervous system regulates gastrointestinal activity. During periods of stress or emotional upset, the sympathetic division of the autonomic nervous system becomes dominant. A sudden emotional upset may lead to a rapid shift from parasympathetic activity to sympathetic activity and cause a person to quickly lose his appetite or become nauseated. For example, if it is before mealtime and an individual is relatively calm, parasympathetic activity causes peristaltic contractions of the stomach, which become progressively stronger as a person's normal eating time approaches. Sensations produced by these contractions are among the internal changes that lead an individual to describe himself as hungry. If immediately prior to mealtime something very exciting or upsetting happens, such as winning a big lottery or learning of a family tragedy, the sympathetic division quickly becomes dominant and the peristaltic contractions rapidly cease. These internal changes are incompatible with hunger and a person may lose his appetite or become nauseated.

In some individuals, prolonged stress may lead to serious gastrointestinal changes. Two examples of the psychophysiological disorders that may result are ulcerative colitis and duodenal ulcers.

ULCERATIVE COLITIS

Ulcerative colitis is an inflammatory disease that primarily affects the colon and the rectum. The clinical symptoms may include repeated attacks of diarrhea, the presence of blood in the stools, painful abdominal cramps, fever, and malnutrition. These symptoms may not reflect the actual severity of pathological changes in the colon. For example, a person may have pronounced toxic manifestations, persistent diarrhea, and frequent bleeding and yet have only minor physical impairment of the colon. Another person may show few clinical symptoms, and appear vigorous and productive, but laboratory studies may indicate severe inflammation and ulceration of the colon (Palmer, 1967).

The course of ulcerative colitis is highly variable. The disorder may develop quickly, spread rapidly, and result in death. In other cases, the disorder may follow a chronic, static pattern, which is occasionally interrupted by intense flare-ups of clinical signs. Sometimes clinical signs are minimal and the person may remain active and productive for many years. The potential for serious structural impairment, however, is much greater than for other gastrointestinal disorders. According to Bacon (1958), "it may be said that in no other disease is tissue so assaulted, ravaged, and completely devastated as is the mucosa of the colon following a severe attack of ulcerative colitis [p. 1]."

The incidence of ulcerative colitis has been estimated at from 5 to 10 patients per 1000 hospital admissions (Bacon, 1958). In about 75% of the cases, the disorder appears in the third or fourth decade of life. At least 3% of the cases, however, begin between 6 and 12 years of age. Although empirical data is lacking, the disorder is thought to be high among Jews and low among blacks. A low incidence has also been postulated for geographical areas that include New Orleans, Italy, Spain, and South America.

The etiology of ulcerative colitis remains unknown. Both organic and psychological variables have been implicated, and evidence supporting sole causation by either class of variables is lacking. Both psychological and organic features are prominent in the disorder. Palmer (1967) calls ulcerative colitis "the gastroenterologic disease that demonstrates more emotional phenomena and more physical phenomena at the same time than any other [p. 110]." Although there is evidence that both emotional and physical factors are involved, the nature of the interaction between these two factors and their relative contributions to the etiology of ulcerative colitis are questions that are still unanswered.

An important early observation regarding the possible role of emotional factors in ulcerative colitis was made by Grace, Wolf, and Wolff (1951). These authors were able to expose a section of ulcerated colonic mucosa in a patient so that visual inspection of changes in the mucosa was possible. Under normal conditions, the mucosa appeared dull pink in color with a thin mucus secretion. When anger was induced by asking the patient pointed questions, the bowel contracted, turned bright red, and secreted heavy amounts of thick mucus. When the patient calmed down, the bowel returned to its original color. Although emotional arousal did produce notable physiological changes, it could not be proved that emotional factors were causing the disease. The demonstration, however, did support the theory that emotional states precipitate flare-ups in patients with established ulcerative colitis.

Another example of the precipitating role of emotional factors was provided by Bacon (1958):

> T.M. was an intelligent married woman of 37 who considered herself neglected by her husband and was certain that he was cavorting with other women. His failure to arrive home at the proper moment, together with her anxiety over frequent trips which he was accustomed to take, was sufficient to incite diarrheal symptoms [p. 26].

Some support for a possible causal role of emotional factors in ulcerative colitis and a similar disorder called Crohn's disease was provided by McKegney, Gordon, and Levine (1970). Both ulcerative colitis and Crohn's disease are severe inflammatory diseases of the lower intestinal tract. Ulcerative colitis primarily involves ulceration and inflammation of the colon; Crohn's disease affects either the large or small bowel. But despite medical differences between the two disorders, findings of psychological significance are highly similar.

In the first phase of an experiment, McKegney *et al.* (1970) obtained data from the charts of 83 patients who had been treated at the clinic for one of these two diseases. In the second phase, similar data and additional measures were collected for 40 current patients, 21 with ulcerative colitis and 19 with Crohn's disease. Patients in both groups were found to have had a high incidence of emotional disturbance prior to the onset of either of the two diseases. In the second phase of the experiment, 86% of the ulcerative colitis patients and 68% of the patients with Crohn's disease had a well-defined, serious life crisis such as divorce, a death in the family, or a business crisis during the 6-month period prior to the onset of the physical disease.

Other findings for subjects in the second phase of the experiment were that 38% of the ulcerative colitis patients and 47% of the patients with Crohn's disease had previously received some type of psychiatric diagnosis. For both disease groups, there was a high positive correlation between the severity of emotional disturbance and the seriousness of the physical disease.

On the basis of these findings, the authors concluded that "similar personality and life event factors contribute to, and may be necessary for, the development and severity of these physical illnesses [p. 165]." Various writers have described patients with ulcerative colitis as hostile, immature, passive, indecisive, and, most of all, highly dependent. In regard to dependency conflicts, Palmer (1967) maintains that "there is always some abnormal psychodynamic process going on in the mother of an ulcerative colitis patient [p. 113]."

Although emotional factors or stress may play a role in the etiology of the disorder, there is no substantial empirical evidence that a particular personality pattern predisposes an individual to develop ulcerative colitis. Whatever personality characteristics are observed by gastroenterologists in ulcerative colitis patients may be a result rather than a cause of the disorder. As Bacon (1958) has suggested, "a toxic, anemic, cachectic patient who passes 8 to 10 diarrheal stools per day for long periods of time cannot be expected to have complete control of his emotions or mental faculties [p. 24]."

Medical treatment of ulcerative colitis is a necessity. Between 20 and 30% of all cases require surgery (Bacon, 1958). Psychotherapy, in conjunction with medical treatment, appears to have beneficial effects for the majority of patients. Karush, Daniels, O'Connor, and Stern (1969) report that the best results were obtained by therapists who were highly interested in their patients, empathic, and optimistic about helping them. Patients most likely to improve were those who were optimistic about being helped and who were able to develop a warm, trusting relationship with their therapists. It was noted that, although "insight therapy" appeared to benefit those patients who were active and well-individuated, dependent patients appeared to benefit more from support, catharsis, and suggestion than from interpretation. Longer therapies (1–3 years) were reported to be almost twice as effective as shorter therapies (a year or less) in promoting and maintaining remissions of the disease.

In brief, ulcerative colitis is an inflammatory disease affecting the colon and rectum; it may range from relatively mild cases to very severe attacks that may result in death. Emotional factors apparently precipitate flare-ups in persons with established ulcerative colitis and may possibly contribute to the etiology of the disorders as well.

DUODENAL ULCER

A duodenal ulcer is a round mucosal defect found in the first portion of the small intestine leading from the stomach (duodenum). The round crater that develops may vary in size from 1 or 2 millimeters in diameter to several centimeters. Duodenal ulcers and ulcers located in the stomach (gastric ulcers) have both been referred to as *peptic* ulcers. Use of the term *peptic ulcer* for both disorders has tended to obscure the fact that duodenal ulcers and gastric ulcers are two distinct entities (Wastell, 1972). In this section, we will discuss only those psychological factors associated with duodenal ulcers. This does not imply, however, that psychological factors play a lesser role in gastric ulcers.

Duodenal ulcers rarely occur before age 15 and the maximum incidence is between the ages of 35 and 45 (Wastell, 1972). It has been estimated that up to 10% of all individuals are either susceptible to ulcers or suffer from ulcers at some time during the life span (Alsted, 1934). The incidence of duodenal ulcers, however, has not remained stable over time. Among men, the incidence continued to increase from 1920 until a peak period between 1950 and 1955. After this period, the incidence gradually declined. The incidence of duodenal ulcers among men has decreased over the last two decades, whereas the incidence among females has remained stable. In 1940, for every 9 males with a duodenal ulcer there were 2 females with ulcers. At present, the ratio is 3 males to 1 female. If we look only at the change in sex ratios we might assume that more and more women are developing ulcers. Palmer (1967), for example, noting that the sex ratio 50 years earlier was 10 males to 1 female and that the present ratio was 3 to 1, suggested that an increase in the number of women entering the working world, with its presumed stresses and strains, might be related to the increasing incidence of ulcers among women. However, as Wastell (1972) points out, the change in sex ratios is *not* due to an *increase* in ulcers among women but to a *decrease* in ulcers among men. Hence, Palmer's speculation that the stresses of working are increasing the prevalence of ulcers among women is not supported.

The etiology of duodenal ulcers is still a subject of controversy. According to Baron (1972), "The simplest explanation for the occurrence of duodenal ulcer is that excess gastric acid strikes the duodenal mucosa, corroding and inflaming it and producing duodenitis and duodenal ulcer [p. 24]." Although some have speculated that susceptibility to developing an ulcer may be a result of individual differences in the resistance of the duodenum to gastric acid, the most important factor appears to be the amount of gastric acid secreted. Baron (1972), in a review of relevant research, concludes that "patients with chronic duodenal ulcers secrete more gastric juice, more acid and more pepsin than normal subjects both at rest and in response to stimuli [p. 19]."

If excess gastric acid is the immediate cause of ulcers, the obvious question is, what causes particular individuals to secrete excessive amounts of gastric acid? There is some evidence that hypersecretion of gastric acid may be influenced by heredity. Parents and siblings of patients with duodenal ulcers have about three times the incidence of duodenal ulcers that a control population has (Baron, 1972). Eberhard (1968) reports that if one identical twin has an ulcer, the likelihood that the other identical twin will develop an ulcer is three times higher than that for fraternal twins (54% as opposed to 17%).

A possible relationship between environmental stress and the development of duodenal ulcers has been postulated frequently. Although stress may not be a primary cause of duodenal ulcers, there is evidence that hypersecretion of gastric acid occurs in response to emotional stimuli and to stress induced by interviews. In fact, Baron (1972) suggests that hypersecretion of gastric acid may occur as a conditioned response to a psychiatrist entering an office. There is also evidence that hypersecretion occurs during the rapid-eye-movement phase of sleep (REM sleep) in which dreams occur regularly.

Another assumption about the etiology of ulcers is that some individuals have so-called ulcer personalities. Alexander and French (1948) theorized that ulcer patients were characterized by strong drives for achievement, independence, and self-sufficiency, which are in marked conflict with strong, unconscious dependency needs. The patient's efforts to appear as a self-sufficient, independent, productive person were construed as defenses against basic dependency needs. Sullivan and McKell (1950), in a study based on 1000 peptic ulcer patients, concluded that there are at least four different categories of ulcer patients: (1) those who possess the "typical ulcer personality," (2) those who are characterized by intrinsic neurotic conflicts, (3) those who have been subjected to pronounced and unusual environmental stress, and (4) those whose ulcers appear to be caused by chemicals, physical trauma, or constitutional factors. They offered the following description of the typical ulcer personality:

> The ulcer personality has been described in terms of drive, multiple attempts at achievement, emotional responsiveness, self-reliance, responsibility, usually normal heterosexual adjustments, independence and determination. The intensity and the wholeheartedness with which these people carry out their self-imposed tasks and strive towards realization of their ambitions cannot be overemphasized. It is our belief that this intensive drive and the tension it creates as well as the inborn cravings for superiority together with the inborn cravings for small failures, particularly the anxiety resulting from anticipated failure or future insecurity, are the emotional patterns which are fundamental in the production of ulcer [p. 36].

Subsequent writers have questioned the existence of an ulcer personality as well as the causative role of anxiety. Baron (1972), after a review of the literature, concluded that "patients with duodenal ulcer are abnormally anxious but do not show specific personality patterns. It is not clear to what extent anxiety precedes and is a prime cause of the ulcer disease, as opposed to the clearer role of anxiety

These impassioned men are buying and selling stocks on the Paris stock exchange. Not long ago, it was widely assumed that such hard-driving businessmen were destined to get duodenal ulcers, but this neat formulation has been undermined by recent studies. (Ken Heyman)

in perpetuating and exacerbating duodenal ulcers [p. 42]." Thus, although psychological factors appear to precipitate ulcer flare-ups, there is insufficient evidence to conclude that they play a primary causal role in the development of ulcers. However, the fact that stress results in a hypersecretion of gastric acid does suggest that psychological factors may have etiological significance.

The classical medical treatment of ulcers includes a special bland diet, antacid medications, anticholinergic drugs, variable sedation, and abstinence from tobacco, alcohol, and coffee. Some gastroenterologists, however, have seriously challenged the effectiveness of classical medical treatment. Palmer (1967), prompted by a facetious comment that his patients would do as well on a diet of pancakes and shaving cream as they would on an ulcer diet, placed 30 ulcer patients on a diet of water, multivitamins, pancakes, and small capsules containing minimal amounts of shaving cream. The patients on this diet did as well as patients on a classical diet "both symptomatically and roentgenologically," the latter referring to evaluation of the ulcer condition by X rays. To further assess the effectiveness of the classical approach, Palmer allowed 230 hospitalized duodenal ulcer patients to choose between a solution containing 2 ounces of dilute hydrochloric acid (equivalent to gastric acid, which, according to the classical approach, should aggravate the ulcer condition) and one containing 2 ounces of aluminum hydroxide, an antacid, which should have beneficial effects. The patients were encouraged to try one and then the other every now and then in order to determine which "worked best." At the conclusion of their hospital stay, 31 patients could see no difference in the effectiveness of the two solutions, 106 reported that they received relief from the aluminum hydroxide (antacid), and 93 reported that they received greater relief from the hydrochloric acid solution. Based on these results and other clinical experiences, Palmer (1967) concludes that a special diet and antacids "is a gesture and a gesture only." A similar conclusion is reached by Baron and Wastell (1972) who end their chapter on medical treatment with the following quotation from Ingelfinger (1966): "Let's face it; no one has yet found a good medical therapy for the patient's tendency to get ulcer. In the meantime, let us not punish the patient and delude ourselves by giving him pap to eat [Baron & Wastell, 1972, p. 129]."

Baron and Wastell (1972) note that research on the effects of psychotherapy with ulcer patients has frequently lacked appropriate controls that would allow a meaningful interpretation of results. A study by Selesnick (1950) was cited as an example of a "controlled" research. Patients on a normal diet were given psychotherapy and compared with a group of patients placed on "sippy diet" (medical treatment). Results were that each group showed essentially the same amount of improvement. Since there was no control group placed on a normal diet but not given psychotherapy, it is not possible to determine whether either psychotherapy or a medical diet would have resulted in improvement over a no-treatment control. Thus, the effectiveness of psychotherapy in the treatment of ulcers has not been established.

Welgan (1974) has attempted to determine whether ulcer patients can employ biofeedback techniques to achieve learned control over gastric acid secretions. Welgan's specific intention was to reduce excessive secretion of hydrochloric acid by the stomach. Since increases in pH[7] are known to be associated with decreases in secretion of hydrochloric acid, the plan was to measure the pH of stomach acid and provide the subject feedback when increases or decreases occurred. Stomach contents were continuously sucked out with a drainage pump through a tube extending from the nose to the stomach. By this means, the pH of stomach contents could be monitored continuously. The primary hypothesis was that an increase in pH would be associated with a reduction in the volume of acid secreted.

In the first of two experiments, the hypothesis received partial support. The feedback technique led to a significant increase in pH and a significant decrease in acid concentration and the volume of acid secreted. But when feedback was withheld and the instructional set was changed, the expectation that these measures would reverse significantly was not supported. In the second experiment, however, withholding feedback and changing the instructional set did lead to a

[7] pH is the negative of the logarithm of hydrogen ion concentration in aqueous solution. A pH of 7 is neutral; a low pH indicates acidity; a high pH indicates alkalinity. Thus, an increase in pH results in a decrease of acidity.

significant increase in both the concentration of acid and the volume secreted. Even though there were problems associated with measurement, the results suggest that biofeedback may be used to alter or control gastric acid secretions in ulcer patients. If measurement of pH can be simplified or adapted for practical application, it is conceivable that biofeedback may be used therapeutically in the treatment of ulcers as well as other psychophysiological disorders.

In summary, the immediate cause of ulcers is persistent irritation of the mucosa caused by hypersecretion of gastric acid. Although the causes of hypersecretion are not yet understood, there is evidence that stress results in an increase in the secretion of gastric acid. There is also partial evidence that the level of gastric secretion may be influenced by hereditary factors. Classical medical therapy involving a "sippy" diet and antacids is of dubious value. The effectiveness of psychotherapy has not been adequately demonstrated. Limited evidence suggests that further development of biofeedback techniques may have potential value in the treatment of ulcer.

Though the gastrointestinal disorders discussed in this section have been limited to ulcerative colitis and duodenal ulcers, there are a number of other gastrointestinal disturbances, including vomiting, diarrhea, constipation, and nausea, in which psychological factors may play a role. However, ulcerative colitis and duodenal ulcers are two of the most thoroughly studied psychophysiological disorders of the gastrointestinal system.

Psychophysiological Genitourinary Reactions

Psychophysiological disorders of the genitourinary system may or may not be related to disturbances in sexual functioning. Frigidity, impotence, and other problems associated with sexual functions are discussed in Chapter 12. With the exception of pseudocyesis, the disorders discussed in this section may occur without identifiable sexual disturbances. Excluding sexual problems, the most widely studied psychophysiological genitourinary disorders involve disturbances related to the menstrual cycle. These include *amenorrhea* (the absence of menstruation, delays in menstruation, or irregular menstruation), *dysmenorrhea* (painful menstruation), and *premenstrual tension*.

The normal menstrual cycle depends upon the interrelated functions of four physiological systems: (1) the central nervous system, (2) the anterior lobe of the pituitary gland, (3) the ovaries, and (4) the uterus. The most important central nervous system structure in the menstrual process is the hypothalamus. The pituitary gland is located in the spenoid bone over the roof of the mouth and is directly connected to the hypothalamus by the pituitary stalk. Hypothalamic stimulation regulates the function of the anterior pituitary lobe, which in turn regulates the output of ovarian hormones by the ovary. Hormonal changes result in uterine changes associated with menstruation.

In addition to its role in regulating pituitary functions, the hypothalamus is the major central nervous system structure involved in the functioning of the autonomic nervous system. As such, the hypothalamus has been referred to as the *seat of emotions*. Damage to the hypothalamus can produce marked changes in emotionality. The hypothalamus, like other subcortical systems of the brain, is partially regulated by the cerebral cortex. Disturbances in cortical functioning, therefore, may also affect functions of subcortical systems. The cortex plays a key role in a person's ability to interpret and respond to external events. Changes in cortical functioning produced by environmental stress may affect subcortical systems such as the hypothalamus. Changes in hypothalamic functioning, in turn, may affect pituitary regulation of ovarian functions, which, in turn, may lead to disturbances of the menstrual cycle. Emotional factors, therefore, via these physiological systems, can play a prominent role in menstrual disturbances. Of course, emotional factors and stress are not the only causes of menstrual disturbances. Organic disturbances in any of the four systems (the central nervous system, anterior lobe of the pituitary, the ovaries, or the uterus) can result in menstrual disturbances. Thus, to attribute all disturbances in menstruation to psychological factors may obscure the role of important and possibly serious organic factors. The present section, however, will focus primarily on the role of psychological factors.

AMENORRHEA

Amenorrhea is the absence of menstruation, which may be of either short or long duration. When menstruation has never occurred and a woman has passed the age of 18, the disorder is called *primary amenorrhea*. If menstruation occurs and then stops, the disorder is called *secondary amenorrhea*. If menstruation occurs every 2 or 3 months, the disorder is called *oligomenorrhea*. Nearly half the patients with primary amenorrhea have either genetic disorders or some type of hermaphroditism (ambiguity of the sex organs). Some patients with oligomenorrhea have a lifelong history of menstruation every 2 months. However, if the menstrual cycle has been normal, then oligomenorrhea may signal the onset of a more serious disorder or the cessation of menstruation (secondary amenorrhea). As we noted, organic disturbances can cause all forms of amenorrhea. The causal role of psychological factors, however, has been most clearly established for secondary amenorrhea. Secondary amenorrhea of psychogenic origin may be grouped into four categories: (1) *emotional amenorrhea*, (2) *amenorrhea and galactorrhea*, (3) *pseudocyesis*, and (4) *anorexia nervosa*.

Emotional amenorrhea may be brought on by intense stress or severe shock. Stress-induced amenorrhea was common in internment camps during World War II. Secondary amenorrhea among interned women reportedly ranged from 15 to 50% during the first 2 months of confinement, when stress was probably the most acute. The rapid onset is significant, because virtually all people held in these camps over an extended period of time became malnourished. Malnutrition is an established cause of amenorrhea and eventually led to amenorrhea in as many as 90% of women confined in the camps. It was not likely, however, that malnutrition could account for the onset of amenorrhea during the first 2 months of confinement. Based on these and other findings, Israel (1967) concludes that "it is now evident that such emotionally induced, psychogenic amenorrhea is, in the absence of physical changes to explain the dysfunction, the most common variety of amenorrhea encountered in medical practice [p. 109]."

Amenorrhea and *galactorrhea* (milky secretion by the breasts) sometimes occur together, chiefly in younger women. A good example is the *Chiari–Frommel syndrome,* which is characterized by amenorrhea, galactorrhea, and a tendency toward obesity. The most prominent symptom of the disorder is persistent lactation or milky secretion of the breasts, caused by an excessive production of lactogenic (milk-producing) hormones in the anterior pituitary. The excessive production of lactogenic hormones is caused by a dysfunction of the hypothalamus, which inhibits release of gonadotropins in the anterior pituitary. The failure to release gonadotropins not only permits excessive production of lactogenic hormones but also leads to a lack of gonadotropic stimulation of the uterus and ovaries. The result is atrophy of the uterus and ovaries and subsequent amenorrhea. In half the patients reported to have amenorrhea and lactation of the breasts, pregnancy had never occurred. In other words, galactorrhea cannot be explained in terms of changes associated with pregnancy that normally lead to lactation. There is some evidence that the hypothalamic dysfunction leading to the sequence of changes just described may have a psychogenic origin. For example, amenorrhea and galactorrhea may follow an anxiety-producing hysterectomy or an episode of pseudocyesis, a disorder that will be discussed next.

Pseudocyesis—false or hysterical pregnancy—is a psychophysiological problem that has fascinated professionals for many years. Hippocrates reportedly treated 12 women who falsely believed they were pregnant (Kroger & Freed, 1956). As we mentioned in Chapter 1, Jones attributed the termination of Anna O's treatment by Breuer to a hysterical pregnancy complete with delivery pains. Israel (1967) describes pseudocyesis as an excellent example of how "the psyche" can affect the functions of the anterior pituitary gland via changes in the hypothalamus. Pseudocyesis is believed to occur primarily among neurotic women who are obsessed with the subject of pregnancy. They have either an intense fear of pregnancy or a compelling need or longing to become pregnant. Pseudocyesis may involve amenorrhea, nausea and vomiting, weight gain, an increase in the fullness of the breasts, and lactation. Virtually every change normally reported by pregnant women may occur. Despite medical evidence to the contrary, a woman may cling tenaciously to her conviction that she is pregnant and use the various physical changes that have occurred as proof of her condition.

In some cases, amenorrhea and galactorrhea may precipitate rather than result from a pseudocyesis episode. That is, rather than psychological factors giving rise to physiological manifestations of pregnancy, the onset of physiological changes may convince a woman that she is pregnant. There is little need to document the fact that women who have had intercourse may become very upset if their period is late. It is conceivable that a woman who is sexually naive and excessively worried about pregnancy (even if she has never had intercourse) may develop pseudocyesis following a sudden onset of amenorrhea and lactation. Thus, it is possible that even if amenorrhea and galactorrhea have a physiological rather than psychological origin, they may contribute to a psychological reaction in the form of pseudocyesis. For example, Cramer (1971) reports a case study in which amenorrhea and galactorrhea caused by chlorpromazine therapy appeared to facilitate a developing delusion of pregnancy. (Chlorpromazine is a drug used in the treatment of psychiatric patients; established side effects include amenorrhea and galactorrhea.)

■   Maria, a 15-year-old Puerto Rican girl, was admitted to the inpatient service after an attempted suicide. On admission she appeared to be very infantile, she was agitated, her speech was illogical, and she had hallucinations and paranoid delusions. Her full-scale IQ score was 75. The results of her physical examination were normal. On November 5 she began receiving 100 mg. of chlorpromazine daily.

She expressed great concern about sexual matters, acted seductively with her physician, and expressed the wish to get married. On November 20 the chlorpromazine dosage was raised to 150 mg. daily, yet she became more withdrawn and paranoid. On November 22 she was found lying on her bed sucking a little doll. She seemed to be hallucinating: when asked where she got the doll, she said, "I took it . . . all for me . . . I have two babies now . . . my doll and one in my stomach . . . my belly is big . . . the spirits gave me a baby. . . ." At this time there was a great deal of talk about pregnancy among the girls on the ward. Maria also said that she hated men: "They are dangerous."

Three days later galactorrhea appeared spontaneously, she was nauseated, and she told everyone that she was pregnant. When asked whether she had had intercourse she responded evasively. A gynecological examination revealed that she was a virgin. Her abdomen was normal but her breasts were distended. The Aschheim-Zondek tests for pregnancy were negative and urine studies for gonadotropins and steroids revealed normal levels.

Chlorpromazine therapy was stopped on December 4: the galactorrhea stopped on December 24, and her menstrual period began on December 27 after a delay of 2 weeks. Chlorpromazine was given again on January 4 (150 mg. daily) and the galactorrhea reappeared on January 17. The delusion of pregnancy subsided. The galactorrhea stopped 4 days after the chlorpromazine was cut.

Her history revealed that Maria had been separated from her parents since infancy. She was described as withdrawn and disturbed. Later she moved in with her father, who had remarried, and witnessed him having sexual intercourse several times. Her mother, with whom she stayed just prior to hospitalization, warned her repeatedly not to let men approach her because of their "evil" sexual intentions. Maria eventually confessed after much reluctance that prior to her hospitalization a 30-year-old cousin had kissed her in the mouth; she said she loved him and hoped she would get pregnant so that he would marry her [pp. 960–961].[8]

As Cramer (1971) points out, the delusion of pregnancy in this case occurred 3 days prior to the appearance of lactation. Thus the side effects of chlorpromazine may not have precipitated the delusion of pregnancy but may have contributed to its development. In other cases, however, the delusion of preg-

[8] *American Journal of Psychiatry*, vol. 127, 1971. Copyright 1971, the American Psychiatric Association. Reprinted by permission.

nancy may be precipitated by amenorrhea and galactorrhea resulting from chlorpromazine therapy.

Anorexia nervosa, which is discussed in Chapter 10, is a disorder that usually occurs among adolescent females and is characterized by prolonged food refusal and subsequent malnutrition. Amenorrhea is frequently associated with anorexia nervosa. It is possible that psychological factors affecting hypothalamic functioning may alter eating behavior as well as induce pituitary changes associated with amenorrhea. It is unlikely that malnutrition resulting from anorexia nervosa causes amenorrhea, since amenorrhea often precedes an extreme reduction of eating behavior.

In summary, alterations of the menstrual cycle may be caused by organic or psychological factors. Even when menstrual functions are altered by physiological disturbances there may be important psychological reactions to these changes. As a final point of interest, it has been noted that a high percentage of patients labeled psychotic may show alterations in menstrual functions. Amenorrhea, for example, occurs in almost a third of female schizophrenics and females in the depressive phase of a manic psychosis (Israel, 1967).

DYSMENORRHEA

Dysmenorrhea is excessive pain associated with menstruation. The disorder is referred to as *primary dysmenorrhea* when there is no identifiable pathological condition of the pelvic organs and as *secondary dysmenorrhea* when the pain appears to be caused by an organic condition of the pelvis.[9] Although psychological factors may play a role in both primary and secondary dysmenorrhea, greater emphasis has been placed on the psychological aspects of primary dysmenorrhea. This section, therefore, will focus on the relationship of psychological factors to primary dysmenorrhea.

The most outstanding characteristic of primary dysmenorrhea is excessive, often disabling, menstrual pain. The pain is typically sharp, intermittent, and usually restricted to the lower abdomen, though it may spread to the back and thighs. Other symptoms may include headaches, nausea, and vomiting. The onset of the menstrual pain is either at the beginning of the menstrual flow or a few hours before. Usually, the intensity of the pain is greatest during the first 24 hours.

It is difficult to estimate the incidence of primary dysmenorrhea. Reports range from 3 to 47% of all patients seeking gynecological treatment. Israel (1967), reviewing a survey of 4000 patients, notes that 8% had sought treatment for primary dysmenorrhea. Primary dysmenorrhea usually begins in adolescence. The pain often starts as discomfort and grows progressively worse over the late adolescent years. The disorder rarely has its initial onset after age 20. Dysmenorrhea beginning after age 20 is typically caused by a pelvic disorder.

The etiology of primary dysmenorrhea is largely unknown. Israel (1967)

[9] Kroger and Freed (1956) used the terms *primary* and *secondary* to refer to two types of functional dysmenorrhea (nonorganic origin). If dysmenorrhea began with the first menses it was called primary. If dysmenorrhea began after a period of normal menstruation it was called secondary.

discusses six organically based etiological theories that have been considered but not adequately supported: (1) an imbalance of normal estrogen–progesterone equilibrium, (2) incomplete disintegration of the endometrium, (3) poor posture, (4) obstruction of the cervical canal, (5) allergic reactivity, and (6) hypoplasia (underdevelopment) of the uterus. In addition to these general theories, efforts have been made to determine the specific conditions of the uterus that are associated with pain. The fundamental basis for the pain is a pathological sensitivity of the nerve endings in the isthmus (cervical area) of the uterus. This hypersensitivity results in exaggerated and uncoordinated uterine contractions, which are the immediate cause of pain. In normal women, the contractions just before and during menstruation are the strongest. In women with primary dysmenorrhea, these contractions are markedly exaggerated. In addition, there is some evidence that women with primary dysmenorrhea have a higher sensitivity to pain in the cervical canal than normal women. One suggested explanation of these findings is that primary dysmenorrhea may be a disorder of the autonomic nervous system, in which the uterine pain is a local "storm" analogous to the localized manifestations in migraine headaches and bronchial asthma.

Although psychological causes of primary dysmenorrhea have been proposed, evidence clearly supporting a psychogenic origin has not been provided. Kroger and Freed (1956) view functional dysmenorrhea as "a symptom of a personality disorder . . . [p. 238]." They suggest that the failure of a general practitioner or a gynecologist to find obvious evidence of emotional problems is due to a facade of poise and maturity constructed by the patient, which conceals an underlying emotional instability. Israel (1967), although suggesting that psychogenic factors may be important contributors to the etiology of primary dysmenorrhea, points out that no psychogenic explanation is sufficiently supported by empirical evidence to warrant universal acceptance. He notes that in most cultures words to describe menstruation "point to inconvenience and disability—unwell, indisposed, sick, the curse, etc. [p. 136]." This leads him to speculate that "an anxiety neurosis regarding menstruation may develop as a result of such linguistic suggestion, coupled with ever-indulgent coddling of the daughter by a mother who herself may have or have had dysmenorrhea [pp. 136–137]."

In short, we may conclude that neither organic nor psychological factors have been clearly identified as primary etiological agents. There is evidence that primary dysmenorrhea is associated with exaggerated uterine contractions and higher sensitivity to pain in the cervical canal. Such findings, however, do not rule out psychological factors that may contribute to the development or continuance of the pain.

PREMENSTRUAL TENSION

About two-thirds of all women are aware of ill-defined symptoms that occur about 4–7 days prior to the onset of menstruation. These vague premenstrual signs include fatigue, difficulty in concentrating, irritability, headache, dull backache, and a sensation of heaviness in the pelvic region. The term for these frequent symptoms is *menstrual molimina*. In some women, these changes are greatly intensified and regularly disrupt their daily activities. When the cyclical pattern of distress assumes such proportions it is referred to as *premenstrual tension*. Frequent symptoms of premenstrual tension include difficulties in concentration, restlessness, annoyance over seemingly trivial matters, crying spells, and emotional outbursts. Complaints of headaches, backaches, and insomnia are also common (Israel, 1967).

As for the other menstrual disturbances we have discussed, the cause of premenstrual tension remains obscure. Both organic and psychogenic etiologies have been proposed. One organic hypothesis is that the premenstrual tension is caused by a menstrual toxin, the source of which may be the endometrium, the tissue in the uterus that is shed during menstruation. A second organic hypothesis is that the disorder is caused by a hormonal imbalance resulting from an endocrine disturbance. Although there is supporting evidence for each of these hypotheses, neither has been confirmed.

Likewise, the hypothesis that premenstrual tension has a psychological origin has not been confirmed. There is evidence, however, that psychological factors are related to premenstrual tension. Gruba and Rohrbaugh (1975) administered the Moos' Menstrual Distress Questionnaire (MDQ) and the Minnesota Multiphasic Personality Inventory (MMPI) to 60 female college students during the first week following their most recent period. The MDQ consists of 47 items, each describing a specific symptom (for example, backache, insomnia, nausea, crying). Subjects rated their experience of each symptom on a six-point scale separately for the premenstrual period (1 week before the onset of menstruation), the menstrual period, and the intermenstrual period (the remainder of the cycle). Forty-six of the 47 items were grouped into eight factor-analytically derived symptom scales: (1) pain, (2) concentration, (3) behavioral change, (4) autonomic reactions, (5) water retention, (6) negative affect, (7) arousal, and (8) control.

Correlations were obtained between distress scores for each of the eight scales and the MMPI clinical scales for the three phases of the menstrual cycle (premenstrual period, menstrual period, and intermenstrual period). Results were interpreted as supporting previous findings of a relationship between neuroticism and premenstrual tension, irritability, and depression. Specifically, scores on the negative affect scale (composed of the following symptoms: crying, loneliness, anxiety, restlessness, irritability, mood swings, depression, and tension) correlated significantly with MMPI indices of neuroticism. Consistently higher correlations were obtained between pain symptoms and MMPI variables during the premenstrual period than during other periods. Gruba and Rohrbaugh suggest that "psychological factors may play a more important role when pain symptoms are experienced before menstruation begins [p. 271]." No evidence was found to support a hypothesis that specific personality factors were related to specific menstrual symptoms. The authors conclude that "the results do not confirm or disconfirm any etiological hypothesis but are congruent with the notion that psychogenic processes may be more important in some areas of menstrual symptomatology than others [p. 272]."

The subjects in the study just described were not selected because of any special complaints or problems associated with menstruation. It is quite possible that a stronger relationship between personality variables and premenstrual symptoms might be demonstrated if subjects were specifically selected because of problems with premenstrual tension. Kroger and Freed (1956) estimate that in at least 40% of women, the signs and symptoms during the premenstrual period are of sufficient intensity to cause considerable distress. Israel (1967) notes that in one prison survey in the United States, 62% of the offenses for which women were imprisoned were committed during the premenstrual week. Tonks, Rack, and Rose (1968) found a significantly greater number of suicides among women during the premenstrual week, particularly among married women. In France, the "temporary insanity or incompetence" associated with the premenstrual week has achieved legal recognition.

In summary, even if the prevalence and severity of problems related to the menstrual cycle have been overemphasized, there is little question that a sizable number of women, particularly in the younger age groups, regularly experience considerable stress and discomfort. It is worth noting that the majority of medical and psychological literature on problems related to the menstrual cycle has been authored by men. A woman's perspective may lead to a different selection of both independent and dependent variables in the assessment of difficulties associated with menstruation. An increasing percentage of women entering the profession of psychology and societal changes related to the women's liberation movement are factors currently affecting research activity in the areas of human sexuality and sex role development. These factors may well affect research pertaining to the menstrual cycle and other experiences unique to women.

Psychophysiological Cardiovascular Reactions

The psychological significance of cardiovascular reactions becomes obvious when we consider the various changes that take place during everyday emotional experiences. Blushing, turning pale, sensations of cold or heat, and "pounding" of the heart are examples of physiological responses to stimuli associated with emotional arousal. Most of these changes are under the control of the autonomic nervous system. When we blush, small vessels dilate and the volume of blood near the skin's surface increases, producing a reddening of the face as well as a sensation of warmth. Conversely, paleness or pallor occurs when these vessels constrict and reduce the volume of blood near the surface of the skin. Sensations of coldness associated with a corresponding drop in skin temperature may accompany vasoconstriction. Changes in heart rate and blood pressure are also prominent signs of emotional arousal.

The common cardiovascular reactions just described illustrate the sensitivity of this physiological system to emotionally arousing conditions. Cardiovascular changes related to pronounced or prolonged stress can result in serious health problems. In this section, two cardiovascular disorders will be discussed: essential hypertension and migraine headaches.

ESSENTIAL HYPERTENSION

Essential hypertension may be defined as consistent elevation of systolic and diastolic blood pressure due to unknown causes. Systolic blood pressure results from contraction of the heart and diastolic blood pressure results from dilation or relaxation of the heart.

Essential hypertension is the most common clinical variety of high blood pressure (Mendels, 1973). In summarizing results of previous research by other investigators, Wolf, Cardon, Shepard, and Wolff (1955) noted that estimates of the incidence of hypertension ran as high as 6% of the general population. A consistent finding across studies was a 60:40 predominance of females. The age of onset ranged from 15 to 50 years with a peak at age 35. Another finding has been that the incidence of essential hypertension is higher among blacks than whites. One suggested explanation is that stresses encountered by minority groups exceed those of the majority. However, it is also conceivable that there may be biological differences between ethnic groups in susceptibility to hypertension. Schachter, Kerr, Wimberly, and Lachin (1974) found that heart rate during

An air traffic controller guides airplanes through the crowded skies around a major airport. The job demands intense concentration; a mistake could cost hundreds of lives. The stress and the responsibility are high, and so is the incidence of essential hypertension among controllers. (Erich Hartmann, Magnum)

sleep among black newborns was significantly higher than the heart rate of white newborns. The authors speculate that since elevated heart rate has been one predictor of hypertension in later life, the higher heart rate among black newborns may relate to the fact that hypertension is more common among blacks than whites.

Symptoms that accompany essential hypertension are, in order of frequency, giddiness; muscle tightness in the neck, back, or extremities; headache; heart palpitations; constipation; and epigastric (upper abdomen) discomfort. The severity and frequency of these symptoms are not directly related to varying levels of elevated blood pressure. About 50% of people with essential hypertension have either tension headaches or vascular headaches, which closely resemble migraine headaches. There is some evidence that headaches may occur years before the discovery of hypertension (Wolf *et al.,* 1955).

As stated earlier, the causes of essential hypertension are not known. A prominent hypothesis is that prolonged psychosocial stress may cause sustained high blood pressure. Although experimental research with animals indicates a causal relationship between stress and sustained high blood pressure, a similar causal relationship has not been demonstrated in humans (Mendels, 1973). However, correlational data suggest that extreme stress may result in a prolonged period of high blood pressure. Wolf *et al.* (1955) cited a study by Ruskin and Beard (1948) in which 57% of patients hospitalized after an oil explosion had elevated diastolic blood pressure. Blood pressure remained elevated in a third of these patients 8 months later.

Although a causal role of stress has not been adequately established for essential hypertension, there is little question that emotional variables play an important role in the elevation of blood pressure. After reviewing psychosomatic research on hypertension, Cochrane (1971) concluded that there is general support for a "link between perceived stress in the environment, a personality overreactive to stress and high blood pressure [p. 61]." Cochrane's review examined four criteria for considering essential hypertension as a psychosomatic disorder: (1) physiological aspects of hypertension should not be incompatible with psychosomatic explanations, (2) there should be evidence that hypertension can be produced experimentally by manipulating psychological variables, (3) there should be evidence of a relationship between environmental factors and the onset of hypertension, and (4) there should be identifiable personality differences between hypertensive and nonhypertensive individuals.

For Cochrane's first criterion, the weight of evidence indicates that "stress and hypertension are related through the autonomic nervous system [p. 62]." The fact that stress can produce autonomic changes such as an elevation in blood pressure suggests that physiological aspects of hypertension are not incompatible with psychosomatic explanations. The second criterion is partially met by the fact that sustained high blood pressure can be produced in laboratory animals by manipulation of psychological variables. Evidence for the third criterion is mostly derived from field research. Various studies have explored the relationship between occupational stress and high blood pressure. Others have looked at the relationship between high blood pressure and unusual stress conditions such as combat or natural disasters. Although the results of such studies lack consistency, evidence tends to support a possible causal relationship between psychosocial stress and sustained high blood pressure. Research on the final criterion, that differences in personality should exist between hypertensives and nonhypertensives, has not been conclusive. Cochrane found little support for a hypothesis that hypertension develops in emotionally labile individuals with neurotic tendencies. A hypothesis that the hypertensive personality is characterized by repression of aggressive and hostile impulses was supported by a number of studies. However, Cochrane was careful to point out that "in many cases the quality of the evidence leaves something to be desired [p. 69]."

One of the most comprehensive and best controlled studies on the relationship between stress and hypertension in humans was part of an ongoing, longitudinal study conducted by Kasl and Cobb (1970). Blood pressure changes were studied over an extended time beginning with a period in which men were faced with the loss of their jobs due to the closing of a plant. Subsequent measures were taken during a 2-year period after the men were originally terminated from their employment. Subjects were married males, aged 35 to 60, with at least 3 years of seniority. A group of men with comparable characteristics, stably employed in a similar work setting, served as controls. The plan of the study included six periods of measurement: (1) a period of anticipation in which the men were still employed but knew that the plant was closing in a month and a half; (2) a period of a little over 1 month after the men lost their jobs; during this period, all men were either unemployed or newly employed but on probationary status; (3) a period 3 months after the second period, during which some men had found stable jobs and others either remained unemployed or had lost their second job; (4) a period 4 months after the third period; (5) a period 1 year after the original job loss, during which most of the men were stably employed but some were still undergoing job changes; and (6) a final measurement period 2 years after the original job loss. Measurements were taken for the same six time-periods for stably employed men in the control group. As the study was still in progress at the time of the first report, complete data for the first year were obtained for 56 men serving in the experimental group and for 39 men serving in the control group.

The major findings were that (1) control subjects showed minor fluctuations in blood pressure but no significant overall trends; (2) blood pressure levels were clearly higher during periods of anticipation of job loss, unemployment, or probationary reemployment than during later periods of stable employment or new jobs; (3) men who had the longest periods of high blood pressure had a more severe unemployment experience, reported that their subjective experience of stress lasted longer, were lower on "ego resilience," and showed little improvement on measures of self-esteem and irritability; (4) there was a clear rise in blood pressure during the period of anticipation when the men knew the plant was going to close; the rise in blood pressure during this period was as high as during the period of unemployment or probationary reemployment; (5) blood pressure variability tended to be higher among men who were relatively rigid and had higher overall mean blood pressure; and (6) preliminary results from a replication on a different sample of unemployed men yielded similar findings.

Viewed collectively, these findings clearly indicate a relationship between psychosocial stress and sustained high blood pressure. Results are particularly impressive in light of the control procedures and the initial replication of findings on a different sample of men.

There is some evidence that hypertensive individuals develop behavioral patterns that permit them to avoid unpleasant interpersonal situations. Sapira, Scheib, Moriarty, and Shapiro (1971) hypothesize that a hypertensive individual "may perceptually screen out potentially noxious stimuli as a behavioral response to his hyperreactive pressor system [p. 239]." Nineteen hypertensive patients and 15 nonhypertensive patients were shown two films involving an interaction between a doctor and a patient. In the first film, the doctor appeared "curt, rude, hurried, disinterested, and annoyed." In the second movie the same doctor was "relaxed, pleasant, courteous, friendly, and appeared pleased." The major finding was that the hypertensive group denied perceiving any differences between the doctor's behavior in the first and second films whereas the control group of nonhypertensive persons readily identified the differences in the doctor's behavior. Sapira *et al*. see these results as supporting their hypothesis that hypertensive persons may perceptually screen out potentially noxious stimulation.

Findings about psychological aspects of hypertension appear to justify the following general conclusions: (1) limited evidence suggests that hypertension among susceptible individuals may be caused by intense or prolonged stress; (2) there is insufficient evidence of a clear relationship between hypertension and a particular type of personality pattern; and (3) there is preliminary evidence to suggest that hypertensive individuals may perceptually screen out stimulation, thereby permitting avoidance of noxious interpersonal situations.

Medical treatment of hypertension involves the use of various drugs known to be effective in lowering both systolic and diastolic pressure. Two well-known antihypertensive agents are chlorthalidone (a monosulfamyl diuretic that increases excretion by the kidneys of sodium chloride and thus reduces arterial pressure) and reserpine (which reduces arterial pressure and also has a sedative effect). These two drugs in combination are very effective in the treatment of hypertension. Although this section will focus on efforts to treat hypertension using biofeedback techniques, we must emphasize that the success of treatment with various drug compounds is well established.

The goal of any treatment approach for essential hypertension is to achieve a clinically significant reduction in blood pressure over a protracted period. Since biofeedback procedures can be used to train human subjects to either lower or raise blood pressure, recent research has tested the use of biofeedback in treating essential hypertension. The major research in this area involves a series of collaborative studies on both normal individuals (Shapiro, Tursky, Gershon, & Stern, 1969; Shapiro, Tursky, & Schwartz, 1970; Schwartz, Shapiro, & Tursky, 1971; Shapiro, Schwartz, & Tursky, 1972; Schwartz, 1973) and hypertensive persons (Benson, Shapiro, Tursky, & Schwartz, 1971; Schwartz & Shapiro, 1973). As summarized by Yates (1975), the major findings obtained by these investigators are that normal subjects who are reinforced for raising or lowering systolic blood pressure are able to do so in a single experimental session, whereas subjects who are given noncontingent reinforcement show no significant changes. Significantly, in one study subjects reinforced for raising and lowering systolic blood pressure did so even though they were unaware that blood pressure changes were being studied. Even after the session, they did not know they had controlled their blood pressure. Similar findings were obtained for control over diastolic blood pressure.

As Blanchard and Young (1973) indicate, studies on instrumental control of heart rate and blood pressure show important methodological problems. For these and other reasons, the leap from laboratory findings to clinical application may be longer than biofeedback enthusiasts believe. Still, the clinical implication of these findings for the treatment of essential hypertension is obvious. The goal of treatment is to condition people with high blood pressure to lower their blood pressure. The hope is that such conditioning eventually can be achieved in a variety of different situations and maintained for extended periods of time. Benson *et al.* (1971) were able to train hypertensive individuals to reduce systolic blood pressure but Schwartz and Shapiro (1973) were unable to train hypertensive patients to reduce diastolic blood pressure. However, Elder, Ruiz, Deabler, and Dillenkoffer (1973) were successful in training hypertensive patients to reduce diastolic presssure. Informational feedback alone produced a significantly greater reduction in diastolic pressure than a no-feedback control, but the greatest reduction in diastolic pressure occurred in a group that was given both informational feedback and verbal praise. Moreover, the reduction in diastolic pressure in the group given both feedback and praise was not only clinically significant but was maintained for at least a week after the training sessions.

Yates (1975), in a review of these and other studies, concludes that essential hypertension is one of three disorders in which the application of biofeedback procedures currently shows "considerable promise." By contrast, Redmond, Gaylor, McDonald, and Shapiro (1974) maintain that biofeedback procedures may be no more useful than merely telling the subject what to do. In their research, they produced consistent directional changes in blood pressure and heart rate merely by giving subjects continuous verbal instructions to concentrate upon. In other words, without the use of biofeedback, subjects raised or lowered their blood pressures and heart rates in response to forceful verbal instruction. These researchers point out that blood pressure changes occurring in biofeedback research are generally no greater than changes produced by manipulation of other variables such as forceful verbal instruction. In addition, they note that the amount of change in blood pressure is usually clinically insignificant even though it may be statistically significant, and such changes tend to be of short duration—too short to have clinically useful effects for patients with essential hypertension. The latter criticisms of the clinical utility of biofeedback are also offered by Blanchard and Young (1973).

These criticisms were made without reference to research by Elder *et al.* (1973) in which clinically significant reductions in diastolic pressure were maintained for at least a follow-up period of 1 week. Perhaps the safest conclusions, based on research cited thus far, are these: (1) There are still methodological problems that hamper interpretation of biofeedback research on blood pressure, and (2) the clinical utility of biofeedback cannot be evaluated without further investigations on the magnitude and duration of blood pressure changes in patients with hypertension.

MIGRAINE HEADACHES

Migraine headaches are acute, recurrent, intense headaches, usually characterized by a deep throbbing or stabbing pain. They are almost always accompanied by either visual disturbances or nausea. The throbbing pain is due to changes in the diameter of certain intracranial arteries; the brain itself is not sensitive to pain. Usually, the headache is unilateral (one-sided), although it may spread over the forehead. The unilateral nature of the migraine headache is sometimes cited to distinguish it from a *tension headache*. A tension headache usually involves pain around the entire head or on the top of the head (Maxwell, 1966). As indicated in the introduction to this chapter, the tension headache is muscular in origin whereas the migraine is vascular in origin. Migraine attacks involve the autonomic nervous system and are usually accompanied by vascular changes leading to an increase of blood flow in the head (Yates, 1975).

Although the causes of migraine have not been clearly established, there is support for the assumption that genetic factors predispose individuals to migraine attacks. Ostfeld (1962) notes that genetic research indicates a high incidence of migraine headaches in families of migraine patients. Data reported by Goodell, Lewontin, and Wolff (1954) indicate that if both parents had migraine, about 70% of the offspring will exhibit migraine. Pearce (1971) reports a positive family history in 65% of 450 migraine patients. As Maxwell (1966) points out, what appears to be inherited is a "migraine constitution" or a predisposition toward migraine attacks. A number of factors appear to bring on migraine attacks. According to data provided by Pearce (1971), the more common precipitating factors reported by patients include (1) anxiety or worry, 73%; (2) relaxation, 45%; (3) fatigue or sleeplessness, 43%; (4) menstruation, 39%; and (5) bright light, 30%. Less common precipitators included specific foods, 13%; alcohol, 10%; and hunger, 7%.

Estimates of the prevalence of migraine range from 5 to 10% of the population (Pearce, 1971). Nearly all studies on migraine report a higher percentage of female patients than male patients. Ostfeld (1962) has suggested that migraine headaches may occur with equal frequency among men and women but factors such as sex roles may lead to a lower percentage of men than women admitting to having headaches or seeking treatment. Although the sex role factor as well as other factors mentioned by Ostfeld (1962) may have exaggerated the magnitude of the sex difference, sex differences have continued to be noted in subsequent investigations. Pearce (1971), for example, reports that 66% of 450 migraine patients who attended a migraine clinic were female. Since migraine attacks are typically very severe, it is unlikely that substantial numbers of men would let their masculine identity prevent them from seeking treatment.

In summarizing research on migraine and personality variables, Rees (1971) notes that persons who suffer from migraines have been described as "tense, anxious self-driving persons who are rigid, ambitious, perfectionistic, and who tend to be highly competitive in their outlook, always trying to excel over their fellows [p. 47]." However, Rees concludes that there is "no specific personality type which is applicable to migraine in general [p. 47]." He notes that part of the problem in studying personality characteristics is that most studies are based on selected groups of patients, such as migraine patients who are attending clinics in order to obtain psychotherapy. Rees suggests that what are needed are reliable measures of personality assessment, applied to a random sample of migraine sufferers in the community and to appropriate control groups (healthy individuals and individuals with disorders other than migraines).

It is generally accepted that emotional factors can precipitate migraine attacks. However, opinion varies on the frequency of emotional factors as precipitating agents and their relative importance in relation to other precipitating agents. A common report is that migraines tend to occur after prolonged periods of work and sustained tension, regardless of whether the work has led to success or to failure (Rees, 1971).

The primary treatment for migraine attacks is the ergot alkaloids (ergotamine). This drug is used not only in the treatment of acute attacks but also as a prophylactic or preventive. An important effect of the drug is vasoconstriction, which presumably accounts for its effectiveness in the treatment of migraine (Berde, 1971).

There is some evidence that biofeedback techniques may prove to be successful in the treatment of migraine headaches. Sargent, Green, and Walters (1973) noticed that an increase in peripheral temperature (temperature of the hands and feet) occurred when a subject was spontaneously recovering from a migraine attack. Following this observation, they attempted to train subjects to raise the temperature of the right index finger, lower the temperature of the midforehead, or do both. They assumed that the greater the blood flow to the periphery, the less the volume of blood in the vessels of the head. A higher temperature of the index finger than of the midforehead would indicate greater blood flow to the periphery, because an increase in the volume of blood results in a higher temperature. Since migraine headaches involve an increase in the blood flow to the head, the headaches might be relieved if subjects could increase the peripheral flow of blood by either reducing the temperature of the midforehead or increasing the temperature of the right index finger.

Their subjects included persons with tension headaches as well as others with migraine headaches. All subjects were given training in temperature control, which consisted of rehearsing phrases suggesting relaxation, an increase in hand temperature, and visualization of the process. Subjects also were given feedback about the difference between the temperature of the midforehead and index finger. Although the difference in temperature could have been due to a drop in midforehead temperature, a rise in finger temperature, or both, subjects indicated that their hands felt warmer but reported no changes in midforehead temperature. Results indicated that a decrease in the frequency and severity of migraine headaches followed increased temperature control. Yates (1975), while noting that temperature control might prove to be a promising treatment technique, points out that no objective data were reported on the temperature changes and appropriate controls were not employed. Interestingly, improvement was obtained in subjects with migraine headaches but not in subjects with tension headaches. Yates adds that such a result is not at all unexpected, considering that specific kinds of training are appropriate for specific kinds of disorders. In other words, a training procedure that produces changes in the vascular system is appropriate for migraine headaches, which are of vascular origin, but inappropriate for tension headaches, which are of muscular origin.

In this section, we have discussed two prominent psychophysiological disorders of the cardiovascular system, essential hypertension and migraine headaches. Other disorders, such as paroxysmal tachycardia (a disorder involving heart rate) and vascular spasms, may also involve psychophysiological factors. The autonomic nervous system plays a major role in regulating cardiovascular functions. Stress that leads to autonomic changes typically has rapid effects on the cardiovascular system.

Summary

Psychophysiological disorders involve both real disturbances in particular physiological systems and psychological concomitants. For many of the disorders discussed in this chapter, there is some evidence implicating constitutional factors. Although some researchers have suggested that stress causes most of these disorders, there is little evidence that stress is the single causal agent in any of them. Instead, stress appears to precipitate attacks or severely aggravate an existing condition.

The major classes of psychophysiological disorders discussed in this chapter were (1) skin reactions, (2) gastrointestinal reactions, (3) genitourinary reactions, and (4) cardiovascular reactions. Representative disorders for each class were discussed and relevant research findings were presented.

Medical treatment is the single most important treatment approach for almost all the disorders discussed. Psychotherapy, in conjunction with medical treatment, may be of value for some disorders but supporting evidence for its effectiveness is minimal. Biofeedback appears to be effective in the treatment of tension headaches and possibly migraine headaches. However, its effectiveness in the treatment of essential hypertension and other psychophysiological disorders has yet to be adequately demonstrated. The clinical applications of biofeedback have stimulated renewed interest in psychophysiological disorders, and preliminary investigations offer some promise for the future role of biofeedback as a treatment approach.

The selection of disorders presented in this chapter is far from exhaustive, but it serves to illustrate both theoretical issues and current conceptions pertaining to the nature of psychophysiological reactions.

8

Central Nervous System Disorders

Although American psychologists have stressed the role of environmental factors in the development of psychological problems, a wide variety of organic disturbances also can produce transient or permanent psychological effects. Any substantial change in the functioning of the central nervous system is likely to be accompanied by psychological changes.

Assuming that few of our readers have any background in neurophysiology, we will present only those technical details that are needed to understand the disorders we discuss. When technical terms are used they will be defined or explained. A brief review of the *central nervous system* (CNS) and the *autonomic nervous system* (ANS) follows.

Most of the disorders discussed in this chapter are disorders of the CNS, which includes the brain and the spinal cord (see Figure 8–1). The entire outer portion of the brain is called the *cerebral cortex*. The cerebral cortex is divided into left and right hemispheres. Each hemisphere consists of four major divisions: (1) the frontal lobes, (2) the parietal lobes, (3) the occipital lobes, and (4) the temporal lobes. Structures beneath the cerebral cortex are referred to as *subcortical areas;* these include such important systems as the hypothalamus, which mediates emotional, sexual, and appetitive behavior—hunger and thirst. A convoluted structure behind the cerebral cortex, called the *cerebellum,* controls body balance and equilibrium. Structures at the base of the brain and the beginning of the

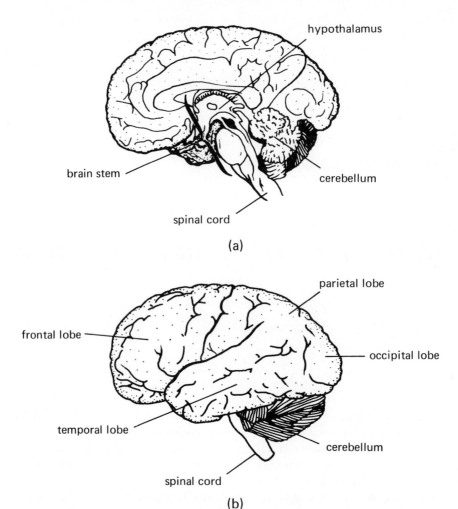

Figure 8–1. Schematic side views of the human brain. Part (a) is a half section of the brain showing major internal structures; part (b) shows the major external structures.

spinal cord compose the *brain stem,* which is critically involved in the regulation of vital processes such as heart rate, blood pressure, and respiration.

Nerves outside the brain and spinal cord constitute the *peripheral nervous system,* composed of the somatic system (which innervates the sense organs and skeletal muscles) and the autonomic system. The autonomic nervous system, ANS, is composed of two divisions: the *sympathetic* division and the *parasympathetic* division. The sympathetic division is generally involved during emotional arousal or response to stress. The parasympathetic division dominates during day-to-day activities of the organism such as eating, sleeping, and digestion. This distinction, however, is an oversimplification in that some behaviors involve activity of both divisions. In male sexual behavior, for example, erection is controlled by the parasympathetic division and ejaculation is controlled by the sympathetic division. The ANS should *not* be viewed as independent of the CNS. The hypothalamus, which is part of the CNS, plays a major role in regulating the functions of the ANS. A disorder of the CNS that involves the hypothalamus can lead to important changes in autonomic activity. Collectively, the CNS and ANS comprise an elaborate, highly complex anatomical unit. When one portion of the nervous system is damaged, the effect rarely is isolated to the specific area that is damaged.

The nature of psychological changes associated with CNS impairment may be influenced by all the following factors: the cause of the impairment, when the impairment occurred, whether the impairment is transient or permanent, and the areas of the brain affected. In addition, the effects of CNS impairment on behavior may vary as a function of an individual's intelligence, psychological adjustment, and the particular conditions of an individual's social environment. For example, if an individual develops seizures following a brain injury resulting from a car accident, his subsequent behavior may be dependent on a variety of personal and social circumstances. If his family and friends believe that seizures signify devil possession, and he lives in a society that places many social and legal restrictions on individuals who have seizures, he may face special problems in adjustment following the accident. In addition, his intelligence and psychological adjustment prior to the accident may significantly influence how well he is able to cope with the changes in his environmental circumstances. There may be, therefore, a complex interaction between the manifestations of CNS impairment and an individual's particular personal and social circumstances. For this reason, it is an oversimplification to assume that brain damage is the cause of all behavioral changes following an injury or disease that affects the CNS. However, it is also erroneous to assume that there are no direct relationships between neurological impairment and psychological functioning. For example, if 30 individuals from diverse environmental backgrounds all show disturbances in memory following damage to the temporal lobes, it is reasonable to conclude that there may be a direct relationship between memory and temporal lobe damage.

There also may be secondary psychological reactions to any changes in specific psychological functions that follow brain damage. For example, the loss of memory associated with damage to the temporal lobes could be a frequent source of frustration for an individual. He might be embarrassed because he is unable to remember names and annoyed because he forgets telephone numbers, or he may have trouble at the office if his work requires him to remember dates, times, and places. The ways in which a particular individual copes with memory loss usually depend on the personal and social circumstances mentioned earlier.

In short, neurological impairment may have relatively direct effects on psychological functioning or highly indirect effects, depending on the nature of the impairment, the environmental context, and the individual's ability to adjust.

In discussing CNS disorders, several general distinctions are useful:

1. Is the disorder temporary and reversible (*acute*), or permanent and irreversible (*chronic*)?
2. Is the disorder confined to a particular brain area (*localized*), or is there general involvement of a number of brain areas (*diffuse or generalized*)?
3. Is the disorder present from birth (*congenital or developmental*), or is it a result of disease, injury, or other factors subsequent to early infancy?
4. Is the disorder genetic or nongenetic in origin?
5. Does the disorder become increasingly severe with time (*progressive*), or does it remain essentially unchanged over time (*nonprogressive*)?

Many conditions can alter the functioning of the CNS and thereby potentially lead to psychological changes. Some conditions that affect the CNS are discussed in other chapters. Neurological impairment associated with certain types of retardation is presented in Chapter 9. A full discussion of the effects of alcohol and other drugs on the functioning of the nervous system is presented in Chapter 14. Chapter 7 describes certain psychophysiological disorders related to disturbances of the hypothalamus.

In this chapter, representative disorders will be discussed in four parts. Part I presents neurological disturbances resulting from traumatic injuries, tumors, and infectious diseases. Aphasia, a particular type of disturbance resulting from multiple causes of CNS impairment, is presented in Part I. In Part II, a variety of toxic agents that may have acute or chronic effects on the CNS are discussed. Part III presents an extensive treatment of epilepsy, a disorder affecting over a million people in the United States. Finally, degenerative neurological disorders associated with aging are discussed in Part IV. As will be apparent, the divisions do not represent four separate classes of disorders. For example, brain injuries or infectious diseases discussed in Part I can be causes of epilepsy discussed in Part III.

Part I. Brain Damage Associated with Injury, Tumors, and Infections

TRAUMATIC BRAIN INJURIES

Traumatic brain injuries are caused by a sudden, severe blow to the head. Four types of traumatic brain injuries are discussed here.

CONCUSSIONS. Concussions are caused by a sudden but blunt blow to the head. A concussion may be mild or severe, depending on the nature of the injury. A frequent cause of a concussion is an automobile accident in which a person's head strikes the windshield or dashboard. In a concussion, the brain may be badly jarred, but there is usually no permanent injury to the neural tissue. If the concussion is mild, the person may not lose consciousness but may experience headaches for several days. In more severe concussions, loss of consciousness may

The boxer Benny Paret hangs on the ropes, unconscious from a blow to the head that ended the fight in the twelfth round. Paret died of massive brain injuries a few hours later; his opponent was awarded the victory. (Charles Hoff, New York Daily News Photo)

continue for hours. Headaches, nausea, dizziness, confusion, and disorientation may persist for days. Recovery, however, is almost always complete.

CONTUSIONS. A contusion is usually caused by a more severe blow to the head than that sustained in a concussion. In a contusion, there is moderate or severe "bruising" of brain tissue. A contusion requires a longer recovery period than that for a concussion and symptoms such as headaches, confusion, and disorientation are more severe. Interestingly, a person struck on the forehead is more likely to sustain damage to the rear of the brain. This is because the brain is bruised when it shifts rapidly to the rear of the cranium. Boxers are far more likely than the general population to show evidence of lesions of the cerebellar, pyramidal, and extrapyramidal brain systems—areas of the brain that are involved in body balance, equilibrium, and motor functions. Such lesions may represent a cumulative effect of frequent minor contusions. Roberts (1969) found that 17% of a randomly drawn sample of British boxers showed evidence of a brain syndrome indicative of traumatic encephalopathy (brain injury result-ing from trauma). Evidence of a chronic brain syndrome was most frequent among boxers who had many fights and long professional careers. Such individ-uals may show what is popularly called the *punch-drunk syndrome,* characterized by grogginess and slowness in speech and muscular movements.

LACERATIONS.　Lacerations of the brain occur when some object, such as a bullet or knife, penetrates the cranium and enters the brain tissue. The effect of such an injury largely depends upon the extent and location of damage. A person may survive massive injury to cortical areas, but a relatively small object penetrating deep brain stem structures can cause sudden death. Likewise, behav-ioral effects partly depend on which brain systems are damaged. This does not mean that there are specific brain centers that directly correspond to specific behaviors. There are, however, brain systems that are known to be important to various categories of psychological functioning. For example, damage to the temporal lobes is known to affect memory functions.

HEMATOMAS.　A hematoma is a collection of blood that eventually becomes enclosed within a fibrous membrane. Hematomas are usually caused by injuries that result in the rupture of small veins; gradual bleeding from the ruptured veins eventually forms a mass of blood. The membrane that forms around the blood tends to restrict the rate of enlargement. A hematoma may take days or weeks to develop. A head injury may result in a form of hematoma called a *subdural hematoma.* In a subdural hematoma, the rupture of small veins leads to an accumulation of blood under the *dura,* a thin, tough membrane encompassing the brain. The buildup of blood causes compression of the brain tissues, and the resulting pressure causes intense headaches. If a subdural hematoma is not corrected surgically, drowsiness, periodic loss of consciousness, and coma may result. Generally, a person recovers if the hematoma is surgically removed. The disorder may occur at any age but is more common among older adults (Agate, 1970).

As is true for other causes of brain damage, it is difficult to assess the effects of traumatic brain injuries on psychological functions. In cases of traumatic injury, what the individual was like before the accident must be determined largely from subjective reports by the patient, his family, friends, and associates. Still, when a similar brain injury is associated with similar psychological changes in a sizable number of people, a cause-and-effect relationship is suggested.

BRAIN TUMORS

Brain tumors (neoplasms) are growths in the brain composed of cells, fibers, and blood vessels. Tumors predominantly composed of cells tend to be soft and spongy; tumors containing a large amount of fibers have a relatively firm tex-ture. Growth is characteristic of all brain tumors. If neurosurgery is performed, any brain tumor that is not *completely* removed will recur after a period of time (Zulch, 1965). There are many types of brain tumors and the prognosis depends on the type of tumor, its size, location, and whether or not surgical removal is possible. Of particular importance to prognosis is whether a tumor is *benign* or *malignant*.

BENIGN BRAIN TUMORS.   A benign brain tumor is *not* likely to recur if it is totally removed by surgery. The growth of a benign tumor is typically slow and partially contained by surrounding brain tissue. A benign tumor does not infiltrate brain tissue although it may severely damage the surrounding brain tissue as it expands. Generally, a benign tumor is likely to contain a predominance of fiber, which results in a firm texture.

MALIGNANT BRAIN TUMORS.   Malignant tumors, even if totally removed by surgery, are likely to recur. Surgical treatment and X ray therapy may delay the spread of destruction, but the prognosis usually is poor. Unlike benign tumors, malignant tumors are characterized by an infiltrating and destructive growth process—that is, they penetrate the surrounding brain tissue. Malignant tumors are likely to be more cellular than benign tumors and therefore softer in texture.

Though the prognosis for benign tumors generally is more favorable than for malignant tumors, a benign tumor can be as serious as a malignant tumor. For example, a benign tumor located near the brain stem may be less accessible to surgery than tumors located in other portions of the brain. In addition, since brain stem structures control vital processes such as blood pressure, heart rate, and respiration, a tumor near this area is more serious than tumors located in other areas.

Brain tumors, like other CNS disorders, do not produce a specific set of psychological changes. As tumors increase in size, the increased pressure inside the cranium usually produces headaches, vomiting, and often ocular disturbances such as blurred or double vision. In addition, convulsions and a variety of sensorimotor changes may occur. Surgery may alleviate the pressure inside the cranium, but the damage to surrounding brain tissue produced by the tumor usually results in a persistence of presurgical defects (Woodburne, 1967).

INFECTIOUS DISEASES OF THE CNS

There are many diseases that can affect the nervous system. One effect on the nervous system that several different diseases can produce is inflammation of brain tissue. When such inflammation occurs, the condition is referred to as *encephalitis*. Other diseases, such as syphilis, may attack brain cells in a more specialized manner and produce a sequence of degenerative changes in the brain.

ENCEPHALITIS.   Encephalitis is an inflammatory process of the CNS that affects the functioning of the brain and spinal cord. Known causes of encephalitis include bacteria, syphilis spirochetes, fungi, protozoa, helminths (parasitic worms), and viruses. In 60% of reported cases of encephalitis in the United States between 1966 and 1971, the cause was unknown (Krugman & Ward, 1973). Of the cases that had known causes, 66% were a result of childhood diseases (mumps, varicella, measles, and rubella); 20% were caused by arthropod-borne viruses, and the remaining 12.5% were caused by several other known agents.

Both immediate and long-term effects of encephalitis partly depend upon the causative agent and the age of the person. For example, encephalitis caused by a mumps virus is fatal in only 1.2% of the cases and rarely is associated with any lasting impairment of the nervous system. However, in St. Louis Encephalitis (an arthropod-borne virus usually transmitted by mosquito bites), the overall mortality ranges from 5 to 30%. If adults are infected, recovery is usually complete. In infants under 6 months of age, permanent brain damage occurs in 10 to 40% of the cases. Subsequent problems in affected infants include seizures, hydrocephalus, and mental retardation (Krugman & Ward, 1973).

As a general rule, the highest frequency and most severe aftereffects occur in people who contracted encephalitis in the first few months of infancy. These aftereffects may involve impairment of motor movements or paralysis, and problems in emotional adjustment and intellectual functioning. Grand mal seizures are a common aftereffect. A child who contracts encephalitis after a year of age is far less likely to suffer from permanent aftereffects. Older children and adults may have a variety of temporary aftereffects, which may last from a few months to 1 or 2 years. During this period they may complain of headaches, sleeplessness, drowsiness, nervousness, depressed feelings, weakness, fatigue, irritability, difficulties in concentration, and speech disturbances. They may also have difficulty in walking and show minor tremors (Fields & Blattner, 1958). Permanent effects may also occur in older children and adults but are far less likely than when encephalitis is contracted in the first few months of life.

In the past, epidemic outbreaks of encephalitis have affected thousands of people. A reduction in the number of cases of encephalitis has been achieved by vaccinations for such causative agents as mumps, measles, and rubella. In addition, more effective techniques for controlling mosquito populations have reduced the incidence of encephalitis caused by arthropod-borne viruses. Outbreaks of viral encephalitis still occur following heavy rainfalls in regions where poor drainage permits ideal breeding conditions for mosquitoes.

GENERAL PARESIS. In 1826, Calmeil described a severe disorder, which he labeled *general paralysis of the insane*. Important characteristics of the disorder included confusion, memory loss, defective judgment, depression, and general mental and physical deterioration. As early as 1854, Esmarich and Jessen suspected that syphilis was a probable cause of this disorder, which came to be known as general paresis (incomplete paralysis). Final proof that general paresis is a result of brain syphilis was provided by Noguchi and Moore in 1913 (cited in Smith, 1969). General paresis, therefore, became one of the earliest types of psychoses with a clearly established organic cause.

Prior to the discovery of penicillin, there was little that could be done to alter the course of syphilis and other forms of veneral disease. During World War II, numerous infected GIs were confined to camps in Italy. With no effective treatment and minimal medical care, the camps became virtual prisons where men suffered without relief and armed guards prevented escape. The arrival of penicillin resulted in the dramatic release of thousands. A literary description of this event was provided by Bourjaily (1960):

> If you should ask me—not that anyone is likely to—my opinions of the scientific achievements of the war, I would reply that radar was an interesting gadget, rocketry a madman's toy, and the atom bomb what humanity deserved to get from the limited minds of its stupid national greeds and tribal prides. But the development of penicillin, which unlocked the gates of that encampment on the fairground, brought five thousand dead men back to life again; having been one of them, I cannot feel that any of the nonmedical achievements were in any way comparable.
>
> It was a tremendous thing for us, the arrival of the medicine; the endless lines, again, but for a reason this time—to receive the huge injections, every four hours for twenty-four; I cannot tell you how gladly I took those needles. Or how gladly I became one of the thousand butts of the final scatological comedy of the second twenty-four hours, when the lines were formed for prostate massages, so that cultures could be made—cultures that showed us, by the hundreds, cured [p. 353].

Despite discovery of the curative powers of penicillin, syphilis continues as a disease with high prevalence in the United States. It has been estimated that in 1972, approximately 140,000 cases of syphilis were treated in the United States; an additional 500,000 Americans might be infected with syphilis without knowing it (Krugman & Ward, 1973). The cause of syphilis is a thin, delicate organism with tapering ends called *Treponema pallidum*. This microscopic organism is usually transmitted by sexual intercourse. In about 10% of the cases there may be a mucous patch or chancre on the lip or tonsil, possibly a result of transmission by oral–genital relations. In addition, a woman infected after the eighteenth week of her pregnancy may transmit the organism to her fetus.

Untreated syphilis may progress through four stages: (1) primary syphilis, in which a chancrous sore may appear 10 to 90 days after contact, (2) secondary syphilis, in which symptoms appear 6 weeks to several months after infection, (3) latent syphilis, during which there may be no discernible clinical manifestations for several years,[1] and (4) late syphilis, which may become apparent several years or more after initial contact.

General paresis is a form of late syphilis in which there is direct involvement of the nerve cells. Pathological changes associated with general paresis include a thickening of the dura mater around the brain and a loss of brain weight due to cortical atrophy, particularly in the frontal or anterior areas. Often the convolutions of the cortex appear to be flattened and abnormally firm.

The clinical symptoms of general paresis usually do not become apparent until at least 10 years after an individual contracts syphilis (King & Nicol, 1969). For this reason, a high incidence of syphilis, such as that occurring during World War II, may lead to an increase in the number of people affected by general

---

[1] After 4 years, latent syphilis is rarely communicable except from mother to fetus during pregnancy (Krugman & Ward, 1973).

paresis 10 to 20 years later. General paresis is associated with a progressively severe sequence of psychological changes. King and Nicol (1969) have described three phases of general paresis: the *period of onset,* the *period of full development,* and the *period of decline.* During the period of onset, a person may appear less motivated to work, show less interest in his personal affairs, become increasingly irritable, and have difficulties in memory and concentration. Behaviors exhibited during this phase sometimes may be labeled as psychoneurotic.

During the period of full development, extensive and irreversible damage to the cortex leads to a variety of psychotic behaviors. The person may make grandiose claims such as being a secret advisor to the President, or designing a new experimental plane for a major aircraft corporation. Feelings that powerful people are plotting against him or other forms of paranoid ideation are common. To focus only on these symptoms may lead to a diagnosis of paranoia or paranoid schizophrenia. However, organic involvement is indicated by such additional symptoms as memory loss and confusion, which frequently indicate dysfunction of the CNS.

During the period of decline, mental and physical deterioration become more and more obvious. Gross memory loss and massive confusion gradually replace any distinctive pattern of psychotic behavior. During the terminal phase, the person becomes incontinent, emaciated, and prone to frequent convulsions. This phase may last for months or years. Without treatment, most patients die within 5 years after developing general paresis.

In summary, general paresis is one of the oldest known organic conditions leading to psychotic behavior. By the time of diagnosis, syphilitic destruction of brain tissue is typically severe and irreversible. The chronic brain syndrome that results is associated with various bizarre patterns of behavior.

APHASIA

Aphasia is any disturbance in the expression or the understanding of written or spoken symbols resulting from impairment of the CNS. Aphasia may result from traumatic injuries, tumors, or other CNS disorders discussed thus far. The damage to the brain underlying aphasia may occur at any time during an individual's life. Aphasia that results from damage before, during, or shortly after the birth process is referred to as *developmental* or *congenital aphasia.* Developmental aphasia may prevent or adversely affect the acquisition of language. If brain injury resulting in aphasia occurs after language has already developed, then the individual's ability to receive and communicate via the symbols of language may be seriously impaired. A person, for example, may be unable to recognize written or spoken words, or he may have difficulties in speaking or writing, or he may have both of these problems at once. The three common forms of aphasia are *expressive aphasia, receptive aphasia,* and *amnesic aphasia.*

EXPRESSIVE APHASIA. Expressive aphasia is a disturbance in an individual's ability to express himself due to difficulties in the production of written or spoken symbols that accurately convey his thoughts. He may "know" what he wants to say or write but he is unable to do so accurately. Another type of expressive aphasia is known as *apraxia*. Apraxia is the inability to guide muscle groups to carry out an intended motor response. In such a disturbance, the individual does not suffer from paralysis or a specific motor incapacity, but impairment of the CNS prevents normal control over voluntary muscle movements. Such a disturbance may interfere with an individual's attempts to write, manipulate objects, or make other responses requiring voluntary coordination of muscle movements. Generally, such disturbances of expressive behavior are a result of damage to frontal or anterior portions of the brain (Osgood & Miron, 1963).

RECEPTIVE APHASIA.   Receptive aphasia occurs when CNS impairment results in a disturbance of a person's perception of auditory and visual stimuli. The individual may be unable to recognize written or spoken words, familiar sounds such as a baby crying or a doorbell, or common objects such as a book or pen. He may perceive such objects clearly, yet they have no significance to him (Longerich & Bordeaux, 1954). Receptive aphasia results from damage to posterior portions of the brain, which include the auditory and visual projection systems in the posterior occipital lobes (Osgood & Miron, 1963).

AMNESIC APHASIA.   Amnesic aphasia involves a disturbance in language patterns resulting from amnesia or memory loss for the right names for various objects. For example, the person may not be able to think of the right word for a table or a chair. Amnesic aphasia rarely occurs in isolation. Both expressive and receptive aphasia typically involve some form of memory loss or amnesia. Amnesic loss may occur whether the lesions are in the frontal, temporal, or parietal lobes (Longerich & Bordeaux, 1954).

As previously stated, expressive aphasia is associated with damage to anterior portions of the brain and receptive aphasia is associated with damage to posterior portions. In addition, most aphasic disorders result from lesions in the left hemisphere. As you may recall, the left hemisphere controls the right side of the body, and vice versa. Most people are right-handed and, in most people, the left hemisphere of the brain plays a critical role in the development of language. Thus it is reasonable to suspect that left-handed people with aphasia might have impairment in the right hemisphere. Although virtually all right-handed aphasics suffer from damage in the left hemisphere, only about 50% of left-handed aphasics suffer from damage in the right hemisphere. Left-handed aphasics, therefore, are more likely to have impairment in the right hemisphere than are right-handed aphasics. However, the fact that 50% of left-handed aphasics have impairment in the left hemisphere rules out any simple one-to-one relationship between handedness and the location of damage in the left or right hemisphere. These findings do suggest that cerebral dominance associated with language functions is less clear among left-handed persons than among right-handed persons (Osgood & Miron, 1963).

If damage to the left hemisphere occurs near the time of birth, then language functions often can be taken over by the right hemisphere. This adaptability generally disappears once language is acquired. For this reason, aphasia resulting from damage to the left hemisphere during infancy or early childhood is more likely to be transitory than similar aphasia occurring during later years (Osgood & Miron, 1963).

To sum up, aphasia is a disturbance in the expressive and/or the receptive aspects of communication, written or spoken. Amnesia, or difficulties in symbolic memory, is a common symptom of aphasia. In most cases, aphasia results from damage to areas in the left hemisphere of the brain that control the production and understanding of symbolic communication. Damage to anterior or frontal portions of the brain is more likely to affect the expressive aspects of communication; damage to posterior portions is more likely to affect receptive aspects of communication. Damage in infancy may hinder the acquisition of language functions. If damage occurs later in life, it may severely disrupt established language functions. Aphasia may result from birth injury, brain tumors, automobile accidents, or a variety of other causes of CNS damage.

SUMMARY OF PART I

The disorders discussed in Part I may produce acute or chronic damage to the CNS. All are known to be associated with transient or permanent behavioral changes. Some of the disorders discussed in this section may also be associated with other conditions discussed later in this chapter. For example, brain tissue may be permanently scarred or overly sensitized by traumatic injuries or infections of the nervous system. If so, recurrent seizures may develop, which would lead to a final diagnosis of epilepsy.

Part II. Toxic Conditions Affecting the Nervous System

Many of the drugs and chemicals abounding in an industrialized society, though they enhance comfortable living, provide potential health hazards. The contemporary emphasis on environmental quality has led to public awareness of such dangers as exposure to high levels of radiation, consumption of fish contaminated with mercury, glue sniffing by children and adolescents, and the consumption of lead-based paint by children living in old homes and apartments. This section will present representative examples of substances that may have direct or indirect adverse effects on the nervous system. Such effects may be mild or severe, temporary or permanent. Some of these substances are readily available in almost every household.

A number of factors determine the severity of a toxic agent's effects on the nervous system. Some of these include the nature of the toxic substance, the quantity entering the body system, and the duration of an individual's exposure to the toxin. In many cases, the effects of a toxic substance vary as a function of how it enters the system—whether it is consumed by mouth, inhaled, or absorbed through the skin or mucous membranes. Another factor related to severity of intoxication is the ease with which symptoms of a toxic agent can be identified and treated. The symptoms may range from subtle to obvious signs of impairment or, in some cases, may be readily confused with similar symptoms produced by other organic or psychological disorders. Bromide poisoning, for example, can produce behavioral changes that may lead to a diagnosis of schizophrenia.

Each of the toxins discussed may be associated with behavioral as well as somatic changes.

COMMONLY AVAILABLE DRUGS

ASPIRIN (ACETYLSALICYLIC ACID). Aspirin, although often regarded by adults as harmless, can be fatal if taken in excess by small children. Since the introduction of candy-flavored aspirins in 1949, the incidence of childhood poisoning by aspirin has increased steadily. In 1959, 19.1% of a total of 25,327 cases of poisoning were due entirely to aspirin overdose (Arena, 1963). Approximately 100,000 children a year suffer from acute oral intoxication caused by aspirin (Deichmann & Gerarde, 1964). An overdose of aspirin leads to a disturbance of the acid–base balance and may cause respiratory and circulatory failure resulting in death. Some people who are hypersensitive to the effects of aspirin may have an intense respiratory disturbance that resembles an acute asthmatic attack.

Symptoms of an aspirin overdose include gastrointestinal upset, perspiration, thirst, fever, and respiratory difficulties. Primary neurological symptoms may indicate permanent neurological impairment, and intellectual and emotional disturbances may be associated with this impairment. Particularly with children, therefore, aspirin cannot be regarded as a harmless drug.

BROMIDES. Bromides used to be a common ingredient in nonprescription sedatives and sleeping pills, and in medications such as Bromo-seltzer that were frequently taken to alleviate headaches and other effects of excessive alcohol consumption. Cases of chronic bromide poisoning are still relatively common despite the fact that bromides have declined in popularity as therapeutic agents (Arena, 1963). Bromides affect the functioning of the CNS by replacing chloride in the fluid surrounding nerve cells. One effect of this physiological change is a depression of sensory and motor areas of the cortex of the brain.

Symptoms of chronic bromide poisoning include weakness, coarse tremors of the hands, incoordination, headaches, staggering gait, disturbed speech, mania, delirium, hallucinations, and coma. About 25% of all bromide cases have some form of skin condition, such as a rash. Often, the victim continues to take medication containing bromides in order to relieve the very symptoms that are produced by the drug. As changes accompanying chronic bromide intoxication may simulate those attributed to schizophrenia, it is not uncommon to find evidence of bromide poisoning among individuals admitted to mental hospitals. It has been estimated that 2–10% of patients admitted to mental hospitals show some evidence of bromide poisoning. In fact, bromide poisoning may simulate almost any functional or organic mental disorder (Arena, 1963).

TOXIC EFFECTS OF HEAVY METALS

LEAD POISONING. Lead is the most important heavy metal that can have adverse effects on the CNS (Aring & Trufant, 1953). The average American is exposed daily to a minimal amount of lead—in his food, his drink, and in the air he breathes. Derman (1970) estimated that the total daily intake of lead in the United States averages around .33 milligrams per person. Lead from the exhaust fumes of motor vehicles has been increasing this daily intake. The presence of minimal amounts of lead in the human system may not be a cause for concern, but high concentrations of lead can produce severe and sometimes permanent effects. There are a number of ways in which children and adults can suffer as a result of lead intoxication.

In children, the most common source of lead poisoning is from chewing or eating paint flakes that contain lead. Since paint companies no longer include lead as an ingredient, this source of lead intoxication will gradually diminish. Paint containing lead, however, is still an important health hazard, especially in old buildings in lower-income neighborhoods. The plaster, wallpaper, and putty in these buildings may also contain lead.

Although most children will not chew paint flakes even when readily available, some children go through an extended period of "pica," an intense appetite associated with a high frequency of chewing inedible substances. Understandably, these children are especially vulnerable to the dangers of lead poisoning (Derman, 1970). There is also some evidence that lead poisoning is most frequent at the time of tooth eruption (Aring & Trufant, 1953). An increase in chewing or biting activity often accompanies the teething process.

Lead poisoning is more severe in children than in adults. Apparently, lead is more actively stored in the bones during the process of growth than in the adult years (Aring & Trufant, 1953). It has been estimated that the mortality rate from lead poisoning in children is between 10 and 15% (Arena, 1963). In children, when the CNS is affected by lead poisoning (encephalopathic form), the mortality rate may be as high as 25%. Survivors often suffer recurring seizures and mental retardation (Derman, 1970).

Lead poisoning in adults occurs almost exclusively in the petroleum industry (Derman, 1970). The danger occurs during the blending process when fumes containing lead are released into the air. A person working in a poorly ventilated area may inhale sufficient quantities of lead to produce severe toxic effects. Temporary exposure to high amounts may have an excitatory effect on the CNS and result in delirium or manic-like states. Continued exposure may lead to inflammatory and degenerative lesions in the brain (Arena, 1963). However, the buildup of large concentrations in the adult brain happens only under unusual conditions.

MERCURY POISONING. The effects of mercury poisoning depend on the type of compound, the concentration, how it enters the system, and how long an individual is exposed to the contaminated source. Mercury can enter the body through the skin or mucous membranes, or it can be inhaled or eaten. Depend-

In the 1950s, fishing families living around Minamata Bay, Japan, were stricken by a mysterious disease of the central nervous system. Eventually it was found that they were being poisoned by the fish they ate. The bay—and the fish in it—were contaminated with chloromethylmercury from a chemical plant. This knowledge came too late to help many of the victims. Sixteen-year-old Tomoko Uemura, being bathed by her mother, was poisoned while still in the womb. (© W. Eugene Smith)

ing on these factors, the effects of mercury may be relatively mild, or death may result in a matter of hours. Mercury is a highly toxic, silver-white metal found in many compounds used in medicine and in the agricultural industry. In medicine, mercury salts are used in antiseptics, diuretics, and cathartics. In agriculture, mercury is used in insecticide powders and fumigants (Arena, 1963). Of the various mercury compounds, mercuric chloride is the most harmful if swallowed. Fish taken from waters contaminated by mercuric chloride can contain concentrations of mercury that are dangerous to human health. In the 1950s, for example, an outbreak of neurological disorders occurred in Japan because people ate fish taken from water contaminated by mercuric chloride (Deichmann & Gerarde, 1964). In recent years, United States citizens have been warned of dangerous concentrations of mercury found in swordfish and tuna.

Metallic mercury, such as that found in household thermometers, is unlikely to have toxic effects when consumed in small amounts because it is not absorbed into the body. For this reason, there is little danger if a child swallows a small amount of mercury because of a broken thermometer (Arena, 1963).

The symptoms of mercuric chloride poisoning occur a few minutes to a half-hour after consumption. Typically, there are complaints of severe gastrointestinal pain, an unpleasant metallic taste in the mouth, intense thirst, and nausea. Vomiting of bloodstained material may occur. The victim may die within a few hours due to vascular collapse. A victim who survives for 1 to 3 days may still die as a result of extensive kidney damage. Generally, the kidneys, liver, and CNS are all highly susceptible to the effects of mercury poisoning (Humes, 1970). The effects on the CNS are usually chronic. Psychological reactions include emotional disturbance, irritability, combativeness, difficulties in concentration, and loss of memory.

OTHER HOUSEHOLD AND INDUSTRIAL HAZARDS

GASOLINE.   The dangers of inhaling lead as one component of gasoline have already been discussed. However, even if all gasoline were leadfree there would still be serious dangers associated with frequent inhalation of gasoline fumes. Mild poisoning from gasoline fumes may occur in industries that use gasoline as a solvent or in filling stations where mechanics may inhale fumes in poorly ventilated areas. Another cause of gasoline intoxication is habitual sniffing of vapors by children and adolescents. Deliberate gasoline sniffing by juveniles produces a "high" that may be accompanied by hallucinations, vague erotic feelings, giddiness, or other pleasurable sensations.

The symptoms of gasoline poisoning depend on the concentration and duration of exposure. High concentrations may lead to sudden unconsciousness, coma, or death. Lower concentrations may produce staggering, mental confusion, awkwardness in movement, blurred speech, and difficulties in swallowing. Repeated exposure to gasoline fumes (chronic poisoning) may result in a loss of appetite, weight loss, nausea, headaches, nervousness, agitation, muscular weakness, and cramps. The person may become very apathetic, unresponsive, and appear confused. He may have tremors, loss of memory, seizures, or other signs of neurological impairment. Generally, adequate ventilation greatly reduces any danger from intoxication by gasoline fumes. If the fumes become concentrated in the air, however, gasoline can be extremely toxic. It has been estimated that about .3% gasoline vapor in the air will make an average adult dizzy in 15 minutes. Exposure to concentrations of 1–2% for over an hour may prove fatal.

GLUE SNIFFING (PLASTIC CEMENT).   Many plastic cements used in model building or household repairs contain a number of potentially toxic ingredients. Some of the more volatile components of glue are toluene, acetone, and isopropanol. Substances found in lesser amounts that can act as CNS depressants are carbon tetrachloride, chloroform, and ethylene dichloride. Intoxication from plastic cement fumes primarily is a result of habitual glue sniffing by children and adolescents. To maximize the concentration of fumes, adolescents sometimes put the glue in a rag or paper bag. Inhalation may produce feelings of exhilaration, euphoria, or excitement. Inhalation of high amounts may cause drowsiness or even hallucinations. It also has been suspected as a cause of kidney damage; some deaths from asphyxiation have apparently resulted. Apparently, as is true with alcohol, some tolerance may develop with repeated use. A chronic glue sniffer may use more than a dozen tubes of plastic cement a day (Oppelt, 1970).

The symptoms of chronic glue sniffing include loss of appetite, weight loss, irritation of the mucous membrane, and a foul breath. Although problems in behavioral adjustment are more frequent among glue sniffers, it has not been established that such problems are a direct result of the ingredients found in plastic cement. Chronic glue sniffing, for example, may be a symptom of already existing problems in adjustment (Oppelt, 1970).

IONIZING RADIATION

Even small amounts of ionizing radiation can cause some degree of damage to cells or tissues. If the dose is not excessive, however, all cells (with the apparent exception of germ cells) recover from radiation effects. Such radiation effects are measured in units called rems. Whenever an X ray or fluoroscope is used for diagnostic purposes, an individual is exposed to ionizing radiation. In a dental X ray, for example, about 5 rems are delivered to the patient's jaw and about .005 rem of stray radiation to the reproductive organs (Deichmann & Gerarde, 1964). Although the potentially harmful effects of radiation depend on which tissues of the body are being X rayed, a single dose of as much as 50 rems may not cause visible symptoms. Repeated doses of radiation, however, have cumulative effects even at levels far below the lethal range of 400 to 500 rems. The most serious effect is an increased risk of cancer. Frequent exposure to X rays, therefore, is dangerous, particularly if the tissue being X rayed is highly sensitive to radiation.

The tissue most sensitive to radiation is the neuroblast (the primitive form of the fetal nervous system, which develops early in the pregnancy period). For this reason, X rays taken in early pregnancy are particularly dangerous to the developing organism.

Despite science fiction stories to the contrary, it is unlikely that sublethal doses of radiation can produce psychological changes by damaging the brain tissue of an adult, since mature nerve cells are among the tissues least sensitive to radiation. Radiation might affect the brain indirectly by damaging the vascular system. The high levels of radiation found near an atomic explosion may directly affect the brain of an adult. However, an individual that close to the blast center would also suffer from the effects of the blast and intense heat, making it difficult to attribute brain damage to radiation only (Hicks, 1953). Because the developing nervous system of a fetus is highly sensitive to radiation, pregnant women near the blast center in Hiroshima and Nagasaki were more likely to give birth to infants with serious neurological defects—such as microcephalism or hydrocephalism.[2]

---

[2] A complete description of these disorders is presented in Chapter 9.

SUMMARY OF PART II

Numerous toxic agents have the potential to affect behavior by altering the functioning of the CNS. Depending on the nature of the toxin and other factors, the effects on the CNS may be transient or permanent, mild or severe. The effects of toxic agents on behavior may be indirect and nonspecific, depending on the nature and extent of neurological involvement. In some cases, such as glue sniffing, problems in adjustment may precede exposure to the toxic agent. In such instances, it is difficult to determine to what extent psychological problems are due to exposure to the toxic agent.

Part III. The Epilepsies

Epilepsy is one of the oldest and least understood disorders. The early Romans regarded it as a sacred disease and assumed that an epileptic attack was a result of seizure by the gods. Hippocrates maintained that epilepsy was a disorder of the brain, but several centuries later, the most frequent explanation was seizure by an evil spirit or devil. A biblical passage that reflects this belief can be found in Luke 9:39:

> And, lo, a spirit taketh him, and he suddenly crieth out; and it teareth him that he foameth again, and bruising him hardly departeth from him.

Although today the word *seizure* may refer only to the manifestation of a neurological disorder, the historical meaning for many centuries was "seizure *by the devil*." Treatment of epilepsy has included castration, arsenic administration, removal of a portion of the skull, and percussion of the spine with a mallet (Guerrant, Anderson, Fischer, Weinstein, Jaros, & Deskins, 1962). It is possible that the historical link between epilepsy and possession by the devil enhanced negative associations with the disorder, which were reflected in sociolegal practices. In 1956, 17 states still prohibited marriage by an epileptic, 18 provided for possible sterilization, and most states prohibited epileptics from driving an automobile. In addition, it was more difficult for an epileptic to secure employment or pursue higher education than it was for people with any other handicapping condition (Barrow & Fabing, 1966).

CHANGES IN SOCIAL ATTITUDES AND
LEGAL RESTRICTIONS SINCE 1956

Although negative attitudes toward epileptics and unnecessary restrictions on their participation in society remain, substantial changes have occurred since 1956. Many of these changes, particularly those involving state laws, were facilitated by the initial publication of *Epilepsy and the Law* by Barrow and Fabing in 1956. According to the late Earl Warren, former Chief Justice of the United States: "*Epilepsy and the Law* probably caused more legislatures to amend more laws in a shorter period of time than any similar research project of the past two decades [Barrow & Fabing, 1966]."

From 1956 to 1966, the number of states prohibiting marriage by epileptics was reduced from 17 to 3, and the number of states providing for sterilization of epileptics was reduced from 18 to 13 (most of which no longer practiced sterilization). In 1956, most states did not allow epileptics to drive an automobile. By 1966, all but one state allowed epileptics to drive, provided there was evidence that seizures had been under control for a reasonable period of time. In more than half the states, epileptics were able to obtain automobile insurance policies. Less substantial gains were made in the area of employment opportunities. In 1960, a survey conducted by the Department of Labor, Bureau of Labor Statistics indicated that only 8% of the employers surveyed said that they would hire epileptics. It was also noted that in the mid-1960s most colleges and universities accepted epileptics only conditionally and many would not accept them at all (Barrow & Fabing, 1966).

By the early 1970s, there were minimal additional changes in the legal and social conditions affecting the epileptic. Sterilization of epileptics under certain conditions was still legal in 10 states. The practice of barring many epileptics from schools and universities continued as well as the practice of rejecting epileptics by the armed services. Up to 25% of medically controlled epileptics of normal intelligence were chronically unemployed (*Data Pak*, published by the Epilepsy Foundation of America, 1974).

INCIDENCE

It has been estimated that 2 out of every 100 persons—about 4 million people—have some form of epilepsy (*Data Pak*, Epilepsy Foundation of America). Livingston (1963) reported that it was a chronic disorder second only to mental retardation. It is more common than cerebral palsy, tuberculosis, or infantile paralysis (prior to the development of the polio vaccine). Of all the neurological disorders discussed in this chapter, epilepsy is the most prevalent.

WHAT IS EPILEPSY?

The public stereotype of an epileptic attack or seizure is based primarily on one type of convulsive disorder called *grand mal epilepsy*. During a grand mal attack, an afflicted individual typically falls to the ground and exhibits intense shaking movements, thrashing of the arms and legs, foaming at the mouth, and a rhythmic biting of the jaws (which sometimes results in injury to the tongue). Although this is a common form of convulsive disorder, there are a number of other types of epilepsy that do not involve this pattern of behavior. Petit mal seizures, for example, often pass unnoticed. Broadly defined, an epileptic attack or seizure is an abnormal discharge of neural activity within the brain.

The abnormal discharge may be localized in a particular brain area or it may be generalized, involving almost all cortical areas. A localized seizure may remain localized for its duration or, if spreading is extensive, it may become generalized. In localized seizures, depending on the brain areas involved, there may or may not be convulsive movements of the body. However, a generalized discharge that involves all areas of the cortex (grand mal attack) is always accompanied by convulsive movements.

It is important to note that epilepsy is a neurophysiological disorder rather than a structural disorder of the brain. That is, it is not like a brain lesion, tumor, or any structural alteration of the brain that can be identified by examining sections of brain tissue. A seizure occurs when an electrochemical disturbance results in a sudden discharge of electrical activity in one or more neural systems in the brain. The same neural systems may function normally most of the time; but if stimulation exceeds the convulsive threshold a discharge and seizure will occur. If the discharge begins in or spreads to motor areas of the brain, which regulate bodily movement, then convulsive movements of the body will occur. If the neural discharge does not affect motor areas of the brain, the individual typically loses consciousness but does not exhibit convulsive movements. Such a seizure may be identified by an instrument called the electroencephalograph (EEG), which records electrical activity of the brain in the form of lines traced on paper. The resulting record is called an electroencephalogram.

A seizure that does not involve convulsive movements but may be identified by EEG recordings is referred to as *subclinical*. A seizure that involves convulsive movements or other observable clinical signs is referred to as a *clinical seizure*. A person with some acting skills who knows the behavior pattern associated with seizures can successfully fake a clinical seizure. An example of such faking is given by Boshes and Gibbs (1972):

> A man, who had paid a "witch-doctor" to help him avoid the draft in the Second World War, had a seizure when he was arrested as a purse-snatcher. Draft examiners, suspicious of the genuineness of his seizures, had done a sensory examination with lighted cigarettes, but the patient had remained unresponsive. In the hospital his electroencephalogram was normal awake and asleep, even during seizures in which his pupils dilated and in which he urinated and foamed at the mouth. In these seizures the electroencephalogram showed only muscle potentials and movement artifacts. After the seizure there was no slow activity, such as usually occurs with postseizure stupor. He could have succeeded in fooling his examiners if he had not been so proud of his ability and had not wanted it recognized. In the midst of a violent tonic–clonic seizure, while a doctor was examining his dilated pupils with an ophthalmoscope, he sucked in a great bubble of saliva and whispered in the doctor's ear, "How am I doing, Doc?" [pp. 82–83].

Although the use of an EEG may help in identifying such instances of fakery, it cannot be relied upon exclusively. One reason is that an accurate recording cannot be obtained during seizures that result in violent convulsive movements. A second reason is that nearly 25% of individuals who have clinical seizures of the grand mal type have normal EEG recordings both when they are awake and when they are asleep (Boshes & Gibbs, 1972).

In defining epilepsy as a neurophysiological disorder, it is important to note that although all epileptics have had clinical or subclinical seizures, the occurrence of a seizure in itself does not warrant a diagnosis of epilepsy. *Any* individual can have a seizure if unusual conditions produce stimulation that exceeds the convulsive threshold of the nervous system. For example, excessive amounts of certain drugs, brain infections, or electric shock can be a potential cause of seizure activity. A diagnosis of epilepsy is generally reserved for individuals who have recurring seizures over a period of time. Epilepsy may begin in childhood, during adolescence, or at any time during an individual's adult life. However, epilepsy is most likely to appear initially in the childhood years. Nearly 90% of epileptics develop their first symptoms prior to age 20 (Livingston, 1963).

GENERAL ETIOLOGY

In most cases, the specific causes of epilepsy cannot be identified. Epilepsy was once thought to be exclusively an inherited disorder, but it is now recognized that although heredity may be a predisposing factor in some individuals, there are multiple nonhereditary causes. The most common causes probably include brain infections, particularly encephalitis, and brain trauma. Trauma may be a result of difficulties during the birth process or later injuries to the brain. Potential causes of epilepsy will be discussed in more detail when specific types of epilepsy are considered.

FACTORS THAT MAY PRECIPITATE AN EPILEPTIC SEIZURE

Most epileptic attacks appear to occur spontaneously without any readily identifiable precipitating factor. In a small percentage of the cases, however, seizures appear to be triggered by some form of auditory, visual, or somatic stimulation. A common example, particularly in children with petit mal epilepsy, is the onset of a seizure following exposure to a bright, flickering light. One source of such stimulation can be a flickering light provided by a defective television. It has been suggested that induction of seizures by flickering lights is more likely in Britain than in the United States because the flicker threshold for the United States television system is five times greater than that for the British system. Television-induced seizures are, in fact, more common in Britain than in the United States (Livingston, 1963).

A well-established factor related to an increase in the likelihood of seizures is degree of arousal. Seizures occur much more frequently during sleep or drowsy states. For this reason, diagnostic procedures for determining the presence of seizure activity often involve natural sleep or the artificial induction of sleep. Other factors known to be associated with a higher probability that a seizure will occur include hyperventilation, menstruation, withdrawal from anticonvulsant drugs, and a stressful environment.

AURAS

In some forms of epilepsy, there may be a warning sensation, called an *aura*, which precedes loss of consciousness. If the aura is long enough, it may give the person time to take precautions, such as lying down to avoid falling as seizure activity spreads. The aura is actually the initial phase of seizure activity rather than a separate process. Examples of auras include abdominal pain, headaches, dizziness, spots before the eyes, humming or buzzing sensations, musical sounds, and peculiar odors or tastes.

SPECIFIC TYPES OF EPILEPTIC SEIZURES

GRAND MAL EPILEPSY.   Grand mal epilepsy is the most common of the epileptic disorders. As we mentioned earlier, the behavioral manifestations of a grand mal attack were described by the early Greeks and Romans. The general public is most likely to equate this type of seizure with epilepsy in general.

Sometimes an individual will give a loud cry or shriek before the onset of a grand mal seizure. If the individual is standing when seizure activity begins, he typically becomes very rigid and falls in whatever direction he is leaning. The rigid muscular extension (*tonic* phase) of the extremities rapidly changes to violent jerking movements of the arms, legs, and trunk (*clonic* phase). The person may bite his tongue as his jaws rhythmically and forcefully move open and shut. Voluntary control over the bladder and bowels may be lost. Breathing may become jerky or temporarily suspended, causing the face to become blue. The seizure may vary in length from less than a minute to 30 minutes or more. It may vary in frequency from many times a day to once in several years. Usually, if the seizure is brief, an individual may return to normal functioning within minutes. If the seizure is long, the person may pass into a very deep sleep, after which he may experience confusion, fatigue, headaches, and nausea. These postconvulsive symptoms may last for a few moments or continue for up to a week (Livingston, 1963).

The causes of grand mal seizures are generally nonspecific and usually unknown. Fortunately, when grand mal epilepsy is not complicated by the presence of any other disorder, the seizures can be controlled or prevented in approximately 85% of the cases by anticonvulsant drugs.

PETIT MAL EPILEPSY.   Petit mal epilepsy is almost exclusively a childhood disorder. It occurs most frequently between the ages of 4 and 8 and almost never after puberty. Although petit mal is regarded as a common type of epilepsy, its actual prevalence would be very difficult to assess. Unlike grand mal attacks, a child during a petit mal attack may show minimal behavioral changes and the disorder may go undetected. Changes occurring during a petit mal attack may involve simply staring with momentary loss of consciousness or rhythmic eye blinking, head nodding, jerking of the arms, or a sudden loss of posture. If standing, a child may stagger or sway but rarely falls. Occasionally, smacking movements of the lips or urination may occur. Seizures are usually very brief, lasting between 5 and 30 seconds, but often occur frequently. A child may have from 5 to 100 seizures a day. After an attack, the child is usually alert and returns immediately to whatever he was doing before the attack (Boshes & Gibbs, 1972).

Petit mal attacks often disappear around the age of pubescence, with or without treatment by anticonvulsant drugs. Children with petit mal attacks may later have grand mal or other types of seizures in the adolescent or adult years. In more than 50% of petit mal cases, however, no other types of seizures develop. Petit mal seizures are rarely associated with subsequent development of psychomotor epilepsy. Children with petit mal epilepsy usually have average or above average intelligence and are unlikely to develop personality disorders.

The causes of petit mal epilepsy, in the majority of cases, are unknown. Encephalitis, however, is the most common presumed cause of petit mal epilepsy. Head trauma, birth injury, and tumors rarely cause petit mal attacks.

Early treatment of petit mal with an anticonvulsant drug may eliminate or greatly reduce seizure activity in approximately 83% of the cases. In addition, a ketogenic diet (a large amount of fat, moderate amounts of protein, and minimal carbohydrates and starches) may also help to reduce seizures in children under 8 years of age (Boshes & Gibbs, 1972).

PSYCHOMOTOR EPILEPSY.   According to Guerrant *et al.* (1962), the introduction of the EEG in the mid-1930s allowed Gibbs and Lennox to delineate the psychomotor type of epilepsy. Studies with EEGs indicated that the area of the brain primarily affected was the temporal lobe—either the left temporal lobe, the right temporal lobe, or both. For this reason, psychomotor epilepsy is sometimes referred to as *temporal lobe epilepsy*. Because the anterior portion of the temporal lobe is the area from which most abnormal activity is recorded, a more precise diagnostic label is *anterior temporal lobe epilepsy*. Horowitz (1970) estimates that approximately one-fourth of all epileptic disorders are of the psychomotor type. Unlike other forms of epilepsy, the disorder occurs almost exclusively in adults. Although the seizure activity originates in the anterior temporal lobe, it often spreads to areas outside the temporal lobe. When this occurs, a clinically evident psychomotor seizure is the result. Psychomotor epilepsy is frequently complicated by seizures of the grand mal type.

Psychomotor seizures may vary in duration from a moment to hours or even days. However, most cases are characterized by frequently occurring seizures with an abrupt onset, brief seizure activity, and sudden termination.

Unlike grand mal and petit mal seizures, the behavioral changes during a psychomotor seizure may vary considerably and may often be confused with alcohol intoxication. The occurrence of various deviant behaviors during an attack may lead to the assumption that the primary difficulties are psychological *rather than* neurological in nature. Note that we are referring to behaviors *during* an actual seizure episode. The general problems of adjustment associated with psychomotor epilepsy during nonseizure periods will be discussed later.

During a psychomotor seizure, an individual may simply stare, drool, smack lips, and mumble, or he may run, jump, dance, sing, cry, shout, fight, or undress. The individual may show evidence of fearfulness or belligerence accompanied by temper outbursts. Occasionally, violent crimes including murder have been committed. It has been speculated that Vincent van Gogh cut off his ear during a psychomotor attack.

The causes of psychomotor epilepsy are largely nonspecific or unknown. Trauma to the brain and encephalitis are assumed to be the most common causes. There is little evidence that birth complications, which may be associated with other types of epilepsy, are associated with the psychomotor type (Boshes & Gibbs, 1972).

Treatment of psychomotor epilepsy generally consists of anticonvulsant drugs. However, in some cases, seizures are not controlled by anticonvulsant drugs. If drug treatment is not successful, neurosurgical lesions in the temporal lobe or total removal of the temporal lobe may be used to reduce or eliminate seizures. Such neurosurgery should be limited to individuals who are both socially and vocationally incapacitated by frequent seizures, however, as it may bring about other handicaps.

PSYCHOMOTOR EPILEPSY AND PSYCHOLOGICAL PROBLEMS. The controversy surrounding psychomotor epilepsy has not focused on deviant behaviors that occur during actual seizure episodes, but on the relationship of psychomotor epilepsy to overall psychological adjustment. Boshes and Gibbs (1972) have drawn this conclusion:

> A high percentage of patients with an anterior temporal focus have more or less continuous personality defects or psychiatric disorder. Despite reports to the contrary, the great majority of patients with what has been called an "epileptic personality" are psychomotor epileptics; patients with other types of epilepsy usually have normal personalities [p. 57].

According to these authors, the psychiatric aspects of adjustment may be more evident and more handicapping than the actual psychomotor seizures. They suggest that continuing psychological problems not associated with specific seizure activity are an independent complication of psychomotor epilepsy. Presumably, these problems stem from a different process of brain functioning and may even become more severe when seizures are controlled by medication. Therefore, Boshes and Gibbs assume that in addition to the problems directly associated with seizure activity, the psychomotor epileptic is much more likely than other epileptics to encounter problems in general adjustment.

Boshes and Gibbs' conclusion that psychomotor epilepsy is associated with more general psychological problems than other types of epilepsy is still subject to controversy. Research on this question has been hampered by complicated methodological problems, particularly those involving the selection of subjects for experimental and control groups. A major problem involves the subjects who are actually available for research. Subjects often are drawn from populations receiving outpatient or inpatient care at a large medical center or charity hospital. But such subjects may not be representative of the general population. They may differ in educational background, social class, willingness to participate as a subject, severity of illness, or other variables that may be related to general problems in psychological adjustment. Such subjects may not be comparable to epileptics from different cultural circumstances and financial means who rely on the care of a private physician.

Guerrant *et al.* (1962) attempted to assess potential differences in personality between psychomotor epileptics, grand mal epileptics, and a chronically ill, nonepileptic control group. All subjects were outpatients in a medical setting. Attempts were made to match the three groups according to age, sex, duration of illness, education, marital status, type of home community, and social class. Extensive neurological evaluations were used to refine classification of the three groups. For example, psychomotor epileptics with other obvious neurological problems, such as a lesion or tumor, were not included in the psychomotor group. Both psychological and psychiatric evaluations were obtained for all subjects. Results were that 90% of the subjects in each of the three groups were viewed by the psychiatrists as having functional emotional disorders. No significant differences in personality disturbances were noted between the three groups. All three groups displayed severe personality disturbances, primarily of a nonpsychotic nature. In general, agreement between psychological and psychiatric evaluations was high except for evaluations pertaining to the incidence of organic brain syndromes. Whereas psychological testing yielded no significant differences between the three groups, results of psychiatric evaluation indicated that 47% of the psychomotor group, 27% of the grand mal group, and only 4% of the chronically ill, nonepileptic group were suspected of having an organic brain syndrome.[3] Results, therefore, failed to support the hypothesis that personality disturbances are more frequent among psychomotor epileptics than among either grand mal epileptics or a chronically ill control group of nonepileptics. However, all three groups were viewed by both psychologists and psychiatrists as having a very high percentage of psychological problems. Guerrant *et al.* readily acknowledge that findings predominantly based on lower-class outpatients in hospital clinics cannot be generalized to dissimilar populations of epileptics. One interpretation of this research is that any group of outpatients with low socioeconomic backgrounds and chronic disorders is likely to have more psychological problems than the general population. But this interpretation rules out any definitive statements about the relationships between various types of epilepsy and personality disturbances.

Horowitz (1970) attempted to discern whether the reduction or elimination of seizure activity among psychomotor epileptics resulted in a corresponding improvement in psychosocial adjustment. The subjects were seriously handicapped psychomotor epileptics with medically uncontrollable seizures who were candidates for neurosurgical intervention.[4] Horowitz recognized that these subjects probably had a much greater tendency toward inadequate control of both behavior and seizures than psychomotor epileptics under the care of a private physician. Neurosurgical treatment consisted of either temporal lobectomy (complete removal of the temporal lobe) or stereotaxic lesions in the temporal

---

[3] The authors acknowledge the fact that the psychomotor group took more drugs than the other two groups. Such factors as recent memory, which are involved in assessing the presence of an organic brain syndrome, may have been affected by the higher drug intake in the psychomotor group.

[4] Medically uncontrollable seizures are seizures that show little or no reduction when treated with anticonvulsant drugs.

lobe (a procedure that allows precision in making relatively small lesions in particular areas of the brain). A reduction or elimination of seizure activity was surgically achieved in approximately 80% of the subjects. The psychosocial problems that were present prior to surgery, such as depression, paranoia, aggressive behavior, and rage, persisted after surgery. In some cases, cognitive impairment such as memory difficulties appeared to be even worse after surgery than before, despite a reduction in seizure activity. In this particular population of psychomotor epileptics, therefore, a reduction or elimination of seizure activity yielded no corresponding improvement in psychosocial problems.

Although psychological problems may remain when psychomotor seizures are reduced by drugs or surgery, this fact does not prove that psychological problems associated with psychomotor epilepsy are derived from an organic brain syndrome. Even a demonstration that psychological problems are more prevalent among psychomotor epileptics than other epileptics would not provide direct evidence that such problems were organically derived. Although all individuals with a diagnosis of epilepsy have the general problem of coping with negative social attitudes toward epilepsy, we cannot assume that environmental factors are similar for individuals with different types of epilepsy. For example, consider the possible differences in social reactions to the following types of seizure episodes: (1) a grand mal seizure, during which the individual suddenly cries out, falls to the ground, and exhibits intense jerking movements of the arms, legs, and trunk; (2) a petit mal seizure, which may involve only momentary staring and loss of consciousness, or minor behavioral changes such as rhythmic blinking of the eyes, head nodding, or a temporary loss of posture; (3) a psychomotor seizure, during which a person may undress in a seductive manner, become violently aggressive, or inappropriately dance and sing. Most people are likely to recognize grand mal attacks as epilepsy, but petit mal and psychomotor attacks may not be recognized as epilepsy. The peculiar, sometimes bizarre, behavior associated with a psychomotor attack may be interpreted as indications of sexual perversion or insanity. Public reaction to a petit mal attack, however, may be minimal or nonexistent. Social reactions, therefore, probably will be very different for different types of epilepsy, but they are all potentially important influences on an individual's psychosocial adjustment.

Where general personality adjustment is concerned, it is not possible to determine the relative contributions of environmental and organic factors. Especially in regard to psychomotor epilepsy, there may be a complex interaction between organic and environmental factors that makes adequate psychosocial adjustment an especially difficult task. Even so, there may be many individuals with psychomotor epilepsy who function quite normally. A case history on psychomotor epilepsy provided by Horowitz (1970) illustrates the difficulty in separating neurological and environmental determinants of behavior. In this particular case, a girl with medically uncontrollable seizures had agreed to participate in research that might involve neurosurgery as a means of reducing or eliminating seizures.

■ Nancy was twenty years old, unmarried, with a twelve year history of psychomotor seizures. An illegitimate child, she had been sexually molested by her stepfather at age twelve. Her mother apparently did not adequately care for her in her early years. She stated that she had a difficult time making friends because everyone was afraid of or was "against" epileptics. In her sophomore year of high school she was prevented from taking the school bus because it was deemed unsafe for the other children to ride with an epileptic. She attended services at a fundamentalist church where the congregation felt that they could cure her of her seizures through prayer. When after a year there was no improvement, they banished her from their congregation, stating that she obviously was possessed by the devil.

In interviews, Nancy presented herself as a chatty, pleasant, moral girl who felt she was maligned by those in her environment because she had epilepsy. The motor components to her seizures expressed, at times, aggressive or seductive behavior. For example, when her family situation was particularly tense during her mid-adolescence, she commonly assaulted her mother during a seizure. She was sent to a home for juveniles because of this aggressive behavior. While there, she had serious arguments with another girl and during one of her seizures ran after the girl with a knife. While at home or at school she occasionally would begin to undress herself seductively during her seizures. It was noted that she had fewer seizures when away from her tense family situation.

Her attitude toward the study was that she was anxious to offer herself as a patient "for the sake of research," even though this might not be of any direct benefit to her. Along with this cooperative attitude, she expressed a great deal of displaced hostility by complaining about doctors who were treating a back injury of her stepfather. She felt that they were not interested in him because he was poor. On the ward during her electrode implantations,[5] she seemed to divide the nurses into "good" and "bad" ones. She appeared always to criticize care that she received elsewhere or from someone else rather than criticizing any personnel directly. After electrode implantation the DVR provided her with secretarial training at a junior college. She moved away from home and her seizures were considerably reduced. She found a boy friend who had a serious physical disability and they mutually supported each other against what appeared to them a hostile environment.

When the neurosurgeon suggested surgery to reduce or eliminate her seizures, Nancy rejected this, stating that she could now withstand what people thought of epileptics. The aggressive component of her seizures continued but was milder and accepted to a greater extent by others. For example, one day, while in class, she entered a psychomotor seizure state and began hitting her teacher on the back. The class and the teacher thought this an amusing situa-

---

[5] The electrode implantations were not a therapeutic procedure. They were used as a diagnostic technique to allow EEG recordings from subcortical areas of the brain. The procedure is a neurosurgical operation during which small electrodes are implanted in brain tissue. Neurological damage resulting from such a procedure is minimal, although patients may take up to 4 weeks to return to their preoperative level of functioning.

tion, since everyone recognized that the teacher was disliked for being too authoritarian [pp. 91–92].

In short, psychological problems are generally thought to be more prevalent among psychomotor epileptics than other types of epilepsy. This contention appears to be based more on clinical impressions than on empirical research. Even so, it has been noted consistently that psychomotor epileptics have a much higher incidence of psychological problems than that found in the general population. The explanation for such problems may lie in a complex interaction between neurological and environmental factors.

SUMMARY OF PART III

There are other types of epilepsy in addition to those presented in this section. The types we have discussed, however, serve to illustrate the special problems epileptics face in regard to social adjustment as well as the complex nature of the disorder. *Most* epileptics are of average or above average intelligence and evidence adequate personal and social adjustment. Except during seizure episodes, *most* epileptics are able to engage in the same kinds of physical activities as the average nonepileptic. Recently, for example, the American Medical Association declared that there is no medical reason why epileptics should be systematically excluded from such contact sports as football. There appears to be little or no relationship between vigorous physical activity and an increase in the frequency of seizures (Livingston, 1963).

In about 50% of all cases of epilepsy, complete control of seizures is possible with anticonvulsant drugs. Another 30% can be controlled to a level permitting rehabilitation. In about 20% of the cases, epilepsy is a disabling disorder (Barrow & Fabing, 1966).

Although notable legal and social progress has been made, most adult epileptics in today's society have had to contend with such obstacles as legal restrictions, negative social attitudes, and restrictive educational and employment practices. As improvement in these areas continues, it appears likely that these potentially important limitations on personal and social adjustment will diminish. Even in psychomotor epilepsy, where there may be at least an indirect relationship between the disorder and psychological problems, an improvement in environmental circumstances is likely to lead to a reduction in problems of adjustment.

Part IV. Degenerative Diseases Associated with Aging

A number of changes are associated with the aging process, such as a tendency to reminisce and forgetfulness. Such changes are typical of the normal aging process. They should not be confused with senility or the more severe psychological changes associated with the organic brain syndromes discussed in this section.

Brain syndromes occurring in later life may be acute or chronic. Acute brain syndromes may produce clouding of consciousness, confusion, delirium, and impairment of recent memory. Memory for remote events, however, is often preserved. Acute brain syndromes generally do not involve structural damage to the brain. They appear to be due to other disorders of the bodily system which may affect brain functioning. If such disorders are corrected, the signs of neurological dysfunction may disappear. It has been estimated that acute brain syndromes account for approximately 10–25% of the brain syndromes among elderly persons who previously appeared to be normal (Kay, 1972).

Chronic brain syndromes are among the most severe and disabling disorders that afflict the elderly. The decline in the birthrate, coupled with an increase in life expectancy, has led to a notable increase in the percentage of older people. In Britain, for example, there are four times as many people over 65 as there were at the turn of the century and eight times as many people over 85. It has been estimated that 4–6% of people over 65 and 20% of people over 80 suffer from a definite chronic brain syndrome. About 75% of the people between the ages of 65 and 74 who are admitted for the first time in state and county mental hospitals in the United States have some form of brain syndrome. About 90% of those over 75 have brain syndromes. The majority of these first admissions is composed of two types of chronic brain syndromes, arteriosclerotic dementia and senile dementia (Kay, 1972).

TYPES OF CHRONIC BRAIN SYNDROMES
OCCURRING IN LATER LIFE

ARTERIOSCLEROTIC DEMENTIA.   The normal functioning of the brain is heavily dependent on a continuous supply of blood from a healthy vascular system. If this blood supply is altered over a period of time, there may be degenerative changes in the tissues of the brain. Thus, a vascular disease that diminishes the supply of blood to the brain may result in progressive, degenerative changes in the brain (Rothschild, 1945). Arteriosclerotic dementia is a type of chronic brain syndrome occurring in later life that is a result of a progressive cerebral vascular disease. It has been estimated that arteriosclerotic dementia accounts for 8–14% of mental disorders occurring among the elderly (Anderson, 1967).

Arteriosclerotic dementia has its origins in a process called *atherosclerosis,* which begins in the arteries. Atherosclerosis is a result of two types of changes in the vascular system. The first is *atheroma,* the depositing of a fatty substance containing a large amount of cholesterol along the internal walls of the arteries. As this substance builds up within the walls of the arteries, it hinders the normal flow of blood. The second change is *thrombosis,* the forming of a blood clot inside the artery. The effect of both these changes is a gradual or sudden blocking of the blood flow through the arteries. As surrounding tissues are increasingly deprived of blood, degeneration occurs. Other disorders, such as diabetes or hypertension, tend to accelerate this process (Irvin, Bagnall, & Smith, 1970). As cerebral structures become affected, a series of minor cerebrovascular accidents (little strokes) may occur. The disorder progressively involves the brain until clinical signs of a chronic brain syndrome lead to a diagnosis of arteriosclerotic dementia.

Behavioral changes associated with arteriosclerotic dementia include emotional instability, disturbances in speech and vision, confusion, disturbances in recent memory, and a general decline in intellectual abilities. Emotional changes may involve frequent outbursts of crying, childlike demands, sulking, moodiness, or depression. Occasionally, a loss of inhibitions may lead to an apparent lack of concern over personal hygiene and inappropriate social behavior. An uninhibited expression of sexual behavior is not uncommon. Usually, personality changes are more obvious to relatives or caretakers who have regular contact with the person. In the presence of strangers, the individual may succeed in presenting himself as intellectually and emotionally normal. However, after longer periods of contact, even strangers become aware of the impaired intellectual and emotional functioning.

Symptoms of arteriosclerotic dementia usually occur after age 50. Memory loss is one of the earliest and most consistent signs. The disorder is more common among men than women (Agate, 1970). There is no cure for arteriosclerotic dementia. Changes typically become progressively worse until the person dies, often as a result of a cerebrovascular accident (stroke).

SENILE DEMENTIA. The behavioral and physical debilitation accompanying senile dementia is similar in many ways to that of arteriosclerotic dementia. The major pathological difference is that people with senile dementia seldom have a history of vascular disease, hypertension, strokes, or other indications of a cerebrovascular disease. It has been difficult to establish specific pathological changes that may accompany senile dementia. Postmortem examination sometimes reveals atrophy of cortical tissue and widening of fissures (sulci); but in most cases the appearance of the brain and cerebral vascular system is normal. Further, some postmortem examinations reveal cortical atrophy and widening of the sulci, and yet there were no signs prior to death of any obvious impairment of mental activity (Agate, 1970). Hence, the presence or absence of obvious pathological changes in the brain cannot serve as the primary basis for a diagnosis of senile dementia.

Generally, the changes that accompany senile dementia begin in the 70 to 80 age range—later than the onset of arteriosclerotic dementia. The disorder appears to be more common among women than men. It is estimated that senile dementia accounts for 19–24% of mental disorders among the elderly (Anderson, 1967).

The primary symptom of senile dementia is a gradual deterioration of intellectual abilities, usually beginning with disturbances in memory for recent events. Other changes involve disturbances in concentration, a tendency to distort the truth or confabulate, deterioration of personal habits and cleanliness, and blunting of emotions. In the later stages, the person may engage in antisocial behavior and atypical forms of sexual gratification. In some cases, individuals may show paranoid ideation, depressive tendencies, and even hallucinations. In the final stages, the person deteriorates to an almost vegetative existence (Agate, 1970).

Arteriosclerotic dementia and senile dementia collectively account for about 23.9–31.4% of all mental disorders among the elderly. Approximately 75% of individuals afflicted with these disorders die within 2 years of admission to state or county hospitals (Anderson, 1967). Drug treatments have proved relatively ineffective for either type of chronic brain syndrome. In most cases, afflicted people appear to fare better in the familiar surrounding of their homes. Removal from their familiar environments tends to produce stress and noticeable deterioration (Agate, 1970).

As the proportion of elderly people in our society is steadily increasing, the prevalence of these disorders will pose greater problems in providing facilities necessary for care and treatment.

PRESENILE DEMENTIAS

In addition to the chronic brain syndromes that occur during the later years of life, some forms of brain syndromes with similar symptoms begin earlier in the adult years. For this reason, they have been categorized under *presenile dementia* or *presenile psychoses*. Like the brain syndromes occurring in later years, deterioration is progressive and ultimately results in death.

ALZHEIMER'S DISEASE. The characteristics of this disorder were first described by Alzheimer in 1907. The disorder is very similar to that of senile dementia except that the pathological changes may be more severe. The onset of symptoms usually begins between the ages of 40 and 65. Like senile dementia, the disorder is more common among women than men. Progressive mental deterioration is very similar to that described for senile dementia.

There is some evidence that hereditary factors may play a role in Alzheimer's disease. In recent years, the same type of pathological changes of the brain occurring in Alzheimer's disease has been identified in the brains of elderly patients with Down's syndrome (mongolism). In an analysis of brains of 35 Down's syndrome cases who had survived beyond age 40, all 35 had signs of Alzheimer's disease. In Down's syndrome, although the nervous system is slow in developing, the aging process is more rapid. This suggests that there may be a relationship between delayed brain development and the early pathological changes in the brain associated with Alzheimer's disease. It has been speculated that longevity may be related to the maintenance of a stable chromosome state in the cells (Malamud, 1972). In other words, there may be a chromosomal factor involved in both the delayed maturation of the brain and its rapid deterioration.

Since the pathological changes are similar to those of senile dementia, there is still a question as to whether Alzheimer's disease is a distinctive disorder or simply an early onset of senile dementia.

PICK'S DISEASE.   Pick's disease was first described by Arnold Pick in 1892. It is a relatively rare disease, which occurs in the same age range as Alzheimer's disease. Its prevalence is no greater for women than men. Unlike other senile and presenile brain syndromes, there is little impairment for memory of recent events. Although there are pathological changes in various areas of the cortex, the hippocampus, a subcortical structure presumed to be important for remembering recent events, is relatively unaffected. Pick's disease, therefore, appears to be a distinctive type of pathological brain disorder that begins in the 40–65-year age range. Although the cause of the disorder is unknown, it has been suggested that genetic factors play a role (Malamud, 1972).

OTHER NEUROLOGICAL DISORDERS OF THE LATER YEARS

The two types of brain disorders discussed next tend to occur more frequently after the age of 30. Variation in the age of onset, however, is considerable and depends partly on the nature of etiological factors. The variation in the age of onset is especially true of Parkinson's syndrome, sometimes called *shaking palsy*.

PARKINSONISM.   Parkinsonism is a pattern of neurological and behavioral changes that may result from several causes. Although it is not infrequent among elderly persons, the primary characteristics of the syndrome may occur at any time during the adult years. However, the most frequent period of onset is between the ages of 40 and 60.

The symptoms of parkinsonism frequently begin with a tremor in one hand. The disorder gradually progresses until both sides of the body are affected. Muscles in the hands, legs, feet, and head are particularly affected. One of the more prominent symptoms is the rhythmic, "pin-rolling" motion of the thumb and fingers, which occurs in conjunction with a very pronounced 3–5-per-second tremor of the hands. Another important characteristic is muscular weakness and rigidity. When the individual attempts to walk, his steps are small and quick. This hurried, shuffling walk can lead to frequent falls; hence the individual often prefers to remain seated rather than risk losing his balance. If the individual attempts to write, the tremor and muscular rigidity of the hand and wrist result in small, difficult-to-read handwriting (Irvin *et al.*, 1970). Frequently there is tremor of the lips, tongue, and head, which make it difficult to comprehend the person's speech. Generally, the tremor becomes worse during agitated states but disappears altogether during sleep.

The face of the patient with Parkinson's syndrome is often described as *masklike*. The individual seldom talks and generally shows little or no sign of emotion. When he does talk, the voice is typically a monotone. The tendency of patients to remain immobile, apparently emotionless, and nonverbal makes it difficult to assess intellectual or psychological changes that may accompany the disorder (Agate, 1970). The time of onset and the prognosis partly depend on which etiological factors are involved. Generally, Parkinson's syndrome is considered a result of damage to parts of the midbrain called the *basal ganglia* (Irvin *et al.*, 1970).

Treatment of Parkinsonism. Until recently, drug treatment of parkinsonism was relatively unsuccessful. Newer drugs have been introduced, which in many cases have led to substantial improvement. Research with Symmetrel (amantadine), a relatively safe drug, has led to notable improvement in about two-thirds of the cases treated (Parsonage, 1971). L-dopa, a more controversial drug, has been the object of considerable research interest. Use of this drug has resulted in substantial improvement in a majority of the cases treated. L-dopa has proved to be particularly effective in the reduction of tremor and rigidity, two of the most unpleasant symptoms of parkinsonism. L-dopa, however, may have serious physiological and psychological side effects. Physiological side effects include hypotension and the development of involuntary abnormal movements (Carlsson, 1970). Riklan (1973) reports that behavioral side effects occur in 10–15% of various populations of Parkinson's patients treated with L-dopa. The critical change appears to involve an increase in arousal, which may lead to either positive or negative behavioral changes. Negative behavioral changes include agitation, restlessness, difficulty in sleeping, depression, and lethargy. Positive changes include an increase in intellectual performance, increased alertness, and alleviation of depression. Riklan concludes that the healthier or more intact patient is likely to show positive changes whereas the less healthy or less intact patient is more likely to show negative changes.

Despite these problems related to side effects, recent drug research provides grounds for optimism about the treatment of parkinsonism. It appears likely that drug therapy will replace procedures such as neurosurgical intervention. Until recently, for example, stereotaxically induced lesions in the thalamus were a fairly common neurosurgical means of achieving reductions in tremor and rigidity.

HUNTINGTON'S CHOREA. Huntington's chorea is a rare, inherited disorder that does not become manifest until the middle adult years. Woody Guthrie, a well-known folksinger and father of Arlo Guthrie, was afflicted with the disorder. Scenes from the movie *Alice's Restaurant* depicted Arlo's visits to the hospital to be with his father during the later stages of the disease. Arlo Guthrie, like other children of a parent with Huntington's chorea, knows there is a 50% probability that he will eventually develop this disorder. The plight of the Guthrie family has served to stimulate scientific investigation of Huntington's chorea as well as public interest.

Chorea refers to abnormal, involuntary bodily movements or gestures. Huntington's chorea, first described by George Huntington in 1872, is a hereditary, progressively degenerative disorder characterized by choreic movements, incoordination, emotional lability, and impairment of memory and concentration (Ringel, Guthrie, & Klawans, 1973). As the disorder progresses, a variety of bizarre personality changes may occur. Often the person requires hospitalization during the final stages of the disease. Like parkinsonism, Huntington's chorea appears to be a disorder of the midbrain, primarily the basal ganglia. The disease is inherited in an autosomal dominant fashion. Because the onset of the disorder occurs between 30 and 50 years of age (Myrianthopoulos, 1973), an individual who carries the dominant gene may marry and transmit the gene to his children before the disorder becomes evident. At present there is no certain way of determining whether a child of a parent known to have Huntington's chorea has received the dominant gene.

The incidence of Huntington's chorea has been estimated to be about 4–7 per 100,000 (Myrianthopoulos, 1966). The disease is found in all races all over the world. In the United States, the incidence appears to be higher in New England. In one New England family, the history of the disease has been traced to two affected brothers who migrated to Boston Bay from Suffolk, England in 1630. The 12 generations that followed over the next 300 years included 1000 known cases of Huntington's chorea (Refsum, 1961).

Children of afflicted parents often suffer from their burden of uncertainty. In one study, 40% of potentially choreic individuals and a similar proportion of their spouses developed symptoms that might be classified as *anxiety neurosis* (Pearson, 1973). The unusual amount of stress in families of an individual at risk is understandable in view of the seriousness of the disorder. In most cases, the individual has witnessed the early death of a parent following years of progressive mental deterioration.

Pearson (1973) has described a typical pattern of reactions by individuals who are finally diagnosed as having Huntington's chorea. Upon being told that he has definitely inherited the disorder, the person's first reaction tends to be one of shocked disbelief. Subsequently, the individual becomes profoundly depressed. He may then go through a period of generalized anger or hostility. Eventually, he may blame others for his unacceptable feelings and actions. A final phase, common among identified victims, is complete denial. The person may claim, for example, that God has freed him from possession of the bad gene. Curiously, despite knowledge of the inherited nature of the disorder, most affected individuals make no special effort to avoid reproduction. The number of children born to diagnosed or threatened individuals is comparable to that of the general population.

At present, there is no cure or preventive therapeutic measure for Huntington's chorea. The abnormal, involuntary movements may be alleviated by several types of drugs (fluphenazine, haloperidol, or perphenazine), and chlorpromazine may be used to control psychotic symptoms (Whittier, 1973).

SUMMARY OF PART IV

As the proportion of elderly people increases in our society, the psychosocial problems accompanying age-related neurological disorders will also increase. Unfortunately, there are no "cures" for the major types of organic syndromes discussed in this section. However, recent advances in drug therapy have led to marked alleviation of the primary symptoms of parkinsonism. Hopefully, the increase in problems posed by age-related disorders will lead to a corresponding increase in research oriented toward prevention and treatment. Until then, unfortunately, many people will spend their final years of life in a state of non-productive dependency.

Summary

The relationship between impairment of the CNS and psychological problems is highly complex. Even when the cause, location, and extent of CNS impairment can be identified, it is often difficult to discern a direct effect on behavior. Two individuals with similar pathology may exhibit very dissimilar behavior.

Psychological problems associated with brain damage may involve a complicated interaction between organismic and environmental forces.

This chapter has described a variety of CNS disturbances which may directly or indirectly affect behavior. A review of these complex disturbances should underscore the fact that psychological problems cannot be adequately explained by considering *only* environmental or *only* organic determinants of behavior.

9

Mental Retardation

Long before the emergence of standardized intelligence tests, there were names for people who appeared unable to achieve the skills necessary to adapt to societal demands. Labels such as *fool* and *feebleminded* were applied to individuals who could not perform the roles expected of them by their culture (Mercer, 1973). The labels have changed, but mental retardation remains as one of the most significant problems in society. In the United States, according to the *Report of the President's Panel on Mental Retardation* (1963), 5.4 million children and adults (3% of the population) are mentally retarded. It is estimated that 126,000 babies who will eventually be labeled retarded are born each year. Of the 5.4 million, an estimated 400,000 need constant care; 5 million have mild disabilities. In every state, there are public schools with special education classrooms, there are institutions, and there are private "homes" for the retarded. In a number of states, people labeled mentally retarded can be sterilized, prevented from marrying, denied the privilege of voting or holding public office, refused a driver's license, and rejected by the military (Mercer, 1973).

Jean Marc Gaspard Itard (1774–1838) was the first to take a scientific interest in the care and training of mentally retarded people. Itard's interest stemmed from his treatment of a very unusual adolescent (McKown, 1961). Many of the issues surrounding the case persist in present discussions of the nature of retardation. In 1799, a newspaper printed a story about a young savage who had been found wandering in the woods by hunters. The youth was described as a wolf-like creature who grunted, trotted like a beast, and dined on raw food and garbage. Billed as the Wild Boy of Aveyron, he was exhibited as a freak to the townspeople. Eventually, news of his wild appearance and strange habits reached scientific circles and he was brought to Paris to be examined by Philippe Pinel, the physician noted for his humane treatment of the insane. Pinel labeled the boy an idiot and declared that he had never been normal. At that time, the word *idiot* referred to anyone considered to be mentally defective. Pinel assumed that all idiots were incurable and incapable of learning; for this reason, his interest in the case ended with the diagnosis.

Itard refused to accept Pinel's opinion. He was convinced the Wild Boy's bizarre behavior and lack of speech were due to a lack of opportunity to learn the expected roles of society. Hence, for 5 years Itard attempted to educate him. Although the youth never learned to talk, he did learn to recognize simple written words, to dress himself, and to perform other low-level skills. To that extent, he was teachable but he never developed the complex abilities necessary to function independently in society. Thus, both Pinel and Itard were partially right. Pinel was right in that the capability of the youth to profit from education had been permanently impaired. He was wrong in assuming that the boy was unteachable. Although Itard's educational expectations for the Wild Boy were unrealistic, he was successful in demonstrating that even a person with severely retarded behavior could be taught a limited range of basic skills. Following his experience with the Wild Boy of Aveyron, Itard devoted the rest of his scientific career to working with people who had been labeled idiots.

The disagreement between Pinel and Itard illustrates the fact that often the causes of mental retardation are not reducible to an either–or choice of environmental versus biological determinants. Mental retardation is not a single condition for which a single cause can be demonstrated. As we shall see, there are different types, as well as different levels, of retardation and there are a number of causes. In some cases, environmental factors appear to play the dominant role, and there is little or no evidence of organic involvement. In other cases, such as Down's syndrome (mongolism), the etiological importance of genetic factors has been clearly demonstrated. In still other cases, it is very difficult to assess the relative etiological contributions of environmental and organic variables; the level of retardation often depends on a complex interaction between the extent of organic impairment and the degree of environmental opportunities. And, in many instances, the causes of mental retardation are unknown.

Regardless of the cause and level of retardation, the importance of remedial training cannot be minimized. As stated in the *Manual of Terminology and Classification in Mental Retardation,*

> We have learned too, that even among the severely disabled, functional performance is a product of the interaction between constitutional and environmental forces, and that it can be modified. The potential for behavior change, i.e., the dynamic nature

A moment of joy in a class for retarded people. Kevin, in the white sweater, has just solved a counting problem. His new-found ability will give him greater independence and self-reliance in the world outside. (Robert Foothorap, Jeroboam)

of retardation, is one of the more significant concepts in the field to emerge in recent years [Begab, 1973, p. ix].

It should be emphasized again that mental retardation is not a unitary disorder. *Mental retardation* is a label applied to individuals who perform substantially below cultural expectations in a variety of environmental settings. Low performance may be associated with cultural or environmental deprivation, brain damage resulting from disease or injury, or genetic disorders such as Down's syndrome. The statement that an individual is mentally retarded actually refers to a level of performance, not to a condition of the organism. A condition of the organism such as brain damage may substantially alter general performance. If so, the individual may be labeled retarded. On the other hand, brain damage may have little effect on a person's overall performance. If so, the person would not be labeled retarded.

Low performance in a *single* environmental setting should not lead to an individual's being labeled as retarded. As we have noted, substantially low performance should be demonstrated in a variety of environmental settings. In some instances the use of the label has been inappropriate and has resulted in undesirable consequences. One example is the reliance on IQ test scores alone to classify an individual as retarded. IQ tests are very useful instruments for assessing and predicting performance in academic settings. However, a low IQ should not be interpreted as indicating retardation unless there are also deficiencies in general adaptive behavior. A Spanish-American child may not perform well on IQ tests or in school because of deficiencies in English. In other environmental settings, such as his home or neighborhood, he may show adequate adaptive behavior. However, a child with Down's syndrome, in addition to achieving low scores on IQ tests, typically shows impaired adaptive behavior in virtually all environmental settings. To label both children as mentally retarded would obscure important differences in behavior.

Despite the fact that the need to assess adaptive behavior has been stressed repeatedly, there are still instances in which too much emphasis is placed on IQs. Such abuses in assessment procedures have contributed to a widespread criticism of psychological testing in the school system, particularly testing of minority children. A full discussion of this problem will be presented later. However, it is not psychological testing per se that causes problems, but the abuse of appropriate assessment procedures.

The material in this chapter will be presented in three sections. The first section will focus on different theoretical conceptions of mental retardation. In the second section, the role of cultural and environmental factors will be discussed. Finally, specific clinical conditions that involve severe alterations of the central nervous system (CNS) will be presented. This separate presentation of environmental and organic factors should not convey the impression that these variables are easily separated. Extreme environmental deprivation may lead to organic complications, and differences in environmental opportunities may result in very different behaviors by people with similar organic conditions.

Contemporary Concepts of Mental Retardation

THE BEHAVIORAL MODEL

Early concepts of retardation were probably based on the failure of some people to show adaptive behavior. If people were unable to perform expected social roles with relative independence, then it was presumed that their minds were weak or feeble (Mercer, 1973). Thus, a weak or feeble mind was inferred to be the cause of inadequate adaptive behavior. The word *mind* has often been used as an explanatory construct with no reference to observable or measurable properties. As we noted in Chapter 2, constructs may play a useful role in theory construction, but their value to science must be assessed in terms of their predictive utility. A construct may be useful if it provides unique, testable predictions that could not be derived solely from observable or measurable events. Unfortunately, the word *mind* is so vague and ill defined that any predictive utility of the construct is dubious. To say that "feeblemindedness" *causes* retarded behavior, therefore, has little scientific utility.

Similar problems can be noted with contemporary constructs such as *mentally defective* and *intellectually defective*. According to Bijou (1963), "the task of behavioral research is to investigate the observable or potentially observable conditions that may produce *retarded behavior*, not *retarded mentality*. The conditions subjected to investigation are the biological, physical, and social interactions, past and current [p. 101]." Although Bijou acknowledges biological variables as one of several classes of variables that limit psychological behavior, he does not conceive of retardation as a condition of the brain that limits the ability to learn. He prefers to view retarded behavior as generated by adverse reinforcement histories, "or simply as the failures of coordinations of stimulus and response functions [p. 109]." More succinctly, Bijou (1968) proposes that the modern view "regards retardation not as a symptom but as a form of behavior: limited behavior that has been shaped by past events in a person's life [p. 47]." In summary, the behavioral approach to mental retardation, as represented by Bijou, questions the scientific utility of constructs such as *mentally defective* as well as the view that retardation is a form of brain dysfunction. Although they recognize that biological factors as well as other variables may limit the range of an individual's responses, the behaviorists view retardation as a *form of behavior* shaped by the events in a person's life history. The primary focus is on engineering the environment so as to maximize learning opportunities regardless of whether the range of an individual's behavior has been limited by biological or by environmental factors.

THE MEDICAL–PATHOLOGICAL MODEL

Generally, the medical approach involves an emphasis on organismic as opposed to environmental explanations for retarded behavior. Despite this orientation, signs of biological impairment may be so ambiguous that other indications of subnormal intellectual functioning must be considered. As suggested by the report of the American Medical Association Conference on Mental Retardation (1965), the physician is frequently unable to make judgments on the basis of a physical examination:

> Over 200 causes of retardation have been identified, yet in most cases the physician can make no specific etiologic diagnosis. He can define retardation only in terms of functional characteristics, of significant impairments in intellectual functioning and in social adaptation of the individual [AMA, 1965, p. 187].[1]

From the standpoint of the medical–pathological model, such a statement should not be interpreted to mean that "most cases" of retardation are caused by environmental factors. The tendency is to assume that biological impairment exists but that it is not possible to verify its existence with current diagnostic procedures.

Contemporary medical conceptions do not exclude environmental causes of retardation. What is assumed, however, is that environmental deprivation, particularly in early infancy, may alter the normal development of neurological

---

[1] From Mental Retardation: A Handbook for the Primary Physician, *Journal of the American Medical Association*, 1965, *191* (3), 183–231. Copyright 1965, American Medical Association.

systems. The assumption, therefore, is that such factors as social or cultural deprivation may alter permanently the normal functioning of the brain. The stress on biological impairment as the major cause of retardation also is illustrated by the American Medical Association's report:

> The primary causes of mental retardation may be considered to originate from the *biological* factors which influence the biochemical and structural organization of the neural matrix, or from *experiential* factors which influence the organization of function in the central nervous system during postnatal maturation, or from varying combinations [p. 4].

In contrast to the behavioral approach in which the focus is on remediation through maximizing learning opportunities, the primary goal of the medical–pathological approach is prevention. Since permanent biological impairment is viewed as the primary cause of retardation, it follows that retardation is generally permanent. Although the importance of remedial learning opportunities is recognized, the medical–pathological model provides less optimism regarding the limits of learning than the behavioral approach.

The behavioral model has led to notable accomplishments in remedial training; research in medical science, on the other hand, has resulted in important contributions involving prevention. Since prevention and remediation are the two most important goals in the field of mental retardation, the different focus of the two models has proved to be valuable.

THE STATISTICAL MODEL

The medical–pathological model has been influenced by the statistical model of retardation derived from the fields of education and psychology. As mentioned earlier, the physician, when unable to discern biological impairment, may use psychological estimates of intelligence and signs of adaptive behavior as a basis for diagnosis.

The statistical model of mental retardation is based primarily upon IQs derived from individually administered intelligence tests. The tests most widely used are the Stanford–Binet Intelligence Scale, the Wechsler Adult Intelligence Scale (WAIS), and the Wechsler Intelligence Scale for Children (WISC). A full discussion of the history, standardization procedures, and variables that affect intelligence test scores is not within the scope of this chapter. Some explanation, however, regarding the origin and use of intelligence tests is necessary for an understanding of the statistical model.

In 1905 Binet and Simon published an "intelligence" scale that was specifically designed to assess the educability of school children. That is still the purpose of this scale and of subsequent intelligence scales. As indicated by Edwards (1971), predictions derived from such tests should be restricted to criteria relevant to school performance:

> Since the scale is designed to assess educability of school children, this is the setting in which intellectual differences must be reflected and measured. Obvious as this may seem, subsequent events and interpretations make it necessary to stress again and

again the original purpose and limitations of tests which have been retained to the present day [p. 24].

The primary success of intelligence tests has been in their prediction of school performance. However, the construct of intelligence, as inferred from scores on various tests, has broader implications than performance in the school setting. For example, as defined by Wechsler (1958), "Intelligence . . . is the aggregate or global capacity of the individual to act purposefully, to think rationally, and to deal effectively with his environment [p. 7]."

If we accept Wechsler's definition, then we must recognize that no existing psychological test has been demonstrated to be a valid measure of such a "global capacity." However, intelligence tests have become the major instruments (and sometimes the only instruments) used in assigning the label *mental retardation*. According to Heber (1970): "In actual practice, in the United States, individuals with measured intelligence at two standard deviations or more below the mean (about an IQ of 70 for most individual tests of intelligence) are classified as being retarded on the basis of their IQ scores alone [pp. 3–4]." Such a practice ignores the assessment of adaptive behavior. The importance of adaptive behavior has been stressed by Heber (1970), Mercer (1973), the report of the American Medical Association Conference on Mental Retardation (AMA, 1965) and the manual published under the auspices of the American Association on Mental Deficiency (Grossman, 1973).

Unfortunately, no standardized tests of adaptive behavior suitable for general use in society have been developed. Assessment of adaptive behavior remains largely subjective. Scales such as the Vineland Social Maturity Scale and the Gesell Developmental Scale are designed primarily for young children or for screening purposes in institutions for the retarded (Mercer, 1973). The absence of adequate objective measures of adaptive behavior may force relatively greater reliance on standardized intelligence tests. At least in educational settings, IQs probably will continue to be the dominant influence on professionals making judgments regarding the label of mental retardation.

The mean IQ of the United States population is assumed to be 100, with one standard deviation equaling 15 IQ points. The normal range within which 68% of the population should fall is between one standard deviation above and one standard deviation below the mean. Hence, IQs of 85 to 115 define the normal range. IQs of more than one but less than two standard deviations below the mean (IQs from 70 to 84) represent 13.6% of the general population. IQs of more than two standard deviations below the mean (IQs of 69 and below) represent approximately 2–3% of the general population.[2]

There has been no consistent agreement as to what the IQ cutoff score should be before considering a label of retardation. Mercer (1973) has noted that at least three different cutoff scores have been used in the past: (1) an IQ of 84 and below, which includes 16% of the population; (2) an IQ of 79 and below,

[2] IQs derived from different tests are not directly comparable and the exact percentage of persons scoring under 69 varies according to the test used.

which includes 9% of the population; and (3) an IQ of 69 and below, which includes about 3% of the population. The cutoff score of 84 was suggested by Heber in the 1961 edition of the *Manual on Terminology and Classification of Mental Retardation* sponsored by the American Association of Mental Deficiency. The cutoff score of 79 is referred to by Mercer (1973) as the "educational criterion" because it has been used frequently in the context of the public school system. The cutoff score of 69 corresponds closely with the cutoff score recommended by test designers and is referred to as the "traditional criterion." The 1973 *Manual on Terminology and Classification* (Grossman, 1973) recommends that *mental retardation* should be used only in reference to "significantly subaverage" performance. In terms of test performance, "significantly subaverage" was defined as an IQ of 68 and below on the Stanford–Binet scale and 70 and below on the Wechsler scale. In short, statistical estimates of the incidence of mental retardation vary considerably, depending on which IQ cutoff is used to define retardation.

The statistical model based on IQs makes no assumption about etiology and prognosis. Nor does it distinguish between individuals with the same IQ who vary in adaptive behavior, social class, ethnic background, or any other behavioral, biological, or social dimension. For this reason, it is not useful to rely exclusively on the statistical model for labeling an individual as retarded.

The statistical model is often used in conjunction with either a behavioral or a medical–pathological approach. In the behavioral approach, an individual's IQ simply indicates a composite score based on the types of behaviors sampled by a particular intelligence test. Behavioral information gained from an IQ test is considered along with samples of behavior from other sources; there is no special reliance on IQs for assessing retardation. In the medical–pathological approach, if there are no apparent signs of biological impairment, low scores on intelligence tests along with developmental lags and deficiencies in adaptive behavior may be used to assign the label *mental retardation*. However, low IQs may be interpreted as a sign of underlying biological impairment.

THE SOCIAL SYSTEMS MODEL

The most recent and most comprehensive model for mental retardation has been structured by Mercer (1973). Basically, the social systems model views mental retardation as an acquired social status. The concept of *normal* in the social systems model is not based on a statistical range nor upon the absence of pathological signs. *Normality* refers only to whether an individual performs the roles expected of him according to the norms of society. Within this model, it is possible that an individual might perform the role expected of him in some social systems but not in others. For example, a child who does not perform the academic role expected of him in the school system might perform all the roles expected of him by his parents, other children, and adults in the neighborhood. In other words, he may be labeled retarded by one social system, but considered normal in other social systems. Mercer (1973) refers to this as *situational retardation* or *quasi-retardation*. If a person does not perform the expected roles in *any* social system at any period in his life, then he is referred to as *comprehensively retarded*.

In the social systems model, mental retardation is characteristic not of the individual but of an achieved status in a particular social system. According to Mercer (1973), "If a person does not occupy the status of mental retardate, is not playing the role of mental retardate in any social system, and is not regarded as mentally retarded by any of the significant others in his social world, then he is not mentally retarded, irrespective of the level of his IQ, the adequacy of his adaptive behavior, or the extent of his organic impairment [pp. 28–29]."[3] A low IQ is not viewed as a symptom of pathology but a behavioral characteristic that is often associated with a higher probability that an individual will be labeled retarded by one or more social systems.

In Mercer's view (1973), a *clinical perspective* has emerged as a result of a partial merger between the statistical model of education and psychology and the medical–pathological model. The clinical perspective has become highly formalized and is considered by Mercer to be the "most important social system in the sociological study of mental retardation [p. 35]." The legal authority to label an individual mentally retarded has been restricted to professional diagnosticians in the medical and psychological professions. The label *retardation* could be a result of an examination by a licensed physician, a legally qualified psychologist, or a collaborative effort of the two disciplines. These professionals are responsible for determining "real" retardation and for training others in diagnostic procedures based upon the clinical perspective.

In comparing the social systems model with the clinical perspective, Mercer (1973) cites six major differences: (1) In the social systems model, mental retardation is an achieved social status, whereas in the clinical perspective mental retardation is considered a pathological condition of the individual. (2) In the social systems model, retardation is specific to the norms of each system. A person is seen as retarded only for the time he is participating in that system. Hence, he may be seen as retarded at one time during the day but not at other times, or for one period of his life but not for other periods. The clinical perspective essentially disregards social systems and seeks to determine whether a person *is* or *is not* mentally retarded. (3) The social systems perspective defines an individual as normal if he performs the expected roles in various social systems, regardless of whatever clinical symptoms are present. In the clinical view, if a person evidences particular symptoms, such as a low IQ or signs of neurological impairment,[4] he may be diagnosed as retarded regardless of various sociocultural factors. (4) A "real" prevalence rate of retardation cannot be determined from the standpoint of the social systems model because retardation is not conceived of as a constant across social systems and time. In the clinical approach a diagnosis is based on the presence of certain symptoms. Hence, it is presumed that the "real" prevalence rate of retardation can be estimated or determined given adequate research and

[3] Copyright © 1973 by The Regents of the University of California: reprinted by permission of the University of California Press.

[4] Neurological impairment may or may not be associated with an individual's ability to function normally. An individual with brain damage and a high IQ would rarely, if ever, be labeled retarded. However, an individual with brain damage and a low IQ is very likely to be labeled retarded.

accuracy of diagnostic instruments. (5) In the social systems model, if an individual performs expected roles in a particular social system, such as his neighborhood, then he is regarded as normal in that system regardless of how he may be viewed in other systems. In the clinical perspective, it is assumed that a skillful, professionally trained individual can detect abnormalities not apparent to others. One function of the clinician is to educate the layman to recognize symptoms of retardation in a person, regardless of how well that person might be performing in particular social systems. (6) In the social systems perspective, IQ tests and clinical instruments used to diagnose mental retardation are viewed as formalized procedures based on the middle-class behavioral norms of the American core culture. It is not considered possible to conceptualize the construct *intelligence* independent of the dominant attitudes of the core culture that created the construct. The clinical approach, however, acknowledges deficiencies in intelligence tests and other clinical measures but assumes that eventual refinement will yield measures that are relatively uninfluenced by social or cultural factors.

In several ways, the behavioral model as proposed by Bijou (1963, 1968) is similar to the social systems model formalized by Mercer (1973). Both systems are primarily empirical; both reject the construct of mental retardation as a condition of the individual that causes other difficulties. The difference between the systems is less conceptual and more a matter of goals and focus. The goal of the behavioral approach is to identify specific behavioral problems or deficits and engineer the immediate environment to maximize learning. The primary focus is on the behavior of an individual. The goal of the social systems approach is to enhance educational and social planning by identifying an individual's strengths and weaknesses with respect to the norms for each of the social systems in which he participates. The focus is on an individual's ability to perform the roles expected of him in each social system.

In summary, four models of retardation have been presented: (1) the behavioral model, (2) the medical–pathological model, (3) the statistical model, and (4) the social systems model. Each model emphasizes different aspects of retardation: The behavioral model focuses on individual behavior; the medical–pathological model, on the role of organic factors; the statistical model, on IQs with respect to established norms; and the social systems model, on performance in relation to expectations of differing social systems. Although the emphasis on environmental and organic variables differs among the four models, none of the models stresses exclusive environmental or organic causation. The role of cultural and biological factors will be discussed in subsequent sections.

The Influence of Culture and the Label Mental Retardation

The values of the white, middle-class core culture in the United States are embodied in the evaluative process that leads to the label *mental retardation*. Mercer (1973) noted that most of the 128 intelligence tests listed in the 1965

Mental Measurement Yearbook by Buros stress verbal skills. Quantitative and abstract conceptual skills are also emphasized. The tests allow little credit for manual dexterity, mechanical skills, artistic or musical abilities, or the ability to establish satisfactory relations with other people.

The traditional academic emphasis in the public school system has been on verbal and quantitative skills. According to Mercer, the public school system, which relies heavily on intelligence test scores, is the number one labeler of mental retardation. For example, of 812 persons in Riverside, California, classified by various agencies as mentally retarded, 429 were labeled as retarded in the public school system. Of the 429, 340 were not labeled as retarded by any other agency. Medical facilities ranked second to the school system in number of persons classified as retarded. However, of the 166 persons classified as retarded by medical facilities, 97 were also classified as retarded by other agencies.

There was a substantial overrepresentation of minority group members among children classified as retarded in the context of the public school. The representation of minorities was lowest among children classified by medical facilities. Assessment procedures used in the school system involving IQ tests and academic performance probably are more susceptible to cultural influences than medical evaluations that focus on organic involvement. Thus, minority children with backgrounds different from the core culture are more likely to be labeled retarded by the school system than by other agencies. Supporting this conclusion is Mercer's (1973) report that out of 429 persons labeled as retarded by the school system, 340 were *not* labeled retarded by any other agency. In other words, many children viewed as retarded in the context of the school system may not be perceived as retarded in other settings. This suggests that indications of adaptive behavior outside the school setting have been ignored in favor of primary reliance on IQs and academic performance.

Of course, serious difficulties in school performance often result in later limitations. Individuals who are *not* retarded but who are *not* successful in school face serious problems in a society organized around educational achievement. The fact that a child with a low IQ shows adequate adaptive behavior in nonschool settings should not be interpreted to mean that he will face no problems in the school setting. The public school system embodies the values and academic expectations of the core culture; so do intelligence tests, which were essentially designed to predict performance in the public school. In other words, a child who does not do well on intelligence tests is not likely to do well in a school situation that demands similar verbal and quantitative skills.

When assessing adaptive behavior, it is important to differentiate children who have not had the opportunity to learn from those who have difficulties in learning. If a black child from the ghetto and a white child from a middle-class family both score 70 on an IQ test, the behavior and prognosis for later performance in society might be quite different for the two children. The black child may not have had the opportunity to learn the type of information sampled by intelligence tests. The white middle-class child may have had the opportunity to learn but failed to acquire or retain the necessary information. Both children would have difficulties in academic performance, but outside the context of the public school, the black child's level of functioning might be far superior to that of the white child. Whereas a white middle-class child with an IQ of 70 usually requires close supervision and special help in a variety of learning situations, the black child from the ghetto with the same IQ often exhibits a wide variety of nonacademic skills. He would be much more likely to develop socially useful skills that would eventually render a label of mental retardation meaningless.

In summary, applying the label *mental retardation* only on the basis of an IQ cutoff can mask highly important differences among individuals that are predictive of later behavior. The importance of sociocultural factors as they relate to performance on intelligence tests has been well established. The assessment of adaptive behavior in a variety of settings may allow finer differentiation of one's current level of functioning and, ultimately, enhance predictability. As indicated earlier, the *mental retardation* label carries important legal and social implications that may critically limit an individual's participation in the social system. The fact that an individual can be legally sterilized or denied the right to vote, drive, or marry should not be based on a casually assigned label of mental retardation. But current labeling practices tend to ignore sociocultural factors related to academic performance. As a result, they support the prejudices and discriminatory practices already prevalent in society.

The influence of environmental factors on the label of mental retardation is not restricted to cultural considerations. The immediate family environment of an individual often has a substantial impact on his ability to perform society's expected roles. For example, an individual may be deprived of physical and social stimulation in any cultural setting. Although family attitudes and practices may be heavily influenced by the surrounding culture, there can be important differences between families within a culture. One such difference involves the amount of physical and social stimulation afforded a person during the first years of development. In the next section, we will examine the possible influence of early stimulus deprivation on retardation.

EFFECTS OF EARLY ENVIRONMENTAL DEPRIVATION

Obviously, an infant totally deprived of care cannot survive. There are situations, however, in which the physical and social stimulation provided by caretakers is minimal. In such situations, learning experiences may be severely curtailed. It is also possible that a substantial reduction in environmental stimulation may alter biological development. The lack of learning experiences, alterations in biological development, or the two combined, could seriously retard behavioral development.

Early research on environmental deprivation involved the plight of infants in certain types of institutional settings. A number of studies reported that deprivation associated with improper institutional care may result in severe retardation (Goldfarb, 1943, 1945, 1947, 1955; Hsu, 1946; Provence & Lipton, 1962; Skeels & Dye, 1939; Spitz, 1945, 1946b). However, Rheingold (1960, 1961) reported that infants up to 3 months of age in well-staffed institutions showed no signs of retardation. It does not appear, therefore, that institutionalism per se results in retardation. The critical variable appears to be the availability of physical and social stimulation. In poorly staffed institutions where stimulation is presumed to be minimal, development is adversely affected. In institutions with an adequate number of caretakers to provide infants with sufficient stimulation, little or no adverse effects on development have been observed. It should be clear that it is not the number of caretakers that is critical for normal development but the quality and level of stimulation provided by the caretakers. Two indifferent caretakers, for example, might provide less physical and social stimulation than one highly affectionate caretaker. The fact that unusual deprivation may seriously retard development appears well established. To what extent such effects are reversible has not been resolved. A number of investigators, though noting serious effects of improper institutional care, reported that such effects were not permanent or were readily alleviated when remedial procedures were instituted (Dennis, 1960; Dennis & Najarian, 1957; Pasamanick, 1946; Rheingold, 1956). However, deprivation of social and physical stimulation during one period of development may be more important than similar deprivation during another period of development. Ainsworth (1962), for example, has proposed that there may be a critical period between 6 and 12 months of age, in which the effects of deprivation are more serious and more likely to be irreversible than comparable deprivation occurring before or after this period. Although some evidence supports this hypothesis, other considerations suggest that conclusive statements regarding the question of reversibility are premature.

Most research involving the effects of deprivation has involved institutional settings. It is virtually impossible to determine the extent to which the quality and level of stimulation are comparable among different institutional settings. For example, cultural differences do not permit direct comparisons between institutions in Lebanon and those in the United States. Further, within the same country, cultural changes between 1945 and 1960 also prevent direct comparisons. Cultural variables may have appreciable effects on attitudes and behavior of caretakers, which may be reflected in the care and handling of institutionalized infants.

In addition to cultural considerations, it is not possible to isolate the variable of *caretaking behavior* from other variables that may account for developmental differences between institutional and noninstitutional settings. For instance, children placed in institutions may not be representative of the general population. Further, children who remain in institutional settings may differ from those who leave the institution because of adoption in early infancy. Mothers of institutionalized children might differ from other mothers in social class, educational attainment, intelligence, general health, or in attitudes toward parental care. Children who remain in institutions may be less healthy and exhibit more handicaps than children who are adopted early in infancy. In other words, the fact that a higher percentage of retarded children are found in orphanages may be due, in part, to variables other than deprivation of social and physical stimulation. Such variables complicate efforts to assess the influence of deprivation. They also complicate attempts to discern critical periods in development, during which the effects of deprivation may be more severe. For these reasons, we do not yet know to what extent the effects of early deprivation are reversible.

An early inference, based on the results of institutional research, was that the presence of a single mother or a mother substitute may be essential for normal development (Ribble, 1943). Such speculation has led to the inclusion of the term *maternal deprivation* in classification manuals as a possible cause of retardation (Grossman, 1973). The fact that infants fare well when cared for by many people in a well-staffed institution indicates that the continuing presence of a single mother-figure is not critical for normal intellectual development. We can presume, however, that the level of social and physical stimulation provided in most homes exceeds that of poorly staffed institutions. Such stimulation can be provided by the mother, father, an older sibling, or any person functioning as a caretaker. *Maternal deprivation,* therefore, is a misleading term that adds confusion instead of clarification.

Although most of our knowledge regarding the effects of deprivation is derived from research in institutional settings, there have been unusual instances in which noninstitutionalized children have been severely deprived of physical and social stimulation. It is important to remember that information regarding the development of such children (sometimes referred to as *attic children*) is necessarily *post hoc*. That is, it has been discovered after the fact that some children, because of various bizarre circumstances, have been reared in almost total isolation. Information about the conditions of such isolation must be obtained from the not-so-normal person or persons responsible for isolating the child. The reliability of such information, therefore, should be considered with regard to the source.

A classic case of the effects of extreme isolation was reported by Davis (1940). Davis learned about Anna, a 5-year-old child, through a news article that described the circumstances of her discovery. The child, according to the article,

> . . . was wedged into the chair, which was tilted backwards to rest on a coal bucket, her spindly arms tied above her head. She was unable to talk or move. . . . "The child was dressed in a dirty shirt and napkin," the officer said. "Her hands, arms, and legs were just bones, with skin drawn over them, so frail she couldn't use them. She never had enough nourishment. She never grew normally, and the chair on which she lay, half reclining and half sitting, was so small the child had to double her legs partly under her [*New York Times,* February 6, 1938, cited in Davis, 1940, p. 554]."

Anna was the second illegitimate child of a rural woman. Although the mother, whose IQ was reported to be 50, did not want to assume responsibility for the child, efforts by agencies to have the child adopted or placed in a foster home were unsuccessful. At the age of 5½ months, Anna was returned to her mother, who lived and worked on her father's farm. According to Davis, Anna was kept in a small, "attic-like" room on the second floor because her grandfather could not tolerate evidence of his daughter's sexual indiscretion. Apparently, Anna remained in a dirty bed and later a chair until she was almost 6 years of age. Her mother gave her little or no attention beyond that necessary to sustain life. For nearly 6 years her diet was primarily cow's milk, which was given to her in a baby bottle. When she was found, she appeared to be both blind and deaf. She was almost totally unresponsive to people and to sights and sounds around her. She could not walk or talk, and showed no signs of intelligent behavior. She did not smile or cry and appeared immobile, expressionless, and indifferent.

Anna was removed from her grandfather's house and placed in a country home. She began to show small signs of improvement almost immediately. Significant progress, however, was slow. When she was 7 years old, 2 years after her discovery, she was able to walk, understand simple commands, and feed herself, and she recognized familiar people. Yet, she still could not talk and behaved more like an infant between 1 and 2 years of age.

A second report (Davis, 1947) describes Anna's progress at age 10. She had developed language skills equivalent to that of a child approaching 3 years of age; she could walk well and run, and appeared to have a pleasant disposition. Unfortunately, Anna died of hemorrhagic jaundice at the age of 10½. Given the slowness of her behavioral development, it is unlikely that she would ever have approached normality. Davis, while noting her progress, concluded that congenital deficiencies as well as extreme environmental deprivation served to limit her development. To an extent, the case of Anna is analogous to that of the Wild Boy of Aveyron. Both may have had some form of genetic or biological deficiency in addition to extreme environmental deprivation. Both improved with training, but neither developed the abilities and social skills required for normal functioning in their societies.

In contrast to the case of Anna, remarkable progress was made by another child who suffered a similar deprivation experience (Davis, 1947). Isabelle, like Anna, was an illegitimate child who spent most of her first 6 years locked in a small room. However, Isabelle's mother was a deaf-mute who apparently spent a considerable amount of time in the room with the child. It is probable that Isabelle received much more physical and social stimulation from her mother than Anna received from hers (Stone, 1954). Thus, the conditions of deprivation may not have been comparable. When discovered, Isabelle had developed no language skills beyond a strange croaking sound. She reacted with fear and hostility toward strangers. Her locomotor skills were notably impaired by a severe case of rickets, a disease caused by a vitamin D deficiency, which softens and distorts bone formation. At first she was thought to be deaf. According to Davis, "the general impression was that she was wholly uneducable [p. 436]." Isabelle underwent an intensive training program. At the end of a week she made her first attempt to vocalize and shortly after the second month of training, she was putting sentences together. By the time Isabelle was 8 years old, 2 years after her discovery, her vocabulary and level of functioning were normal for a child of her age. At age 14, she had passed the sixth grade in the public school. Although she was somewhat older than her classmates, her teachers observed that she participated in all school activities as normally as other children.

It is difficult to say whether Isabelle's rapid and extensive progress, as compared to Anna's slow and minor progress, was due to differences in the extent of environmental deprivation, to congenital organismic differences, or to both. Although Isabelle may have received more social and physical stimulation than Anna, it is impossible to determine how much more. Even less can be said about possible qualitative differences in caretaking by the two mothers. It is also possible that children may differ in susceptibility to the effects of environmental deprivation. What was demonstrated, however, was that even though the effects of environmental deprivation were profound, remedial training resulted in notable improvement. The degree of such improvement may be determined by the nature of the deprivation, organismic factors, or both.

In our society, attic children like Anna and Isabelle are rare. Frequently, however, responsibility for the care of a young child may be shifted to an agency, to a foster home, or to adopting parents because of parental abuse or neglect. In many such cases, learning opportunities have been so restricted that social and intellectual development have been affected.

Assessment of the relative contribution of environmental and organic factors is complicated. Neurological examinations frequently give no clear indications of neurological impairment. However, developmental lags, deficits in perceptual–motor functions, and other "soft signs" of this sort may indicate the possibility of minimal damage or dysfunction of the CNS. Still, in the majority of cases, the etiological roles of environmental and organic factors are either ambiguous or unknown. Heber (1970) estimated that 80–90% of individuals labeled retarded in the United States have no obvious neurological impairment and the majority appear normal physically.

Assessment procedures require sampling of a broad range of behaviors. In making an evaluation, the clinician should consider the person's medical reports, cultural influences, opportunities for learning experiences, developmental history, and data from psychological testing. Although an individual's present abilities can be described with some degree of accuracy, specific predictions regarding ultimate levels of functioning always should be qualified. The goal of psychological assessment is to provide parents and teachers with a realistic appraisal without instilling false hopes or undue pessimism.

CULTURAL INFLUENCES: A SUMMARY

Some persons who will later become independent, productive citizens may be inappropriately labeled retarded because of primary reliance on IQs and school performance. Virtually all professionals emphasize the need to consider adaptive behavior as well as test scores before classifying an individual as retarded. Assessment and predictability may be improved if evaluations are based upon behavior in all the individual's customary environmental settings. The social systems perspective, as proposed by Mercer (1973), appears to be a promising model for assessing the multivariate aspects of an individual's abilities.

Biological Aspects of Mental Retardation

Thus far, we have examined the influence of environmental factors on mental retardation. However, any disease, injury, metabolic disturbance, or genetic abnormality that impairs the functioning of the CNS may alter the learning process and retard development. Psychologists have tended to stress the role of environmental factors while deemphasizing organismic variables. The tendency among medically trained individuals has been just the opposite. For example, Rundle (1970) refers to the "minimal" contribution of socioeconomic factors to mental retardation. Carter (1966) states that "mental retardation due to environmental or cultural deprivation is not a true form of the condition but is simply a manifestation of lack of opportunity to develop [p. 147]." As we noted earlier, these differences are reflected in the different models of mental retardation favored by the two professions.

A preference for an organismic or an environmental emphasis also may be influenced by such factors as when a child is seen and for what. For example, a child who is not viewed as retarded until the school years and is then referred because of academic difficulties is more likely to be labeled as retarded on the basis of IQ. Such children are more likely to be seen by a psychologist and less likely to evidence any obvious form of biological impairment. A child labeled as retarded during the preschool years is more likely to evidence obvious biological impairment and to be classified as retarded on the basis of a medical examination (Mercer, 1973).

Research reported by Mercer indicates that middle-class white children labeled as retarded were more likely to have notable physical disabilities and to be labeled by physicians in the preschool years than either Mexican-American or black children. Minority children, on the other hand, were more likely than white children to be labeled retarded on the basis of IQs obtained during the school years. According to Mercer's research, physicians are more likely to encounter preschool white children with biological impairment, whereas educators and psychologists are more likely to have experience with physically normal, culturally disadvantaged children. Thus, the biological orientation of the physician and the environmental orientation of the psychologist may well be reinforced by the population of clients to which they are exposed.

These differences between professionals center around cases where the subject exhibits no readily discernible signs of physical impairment, but functions substantially below the norms of society. Disorders that will be presented in this section, on the other hand, are readily definable organic disorders associated with retardation. For convenience, such disorders will be referred to as *distinctive clinical types* of retardation, meaning that there are distinctive organic signs that allow a reliable medical classification. It is important to stress that distinctive clinical types represent a relatively small proportion of persons who are labeled mentally retarded. Dunn (1973), for example, points out that even if one uses a conservative sociolegal definition of retardation (1% of the population), causes of retardation will be unknown for 85% of the people in this group. Cases with unknown etiology have been assigned such labels as *aclinical, nonpathological,* or *cultural–familial.*

The distinctive clinical types that will be discussed do not include the whole range of diseases, genetic abnormalities, injuries, or other causes of organic impairment that may be associated with retardation. The selection of disorders in this section has been based on frequency of occurrence and the amount of available research. In addition, some disorders will be omitted because medical advances in treatment and prevention have rendered them unimportant as causes of retardation. For example, *cretinism* is a thyroid disorder that can lead to severe retardation. But because it now can be detected and treated in early infancy, it is becoming rare in the United States.

When possible, the cardinal symptoms and etiological factors will be discussed for each disorder. Particular attention will be devoted to the chromosomal disorder known as Down's syndrome, the most frequent of all the distinctive clinical types.

DOWN'S SYNDROME

The physical characteristics of Down's syndrome (also referred to as *trisomy 21* and *mongolism*) were first described in 1866 by Langdon Down. Because of the broad nose and the seemingly slanted eyes, Down referred to the disorder as mongolism. Gustavson (1964), noting that the term *mongolism* implied inappropriate racial connotations, supported the suggestion that the disorder be referred to as either Down's syndrome or trisomy 21.

CARDINAL SYMPTOMS. Since Langdon Down's original recognition of the syndrome, various physical characteristics associated with the disorder have been noted. Some of the more readily observable signs include a skin fold covering the corner of the eyes, giving them a slanting appearance; a single, transverse crease across the palm of a small hand with short fingers; inward curving of the little fingers; a frequently open mouth with a protruding fissured tongue; a nose with a flat bridge and nostrils turned slightly upward; a skull that appears relatively small and somewhat flattened (*brachycephalic*); ears that seem square-shaped because of fused ear lobules; smooth, soft hair that tends to become sparse as a child grows older; a short, broad neck; legs that are short in proportion to the body trunk; and a notable space between big and little toes (Gustavson, 1964; Dunn, 1973). Dunn notes that not all persons with Down's syndrome have all these characteristics, and a number of the features can be observed in normal individuals. Diagnosis of Down's syndrome made early in infancy on the basis of observable signs alone has generally proved to be accurate. Still, according to

Dunn, "the only certain means of diagnosis" is confirmation of the various physical signs by chromosomal analysis.

INCIDENCE.   Down's syndrome is the most frequent of all clinical types of retardation. Carter (1966), defining retardation strictly in terms of the medical–pathological model, refers to Down's syndrome as "the greatest single cause of mental retardation   [p. 126]." He notes that, according to some estimates, Down's syndrome may account for as much as 25% of all the distinctive clinical types of retardation. Dunn (1973) suggests that the syndrome represents one-third of all moderately retarded individuals.[5] According to Heber (1970), in 1968 8.1% of all residents at public institutions were afflicted with Down's syndrome. In the same year, Down's syndrome accounted for 9.4% of all new admissions to public institutions for the retarded.

There are many variables that make it difficult to estimate how frequently Down's syndrome occurs in the general population. Gustavson (1964) notes that, in addition to other factors, the incidence of Down's syndrome will vary according to whether investigations are based on populations of newborns, mental defectives, or the total population. In studies of newborns, the incidence per 1000 varied from .45 to 3.4. Other studies estimated the incidence at birth as between 1.5 and 1.7 per 1000.

Two important discoveries pertaining to Down's syndrome have made such general estimates of the incidence at birth less meaningful. According to Richards (1970), it was clearly established in the 1930s that the risk of having a child with Down's syndrome greatly increased in mothers nearing the end of their childbearing years. The age of the mother at the time of birth, therefore, is an important factor to consider when estimating the incidence of the disorder among newborns. The second discovery was the finding of a chromosomal abnormality in persons having Down's syndrome (Lejeune, Gautier, & Turpin, 1959). This finding suggests that incidence at birth may be a misleading estimate of the actual incidence of the syndrome. For example, aborted fetuses may have a higher incidence of the chromosomal abnormality than newborn infants. If so, the incidence of the syndrome may be greater than that calculated on the basis of a sample of infants born at full term. A chromosomal abnormality, although not necessarily an indication of an inherited disorder, indicates the importance of considering variables such as family history and ethnic or racial origins.

Maternal Age as a Factor.   Heber (1970) notes that over one-half of all children with Down's syndrome were born to mothers in their late thirties and older, even though only one-sixth of all children are born to mothers in this age range.

[5] Presumably, *moderately retarded*, in this instance, refers to persons with an IQ range of 35 (plus or minus 5) to 60 (plus or minus 5). Heber's (1961) definition of moderately retarded was an IQ range of 36–51 for the Stanford–Binet scale and an IQ range of 40–54 for the Wechsler scales. Traditionally, *moderate retardation* has referred to persons within the IQ range of 25 (plus or minus 5) to 50 (plus or minus 5).

Collmann and Stoller (1962) found the incidence of Down's syndrome among mothers under 20 to be 1 in 2300 births, whereas in women over 45 the incidence was 1 in 46. Lilienfeld and Benesch (1969) suggest that a decrease of 20–45% in the frequency of Down's syndrome could be expected if women over 35 practiced birth control. According to Lilienfeld and Benesch, there is little or no evidence to indicate that age of the father is an important variable related to the incidence of Down's syndrome. It may be concluded, therefore, that mothers in their last years of childbearing have a substantially higher risk of giving birth to an infant with Down's syndrome than have younger mothers. As will be discussed later, however, there are certain types of Down's syndrome that appear to be unrelated to maternal age.

Incidence among Aborted Fetuses. The discovery of a chromosomal abnormality underlying Down's syndrome made it possible to identify the disorder in pregnancies terminated prior to full term. Spontaneous abortions (as opposed to induced abortions) are of particular interest in that a higher incidence of chromosomal abnormalities among spontaneous abortions might indicate that the abnormality itself is a factor contributing to the abortion.

From a review of relevant research, Lilienfeld and Benesch (1969) note that of 261 spontaneously aborted fetuses, 28% had chromosomal abnormalities. Four percent of the abnormalities (10 out of the 261) were of the type called trisomy 21, which accompanies Down's syndrome. Lilienfeld and Benesch suggest the following procedure for estimating the incidence of Down's syndrome for *all* conceptions: Assume that 15% of all conceptions terminate in fetal death and that 4% of these have trisomy 21. Next, assume that 1.5 per 1000 of all live borns have trisomy 21. Based on these figures, we would expect 1000 conceptions to yield 850 live births and 150 fetal deaths (15%). Of the 850 live births, 1.3 infants (1.5%) would have trisomy 21. Therefore, the 1.3 infants of the 850 live births plus the 6 fetuses of the 150 fetal deaths would yield an incidence of 7.3 trisomy 21 cases per 1000 conceptions.

Based on these figures, it can be determined that approximately 80% of all pregnancies in which the fetus has trisomy 21 terminate in spontaneous abortion. Only 20% of conceptions with trisomy result in a live birth. As Lilienfeld and Benesch state, to consider the incidence of trisomy 21 only among live births would be "merely studying the top of the iceberg." Their inferences are based on limited data, but if the estimates are supported by research employing larger samples, the true incidence of Down's syndrome may be four to five times that calculated on the basis of live births. At the very least, it appears that Down's syndrome is more common than indicated by traditional estimates based on full-term pregnancies. It would be of interest to have data on the incidence of trisomy 21 among spontaneously aborted fetuses for mothers at varying age levels.

Ethnic or Racial Factors. At one time, it was thought that Down's syndrome was less common among blacks than whites. More recently, however, Lilienfeld and Benesch (1969) and Heber (1970) have concluded on the basis of previous research that the incidence of Down's syndrome differs very little between black and white samples. Heber (1970), in a summary of previous research, notes that the lowest incidence of Down's syndrome was in Japan. Lilienfeld and Benesch (1969), however, citing studies done in Bombay, Calcutta, and Kuala Lumpur, observe that in 66,000 births to Indian and Malaysian mothers, only one case of Down's syndrome was reported. In Alexandria, Egypt, no cases of Downs syndrome were reported for 9598 births. Based on a frequency of 1.5 per 1000, one would expect 99 cases in the Indian sample and approximately 14 in the Egyptian sample. Possible differences in diagnostic and sampling procedures may have obscured a higher incidence than that reported for these two countries. Still, the data suggest potential variations in susceptibility associated with the genetic histories of different racial and ethnic groups. Down's syndrome, however, occurs in the great majority of all countries in which statistical surveys have been conducted.

THREE TYPES OF DOWN'S SYNDROME.

Standard Trisomy 21. The most common form of Down's syndrome involves the presence of a 47th chromosome such as originally observed by Lejeune *et al.* (1959). Basically, normal individuals have 46 chromosomes (23 pairs). In trisomy 21, the 21st set of chromosomes contains 3 rather than 2 chromosomes. The trisomy is a result of nondisjunction—a failure of one pair of chromosomes to separate during meiosis. Normally, one pair of chromosomes in the 21st set would end up in each of two gametes. In nondisjunction, 3 chromosomes end up in one gamete and 1 chromosome ends up in the other gamete. Fertilization of the gamete with 3 chromosomes results in trisomy 21.

According to Dunn (1973), standard trisomy 21 does not appear to be an inherited disorder. Richards (1970), however, has suggested that genetic factors might increase the likelihood of the chromosomal error occurring. For mothers who give birth to a child with standard trisomy 21, the risk of having a second child with the same disorder is less than 1 in a 100 (AMA, 1965). A significant fact regarding standard trisomy 21—a fact that has bearing on the risk of recurrence— is that the disorder is clearly related to maternal age. Since the incidence of the syndrome is much greater for older mothers, the risk of a second trisomy 21 birth will be higher among older mothers than among the total population of childbearing women. However, the risk of an older mother having a second child with trisomy 21 appears to be no greater than that for an older mother who has not had a trisomy 21 birth. In standard trisomy 21, therefore, the age variable appears to be considerably more important than variables associated with heredity.

Richards (1970) has estimated that of all Down's syndrome births, 94% are of the standard trisomy 21 type. The chromosomal error associated with the disorder, however, may have little to do with hereditary factors. Lilienfeld and Benesch (1969) propose what they call the most tenable hypothesis regarding etiology: Progressive deterioration of the egg cell due to aging may increase the chance of a chromosomal error. Exactly how the presence of the 47th chromosome leads to the alterations in physiological development that underlie retardation remains unknown (Grossman, 1973).

Translocation Types. In standard trisomy 21, in which there are 47 rather than the normal 46 chromosomes, the extra chromosome is clear and distinct. In the translocation types, the extra chromosome attaches itself to another chromosome so that an individual appears to have a normal count of 46 chromosomes. The extra material of the 47th chromosome, however, can still be identified. Two types of translocations can occur. In the first type, the extra chromosome may be fused with the D group, which consists of chromosome pairs 13–15. This type of translocation is referred to as a D/G translocation. In the second type of translocation, the extra chromosome becomes fused with a chromosome in the G group (pairs 21 or 22). This type of translocation is referred to as a G/G translocation. Both types of translocations are rare and each type accounts for only about 2% of all forms of Down's syndrome (Richards, 1970).

Whereas standard trisomy 21 occurs far more frequently in older mothers, the translocation types do not appear to be related to maternal age. Although standard trisomy 21 is far more frequent at all maternal ages than the translocation types, the translocation types account for a higher proportion of Down's syndrome at the younger maternal ages. However, this reflects the rarity of standard trisomy 21 cases at the younger age groups rather than an increase in the translocation types. About 15% of Down's cases in mothers under 20 are of the rare translocation type, whereas only 1.5% of Down's cases in mothers over 45 are of the translocation type (Richards, 1970).

There is direct evidence that, unlike standard trisomy 21, the translocation type of Down's syndrome may be inherited. Parents of children with trisomy 21 show no chromosomal abnormalities, but parents or relatives of children with the translocation type are sometimes the carriers of the translocated chromosomes. If one parent carries the translocated chromosome, the risk is about one-third for a Down's child of the translocated type, one-third for a normal child who carries the translocated chromosome, and one-third for a normal child who does not carry the translocated chromosome. In about one-third of the families who have two or more children with Down's syndrome, a translocation is the cause (AMA, 1965).

Although the translocation type of Down's can be inherited, the majority of translocation cases appear to be sporadic or noninherited. In such cases, no chromosomal abnormalities can be found in relatives. Lilienfeld and Benesch (1969) have estimated that 41% of all D/G translocations and 8% of all G/G translocations are inherited. In such cases, chromosomal abnormalities can be identified in one or more relatives.

In summary, the major differences between the translocation type of Down's and the standard trisomy 21 are that (1) the translocation types are rare and account for only 4% of Down's cases; (2) the translocation types do not show a significant increase with maternal age; and (3) in the translocation types, the importance of hereditary factors has been demonstrated.

Mosaic Type. The major characteristic of the mosaic type of Down's syndrome is the presence of an extra chromosome in some body cells but not in others. In other words, some of the body cells contain a normal number of 46 chromosomes whereas others contain 47. The mosaic type, like the translocation type, is rare and accounts for about 2% of all forms of Down's syndrome. Mosaicism may be of two types. One type may start as a normal zygote (fertilized ovum with 46 chromosomes), with nondisjunction occurring during mitosis; the other may begin as an abnormal zygote with trisomy. Maternal age does not appear to be related to the first type of mosaicism, which originates from a normal zygote. Maternal age is, however, related to the second type, which originates from abnormal, trisomic zygotes. Like standard trisomy 21, the incidence of the second mosaic type is higher among older mothers. The role of heredity in mosaic types of Down's syndrome has not been established. Lilienfeld and Benesch (1969) stress the importance of studying mosaicism among normal-appearing mothers of children with Down's syndrome, particularly since previous research indicates that as many as 10% of normal-appearing mothers of Down's syndrome cases may have chromosomal mosaics.

Persons who are mosaic types tend to have fewer physical signs characteristic of Down's syndrome and obtain higher scores on IQ tests. Dunn (1973), citing previous research, notes that the mean IQ for 30 cases of mosaicism was 65, whereas the mean IQ for both the standard trisomy 21 and translocation types was in the low 40s. Mosaic types, therefore, show less severe physical and behavioral effects than other types.

OTHER FACTORS RELATED TO DOWN'S SYNDROME. Children with Down's syndrome frequently show delays in motor and behavioral development. The majority do not walk until 2–3 years of age—at least a year later than normal children (Gustavson, 1964). Down's cases have poor muscle tone (hypotonia) in infancy, but muscle tone tends to improve as they grow older.

Behaviorally, children with Down's syndrome have sometimes been described as cheerful, affectionate, cooperative, and skilled at mimicry. Such observations are not supported adequately by research. It is possible, however, that pleasant behavior may characterize younger children with Down's syndrome but may not be typical of adolescents and adults (Dunn, 1973).

Performance on IQ tests of persons with Down's syndrome falls within the 25–50 range in about 71% of the cases (Gustavson, 1964). There is some evidence that as children grow older, their IQs decrease.

At least 13 cases have been reported in which persons with Down's syndrome and the associated physical signs of the disorder have IQs ranging from 80 to 120 (Carter, 1966). Several of these cases were verified as true Down's syndrome on the basis of chromosomal analysis. Although normal performance on IQ tests is extremely rare, it would be erroneous to conclude that Down's syndrome invariably leads to retardation (if retardation is defined by IQ).

In general, the mortality rate for Down's syndrome is high. Until 1941, no institutionalized person with Down's syndrome survived past the age of 45 (Rundle, 1970). Improved health care, however, has extended the life expectancy considerably. Two of the most frequent health problems are congenital heart disease and bronchopneumonia (Richards, 1970). Because of control by antibiotics, death caused by pneumonia is less likely than death caused by cardiac problems. Gustavson (1964) reported that two-thirds of all cases dying in the first 3 years had congenital heart defects. Approximately one-fifth of those dying between 4 and 10 years had congenital heart defects. Reports on the incidence of cardiac defects among all cases of Down's syndrome range from 40% to 60% (Carter, 1966).

There is also evidence that leukemia may be 8 to 19 times more prevalent in persons with Down's syndrome than would be expected on the basis of norms for the general population (Carter, 1966). A person with Down's syndrome, therefore, is frequently handicapped by health problems that decrease his chance for survival.

TREATMENT AND PREVENTION.   Once an individual with Down's syndrome is born, there is no treatment that can cure or even alleviate the condition. Because of recent advances in the area of genetics, however, preventive measures are becoming increasingly feasible. Since heredity is known to play a role in the translocation type, it is possible for suspected carriers to have a chromosomal analysis of tissue to determine the presence or absence of a translocated chromosome. Depending on the results, parents can be advised more precisely regarding the risk of having a Down's child. Information on some forms of chromosomal abnormalities can also be obtained by analyzing cells present in the amniotic fluid during the third to fourth month of pregnancy. Presumably, all types of Down's syndrome may be detected in this manner, but the procedure, known as *amniocentesis*, involves a slight risk and is currently expensive. Recent research involving a computer-assisted chromosome analysis may yield a more practical, less expensive, 5-minute heredity analysis (Dunn, 1973). In the future, therefore, many mothers may be advised early in their pregnancy about the risk of Down's syndrome and other chromosomal abnormalitites as well. Mothers may decide to have abortions. Such preventive measures may reduce the prevalence of Down's syndrome in the future. At present, however, it is the most common of all the distinctive clinical types of retardation.

HYDROCEPHALY

GENERAL CHARACTERISTICS.   Hydrocephaly is not a disease, but a condition that may result from a variety of causes (Carter, 1966). The normal brain contains several spaces called ventricles, which are filled with a clear fluid called *cerebrospinal fluid*. The ventricles are connected by passages so that cerebrospinal fluid may circulate from ventricle to ventricle. Two large ventricles, called the lateral ventricles, and smaller ventricles referred to as the third and fourth ventricles, contain structures called *choroid plexuses,* which secrete about 150 cubic centimeters of cerebrospinal fluid every 24 hours (Benda, 1952). Normally, cerebrospinal fluid continuously flows out of the ventricular system into spaces at the base of the brain, where the fluid is absorbed into the bloodstream.

Within the ventricles, a certain amount of pressure is maintained by the cerebrospinal fluid (expressed in millimeters of water, the normal pressure is about 60–120). Basically, hydrocephaly occurs when an excessive amount of cerebrospinal fluid accumulates in the ventricular spaces. Because of the abnormal accumulation of fluid, the ventricles, particularly the lateral ventricles, are forced to expand beyond normal size. As a result, the surrounding brain tissue is pressed outward against the skull. In the fetus or the newborn infant, the sections of the skull or cranium have not become fused and the internal pressure of the fluid causes abnormal expansion of the head. Expansion is greatest at sites called *fontanelles,* where sections of the cranium intersect. If the buildup of fluid is unchecked, the head may enlarge as much as 1 inch each week (Benda, 1952). Primarily because of the abnormal enlargement of the head, hydrocephaly, like Down's syndrome, can be diagnosed before 12 months of age (AMA, 1965).

The physical appearance of the hydrocephalic is usually unattractive. Often the forehead is huge, causing the face to appear relatively small. The skin may be stretched so tight that the child is unable to close his eyes. Frequently, the eyes appear to be turned downward and a variety of visual defects may accompany the disorder (Benda, 1952; Carter, 1966).

The physical appearance of the hydrocephalic and the level of behavioral function depend on the extent of the cerebrospinal fluid buildup. In some cases, the buildup of fluid may be minimal or may occur for only a short period of time. Although the individual's external appearance may be normal, a pneumoencephalogram (in which the lateral ventricles are filled with air and X rays are taken) might still reveal enlargement of the lateral ventricles. Similarly, if the damage to the CNS is minimal, there may be no evidence of intellectual or behavioral impairment. Unfortunately, most untreated cases are severely impaired intellectually because of extensive damage to the nervous system.

INCIDENCE. Hydrocephaly is the most common of the cerebral–cranial disorders—disorders associated with impairment of the nervous system as well as the size and appearance of the skull (Carter, 1966). Studies reviewed by Heber (1970) suggest that the incidence of hydrocephaly in various countries ranges from .3 to 3.5 per 1000. In the United States, the incidence reported in seven studies ranged from .3 to 3.2 per 1000. In four of these seven studies, however, the range was restricted to .8 to 1.0 per 1000. Although Heber advises caution in interpreting these statistics, the overall incidence of hydrocephaly would seem to be slightly less than 1.0 per 1000 births.

There is little evidence that hydrocephaly is unusually frequent among any particular ethnic or racial group. Factors related to geographical areas may be associated with higher incidence rates (Pratt, 1967), but the evidence to date is inconclusive.

TYPES OF HYDROCEPHALY AND ETIOLOGICAL FACTORS.   There is no substantial evidence of any genetic cause of hydrocephaly (Pratt, 1967).[6] However, if a mother has one hydrocephalic child, the risk of having a second hydrocephalic child, at least in some families, may be greater than that for the general population. The risk of having a hydrocephalic child may increase with maternal age.

As previously discussed, hydrocephaly is caused by an excessive buildup of fluid in the lateral, third, and fourth ventricles of the brain. In the past, hydrocephaly often has been divided into subcategories of *communicating* and *noncommunicating* hydrocephaly. In communicating hydrocephaly, there is an adequate flow of the fluid between the ventricles but the reabsorption of the fluid is too slow. "Spontaneous" normal absorption of fluid frequently occurs in communicating hydrocephaly before the child reaches 2 years of age. Thus, even though extensive damage to the nervous system may have already resulted, further damage or enlargement of the head may not occur. Noncommunicating hydrocephaly occurs following blockage or obstruction of the flow of cerebrospinal fluid in the small openings that connect the ventricles. Thus, fluid that cannot pass through these small openings accumulates in the ventricles and causes expansion (Carter, 1966).

Disregarding distinctions between communicating and noncommunicating hydrocephaly, we can distinguish at least three causes of excessive accumulation of fluid:

1. Overproduction of cerebrospinal fluid by the choroid plexuses due to tumors in that area or to other causes.
2. Underabsorption of cerebrospinal fluid due to such factors as meningitis or encephalitis.
3. A block in the flow of the fluid in one or more of the small spaces connecting the ventricles due to tumors or diseases such as meningitis (Carter, 1966).

The most severe cases of hydrocephaly are due to the obstructive type in which the passageways (the small spaces or ducts between the ventricles) are blocked (Benda, 1952).

Hydrocephaly may occur prenatally or it may begin after birth. A number of factors such as brain injury, tumors, and diseases such as meningitis, encephalitis,

---

[6] An exception may be a form of sex-linked hydrocephaly involving stenosis (narrowing) of the aqueduct of Sylvius. This particular form of hydrocephaly may explain the fact that in some families, if the first child is hydrocephalic, the risk of hydrocephaly for subsequent children may be greater than that of the general population (Pratt, 1967).

and toxoplasmosis, may lead to hydrocephaly. There is some statistical evidence that hydrocephaly increases in frequency if mothers have been exposed to Asiatic flu during the first trimester of their pregnancy. Others have suggested a possible role of particular kinds of vitamin deficiencies, especially riboflavin (vitamin B_2). In many cases, however, the causes are not known (Carter, 1966).

TREATMENT AND PREVENTION.   At present, there is no real cure for hydrocephaly. There are procedures, however, that can substantially reduce the severity of the disorder. According to Carter (1966), the most successful treatment for all types of hydrocephaly is surgery. In the most frequent form of surgery, a shunt (hollow tube) is inserted inside the brain to continuously drain off the excess cerebrospinal fluid. The preferred type is a ventriculo–auricular shunt. (One end of a synthetic tube is inserted in the lateral ventricle of the brain; the other end is run under the skin into a large vessel of the neck and from there into the auricle of the heart.) The shunt may be constructed so that it will stretch as the patient grows, thus making frequent replacement unnecessary. If such surgery is performed very early, damage to the nervous system and enlargement of the head may be minimized. Even with early treatment, the damage is often severe enough to cause some retardation. Generally, hydrocephalics who have had surgery function at a higher level than those who have not had surgery, but the mortality rate associated with surgical intervention is fairly high (Carter, 1966). Surgery helps to prevent further damage from hydrocephaly, but it cannot cure the damage that has been done.

MICROCEPHALY

GENERAL CHARACTERISTICS.   Microcephaly, like hydrocephaly, cannot be considered a disease. A variety of causes may lead to the condition. The major characteristic of the disorder is the failure of the brain to grow to a normal size. Alterations in brain size may vary from only a slight degree of arrested growth to a marked decrease in the size of the brain (Benda, 1952). Because the brain is undersized, the sections of the cranium (skull) do not expand normally. Thus, the head size is typically much smaller than normal. Often, the forehead recedes because of a reduction in size of the frontal lobes of the brain. The back of the head tends to be flattened and the scalp is sometimes wrinkled. One criterion for microcephaly is a head circumference smaller than three standard deviations below the mean for age and sex. However, a diagnosis of microcephaly should never be based on head size alone (Warkeny & Dignan, 1973). There are persons with small heads who are quite normal.

Microcephalics usually are severely retarded, but occasionally they may be found in special education classrooms for retarded children who are functioning at a higher level (Dunn, 1973). The severity of retardation may vary according to the cause of the condition.

There are no general behavioral characteristics that distinguish the microcephalic from other clinical types of retardation. In one form of microcephaly the individual may make peculiar sounds resembling the cry of a cat. The distinctiveness of such sounds has led to the use of the label *cat-cry syndrome* (Pratt, 1967).

INCIDENCE. Although Dunn (1973) refers to microcephaly as a "rare condition," Carter (1966) considers it a "very common abnormality." Like other clinical types of retardation, the true incidence remains speculative because of differences in population sampling and diagnostic procedures. Warkeny and Dignan (1973) noted previous estimates ranging from 1 per 1000 in Louisiana, to 1 per 6200 in Sweden, to 1 per 8500 in Germany. Microcephaly is not as common as Down's syndrome or hydrocephaly, but its occurrence is sufficiently frequent to warrant its inclusion as a major and distinctive type of clinical retardation.

TYPES AND ETIOLOGY OF MICROCEPHALY. Two forms of microcephaly have been generally discussed, a primary and a secondary form. Primary microcephaly is inherited and may be transmitted as in an autosomal recessive gene (Grossman, 1973). Secondary microcephaly may result from several prenatal and postnatal causes. One of the earliest factors identified as a probable cause of secondary microcephaly was X ray exposure during pregnancy, particularly during the first trimester (Benda, 1952). In some cases, the X ray treatment was performed because the pregnancy had been mistaken for a uterine tumor. In other cases, a uterine tumor may have obscured the presence of pregnancy (Benda, 1952). Women 15 to 17 weeks pregnant who were as close as 1500 meters to the hypocenter of the atomic explosions in Hiroshima and Nagasaki were more likely to give birth to microcephalics. Microcephaly caused by X ray exposure is now rare because the dangers have been recognized (Warkeny & Dignan, 1973). Other causes of secondary microcephaly include prenatal infections such as rubella and toxoplasmosis and traumas such as neonatal asphyxia and birth injury (Grossman, 1973). There is also some evidence that the incidence of microcephaly is higher when the mother has had cytomegalic inclusion disease (a viral infection in the mother's salivary glands, which may be passed on to the fetus later in pregnancy). A higher incidence has also been noted among mothers who are carriers of phenylketonuria, a genetic disorder that will be discussed later in this chapter (Warkeny & Dignan, 1973).

The role of genetic factors in primary microcephaly has been recognized for some time (Benda, 1952). More recent cytogenetic research has led to the discovery of a number of chromosomal abnormalities present in various microcephalic populations (Warkeny & Dignan, 1973). Genetic factors, therefore, may play a more important role than was once thought. As was noted in the discussion of Down's syndrome, the identification of a chromosomal disorder does not mean that a condition is inherited. Chromosomal errors may occur for various reasons after fertilization has taken place.

A type of cranial disorder called *pancraniostenosis* is sometimes referred to in discussions of microcephaly (Carter, 1966). Although this condition may result in a small head and extensive brain damage, it is not caused by the failure of the brain to grow normally. In pancraniostenosis, all of the suture lines dividing sections of the cranium are fused either before or soon after birth. Normally, these suture lines are open at birth and allow the cranium to expand with growth of the brain. In pancraniostenosis, the fusion of all cranial sections prevents the brain's normal expansion. If untreated, the condition typically results in death or severe retardation. It is possible, if the condition is detected early, to open the closed sutures or remove strips of bone surgically (Carter, 1966). Such surgery allows the brain to expand and neurological damage may be avoided or minimized. Although untreated pancraniostenosis may result in a small head and severe retardation, it is really a very different kind of disorder than microcephaly. Therefore, reference to pancraniostenosis as a form of secondary microcephaly is inaccurate.

TREATMENT AND PREVENTION.   Once the growth of the brain is arrested by microcephaly, there is no effective cure or treatment. Genetic counseling, based on chromosomal analysis of the parents or identification of chromosomal errors by amniocentesis during pregnancy, may permit preventive measures to reduce the incidence of some types of microcephaly. Genetic counseling, however, cannot prevent other causes of microcephaly, such as asphyxia at birth.

CEREBRAL PALSY AND MENTAL RETARDATION

Approximately 700,000 children and adults in the United States are victims of cerebral palsy. Many are intellectually normal and lead productive lives. Though cerebral palsy is *not* a form of retardation, it represents a class of neurological disorders that frequently lead to retardation. Unlike other distinctive clinical types, cerebral palsy shows little uniformity in physical and behavioral characteristics. Cerebral palsy is defined as a *nonprogressive* brain lesion that usually occurs before birth, during birth, or in infancy or early childhood. About two-thirds of cerebral palsy cases are due to prenatal and perinatal (during birth) complications. The most common clinical symptom of cerebral palsy is a motor deficit—that is, a limitation on physical movement. A major cause of cerebral palsy is anoxia associated with prematurity (Molnar & Taft, 1973). Anoxia, or prolonged deprivation of oxygen to the brain, may occur as a result of such factors as temporary respiratory failure at birth, prolonged high fever, or a disturbance in the supply of oxygen from mother to fetus.

Frequently, the actual extent of brain damage associated with complications at birth cannot be determined until late infancy or early childhood, largely because cortical control over many muscular movements is not present in early infancy. Hence, the effects on motor abilities of a cortical lesion in early infancy may not become obvious until the relevant motor systems mature. Similarly, it is very difficult to predict the extent to which intellectual processes may be impaired (if they are impaired at all). Even in later childhood, assessment of intellectual functioning is often seriously complicated, because there may be impairment of the various motor and sensory systems necessary for performance on intelligence tests or in school. In other words, a cerebral palsy child may "know"

Esme, trying not to spill food from her spoon, has cerebral palsy as a result of a brain injury at birth. Because her speech and hearing are impaired, she was originally diagnosed as retarded (IQ 75). Her parents rejected this evaluation and concentrated on nonverbal communication with her. Recently, she scored 147 on the nonverbal part of the IQ test. (Nathan Farb)

material, but be unable to demonstrate this knowledge because he is unable to make the required motor or sensory responses. In addition, speech disturbances often complicate attempts to administer tests. For these reasons, assessment of intellectual abilities is difficult, particularly in borderline cases where IQ estimates are inconsistent. While recognizing these difficulties, Molnar and Taft (1973) estimate that about one-third of cerebral palsy cases score in the normal range, one-third score in the educable range, and the remainder score below the educable range. Intellectual impairment, therefore, is a handicap frequently associated with cerebral palsy.

METABOLIC DISORDERS AND MENTAL RETARDATION

A number of metabolic disorders can severely affect the development of the nervous system and lead to retardation. Metabolic disorders, however, account for a relatively low percentage of persons labeled mentally retarded. In some disorders, such as Tay-Sachs disease, the onset of symptoms occurs rapidly and an early death is inevitable. Thus, the child does not survive long enough to be placed in an institution or require special education and care. In other disorders, notably phenylketonuria (PKU), early diagnosis and treatment may prevent retardation.

The incidence of the various metabolic disorders is considerably less than that of other clinical types, such as Down's syndrome or hydrocephaly. A conservative estimate for phenylketonuria, for example, is about 1 per 10,000. Before we discuss the differences among the various metabolic disorders, the following general similarities should be noted: Except in cases where treatment is effective, retardation is typically severe and an early death is the rule; most of the disorders involve a recessive, autosomal type of inheritance; most of the disorders are characterized by a progressive increase in the severity of symptoms. These disorders are associated with three basic types of metabolic abnormalities—abnormalities of lipid metabolism, of amino acid metabolism, and of carbohydrate metabolism.

ABNORMALITIES OF LIPID METABOLISM. Disorders in this category involve an abnormality of the enzyme system that metabolizes lipids (fats). This pathology is characterized by an accumulation of lipid substances in the cytoplasm of nerve cells, causing swelling and distortion of the nerve cells (Carter, 1966). The storage of lipid substances in the nerve cells eventually leads to massive neurological impairment. Four forms of cerebral lipoidosis, all inherited, are commonly recognized:

Early Infantile Cerebral Lipoidosis (Tay-Sachs Disease). This form of cerebral lipoidosis is transmitted by a single autosomal recessive gene. It is more prevalent in people of Jewish ancestry from northeastern Europe (Grossman, 1973). The development of the infant appears normal until about the third to the sixth month. Initially, the infant becomes hypersensitive to sound and light stimulation (Robinson & Robinson, 1965). The child gradually becomes weak, blind, and increasingly apathetic. Often a cherry-red spot appears on the macular area of the retina. Typically, the child dies by 3 years of age (Zacks, 1971). A child with Tay-Sachs disease, therefore, is not likely to live long enough to be labeled as mentally retarded.

Late Infantile Cerebral Lipoidosis (Bielschowsky–Jansky Disease). In the late infantile form, the clinical picture is similar to that of the early infantile form except that the onset of the disease is not evident until between the second and fourth year. It does not appear to be as common as Tay-Sachs disease among Jewish families. Although there is retinal degeneration that eventually leads to blindness, there is no red spot on the macular area of the retina. Retardation becomes progressively severe and death is inevitable at around 5 or 6 years of age (Carter, 1966).

Early Juvenile Cerebral Lipoidosis (Spielmeyer–Vogt Disease). In this form, the onset of the disease does not become obvious until around the sixth to eighth year of life. The pathology is similar to the infantile forms but progresses more slowly. Retinal degeneration leads to eventual blindness, and the child becomes more and more spastic. Retardation increases in severity as the disease runs its course. The child usually lives until around 10 to 14 years of age (Carter, 1966).

Late Juvenile Cerebral Lipoidosis (Kuf's Disease).   The major difference between the late juvenile form and other forms is that the onset of symptoms in the late juvenile form does not occur until 20 to 30 years of age. In addition, because the disease usually progresses much more slowly than other forms, the affected individual may live to 40 or 50 years of age. Because of this longer survival period, both early and late juvenile forms of cerebral lipoidosis are more likely to lead to institutionalization than are the infantile forms. There are no effective treatments for either the infantile or juvenile forms of cerebral lipoidosis.

ABNORMALITIES OF AMINO ACID METABOLISM.   Although there are several forms of amino acid metabolism abnormalities, the most widely known is phenylketonuria (PKU). It is the most widely studied and best understood of all the metabolic disorders potentially associated with retardation (Carter, 1966). Basically, the disorder is genetically transmitted as an autosomal recessive defect of phenylalanine metabolism. The affected individual lacks a particular liver enzyme necessary to convert phenylalanine to tyrosine (Grossman, 1973). As a result of this metabolic failure, an excess of phenylpyruvic acid, hydroxyphenylacetic acid, and other abnormal metabolites collects in both the blood and the urine. Phenylpyruvic acid has a distinctive odor. The peculiar smell of affected infants was the first clue that eventually led investigators to discover the causes of PKU. In addition to the peculiar odor, other characteristics of PKU include an early onset of irritability; a lack of pigment (melanin), which results in very blonde children; and eventual retardation (Carter, 1966).

Unlike cerebral lipoidosis, PKU can be treated effectively. When an affected child eats a normal diet, the failure of the liver enzyme to metabolize phenylalanine into tyrosine leads to a surplus of phenylalanine and a shortage of tyrosine. Treatment, therefore, consists of a diet low in phenylalanine and high in tyrosine. If the diagnosis is made early, the child may be placed on this diet in the first month. The effect of the diet is to prevent major damage to the nervous system during the critical period of rapid development. Authorities disagree as to how long the diet should continue, but the range is anywhere from 3½ to 9 years of age (Carter, 1966). Although untreated cases of PKU usually result in retardation, there are some untreated individuals who are of normal intelligence. If the treatment diet is begun prior to 6 months of age, most children with PKU will develop normally (Heber, 1970).

ABNORMALITIES OF CARBOHYDRATE METABOLISM.   Two abnormalities of carbohydrate metabolism, *Hurler's syndrome* and *galactosemia,* have often been discussed in relation to mental retardation. An effective treatment has been developed for galactosemia but not for Hurler's syndrome (Carter, 1966).

Hurler's syndrome, therefore, is currently a more important contributor to retardation than galactosemia.

Hurler's Syndrome (Gargoylism).   Hurler's syndrome is inherited via an autosomal recessive gene. Errors of metabolism cause deposits of a mucopolysaccharide to accumulate in various organs of the body, particularly in the liver, heart, lungs, and spleen. This same substance, along with a lipid substance, accumulates in the gray matter of the brain and produces lesions (Robinson & Robinson, 1965). The onset of symptoms may occur shortly after birth or at any time up to 5 or 6 years of age (Carter, 1966). Typically, skeletal growth is stunted and deformed and visual processes gradually deteriorate. Facial features appear coarse; the nose is broad and the eyebrows are bushy. The mouth, lips, and tongue all tend to be enlarged. In the later stages, the cornea of the eye clouds over. Another characteristic is a swollen abdomen (Clarke & Clarke, 1965). Although most individuals show a progressive deterioration until death (usually prior to the teens), some individuals survive to the adult years and evidence no further deterioration. Most affected persons are severely retarded, but individuals with mild forms of the disorder have been known to function at a normal or near-normal level (Hilliard & Kirman, 1965). Hurler's syndrome, like other metabolic disorders, is relatively rare, probably about half as common as PKU (Robinson & Robinson, 1965).

Galactosemia.   Galactosemia is caused by a defect in carbohydrate metabolism that leads to a gradual accumulation of galactose in the bloodstream. The role of genetic factors has not been established (Heber, 1970). Generally, the disorder becomes evident shortly after birth. As soon as the child is able to ingest milk, various symptoms such as vomiting, diarrhea, and colic become apparent. The infant shows poor weight gain and extreme malnourishment. Diagnosis is based on the identification of galactose in the urine. As soon as the disorder is identified, the infant can be placed on a diet that is free of lactose and galactose. Unlike the dietary treatment of PKU, the galactosemia diet is usually a lifetime necessity. If no treatment is undertaken, mental retardation is usually progressive and severe. If treated early, however, a large proportion of the cases develop normally (Carter, 1966).

Summary

Throughout history, various derogatory words have been used to label those who cannot or do not function at the level expected by their society. In our achievement-oriented society, which places a high value on verbal and quantitative skills, there are many derogatory connotations associated with the label *mental retardation.* Persons labeled retarded, like persons labeled mentally ill, are subject to a variety of social and legal restrictions. The tendency in the past has been to use the label *mentally retarded* too freely, sometimes including individuals who function adequately on all criteria except performance in the school setting and on intelligence tests. Most professionals now label as retarded only those people who function *substantially* below the norms on *multiple* criteria.

The distinctive clinical types of retardation presented in this chapter represent some of the more frequently occurring physical disorders that may lead to retardation. There are, however, many other disorders that can impair the nervous system and lead to retardation. Disorders involving extensive damage to the nervous system are likely to lead to a label of retardation in almost all settings in which an individual functions. Distinctive clinical types of retardation are often identified by medically trained individuals prior to the school years. These clinical types represent a relatively small proportion of individuals who acquire the label of mental retardation. The majority of individuals who are labeled retarded have no obvious neurological or physical impairment.

10

Disorders of Childhood

The field of child psychopathology has been hampered by a tendency to extend to child populations diagnostic classification systems devised for adult populations. Professionals adhering to a model of psychopathology that stresses the childhood origins of adult disorders understandably expect to find early childhood symptoms that resemble symptoms of adult disorders. For example, on the basis of behavioral characteristics attributed to adult schizophrenics, some have predicted that childhood precursors of the adult disorder would include withdrawn behavior and blunted or inappropriate affective behavior. In fact, some psychiatrists have made a diagnosis of childhood schizophrenia solely on the basis of these symptoms (Robins, 1972).

Robins, in a summary of longitudinal research findings, suggests that childhood schizophrenia may portend later identification of neurological impairment but not adult schizophrenia. Robins also cites findings by Morris, Escoll, and Wexler (1956) in which one-fourth of a group of children who were initially hospitalized for serious antisocial behavior were diagnosed as schizophrenics in their adult years. As children, they were viewed as nonpsychotic, non-brain injured, and intellectually normal. Robins concludes that "while childhood *psychosis* may not be an early form of schizophrenia, antisocial behavior serious enough to lead to hospitalization may sometimes forebode schizophrenia [p. 437]." These findings serve to emphasize that although serious childhood problems may be predictive of adult problems, the *type* of behavioral problem displayed in child-hood may not resemble the type of behavioral problem displayed in adulthood. In other words, a classification system for childhood disorders should not be based on an adult classification system. Instead, the relationship between child and adult disorders should be established empirically, ideally through longitudinal research. Such a relationship cannot be presumed on the basis of an apparent similarity of child and adult behavioral problems.

A meaningful classification system for childhood disorders should be based on developmental norms established for a child's culture. Within such norms, factors of age, frequency, and intensity of behavior can be established. The age variable has obvious importance. For example, thumbsucking among 3-year-olds is far more likely than thumbsucking among 10-year-olds. The importance of the frequency of behavior is also apparent. Problems associated with a 6-year-old wetting his bed every night are much greater than those for a 6-year-old who wets his bed every 4 or 5 months. Establishing norms for intensity of behavior may be more difficult because judgments about this dimension of behavior are relatively subjective. For example, it may be hard to determine whether a child's fear is mild or intense.

Ross (1974) suggests that the primary data for classifying psychological disorders should be obtained from teachers, parents, and other adults who are in daily contact with the child. These adult judgments about child behavior reflect the demands made upon a child by his environment as well as the tolerance level of the child's culture for various forms of behavior.

In this chapter, though frequent reference will be made to a classification system proposed by Ross (1974), different categories will be used for the various disorders under consideration.

Child Behavior in Clinic and Nonclinic Populations

If we study only the problem behaviors of children referred to a psychological or psychiatric clinic, we will never know the base rate for these behaviors in the general population. But if a clinician perceives a behavior problem as uncommon among children in the general population, the clinician's perception will influence his attitudes toward the seriousness of the problem and the treatment process. The clinician's concern about a problem may be transmitted to the parents or teachers and thereby affect adult expectations. To this extent, the clinical significance assigned to a problem may be influenced by whether the base rate for the behavior in the general population is 1% or 50%.

One might argue that a high frequency of occurrence in the general population does not make a problem behavior any less of a problem. To use a medical analogy, teenage acne may still be regarded as a problem whether it affects 1% or 50% of the population. This reasoning, however, obscures the fact that expectations of clinicians, parents, teachers, peers, and the social environment in general are partly based on how closely behavior conforms to cultural norms. Behavior that occurs with a high frequency is more likely to be accepted or tolerated. Behavior that is very unusual with respect to base rates may incur negative adult reactions and peer rejection. The frequency of a behavior within a culture, therefore, is probably related to the tolerance level for that behavior.

Nonetheless, Ross (1974), citing reports by several different investigators, notes that "the prevalence of the kind of behavior which brings children to the attention of relevant clinics and agencies has been shown to be remarkably high in unselected samples of the so-called normal population [p. 19]."[1] Werry and Quay (1971), for example, administered to teachers a 55-item checklist of childhood problems found among children who were referred to a child guidance clinic. For nonselected schoolchildren, teachers checked an average of 11.4 problems for each boy and 7.6 problems for each girl.

Conners (1970), using a list of 73 problem behaviors, compared the incidence of problems among 316 children attending a psychiatric clinic with that of problems reported among 365 normal children by parents attending a PTA meeting. Although children attending the clinic had a significantly greater number of problems than the nonclinic sample, several problem behaviors were reported by parents of the nonclinic sample to have a high frequency of occurrence. These included restlessness (65%), bed-wetting (15%), nightmares (24%), overeating (11%), and biting, chewing, or sucking objects (20%). Ross (1974) notes that Lapouse and Monk (1959) obtained similar findings with a sample of parents who were carefully selected to represent the general population of a city in New York State. Of 482 children between the ages of 6 and 12, bed-wetting was reported for 17%, nightmares for 28%, and nail-biting for 27%. Collectively, these findings emphasize the fact that some behavior problems found in clinic populations also have relatively high frequencies of occurrence in nonclinic populations. Knowledge of these base rates might affect how parents and teachers, as well as clinicians, judge the significance of various childhood problems.

How a Child Comes to the Attention of a Clinician

An important difference between problem behaviors of adults and children is that children rarely—if ever—refer themselves for psychological assessment or treatment. An adult experiencing psychological discomfort can decide whether to seek professional help, but the child's feelings about his situation are often irrelevant to the referral process. From the preceding section, it is obvious that many nonclinic children are perceived by parents or teachers as having the same

[1] This and all subsequent quotes cited to Ross, 1974 are from A. O. Ross, *Psychological Disorders of Children* (*A Behavioral Approach to Theory, Research and Therapy*), © 1974 by McGraw-Hill Book Company. Reprinted by permission of McGraw-Hill Book Company.

problems as children who are referred to clinics. A logical question, assuming the availability of treatment services, is why some children are referred for treatment and some children are not. One logical answer is that individual parents and teachers have different tolerance levels for various types of childhood behaviors. For example, a very active child who is "into everything" may be viewed as a behavior problem by one individual but as energetic and curious by another individual. In this sense, the child may be considered as having a problem only if significant adults have a low tolerance level for this form of behavior.

Such variations in tolerance may explain why many children are not referred for psychological services until they enter the public school system. Generally, school referrals are three times higher for boys than for girls. This finding appears to be consistent for both informal reports and systematic investigations (Ross, 1974). One possible explanation is that males and females react differently to difficulties associated with the learning process. Miller, Hampe, Barrett, and Noble (1971) suggest that female reactions to learning difficulties or failure to learn may take the form of social withdrawal, sensitivity, and fear. Male reactions are more likely to involve aggression, hyperactivity, and asocial behavior. When children enter the elementary school system they may be expected—perhaps for the first time—to remain quiet and inactive for extended periods. Aggression and hyperactivity are incompatible with this expectation whereas social withdrawal and sensitivity may not be perceived by teachers as sufficiently serious to warrant referral for psychological services. Werry and Quay (1971), reported that, of public school children enrolled in kindergarten, first grade, and second grade, 49.7% of the boys were perceived by teachers as restless and unable to sit still. In the same survey, 48.2% of the boys were perceived as distractible and 46.3% were perceived as disruptive. In relation to these findings, Ross (1974) concludes:

> It makes little sense to speak of behavior problems when nearly half of an unselected population engages in that form of behavior. If one uses the statistical concept of normality, the restless, distractible, and disruptive behavior of the children in this school system would have to be viewed as normal behavior. But the teachers check it off on a problem ("symptom") checklist. Whose problem is it? Could it be that classrooms in elementary school are so structured and teacher behavior so programmed that the "normal," to-be-expected behavior of male children is to emit responses the teacher identifies as restlessness and distractibility? If this is the case, the modification called for is situational–environmental and should not have its focus on changing the behavior of boys so that they "adjust" to what may be an intolerable situation [p. 24].

On the basis of this discussion, it seems important to distinguish between "problem" behaviors that are statistically normal and appear to result from low tolerance levels, and problem behaviors that are statistically abnormal and appear in a number of environmental settings with varying tolerance levels. As we will see later in this chapter, there are serious childhood behavior disorders that are not a result of unrealistic expectations of the educational system or low tolerance levels in the child's culture.

Childhood behavior disorders discussed in this chapter will be divided into four major categories: (1) conduct and personality problems; (2) psycho-physiological disorders; (3) learning difficulties in the school situation; and (4) psychotic disorders of childhood. The first category, conduct and personality problems, represents broad classifications that are primarily a result of factor analytic studies. These labels were proposed originally by Ackerson (1931) and were later discussed as major categories of childhood behavior by Peterson (1961). Some of the behaviors included under personality problems have been classified traditionally as *psychoneurotic disorders*, a category that has questionable usefulness for children. Childhood problems classified as neurotic are often transient and bear only superficial resemblance to adult problems labeled as neurotic.

Conduct and Personality Problems

In summarizing findings of factor-analytic research, Ross (1974) notes that one bipolar dimension of maladaptive behavior has been reported consistently. Basically, two clusters of behavior comprise this dimension—those in which the maladaptive behavior is directed toward the environment (excessive approach behavior) and those in which maladaptive behavior is directed toward the child (excessive avoidance behavior).

Ackerson (1931) and Peterson (1961) refer to problems associated with excessive approach behavior as *conduct problems* and problems associated with excessive avoidance behavior as *personality problems*. These labels correspond closely to the manner in which parents, teachers, and many clinicians construe the significance of these behaviors. For example, fighting or disruptive behavior is likely to be referred to as *misconduct*, whereas shyness or timidity would probably be considered attributes of *personality*.

CONDUCT PROBLEMS

As already indicated, conduct problems are behaviors directed toward the environment. Generally, factor analysis allows us to isolate those groupings of teacher and parental judgments about behavior that are statistically related. In Peterson's (1961) study, for example, the following teacher judgments about behavior were highly interrelated: fighting, disobedient, boisterous, attention-seeking, disruptive, and restless. In other words, the teacher who attributes any one of these characteristics to a child is likely to attribute all or most of the other characteristics to the same child. Peterson also found that the incidence of conduct problems was consistently higher for males than for females from kindergarten until the sixth grade. Again, it is important to point out that the data for this particular study consisted of teacher judgments about child behavior rather than direct observations of actual child behavior.

Teacher judgments about behavior may not be truly descriptive of actual behavior. For example, a child may not be concerned about a teacher's attention. Yet, if he is disruptive the teacher may infer that he is engaging in these behaviors *because* he is seeking attention. Thus, a teacher who checks "disruptive" as a problem may also check "attention-seeking" as a problem without any actual evidence of attention-seeking behavior. This point is critically important because parents and teachers initiate most referrals of children to agencies. If the reasons for referral contain inaccurate statements about a child's behavior, then subsequent judgments by clinicians may be biased.

As we noted earlier, behaviors that teachers label as conduct problems may often reflect more fundamental difficulties in meeting academic expectations. If this is the case, behaviors the teacher observes in the classroom may not be observed in a clinical setting or in a home setting, as they make few academic demands on a child. Such a situation may lead a parent or a clinician to challenge observations made by a child's teacher. It is not uncommon to hear statements from parents such as, "He behaves well at home—I don't know why he has so many problems at school." Similarly, a clinician who sees a child for an hour in an office or an unstructured playroom may observe none of the behaviors reported by teachers in a structured situation involving academic demands. Under such circumstances, a less experienced clinician may be tempted to dismiss teacher observations as groundless and conclude that the child has *no* problems. What sometimes becomes obscured, therefore, is that the primary source of a child's difficulties in meeting behavioral expectations in the classroom may be problems of an academic nature. Factors associated with such learning difficulties will be discussed later in this chapter.

Though conduct problems may often stem from academic difficulties, we cannot conclude that all such problems are a result of academic difficulties. Both males and females who perform adequately by academic standards may display any or all of the behaviors clustered under the label of conduct problems. Other factors—disturbances in the home environment, peer influences, or neurological impairment—may also lead to conduct problems involving aggressive behavior, restlessness, and so on.

Aggression is probably the most important form of behavior considered a conduct problem. Aggressive behavior, however, may not be perceived as a problem in our society unless laws or social norms are violated and harm occurs to other persons. For example, aggression associated with a contact sport or self-defense has always been acceptable behavior in our society. To a considerable extent, physical aggression is part of our sex-role expectations for young males. A boy may be encouraged to stand up for himself, to fight back, or to develop skills in boxing, judo, or karate. However, picking on smaller children, being a bully, or fighting others without provocation are negatively sanctioned. Depending on the circumstances, therefore, aggressive behavior may be acceptable or unacceptable.

Aggressive behavior by a child may result in referral to a clinic if it is perceived as a problem by parents, teachers, or legal authorities. Since adult individuals have varying tolerance levels, the perception of aggressive behavior as a problem warranting referral will vary as a function of different tolerance levels among individual adults. The perception of aggression may also vary as a function of different tolerance levels associated with different environmental settings. For example, aggression may be perceived as a problem at school but not at home. In the school setting, one teacher may perceive a child as having a problem with aggression whereas a teacher with a higher tolerance level may consider the same behavior as falling within normal limits. Similar behavior, therefore, may lead to a referral in one instance but not in another.

It is undoubtedly true that individual adults in various environmental settings have different tolerance levels, but it would be a mistake to conclude that problems associated with aggressive behavior are all in the eyes of the beholder. There are children who respond so aggressively that virtually all persons who come into contact with them can agree that they are overly aggressive. Such children typically initiate frequent fights and display intense anger in a variety of different settings.

Clinical explanations for aggressive behavior are usually made after the fact; they often involve the assumption that factors correlating with the behavior are its primary causes. For example, if a child with neurological impairment displays violent aggressive behavior, it is tempting to conclude that the brain damage causes the aggressive outbursts. Similarly, when Bandura and Walters (1959) found that parents who use physical punishment (a form of aggression) to control aggressive behavior tend to raise aggressive children, their findings led to a tenable hypothesis that the cause of the child's aggression is his modeling of aggressive behavior by his parents. It is also possible, however, that children who are frequently aggressive may "cause" parents to use more severe measures to control behavior.

Perhaps the safest conclusion about the etiology of high levels of aggressive behavior is that there may be multiple causes. Some cases apparently represent an interaction of neurological and environmental determinants. In other cases, environmental factors involving modeling of aggressive behavior or reinforcement for aggressive acts appear to be the most important causes of aggressive behavior. In addition, there may be important temperamental differences that predispose some children to respond to stressful situations by aggression and others to respond by withdrawal. *Temperament* refers to the behavioral style of a child and includes such characteristics as activity level, approach or withdrawal tendencies, adaptability to new situations, intensity of reactions, and quality of mood, such as pleasant versus unpleasant or friendly versus unfriendly. An extensive analysis of the role of temperament in patterns of childhood behavior can be found in Thomas, Chess, and Birch (1968).

Although the causes of high levels of aggression among children may not be clearly defined, behavioral modification techniques have been successfully used to reduce levels of aggressive behavior (Ross, 1974). For example, if a child gains a teacher's attention by being disruptive or aggressive, then teacher attention is a social reinforcer that serves to maintain the disruptive behavior. To reduce aggressive behavior the teacher may ignore aggressive or disruptive acts and attend to the child only while he is emitting positive behaviors. Eventually, disruptive behavior should undergo extinction while positive behaviors should occur more frequently. It is also likely that a child may be receiving social reinforcement for disruptive behavior from his peers as well as the teacher. If so, the child may be removed from the class or isolated from both his peers and the teacher immediately following an aggressive act. In this case, the purpose of removing the child is not to punish him but rather to prevent him from receiving reinforcement from other children for his aggressive behavior. This particular procedure is often referred to as *time out from reinforcement*. If the child is unable to receive reinforcement from his peers, then aggressive acts should undergo extinction. Another procedure involves the use of a token-economy system. Tokens, which can be exchanged for rewards, may be handed out for any number of carefully defined acceptable behaviors that are incompatible with disruptive or aggressive acts.

Fundamental to the success of such techniques is the accurate identification of the major sources of reinforcement for a child's aggressive or disruptive behavior. Teacher attention and peer approval are among the most likely sources of reinforcement in the classroom. Parental approval or other sources may maintain disruptive behavior in the home. One of the advantages of behavioral modification procedures for reducing a variety of undesirable behaviors is that parents, teachers, or institutional workers can be trained to use the techniques in the particular settings in which the problems arise. As mentioned before, a child seen in a clinic may not exhibit the type of behavior emitted at school or at home. Even if similar behavior did occur in a clinical setting, behavioral modification procedures used only in the clinical setting may have little effect on behavior emitted at home or in the classroom. In other words, there may be minimal generalization to other settings in which the behavior is perceived as a regular problem.

In summary, behavior modification appears to be a practical and effective approach for coping with conduct problems in a variety of settings. However, a reduction in behavioral problems achieved by the application of learning principles does not warrant the conclusion that all such problems are caused by environmental factors. As we noted in Chapter 8, a wide range of organic factors can have direct or indirect effects on behavior. In addition, individual differences in temperament may predispose children to respond in different ways to environmental demands.

PERSONALITY PROBLEMS

Peterson (1961) uses *personality problems* as a factor label for a dimension of behavior in which the heaviest factor loadings are on items such as shyness, anxiety, lack of self-confidence, feelings of inferiority, social withdrawal, self-consciousness, and a tendency to become flustered. Ross (1974), noting that a similar dimension of behavior has been isolated in other factor-analytic studies, suggests that the common pattern of maladaptive behavior is excessive avoidance

Feeling lonely and unwanted, a child has withdrawn from his group during a play period. Such behavior is typical of children with personality problems. The counselor, knowing this, is reassuring him and encouraging him to rejoin the group whenever he feels ready. (Charles Biasiny)

behavior. Aggressive behavior is directed toward the environment, avoidance behavior is apparently directed inward, toward the self.

Although Peterson (1961) reports that conduct problems are consistently higher among males over all ages, personality problems are higher only for younger males. After the third and fourth grades, personality problems are higher among females. A probable explanation is that passive, withdrawn forms of behavior are more compatible with society's expectations for the female's sex role than for the male's. The delineation of male and female roles may become sharper with increasing age. Achenbach (1966) found sex-related problems among children referred to clinics by parents. On the basis of Achenbach's findings, Ross (1974) concludes that parents will bring male and female children to a clinic for different reasons:

Thus, "breathing difficulty," "excessive talking, chattering," "fainting," "inappropriate indifference, e.g. to physical complaints," "over-eating," and "picking" had been reported only for girls, while only the records of boys contained "cruelty, bullying, meanness," "firesetting," "loudness," "sexual perversion, exposing self," "showing off," "sleepwalking," and "vandalism." These differences, which reflect differential tolerance levels on the part of society, as well as differential sex-role expectations, are the most likely reasons for the differences in factor structure. These data should not be interpreted as reflecting genetic sexlinked differences in behavior or in susceptibility to psychological disorders [p. 36].

At the very least, many of the problems experienced by males in meeting the expectations of adults are different from those experienced by females. Both parents and teachers are more likely to report conduct problems for males than for females. For females, maladaptive behavior in the late elementary grades is more likely to take the form of personality problems.

There is no single explanation why some children tend to establish patterns of withdrawal. The dominant psychological thought in the United States has been that such behaviors have an environmental origin. This is true of systems that emphasize the role of conflict, and it is true of those behavioral approaches that stress S–R (stimulus–response) learning explanations. However, longitudinal research findings show that temperament patterns observed in early infancy remain relatively stable until at least the first grade. Thomas *et al.* (1968) note that both withdrawal and approach patterns in infancy are predictive of later temperament differences. Their longitudinal evidence indicates that initial negative reactions to new situations in infancy and early childhood are predictive of similar behaviors in later childhood. The child who is shy in new situations or "slow to warm up" may have a basically different temperament than more outgoing children. This, of course, does not mean that such behaviors are not influenced by experience, but it does suggest that environmental factors alone may not be sufficient to account for the behavior. Childhood problems involving shyness or fearfulness may result from an interaction between temperament variables and environmental factors. For example, parents who attempt to force a shy child to interact immediately with new friends may be unwittingly facilitating a child's aversion to social situations.

In a similar vein, it should be recognized that normal children have fears—even intense, unrealistic fears. In some cases, fears may be a problem for the child. In other cases, fears may not be a problem for the child but may be perceived as a problem by the child's parents. For example, in our society an aspect of sex-role expectations is that males should be brave. Given this expectation, it is not surprising that some fathers may make unrealistic demands on a male child to approach rather than to avoid fear-evoking stimuli. For a child who is by temperament somewhat shy and withdrawn, such demands may prove to be unduly stressful and thus will aggravate rather than alleviate his fearfulness.

Numerous, unrealistic fears may limit a child's world to a narrow range of pleasurable activities. A child who is intensely afraid of dogs, for example, may be afraid to visit friends or even go out in his own yard. In such cases, behavioral approaches designed to reduce or eliminate specific fears have been quite successful. Methods such as *participant modeling*, described in Chapter 15, have proved to be highly effective in reducing or eliminating such fears.

To summarize, conduct and personality problems are not labels for specific kinds of childhood disorders. Rather, they represent two broad categories of behavior that have been determined empirically by factor-analytic studies of parental and teacher judgments about childhood behavior. In subsequent sections, specific types of behavioral problems, as well as behavioral syndromes or patterns of symptoms that are presumed to define more pervasive disorders, will be discussed.

Psychophysiological Disorders of Childhood

Psychophysiological disorders are disorders that appear to involve both physiological and environmental factors. Since psychophysiological disorders were presented in detail in Chapter 7, this section will cover only those psychophysiological disorders that have a higher frequency in the childhood years than in the adult years. Some disorders, such as asthma and obesity, also occur frequently in the adult years. Other disorders, such as enuresis (urinary incontinence), and encopresis (involuntary defecation) rarely occur in the adult years.

Some of the disorders in this section have been discussed by other authors as types of habit disorders. Bakwin and Bakwin (1966), for example, include in their discussion of problems of habit and training such problems as tics, obesity, anorexia nervosa, and encopresis. The implication is that these disorders are traceable to the child's learning experiences. As will be made clear, the role of learning may vary in importance for different children with similar problems. The heading "Psychophysiological Disorders of Childhood," therefore, simply indicates that there are physiological as well as psychological factors associated with the disorders presented in this section.

OBESITY

Obesity is a result of excessive weight gain primarily due to accumulation of adipose (fat) tissue. Many children show transient weight gains, particulary around the pubescent period. In fact, some weight gain between the years of 10 and 15 typically precedes the growth spurt characteristically associated with the onset of puberty. Basing their conclusions on research by Mayer (1966), Bakwin and Bakwin (1966) suggest that obesity before age 9 and after age 15 is far more likely to be predictive of obesity in the adult years. The prognosis is especially poor for a child who has a chronic history of obesity prior to age 10. The likelihood of later weight reduction is more favorable for boys than for girls. Abraham and Nordsieck (1960) found that 80% of children who were markedly obese during childhood were overweight as adults. Thus, the persistence of problems associated with obesity into the adult years appears to be related to chronicity, age of onset, the extent of childhood obesity, and the sex of the child.

The etiology of obesity is subject to much disagreement. Very few cases of obesity have a demonstrable organic cause. In most instances, the primary causes appear to be *eating too much* or *exercising too little* (Werry, 1972c). Since there is some evidence that obese children seldom eat more than nonobese children (Mayer, 1966), it is possible that inadequate consumption of energy may be a more important etiological factor than overeating.

It is also possible that genetic factors may affect physical activity, metabolism, or both. For example, Bakwin and Bakwin (1966) note that approximately 80% of children are obese if both true parents are obese. However, there is only a modest correlation between the weights of adopted children and their foster parents.

The relative importance of psychological variables is difficult to evaluate, but it is conceivable that psychological factors may interact with eating behavior, physical activity, or metabolic functions.

Whatever the causes of obesity in children, obese children are likely to have psychological problems. Kessler (1966), citing research by Bruch (1941), notes that 40% of 225 obese children over 6 years of age were classified as enuretics (bed-wetters). Mayer (1966) suggests that the problems of obese children are similar to those of minority groups who are the object of prejudice by the larger society. How a person looks affects how others react to him. Negative reactions by peers clearly may have adverse effects on self-concept and general social development.

At present, there are no simple solutions to problems of obesity. Werry (1972c) notes that both anorexic (appetite-reducing) drugs and placebos usually result in initial weight reduction but are relatively unsuccessful for long-term weight reduction. Likewise, the long-term effectiveness of various behavioral approaches in treating obesity has yet to be demonstrated (Yates, 1975).

FOOD REFUSAL

According to Kanner (1972), "it may be safely assumed that at least one-fourth of all children present feeding difficulties [p. 452]." Although Kanner provides no data to support this statement, he echoes the views of other clinicians. Bakwin and Bakwin (1966) note that parental concern over a child's poor appetite is one of the most frequent complaints heard by physicians. Verville (1967) suggests that many preschool children eat well only once a day—usually at noon.

Kanner (1972) suggests that food refusal is peculiar to our modern civilization and that similar problems are rare or nonexistent among primitive cultures. There is little doubt that dinner time in our culture requires far more of a child than simple ingestion of food. A child must eat neither too slowly nor too fast, chew with his mouth closed, avoid touching his food with his hands, use eating utensils in a proper manner, repress belches and burps, and never vomit. When these normal social expectations are supplemented by stress and excessive demands, it is not surprising that eating problems are so frequently reported for young children.

Problems of food refusal range from very mild, temporary reductions in food intake, quite common among preschool children, to extreme and prolonged reductions that may result in death. Serious problems associated with food refusal are relatively rare and are typically discussed under the label of *anorexia nervosa*.

ANOREXIA NERVOSA

In 1868, Sir William Gull, a British physician, described a condition of extreme emaciation that appeared mostly in young women between the ages of 16 and 23. The most notable feature of the disorder was a severe reduction in food intake. Gull was unable to discern any obvious organic cause, such as illness or gastrointestinal disturbances, that could account for the apparent loss of appetite. For this reason, he considered the possibility that the loss of appetite (*anorexia*) was due to some disturbance in mental processes related to a disturbance in CNS activity (*nervosa*). Hence, in 1874, Gull referred to the disorder as *anorexia nervosa*. In addition to loss of appetite, Gull noted that in two cases involving adolescent girls there was amenorrhea (menstrual disturbances), a very slow pulse, depressed respiration, and the appearance of premature aging.

The predominance of the disorder among young females, together with amenorrhea and slow pulse have also been reported by contemporary writers. Bakwin and Bakwin (1966) list a number of additional characteristics: dryness of skin, brittle nails, intolerance to cold, low basal metabolic rate, subnormal temperature, reduced blood pressure, gastrointestinal syndromes with hyperacidity common, and abnormal blood sugar curves—usually flat. The higher prevalence of anorexia nervosa among females, particularly adolescent females, has been consistently reported since the original observations by Gull. Bliss and Branch (1960) in a review of 473 published case histories, note that females outnumbered males nine to one.

The definition of anorexia nervosa has varied because there is no well-defined line between a transient loss of appetite, a diminished appetite, and true anorexia. A typical pattern, however, is a sudden and sharp reduction of food intake sometime during the adolescent period. As the individual loses weight, aversion to food becomes prominent. When starvation becomes advanced, concomitant physiological changes associated with malnutrition make the process very difficult to reverse. The patient resists forced feedings, often hides food and pretends that she has eaten, sometimes wears bulky clothes to conceal the amount of weight loss, and if these tactics are not successful, she may induce vomiting or take laxatives to rid her system of food (Kessler, 1966). Usually, the patient exhibits good behavior at school and is sometimes compulsively conscientious about her studies (Bakwin & Bakwin, 1966).

Although there appears to be no predominant etiological factor associated with anorexia nervosa, most writers stress the role of environmental factors. Kanner (1972) claims that anorexia nervosa is "always a manifestation of severe emotional conflicts [p. 457]" but adds that it is difficult to classify the condition in specific terms. Bakwin and Bakwin (1966) maintain that anxiety about the sex role is prominent in many patients and that the parents are often emotionally unstable. Harrison and McDermott (1972) stress the patients' fears of assuming an adult role—including the sex role. Kessler (1966) lists four factors associated with anorexia nervosa: (1) one or both parents drink or eat too much or exhibit some type of gastrointestinal symptoms; (2) the ingestion of food has unique significance to the patient long before anorexia becomes prominent; others often note that the patient has a past history of overeating and problems associated with excessive weight; (3) a resistance to growing up and assuming a mature heterosexual role; Kessler notes that the excessive weight loss often leads to the disappearance of secondary sex characteristics and sometimes interrupts menstruation as well; and (4) a tendency toward emotional regression.

Ross (1974) favors a behavioral explanation, assuming that individuals must learn appropriate labels for various bodily sensations that eventually "come to guide behavior that is relevant to these sensations [p. 66]." In other words, a person must learn to label correctly those sensations that normally precede eating behavior. Children who fail to learn the appropriate labels for these sensations may not know when they are hungry or satiated. Ross suggests that during the childhood years, some parents may take primary responsibility for determining what and *how much* a child should eat. If a child has not learned to respond to internal cues indicating satiation or hunger, she is likely to overeat if parents insist that she "clean her plate." The responsibility for controlling eating behavior may then shift to the child as she approaches adolescence. But if she has not learned to respond to internal hunger cues, she may cease to eat.

Alternative hypotheses can be derived from learning theory. For example, it might be proposed that the social attention gained by failing to eat may serve to maintain noneating behavior. Leitenberg, Agras, and Thomson (1968) note that food refusal did not cease when positive reinforcement for other complaints (e.g., headaches, nausea, cramps) was withheld. The complaints, however, showed a marked reduction. Ross (1974) interprets this finding to mean that food refusal appears to be an avoidance behavior, not a response pattern maintained by positive reinforcers such as social attention. Significantly, when Leitenberg *et al.* made pleasurable activities such as television watching contingent upon eating and weight gain, and gave verbal praise for food intake, the anorexic patients ate more and gained weight. Regardless of the cause of anorexia nervosa, therefore, behavioral approaches to treatment are effective.

ENURESIS

Enuresis may be defined as frequent accidental urination after the age at which most children in a particular culture have been successfully toilet trained. A substantial number of children occasionally have such wetting accidents. Werry (1972c) notes that recent estimates run " as high as 20% for children at age six depending on the thoroughness of survey of the population, the definition of dryness, and the country studied [p. 147]." Among children referred to a clinic for psychiatric or psychological services, Kanner (1972) reports that not less than 26% were enuretic. Of these enuretic children, 62% were male and 38% were female. Verville (1967) cites earlier research by Powell (1951) in which 15% of *all* children were considered enuretic and over two-thirds of these were boys.

We should emphasize that the criteria for labeling a child enuretic vary from author to author. High estimates of the frequency of enuresis may reflect less stringent criteria. For instance, occasional bed-wetting by a preschool child is little cause for concern. However, when a school-age child wets the bed virtually every night and is obviously ashamed of his "babyish" habit, or refuses to spend the night with peers because he fears his embarrassing secret will be disclosed, then the problems associated with the wetting behavior are clearly significant. In such cases, few professionals would be reluctant to use the label *enuresis*.

The majority of enuretic children stay dry during the day but wet their bed at night (*nocturnal enuresis*). Kanner (1972) reports that 63% of enuretics wet only at night, 30% wet during the day as well as night, and 7% wet only during the day.

A major theoretical issue pertaining to enuresis has been whether enuresis is itself the primary problem or whether it is merely a symptom of a more deeply rooted psychological problem.[2] Those who view enuresis as a primary problem may assume either organic or environmental causation or an interaction of the two. Explanations for enuresis given by physicians are likely to emphasize dysfunctions of the urinary tract or the failure of cortical control in the neurological regulation of eliminatory processes. Behaviorally oriented psychologists are likely to assume that the primary cause can be traced to specific learning experiences. Those who consider enuresis to be a symptom of underlying psychological problems are generally proponents of a psychodynamic approach derived from psychoanalytic theory.

If enuresis is a symptom of deeper psychological problems, one would expect to find that enuretic children have other kinds of psychological problems, which will persist even if the specific symptom of enuresis is eliminated. If enuresis is the primary difficulty, one still might expect to find other kinds of problems, but such problems would be considered consequences of enuresis rather than causes. In this case, elimination of enuresis should lead to a reduction in whatever other problems presumably developed as a result of enuresis.

Research supporting a higher incidence of other types of psychological problems among enuretics is not convincing. There appears to be a small correlation between psychopathology and enuresis, but the majority of enuretic children do not have any apparent emotional disturbance. Of those who do have other problems, there is no evidence that these problems are causally related to enuresis.

There is some evidence that enuretic children have lower self-concepts than normal controls. Ross (1974) cites research by Compton (1968) in which 40 enuretic children scored significantly lower than 40 normal controls on measures of self-concept. Ages of subjects ranged from 8 to 18. Following successful treatment of 33 of the 40 enuretic children, scores on the self-concept measures rose

---

[2] As has been noted in previous chapters, this theoretical issue is by no means confined to the problem of enuresis.

to the level of normal controls. When enuresis was controlled or eliminated, therefore, the children generally felt more positive about themselves. This finding cast doubt on the psychodynamic view that enuresis is a symptom of deeper problems, to be treated by more global attempts to modify personality.

Investigations on the etiology of enuresis have not led to the identification of any single cause of the problem. There is evidence to suggest the influence of both physiological and environmental factors.

Summarizing psychophysiological research by several investigators, Werry (1972c) notes that both sleeping patterns and aspects of bladder functioning appear to be relevant to enuresis. Although bed-wetting can occur at any stage of sleep, electroencephalogram (EEG) studies indicate that it typically occurs during deep sleep. However, there does not appear to be any difference in the ease with which enuretic and nonenuretic children can be aroused from sleep. Thus, a hypothesis that enuretics are deeper sleepers has not been supported. There is evidence that enuretics show more extreme psychophysiological reactions to being aroused from deep sleep. One of these reactions appears to be larger and more frequent contractions of the bladder. There is also a relationship between nocturnal enuresis and the following factors: frequency of urination during the day; urgency—some children must hurry to get to the bathroom on time; and a small bladder capacity.

It should be emphasized that, although there are physiological factors that correlate with enuresis, no single physiological variable has been identified as a primary cause. There also appears to be a relationship between social factors and enuresis. A higher incidence, for example, occurs under conditions of social disorganization such as broken homes, mother–child separation and maternal incompetence. Considering the causes of enuresis, Werry (1972c) concludes,

> Enuresis appears to be a multifactorily determined condition or, in short, a phenotype in which a multiplicity of physiological, psychological, and social factors can be etiological either singly or in combination [p. 152].

If untreated, all but about 2% of enuretic children will cease to have problems with wetting by the age of 14. This fact, however, should not alter the importance of treatment. As already stated, enuresis is an unpleasant experience for both child and parent. As long as the problem persists, the child's feelings about himself may be unduly negative. His relationship with his peers as well as with his family may be adversely affected.

The most successful treatment approaches involve conditioning procedures that were originally introduced in 1904 by a German pediatrician named Pfaundler, but were rediscovered and popularized by Mowrer and Mowrer in 1938 (Werry, 1972c). An apparatus for this procedure is now available commercially. Basically, the apparatus is a bed pad that consists of two aluminum-foil sheets connected to a battery. The aluminum sheets are separated by a sheet of absorbent cloth. If a child wets his bed at night, the dampening of the absorbent sheet creates an electrical connection that activates a loud buzzer. The rationale for the development of the apparatus was based on the classical conditioning model. The basic assumption is that a child has not learned to respond by awakening to internal cues associated with bladder pressure (the conditioned stimuli or CS) that precede urination. The desired conditioned response (CR) is *waking up to bladder-pressure cues* so that bed-wetting can be avoided. The loud buzzer connected to the pad is the unconditioned stimulus (UCS), which evokes an unconditioned response (UCR) of *waking up* to the sound of the buzzer. Thus, bladder pressure (CS) precedes urination, which dampens the sheet and activates the buzzer (UCS). After awakening a number of times to the buzzer (UCRs), the child should eventually awaken to the bladder-pressure cues that precede the buzzer. The child's awakening to the bladder-pressure cues is the conditioned response. According to Azrin, Sneed, and Foxx (1974), various authors have reported that the urine-alarm system has been initially effective for 80–90% of enuretics. However, the procedure has required several weeks or months and is associated with a relatively high relapse rate.

Recently, Azrin, Sneed, and Foxx (1973) introduced a new procedure called the *dry-bed procedure*, which requires one night of intensive training followed by the use of the urine-alarm procedure "for as little as 1 week." According to Azrin *et al.* (1974), the major features of the intensive training procedure are "(1) large fluid intake to increase the desire to urinate, (2) hourly awakenings, (3) teaching the client to awaken to mild prompts, (4) practice in going to the toilet, (5) reinforcement for urinating in the toilet at night, (6) use of the urine-alarm apparatus to signal bedwetting, and (7) training in the awareness of the dry versus wet condition of the bed [p. 147]." The procedure developed by Azrin *et al.* (1973) was developed around an operant model rather than a classical conditioning model.

Azrin *et al.* (1974) found the dry-bed procedure to be significantly superior to the urine-alarm method. Enuresis was eliminated for all 24 children studied (all were over 3 years of age and the average age was 8 years). All but two of these children had been wetting the bed every night since infancy. During a 6-month follow-up, no major relapses occurred. If a child had more than two accidents within a week during the follow-up period, then the urine-alarm system was reinstituted. In only seven instances did two such accidents occur and in each instance there were no further accidents during the 6-month period after the urine-alarm system was reintroduced for 1 week.

In summary, although issues pertaining to the etiology of enuresis are still unresolved, a behavioral approach to treatment has proved to be very successful.

ENCOPRESIS

Encopresis refers to "involuntary defecation after the second year of life which is not due to gross disease of the muscles or nerves [Bakwin & Bakwin, 1966, p. 493]." Although persistent "soiling" after the second year is referred to as encopresis, only about 50% of children achieve bowel control by 2 years of age, whereas over 90% have achieved control by age 4. At 8 years of age, only 2.3% of boys and .7% of girls have not achieved bowel control. Bowel control usually occurs prior to urinary control and, unlike urinary control, nighttime control is typically achieved before daytime control (Werry, 1972c).

Encopresis is rarer than enuresis and is generally regarded as more serious. There is little question that negative social reactions are stronger for soiling than for wetting. Soiling is more closely linked to uncleanliness as evidenced by words such as *dirty* and *stinky* used by some parents in connection with toilet training. Occasionally, mothers who are unsuccessful in their bowel training efforts have been known to resort to techniques usually reserved for dogs. Kanner (1972) provides the following example of parental reactions to encopresis:

> He (8 years old, IQ 90) had the bad habit of doing something in his clothes, and I whipped him and rubbed his nose in it and made him wash them, and the next day he'll do it again [p. 398].

Research has led to a distinction between two kinds of encopretic children– *nonretentive* and *retentive*. Both types continue to soil well after toilet training is normally accomplished. In nonretentive encopresis, which represents only a small percentage of encopretic cases, the child produces a soft, fully formed stool. In retentive encopresis, the soiling primarily consists of a constant leakage of fecal-stained fluid from the rectum. In this type, retention of the stool eventually leads to accumulation of mucoid material, which flows around the fecal mass and gradually leaks out the rectum (Bakwin & Bakwin, 1966). As a result of retaining the feces, the rectum typically becomes distended because of the accumulation of hard fecal matter. Fecal retention may persist until the normal defecatory reflex extinguishes. The fecal material may become so impacted that medical intervention is required to cause evacuation. It is also possible that retention over an extended period can lead to an enlarged colon (megacolon). Extreme retentive behavior, therefore, can become a serious medical problem.

The etiology, prognosis, type of treatment, and correlation between encopresis and other kinds of psychopathology probably vary for nonretentive and retentive forms. In the nonretentive form of encopresis, the causes may be coercive measures that have led to anxiety surrounding the toilet training situation or parental neglect—the child may not have been encouraged to learn bowel control. The use of coercive measures may be suspected if the child refuses to sit on the toilet or displays strong, negative emotional reactions to the toilet situation.

There may be several causes of retentive encopresis. A prominent pediatric view is that constipation developing in infancy may be associated with painful defecation. In other words, retention becomes a means of pain avoidance. The psychiatric and psychological views of the etiology, derived from psychoanalytic conceptions, stress disturbances during the anal-retentive phase of psychosexual development or disturbances in parent–child relations. For example, according to Kessler (1966): "The child retains the feces as his property, in defiance of the parents' wish to take it away [p. 123]," and "it is readily linked with unconscious aggressive wishes towards the parent, and can become a weapon for the child [p. 123]." Empirical support for such assumptions is lacking but some case histories point toward difficulties in parent–child relations. Ross (1974) offers a behavioral explanation of retentive behavior and subsequent soiling, suggesting that the child may have learned only the "hold" part of the "hold–wait–seek toilet–defecate" sequence. Perhaps, it is best to conclude that etiological factors associated with encopresis have not been clearly identified.

Different treatment approaches have been proposed for nonretentive and retentive encopresis (Werry, 1972c). For nonretentive encopretics, the goal of treatment should be either to extinguish anxiety associated with the toilet situation or to make it rewarding to go to the toilet. In retentive encopresis, medical treatment involving enemas and laxatives appears to be successful in 80–90% of the cases. A behavioral program involving an incentive system for going to the toilet may be used in conjunction with a medical treatment approach.

The majority of retentive encopretics appear to have no other prominent psychological problems. However, nonretentive encopretics (who represent a small minority of encopretics) often have various types of psychological problems. The relationship of these problems to encopresis remains unclear. It is not known, for example, whether such problems *cause* encopresis or whether they are a *result* of parental and social reaction to continual soiling.

ASTHMA

Purcell and Weiss (1970) define asthma as "a symptom complex characterized by an increased responsiveness of the trachea, major bronchi, and peripheral bronchioles to various stimuli, and . . . manifested by extensive narrowing of the airways which causes impairment of air exchange, primarily in expiration, and wheezing [p. 597]." The same authors conceptualize asthma as arising from a respiratory system that is overreactive to many different stimuli including infections, allergies, and psychological influences. The vulnerability of the respiratory system to various forms of stimulation is probably influenced by genetic factors but in some cases there is no family history of asthma. Estimates of the incidence of asthma in the general population range from 2.5 to 5%. Approximately 60% of asthmatics are below the age of 17. The incidence among males is twice that among females. Although asthma has been diagnosed during the first few months of life, its occurrence in early infancy is uncommon.

The majority of asthmatic children (71%) show significant improvement sometime before or during the adult years. Asthma, however, is a serious disorder. The fatality rate has been estimated at 1.5 deaths per 1000 asthmatics per year. In each year since 1949, 4000–7000 deaths in the United States have been caused primarily by asthma. Approximately 25% of all school absences caused by chronic illness among children are due to asthma (Purcell & Weiss, 1970).

Like other psychophysiological disorders of childhood, asthma has stirred a variety of speculation regarding its etiology. There are three broad classes of potential etiological agents: (1) allergens such as dust, (2) infections of the respiratory tract, and (3) psychological factors. The relative contribution of each of these sources is often difficult to establish.

Werry (1972c) summarizes specific and nonspecific etiological theories. Two theoretical formulations specific to asthma are: first, that asthma is associated with a specific personality type characterized by anxiety, dependency, and difficulty in expressing emotions—particularly grief and aggression, and second, that asthma is associated with a specific conflict in which the asthmatic attack symbolizes a suppressed cry for help originating from separation anxiety feelings. In addition to these specific formulations, nonspecific hypotheses may be derived from learning theory. One hypothesis is that the asthmatic response is classically conditioned. A second hypothesis is that asthma may be best explained by an operant paradigm. A good example is the explanation offered by Ross (1974) for the fact that many asthmatic children appear to show marked improvement when separated from the mother:

> Since breathing is one of the most frequently occurring responses and inasmuch as changes in rate of breathing are reflexive reactions to sudden changes in stimulation, it would not be unexpected that for children with an atypical breathing pattern, maternal behavior can come to be associated with respiratory distress, since such behavior would have countless opportunities to become contingent on respiratory responses of the child [p. 164].

As Purcell and Weiss (1970) indicate, there have been few methodologically sound investigations undertaken to test any of these propositions. Generally, research has failed to identify personality characteristics of asthmatic children that clearly distinguish them from control groups. Etiological hypotheses derived from learning theory would receive support if conditioning procedures were successful in establishing an asthmatic response. Summarizing various attempts to condition asthma, Purcell and Weiss (1970) conclude that: "with either animals or human beings, the successful conditioning of asthma remains to be demonstrated [p. 607]."

An important observation about asthma is that some children show dramatic improvement when removed from the home, and others show little improvement. For those children who show improvement, it is quite possible that psychological variables having to do with family interactions might be precipitating asthmatic attacks. Another possibility is that if a child is removed from the home, he may also be removed from many possible allergic agents in the home such as dust, animal fur, grass, molds in the basement, and so on.

Purcell, Brady, Chai, Muser, Molk, Gordon, and Means (1969), in an exceptionally well designed study, were able to isolate the effects of separation by removing the family from the home and leaving the child with a substitute mother. Subjects were 25 asthmatic children ranging in age from 5 to 13 years, with a mean age of 8 years, 4 months. The design of the study allowed for four measures of asthma to be taken over the following time periods:

1. *Qualification period.* During this period, not even the parents of the asthmatic child knew that the investigators were planning to separate the family from the child. Thus, there was no threat of separation to aggravate the asthmatic condition. This period, therefore, allowed for base rate measures of asthma.

2. *Preseparation period.* During this period, parents were informed of the plan to move out all family members except the asthmatic child for a period of 2 weeks. Twenty-five asthmatic children and their parents consented to continue their participation and to undergo the separation period. Because the participating child was told that his family would be leaving for 2 weeks, this period allowed the investigators to determine the effects of impending separation on asthma.
3. *Separation period.* During this period, all family members left the home for 2 weeks while a carefully selected substitute caretaker moved in. Parents and siblings were instructed not to telephone or otherwise contact the asthmatic child. The only contact with family members occurred when a few children saw their siblings at school.
4. *Reunion period.* When the family returned at the end of 2 weeks, the same four measures of asthma were made daily. This period allowed the investigators to determine if return of the family members resulted in asthma similar to that of the base rate (qualification period).
5. *Postreunion follow-up period.* This period was later added for most subjects.

On the basis of information obtained prior to the period of separation, the authors identified two groups of asthmatic children. Thirteen of the 25 children appeared to have asthmatic attacks associated with some form of emotional arousal, such as anger or grief. The remaining 12 children did not appear to have asthmatic attacks associated with any particular emotional state. Purcell *et al.* predicted that the 13 children for whom emotional arousal appeared to precipitate attacks would show significant improvement when separated from the family. No change was predicted for the 12 children for whom asthma appeared to be unrelated to emotional arousal. It is important to note that all the asthmatic subjects remained in the family home during the 2-week separation period. Thus, if allergic agents such as dust, pollen, or pets were important precipitators of asthmatic attacks and psychological variables associated with family interaction were of minimal importance, then no changes in asthma should occur during the separation period. The four measures taken during the five time periods were as follows: (1) expiratory peak flow rates—a pulmonary function index involving the speed with which a child can expel air, (2) daily amount of medication required—which indirectly indicates the frequency or severity of asthma, (3) daily history of asthma—the perception by the caretaking adult of the child's daily asthmatic problems, and (4) daily clinical examination for sounds of wheezing.

The major finding was that the 13 children whose asthmatic attacks appeared to be precipitated by emotional arousal showed significant improvement on all four measures during the separation period.[3] The remaining 12 children showed significant improvement on only one measure, the daily history of asthma. There were no significant differences for either group of children be-

---

[3] The p value for one measure (daily clinical examination) was at the .10 level. Generally, $p < .05$ is required for statistical significance.

tween the qualification period (base rate) and the preseparation period. Thus, the fact that the children knew that they were going to be separated from their families did not appear to have any significant effect on their asthmatic condition. When the families returned after the 2-week separation period, the children's asthmatic conditions returned to the levels of the qualification and preseparation periods. We may conclude, therefore, that psychological variables involving family interactions affect the asthmatic condition of children whose asthma is associated with emotional arousal. Although these findings clearly indicate a relationship between psychological factors and asthma, they should not be interpreted to mean that psychological factors alone are responsible for asthma. One important finding of the study is that asthmatic children may vary in response to psychological treatment depending on the relationship between asthmatic attacks and states of emotional arousal. According to Purcell and Weiss (1970), the assessment of emotional states should focus on the patient's and/or parents' perceptions of the immediate antecedents of asthmatic attacks and on the patient's response to separation from family members.

Psychological treatment of asthma should be combined with medical treatment. The beneficial effects of medication in the treatment of asthma are well substantiated. Purcell and Weiss (1970) note that various forms of psychological treatment, including psychoanalysis, group therapy, and behavioral therapy, have all had some success. The effectiveness of psychological treatment may be improved if the relevance of emotional factors can be determined.

In summary, asthma is associated with both physiological and psychological variables. The classes of conditions that affect asthma (allergens, infections, psychological factors) may vary considerably from child to child. Asthmatic children do not appear to vary in personality characteristics from nonasthmatic children. However, in some children, emotional states appear to precipitate or aggravate asthmatic attacks.

Learning Difficulties in the School Situation

In Chapter 9, school problems associated with minority status were discussed. We pointed out that low performance on intelligence tests and academic problems should not lead to the label *mental retardation* unless supported by additional indicators of a child's inability to adapt to other social systems. In this section, the focus will be on children who appear to have adequate intellectual potential, yet for some reason perform poorly in one or more academic areas. Estimates of learning difficulties run as high as 20% of the entire school-age population. Learning difficulties appear to be the most frequently cited problem of children referred for psychological services (Ross, 1974).

The term *learning difficulty* should not be applied to children whose academic problems stem from ineffectual teaching methods. A learning difficulty may be defined as a discrepancy between a child's learning potential and his actual level of performance. Basic to this definition is the assumption that learning potential can be measured. According to Ross (1974), "To determine learning potential one would need a measure of the child's inherent endowment: *there is no such measure* [p. 98]." The assessment of a learning difficulty usually involves comparing scores on IQ tests with those obtained on tests specifically designed to assess academic achievement. As discussed in Chapter 9, cultural factors associated with minority status may result in low scores on both types of tests and may lead to the inappropriate inference that a child *lacks the ability* to learn. Often, however, a child may score within or above the normal range on an IQ test (usually a good predictor of academic performance), yet he may still have notable difficulty in mastering one or more academic subjects. A number of factors may account for this discrepancy.

One explanation for academic difficulties is that other psychological problems may be interfering with the child's overall school adjustment. For example, emotional disturbance associated with acute stress reactions or long-standing problems in adjustment may interfere with the social and academic demands of the school system. In such cases, academic difficulties may be viewed as secondary to more basic problems in adjustment. If such problems are not resolved, the child may fall farther and farther behind in his schoolwork and may require remedial tutoring to catch up.

In most cases, however, the child's academic difficulties appear to be a result of problems directly or indirectly related to the performance of academic tasks. The teacher may complain that the child is easily distracted from his work, disrupts other children, never completes his assignments on time, frequently gets out of his seat, or is "fidgety." The child may do well in some subjects but poorly in others. He is most likely to have difficulties with such subjects as reading and math, which require fine perceptual–motor skills and sustained attention. The educational label most likely to be assigned to such problems is *learning disabilities,* a term introduced by Samuel Kirk in 1963 to describe children who have disorders in language development, speech, reading, and associated communication skills but who are free from any sensory defects such as blindness or deafness (Hallahan & Cruickshank, 1973). Kirk also excluded from this group children who are comprehensively retarded, that is, children who function substantially below the norms in every social setting in which they participate. Adoption of the term *learning disabilities* was based on the premise that the label should reflect educational need rather than the results of a medical examination. Kessler (1971) offers an example of a definition of learning disabilities taken from the *North Carolina Guidelines for Special Education* (1969–1970):

> The child with a learning disability exhibits a disorder in one or more of the following basic psychological processes involved in understanding or using spoken or written language. These may be manifested in disorders of listening, thinking, talking, reading, writing, spelling, or arithmetic. They include conditions which have been referred to as perceptual handicap, brain injury, minimal brain dysfunction, dyslexia, developmental aphasia, etc. They do not include learning difficulties which are due primarily to visual, hearing, or motor handicaps, to mental retardation or to emotional disturbance. A learning disability may be caused by external as well as internal factors or may result from a

combination of both factors. In any event the child will show a strong contrast between his level of academic achievement and measured intellectual potential[4] [p. 20].

Such a definition is so broad that a large variety of school-related problems are included. Hallahan and Cruickshank (1973) note that "classes for mentally retarded have often been criticized as being 'dumping grounds' for the benefit of school personnel who could not solve certain problems in children. This criticism could apply a hundred fold to the typical public school program for learning disabilities [p. 8]."

Despite difficulties associated with the use of the term *learning disabilities* Hallahan and Cruickshank (1973) speculate that "the problems of the great majority of children described as 'learning disabled,' in our opinion, are fundamentally based in neurological function or dysfunction. In large part, the confusion characteristic of the field of education for children with learning disabilities is due to the failure of professional persons to circumscribe the problem and relate it to the neurological system [p. 12]." This contention is partly based on the authors' faith that present failure to find any evidence of neurological dysfunction in a majority of children considered to have learning disabilities is due to the lack of "new instrumentation to determine yet undiagnosable brain lesions [p. 252]." Although they acknowledge that some learning problems are caused by environmental factors, Hallahan and Cruickshank regard children who exhibit a pattern of behavior similar to those children with known neurological impairment as "suspect cases." For this reason, they "readily include these *suspect* cases among those where positive findings are available." Ross (1974) points out the logical difficulty inherent in this type of reasoning:

> The assumption of neurological impairment in children who manifest learning dysfunctions is, at least in part, based on the unsound syllogism: Children with learning dysfunctions often display hyperactivity and distractibility; children with demonstrable brain damage often display hyperactivity and distractibility; therefore, children with learning dysfunctions have brain damage, even if it is not otherwise demonstrable [p. 105].

Ross concludes that the use of the label *minimal brain dysfunction* for children in whom no real neurological dysfunction can be demonstrated adds "nothing to the understanding of the problem and largely serve[s] to give the misleading impression that there is a medically identifiable syndrome—and a known (and irreversible) cause of the difficulty [p. 105]." Basically, learning disabilities as

---

[4] "Measured intellectual potential" probably refers to performance on conventional intelligence tests. As indicated in Chapter 9, performance on intelligence tests may be influenced by a number of environmental factors. Although IQ tests are useful in predicting school performance, they cannot be regarded as a measure of native potential.

[5] Reproduced by permission from "Nosology in Child Psychopathology," by J. Kessler, in Herbert E. Rie, editor, *Perspectives in Child Psychopathology* (Chicago: Aldine Publishing Company), p. 109. Copyright © 1971 by Aldine–Atherton, Inc.

defined by Hallahan and Cruickshank (1973), are largely indistinguishable from the disabilities labeled as *minimal brain dysfunction*.

MINIMAL BRAIN DYSFUNCTION AND THE HYPERKINETIC SYNDROME

The labels *minimal brain dysfunction* and *the hyperkinetic syndrome* have been subsumed under the category of learning disabilities and so an extensive, separate treatment is unnecessary. Wender (1971) maintains that children with minimal brain dysfunction (MBD) "manifest dysfunction in the following areas: motor activity and coordination; attention and cognitive function; impulse control; interpersonal relations, particularly dependence–independence and responsiveness to social influence; and emotionality [p. 12]." The neurological signs supposedly characteristic of the MBD syndrome are referred to as *soft signs.* (*Hard signs,* in classical neurology, refer to clear indices of neurological impairment such as paralysis, anesthesia [loss of sensation], and reflex changes.) Soft signs, according to Wender (1971), include poor fine motor coordination, impaired visual motor coordination, poor balance, clumsiness, poor speech, strabismus, and choreiform movements. (Strabismus is a visual disorder—e.g., cross-eye—in which the turning of one or both eyes makes it difficult to direct both eyes toward an object. Choreiform movements are abnormal or involuntary movements or gestures.) Though many of these soft signs occur in apparently normal children and adults, they are more frequent among children classified as having MBD. However, a child may be classified as having MBD even if there are *no* neurological signs, soft or hard. According to Wender (1971), "many MBD children (approximately one-half) are neurologically intact: there is no doubt that the syndrome can appear with the total absence of neurological signs or symptoms or EEG abnormalities [p. 28]." Wender suggests that improvement following amphetamine treatment may serve as one indicator that a child, in fact, has MBD.

For the most part, *minimal brain dysfunction, minimal cerebral dysfunction, minimal brain damage,* and *the hyperkinetic syndrome* all may be regarded as synonymous terms.

The hyperkinetic syndrome has been postulated to label a behavioral complex of hyperactivity, short attention span, impulsiveness, irritability, clumsiness, and poor schoolwork. According to Werry (1972b), "empirical studies of clinical symptomatology have thrown considerable doubt on the specificity of hyperkinetic syndrome as apart from behavior disorders in general and have failed to demonstrate clear or invariant relationships between the hyperkinetic syndrome and other so-called 'organic indicators' [p. 105]." Werry also notes that a "significant number" of children exhibit one or more of the behaviors that define the hyperkinetic syndrome, yet have no other problems in any area or any signs of brain dysfunction. He concludes that these behavioral symptoms should not be taken in themselves as indicators of brain dysfunction.

The major problem associated with the term *minimal brain dysfunction*, as well as with its synonyms, is the willingness of diagnosticians to include in this diagnostic category children who have neither hard nor soft signs of neurological impairment but who show a pattern of behavior similar to that of neurologically impaired children. Rather than seriously entertain nonorganic explanations for such cases, writers such as Wender (1971) elect to advance the position that brain dysfunction is the most likely etiological agent. Hence, 50% of children with *no evidence* of *any* neurological impairment are classified as MBD.

Psychologists and educators have too often insisted on environmental explanations for behaviors in the face of compelling evidence that organic explanations are more tenable. Medically trained individuals, however, seem just as likely to underestimate the potency of environmental forces. There are children who exhibit soft signs of neurological impairment in varying degrees and there are children with similar behavior who exhibit no neurological impairment. *Minimal brain dysfunction* may be a useful label for the former but not for the latter. Assigning the same label to both groups tends to obscure possible differences in etiology, prognosis, and response to medical and/or psychological management. Separating these two groups would at least allow for these assessments.

As discussed earlier in this chapter, problems under the label *conduct problems* often do not appear until the child enters the school system. Some of the behavior problems described as conduct problems are indistinguishable from those described as learning disabilities. These include aggressive or disruptive behavior, restlessness, and academic problems. Teachers may also describe such children as overactive and distractible. Behavior that leads teachers to label children as distractible, restless, or overactive may well be a result of academic problems rather than a cause. There is little evidence to support a widely held assumption that children perceived as hyperactive and distractible are easily distracted by *external* stimulation. For example, research with 24 first grade males perceived by teachers as easily distractible by external stimulation indicated that these children had significantly greater problems in performing perceptual–motor tasks than 24 nondistractible controls with comparable IQs. However, their performance was *not* impaired by very high levels of external stimulation. Nor was their performance facilitated by a marked reduction in external stimulation (Somervill, Warnberg, & Bost, 1973). Distraction by external stimulation, therefore, does not appear to be the cause of the children's poorer performance. In a follow-up study, when the children were in the third grade, different teachers also perceived the original distractible group as significantly more distractible (as well as more active) than nondistractible controls. The distractible group obtained significantly lower scores on measures of reading and arithmetic achievement. Seven of the distractible group and none of the nondistractible controls were receiving remedial services (Somervill & Brophy, 1975). The authors suggest that the fundamental problem appears to be academic difficulty and inattentive behavior may be a consequence rather than a cause of academic problems.

That many problems of childhood are not noticed until the school years suggests that the educational system may make special demands to which many children, particularly males, have difficulty in adjusting. A child regarded by his parents as healthy and active or "all boy," may find a school environment that stresses quietness and inactivity intolerable. In addition, his social background may not have allowed him to develop skills in performing the fine perceptual–motor tasks required to master basic academic subjects, such as writing. The emergence of behavioral problems and/or learning difficulties may be partly a function of behavioral expectations that are unique to the school system. This point has led to the question of whether the goal should be to change the child or change the system. Such a question, however, oversimplifies the issues. In some cases, children have problems that originate outside the school that may seriously affect school adjustment and academic performance. In other cases, the problems may be associated with the child's inability to accomplish academic tasks despite appropriate teaching methods. In still other cases, the problems may be produced or aggravated by unrealistic and inflexible demands of particular classroom situations. Unfortunately, the label *learning disability* tends to obscure rather than clarify the particular nature of a child's problem in the educational system.

TREATMENT OF LEARNING DIFFICULTIES

The treatment of school-related problems, of course, depends on the type of problem. Wender (1971) gives evidence that medical treatment involving the *discriminate* use of amphetamines or methylphenidate (CNS stimulants) may lead to behavioral improvement in one-third to one-half of MBD children. Wender strongly advocates medical treatment with stimulants, but he also acknowledges both the limitations of drug therapy and the problems associated with side effects. Although he belittles psychological intervention and even suggests that "we must be particularly cautious lest we have placed our faith in new superstitions, formulas, and rituals [p. 132]," there is increasing evidence that behavioral approaches are successful. Werry (1972b), citing his own research as well as the research of others, maintains that hyperactive, aggressive children, in a behaviorally engineered classroom, "can be made to exhibit classroom behavior (notably attention) similar to that of normal children [p. 111]." He concludes that "a more pragmatic behavioral approach to so-called minimally brain-injured children is preferable to neurologically derived concepts [p. 111]."

Despite the conflict between medical and psychological treatment approaches, there is evidence that both drug therapy and behavioral techniques are effective. For some children, a combination of the two approaches may be more effective than the use of either approach alone. A dispute over which treatment is best may prevent professionals from engaging in potentially important collaborative research.[6]

To summarize, there is a sizable group of children whose actual level of

[6] Perhaps an additional point should be made. Drug therapy involving the use of CNS stimulants in children is currently far less popular than psychological management. It may be tempting for some psychologists to ignore a rapidly growing body of research literature (particularly studies involving treatment with methylphenidate) and prematurely conclude that drug therapy is not desirable.

academic performance (for various reasons) appears to be below that of their estimated potential. Such children are considered to have *learning disabilities.* Included are children who have problems referred to by the following labels: *hyperkinesis, hyperactivity, minimal brain damage, minimal cerebral dysfunction,* and *minimal brain dysfunction.* Excluded are children with specific sensory defects such as blindness or deafness and children with generalized retardation. Some of the children evidence soft signs of neurological impairment. In a majority of cases, however, there is no evidence of neurological impairment.

Psychotic Disorders of Childhood

Psychotic disorders of childhood account for less than 10% of child referrals to psychiatric clinics. Kessler (1966) reports that of 6869 children evaluated at various psychiatric outpatient facilities in Ohio, only 2.7% were diagnosed as psychotic. Werry (1972a) notes that there has been an "inordinate amount of attention given childhood psychosis" and suggests that such attention is a "reflection more of its severity and obdurateness than its actual frequency [p. 188]." Several diagnostic terms such as *childhood schizophrenia, atypical children, autism,* and *symbiotic infantile psychosis* have been used for profoundly disturbed children. Diagnostic assessment, however, has been seriously hampered by lack of agreement on criteria for childhood psychosis. Still, there is sufficient evidence to warrant a distinction between a severe disorder labeled *early infantile autism* and other types of psychotic disorders. For this reason, a separate treatment of early infantile autism will be presented after a general discussion of childhood psychosis.

It is doubtful that meaningful distinctions can be made between childhood schizophrenia, atypical children, and symbiotic infantile psychosis. Because the labels *atypical children* and *symbiotic psychosis* are seldom used in the current literature, they will not be discussed in this chapter. *Childhood schizophrenia* is the most common label for severe childhood disorders and is often used interchangeably with *childhood psychosis.* In this section, therefore, the terms *childhood schizophrenia* and *childhood psychosis* will be treated as synonomous.

Children who are labeled psychotic tend to be withdrawn, aloof, distant, and generally uninvolved with people. However, some psychotic children may show extreme clinging behavior toward one person. According to Ross (1974), careful observers of psychotic children are able to agree on a series of characteristics such as those proposed by a British committee of psychiatrists cited by Goldfarb (1970):

1. Distorted interpersonal relationships, including aloofness and withdrawal
2. Disorientation with respect to the child's own person and body in relation to the environment, including self-injurious and bizarre explorations of his body
3. Bizarre preoccupation with specific objects without regard to their accepted function
4. Demand for sameness in the environment and a concomitant resistance to change

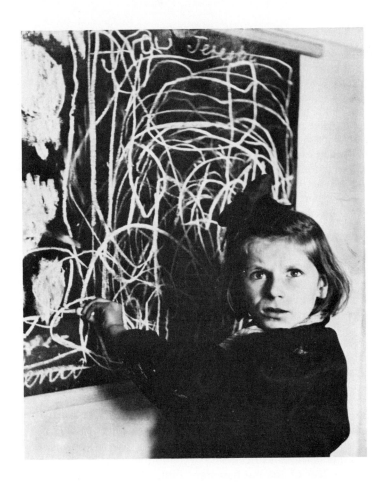

Three years after World War II ended, this Polish girl was still traumatized by her wartime experiences. When asked to draw a picture of her home, she scrawled these lines on the blackboard. In her case, overwhelming experiences clearly led to her disorder; ordinarily, the origins of childhood psychosis are rarely identifiable. (David Seymour, Magnum)

5. Atypical response to sensory stimuli, such as apparent insensitivity to pain or excessive responses to stimulation

6. Distorted and excessive fears in the absence of objective danger with a concomitant absence of fear in the face of real danger

7. Use of speech to communicate bizarre and meaningless content; absence of or greatly immature language

8. Poor coordination, locomotion, and balance; body whirling and toe-walking; and excessive motility, immobility, bizarre posturing, or rocking

9. Extensive retardation with occasional "islands" of normal or near normal intellectual function   [Ross, 1974, pp. 222–223].

Not all psychotic children evidence all nine characteristics and two of the nine (numbers 4 and 7) are typically associated with early infantile autism. Ross (1974) presents a description of a "schizophrenic child" in which almost all the characteristics are exemplified:

■ The boy was brought to the clinic at age 5 years, 11 months, when his mother sought help because the child embarrassed her by his peculiar behavior, and because of certain purposeless movements of the upper extremities. She stated that there was something definitely wrong with him because he did not act like other children his age. She mentioned his fondness for examining women's purses, his running into rest rooms looking under commodes to explore the pipes, his getting on his knees to examine women's legs, and his desire to rub his hands over the hair of other children and then smelling his hands. Because of these actions, as well as a tendency to strike other children on the head, the mother stated that he needs "watching all the time." She added that the boy prefers to remain at home and to play by himself. When he occasionally joins other children, the shooting of a cap pistol creates intense fear in him. In playing hide-and-go-seek, he screams when the other child comes out of hiding and when it is his turn to hide, he insists that his mother accompany him.

During subsequent interviews with the mother, further "strange behavior" was reported. The boy likes to listen to the radio and seems to prefer popular music with a pronounced rhythm. He is extremely preoccupied with the daily mail delivery and will ask constantly whether the mail has come and accosts the mailman when he arrives at the house. Fender aprons of trucks are of particular fascination to him and he will crawl under trucks to examine them. He calls these aprons "rainwater" and when he sees a vehicle without them, he'll get upset and cry, "Put the rainwater on, Mommy, put the rainwater on."

The mother dated the onset of the child's difficulties as occurring when he was 2 years old, although at another time she claimed that she first noticed something strange about the time a younger brother was born when the boy was 1 year old. As an infant, he was said to have shown anticipatory posture at feeding, reaching out for bottle and mother. He was friendly, would coo and look at everybody and notice everything so that the parents thought that he was a bright baby. His first smile is dated as occurring at 3 months; he took his first unassisted step around 1 year of age but had some difficulty in this area, and when seen at the clinic was wearing corrective shoes because of his "habit of walking on his toes." The child began to utter single words before he was 13 months old, and spoke in short sentences by 2 years although his speech remains difficult to understand even at this time, in part, because he has a high-pitched, squealy voice.

During a 20-minute interview with the boy he showed no evidence of any interpersonal contact. He ignored the psychiatrist and played oblivious to all distractions and external stimuli. He put strange objects into his mouth and evidently explored them in this way rather than by looking or with his hands. He was rather clumsy but there was no gross disturbance of motor behavior. Whenever he became excited, which was rather frequently, he would jump up and down and move his arms in a rapid, apparently purposeless, repetitive movement. He whirled about several times whenever his body was turned by the doctor. On two or three occasions he became interested in the doctor's foot or hand if one of these was placed directly in front of him, but there was no evidence that he recognized it as a part of someone else's body [pp. 224–225].

Like most childhood disorders, psychosis of childhood is much more common among males than females. Werry (1972a), in a summary of research findings, reports that the higher incidence among males ranged from a low of 1.7:1 to a high of 9.5:1. On the average, three to four times as many males were labeled psychotic as females. The higher incidence of psychosis among males is probably unrelated to sex-role expectations. Reports indicating frequent signs of neurological impairment among psychotic children suggest the possible role of sex-linked biological factors.

Excluding early infantile autism, the onset of psychosis in childhood is typically after age 2. As we will see, the onset of severe disturbance in the first 2 years usually signifies early infantile autism rather than childhood psychosis.

Theories about the etiology of childhood psychosis have varied in the relative emphasis placed on environmental and organic explanations. A popular environmental view is that the primary cause of childhood schizophrenia is a pattern of maternal behavior; this view has led to the term *schizophrenogenic mother*. Clinical observations of mothers of psychotic children suggest that they are often tense, anxious, and preoccupied with their child's problems. Hence, it has been assumed that such behavior may be the *cause* of childhood schizophrenia. Such a conclusion is based upon the fallacy of mistaking correlation for causality. Klebanoff (1959) found that mothers of schizophrenic children and mothers of children with cerebral palsy both evidenced more "pathological" attitudes than mothers of normal children. But mothers of schizophrenic children showed fewer pathological attitudes than mothers of cerebral palsy children. Cerebral palsy clearly results from neurological impairment and is *not* a result of deviant behavior by the mother or father. Thus, the most feasible interpretation of this research is that any severe childhood disturbance may affect the behavior and attitudes of the parents. In other words, severe psychotic disorders among children may well lead to parental behavior characterized by tenseness, anxiety, and preoccupation with the child's problems. Summarizing research findings, Ross (1974) concludes that "nothing in available research lends support to the notion that psychotic or schizophrenic children are basically normal children who 'were made psychotic' by some peculiarity in the behavior of their 'schizophrenogenic' mother [p. 233]."

Research on the causes of childhood psychosis, while far from definitive, suggests that impairment of the CNS may be a primary etiological agent. Werry (1972a) notes a general research finding that psychotic children have more neurological and EEG abnormalities than normal children and possibly more than neurotic children. Observing that minor abnormalities are also found among normal children, mentally retarded children, and children with behavioral disorders, learning problems, and so-called MBD, Werry goes on to suggest that EEG abnormalities may be more severe among psychotic children.

Ross (1974), reviewing findings by Rutter and Lockyer (1967) and by Rutter, Greenfeld, and Lockyer (1967), concludes that the most noteworthy finding was that the majority of psychotic children who are labeled psychotic eventually show signs of brain damage. Of 63 psychotic children who showed no substantial signs of CNS impairment on first admission to a hospital (mean age at first admission was 5 years, 11 months), only 20 showed no evidence of brain damage when reexamined about 9 years later.

The prognosis for children labeled psychotic is poor. According to Werry (1972a), less than a third of such children are capable of any kind of independent life and "most are and will remain at least functionally mentally retarded with the added handicap of severe behavioral disturbance [p. 222]." In general, most attempts at treating psychotic children have not been very successful. The approach that appears most promising involves systematic, individualized educational efforts (Ross, 1974).

A relationship between childhood psychosis and adult psychosis has not been adequately demonstrated. There is no relationship between child and adult psychosis if the onset of childhood psychosis is before 5 years of age, but there appears to be some relationship if the onset is after 5 years (Werry, 1972a). It is probable that many children labeled as psychotic in the childhood years will be labeled mentally retarded or brain damaged in their adult years. In short, childhood schizophrenia and adult schizophrenia appear to represent two different disorders with little more in common than the label *schizophrenia*.

EARLY INFANTILE AUTISM

Early infantile autism is perhaps the most baffling of all childhood disturbances. In 1943, Kanner described 11 children who exhibited severe withdrawal tendencies in the first year of life. At that time he suggested the label *early infantile autism* (Kanner, 1972). Although it is virtually impossible to make an accurate diagnosis in the first year, Wing (1966) presents the following behavioral signs based on retrospective maternal descriptions:

The infant often has difficulty in developing routines of feeding, sleeping and elimination from the moment of birth. Motor milestones are usually normal and the smiling reflex develops as usual, but the baby appears unresponsive to the environment. He does not lift up his arms in anticipation of being picked up and does not adapt his posture to his mother's. The mother complains that he is not cuddly. The baby does not point to things in the room that he wants or is interested in and may be happiest when left alone. He may spend an undue amount of time scratching with his fingernails at the pram cover (as blind babies do) or make odd movements with his fingers held at the periphery of vision. He may dislike certain noises, but at the same time be unresponsive to sounds in general so that people wonder whether he is deaf. Some babies are described as unusually quiet and good but there is often inordinate screaming, particularly at night or when waking from sleep, and the child is then quite unconsolable. At other times he can laugh happily, particularly when tickled or swung around or taken riding in a pram or a car. Rocking and headbanging are very common [p. 5].

Professionals appear to agree on the following major characteristics of early infantile autism: (1) early onset of autistic aloneness, (2) absence or distortion of language, (3) stereotyped insistence on sameness, and (4) lack of demonstrable physical defect.

Autistic aloneness is the most striking symptom of autism. Autistic children are unable to relate normally to people and situations. Usually they seem obvious to the actions and conversations of other persons and rarely respond to questions except in a very perfunctory way. They prefer objects to people. The autistic child may play for hours with a simple toy but rarely respond to other children or adults.

The absence of language development may take the form of apparent mutism, parrotlike repetition of speech, or confusion in the use of personal pronouns such as the use of *you* instead of *I*. The mutism, which characterizes about a third of autistic children, is not *true* mutism in that many of the children are able to speak words or sentences in special circumstances. Generally, they seem to have little need for speech or derive no enjoyment from using or responding to language.

The stereotyped insistence on sameness often takes the form of obsessiveness over maintaining the same routine and an intolerance of any changes in their environmental surroundings. An autistic child, for example, may resist any changes in the arrangement of his toys and furniture, or other minor alterations of his immediate environment (Bakwin & Bakwin, 1966).

Autism is considered extremely rare. Kessler (1966), noting that Kanner saw only 150 cases of autism out of 20,000 clinic cases over a period of 20 years, estimates that less than 1% of the clinic population fit the criteria for autism. Like childhood psychosis, the ratio of males to females is about four to one. The rarity of the disorder has probably tempted some investigators to stretch the criteria in order to obtain sufficient numbers of children for research purposes. Thus, some reports seemingly include in their "autistic" sample subjects with neurological impairment or other characteristics that do not fit the major criteria of autism. Such a practice can only adversely affect efforts to understand the nature and causes of the disorder originally described by Kanner.

Despite its rarity, early infantile autism has received considerable attention—perhaps because it is such a puzzling disorder. Kessler's (1966) remarks probably typify the feelings of many professionals:

> In spite of research and study, the essential mystery remains: how is it that a very young child will exclude the stimulation of human contact but still respond alertly and retentively to objects. It is not a matter of general withdrawal; it is a highly selective exclusion which sometimes entails great discrimination between the animate and the inanimate [p. 292].

The cause of autism remains unknown. A number of etiological theories have been proposed. It is beyond the scope of this chapter to present a detailed description of each etiological theory. Generally, they fall into three categories: those that emphasize environmental determination, those that emphasize some form of CNS dysfunction, and those that postulate an interaction between these two determinants.

Kanner (1972) considers autism to be a result of an inborn affective disturbance, but his early observations pertaining to parental characteristics seem to have encouraged others to seek environmental explanations. Kanner notes that parents of autistic children have a higher educational and professional status than a control group of parents drawn from the same clinic population who had children with other types of problems. Rimland (1964), emphasizing that Kanner did employ an appropriate control group, dismisses as unfounded the criticism that persons of high educational and professional status were the only group seeking Kanner's services. Rimland, like Kanner, rejects environmental explanations for autism, and strongly supports Kanner's contention that parents of autistic children are superior to parents in the general population:

> Keeler (1957), who has done as yet unpublished research on this problem, reports that his "most detailed appraisal" indicates the parents ". . . truly do have high IQ's . . . too high to be tested with presently available IQ tests." Kanner states that parents of autistic children are "indisputably intelligent" and "function in society with such distinction that they are often at the top of scientific, artistic, or commercial enterprises . . . [Rimland, 1964, p. 29]."

Rimland concludes that it "seems inescapable that we are not simply dealing with a random sample of parents astute enough to realize their child is ill, or articulate enough to describe the symptoms. The parents form a unique group [p. 30]."

Parents of autistic children have also been described as emotionally cold, introspective, detached, and excessively objective. Wolff and Morris (1971), however, failed to confirm the hypothesis that parents of autistic children were highly intelligent or cold. It is possible that parental coldness may be a result of having a severely disturbed child; the question of why such parents are often superior in professional and educational attainment remains unanswered.

As we noted in the section on childhood psychosis, the observation that parents of autistic children are different from parents of normal children does not justify a conclusion that autism is *caused* by certain types of parental behavior. However, several different investigators either view parental behavior as the primary cause of autism or hold that autism can be prevented if the parents provide ample stimulation and nurturance. Ross (1974) presents the views of Bettelheim (1967) and the operant formulations of Ferster (1961) as examples of the thinking of individuals who consider parental behavior to be the primary cause of autism. Ward (1970) though postulating two types of organic causation, lists a third cause involving lack of stimulation, which "may result from either the physical absence or the psychological absence of a mothering figure [p. 361]." Bakwin and Bakwin (1966), although they do not stress the causative role of environmental factors, intimate that a warmer relationship between mother and infant may delay, if not prevent "the emergence of the full-blown syndrome [p. 597]."

Most contemporary writers on autism are skeptical of views that emphasize environmental factors as a primary cause. L'Abate (1972), in response to Ward's speculation that there may be environmental as well as organic causes of autism, claims that there is not "a single piece of evidence to support his conclusion [p. 49]." According to L'Abate, most of the evidence favors a transactional hypothesis in which constitutional and environmental factors interact. L'Abate suggests that failure to acknowledge the role of constitutional factors results in making parents scapegoats for the condition of their child. Kanner (1973) is especially critical of writers who stress environmental causation, According to Kanner, "making parents feel guilty of responsibility for their child's autism is not only erroneous, but cruelly adds insult to injury [p. 139]."

There are several theories that assume a constitutional or organic basis for autism. As already stated, Kanner (1943) suggests that autism results from an inborn affective disturbance. Rimland (1964) hypothesizes that damage to the reticular formation of the brain stem results in an impaired ability to relate new stimuli to remembered experience. Because of this difficulty in integrating current perceptions and memory, the child is unable to assimilate sensations into a meaningful whole and his world is perceived as vague and frightening. Each minor change evokes panic and leads to an insistence on sameness and a stereotyped preoccupation with particular inanimate objects.

Lovaas, Schreibman, Koegel, and Rehm (1971) assume that the basic deficit involves the inability of the child to respond to a stimulus complex. When several stimuli are presented simultaneously, the child is only able to respond to one aspect of the stimulus pattern. This *stimulus overselectivity* prevents the child from learning to respond appropriately to complex patterns of stimulation. The ultimate effect is a greatly impoverished behavioral repertoire.

DesLauriers and Carlson (1969) hypothesize that autism is a result of an imbalance between two arousal mechanisms in the brain, one located in the reticular formation and the other located in the limbic system. The arousal system in the reticular formation is the source of activation and energy; the arousal system in the limbic area mediates reward functions. The imbalance resulting from too high or too low activity of these systems impairs the association of responses with rewards. Thus, the autistic child can attend to stimuli and emit responses, but learning is severely curtailed. Most incoming stimuli are perceived as new and unfamiliar. However, the child may display learning under conditions involving a high degree of repetition and strong affective arousal.

DesLauriers and Carlson use a treatment approach that is consistent with their neurophysiological model. They emphasize intense affective stimulation and direct bodily contact to stimulate near receptors. The near receptors (those involving direct bodily contact) are assumed to be more primitive in origin than far receptors (sight, hearing, and smell). Parents of autistic children are urged to forcefully and playfully interact with their children as well as to control disorganized, purposeless activity. Remarkable success is claimed with a small group of five children who underwent this form of treatment.

Zaslow and Breger (1969) hypothesize that the basic factor underlying autism is the failure to form an attachment to the mother. They observe that autistic children are less "cuddly" in early infancy. If the mother, in response to this lack of cuddliness, increases her efforts to establish affectionate physical contact, then attachment to the mother may develop. If, on the other hand, the mother reduces her efforts at physical contact, then the infant may fail to form an attachment. As a result, the child may not develop social smiling, and may fail to learn language or to relate to his social environment. The basic theoretical assumption is that autism results from an interaction between constitutional factors and primary social forces. By nature the autistic child is not very responsive; unless unusual efforts are made by the mother to maintain physical contact, attachment to the mother does not occur.

The treatment by Zaslow and Breger, like that of DesLauriers and Carlson, emphasizes physical interaction involving affective stimulation and bodily contact. One aspect of their treatment program is the "rage reduction method." When the autistic child has a rage episode, he is held very close until the rage episode subsides. The long-range effectiveness of this technique has not been demonstrated.

The operant approach used by Lovaas (1966) also involves a great deal of direct physical contact or stimulation of near receptors. For example, the "teacher," when rewarding the child, places food directly in the mouth. Direct physical contact is provided by holding the child's legs between the teacher's legs.

According to Ross (1974), "operant approaches view the autistic child as one who has failed to learn socially adaptive response patterns and therapists working in this frame of reference set up systematic contingencies of behavior control designed to build small response units through the immediate use of powerful reinforcers [pp. 95–96]." Using this approach, Lovaas, Freitag, Kinder, Rubenstein, Schaeffer, and Simmons (1966) have been successful in establishing responses to social stimuli as well as developing language skills.

In summary, a distinction between early infantile autism and other severe childhood disorders appears to be warranted. The primary criteria for autism are an early onset, absence or disturbance of language, autistic aloneness, and stereotyped insistence on sameness. The etiology of autism remains a mystery but contemporary emphasis is on the interaction between constitutional and environmental factors. There is little support for the premise that parental behavior is a primary cause of autism. Although much has been written on the subject of autism since Kanner's original observations in 1943, it is an extremely rare disorder. Some authors have reported remarkable success using certain treatment techniques, but there is no substantial evidence favoring one approach over another. However, physical contact and strong affective stimulation appear to be important aspects of treatment.

Summary

A meaningful classification system for childhood disorders cannot be based on an adult classification system. The focus of a classification system for children should be on developmental norms established for a child's culture. Three important variables to consider are age, frequency of behavior, and intensity of behavior. Unlike adults, children rarely seek psychological services. Referral of a child to psychological or psychiatric clinics is most frequently initiated by parents or teachers who perceive the behavior of a child as a "problem." Frequently, the perception of behavior as a problem is related to the tolerance level for that behavior in a particular environmental setting. In other cases, such as childhood psychosis or early infantile autism, the behavior of the child would be defined as a problem in virtually any environmental setting, regardless of the tolerance level. With few exceptions (e.g., anorexia nervosa), almost all disorders discussed in this chapter have a higher prevalence among males than females. In many cases, such as *conduct problems,* the higher incidence of problems among males may be related to sex-role expectations. In other cases, like childhood psychosis or early infantile autism, the higher incidence may be due to sex-linked biological factors.

In this chapter, childhood disorders were divided into four major topics: (1) *conduct and personality problems,* which represent two broad categories of behavior identified by factor-analytic research; (2) *psychophysiological disorders,* which are characterized by physiological as well as psychological manifestations; (3) *learning difficulties in the school,* which primarily involve problems related to performance in a structured academic situation; and (4) *psychotic disorders of childhood,* in which severe disorders with a relatively poor prognosis were presented.

III

AREAS OF
CURRENT INTEREST

11

Criminal and Dangerous Behavior

STANLEY L. BRODSKY
University of Alabama

What is Criminal Behavior?

A 35-year-old deaf and mute man is arrested and charged with murder. He can neither read nor write and he does not understand sign language. The decision of the court is to commit him as mentally incompetent to a security ward of a psychiatric hospital because it cannot be determined whether he understood the court proceedings.

Police discover over 500 pairs of trousers and 1000 shirts, all unsold and in their original packages, in the closets and back room of a young mechanic. The psychologist at the forensic (legal) diagnostic center asks what the man was feeling at the time of the thefts. "Nervous sometimes, total disgust sometimes," the man replies.

A well-to-do bank officer is caught embezzling a half-million dollars from her bank. Her community and family are shocked. She professes terrible shame, and explains that she has done a stupid, foolish thing. She is sentenced to the state prison, serves 6 months as a clerk typist, and is then released on parole. Her classification officer describes her motives for the crime as being "transient and situational."

A 21-year-old man breaks into a house and is apprehended with stolen jewelry as he leaves. He shrugs his shoulders and expresses his regret at being caught, but has no guilt or shame about the crime. His pre-sentence investigation labels him as callous and psychopathic.

A 40-year-old man is arrested for having had an incestuous relationship with his 12-year-old daughter for the past 2 years. When asked how he could do it, he cries sorrowfully, then explains that she sought it out and enjoyed it. After sentencing, he is sent to a sex-offender treatment program in the state hospital.

What do these people have in common? They represent cases in which psychological intervention is subordinate to the juridical system. All of them have been apprehended for law violations and have been confined as criminals or as dangerous individuals—or as both.

One traditional approach to the etiology of crime has been to search for a single personality type or set of psychodynamics that adequately explains narcotics addiction and drug peddling, embezzlement and robbery, murder and rape, purse-snatching and ticket-scalping at football games. The search for the criminal personality or the seed of maladjustment that causes crime has been simplistic and futile. A more promising route to understanding law violations and criminals is based on distinguishing between the many types of people who acquire the formal status of offender. Criminality is a *legal* status, whereas social deviance and law violation are *behavioral* dimensions. A person becomes a criminal as a result of legal processes and a formal societal decision to transform his status from that of citizen to that of offender. Many law violators never come to the attention of legal authorities; think of those who cheat on tests, go for joyrides, or use illicit business practices and who have never been discovered. Still others who do come to the attention of authorities do not fit into conventional categories of offenders—draft resisters and political prisoners, for example.

Criminal and dangerous behavior has been examined in detail by the disciplines of psychology and sociology. Some antagonism exists between the practitioners and theorists of the two disciplines. Nonetheless, many psychologists have adopted substantially sociological perspectives of social labeling (e.g., Gottfredson, 1973), and many sociologists have adopted psychological viewpoints about learning and about bonds to society and in family relationships as well (e.g., Hirschi, 1970).

Let us examine how psychology tends to view criminal behavior. (An excellent summary of sociological views can be found in Shrag, 1971.) Psychological studies usually are directed toward understanding the most disturbed and serious offenders, such as the psychopath and the murderer. Sociological theories of criminality ask questions about such matters as what opportunity exists for people to achieve their goals through legitimate channels and behaviors, whereas psychological theories are directed toward individual psychodynamics and causes.

Are offenders more likely to be psychologically disturbed than nonoffenders? In other words, are there behavioral difficulties or psychodynamics that lead people to crime and to being caught? The answer would appear to be yes, but only to a limited extent. Not all offenders are disturbed, any more than all disturbed people are offenders.

A false syllogism lurks beneath much of the thinking about the relationship between mental disorders and law violation. The syllogism goes like this:

> Most people are not mentally troubled.
> Most people are not law violators.
> Thus most law violators are mentally troubled.

The error in this logic becomes clearer if we change one of the premises in the syllogism:

> Most people are not swallowed by giant clams.
> Most people are not law violators.
> Thus most law violators are swallowed by giant clams.

The best evidence indicates that *all* the statements in the first syllogism can be challenged. Survey studies of psychological adjustment in Manhattan and other communities have indicated that over 40% of studied individuals had moderate or severe maladjustment problems (Srole, Langner, Michael, Opler, & Rennie, 1962b). The rate of law violation is equally high; asking individuals whether they have committed any felonies, when a list of crimes is presented to them, elicits rates of up to 75% acknowledgment of personal lawbreaking.

The third statement, that most law violators are mentally troubled, has been investigated in studies of large numbers of prisoners. A limitation of such studies is that prisoners are different from law violators at the time of the offense; they have been caught, arraigned, convicted, sentenced, and imprisoned, a selective filtration process through which only a handful of offenders pass. Furthermore, they have suffered the effects of confinement. Rates of mental disturbance in prisoners ranging from 20 to 80% have been found. In one review of over 32,000 assessments by army psychiatrists of military prisoners, S. L. Brodsky found that 78% of the prisoners were diagnosed as having character or behavior disorders, groupings used to describe persons who manifest their disorders externally through antisocial actions rather than maintaining them internally as phobics and compulsives do (Brodsky & Eggleston, 1970). The numbers are not important in themselves, since the coarser the screening one uses, the less psychopathology is found. The finer and more detailed the examination, the greater is the likelihood that mental disturbance will be found. Moreover, we tend to find what we seek; searching for disorders produces the discovery of disorders. Searching for strengths and positive functioning—a process much more common in college counseling than in prison diagnoses—produces the discovery of strengths and positive functioning. A survey of nine studies of law violators (S. L. Brodsky, 1973) did find that psychosis was rare, occurring less than 2% of the time. However, the absence of psychological impairment was also rare, typically occurring less than 20% of the time compared to base rates for nonviolators (Dohrenwend & Dohrenwend, 1965).

The law-violating act for which a person is arrested and imprisoned makes up a tiny proportion of the person's life experiences. As the clinical psychologist or psychiatrist works toward a diagnosis, this distortion is compounded by the

Convicts are frisked at the prison gate after a day's work on the road gang. Searches are a common experience for prisoners, along with overcrowding, boredom, and the fear of violence. Psychological impairment is common too—but psychosis is surprisingly rare among convicts. (Danny Lyon, Magnum)

already noted self-fulfilling prophecies in diagnosis, by the harmful effects of imprisonment, and by the low reliability of psychiatric diagnoses. However, the difficulty of the task does not mean that the results are without value. The clinician at best is like a detective, a Sherlock Holmes attending to subtle cues and putting them together in ways that reveal hidden information. For instance, a positively Holmes-like use of diagnostic insights led psychiatrist James Brussel (1968) to accurately predict from written threats that the Boston Strangler was a middle-aged man of eastern European descent who wore double-breasted suits. Alas, all psychologists and psychiatrists are not Brussel or Sherlock Holmes. There are some very consistent findings, nevertheless.

First, the mad-villain image of the criminal does not apply. Psychotic offenders, leering with unspeakable evil, are rarely found outside of horror movies.

Second, the largest number of criminals are doers, people who annoy or harm others in the world. This behavior-disorder category is made up of people who practice unusually well the axiom, "Action is the natural antidote for anxiety." They may steal a car, break into a house, or pass a bad check, all impulsively and without thinking much about the future consequences. Carried to an extreme, this pattern becomes psychopathy, which will be discussed later.

Finally, many altogether normal individuals are law violators. This category includes numerous citizens who have simply found themselves in tempting situations that led to crime or encouraged antisocial behaviors. As we stop grouping all criminal behaviors together as if they were identical—they are not—we can begin to examine one particular cluster of beliefs and behaviors, those associated with dangerousness and violence.

Dangerous and Violent Behavior

The word *dangerousness* has its origin in the Latin word *dominium*, which suggests relationships of power and esteem between persons at different positions in a social structure. Sarbin (1967) has elaborated on this perspective, advancing the thesis that the label of *dangerous* is acquired by a person becoming degraded and brutalized and thus changing his social identity. This person is then "faced with the choice of accepting the identity of a non-person, a brute, or engaging in instrumental behavior that radically alters the social system, and reverses the *dominum*, the power relationship, thus affording him a more acceptable social identity [Sarbin, 1967, p. 286]." This upsetting of the role structure is experienced as a danger by those at the top. Such a transformation is commonly seen in protests and riots in prisons and other totally controlled institutions. The key element of this perspective is that dangerousness is not a trait that lies within the individual but rather a power relationship with potential for changing the pecking order in social roles of dominance–submission.

Social identities were transformed to dangerousness in the Stanford prison experiment (Haney, Banks, & Zimbardo, 1973). Ten Stanford University undergraduates, selected as being especially stable, mature, and without antisocial tendencies, were randomly assigned the roles of prisoners in a simulated prison. Other students, similarly selected, were assigned the roles of guards. As some of the students playing guard roles became aggressive, five of the student–prisoners had to be released because of extreme emotional reactions to their dependent and depersonalized status. The guards came to see the prisoners as dangerous because they refused to accept their degraded status passively. The need for control of the prisoners and the threat of a possible riot became central concerns of the guards. A major implication of this experiment is that dangerousness and pathology may be situationally induced even in persons without traits of aggressiveness or maladjustment. Because the word *dangerousness* tends to be used to describe traits within individuals, we will follow Megargee's (1976) recommendation and use the description *dangerous behavior* to allow consideration of the situation and personal changeability.

The prediction of dangerous behavior by psychologists and psychiatrists has been vastly overdone; the predictors identify huge numbers of false positives, or people who are predicted to be violent and subsequently are not. The 1966 Supreme Court *Baxstrom* v. *Herold* decision ruled that persons psychiatrically assessed as potentially violent and committed to a state security hospital were entitled to the full due process of civil hearings. The "Baxstrom patients" were released to civil hospitals or to their communities. In a 4-year follow-up of 967 Baxstrom patients (Steadman & Cocozza, 1974), 13 of these people were returned to security hospitals because they behaved dangerously. Four of them had made threats of violence; the others committed acts of violence, with one committing an assault that resulted in a death. Eleven other patients, totaling 2.6% of the original confined group, were returned through criminal procedures (Steadman & Cocozza, 1974). Only 20% of the original group showed any dangerous or assaultive behaviors—a figure that includes the returned 2.6%. Such data have led many courts to discard clinical definitions of dangerousness when considering involuntary commitments to mental hospitals, and to substitute such criteria as recent and demonstrated acts of physical harm.

Monahan (1975) has reviewed four other attempts to predict dangerous behaviors and has found false positive rates that run from 65.3 to 99.7%. Although there are many causes for these predictive failures, one major contribution is the low base rate of violence. Megargee (1976) postulates that if one tries to predict violent crime among 100,000 people in the general population—a behavior that has a base rate (or normal occurrence) of 187 per 100,000 persons—even with an unattainably good false positive rate of 10%, 9981 persons would be mislabeled as potentially violent. Given these figures, is it *ever* justifiable to predict dangerous behavior? One answer lies in the possible consequences to the people incorrectly predicted to be violent. Megargee comments:

> Who can calculate the false positive rate of the psychological screening profiles used by airlines to identify potential hijackers or by the secret service to spot potential assassins? But if the only consequences of being classified as a potential air pirate or presidential assassin are being denied access to an aircraft or proximity to the President then the writer feels it is better to have a thousand false positives than a single false negative [p. 17].

Much of the research conducted on violent persons and criminals has taken place after the fact. The types of offenders described in this chapter represent patterns and syndromes identified in convicted persons, usually while they are incarcerated. Far less information is available about apparently law-abiding or suspected but uncaught law violators. The assumption of potential violence cannot always be made about the persons and syndromes to be considered. It is only in the context of the situation itself, the nature of the person, and the serious limitations on successful clinical prediction that such evaluations and judgments can be made. With those qualifications firmly in mind, we can begin to examine psychopathology specific to crimes and to types of criminals.

Crime-Specific Psychopathology

MURDERERS

Murders and other cases of extreme aggression may serve the purposes of either instrumental aggression or angry aggression. *Instrumental aggression* (Buss, 1961) is purposefully committed to achieve a positive goal, as when a soldier fights in battle or a boxer in competition. On the other hand, *angry aggression* is triggered by events that annoy or infuriate the attacker. Not surprisingly, it is the angry aggressor who is more likely to show symptoms of psychopathology and therefore will be of interest to us here.

Three factors interact in extreme angry aggression. The first is the situation itself, which may elicit or promote the assault. The second factor is the amount of aggressive drive and potential within the person—the self-contained instigation to aggression. The third factor is the amount of inhibition of aggression felt by the person. Some people may be highly instigated to aggress from both within and without, and yet their lifelong inabilities to aggress will lead to a mild-mannered, ingratiating set of behaviors (Megargee, 1971).

Investigators usually consider the situation itself in a very short time-frame. Was there a weapon present at the moment of aggression? Did someone antagonize or thwart the person immediately before the assault? However, Wolfgang and Ferracuti, in their book *The Subculture of Violence* (1967), note that long-term situational influences to aggress may also be present in the form of widespread peer support and norms for overt expression of aggression—the "everybody's doing it" phenomenon.

Although many murderers are indeed uninhibited persons who are repeatedly involved in fights, assaultiveness is not descriptive of all murderers. Megargee (1971) observes that "there would appear to be some drawbacks to the notion that the violent person is invariably someone with 'all id and no lid' [p. 132]." Megargee conducted a series of studies over a 15-year period on levels of inhibition and assaultiveness, including murder. Two very distinct groups of murderers appeared. The first was the *chronically undercontrolled person,* whose aggressive potential is high and near the surface and whose internal restrictions against aggression are low. Thus the chronically undercontrolled person needs little situational provocation to assault or murder; he is primed all the time.

The second type of murderer observed by Megargee is the *chronically overcontrolled person,* characterized by high aggression levels, but even higher, broad-ranging inhibitions against showing aggression, anger, or negative feelings. Such persons usually have only one instance of assault or murder, which occurs after a cumulative buildup of aggressive drive and a sudden, total inability to maintain the resistance to drive to aggress. When newspapers report a quiet, well-behaved, shy, good citizen who murders a close relative or even several people without apparent provocation or reason, it is likely that this murderer is a chronically overcontrolled person.

RAPISTS AND OTHER SEX OFFENDERS

Brownmiller (1975) argues that rape has a long history as a pathway for vengeance and power struggles between groups of men. Rape also serves the purpose of "male bonding"; that is, it may be seen by the men as a shared adventure that unites the group, whether it is a street gang or a squad of soldiers in enemy territory. In such cases, responsibility for the rapes may be attributed to disordered, society-wide attitudes toward women and sexuality. A fuller presentation of this perspective is found in the book *Against Our Will* (1975) in which Brownmiller describes the nature and consequences of rape from a sociological and feminist view.

Psychologists generally are less concerned with historical perspectives. They tend to focus on treatment programs for sex offenders—and for their victims as well, as we shall see later. Sex-offender treatment programs associated with state mental hospitals deal primarily with convicted rapists and, to lesser degrees, with child molesters and exhibitionists. By contrast, note that there are no bad-check-passer treatment programs, murderer treatment programs or other crime-specific programs. One exception is that Sweden has treatment programs for persons incarcerated for driving while intoxicated, indicating how negatively drunken driving is evaluated in Scandinavian countries.

It is simplistic to think that rapists are all alike. Pacht (1976) and S. L. Brodsky (1976) independently observed persons convicted of rape and found a wide variety of overall behavior patterns. The persons observed ranged from the generally well adjusted to the severely disturbed. In general, studies of rapists have produced the following findings:

1. Over 40% of all rapists were drinking heavily at the time of their offense. These men usually do not remember the offense and it seems likely to be a one-time event for them.
2. About 50% of the victims were known to the offenders. Many of these rapes resulted, at least in part, from bad communication, incorrect expectations, or self-righteous attitudes of the rapist.
3. Rapists can be divided by their motives into three groups: (a) those who are aggressive–dominant in their motives and behavior; (b) those predominantly sexual–erotic in their rapes; (c) those who are confused and disturbed.
4. Rape tends to be an intraracial event. Black men most frequently rape black women; white men most frequently rape white women. The rape rate is higher among blacks than among the population as a whole. However, rape rates of minority groups seem to be closely proportionate to the rates of whites at similar economic and social levels.

Treatment programs for rapists consist of teaching them fundamental social skills. These programs grew from the observation that some sex offenders had never successfully dated women. Social skills training, with rehearsals of social interchanges, are designed to teach adequate and proper ways of achieving sexual–social satisfaction. Nevertheless there are many rapists who are married or sexually active; for them, obviously, such a program does not apply.

The social skills teaching approach has been applied more widely to exhibitionists and child molesters. The self-exposure of exhibitionists almost always occurs because the man is unable to form normal relationships with women. The exposure is a desperate, inadequate attempt to make contact with a female and to demonstrate his sexuality. Exhibitionism is a disorder attributed to men. There are interesting differences in public reactions to men and women who repeatedly expose themselves. A man is likely to be labeled a criminal and processed through the criminal justice system, unless he is obviously very disturbed. A woman who repeatedly undresses in public is more likely to be labeled as mentally ill and referred to a clinic for psychiatric treatment. This differential societal reaction is characteristic of the handling of deviance in general; men are prone to be characterized as bad and women are likely to be seen as sick.

Typologies of Criminals and Delinquents

The search for personality typologies has involved attempts to match every crime with a set of accompanying, crime-specific psychodynamics (Roebuck, 1966). Such efforts have been unsuccessful, for the more widespread the behavior, the more the offenders reflect the varied nature of the general population. An alternative, more accepted approach tends to be person-specific rather than crime-specific. We will now consider this approach to finding typologies of offender living and behaving.

A *typology* refers to a cluster of related phenomena. There are dozens of schemes and methods of classifying and typing offenders, most of which are presented with the provincial belief that this is the one truth. These include sociological and psychological approaches, approaches that arise inductively and empirically from data, and approaches that descend deductively and with hypothesis testing from broad theoretical constructs (Ferdinand, 1966). Some of these constructs are part of common folklore. When a mental health expert is testifying in court about a typology, resorting to folklore is a frequently successful cross-examination method. Following the testimony by a psychologist about a hostile and aggressive borderline psychotic, an attorney asked, "Tell me, doctor, don't you believe there is such a thing as just plain mean people?" In this case, the jury found the commonsense typology used by the attorney (mean and not-mean persons) to be more understandable and sensible than that presented by the rattled expert. Warren (1971) and Gottfredson (1973) reviewed 16 major systems of classification, which have a total of 85 subtypes; they found only 6 subtypes that appear consistently. These subtypes are the asocial (or garden-variety meanness), the conformist, the antisocial-manipulator, the neurotic, the subcultural identifier, and the situational offender. We will consider some of these systems and subtypes in more detail.

Two typologies that specify treatment methods to accompany classification of offenders are the I-Level System and the Behavior Classification System. *I-level* stands for "interpersonal maturity level." I-levels are determined from clinical interviews in which youthful offenders are classified into one of four maturity levels and nine subtypes. The I-Level System and differential treatment approach were developed by Warren and her colleagues in the California Community Treatment Project, which was started in the late 1950s and is still in operation. The case loads were very small, with each treatment agent seeing as few as 6 or 8 youths. (A typical probation officer's case load would be 50 to 75 youths.)

The treatment personnel were themselves divided into types and then matched to the types and needs of the offenders. Delinquents treated under the I-Level System, when compared with institutionalized control groups, yielded a low rate of recidivism (return to criminal patterns of behavior). Particular success was achieved with neurotic–anxious youths on probation.

The second typology is the Behavior Classification System developed by Quay (1964a, 1964b, 1970). In this system, three sources of information are used in categorizing:

1. A 100-item self-report questionnaire called the *Personal Opinion Survey*. Sample items from this questionnaire follow:
   - When a group of boys get together they are bound to get in trouble sooner or later.
   - When I was going to school I played hookey quite often.
   - I often get so nervous I have to get up and move around to calm myself down.
   - Sometimes I have stolen things I really didn't want.

2. A 44-item checklist, used to assess current behavior problems. Some of the behaviors rated include the following:
   - Crying over minor annoyances and hurts
   - Incoherent speech
   - Tension, inability to relax
   - Impertinence, sauciness
   - Irritability; hot-tempered, easily aroused to anger

3. A 36-item checklist, used to examine life-history records and analyze and rate problem behaviors found in the history. Here are some sample items:
   - Assaultive, attacks others with little or no provocation
   - Loses interest quickly
   - Habitually truant from home
   - Feels persecuted, believes others unfair
   - Restlessness, inability to sit still

Quay's statistical studies use the technique of factor analysis to identify four reliable behavior dimensions for delinquents: inadequate–immature, neurotic–conflicted, unsocialized–aggressive (or psychopathic), and socialized (or subcultural) delinquency. In this system, data from all three sources are collected on each individual and the person receives scores on all four dimensions. Thus it is recognized that these are not mutually exclusive categories, but rather potentially overlapping dimensions that exist to varying degrees in each youth.

Recognizing that the labels themselves sound pejorative, Quay substituted neutral labels. The youths were referred to as BC-1 (behavior category 1), BC-2, BC-3, BC-4. However, the actual understanding by staff members of these terms was hardly neutral or positive. If the labels were neutral, the meanings were negative. For example, inadequate, immature youths called BC-1 were described by the staff as lazy, inattentive, childish, weak, and naive (Bureau of Prisons, 1970). The neurotic clients, BC-2s, were seen as feeling guilty and sorry, nervous and unhappy, willing to talk, and likely to repeat their same acts the next day in spite of their guilt. Psychopathic offenders, BC-3s, were described as hostile, verbally and physically aggressive, lying readily, and seeking to create excitement. The subcultural delinquents, BC-4s, were described as gang members with high loyalty to peers, who appeared normal except for the delinquent acts. In one application of this system at the Kennedy Youth Center in Morgantown, West Virginia, a BC-5 category was constructed from the offenders who scored high on BC-1 and BC-4 and shared traits of the two groups. When 289 youthful offenders were categorized by this system, the distribution was as follows:

BC-1	18%
BC-2	25%
BC-3	11%
BC-4	22%
BC-5	19%

An additional 6% were not classified (Bureau of Prisons, 1970).

The treatment agents who work with each of these groups assume different goals and are selected to fit into the treatment plan relevant to those goals. This is the principle of differential treatment. Thus the BC-4 treatment agents are described as follows:

> Personnel who work best with these youths have a real sense of integrity; they never cut corners when it comes to following rules. They have very strong feelings about their beliefs and will adhere to them even when this results in their own discomfort. Such adult models are needed to work with the BC-4s because of these youths' contempt for "phonies"—those people who violate their own standards.
>   . . . This type of youth does not help the counselors learn what is "really" going on in the living unit. Therefore, the counselor must be exceedingly sharp in getting at the bottom of things. He must be willing to establish close, friendly, one-to-one type relationships which can be used to break through the peer group influence. Once this is done, the counselor must feel that direct confrontation will result in positive behavior changes [Bureau of Prisons, 1970, p. 10].

The Quay Behavior Classification System is important for several reasons. It is empirically based. It does not require absolute, either–or classification, although for practical treatment purposes, such decisions are made. It lends itself to replication. It is in use in a number of applied settings. And it provides a base of shared knowledge into which program developments and new information may be comparatively and usefully accumulated.

The Psychopath

Psychopath is a diagnostic term used for the most severe, guiltfree, "pure" criminal. The serious social consequences of psychopathy have led many psychologists to study this behavior disorder. The terms *sociopath* and *antisocial personality* are often used synonymously with *psychopath*. Several behavioral signs have been identified by McCord and McCord (1964) and others as characteristic of the psychopath; they are antisocial behavior, impulsivity, hedonism, aggressiveness, guiltlessness, a warped capacity for love, and the ability to appear superficially adequate.

ANTISOCIAL OR ASOCIAL BEHAVIOR.   The psychopath breaks rules and laws, is identified as deviant in this process, and therefore is viewed negatively by society. Thus, institutionalized psychopaths usually are found in prisons or in security units of mental hospitals.

IMPULSIVITY.   It is the personal, immediate moment that preoccupies the psychopath. He is not concerned about or considerate of the well-being of others. If a fancy or whim passes through his mind, it becomes quickly converted to action. Possible negative consequences of his acts do not concern him. Rather he has a high need for stimulation and acts recklessly, thoughtlessly taking risks, sometimes harming others, and not thinking about future consequences.

HEDONISM.   The psychopath is a hedonist, a pleasure-seeker. Self-pleasures and satisfactions are very important to him. Rather than drawing pleasure from reciprocal and mutually satisfying relationships with others, the psychopath strongly seeks physical satisfaction. Pleasures are not planned ahead, but actively and impulsively pursued, often in sensational ways that interfere with others' lives.

AGGRESSIVENESS.   Physical and verbal aggression repeatedly occur in the psychopath's life. He becomes aggressive when his satisfaction is thwarted, when he faces a confrontation, when he is unable to defer action, or at times for no obvious situational reason.

GUILTLESSNESS.   No sense of conscience, guilt, or remorse is present. Harmful acts are committed without discomfort or shame. Though the psychopath, after being caught or confronted with a brutal act, may verbalize regret, he typically does not display true remorse.

WARPED CAPACITY FOR LOVE.   The psychopath uses people and takes advantage of them. He will often have many passing acquaintances, but he is unable to form and maintain any deep or lasting relationship. His ability to feel and express affirmative and affectionate feelings is minimal. He will discard people who feel very attached to him, with little concern or feelings of his own.

SUPERFICIAL ADEQUACY.   Psychopathy is sometimes not obvious because the psychopath shows a superficially adequate adjustment. He is not anxious or distressed. He shows no blatant irrational thinking and displays no bizarre behaviors. His initial charm and verbal ability distract attention from his deviant and unfeeling behaviors. Cleckley (1964) has called these superficial adjustments "the mask of sanity."

Much psychological attention has focused on psychopaths, usually drawing on the six-point definition formulated by the McCords or on Cleckley's definition, which includes superficial charm and high intelligence. Psychopathy has become a special province of psychological research and theory. On any scale of antisocial behaviors, psychopathy is at the extreme; it is the distilled essence of guiltlessness and antisocial acts. Moreover, factor-analytic studies (e.g., Quay, 1964a, 1964b) consistently find one factor that fits the description of psychopathy. And Warren (1971) reports psychopathic symptoms and behaviors as one of the regularly appearing typologies of delinquents.

What makes psychopaths the way they are? One theory is that they do not learn from negative experiences and punishment because they never become anxious when they should. Lykken (1957) demonstrated that psychopaths do not develop the fear necessary to avoid a noxious stimulus. They simply do not learn well from punishment, an observation that indicates imprisonment will not change their behaviors and personal traits. Eysenck (1964) attributes the psychopath's deficits in societal adaptability to difficulty in being conditioned. The psychopath is classified by Eysenck as an extrovert, characteristically very slow to acquire conditioned responses and quick to extinguish them. The psychopath does not condition well and therefore he does not socialize well. In a related vein, Hare (1970) identifies an impairment in the anticipation of punishment as central to psychopathic behavior:

> . . . the psychopath's relative inability to avoid punishment is related to the failure of cues associated with punishment to elicit sufficient anticipatory fear for the instigation and subsequent reinforcement of avoidance responses. In a social context, ability to inhibit responses that have previously been punished may be analogous to the concept of conscience or more specifically to resistance to temptation [p. 81].

TIME PERSPECTIVE

> You see: The opposite of craving is saying, Baby, this is the way it is. Yeah. OK. Here and Now. This is it. I accept the Here and Now fully. As. It. Is. Right at this moment [Baba Ram Dass, 1971, p. 3:37].

Living fully in the "here-and-now" has become a positive goal and peaceful outcome of many Eastern meditation processes and American sensitivity groups. Most Western participants, however, are initially underinvested in immediate experiences. They tend to be future oriented and internally controlled. It is often difficult for them to accept the notion that shortened time perspectives can lead to more pleasurable life experiences. The psychopath has the opposite pattern: an overcommitment to here-and-now experiencing, with little value placed on future pain and discomfort. Both the Zen monk and the psychopath may be said to have time perspectives that differ from American norms. But the quiet reflection of the monk and the active aggression of the psychopath lead us to place very different values on their perspectives.

Time perspectives of prisoners and criminals yield indirect support for the theory that time experiences of psychopathic populations are deviant. Prisoners have shorter future time perspectives—measures of planning ahead—than do other groups of men (Landau, 1975). The judgment of the speed at which time passes is different as well. Groups of psychopaths seem to experience time passing rapidly. If asked to close their eyes and judge how many seconds have passed in a given interval, they will typically report average scores much higher than control groups.

You may wish to judge your own time experience. Ask a partner to time your eyes-closed judgment of when 60 seconds have passed. Though unrelated to psychopathy in normal persons, such a judgment does indicate your subjective experience of speed of time passing.

OTHER FINDINGS ON PSYCHOPATHY

Reviews of psychopathy research have found several other consistent patterns (Hare, 1970) in addition to deviant experience of time:

1. If one includes psychopaths who are not incarcerated, their average level of intelligence is higher than that of the general population.
2. In personality assessments through projective techniques, psychopaths have been found to perceive aggressive, sexual, unsocialized, impulsive content; this finding supports the theory that psychopaths are aggressive, sexual, unsocialized, and impulsive.
3. Electroencephalogram (EEG) research shows differences between psychopaths and normals. These differences are most marked in measures of (a) localized slow-wave activity, in which psychopaths have seven times the rates of occurrence of normals; and (b) positive spikes, in which psychopaths show rates of 40% compared to less than 2% in the general public. There are difficulties in interpreting any such research, but one suggestion is that psychopaths show *cortical immaturity*, with EEG patterns similar to those of children.
4. Psychopaths tend to have strong needs for stimulation. They appear to live in a state related to that of sensory deprivation. Their risk taking and the incessant activity revolving about themselves are intended to produce high levels of experiencing. Being bored is intolerable to the psychopath.
5. Parental and early home rejection appear to be linked with psychopathy. In particular, an antisocial father and inconsistent and delayed parental discipline are factors often associated with the development of psychopathy. Nearly all such child-rearing information on psychopaths is retrospective, however, and therefore of uncertain reliability.

The Victim

My machine will take a head off in a twinkling and the victim will feel nothing but a slight sense of refreshing coolness on the neck [Dr. Joseph Guillotin, to the National Assembly of France, 1789][1]

[1] Dr. Guillotin was later a victim of his own invention.

Dr. Guillotin's attitude could be described as humanitarian benevolence toward the beheaded victim. For many modern citizens as well, no one becomes a victim without just cause. This "just-world hypothesis" holds that we live in a just and fair world; if one suffers, it is because he or she deserves it; if the search is exhaustive enough, the reason for the just punishment will always be found. The victim of a crime must therefore have provoked the offense, subtly or obviously, or deserved to be harmed for any number of reasons. This common reaction to victims has been called *blaming the victim* (Ryan, 1971a). The illogical extent to which such blame can be carried is mocked by the comedian Zero Mostel, playing a senator looking into the origins of World War II, asking "What was Pearl Harbor *doing* in the Pacific? [Ryan, 1971a]."

This kind of social blame, combined with persistent fear, may psychologically transform a victim of a crime. Previously satisfactory ways of living and adjusting may be replaced by anxiety, feelings of catastrophe, and impaired abilities to be effective and gain happiness. This process is often observed in victims of muggings, rape, and other personal crimes.

A mugging is a robbery that involves physical assault. Le Jeune and Alex (1973) studied 24 mugging incidents in New York City. Until they were assaulted, the victims had carried on their daily lives comfortably because they had preserved their personal assumptions about their invulnerability and the impossibility of their own deaths. Their being mugged evidently shattered these assumptions. "However minor the material loss or physical injury, whatever the class or race of the respondent, the psychological impact of having been mugged is traumatic [Le Jeune & Alex, 1973, pp. 271–272]." In 12 cases of men mugged at work, C. M. Brodsky (1976) reported strong fears of being alone or walking on city streets. These men all avoided other people, had nightmares, and experienced prolonged periods of sexual dysfunctions. The male victim of a mugging may feel a loss or threat to his masculinity. This is a self-blame process parallel to that often found in the rape victim.

One mugging victim reported this reaction: "Entirely too much of my thinking goes to devising ways to avoid getting robbed. I turn to see who's behind me. I tend to classify all approaching men as to whether they are or are not aggressors [Le Jeune & Alex, 1973, p. 276]." Such reactions sometimes dissipate with time. In other cases, a habituation is made. The victim becomes more vigilant, less at ease, more suspicious, and with discussion of the event may gain much social support from friends and fellow workers.

The victim of rape suffers one additional blow beyond that felt by the mugging victim: She may encounter openly victim-blaming negative attitudes among officials and even acquaintances. Burgess and Holmstrom (1974a, 1976) have identified a rape trauma syndrome among most victims. The syndrome, described as a crisis reaction to a life-threatening situation, is characterized by a disruption of both life-style and work performance. Of 146 sexual-assault victims studied by Burgess and Holmstrom (1976), 79% suffered from rape trauma. Forty percent of the adolescent victims left school or changed schools. More than half the adult victims changed or quit their jobs. Even larger proportions were unable to resume sexual relations with husbands and could not manage home-making tasks.

Out of an awareness of the traumatic impact of rape, rape crisis centers have been established in every major city and most university communities in the United States. The services include immediate counseling of the victim, mobilizing personal and social support services for her, and assisting her in dealing with hospital and criminal officials. Unfortunately, similar attention has not yet been focused on the needs of other crime victims, many of whom are also deeply traumatized and in need of help.

Competence and Sanity

Union Station in Washington, D.C. is like metropolitan railroad stations all over the country. Built to handle tens of thousands of people, Union Station today is filled mostly with fleeting shadows of people and events long past. One Union Station encounter that casts strong shadows is the meeting of President Garfield and Charles J. Giteau on July 3, 1881. On that day, Giteau shot and fatally wounded the president (Rosenberg, 1968).

It was not a clean death for the president. Garfield's health slowly deteriorated during the sweltering summer of 1881. It was not a clear case of criminal responsibility for Giteau; his trial represented the prototypical dilemma of what courts should do with psychologically disturbed defendants. Giteau will be considered again shortly, but our discussion must begin with the first decision point: Is a client mentally competent to stand trial? For incompetence means there can be no trial.

Common law has long required that a person must be physically present to be tried. From that point, the law gradually has been extended to ensure that an individual is mentally present as well. Competence to stand trial is made up of three components. The defendant must (1) be able to understand the nature of the charges against him; (2) be able to understand the proceedings; and (3) be able to assist his attorneys in his own defense. In some jurisdictions, the individual is considered not competent if he is likely to deteriorate substantially during the trial. The determination of mental competence is increasingly made at regional or state forensic clinics that operate under provisions guaranteeing due process for the defendant. Defendants in some states have the right to have attorneys present during the psychiatric or psychological competence evaluation, if they choose.

Competence often has been confused with the legal concept of insanity and the psychological diagnosis of schizophrenia. These are separate and independent issues. A person may be schizophrenic, yet fully competent to stand trial. If found incompetent, the defendant is involuntarily committed to a mental institution until either the charges are dropped or he is restored to competence. The long-term, involuntary commitment of such persons is inappropriate and harmful (Group for the Advancement of Psychiatry, 1974). In a landmark decision in

1975, the Supreme Court held that directors of mental hospitals are personally responsible for inappropriate commitment without treatment. Kenneth Donaldson was confined without treatment for 15 years in a Florida state hospital and the superintendent and director were held to be financially and professionally responsible—a major event for the patients' liberation movement.

Four remedies have been proposed by the Group for the Advancement of Psychiatry to correct injustices following a person's being found incompetent and his subsequent involuntary commitment. (1) Only the defense attorney should assess competence, since the attorney has to work with the person and knows best if he understands the trial procedures and can aid in his defense. (2) All persons should be locally screened for competence rather than being routinely sent to hospitals for evaluations. The hospitalizations are often unnecessary and too lengthy; they also promote institutionalization of the defendants. (3) Psychological treatment should be designed specifically for restoration to competence. This is a treatment goal quite different from traditional therapeutic objectives. Treatment for restoration to competence usually emphasizes training the defendant to cooperate with the attorney. (4) Release or return for trial should be required for all accused persons after a year of involuntary hospitalization because of mental incompetence. In this way, such persons would not be subjected to indefinite, perhaps permanent, commitments because of their status.

Insanity: The Legal Concept

In the eighteenth century, the "wild beast" test was used for criminal responsibility. A person was not considered criminally responsible for his acts if he did not know what he did, any more than "a new born babe or a wild beast in the woods" would be considered responsible (Allen, Ferster, & Rubin, 1975). Insanity as a legal defense changed in the nineteenth century. A person could successfully plead not guilty by reason of insanity only if he was unable to understand the nature and quality of his act, or if he did not understand that what he was doing was wrong. This M'Naghten Rule was more restrictive than prior rules since it focused on the ability to know what one was doing; the emotional components and issues of self-control were purposefully devalued.

Insanity is an official, legal definition of abnormal behavior; it tends to get redefined in the context of political events of the day. The more restrictive definitions of the M'Naghten Rule followed an assassination attempt on Lord Peel, Prime Minister of England, by Daniel M'Naghten, a man suffering from delusions of persecution. Similarly, the trials of assassins from the 1880s to the present frequently have centered about the meanings of insanity pleas. The trial of Charles Giteau was a great public spectacle, like the Daniel M'Naghten, Sirhan Sirhan, and Jack Ruby trials. Giteau held paranoid beliefs about his great worth and mistreatment by the Garfield administration and repeatedly interrupted his trial with inappropriate declarations and rambling statements. The expert witnesses were divided. Some described Giteau as bad but not sick—a label that becomes translated into conduct disorder or psychopathy in current trials—and others diagnosed him as clearly insane and not responsible (Rosenberg, 1968). Giteau's insanity defense failed; he was found guilty and executed.

The plea of not guilty by reason of insanity falls in an area of overlap between criminal justice processes and the study of psychopathology. The more significant observations in this area of overlap are as follows:

1. The diagnosis of dissociative reaction, which is very rare in general psychiatric practice, is given in over half the insanity defenses in some jurisdictions.

2. Insanity defenses are entered only for serious offenses, particularly for murder charges. They are considered a plea of last resort by experienced defense attorneys.

3. The public and juries alike are reluctant to believe even unanimous expert diagnoses supporting an insanity defense. About 95% of all such pleas are followed by convictions.

4. The most seriously disturbed offenders never reach trial to make such pleas; they are found incompetent to stand trial and are shunted off to security hospitals.

5. A continuing debate rages in legal criminological groups about what definitions should be applied to insanity. The Durham Rule, once considered psychiatrically ideal, made a brief appearance in the District of Columbia for less than two decades. The Durham Rule allowed a successful defense to be based on the offense being the product of a mental disorder, and was seen as a very liberal rule.

6. The "irresistible impulse" statement is used as part of several legal rulings. It provides nonculpability if the defendant could not stop himself from committing the act, even if he knew it to be wrong. The question is asked, would he have gone ahead even if a policeman were standing by his elbow?

7. The American Law Institute rule is being increasingly adopted. It reads: "A person is not responsible for criminal conduct if at the time of such conduct as a result of mental disease or defect he lacks substantial capacity either to appreciate the criminality (wrongfulness) of his conduct or to conform his conduct to the requirements of law [p. 689]." This rule is of particular interest because the use of the word *substantial* permits leeway for the experts. They can testify about a defendant without having to state if he is *totally* without awareness of what he did. This conforms to the relativistic nature of psychological judgments.

8. Many psychiatrists and psychologists are gun-shy of testifying in court. The cross-examination process reveals some of the underlying conceptual weaknesses of their fields (Ziskin, 1975) and at its most severe makes them appear foolish and inept.

9. A concerted effort is underway to abolish the insanity defense, in the belief that this legal labeling process wastes professional time and does

not fit with existing scientific information. Allen (1975) observes that "the defense of insanity works directly against both the goals of protection of society and reformation of the offender [p. 709]." From this point of view, psychologists should intervene only after findings of guilt or innocence on the facts.

Summary

Criminality is a legal status and not a behavioral one. Research indicates that whereas up to 80% of prisoners may be diagnosed as maladjusted, law violation does not necessarily indicate the existence of psychopathology. Though dangerousness is often related to criminality, it is very difficult to predict who may be dangerous. Dangerousness may be described as a threat to the existing social structure; it often exists more in the eyes of the beholder than in the potentially harmful person.

Personality research on angry aggression has concentrated on the murderer and the rapist. Persons convicted of murder and assault have been divided along the dimension of overcontrol versus undercontrol of aggression to account for the "meek murderer." Historical, sociological, and psychological theories have all been used to interpret the behaviors of rapists. Though rapists are not all alike, several factors have been identified that are common to a large proportion of all instances of rape.

One useful empirically based typology of offenders is the Quay Behavior Classification System. It classifies youthful offenders into four groups: inadequate–immature, neurotic, psychopathic, and subcultural. This classification system is used as part of a program of differential treatment, a procedure in which types and techniques of correctional counselors are matched with types and needs of offenders.

Because of the severity of the social harm caused by the psychopath, understanding of the disorder is important. The word *psychopath* has acquired many vague popular meanings, but there are several accepted descriptions of psychopathic behavior. The psychopath uses and manipulates other people. He is aggressive and antisocial, impulsive and guiltless, ruthless, and frequently a chronic criminal, unable to love and relate well. At the same time he is often clever, charming, and superficially well-adjusted.

The victim of a mugging or rape may suffer prolonged psychological consequences. Avoidance behaviors and disruptions in the performance of normal life tasks are frequent patterns among the victims of such personal crimes.

Legal issues related to psychopathology include the question of mental competence to stand trial and the insanity defense. Mental incompetence refers to the inability to understand the nature of the trial proceedings and inability to aid in one's defense. The most important insanity criterion is that of the American Law Institute. Under this criterion, a not-guilty verdict indicates a lack of substantial capacity to appreciate the wrongfulness of one's act or to conform one's behavior to the law.

12

Sexual Deviance and Dysfunction

JOHN P. WINCZE
Brown University Medical School

The scientific study of sexual behavior is a relatively new development. It began in earnest when the monumental studies of Kinsey and his associates were published in 1948 and 1953. These researchers were the first to provide empirically based descriptions of human male and female sexual behavior. Prior to Kinsey, sex research and open discussion of sexual behavior were considered taboo; as a result, false and harmful beliefs were common. For example, during the eighteenth and nineteenth centuries, it was accepted medical dogma that excessive masturbation caused a wide variety of disorders including failing eyesight, melancholy, imbecility, hemorrhoids, impotence, and insanity. Although these false beliefs seem amusing now, they are also horrifying—for in the name of treatment thousands of men and women were subjected to castration, clitoridectomy (removal of the clitoris), and ovariotomy (removal of the ovaries). Before we smugly condemn the ignorance of our forefathers, we should note that our own attitudes toward homosexuality, female sexual expression, and masturbation have undergone tremendous changes in the 1970s. The purpose of this chapter is to bring together recent scientific information that will give the reader a general understanding of the field. Among the topics discussed will be the concept of normal sexual behavior, the assessment of sexual behavior, the evolution of sexual behavior, sexual deviance, and sexual dysfunction.

Normality and Sexual Behavior

Our present knowledge and the scientific study of human sexual behavior began with Alfred Kinsey. Kinsey was a biology professor at Indiana University in 1937 when he was assigned to teach a course on marriage—a new experience for a man whose expertise was in birds and gall wasps. When he began teaching the course, he realized that he could not answer many of his students' questions concerning sexual behavior. To his disappointment, he found few scientific studies concerning sexual behavior. In an attempt to gather empirical information, he began interviewing people about the sexual aspects of their lives. Pomeroy (1966) reports that this was the beginning of Kinsey's career in sex research. In all, Kinsey and his associates interviewed over 18,000 men and women during a 20-year period and thereby provided the most comprehensive statistical survey on human sexual behavior to date. Although Kinsey's work has been criticized for methodological weaknesses in the interviewing approach, his research allows us to look at many questions, including this one: What is normal sexual behavior?

Kinsey's studies make it clear that normality is relative to culture, social class, the laws of a society, religion, and a host of other parameters. In short, Kinsey's work above all else emphasizes the incredible diversity of sexual behavior. What is considered normal sexual practice in one culture, social class, or region of a country may be considered abnormal, bizarre, and illegal elsewhere. For example, Brecher and Brecher (1966) cite a wedding custom in the Marquesas islands, reported by French anthropologist L. F. Tautain, in which all the men present at the wedding ceremony have sexual intercourse with the bride. Furthermore, "the more men a bride had satisfied, the prouder she was [p. 49]." Though this South Seas wedding ceremony would be unacceptable in our North American culture, it illustrates the profound differences in sexual practices that exist in different cultures. Even within our own culture there are numerous legal and social class differences governing acceptable sexual behavior. Because sexual beliefs and behavior are molded by rather narrow sociocultural influences, it is difficult if not impossible to talk about "normal" or universal patterns of sexual behavior or systems of sexual beliefs. Kinsey's careful reporting of sexual behavior in various segments of our society reveals the tremendous diversity of sexual behavior that normal adults in our society engage in. To understand the reasons for this diversity, we shall examine the development of sexual behavior.

Development of Sexual Behavior

In general, as we move up the phylogenetic scale, we find sexual behavior less related to fertilization and increasingly related to social behavior. In less complex animals, sexual behavior is almost entirely determined by genetic and hormonal influences. In more complex animals, especially humans, sexual behavior is largely determined by postnatal environmental influences. As Rosenberg and Sutton-Smith (1972) point out, vast differences in sexual behavior do exist even among different species of animals of equal phylogenetic development. Thus, the relationship between phylogenetic development and sexual behavior may be stated only as a general guideline and not as a law of nature. In humans, the influence of the social environment is unquestionably of major importance in determining one's sexual behavior, whereas genetic and hormonal influences appear to be less important.

GENETIC AND HORMONAL INFLUENCES

Although there is widespread agreement among researchers that genes are important in lower animals for determining sex-role behavior, the exact processes by which they control sexual behavior are not entirely understood. Most researchers agree, however, that genes exert a complex influence on the developing nervous system. This genetic influence may predispose structures in the brain to control hormonal influences.

In humans, a great deal of our knowledge of genetic and hormonal influences on sexual behavior has come to us indirectly through the study of chromosomal errors. Money (1965), who has studied a number of people with anomalies of psychosexual differentiation, points out several incongruities that may exist in hermaphrodites (people possessing some primary genital characteristics of both sexes). These are

1. atypical chromosome count
2. hormonal imbalance that is predominantly androgenic or estrogenic
3. ovaries or testicles abnormally developed or mixed
4. internal structure of reproductive organs abnormally developed
5. external structure of genitals abnormally developed [p. 10]

Money's research shows that, despite such pronounced genetic and hormonal abnormalities in sexual differentiation, environmental influences determine an individual's sex-role identification and subsequent sexual behavior. In a now-classic study, Money (1965) found that hermaphrodites could develop the normal identity and behavior expected of either sex, depending on how they were raised by their parents. This research strongly supports the notion that the environment—not genetics or hormones—is the determinant of sexual identity and behavior.

This is not to say that chromosomes and hormones have no influence on the development of human sexual behavior. The structure of a person's body, especially the genitals, greatly influences how the person and society will feel about the person's sex role. If chromosome anomalies have caused abnormal genital appearance, necessary corrective surgery should be accomplished very early in a person's development, so that the external appearance coincides with the gender role in which the person is being raised. It is vital that sexual identity be established very early in life.

The acquisition of a native language is a human counterpart to imprinting in animals. So also is the acquisition of a gender role and psychosexual identity. The critical period in establishing psychosexual identity appears to be approximately simultaneous with the establishment of native language. . . .

. . . By school age, psychosexual differentiation is so complete that a sex reassignment is out of the question save for rare instances of ambiguous psychosexual differentiation [Money, 1965, pp. 12–13].

Hormones may have other important influences on the developing human. Kane, Lipton, and Ewing (1969) conclude that hormones may play two roles in human female sexuality. First they guide the early development of the neural substructures that will underlie adult sexual behavior. Then at puberty, they activate those substructures to adult functional levels. Once a person has developed to adulthood, however, female hormones (estrogen and progesterone) can do little to influence a person's psychosexual identity. Masters and Johnson (1966) see supplementation of the female hormone estrogen as important only for nourishing sexual tissues and precluding discomfort in the adult female.

Money and Erhardt (1972) theorize that all fetuses would develop into females if it were not for the presence of the hormone androgen during fetal development. Recent studies of androgen and the other male hormone, testosterone, have revealed the profound importance of these male hormones in the development of the fetus. In both the adult male and the adult female, the addition of male hormones usually produces increases in sexual arousal. Kaplan (1974) cautions, however, that there are sometimes undesirable side effects from male hormone supplements, such as increased aggression and masculinization in women. The effects and side effects of hormone supplements are not yet entirely understood and they certainly should be used with caution.

ENVIRONMENTAL INFLUENCES

The research of Money and others has underscored the importance of environmental influences in the development of psychosexual identity and behavior. Harlow has also contributed greatly to our understanding of environmental influences on sexual behavior through ingenious studies with rhesus monkeys. These studies demonstrate the importance of early environmental experiences on later sexual behavior (Harlow & Harlow, 1965). Monkeys reared in isolation from their mothers and peers showed marked disturbances in their sexual behavior when later introduced to other monkeys; the longer the isolation, the more profound was the disturbance. Monkeys isolated for the first 2 years of their lives showed no sexual behavior whatsoever; monkeys isolated for the first 80 days of their lives showed sexual behavior characterized by inadequate mounting and unsuccessful copulation.

The work of Money and Harlow demonstrates the importance of environmental influences on sexual behavior. It is logical to extrapolate from this research to the normal human infant. The child raised in a family without affection will find it difficult to show affection as an adult; the child raised in a family that condemns any expression of sexual behavior will feel uneasy expressing sexual behavior as an adult. There are exceptions to these examples, but in general, family and peers are the major influences on later sexual behavior. Since sex is still a somewhat taboo area in our society, accepted sexual practice is not openly discussed or observed. Therefore, children must rely on a relatively narrow set of experiences to shape the intensity and direction of their own sexual beliefs and behavior.

Of course, other environmental influences may direct the feelings and expression of sexuality. Traumatic experiences such as rape, or more subtle sexual experiences, may dramatically change an otherwise healthy sexual development. For example, McGuire, Carlisle, and Young (1965) emphasize the importance of ejaculation as a learning experience:

> It is in accordance with conditioning theory that any stimulus which regularly precedes ejaculation by the correct time interval should become more and more sexually exciting. The stimulus may be circumstantiated (for example, the particular time or place in which masturbation or intercourse is commonly practiced) or it may be deliberate (for example, any sexual situation or a fantasy of it, be it normal intercourse or wearing female apparel). It is hypothesized that the latter process is the mechanism by which most sexual deviations are acquired and developed [p. 186].

Thus, according to these researchers, the repeated association of orgasm with a specific fantasy or real stimulus may strengthen the importance of that fantasy or stimulus as a part of a person's sexual expression. The fact that specific patterns of sexual behavior may have unique learning histories will be discussed in more detail in the sections on deviance and dysfunction.

Problems of Research and Assessment of Sexual Behavior

The scientific study of sexual behavior has experienced unique stumbling blocks. The biggest problem has been the general taboo associated with the field of sexual behavior. When Kinsey began his research at Indiana University in 1937, some of his fellow faculty members urged the president of the university to put a stop to such a disgraceful academic undertaking (Pomeroy, 1966). Fortunately, the president and the board of trustees supported Kinsey, but he still had to suffer the humiliation of having some faculty members deliberately not speak to him. Even in today's more open and liberal times, sex research is sometimes faced with similar problems, though these problems are usually of a lesser degree. For example, most researchers in the field are continuously asked by friends and colleagues how and why they became interested in this area of research, and almost always encounter jokes and off-color remarks even when attempting to discuss their research on a scientific level.

Another problem unique to this field has been the assessment or measurement of sexual behavior. Accurate assessment is extremely important for every behavioral scientist and clinician. Without accurate assessment, behavioral science could easily be led astray by false impressions. Therefore, it is crucial for all behavioral scientists to use the most accurate measurement procedures available.

Sex researchers, unfortunately, face the problem of trying to measure extremely private behavior that is permeated with taboos and sacrosanct beliefs. There are few objections to recording the typical behavior of a retarded child, for example, but there have been *extreme* objections to recording the typical sexual behavior of two adults.

In the early days of sex research, researchers and clinicians relied almost exclusively on interviews to obtain information, mostly through indirect and subtle questioning. Unfortunately, this technique did not yield much useful information about sexual behavior. It was not until Kinsey began doing research that experimental rigor was added to the field and concern for more direct and accurate interviewing procedures developed.

Interviewing procedures have their shortcomings; even at their best, they are almost always subject to questions of validity and reliability. Self-reports provided by patients and experimental subjects during interviews may not correlate with other levels of assessment. Furthermore, patients and subjects may try to please the therapist or researcher by responding in the direction they think is expected of them. A study by Conrad and Wincze (1976) found that males who wished to change their sexual orientation from homosexual to heterosexual all reported to the therapist at the conclusion of therapy that their orientation had changed and that they felt therapy was successful. Behavioral records and objective physiological measures failed to support the interview report, and no changes in sexual orientation were found on these other, more objective levels of assessment. This study dramatically shows the need for multilevel assessment to counterbalance this potential shortcoming in interview procedures. In an effort to increase the objectivity of assessments of sexual functioning, researchers have turned to (1) the use of questionnaires, (2) direct and indirect behavioral observations, and (3) the use of physiological recording devices. Each of these three methods will be discussed briefly.

Many statistically valid questionnaires have been developed that have yielded information about the occurrence of various types of sexual behavior and about attitudes toward sexual behavior. Udry and Morris (1967) and Thorne (1966) have presented evidence suggesting that direct questioning about sexual behavior via a questionnaire is a reliable source of information. In a similar vein, Barker and Perlman (1975) show that volunteers for sex questionnaires are not atypical or deviant as a group. These studies present a compelling argument against the most common criticisms of sex questionnaires and support this method as a useful assessment tool.

Perhaps the most dramatic development in the field of sex research has been the work of Masters and Johnson (1966, 1970). These researchers pioneered in the scientific study of sexual behavior by directly observing and recording it in their own laboratory. During their initial research project, they observed over 690 couples engaging in intercourse or masturbation under laboratory conditions. These observations provided the scientific world with the most comprehensive and accurate information ever compiled about human sexual response. In addition, their method of direct observation coupled with physiological recording has proven to be an objective and workable laboratory method of collecting data. Their method is limited in its usefulness since there are few laboratories set up for such research. Some researchers have used indirect behavioral records in place of direct behavioral observation, but such records rely on the subject's honesty and are therefore susceptible to criticisms of responder bias.

One of the most promising new areas in assessment involves the use of physiological recording devices. A variety of devices for measuring sexual arousal in both males and females have been developed and validated. Freund (1963) was the first to develop a useful instrument for directly assessing male sexual arousal by measuring penile volume changes. This device consists of a glass cylinder fitting over the penis. Volume changes, signaled by air displacement, are transmitted mechanically to a sensitive measuring device. Barlow, Becker, Leitenberg, and Agras (1970) and others have developed instruments for measuring penile circumference changes rather than penile volume changes. These newer devices are less cumbersome and more comfortable. Barlow's device consists of a flat metal spring that fits around the penis. A strain gauge connected to the spring measures changes related to the expansion of the metal. There was some question as to which method of recording sexual arousal in males is most accurate, until a collaborative study by Freund, Langevin, and Barlow (1974) demonstrated the greater sensitivity of the volumetric measure.

Only recently have researchers developed instrumentation to measure sexual arousal in females. In 1971, Zuckerman concluded that there were no reliable physiological measures of female sexual arousal. Geer, Morokoff, and Greenwood (1974) and Sintchak and Geer (1975) were the first to develop a device that was easy to use and seemed to give a valid measurement of sexual arousal in women. The device is a clear acrylic probe with an incandescent light source mounted on one end and a selenium photocell light detector mounted on the side. The probe measures the amount of light reflected by vaginal wall tissue. The development of this device was largely influenced by the work of Masters and Johnson, who noted a darkening of color (as a result of increased blood flow) of the vaginal wall during periods of reported sexual arousal. In Geer's study, women were exposed to erotic or neutral stimuli; they reported their feelings while vaginal capillary blood flow measures were taken. Geer found significant reflected light changes during the sexually arousing stimulus condition. Hoon, Wincze, and Hoon (1976) developed an improved probe device, which uses an infrared light source and phototransistor detector cell. These investigators have demonstrated that their device is valid since it can discriminate between sexually arousing, unpleasant, and neutral emotional conditions in women.

The development of physiological measuring instruments for recording sexual arousal in males and females has added a dimension of objectivity to the field that previously did not exist. These devices have tremendous potential for helping the practicing clinician diagnose sexual problems and evaluate the progress of therapy. For the researcher, these devices have opened new frontiers of study. We can anticipate scientific answers to such questions as the following: What is the relationship between cognitive and physiological levels of sexual arousal? Are people always aware of their sexual feelings? How does fear affect sexual arousal? What happens physiologically during sexual arousal? These and even more interesting questions will be asked and answered largely because of the technical advancements in the field.

Sexual Deviance

In our discussion of normality and sexual behavior we suggested that normality is related directly to the social class, culture, and legal environment in which one lives. In Western cultures, many sexual behaviors are labeled as deviant. These will be the focus of our discussion. Although many sexual problems can develop secondarily to other problems, our concern is with sexual problems that are the primary problems of an individual. The American Psychiatric Association placed such sexual problems in DSM II (1968) in the same category as personality problems:

> This category is for individuals whose sexual interests are directed primarily toward objects other than people of the opposite sex, toward sexual acts not usually associated with coitus, or toward coitus performed under bizarre circumstances as in necrophilia [with dead bodies], pedophilia [with children], sexual sadism and fetishism. Even though many find their practices distasteful, they remain unable to substitute normal sexual behavior for them. The diagnosis is not appropriate for individuals who perform deviant sexual acts because normal sexual objects are not available to them [p. 44].

According to DSM II, there are eight classifications considered in the category of sexual deviance:

1. homosexuality
2. transvestism
3. fetishism
4. pedophilia
5. exhibitionism
6. sadism
7. masochism
8. voyeurism

Regardless of which behaviors are classified as deviant, it must be emphasized that problems come to the attention of mental health professionals only when they are disturbing to an individual or to society. In the case of sexual behaviors, it is most often society that has objected to an individual's deviant behavior and has pressured an individual to seek "help." This pressure may be through subtle influence, such as pointing out to an individual that his or her behavior is offensive, or it may be through direct influence such as legal action. Because individuals committing sex offenses are often coerced into therapy, therapy success rates with sexual deviance have been comparatively poor. Many individuals who practice offensive and unacceptable sexual behavior are happy with their own behavior and do not feel they need to change. Child molesters, for example, often feel they relate well to children and that fondling a child is merely a show of affection on their part and is something the child enjoys. The violent reaction by a child's parents is often very confusing to the child molester. In this section we will look at some of the more uncommon sexual behaviors, most of which are classified as deviant, and attempt to gain some understanding of the behaviors and the types of individuals engaging in them.

HOMOSEXUALITY

Perhaps no other behavior discussed in abnormal psychology textbooks raises so many controversies and heated arguments as homosexuality. There are some who question whether a discussion of homosexuality should even be included in an abnormal psychology textbook (Davison & Neale, 1974), because such an inclusion may prejudice people's attitudes toward homosexuality. On the other hand, there have always been laws prohibiting homosexual behavior. For example, in nineteenth-century England the death penalty was in effect for specific homosexual acts. In the United States, there are no specific laws against being a homosexual, but homosexuals are subject to arrest under a variety of laws covering such behaviors as disorderly conduct, lewd and lascivious behavior, sodomy, and vagrancy. There are also many subtle problems that homosexuals must face, such as difficulties in renting or buying housing and obtaining membership in clubs and organizations.

Currently, traditional ideas about homosexuality are being challenged by scientific evidence suggesting that homosexual behavior is not harmful to those who engage in it. In addition, a number of groups such as the Mattachine Society and Gay Liberation have brought tremendous pressures on legislators and health professionals to change their thinking toward homosexuality. As a result of these influences, the American Psychiatric Association voted in 1974 to remove homosexuality from its list of mental disorders. Another significant occurrence was the 1974 presidential address by Gerald Davison, president of the Association for the Advancement of Behavior Therapy, in which Davison strongly supported the position that individuals engaging in homosexual behavior should not be treated in psychotherapy for sexual orientation change. Davison stated that "the very existence of sexual reorientation programs might very well impede social change towards a lessening of cultural prejudice and of legal oppression [Davison, 1974, p. 1]." In other words, Davison feels that by offering therapy for homosexuality and by conducting research on homosexuality, therapists and scientists are viewing homosexuality as a problem and thus reinforcing this belief in society as a whole. Davison believes that homosexuality is not a problem in a pathological sense, but because therapists and society consider it a problem, homosexuals are pressured against their will into seeking change in their behavior. One of Davison's suggestions is that "as behavior therapists and clinicians, we might perhaps pay more attention to the quality of human relationships, to the way people deal with each other rather than to the particular gender of the adult partners [Davison, 1974, p. 7]."

Militants march in favor of gay rights, New York, 1972. Public demonstrations by homosexuals would have been unthinkable only a few years earlier. Now they are increasingly common as homosexuals seek equal treatment under the law. (Charles Gatewood)

Davison's address was carefully written and well timed in the face of rising and increasingly vocal opposition to behavior therapy by homosexual pressure groups and by the American Civil Liberties Union. It is still too early, however, to measure the exact impact of this speech and of the American Psychiatric Association decision. Certainly, articles are still appearing in psychiatric as well as behavioral journals outlining treatment of and research on homosexuality. It may be that in the future, fewer and fewer individuals will seek treatment for homosexuality and those who do seek help will be encouraged to reduce their anxiety about the problem rather than change their sexual orientation. This is perhaps an overly optimistic prediction since as early as 1948, Kinsey, Pomeroy, and Martin expressed concerns similar to Davison's:

> . . . but psychiatrists and clinicians in general might very well re-examine their justification for demanding that all persons conform to particular patterns of behavior. As a matter of fact, there is an increasing proportion of the most skilled psychiatrists who make no attempt to re-direct behavior, but who devote their attention to helping an individual accept himself, and to conduct himself in such a manner that he does not come into open conflict with society [Kinsey *et al.*, 1948, p. 660].

Today, prejudices toward homosexuality still exist among professionals and nonprofessionals even though homosexuality is no longer officially recognized as a deviant or an abnormal behavior. Thus, the topic of homosexuality is included in this textbook, not in opposition to the spirit of Davison and Kinsey, but in order to give the reader a clearer understanding of the behavior and to challenge any lingering misconceptions and prejudices. Through the factual presentation of knowledge, prejudices can be removed and new ways of thinking generated.

HOMOSEXUAL BEHAVIOR.   The term *homosexuality* is derived from the Greek root *homo-*, which emphasizes the sameness of the two individuals involved in sexual activity. Thus, the term applies to two women as well as to two men involved in sex, although female homosexuality is usually referred to as lesbianism. The term *lesbian* comes from the classic Greek poet Sappho, who described sexual relations between women of the island of Lesbos. Although we usually talk of individuals as being homosexuals, it is more correct to talk in terms of an individual's homosexual behavior. By so doing, we recognize the fact that an individual is capable of engaging in both homosexual and heterosexual behavior. More important, describing an individual's homosexual behavior rather than labeling the individual as homosexual should minimize the disease connotations.

Traditionally, the stereotype view of the homosexual male has been that of the "limp-wristed faggot" engaging exclusively in homosexual activities. But the work of Kinsey and others overwhelmingly supports the diversity of all sexual behavior, including homosexuality. Individuals engaging in homosexual behavior are as diverse in their interests, intellect, appearance, and sexual behavior as are individuals engaging in heterosexual behavior. There are limp-wristed, effeminate-looking men who are exclusively heterosexual and there are herculean, athletic-looking men who are exclusively homosexual. In spite of this diversity in appearance and behavior among adult male homosexuals, Saghir and Robins (1973) found that about two-thirds of adult male homosexuals reported being teased for effeminate appearance and behavior during adolescence.

In order to aid in the description of homosexual behavior, Kinsey *et al.* (1948, p. 638) developed a simple heterosexual–homosexual rating scale from 0, exclusively heterosexual, to 6, exclusively homosexual (Figure 12-1).

One of the most controversial discoveries of the Kinsey survey was that 37% of the total male population has at least some overt homosexual experience to the point of orgasm between adolescence and old age. Thus, if we accept the notion that one incidence of homosexual behavior makes a person a homosexual, then over one-third of the male population is homosexual. Obviously, it is much more meaningful to speak in terms of degrees of homosexual behavior.

Saghir, Robbins, and Walbran (1969a, 1969b) and Hooker (1966) describe the types of behaviors and life-styles of individuals who engage in homosexual behavior. It is clear from their work and from Kinsey's that there is great diversity in behavior and life-styles. Although some individuals always play the active or passive sexual role, the majority prefer varying roles and activities:

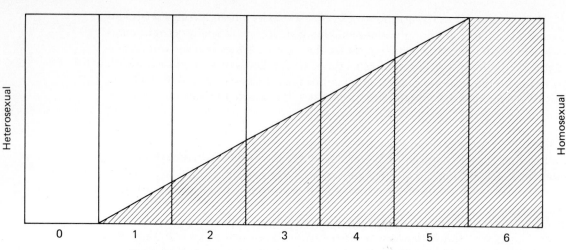

Figure 12-1. Heterosexual–homosexual rating scale developed by Kinsey *et al.*
(1948, p. 638):

0 Exclusively heterosexual with no homosexual behavior
1 Predominantly heterosexual, only incidentally homosexual behavior
2 Predominantly heterosexual, but more than incidentally homosexual behavior
3 Equally heterosexual and homosexual behavior
4 Predominantly homosexual, but more than incidentally heterosexual behavior
5 Predominantly homosexual, but incidentally heterosexual behavior
6 Exclusively homosexual behavior

The range of erotic sensitivity, the preferred or accepted mode and conditions for
achieving sexual gratification, the nature of sexual gratification, and the frequency
with which it is sought vary from one individual to another [Hooker, 1966, pp.
30–31].

Saghir *et al.* (1969b) observed that male homosexual activity seems to evolve
through various stages. Adolescence and preadolescence are characterized
largely by casual relationships involving mutual masturbation and, to a much
lesser degree, mouth–genital contacts and anal intercourse. As an individual
matures, there is a tendency to decrease the activity of mutual masturbation and
increase oral–genital contacts and anal intercourse. Lasting relationships may
develop between homosexuals, although this practice is more common among
females than among males. Saghir *et al.* (1969a, 1969b) make another observation that contradicts a widely held belief: Ninety-eight percent of the homosexuals interviewed stated that their first experience with an adult was of *no* significance in relation to their homosexual desires and orientation. Almost all males
and females felt that their desires preceded their first experiences.

Females begin their homosexual activities later in life than males, and usually favor oral–genital and manual–genital activities. Homosexually oriented
females rarely use a penis substitute for sexual gratification. Inserting an object
into the vagina is also a rare masturbatory activity of heterosexually oriented
females.

THEORIES OF HOMOSEXUALITY.   Many different theories have attempted to explain the origins of homosexual behavior. Because of the diversity and complexity of the behavior it is no surprise that so many theories exist. Feldman and MacCulloch (1971) suggest that one theory may explain one degree of homosexual behavior whereas another theory may explain another degree. Certainly the evidence is inconclusive at this point.

Biological Theories.   Because homosexual behavior seems so resistant to change, many have felt that the only feasible explanation is a biological one. Kallmann (1953), in one of his many twin studies, reports 100% concordance rates for homosexuality in monozygotic (identical) twins and less than 15% concordance for dizygotic (fraternal) twins. Twin studies are subject to criticism, however, and others have not been able to replicate Kallmann's findings. The determination of fraternal versus identical twins is sometimes technically very difficult, requiring sophisticated chromosomal analysis. Kallmann did not follow the accepted procedures for determination of zygosity, thus raising doubts about his findings. Other researchers have looked toward hormonal differences between homosexual and heterosexual populations. Some recent studies have suggested that males who are exclusively homosexual have a lower sperm count and a lower level of testosterone compared to a control group of heterosexual men (Kolodny, Masters, Hendryx, & Toro, 1971). This could be interpreted as either a cause or a result of homosexual behavior. A study by Money and Alexander (1969), which complements the Kolodny *et al.* (1971) research, suggests a relationship in human males between excessive production of masculinizing hormones during fetal development and childhood years and a total absence of homosexual interest in adolescent years. Most resarchers feel it is too early however, to draw any conclusions about the role of biological factors in determining homosexual behavior.

Psychological Theories.   Psychoanalytic theorists have advanced a number of possible explanations for the development of homosexual behavior. One prominent theory suggests that the male homosexual is fearful of the female genitals and therefore seeks male sexual relations:

> The sight of female genitals may arouse anxiety in a boy in two ways: (1) the recognition of the fact that there are actually human beings without a penis leads to the conclusion that one might also become such a being; such an observation lends effectiveness to old threats of castration. Or (2) the female genitals, through the connection of castration anxiety with old oral anxiety, may be perceived as a castrating instrument capable of biting or tearing off the penis. Quite frequently a combination of both types of fears is encountered [Fenichel, 1945, p. 330].

Some psychoanalysts believe that castration shock is common in many boys, but only those who overreact to the shock develop homosexual tendencies. Another prominent analytical theory is that the male homosexual has an unresolved Oedipus complex, which leads to an intense fixation with his mother. The relationship with his mother is openly recognized by the homosexual and is not unconscious. According to Fenichel, "the homosexual man identifies himself with his frustrating mother in one particular respect: like her, he loves men [p. 331]."

Any therapist who has talked with a large number of homosexually-oriented men will remember many examples that support these two hypotheses. There is little doubt that many male homosexuals fear genital contacts with females and are often intensely emotionally involved with their mothers. But what about female homosexuals? Psychoanalysts feel that similar factors are important for the development of female homosexual behavior:

> The sight of a penis may create a fear of an impending violation; more frequently it mobilizes thoughts and emotions about the differences in physical appearance. These fears, thoughts and emotions may disturb the capacity for sexual enjoyment to such a degree that sexual pleasure is possible only if there is no confrontation with a penis [Fenichel, 1945, p. 338].

The sight of the genitals of the opposite sex is seen by psychoanalysts as a potentially disturbing experience for both males and females. This "shock" can lead not only to homosexuality but to frigidity as well. Thus, some analysts caution against letting a child observe his or her father's penis (Greenhill, 1952). Female homosexuality may also develop following an emotional fixation on the mother. In order to love the mother intensely, the female child identifies with the father's role and loves "mother in the way the father loved her [Fenichel, 1945, p. 338]."

Behavioral theorists use a different language to describe the origins of homosexuality. Behaviorists talk about homosexuality as an avoidance of sexual behavior with members of the opposite sex because of disturbing experiences with such individuals. Behaviorists may also talk about being sexually attracted to the same sex because of the role one has been reinforced to play in life. Many clinicians, including the present author, have interviewed males involved in homosexual behavior who have described heterosocial and heterosexual anxieties. It is apparent from these case histories that anxieties developed following punishing experiences with females. This is one of many possibilities, however, and it is unwise and perhaps naive to attempt to explain such a diverse behavior as homosexuality in terms of a single theoretical orientation.

Feldman and MacCulloch (1971) present a theory that includes both biological and learning theory components; it divides homosexuals into primary and secondary groups. *Primary homosexuals* are those individuals who have never had heterosexual experiences and would therefore be rated on the Kinsey scale as 6. These individuals, according to Feldman and MacCulloch, probably develop homosexual behavior because of biological determinants. The exact determinants are unknown but they may be prenatal hormonal influences. Secondary homosexuals are individuals who are born possessing normal biological makeup and therefore have the potential to develop heterosexually, but because of environmental factors they develop homosexual interests.

TREATMENT OF HOMOSEXUALITY. A storm of controversy surrounds the treatment of homosexuality. Many emotional opinions have been expressed opposing psychotherapy for homosexuality. Some of the opinions are justifiable, but others are based on incomplete or inaccurate information. In many cases, homosexuals have been forced into aversion therapy by court order. Even when the prescribed therapy is not aversion therapy it is offensive, since it is not being entered by choice. If you doubt this, just imagine for a moment that a court has ordered you to seek psychotherapy to "cure" your sexual orientation. As you might guess, therapy under such conditions is rarely successful.

In fact, the vast majority of homosexuals never seek psychiatric help. Furthermore, most of these individuals do not look upon themselves as sick, and Saghir and Robins (1973) found no greater occurrence of psychiatric disorders in a group of homosexual men than in a control group of heterosexual men. Similarly, they found no difference between homosexual women and heterosexual control women in terms of neuroticism or psychosis, although homosexual women tended to have a higher incidence of alcoholism.

When homosexual men and women do seek psychotherapy, it is most often for depression and anxiety associated with the pressures placed on them as homosexual individuals in this society. Such therapy may attempt to change the person's sexual orientation, or it may focus on helping the individual to be more comfortable with his or her homosexual behavior. In either case, the major treatment approaches have come from the psychodynamic and behavioral schools.

Psychodynamic Treatment. Psychodynamic therapy for homosexual behavior has undergone considerable change over the years. Earlier dynamic therapy programs focused on resolving underlying narcissistic, oedipal, or castration conflicts in order to effect a complete cure. A complete cure meant that an individual's sexual interests had been redirected toward members of the opposite sex (Hadfield, 1958). This more global goal has not met with much success. Therefore many contemporary dynamic therapists are concentrating more on the homosexual individual's adjustment to life, rather than attempting a complete sexual orientation change (Mayerson & Lief, 1965). These more limited goals are reported to be successful although objective measurement of change is a problem.

Behavioral Treatment. Behavioral approaches to the treatment of homosexuality have also undergone change. Some of the earlier attempts at treatment appear more like fraternity initiation rites than serious therapeutic interventions. For example, a case study described by James (1962) contains many untested yet upsetting ingredients:

> Treatment was carried out in a darkened single room, and during this time no food or drink other than the prescribed alcohol was allowed. At regular two-hourly intervals he was given an emetic dose of apomorphine by injection followed by 2 oz. (57 ml.) of brandy. On each occasion when nausea was felt, a strong light was shone on a large piece of cardboard on which were posted several photographs of nude or near-nude men. He was asked to select one which he found attractive, and it was

suggested to him that he re-create the experiences which he had had with his current homosexual partner. His fantasy was reinforced verbally by the therapist on the first two or three occasions [p. 769].

In addition, this individual was repeatedly subjected to a tape recording describing his homosexuality as nauseating. There were several other components to this grueling therapy. Not surprisingly, therapy had to be terminated twice because the patient was experiencing a metabolic imbalance that could have resulted in a coma. Fortunately, this treatment approach is not representative of current behavioral approaches. In fact, it is not representative of aversion therapy since it incorporates crude and untested methodology. It is an example of the type of poorly thought-out treatment that has outraged civil libertarians and homosexual groups.

A more scientifically based aversion therapy is being used by many researchers and therapists today (Bancroft, 1970; Feldman & MacCulloch, 1971). By *scientifically based* is meant a technique, premised on strict learning theory principles, that has been thoroughly tested in controlled research. Aversion therapy is aimed exclusively at decreasing homosexual behavior, however, and as Barlow (1973) points out, increasing heterosexual responsiveness may be the more important factor in treatment.

Therapists attempt to increase heterosexual responsiveness by associating the existing homosexual arousal with heterosexual stimuli in the form of slides and movies. In an ingenious study, Barlow and Agras (1973) superimposed a slide of a nude male over a slide of a nude female. Male homosexuals viewing the slides would become sexually aroused by the male slide, which was initially at a much greater light intensity. The experimenters slowly increased the light intensity of the female slide, while simultaneously decreasing the intensity of the male slide over a number of trials. Homosexual clients were finally able to show arousal to female slides. The results are more impressive since all three clients involved in the study later were able to experience heterosexual arousal in real-life situations. Although these results are encouraging, Barlow and Agras's (1973) methodology has not yet been widely used and thus its clinical usefulness is still untested. Barlow (1973) points out that little controlled research has been accomplished for other methods aimed at increasing heterosexual arousal; consequently, there are no proven techniques available to therapists seeking to increase heterosexual arousal.

Some common background factors in homosexual patients have proved to be reliable predictors of successful treatment by either psychodynamic or behavioral therapy:

1. First and most important, patients must enter therapy totally voluntarily and show strong evidence of wanting to cooperate in therapy.
2. Patients and therapists should be clear on the purpose of therapy, whether it is increasing heterosexual responsiveness, becoming exclusively heterosexual, or feeling more adjusted with one's homosexuality.

3. For those patients who wish to change sexual orientation, a prior history of heterosexual experience is very important.
4. For those patients who wish to change sexual orientation, the younger one is, the more likely is change.

TREATMENT FOR BETTER ADJUSTMENT AS A HOMOSEXUAL.   We have described some treatment methods used by therapists to bring about a sexual orientation change. But most therapists today believe strongly that homosexuals who seek treatment should have the alternative of learning how to accept their homosexuality and live with it. Furthermore, homosexuals should feel free to seek therapy for problems of living, without having their homosexuality brought up as a concern and made the focus of treatment. A homosexual who is seeking psychiatric or medical treatment can usually consult local gay organizations to get information on how he or she might be treated by various health professionals.

For those individuals who wish to become more comfortable with their homosexuality, treatment involves such behavioral procedures as systematic desensitization and assertive training. That is, the homosexual individual is presented, either in imagination or during role playing, with scenes and situations that make the individual uncomfortable as a homosexual. The individual then works through these uncomfortable situations by using learning strategies to reduce anxiety and cope with the problems. A great deal of the treatment involves the building of confidence through discussion with a therapist who is understanding and supportive of the individual's homosexuality. Some therapists hold group therapy sessions with homosexuals, so that the support can also come from the group process. Therapists who are fully supportive also offer treatment for various sexual dysfunctions, such as rapid ejaculation, delayed ejaculation, and impotence.

TRANSVESTISM

Transvestism is dressing in the clothing of the opposite sex in order to achieve heightened sexual excitation. Typically, a male will cross-dress in female clothing including undergarments and makeup and masturbate while observing himself in a mirror. Sometimes the cross-dressed individual will walk in public in order to obtain the "admiring" glances of strangers and then later masturbate to this fantasy. Some individuals may cross-dress for the purpose of inviting a homosexual experience. A vivid example is Miss Destiny in John Rechy's book *City of Night* (1963):

> . . . I went to Philadelphia. And the first thing I did, why, I bought myself a flaming red dress and high heeled sequined shoes and everyone thought I was Real, and Miss Thing said, "Hurray, honey! You've done it—stick to it"; and I met a rich daddy, who thought I was Real, and he flipped over me and took me to a straight cocktail party [p. 106].

In this case of a young male transvestite, Miss Destiny has a strong desire to be a "Real" female. This is also an example of transsexualism, which is discussed

Miss Holly Woodlawn relaxes with a scrapbook of her theatrical successes. Miss Woodlawn is actually a male who has built a show-business career around female impersonations that include elaborate cross-dressing. (Dick Frank)

in the next section. It is important to understand that transvestism may occur with or without homosexual intentions. Many male transvestites are married and seek only heterosexual gratification, in addition to the gratification obtained through cross-dressing. Often, the wife is fully aware of her husband's cross-dressing and participates in heterosexual intercourse with her husband only when he is cross-dressed.

It is interesting that in the background of transvestites there is sometimes strong evidence of family support for this behavior (Stoller, 1967). Mothers, fathers, aunts, or uncles may openly encourage a child to dress in clothing of the opposite sex. In one case, the mother bought women's jewelry for her son and left her own clothing or her daughter's clothing on his bed for him.

The exact incidence of transvestism is unknown, since individuals without homosexual involvement are rarely compelled to seek treatment. The level of public condemnation for this behavior is very low. It is quite possible for an individual to participate in private cross-dressing all his life without ever having this behavior in any way interfere with his life. Transvestism is an exclusively male problem today, since man-tailored clothes are not only acceptable for women but fashionable.

TRANSSEXUALISM

Transsexuals differ from homosexuals and transvestites in their feelings of gender identity. That is, they feel and act as if they were of the opposite gender. Male transsexuals, for example, often describe themselves as being a female "trapped" in a male body. The desire to be identified as a member of the opposite sex appears very early in the development of transsexuals, often as early as age 2 and almost always before age 5 (Green, 1974). The transsexual describes himself or herself as feeling more comfortable in the opposite gender role. This feeling contrasts with the feelings of the transvestite who experiences sexual pleasure from cross-dressing.

Early signs of transsexualism in children often appear in their play activity as well as in their dressing. A boy, for example, may insist on playing with dolls or being the mother while playing house. Other children often brand such a child as a sissy and make him the target of social ostracism and abuse.

Many factors may enter into the etiology of transsexualism. It is not clear exactly how important biological factors are but Money, Hampson, and Hampson (1957) feel that "neither a purely hereditary nor a purely environmental doctrine of the origins of gender role and orientation is adequate [p. 334]." According to Green (1974), some environmental variables commonly appear in the background of transsexual boys, although no one factor seems to stand out as most important:

1. Parental indifference to feminine behavior in a boy during his first years.
2. Parental encouragement of feminine behavior in a boy during his first years.
3. Repeated cross-dressing of a young boy by a female.
4. Maternal overprotection of a son and inhibition of boyish or rough-and-tumble play during his first years.
5. Excessive maternal attention and physical contact resulting in lack of separation and individuation of a boy from his mother.
6. Absence of an older male as an identity model during a boy's first years or paternal rejection of a young boy.
7. Physical beauty of a boy that influences adults to treat him in a feminine manner.
8. Lack of male playmates during a boy's first years of socialization.
9. Maternal dominance of a family in which the father is relatively powerless.
10. Castration fear [pp. 212–213].

Transsexuals do not grow out of the condition and as adults they usually request sex-change operations. For both males and females, this involves extensive counseling and hormone therapy before surgery as well as a trial period when the individual is encouraged to live as a member of the opposite sex. The sex-change operation should be performed only if it is still indicated following these procedures. For a male, the operation involves castration and creation of a vaginal opening and breasts. For a female, the operation involves removal of the ovaries, uterus, and breasts and the creation of a penis. The creation of a penis is far more difficult and the aesthetic and pragmatic results are less satisfactory than the surgical creation of a vagina. Postoperatively, there is extensive psychotherapeutic counseling to help the individual adjust to a new sex role. Hormones for opposite gender characteristics are also administered to transsexuals.

Surgical intervention has for over 40 years been the only truly successful strategy for treating transsexuals. Psychotherapeutic intervention, in which individuals are encouraged to accept their inherited gender, has been unsuccessful. The single exception to this has been an ingenious study by Barlow, Reynolds, and Agras (1973) in which behavioral procedures were systematically applied to the behavior patterns of a 17-year-old male transsexual. These researchers carefully identified masculine and feminine components of walking, sitting, talking, standing, and social behavior. Then, using modeling and videotape feedback, they treated each behavior separately. Independent behavioral and physiological assessments revealed significant changes from feminine to masculine orientation. One year later, the individual was still manifesting dominant patterns of masculine behavior; he was dating females and showing strong penile erections to slides of nude females. Barlow (1975) reports success in two other cases using similar behavioral interventions. All Barlow's research with transsexuals is made more impressive by his careful and objective assessment procedures. So far, his procedure offers the only encouraging alternative to surgery.

FETISHISM

Some people become sexually attracted to objects instead of people. Ullmann and Krasner (1969) look upon this unusual condition as an error in discriminative stimulus control. The same degree of sexual excitation that one young man might experience at the sight of a nude female may be experienced by another individual at the sight of boots, handbags, panties, or even baby carriages. The young man who is sexually attracted to women's boots or to other objects displays behavior described as *fetishism*. The object of his attraction or affection is the fetish. Men more than women display this unusual behavior, which is the source of much humor for those with normal sexual orientation, but a source of extreme consternation for most fetishists. Some fetishists can carry on their behavior in secret; this usually involves masturbation while holding, wearing, or just looking at the fetish object. Problems arise when someone else is holding, wearing, or in possession of the desired object and the fetishist openly displays sexual behavior or steals the object for later gratification. It is quite common for a fetishist to be arrested for stealing panties from a clothesline or shoes from a pedestrian. An example of this type of encounter was reported in San Antonio, Texas.

Foot fondler tripped up?

San Antonio, Tex.—Police said yesterday they believe they have nabbed the phantom female foot fondler.

Several women residents on the affluent north side of the city have reported being attacked by a young man who grabbed their feet, slipped off their shoes then kissed and carressed their toes.

Thursday, officers said a man pushed a 30-year-old woman shopper against her car, grabbed her ankle and removed her shoe. But he ran away, with her shoe still in his hand, when the woman struggled and screamed.

An off-duty officer and passerby subdued the man, who was charged with stealing a shoe and jailed in lieu of $10,000 bond.[1]

Although fetishists are capable of carrying on normal heterosexual relations, their arousal often depends on fantasies of the fetish object or the actual wearing of the fetish object. In many cases, the heterosexual partner is aware of the fetishism and participates by wearing the fetish object.

The etiology of fetishism is explained by behaviorists as the result of unfortunate classical conditioning, in which certain objects rather than people are associated with sexual excitement or arousal. Rachman (1966a) developed an experimental analog of this condition. He asked male subjects to sit passively as they were shown boots and then pictures of nude females. Over a series of trials, the males demonstrated sexual arousal to the boots alone though they previously had been neutral, nonarousing stimuli. It is unlikely, however, that one could play a cruel joke on friends by repeatedly presenting them with old sneakers and *Playboy* centerfolds. The Rachman study was conducted under controlled experimental conditions and is merely a demonstration of a conditioning process. Certainly a host of other factors influence fetishism, including personality variables and the availability of alternative sexual experiences.

Treatment for fetishism and transvestism may follow the same course when transvestism is not complicated by homosexual or transsexual interest. Marks and Gelder (1967) employed aversion therapy in which electric shock was administered to the arm or leg of patients while they imagined their deviant sexual objects, i.e., boots or cross-dressing. Following 2 weeks of therapy, all five patients showed marked improvement in their deviant fantasies and behavior. Other therapists and researchers have reported similarly successful results using aversion therapy when the patients possessing the deviant behavior were otherwise well adjusted. When severe neurosis or other complicating factors are present, then aversion therapy may be used as an adjunct to a more comprehensive therapy program.

PEDOPHILIA

When the sexual stimulus for an adult is a child, then the sexual act is classified as *pedophilia*. Usually the pedophiliac caresses the child's body, manipulates the child's genitals, or induces the child to manipulate his or her genitals. Although most offenders are males and most victims are females between the ages of 2 and 12, pedophilia can be a heterosexual or a homosexual act and most often involves a child known to the offender. Pedophilia is a serious criminal offense in any case. Pedophiliacs show a broad range of personality types and patterns of sexual intimacy, as illustrated by the two very different cases that follow:

[1] Reprinted from the *Providence Journal Bulletin*, October 9, 1975, by permission of United Press International.

■ Case 1: The offender, Mr. Branch, was a 55-year-old laborer who had been divorced and had remarried. Mr. Branch had always had an active heterosexual life in marriage although he complained of impotence on a number of occasions. Mr. Branch had three daughters by his first wife and two daughters and a son by his second wife.

He came to the attention of our clinic because of a pedophiliac offense against one of his stepdaughters, age 6. The sexual act consisted of Mr. Branch caressing his daughter's stomach for about 20 minutes while she sat on his lap. There was no attempt at genital manipulation and although Mr. Branch reported sexual excitement he did not achieve orgasm. He was discovered in the act by his wife and later admitted engaging in this same behavior with his other daughters. The offensive behavior only occurred two or three times a year and did not involve any force or coercion.

Case 2: Mr. Stone was 26, single, and a salesman in a department store. He had never had a successful heterosexual relationship and was sexually attracted to boys aged 8 to 10. He would ride around shopping centers in his car until he spotted a boy in the appropriate age range. He would then approach the boy, strike up a friendly conversation, and usually buy the boy some small object such as flashlight batteries. Mr. Stone would then offer the boy a ride in his car and during the journey he would place his hand on the boy's thigh and ask him if he liked to fool around. According to Mr. Stone, about 50% of the boys he approached would go for a ride with him and of those, 75% would allow him to manipulate their genitals. Following the car ride with a boy, Mr. Stone would masturbate to the fantasy of manipulating a boy's genitals. This pedophiliac behavior was of an extremely high frequency, occurring as often as 3 times a day and usually at least 10 times a week. Mr. Stone was arrested following a complaint by one of the victims, and was released on bail. As evidence of the compulsive nature of his behavior, he was arrested a second time on the way to the court hearing for the first offense after accosting two boys in a shopping center near the courthouse.

The cases of Mr. Branch and Mr. Stone illustrate the diversity of pedophiliac behavior. Regardless of the frequency or nature of the act it is condemned by society. Most offenders are imprisoned or ordered into treatment by the courts. Treatment often involves group therapy although behavior therapy offers a great deal of promise. Since many pedophiliacs are inadequate heterosexually, treatment often includes training in heterosocial and heterosexual skills as well as aversion therapy for the pedophiliac act.

Some cases of pedophilia are incestuous and include actual sexual union between members of the same family, most often between a father and daughter. Mr. Branch did not have sexual union (penetration) with his daughter and so technically he did not commit incest. The actual incidence of incest is unknown, although Kinsey *et al.* (1948) report an incidence of about .05%. Incest is prohibited in almost all cultures, presumably because the dangers of genetic inbreeding are generally understood. A sexual relationship between family members usually represents profound psychopathology; it often results in disturbed sexual functioning in men and women who were victims as children.

EXHIBITIONISM

Exhibitionism is the deliberate exposure of the genitals to another person or persons for the purpose of sexual excitation. According to police records, it is the most commonly reported sexual offense. The exhibitionist often masturbates while exposing himself or masturbates after the act to the fantasy of genital exposure. Sexual excitation is often heightened for the exhibitionist if the victim or victims scream or run, but exhibitionists rarely assault their victims. In fact, sexual gratification is achieved mainly through exposure. Although some exhibitionists are married and carry on successful heterosexual relationships, the majority are inadequate heterosocially and heterosexually.

Exhibitionists who obtain sexual pleasure by exposing their genitals in public have always been male. It is true that women have socially acceptable outlets for exhibitionism as stripteasers or nude models but apparently this behavior rarely if ever leads to their own sexual arousal. There is no female counterpart to the male street-flasher. In a study of the background and motivation of striptease artists, Skipper and McCaghy (1969) found that strippers came from varied backgrounds and stripped mainly for economic gain. There is no mention of sexual pleasure associated with stripping.

Therapy for the exhibitionist often includes training in heterosocial and heterosexual skills as well as aversion therapy to suppress the exposing behavior. In cases where there is a great deal of compulsiveness and anxiety associated with exposing, systematic desensitization has proved helpful (Bond & Hutchison, 1960).

SADISM AND MASOCHISM

Sadism means obtaining sexual excitement and gratification by inflicting physical and mental pain on others. The term comes to us from the writings of the Marquis de Sade (1740–1814). In his novel entitled *Justine and Juliette,* he describes in lurid detail many episodes of forced and violent sexual gratification with unsuspecting young women.

Sadism is seen by psychodynamic theorists as a means of relieving anxiety associated with sexual pleasure:

> If a person is able to do to others what he fears may be done to him, he no longer has to be afraid. Thus anything that tends to increase the subject's power or prestige can be used as a reassurance against anxieties. What might happen to the subject passively is done actively by him, in anticipation of attack, to others [Fenichel, 1945, p. 354].

Psychoanalysts see exhibitionism as a form of sadism because the threatening behavior of the exhibitionist makes his victims powerless. In actual practice, however, exhibitionists rarely evolve into sadists and seem to be content with exposure alone. Some psychoanalysts also believe that sadism evolves into masochism, which means obtaining sexual excitation and gratification by inflicting self-injury. According to this view, masochism is merely an expression of sadism that has turned inward. In clinical practice, it is common to find both sadistic and masochistic behavior within the same individual.

Behaviorists theorize that sadistic and masochistic behaviors develop when sexual excitation and orgasm became associated with viewing or participating in painful behavior. For example, the early history of a masochist may include the experience of being spanked on the naked bottom while being caressed on the genitals by a perverse mother or father. The literature of psychology presents many animal learning models of masochistic behavior. For example, Masserman and Jacques (1948) trained cats to punish themselves by using a blast of air as a discriminative stimulus for food reward. Similarly, Schaefer (1970) conditioned monkeys to inflict serious injury on themselves by feeding them when they repeatedly struck their heads with their fists. Although food reward was used in these animal experiments, there is no reason to doubt that sexual reward, theoretically at least, could also be used to shape injurious behavior.

The incidence of seriously harmful sadistic and masochistic behavior seems to be quite low. Often a victim may be injured incidentally during a sex crime, but deliberate injury for the sake of injury during a sex crime occurs less than 5% of the time. Mild or relatively harmless sadistic and masochistic behavior may be prevalent in the general population. Some sex manuals advise mild forms of sadistic and masochistic behavior for enhancing sexual pleasure. For example, *The Joy of Sex* by Alex Comfort (1972) suggests the use of "bondage" (tying the partner's hands and feet) to increase sexual arousal and satisfaction. Comfort carefully warns against dangerous and coercive bondage and distinguishes between real and feigned pain. Thus, although such bondage resembles a sadistic act, it lacks the ingredient of forcibly rendering a victim powerless. Many sex shops also cater to sadomasochistic behavior by selling shackles, chains, tethers, and whips. In addition, there are movies, books, and magazines catering exclusively to sadomasochistic interests. The number of patients actually treated by professional therapists for sadistic and masochistic behavior is quite low and only a small number of applied studies have presented treatment strategies.

RAPE

A far more serious form of sadistic behavior is rape. Rape is legally defined as sexual intercourse with a woman other than one's spouse under conditions of force or threat of violence. The legal definition of rape also includes sexual intercourse with a woman who is drugged, mentally unsound, unconscious, or under age 18 (statutory rape). Forcible rape is a very serious crime and, in fact, is punishable by death in 16 states and punishable by 20 years to life in prison in 27 other states. Between 1930 and 1948, 316 men were executed for rape in the United States.

Although the actual incidence of rape is unknown it is estimated that the rate is between 28 and 70 victims per 100,000 women per year. The actual rate is estimated to be three and a half times higher than the reported rate because of the reluctance of many victims to report the crime (Sutherland & Scherl, 1970). Since 1960, the incidence of rape has been increasing dramatically and is currently anywhere from 84 to 121% higher (Burgess & Holmstrom, 1974b; Zussman, 1972). The reasons for this increase are poorly understood. Certainly crime in all our major cities has increased since 1960 and rape is influenced by many of the same contributory factors: overcrowding, increasing use of drugs and alcohol, unemployment, availability of firearms, and poor living conditions. In addition to these factors, the *reported* incidence of rape may be increasing because victims are more willing to come forward and press legal charges. Most major cities now have rape crisis centers and women's groups to support rape victims. Furthermore, supportive procedures have been developed to help the rape victim adjust to her traumatic experience and even to help her legally (Medea & Thompson, 1974; Oliver, 1974). The purpose of the centers is mainly to provide psychological support, although a large number of victims need medical attention for lacerations and other injuries and about 1% of all victims become pregnant as a result of the assault.

Men who commit rape are most often classified as psychopaths: cold, impulsive men who have little concern for the feelings of their victims. A number of studies have found that rapists can be classified into descriptive subcategories. In perhaps the most widely cited study in this area, Cohen, Seghorn, and Calmas (1969) divide rapists into four categories according to the roles that aggression and sexual desire play in the rapist's behavior:

1. Rapist, displaced-aggression type: Aggression and not sexual behavior is the primary motive of this type. Although the focus of the assault may be on a woman's breasts or genitals, the behavior is a result of displaced aggression and is not primarily sexually motivated.
2. Rapist, compensatory type: The recurrent fantasy of these offenders is that the victim will yield to their force, submit to intercourse, and enjoy it. These offenders are often passive and submissive and may flee if the victim struggles too much.
3. Rapist, sex aggression diffusion type: These offenders are unable to experience or even fantasize sexual desires without a concomitant arousal of aggressive thoughts and feelings. They are often loud and assertive and many of them believe that women enjoy being roughed up.
4. Rapist, impulsive type: This type of offender often commits rape while involved in another crime. He has a history of antisocial behavior and neither sexual nor aggressive desires play a significant role in his behavior.

Abel, Barlow, Blanchard, and Guild (1975) have provided some physiological evidence to help discriminate rapists from nonrapists and to help identify subcategories of rapists. They used audio descriptions of various rape and non-rape sexual scenes and measured penile circumference changes in rapists and nonrapists.

They found that rapists as a group responded to both rape and mutually enjoyable intercourse scenes, whereas nonrapists only responded to the mutually enjoyable intercourse scenes. A "rape index" was compiled by dividing erection-to-rape cues by erection-to-mutually-enjoyable-intercourse cues. This index was useful not only in distinguishing rapists from nonrapists but also in identifying rapists with a high frequency of rape, rapists who commonly injured their victims, and rapists who chose children as victims. Such a specific identification of a rapist's arousal pattern may be helpful in understanding the rapist and in designing treatment programs. Abel *et al.*'s technique may also be useful as a preventive measure for identifying and treating potential rapists.

Treatment for the rapist is usually not available; when it is, it is lengthy and difficult. Cohen *et al.* (1969) point out that their subcategory classification of rapists is useful in developing specific treatment programs. However, the main focus of most programs is in the direction of socialization and impulse control.

VOYEURISM

Voyeurs pursue sexual excitement and gratification through the secret observation of others. Most frequently, voyeurism is performed by males who observe females undressing or observe couples engaging in sexual relations. Though the voyeur may frighten or anger the victim, he is not likely to cause harm. In fact, voyeurism is usually the only sexual behavior that such individuals participate in. Furthermore, there is no evidence of any progression from minor sexual offenses such as voyeurism to more serious sexual offenses such as forcible rape.

Some degree of voyeuristic behavior exists in most normal individuals, but it is not considered deviant unless it is the person's exclusive or dominating sexual outlet. Voyeurism or "peeping" is one of the sexual offenses most commonly reported to the police. Psychoanalysts explain voyeurism as an attempt by an individual to reduce castration anxiety, which was originally generated by the sight of adult genitals. The voyeur is repeating the behavior that produced the original fright, so that he can be reassured that there is nothing to fear (Fenichel, 1945). Behaviorists, on the other hand, explain voyeurism as a learned behavior most likely generated from the chance and clandestine observation of a sexually arousing scene. This experience may have been repeated on a number of occasions and associated with orgasm through masturbation. Most people have on occasion, either intentionally or unintentionally, observed a woman or man undressing or even observed a couple making love. Most people do not become voyeurs, however, and thus personality variables must also be considered in the etiology of voyeurism. Voyeurs, like most sexual deviates, have inadequate heterosexual patterns of behavior. They are often immature individuals who possess few social skills and may have a high degree of heterosexual anxiety. Treatment usually aims at reducing heterosexual anxiety and increasing heterosexual skills as well as suppressing the voyeuristic behavior.

Sexual Dysfunction

Through the research and clinical experience of Masters and Johnson (1966, 1970), our knowledge of sexual dysfunction and treatment strategies has emerged from the Dark Ages. Professionals and laypersons alike are becoming more aware of the problems and the possibilities of treatment. As a result, centers for treatment of sexual dysfunction are being burdened to the limit. A number of influences outside of professional circles have also contributed to this new area. Certainly the women's liberation movement has been instrumental in changing attitudes involving many spheres of life, including sexual behavior. No longer are women content to be the passive recipients of wanted or unwanted advances of males; rather they are concerned more with the development and free expression of their own sexuality. They want to get something out of sex too, and not be mere receptacles for the pleasures of men. Wanting to get more out of sex leads many women to compare their own experiences with that of others. Consequently, some women become more aware of any existing inadequacies in their own and their partner's sexual behavior. The women's liberation movement may, in fact, be a reflection of a more general change in the sexual mores of North American society. Certainly there is more freedom of sexual expression in literature and movies, which again could lead individuals to be more aware of their own sexual adequacies or inadequacies. Unfortunately, dissatisfaction with one's own sexual performance is often generated by attempts to match the unrealistic sexual achievements of literary and cinematic characters. Regardless of the contributing factors, there is no doubt that sexual dysfunction in men and women is a common problem demanding professional attention.

DESCRIPTION AND ETIOLOGY OF SEXUAL DYSFUNCTION

The term *frigidity* has been used as an all-encompassing label for sexual dysfunction in women. It can include one or more of the following concepts: complete or partial absence of sexual arousal, loss of sexual interest before reaching orgasm, disgust during foreplay, inability to achieve orgasm, absence of pleasure during foreplay, absence of pleasure during intercourse, discomfort during intercourse, pain during intercourse (dyspareunia), disgust during intercourse, and inability to tolerate penetration (vaginismus) (Caird & Wincze, in press). In men, sexual dysfunction usually involves one of the following components: the inability to achieve or maintain an erection, premature ejaculation, and delayed or absent orgasm. It is important to understand from the outset that any of these conditions can occur occasionally in the behavior of perfectly normal women and men. In fact, it would be more unusual if a woman or man never experienced any of these problems. Only when unpleasant or disappointing sexual experiences like those described become the rule, rather than the exception can sexual behavior be classified as dysfunctional.

Many factors can contribute to the development of sexual dysfunction. Our scientific knowledge is not complete in this field but we can note a number of conditions commonly reported by individuals experiencing sexual dysfunction. Surprisingly, many of these same conditions can be experienced by individuals functioning perfectly normally, and it is not clear why one person is crippled for life by certain learning conditions but another person is left unscathed by them. Some of the common factors found in the background of sexually dysfunctional individuals are discussed next.

SEXUAL TRAUMA. This category includes incidents of rape, sexual assault, incest, and other physically or mentally painful sexual experiences. Very often such experiences have occurred in childhood or early adolescence. An example of this is the case of Norma:

■   Norma at age 19 has been married 2 years. Her childhood was marred by various forms of sexual abuse from her alcoholic father. From age 12 on she was warned by her father of the evils of sex; he threatened to kill her if she ever masturbated, even though he never bothered to explain what masturbation was. In spite of the father's misguided moralistic preaching, he attacked Norma on a number of occasions and openly fondled her breasts and genitals in the presence of her siblings, mother, and friends. On some occasions he dragged her to his bedroom and threatened to have intercourse with her if she walked around in a nightgown. Norma married at age 17 to escape the family situation, but quickly found marriage difficult because of the continual demand for sex by her husband. She came to the sexual dysfunction clinic in order to be able to accept sexual relations with her husband.

For males, sexual trauma rarely involves forceful sexual assault or any physically painful experience. Rather, trauma for males usually means failure to perform followed by belittlement. As Kaplan states, "there is probably no other medical condition which is as potentially frustrating, humiliating and devastating as impotence. In almost all cultures and socioeconomic groups a great deal of male self-esteem is invested in the erection [Kaplan, 1974, p. 257]." An example of sexual trauma in males is the case of a 25-year-old man named Ken:

■   On Ken's wedding night he was somewhat nervous with his new bride and although he managed to achieve a partial erection during foreplay, he rapidly lost this when penetration was attempted. His wife became very angry with his failure and blamed it on his small penis size. From that time on she reminded him of his inadequate performance and penis size whenever an argument erupted. Subsequently, attempts at sexual activity always ended in failure, which reinforced his and his wife's belief in his inadequacy. Ken sought help for his condition after 1 year of marriage; he entered a large mental hospital showing symptoms of depression and anxiety and expressing suicidal intentions.

OBSERVATION OF PARENTAL SEXUAL BEHAVIOR.   Children sometimes observe their parents engaging in sexual intercourse. If a child is frightened by this, it can seriously damage his or her attitude toward sexual activity. Since moans and cries often accompany even wanted sexual relations, a small child can easily be misled into believing that his or her parents are hurting each other. When a drunken, aggressive father is forcibly having intercourse with an unwilling wife, the sight and sounds can be even more profoundly traumatic for a small child. It is unlikely, however, that a single experience would cause damage. In cases where such experiences have been a factor, observation of parental sexual relations has occurred on many occasions over a number of years.

LACK OF AFFECTION FROM PARENTS.   It is very common for a woman who is sexually unresponsive to report that she has never experienced any verbal or physical affection from her parents or between them. This type of environment may even lead a person to feel uncomfortable holding hands or greeting people warmly.

RESTRICTIVE MORAL OR RELIGIOUS TEACHING.   Many religious sects warn of the sinful nature of sexual behavior before marriage. Girls in these groups are often given repeated warnings about sexual misadventure and about the animalistic intentions of all boys. In families in which this type of indoctrination is pervasive (and lacking more moderate reference points), a woman may have extreme difficulty in trying to accept sex after marriage. What was thought sinful before marriage is thought sinful after marriage.

IGNORANCE OF SEXUAL BEHAVIOR.   Though we live in a changing, more open, and increasingly sophisticated society, not everyone is aware of these changes. In spite of openness and sophistication there is an appalling amount of ignorance surrounding sexual behavior. Many young people enter marriage thinking that sexual relations will blossom even when evident problems and misunderstandings exist before marriage. Nothing could be further from the truth. Continual confrontations during sexual behavior due to inadequate or nonexistent understanding more likely will lead to frustration, anger, and sometimes divorce. Some couples have participated in unsatisfactory sexual relations for years due to misunderstandings about sexual response. One irate husband, for example, brought his wife to a sexual dysfunction clinic because she was not ejaculating sperm during intercourse. He was surprised, but not apologetic, upon learning that this was only a male function. Another couple sought help at a sexual dysfunction clinic because of the wife's "frigidity." It turned out that she would not tolerate intercourse in any position other than the male superior position, because of her firm belief that other positions would cause damage to her uterus. Sex counselors are confronted with hundreds of such examples of sexual ignorance.

HOMOSEXUALITY.   In some cases, a person with homosexual interests will enter into a heterosexual marriage because of social pressures. This usually turns out to be unsatisfactory when homosexual interests continue to be strong. The unsuspecting marriage partner is often left wondering why his or her spouse finds sex uninteresting or distasteful.

PHYSICAL CAUSES. In addition to the numerous psychological causes of sexual dysfunction, there are a number of physical problems that can make sexual relations uncomfortable or even impossible. Among the more common physical problems are lesions and infections in the genitals or various other pathologies such as warts, cysts, or polyps. Certain drugs may cause impotence in males. Although physical causes of sexual dysfunction are far less common than psychological causes, every person involved in sexual dysfunction therapy should undergo a complete examination to eliminate the possibility of physical causes of dysfunction.

PRIMARY VERSUS SECONDARY SEXUAL DYSFUNCTION. In every complaint of sexual dysfunction it must be established whether the problem is of a primary (essential) nature or of a secondary nature. Primary sexual dysfunction means that the sexual problem is not related to a particular partner or place; rather, the sexual problem exists within a person regardless of the particular partner. The problem is usually of long duration. A secondary sexual problem is a problem related directly to a particular partner or circumstance. Thus, if a person is turned off by one sexual partner, but is quite capable of enjoying sex with another partner, then this is classified as a secondary sexual dysfunction. Changes in the partner's behavior, or a change to a new partner, often remedy secondary sexual dysfunctions.

MISCONCEPTIONS AND SEXUAL BEHAVIOR

Many men and women come into a sexual dysfunction clinic and ask the therapist what frequency and type of sexual behavior is normal. Therapists answer by explaining that both partners should be comfortable and satisfied with what they are doing, rather than behaving according to some set of norms. Thus, some couples are perfectly happy with sex once a month, whereas other couples prefer sex one to three times a day. Problems arise when couples have very divergent views on what constitutes a satisfying pattern of sexual behavior. One partner may then pressure the other partner into adapting his or her sexual norms—often with the firm conviction that there is only one right way to behave sexually and there must be something wrong with a partner who is not behaving that way. Therapy often involves educating a couple so they can compromise in their behavior.

Misconceptions about sexual behavior often arise from exposure to books, magazines, and movies about sex. Popular literature often gives the impression that everyone enjoys sex all the time and a truly sensuous woman has an orgasm easily every time. Many women have come to sexual therapists complaining of orgasmic dysfunction because their experiences did not match those described in the literature or did not match their husband's expectations. In real life, few women have orgasms every time. In fact, orgasmic ability depends on many factors, including age, health, arousability, and type of stimulation.

Popular literature often misleads individuals into believing that simultaneous orgasm is necessary for true sexual fulfillment. This again is a personal preference; it may be fulfilling to some individuals but not to others. In fact, most sex manuals point out that orgasm should occur under the conditions most comfortable for the individuals involved (e.g., *SAR–Sexual Attitude Restructuring–Guide,* 1975).

One of the most common misunderstandings has come to us through professionals rather than popular literature. This is the confusion about whether there are one or two distinct types of orgasm that the female can experience. Freud is responsible for raising the issue, since he claimed that a truly mature female experienced vaginal orgasm rather than clitoral orgasm. Clitoral stimulation was equated to masturbation, which Freud believed was an infantile response. Kinsey, Pomeroy, Martin, and Gebhard (1953) were the first to question this theory by observing that the vaginal walls were composed of comparatively few nerve endings and were insensitive when stroked or touched lightly. Masters and Johnson (1966) added further support to Kinsey's observations and it is now widely accepted that the female is capable of only one type of orgasm, which is seated in the clitoris and the surrounding area. Even though women can experience qualitatively different types of orgasm at various times, the physiological mechanism of orgasm is always the same.

TREATMENT OF FEMALE SEXUAL DYSFUNCTION

Treatment techniques for sexual dysfunction have come to us from many sources, including psychiatrists, gynecologists, and psychologists. Many psychotherapeutic interventions use procedures based on research, while others are based largely on clinical inference. Because of the comparatively new status of sexual research, many of the treatment strategies for sexual problems have yet to be scientifically tested. Compounding the problem is the recent proliferation of sexual treatment centers and guidebooks for self-treatment. Many of these sources of "help" are simply moneymaking operations and must be looked upon with great caution. There is little concern in these enterprises for evaluation of treatment procedures and many untested or ill-advised procedures are imposed on unsuspecting clients, sometimes with disastrous effects. Any person in need of professional assistance for a sexual problem should seek help from sexual treatment clinics connected with hospitals or universities. If there is any doubt about the legitimacy of a therapist or clinic, one should ask a local medical society.

It is important to involve a client's sexual partner in any treatment of sexual dysfunction. This is true for both women and men who seek help. Without the close interest of the sexual partner, changes in sexual attitudes and behavior are extremely difficult. Many hours of therapy progress can be undermined by a single episode with an insensitive partner. In most cases, the behavior and attitudes of the partner also have to change in order for progress to be made. Intervention strategies for both males and females often include repeated practice sessions in sexual and nonsexual behavior. The environment for practice sessions must include complete cooperation and understanding from the partner so that anxiety and pressure are not present.

Treatment procedures for sexual dysfunction have come mainly from behaviorists and Masters and Johnson. Relatively little, other than case studies and a great deal of theoretical speculation, has been contributed by psychoanalytically oriented therapists (Meikle, 1972). For these reasons, the discussion of treatment approaches for sexual dysfunction will concentrate entirely on behavioral procedures and on the heavily behavioral procedures developed by Masters and Johnson.

PRIMARY SEXUAL DYSFUNCTION.   In both primary and secondary sexual dysfunction, any or all of the following problems may be present: (1) arousal dysfunction (lack of sexual arousal); (2) anxiety reaction associated with sex; and (3) orgasmic dysfunction (total or almost total absence of orgasmic ability).

When assessing a woman for sexual dysfunction it is necessary to explore each of these problem areas in order to formulate the best treatment strategy. *Arousal dysfunction* is usually indicated if a woman describes herself as being very bored or uninterested in sex. She is not upset with sex, but views it as a waste of time and would really rather be doing something else. Many of these women report these feelings in spite of the fact that they achieve orgasm during intercourse. Treatment for primary arousal dysfunction is often extremely difficult. Some sex manuals naively suggest reading erotic literature, masturbating, performing coitus in new and interesting ways, and fantasizing erotic images. These treatment remedies may be adequate for sexually well-adjusted but unimaginative women, but they fall far short of what is needed for the woman who has never experienced sexual arousal. Much more research into the physiological and cognitive development of sexual arousal is needed before more efficient treatment procedures can be formulated.

In an *anxiety reaction associated with sex,* a woman usually describes her sexual experiences as extremely upsetting, disgusting, or maddening. She may enjoy certain parts of sexual behavior and then suddenly become extremely anxious when intercourse is about to occur or when genital stimulation occurs. The exact stimulus that sets off the anxiety reaction is a very individual experience. For example, there are women who fear breast stimulation, others who fear genital stimulation, and still others who fear touching the male's penis.

Treatment for anxiety reaction usually involves anxiety reduction through relaxation training and systematic desensitization. Wincze and Caird (1976) have also found video desensitization very effective in reducing sexual anxiety. Instead of presenting a hierarchy of sexual material in imagination, these authors present graduated scenes of sexual behavior via videotapes. Another technique is *sensate focus,* developed by Masters and Johnson, which encourages couples to touch each other in a nonsexual, nondemanding way. This procedure may also be helpful in reducing sexual anxiety. For the most part, treatment for this problem is successful when there are no other complicating factors.

Some women can experience a wide range of sexual excitation but never achieve orgasm. This condition is called *primary orgasmic dysfunction*. Also included in this category are women who can achieve orgasm through masturbation but not through intercourse. A great deal of misunderstanding exists on the part of both males and females concerning female orgasmic response. In counseling a woman who has never experienced orgasm, it is sometimes difficult to explain exactly what she is supposed to experience. This is especially true because orgasmic experience differs not only from person to person but also within a single person from orgasm to orgasm. Therefore, counseling usually begins by discussing the physiology and mechanics of female orgasmic response with the woman and her partner. This educational experience is important for couples who have had a misunderstanding of the orgasmic response. Many couples believe, for example, that penile penetration is all that is necessary for orgasm to occur.

In interviewing many couples it is quite obvious that changes in their approaches to sexual behavior are needed for orgasm to occur; for other couples specific training in orgasmic behavior is needed. Lopiccolo and Lobitz (1972) have developed a step-by-step program for orgasmic training through progressive genital stimulation and masturbation. This program is widely used and reported to be successful. Kohlenberg (1974), in a controlled study, demonstrated successful treatment of three inorgasmic women using this procedure. Following therapy, all three women were able to achieve orgasm during masturbation sessions and during intercourse. Moreover, all three women reported systematic increases in their subjective arousal once masturbation training began. A 6-month follow-up showed that treatment gains had been maintained. Many women reject the idea of masturbation even in this therapeutic context, however, and alternative strategies must be employed. Anxiety reduction alone does not seem to improve the inorgasmic condition significantly (Wincze & Caird, 1976).

SECONDARY SEXUAL DYSFUNCTION. In secondary sexual dysfunction, the symptoms can be identical to the three categories described previously, but represent a reaction to the specific circumstances under which sexual behavior occurs or to the specific sexual partner. Many women have come to a sexual treatment clinic with a complaint of frigidity only to realize that their reaction is specific to their husband. There may be a subtle communication problem or there may be a more obvious problem involving open hostility. In one case, a woman was offended by her husband's dirty, unkempt appearance and generally malodorous condition. Her husband's unsavory nature was further degraded in her mind by his abrupt approach to lovemaking. Apparently, the same aplomb with which he worked over a car engine was present in the bedroom; furthermore, he could not appreciate that any change was needed in his behavior. Rather than try to teach the old dog new tricks, the woman chose to separate because of this and other problems.

In many cases, a woman may feel very aroused by other men and engage in sexually satisfying extramarital affairs. These cases are easy to distinguish as secondary sexual dysfunction. But it is difficult to determine if a reaction is primary or secondary if a woman has never had sexual experiences with any other partner. Careful questioning must then be pursued to determine a woman's feelings toward her husband and toward sex in general. Treatment for secondary sexual dysfunction is usually referred to marriage counseling.

DYSPAREUNIA AND VAGINISMUS.　Dyspareunia is the term used to describe painful intercourse in both women and men. In women this may mean actual physical pain in the vagina during intercourse or it may mean burning sensations in the genital area during intercourse or hours after. There are many physical causes of painful intercourse, but a large percentage of complaints are of psychogenic origin. It is often a conscious defense against unwanted sexual advances and may take the form of facial grimacing during intercourse or screaming, tears, and hysteria. Needless to say, this usually has its intended effect of reducing the frequency of sexual advances in all but the most callous husbands. When a woman frequently finds intercourse painful, it may develop into *vaginismus,* which is the inability to accept intromission because of involuntary, painful muscle spasms and contractions in the outer third of the vagina. Quite often, however, vaginismus is present without first evolving through dyspareunia. In many such cases, marriages have gone on for years unconsummated; couples continue to have sexual contacts, but whenever penetration is attempted there is abrupt and complete failure and the male usually ejaculates extravaginally. If this experience is repeated often enough, males quite commonly respond to even mild levels of sexual stimulation with premature ejaculation.

Some women experiencing vaginismus are able to insert tampons or their fingers into the vagina but go into spasm when penis insertion is attempted. Other women are unable to tolerate any insertion and must be anesthetized for even a routine pap smear. Masters and Johnson (1970) have developed treatment procedures reported to be highly successful for cases of dyspareunia as well as vaginismus. Their basic procedure involves extensive explanation of the nature of the condition, including demonstration of the muscle spasm by attempting digital insertion during a pelvic examination. During actual sexual activity, a couple is encouraged to attempt digital and penile insertion gradually and for longer periods of time until full thrusting of the erect penis can be tolerated. Relaxation training can be an important adjunct to this therapy procedure.

TREATMENT OF MALE SEXUAL DYSFUNCTION

The patterns and problems of sexual behavior in the male are as varied and complex as those in the female. Unlike females, however, males cannot "fake" sexual involvement when arousal is not present. Males have to achieve an erection for intercourse to occur and they must not ejaculate until after penetration. Although there are many similar etiological factors in the background of sexually dysfunctional males and females, the first coital experience seems to be more important for males as a potentially threatening experience. Many males with erectile or ejaculatory problems report their initial sexual experience was a traumatic event. As a result, subsequent sexual opportunities were flooded with thoughts of disaster and these worries led to more failures. In some cases, males enjoyed a number of successful sexual experiences, but then for a variety of possible reasons, failed to perform on one occasion. Again, worry over subsequent performance led to a vicious cycle of failure because of anxiety and then anxiety because of failure.

Men, like women, can be afflicted with a variety of physical causes of sexual dysfunction and therefore should always undergo a complete physical exam if sexual dysfunction is present. In almost 95% of the cases, however, the problem is of psychological nature (Shusterman, 1973).

IMPOTENCE. Impotence may mean either failure to achieve an erection or loss of an erection before coitus is completed. In rare cases, individuals have never achieved an erection. More commonly, individuals sometimes can achieve an erection, but find that in certain situations, erection is lost or unobtainable. With some men, loss of erection occurs only with certain women or under certain circumstances. For example, one patient treated in a sex clinic was able to achieve an erection with any woman as long as she did not become aggressive in her lovemaking. As soon as a woman initiated sexual contact or became sexually aggressive he immediately lost his erection. Evidently, such sexual aggression made him feel under pressure to perform, which in turn heightened his anxiety to a critical level.

Many different personal histories can lead to this same condition: restrictive moral and religious training, incest, personal devaluation during sexual experience, and repeated masturbation to ejaculation without erection, to name a few. Regardless of the etiology of the condition, it can usually be successfully treated if there is a willing female sexual partner available to assist in therapy. This is almost always a wife or girlfriend although some therapists have enrolled the assistance of paid surrogates. Therapy usually begins by instructing the couple that all future sexual contacts should occur under relaxed, nondemanding conditions. The demand for performance is antitherapeutic and usually diastrous. In essence, the therapy procedure outlined by Masters and Johnson (1970) encourages the couple to proceed slowly in all nonsexual and sexual contacts and to progress to a more intimate stage of contact only when the male feels perfectly confident and successful in the stage he is operating in. For example, a male may achieve erection while his wife gently strokes his body, but intercourse should not be attempted until erection can also be achieved while the penis is directly stimulated. Intercourse too should be attempted gradually and in stages of intimacy and activity. The Masters and Johnson approach (or any therapy approach) must be achieved under the guidance of a professional therapist. All too often, a person may attempt self-treatment by hiring a prostitute, but almost always this is an unsatisfactory experience and turns out to be yet another sexual trauma.

PREMATURE EJACULATION. The definition of premature ejaculation is not widely agreed upon. Some researchers define it in terms of coital time prior to ejaculation; others define it in terms of the number of strokes prior to ejaculation. Still others, like Masters and Johnson (1970), define it in terms of the percentage of time the male is able to sexually satisfy his female partner; less than 50% constitutes premature ejaculation. Each of these definitions has some interpretation problems and in actual therapy, it is best to try to define very carefully with the patient his exact complaint. Through careful questioning it is sometimes learned that the male is functioning adequately and his female sexual partner is inorgasmic. Most commonly, however, males describing their problem report ejaculation prior to intromission or within 60 seconds following intromission.

Most therapists agree that the major problem in premature ejaculation is the inability of the male to detect all the warning signs of forthcoming ejaculation. There is a point of heightened sexual arousal, described by Masters and Johnson (1970) as *ejaculatory inevitability,* which precedes ejaculation by 2 to 4 seconds and is the point when a man can no longer prevent ejaculation. The focus of therapy is centered on teaching patients to be able to detect the point preceding ejaculatory inevitability, so that they may act to postpone the automatic response. Most males experiencing premature ejaculation also show high levels of anxiety associated with sexual behavior, which in turn develops into the vicious circle of anxiety causing premature ejaculation and premature ejaculation causing further anxiety. As in the case of other sexual problems, there are many etiological factors that could contribute to the problem. One behavioral theory is that young boys who continually masturbate hurriedly to avoid parental detection fail to learn ejaculatory control.

Treatment for premature ejaculation is most often successful using either the "semans" (Semans, 1956) or the "squeeze" (Masters & Johnson, 1970) technique. Both these techniques require the patient to focus on the sensations experienced preceding ejaculation. A heightened awareness and control of these sensations is the goal of therapy. When either procedure is used under the direction of a therapist, there is almost always successful remediation of the premature ejaculation symptoms. As in the problem of loss of erection, it is essential for the female partner to be involved in the treatment procedure.

DELAYED EJACULATION OR EJACULATORY INCOMPETENCE. Some men are able to achieve and maintain an erection throughout heterosexual intercourse, but are unable to ejaculate intravaginally. This is a very rare condition for which there are no dependable treatment procedures (Masters & Johnson, 1970). The condition can also exist in men participating in homosexual genital stimulation; it seems to involve high levels of anxiety. Razani (1972) presented a case study in which he postulated that anxiety was an important factor in the etiology of this disorder and successfully treated a patient using systematic desensitization. The specific etiological conditions for this problem remain unknown and each new case brings with it new possibilities.

Summary

This chapter has discussed a wide range of topics in sexual behavior under the general headings of deviance and dysfunction. It emphasizes that ideas about deviance and dysfunction are determined by cultures and by individuals within cultures. If an individual is identified as having a sexual problem it is because the individual is distressed by the behavior or people around the individual are distressed by the behavior. Moral and legal acceptance of sexual behavior is subject to a multitude of changing societal influences. For example, many people who would have agonized over their homosexuality 50 years ago find organized support in society today for the same behavior. Certainly there are still large numbers of individuals who are faced with difficulties because of their homosexuality, but increasing numbers of homosexuals are finding contentment with their behavior. On the other hand, some sexual behaviors have always been unacceptable, such as rape and pedophilia. The understanding of these behaviors, and of sexual behavior in general, is extremely important for relieving the distress associated with all behaviors labeled as sexually deviant.

Attitudes toward sexual dysfunction have changed dramatically since the 1960s. Many individuals who would have endured the absence of sexual pleasure are seeking professional help to increase their sexual fulfillment. In fact, there is perhaps no other area in clinical psychology where change is so evident as in our approach to sexual dysfunction. All too often, however, the conceptualization of sexual dysfunction is too simplistic: A woman is frigid and unable to have an orgasm, or a man is impotent and cannot achieve an erection. That is why we have repeatedly stressed the complexity of the problems confronting therapists. Because the field of sex research is so new, problems are still being defined and treatment approaches are still being developed. At this stage in development, there are very effective treatment approaches for some problems, such as the squeeze technique for premature ejaculation; other problems, such as arousal dysfunction in women, still await more effective solutions.

It is clear that there is a high incidence of sexual dysfunction in both men and women. Perhaps as high as 50% of all marriages are confronted with sexual discord at one time or another. Often, problems are solved by a patient, understanding partner, but in all too many cases this remedy does not help and the couple seeks outside counseling. Sometimes the solutions for sexual dysfunction are simple, requiring only education and instruction on the part of a therapist. More often, the problems are complex and involve intensive therapy for both partners. There is no question that many sexual problems are caused or maintained by an unskilled, uninformed, or insensitive partner and must be solved with the cooperation of this same partner in therapy.

13

Sleep, Disorders of Sleep, and Hypnosis

THOMAS D. BORKOVEC, KATHERINE M. SLAMA, JONATHAN B. GRAYSON
University of Iowa

Any activity that fills a full third of our lives must be an important human behavior. You might assume that scientists would have determined long ago the causes and functions of that activity. Sleep is such a behavior, yet despite hundreds of experimental studies during the last two decades, the phenomenon of sleep remains something of a mystery. Those of us who obtain sufficient and restful sleep take our slumber for granted. If we are among the millions of people whose sleep is disturbed, sleep is more than a mystery; it may represent one of the most important lacks in our lives.

This chapter will describe what is known about sleep and the kinds of disorders that disrupt this ordinarily pleasurable activity. Sleep disturbance is relevant to abnormal psychology for at least two reasons. First, as you may have noticed from preceding sections of this book, disturbed sleep often accompanies other psychological disorders, such as depression. Such sleep disturbance is often called secondary; the sleeping difficulty represents only one of the many behavioral problems manifested by the individual and it is considered to be symptomatic of a crisis in living or a more basic psychological maladjustment. It is hardly surprising that if a person's day is filled with hallucinations, delusions, crushing depression, or debilitating anxiety, these problems will intrude on the quantity and quality of nighttime sleep. Treatment of secondary sleep disorders ordinarily focuses on the presumed underlying problems rather than on sleep itself. We will therefore devote only passing attention to such secondary disorders.

Some sleep aberrations, however, occur when no other psychological disturbance is evident. Nothing in the individual's current environment or psychological makeup suggests a reason for the disorder. Yet, the frustration and misery emanating from the sleep difficulty may well cause additional maladjustment, such as difficulty in performing job or social functions, or anxiety and depression over the inability to sleep and the presumed consequences of sleeplessness. DSM-II categorizes these sleep disturbances under the heading of Special Symptoms, Disorders of Sleep. We will examine these primary sleep disorders and their direct treatment in some detail.

Like sleep, the hypnotic trance has long been considered a psychological state that is qualitatively different from the normal waking state. Thus, it is no wonder that hypnosis and sleep have often been related to one another. Indeed, the Greek word *hypnos* literally means "sleep." Because of similarities between hypnotic and sleep states, and because of the characteristically "abnormal" behavior apparently produced by hypnotic procedures, the final section of this chapter will discuss hypnosis, its relationship to sleep, and some possible explanations of hypnotic phenomena.

The Phenomena of Sleep

The experience of falling asleep is a familiar one to all of us. One moment we are aware of our surroundings; the next we are not. It turns out, however, that sleep is not a simple state but rather a complex and cyclical sequence of events. Indeed, with the aid of a polygraph to record electrical activity of brain cells, eye movements, and muscle activity, researchers have identified at least *five* distinct stages of sleep (see Figure 13-1 for first four stages). As a person lies quietly with eyes closed, the EEG records show low-voltage, mixed-frequency brain waves often accompanied by a regular pattern known as *alpha activity*. When the subject enters Stage 1 sleep (usually within 1–7 minutes), alpha disappears, the muscles begin to relax, and the EEG is characterized solely by low-voltage, mixed-frequency waves. Sensory perception ceases, and the eyes begin to roll slowly from side to side. The remainder of the evening's sleep alternates in rhythmic cycles between two kinds of sleep: non-REM (NREM) and REM sleep.

NREM SLEEP

If the subject continues to sleep, Stage 1 is replaced by as many as three succeeding stages of NREM sleep. Stage 2 sleep is distinguished by the appearance of sleep spindles and K-complexes on the EEG (see Figure 13-1). The onset of later stages is characterized by moderate (Stage 3) and then large (Stage 4) amounts of high-amplitude, slow-wave activity. Because the latter two stages involve the largest and slowest waveforms, they are often called *slow-wave sleep*.

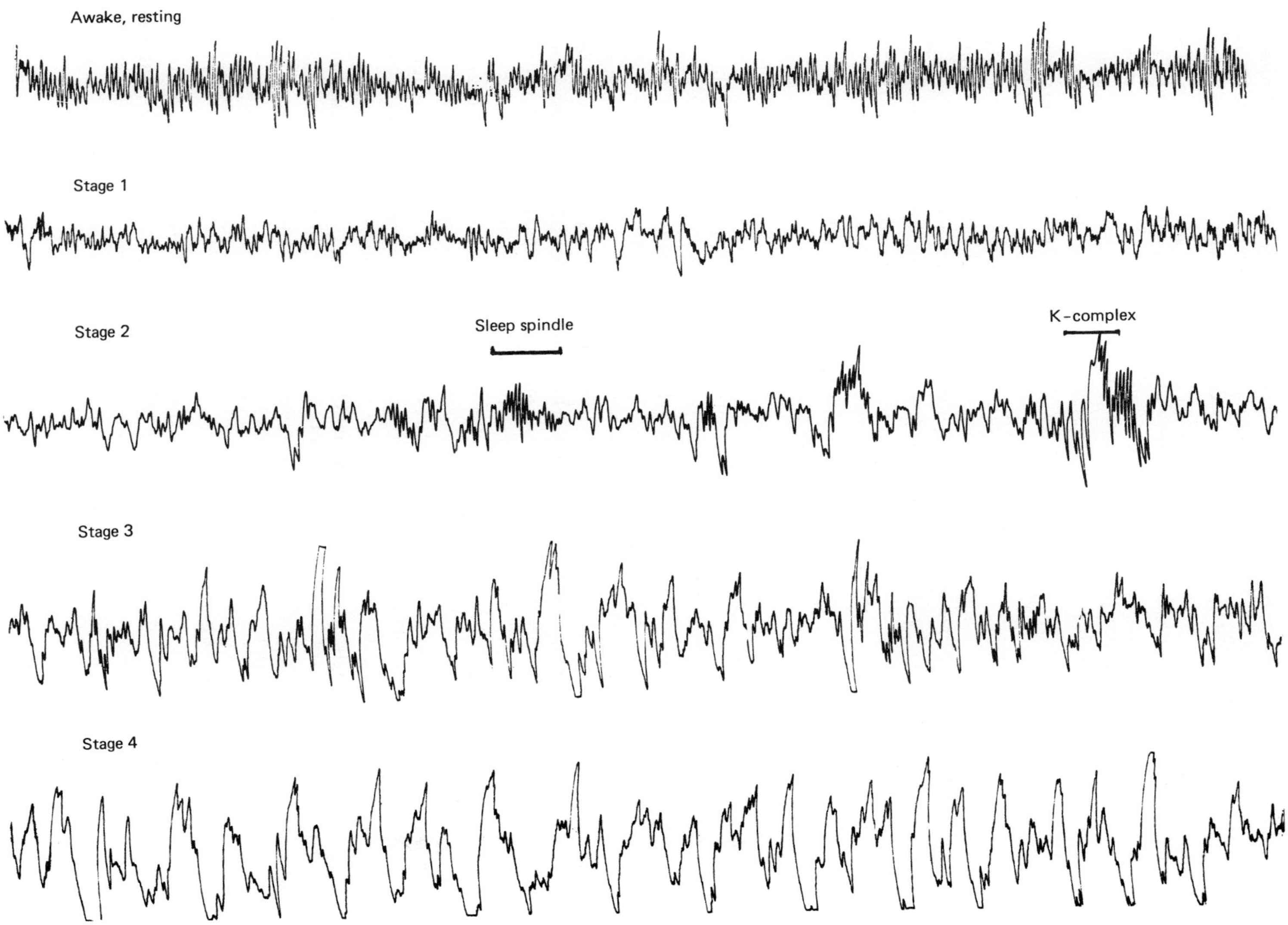

Awake, resting

Stage 1

K–complex

Sleep spindle

Stage 2

Stage 3

Stage 4

Figure 13-1. Electroencephalographic activity during resting state and during the four stages of NREM sleep.

Stages 1 to 4 are collectively called NREM sleep, to distinguish these periods of sleep from the REM stage discussed next. The difficulty experienced in arousing a subject from Stage 4 sleep suggests that it represents the deepest stage of NREM sleep.

The body's physiological reactions during NREM sleep include a decrease in heart and respiration rates, body temperature, and muscle tone, and an increase in GSRs (galvanic skin responses). A subject awakened during any stage of NREM sleep seldom recalls the occurrence of imagery or thoughts. Any material that is recalled is usually quite vague and does not incorporate recently presented external stimuli.

Approximately 50% of an average adult's time asleep is spent in Stage 2 sleep; about 5, 7, and 16% are spent in Stages 1, 3, and 4, respectively (Johnson, 1973). Physical exercise during the day preceding sleep produces a higher proportion of slow-wave sleep (Baekeland & Lasky, 1966), and drugs such as amphetamines can drastically decrease it (Rechtschaffen & Maron, 1964). In addition, slow-wave sleep is reduced in depressives (Mendels & Hawkins, 1967) and schizophrenics (Feinberg, Braun, Koresko, & Gottlieb, 1969) and is usually absent in alcoholics (Gross & Goodenough, 1968).

REM SLEEP

Until the 1950s, most researchers assumed that sleep consisted of the four stages we have just described. However, the important subjective experience of dreaming could not be related to such a picture; it remained in the realm of the mystical. Then Aserinsky and Kleitman (1953) discovered that there is a second type of sleep, characterized by rapid movements of the eyes (hence the term, REM). During REM sleep the EEG resembles either an awake or a Stage 1 record. However, the skeletal muscles have almost no tone, even less than in slow-wave sleep. Spontaneous GSRs and spinal reflexes disappear, and heart rate and respiration become irregular. Twitches appear in many muscles, and penile erection in males is common. Oxygen use in the brain becomes very high, and the pituitary gland is activated. In cats, a distinctive spike phenomenon (a rapid increase and decrease in amplitude) begins shortly before the sleeper enters the REM stage and continues to occur throughout REM sleep at the rate of about 60 spikes per minute. Jouvet (1969), the French researcher who discovered the spikes, speculates that they may be the electrical signs of a memory mechanism playing upon the central visual system. In humans, a similar wave known as the *sawtooth wave* appears just before the onset of REM sleep and continues throughout the REM period (Berger, Olley, & Oswald, 1962).

REM sleep is intriguing because the EEG and most physiological signs indicate that the person is aroused as if awake. Yet the complete relaxation and loss of reflexes, as well as the difficulty encountered when attempting to awaken a sleeper from REM sleep, suggest that REM is a deep or quiet sleep. For these reasons, the REM stage is also known as *paradoxical sleep*.

Young adults generally spend about 20–25% of their sleeping time, or about

90–110 minutes, in REM sleep every night (Hartmann, 1973). There is some evidence that more intelligent people spend more time in REM sleep than do less intelligent people (Feinberg, Koresko, & Heller, 1967). Most sleeping pills, such as hypnotics, decrease REM sleep (Kales & Kales, 1973); some may block it out entirely, which can complicate drug treatment for sleep disturbances, as we shall see.

Excitement grew when experimenters discovered that subjects awakened from REM sleep usually reported that they were experiencing vivid dreams (Aserinsky & Kleitman, 1955; Dement & Kleitman, 1957). Although these dreams often incorporated outside stimuli into their imagery, dreams could not be initiated by these stimuli. Rather, dreaming seemed to follow a cycle, inherent in the organism, which occurred every 90 minutes or so. People who believe themselves to be nondreamers thus dream as much as other people; they simply do not remember any of their dreams. Moreover, dreams do not run their course instantaneously. They take about as much time as it would take for the dreamed events actually to occur. Dreamers are able to estimate the duration of their dream quite accurately (Dement & Kleitman, 1957). Contrary to what Freud (1915/1955) hypothesized, the content of dreams often comes from sources outside the previous day's experiences. The later in the night the dream occurs, the more it tends to draw on stored images that have little relationship to the previous day's events (Dement, 1972).

SLEEP CYCLES

Within the larger 24-hour sleeping–waking cycle, normal young adults usually go through four to six NREM–REM cycles during the night, as shown in Figure 13-2. A single cycle averages about 90 minutes, so the first REM period is usually entered about 1½ hours after falling asleep. Note that most of the slow-wave sleep (Stages 3 and 4) occurs during the first part of the night, while the majority of REM sleep occurs toward morning in increasingly longer periods.

CHANGES IN SLEEP PATTERNS WITH AGE

Infants obviously sleep differently from adults. Just how differently was not discovered until EEG research provided comparative data. The most immediately obvious contrast is in length of total sleep time, which becomes shorter as a person grows older, from about 16–18 hours in the newborn child to 7–8 hours in the average adult (Hartmann, 1973). The decreases occur mostly in the period from birth to adolescence and again in old age.

The time required to fall asleep after retiring also declines from the age of about 2 years until the age of 60, when it becomes more difficult to fall asleep rapidly (Feinberg, 1969). At the same time, with increasing age, awakenings during the night and the proportion of time in bed spent awake increase. Apparently, the soundness or depth of sleep decreases throughout life.

A child is born with a cerebral cortex that is still growing and gaining its

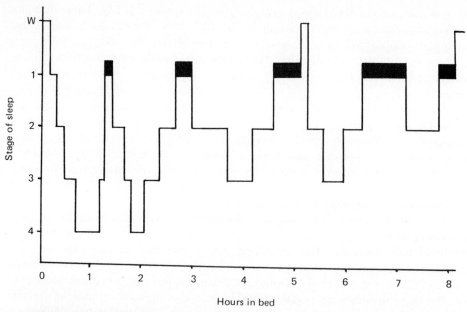

Figure 13-2. A typical nocturnal sleep pattern of a young adult. (Solid lines indicate REM periods.)

functions. For this reason, a newborn infant's EEG patterns show much less distinct stages than an adult's (Ames, 1964). However, it is possible to distinguish REM sleep from other sleep stages in the infant. Surprisingly, about half of a newborn child's sleep is REM sleep, and this figure is even higher for premature infants (Feinberg & Carlson, 1968). Slow-wave sleep, on the other hand, is not fully present in an infant until around the age of 3 months; it then remains at a fairly constant level until the age of 30, when it slowly begins to decrease; the EEGs of many older persons show no Stage 3 or Stage 4 sleep at all (Feinberg *et al.*, 1967).

Newborn infants sleep in several separate periods per day. Gradually children learn to sleep in two periods, and then in the one period characteristic of adult sleep. Older people often begin to sleep in two or more periods once again. Within a sleep period, the cycle from slow-wave sleep to REM requires an average of 50–60 minutes for young children, compared with the 90-minute adult cycle (Hartmann, 1973).

SLEEP DEPRIVATION EFFECTS

Animals kept continually awake die within 4–13 days (Kleitman, 1963), which suggests that sleep must include some physiological process necessary to life. Although research thus far has been unable to identify this process, suggestive evidence has been obtained from experiments in which subjects are deprived of sleep or of particular stages of sleep.

The record for a human remaining continuously awake is 264 hours (Dement, 1972). Like most sleep-deprivation subjects, the record holder showed no detectable long-term effects, despite occasional reports of psychotic reactions presumably induced by long periods without sleep. Only individuals who were previously predisposed to psychosis appear to develop such reactions to sleep deprivation and these reactions occur early in the experiments, usually after 60–70 hours of sleep deprivation.

Behavioral changes that occur during extended sleep deprivation (e.g., fatigue, irritability, feelings of persecution, inability to concentrate, disorientation) tend to be worst in the early morning hours (Kleitman, 1963). Illusions and hallucinations, if present, are mainly visual and tactile, unlike the principally auditory phenomena characteristic of schizophrenic reactions.

Neurological changes occur as well (Kleitman, 1963). After 3 days, drooping eyelids are common, along with a mild eye-muscle dysfunction. After 7–8 days of sleep deprivation, slurring of speech and mild tremors are usually present. EEG changes include an increase in discharges associated with convulsive seizures and a decrease in the relaxed waking pattern of alpha activity.

Performance tests must measure quite subtle changes in order to detect the effects of sleep deprivation, for it seems that a properly motivated sleep-deprived subject can perform as effectively as a rested subject on short tests of almost any type. The main performance deficits are found on tasks that require focused and sustained attention. Performance tends to be worst when (1) the subject cannot control the pace of the task, (2) long-term attention is required, and (3) the subject's motivation is low, such as a situation in which he receives little feedback about his performance (Johnson, 1969). A sleep-deprived subject's performance follows the same cycle as a rested subject's performance—best in the evening and worst toward dawn.

When subjects are allowed to sleep after a long period of deprivation, they display a characteristic rebound phenomenon for Stage 4 and REM sleep: A much larger proportion of their sleep than usual consists of these two stages (Berger & Oswald, 1962). The first night shows mostly Stage 4 rebound, and Stage 4 sleep is normal thereafter. The next 2–3 nights show unusually large proportions of REM sleep. The alpha activity in the subject's EEG also recovers within 3 days, but shows no rebound effect. Interestingly, addicted patients undergoing alcohol or barbiturate withdrawal also display a large REM rebound, which may provide the basis for the hallucinations that are a characteristic of such withdrawal (Williams & Karacan, 1973).

By sounding a buzzer or tone whenever a subject enters a certain stage of sleep, the subject can be sufficiently aroused to be selectively deprived of only that stage of sleep. REM sleep shows a rebound effect after such selective deprivation, even when total amount of sleep remains constant (Agnew, Webb, & Williams, 1967). In fact, deprivation of REM sleep alone can result in some of the effects of total sleep deprivation: a decreased convulsion threshold, irritability, disorientation, hallucinations and paranoid delusions, and possible effects on learning and long-term memory. Some researchers believe that the phasic brain activity (e.g., the phasic spikes in cats) is the core of the REM phenomenon, since deprivation of this activity produces larger REM rebound than that induced by REM deprivation alone (Ferguson, Henricksen, McGare, Belensky, Mitchell, Gonda, Cohen, & Dement, 1968).

Sleep Needs and Functions

It seems certain from the research on sleep deprivation that we do indeed need sleep, but how much sleep we need and what functions sleep and its stages provide remain unclear. The adult average is between 7 and 8 hours, but the need for sleep varies widely both across and within individuals and across different environmental conditions. For instance, women need about 2 more hours of sleep when they are pregnant. Two Australian men, however, sleep an average of only 3 hours per night and have been found to be completely healthy, both physically and psychologically (Jones & Oswald, 1968). Like most short sleepers, these men compressed as much Stage 4, and possibly REM sleep as well, into their shorter sleep time as longer sleepers obtain. Apparently the amount of sleep required is a complex function of several variables: (1) genetic–constitutional factors; (2) early experience, especially parental attitudes and behavior controls; (3) physiological differences, such as nutrition, endocrine function, and blood-system factors; and (4) psychological and physical stress, such as anxiety or work demands (Webb, 1969).

Dozens of theories regarding the functions of sleep have been proposed, but many have been either untestable or contradicted by what we have already learned about sleep. In one of the best known early theories of sleep and dreaming, developed by Freud (1915/1955), dreams were presumed to be "guardians of sleep," incorporating outside stimuli into a dream story and thus preventing the stimuli from awakening the sleeper. More important for psychoanalytic theory, Freud also hypothesized that dreams served as a safety valve for the unconscious, allowing repressed psychic material to be expressed in disguised and acceptably sublimated form. Sleep disturbances, of course, would be viewed in terms of unconscious conflict and failures to resolve it.

Recent EEG research has helped to eliminate several erroneous theories, including Freud's, and to point researchers in directions more likely to provide an adequate understanding of sleep functions. For example, we now know that many forms of animal life never sleep. Not until the development of the cerebral cortex (past the reptiles and birds on the phylogenetic scale) does sleep appear (Hartmann, 1973). Whatever functions are served by sleep, they appear to be most important for higher brain processes.

Furthermore, the documentation of two kinds of sleep suggests that different functions may be performed by NREM and REM sleep. Evidence gathered so far, although scanty, suggests that NREM may provide some form of physical restoration process as well as a necessary preparation period for the occurrence of REM sleep (Jouvet, 1969). The majority of recent research and theorizing has focused on the possible functions of the REM stage. From the high incidence of REM sleep in premature and newborn infants, one might assume that REM sleep provides stimulation necessary for the development of certain cortical functions. Reviewing several theories and evaluating a large amount of data from his own and others' laboratories, Hartmann (1973) has presented a well-conceptualized, if not completely accepted, statement regarding the apparent role of REM sleep in psychological functioning:

> Functions of D (REM) . . . appear clearly to involve the central nervous system and to be more complex than the functions of S (NREM). From the studies of sleep deprivation and the studies of tiredness we have concluded that sleep, and probably D-sleep specifically, may have a restorative function with respect to systems of focused attention (especially the ability to focus on one item while ignoring others); systems involving the ability to maintain an optimistic mood, energy, and self-confidence; and systems involving processes of emotional adaptation to the physical and social environment.
>
> From the studies of long, short, and variable sleepers we have concluded that sleep, especially D-sleep, is needed in larger quantities after days of stress, worry, or intense new learning, especially if the learning is in itself somewhat stressful. D-sleep thus may have a role in consolidating learning or memory, but there is a strong hint that stress is important and that more D is needed when there have been emotionally involving changes during the day. In other words, those who require more sleep are not so much persons who have learned a lot of new facts during the day, but rather persons who have disrupted their usual ways of doing things, who have, often stressfully, reprogrammed themselves during their waking hours. Thus sleep and D-sleep may have a role in consolidating or reconnecting these important alterations made during the day [p. 147].

Sleep Disturbances

Our knowledge of sleep disturbances depends on how well we understand sleep itself. Until we know more about the mechanisms and functions of sleep, explanations and treatment of its disorders will remain inadequate. What has been learned about sleep so far has provided some interesting clues to this complex area, as you will see.

Until recently little attention has been devoted to the diagnosis and treatment of sleep disorders, a surprising fact considering that a large percentage of the population has some kind of sleep problem—14% in a recent survey by Karacan of an urban area (cited in Kales, 1972). The present discussion of each sleep disturbance will include its description, data on its incidence or rate of occurrence in the general population, theories of causation, and currently recommended treatments.

INSOMNIA

The most common of adult sleep disturbances, insomnia, may include frequent awakenings, inability to go back to sleep after nighttime or early morning awakenings, and inability to fall asleep rapidly at bedtime. Insomnia is very rare in children. A child who takes a long time to get to sleep is almost always the victim of poor habit training by parents who reinforce the child's talking, leaving the bedroom, and requests for food and drink. Surprisingly, perhaps half the adults who complain of insomnia show a normal amount of sleep measured on the polygraph; they only *believe* that they get very little sleep (Schwartz, Guilbaud, & Fishgood, 1963). The question of why such people feel that they sleep only an hour or two each night remains unanswered; perhaps they retain impressions of consciousness into Stage 1 or even Stage 2 sleep (Rechtschaffen & Monroe, 1969).

Because of the wide variation among individuals in the amount of sleep required, any definition of insomnia must be viewed with caution. You may recall a sequence of television commercials produced for a supposedly sleep-inducing product. The initial commercial suggested that if *15 minutes* (!) is required to fall asleep, you need their product. Later, perhaps under pressure from medical or research professionals, the commercial added, "and if you feel you have a sleeping problem. . . ." Still later, mention of the 15-minute period was deleted.

A commonly used research criterion characterizes true insomniacs as those who obtain less than 6 hours of sleep per night (simply because the majority of the population obtains 7–8 hours) *and* are sleepy enough in the daytime to show a need for more sleep. Such people are one of the few types of sleep-disturbed patients who have been reliably demonstrated to show additional psychopathological symptoms, often including depression and anxiety; the symptoms tend to vary with the age of the patient. Many poor sleepers fall asleep with difficulty, awaken often during the night, have EEGs showing activity characteristic of waking states mixed in with more normal sleep activity, and display heightened autonomic activity prior to and during sleep (Monroe, 1967).

With the apparent exception of Dalmane (Kales & Kales, 1973), sleep-inducing drugs prescribed by most doctors for insomnia frequently worsen the patient's problem. They may create chronic insomnia even though the medication was initially taken to relieve periodic sleep disturbance. For a while these drugs may indeed help the patient, but frequently a dependence on the drug develops and habituation occurs—more and more of the drug is required for the same effect. Worse, most of the hypnotic (sleep-inducing) drugs decrease both Stage 4 and REM sleep (Kales & Kales, 1973). The patient is not only robbed of the most restful sleep, but should he or she try to stop taking the pills, vivid nightmares due to REM rebound may occur. Soon the insomniac is taking many pills in combination with one another and is still unable to get to sleep easily. Drug-dependency insomnia is recognized by sleep researchers as the most serious type of insomnia, and only very gradual withdrawal from all sleeping medications can again give the patient a chance at truly restful sleep.

Because of the problems associated with using drugs to treat insomnia, much recent research has concentrated on nondrug therapy. Regardless of the presence or absence of other psychological problems, symptomatic treatment of insomnia can apparently be readily effected via relaxation training or stimulus control procedures. The general principles underlying these techniques will be described in Chapter 15. Relaxation training apparently enables poor sleepers to reduce their characteristically heightened physiological activity and to focus their attention on pleasant, monotonous internal sensations, thus precluding intrusive and sleep-preventing thoughts. Stimulus-control procedures (Bootzin, 1973), on the other hand, assume that sleep is a conditioned behavior that will or will not occur depending on the association of bed-related stimuli with behaviors that are either compatible or incompatible with sleep. The patient is instructed to observe a regular sleep schedule (retiring and awakening at the same time each day, avoiding daytime naps) and to avoid engaging in sleep-incompatible behaviors in the presence of bed-related stimuli (e.g., watching television, eating, or studying in bed). Sometimes the patient is also told to leave the bedroom within 10 minutes after retiring if he or she has not yet fallen asleep, return when drowsy, and repeat this procedure as often as necessary. This latter technique guarantees that only sleep-compatible behaviors are occurring in bed and that rapid sleep onset becomes associated with bed stimuli.

In recent years, numerous experimental studies have documented the effectiveness of both relaxation training and stimulus-control approaches for reducing sleep-onset time (Bootzin, 1973; Borkovec, Kaloupek, & Slama, 1975; Nicassio & Bootzin, 1974; Steinmark & Borkovec, 1974; Tokarz & Lawrence, 1974). Such treatment is often sufficient in primary cases of the disorder. If the sleep disturbance is secondary (i.e., due to other psychological problems), symptomatic treatment may be helpful in ameliorating one of the patient's difficulties, but ultimately the main source of the problem must be removed.

Borkovec treated a common example of the latter type with a combination of therapeutic techniques. A young woman complained of chronic insomnia for the previous 2 years; sleep onset regularly occurred 2–3 hours after she retired. The sleep problem developed just after she began to perform piano recitals in front of large audiences. The anxiety associated with public performance, combined with the rigors of her academic program and an overdemanding music instructor, provided multiple sources of stress that undoubtedly served as the basis of her sleep disorder. Treatment began with relaxation training and stimulus-control procedures to improve her sleep. Although this treatment in and of itself might have been successful in temporarily relieving the disordered sleep, inattention to the stress reactions occurring in the woman's daily life would probably have resulted in a recurrence of those difficulties at some future time. Consequently, various strategies were adopted during the remainder of the therapy sessions: systematic desensitization of recital performance, assertion training aimed at gradually changing her instructor's unrealistic demands, and differential relaxation to provide a method for reducing general tension and arousal throughout the day. The outcome of this case was quite successful—

reduction of sleep-onset time to 20 minutes, greater enjoyment and effectiveness in pursuing her career, reduced general anxiety. Although direct treatment of the secondary sleep problem no doubt facilitated the entire therapeutic enterprise, amelioration of the problems in living that caused that difficulty was of primary importance.

NARCOLEPSY AND HYPERSOMNIA

Some people have problems falling asleep; others have difficulty staying awake. Part of the phenomenon is due to normal individual differences in sleep requirements. Just as there are a few people who function normally and well with 3 hours of sleep, there are probably people who need a great deal of sleep to feel and act their best.

Narcolepsy, however, consists of daytime attacks of irresistible drowsiness and fatigue, leading to periods of sleep lasting from a few minutes to 20 or 30 minutes. A narcoleptic attack may occur anywhere and at any time, but is most likely during boring, monotonous, and understimulating activities (Yoss & Daly, 1960). Most narcoleptics experience one or more of three auxiliary symptoms. Most common is *cataplexy* (complete loss of muscle tone) which often occurs following some strong emotion. The narcoleptic person often needs only to see a humorous situation or feel angry or frustrated to lose control of his or her muscles and immediately topple in a heap wherever he or she happens to be. The narcoleptic may also experience hypnagogic hallucinations, vivid and often horrifying, or sleep paralysis, the inability to move while conscious at the beginning or end of a sleep period.

EEG studies of narcoleptic patients have pointed toward the likely explanation of narcolepsy (e.g., Rechtschaffen, Wolpert, Dement, Mitchell, & Fisher, 1963). Surprisingly, narcoleptics falling asleep often enter immediately into REM sleep. Thus the narcoleptic symptoms of cataplexy and sleep paralysis appear to emanate from the muscular inhibition associated with the onset of REM sleep, and the hypnagogic hallucinations may reflect the REM dream. The cause of narcolepsy was formerly thought to involve a neurotic or psychotic process, but researchers now hypothesize an injury or abnormality of the brain's REM sleep system. The fact that narcolepsy tends to run in families partially supports such an organic view.

Estimates of the incidence of narcolepsy in the population are generally under 1%, but most researchers believe that unidentified mild cases would push this number even higher. Some researchers (e.g., Kanner, 1972) claim that narcolepsy is an exclusively male disorder; others merely find a male predominance (e.g., Sours, 1963). Unfortunately, narcolepsy, which usually appears in late adolescence and may occasionally remit temporarily, never entirely disappears and is incurable at present. The only treatment that mitigates the frequency of attacks is regular intake of stimulants, such as Ritalin.

In contrast to narcolepsy, hypersomniac sleep is not usually quite so irresistible, but it ordinarily lasts much longer. Chronic hypersomniacs also tend to display marked confusion on awakening, as well as the absence of sleep-onset

REM periods and the narcoleptic auxiliary symptoms (Rechtschaffen & Dement, 1969). Most types of hypersomnia are thought to be caused by some abnormality in the hypothalamus, and, like narcolepsy, can only be treated with stimulants, and then only with partial success. Unlike narcolepsy, which is a chronic disease, hypersomnias may be either chronic or periodic.

The best-known periodic hypersomnia is the Kleine–Levin syndrome, consisting of recurrent episodes of excessive sleeping, often lasting several days and involving 18–20 hours of sleep per day. Bulimia (great hunger), hyperphagia (overeating), and, occasionally, hypersexuality are additional symptoms of the syndrome. The sleep seems to be normal in every respect except duration. Researchers disagree on incidence and associated psychological symptoms. Fresco (1971), for example, suggests that the syndrome is specific to adolescent males and includes no psychological abnormalities; on the other hand, Gallinek (1967) has found no specific age or sex factors but reports psychological symptoms such as decreased sensory awareness, amnesia for episodes, and the classic depressive syndrome. Both sources, however, agree that the cause is probably some dysfunction in the hypothalamus.

Hypersomnia and narcolepsy present their victims with several kinds of psychological stress. If the symptoms include cataplexy, victims must make every effort to keep their emotions under control at all times. There is the constant danger of physical injury, and patients may wrongly feel guilty about a laziness that is not at all their fault. For these reasons, diagnosis of the disorder is important. Once the patient understands the biological nature of the disorder, he or she can then be helped in adjusting to the problem.

SLEEP APNEA

Sleep apnea is a curious disorder because some patients with this problem complain of insomnia whereas others complain of hypersomnia. Apnea is an inability to breathe. Studies recording respiration and EEG patterns of patients with sleep apnea (e.g., Drachman & Gumnit, 1962) found that, remarkably, the patients stop breathing as soon as they fall asleep. After 1 or 2 minutes, the amount of carbon dioxide in the blood increases to such a degree that the patient becomes aroused, takes several violent breaths, and falls asleep again. Individuals aware of the frequent arousals interpret their problem as insomnia. Others, though oblivious to the awakenings, are still always tired and must sleep 10 or 12 hours per night to feel at all rested. In addition to adult sleep disturbance, sleep apnea has been implicated as a possible cause of crib death—the sudden death of apparently healthy infants during sleep. No known drug treatment affects the disorder.

NIGHTMARES

The EEG evidence indicates that vivid nightmares take place during REM sleep (Jacobson, Kales, & Kales, 1969). Most prevalent in children, nightmares may continue to occur occasionally throughout most people's lives. Hypothesized causes of nightmares range from fairly normal childhood fears (Kessler, 1966) to poor home environments and emotional stress (Bakwin & Bakwin, 1972). Most authors feel that no treatment is necessary, although Jacobson *et al.* (1969) recommend "measures to encourage a feeling of security" in the child. Drugs that eliminate REM sleep may control nightmare occurrence (Bakwin & Bakwin, 1972), but such treatment ignores the possibility of worse nightmares occurring when the drug is withdrawn. Behavioral treatments may be more promising. Geer and Silverman (1967), for example, successfully terminated a recurrent nightmare in a young adult using systematic desensitization to the content of the nightmare (see Chapter 15).

SLOW-WAVE SLEEP DISTURBANCES

Sleepwalking, *pavor nocturnis,* and nocturnal enuresis all occur primarily in Stage 3 and Stage 4 sleep; thus they are categorized as slow-wave sleep disturbances. These disorders occur mostly in children, tend to run in families, predominate in males, and are generally outgrown by adolescence. A further characteristic shared by all three syndromes is that they disturb the child's parents more than the afflicted child, who usually has no memory of the episode the next morning. None of the three phenomena have been reliably linked to any type of psychopathology in the children who exhibit them. However, some evidence suggests that their occurrence in adults may reflect psychological maladjustment (Kales, Paulson, Jacobson, & Kales, 1966).

Sleepwalking, or somnambulism, probably has more folklore surrounding it than has any other sleep disturbance. For example, two common beliefs were that the full moon shining on a sleeping child caused sleepwalking and that a woman ceased sleepwalking once she conceived her first child. Sleepwalkers supposedly performed amazing feats, such as walking tightropes, climbing walls, and reading letters through closed envelopes. Early psychologists believed that sleepwalking was caused by childhood sexual experiences—seeing a parent's nude body, sleeping with a parent, sexual stimulation by a parent, sexual play with other children, and so on. Many psychoanalysts still adhere to this concept. Later investigators believed somnambulism to be the motor enactment of a dream.

Sleepwalking usually takes place in the early hours of sleep (Kales, Jacobson, Paulson, Kales, & Walter, 1966). The somnambulist moves with open eyes, a bland expression, and an often unsteady gait. His movements are rigid and generally appear quite purposeless, if sometimes complicated. Although his senses appear dulled, he avoids most obstacles. He seldom awakens of his own accord, and usually returns to bed or lies down in some other place.

Recent EEG sleep research has eliminated many of the myths associated with sleepwalking. Kales and his associates have studied the EEGs of somnambulist children and compared them with the EEGs of nonsleepwalkers (Kales, Jacobson, Paulson, Kales, & Walter, 1966). The sleepwalkers showed more slow-wave activity throughout the night, as well as more body movement. Arousing the sleeper was equally difficult regardless of the sleep stage. When the experimenters attempted to induce sleepwalking by standing the subjects on their feet during various stages of sleep, none of the nonsleepwalkers were able to remain upright. However, the maneuver induced sleepwalking in the somnambulists, but only in Stages 3 and 4. Interestingly, when awakened during REM sleep, somnambulists recalled dream content less often and less clearly than nonsleepwalkers.

Estimates of the incidence of sleepwalking vary from 6 to 20%, and some authors (e.g., Jacobson *et al.*, 1969) suggest that the phenomenon probably occurs in most children at some time in their lives. On the other hand, two studies have found a genetic factor in sleepwalking (Abe & Shimakawa, 1966; Bakwin, 1970). In the latter investigation, identical twins were concordant for sleepwalking six times more often than fraternal twins. Finally, fewer psychotics than normals, but about the same number of neurotics as normals, have histories of somnambulism (Winokur, Guze, & Pfeiffer, 1959).

Although drugs that suppress Stage 4 sleep have at times been found effective in reducing sleepwalking (e.g., Pesikoff & Davis, 1971), most authorities discourage the use of drugs, and few recommend psychotherapy. The only general recommendation is to lock doors and remove dangerous objects at night if there is a known sleepwalker in the house.

Borkovec's younger brother was a frequent childhood sleepwalker. The activity produced no problems, and in fact saved him once from a terrible fate. Early adolescence heralded the beginnings of typically innocuous deviance, including escapes from his second-story bedroom window for midnight jaunts with his peers. After observing him dangling from the rope ladder one night, his father, a light sleeper himself, locked the bedroom window. Upon returning home and anxiously discovering that the game was lost, he retired to the family car for the rest of the night. His mother found him there in the morning, and he offered his convincing sleepwalking explanation. Punishment was averted; his father never said a word. The window-locking contingency did have interesting effects, however: Neither midnight jaunts nor sleepwalking occurred again.

Pavor nocturnis, also known as night terrors in children and incubus attacks in adults, involves "apparent arousal (during sleep) with expressions of intense fear and emotion [Kales & Kales, 1970, p. 2232]." It is an unforgettable experience to witness a child screaming in fear, vigorously fighting with or running from an invisible enemy for 15 or 20 minutes and unaware of any help or consolation an adult tries to give. However, for the victims of *pavor nocturnis*, the experience is eminently forgettable; even if awakened during an attack, they are unable to recall more than a feeling of intense fear, and no memory of the experience remains in the morning.

On EEG records, *pavor nocturnis* is indistinguishable from a sleepwalking episode (Jacobson *et al.*, 1969). However, observers can distinguish it easily by the signs of distress and the large autonomic reactions that accompany it. Heart rate increases dramatically, often doubling or tripling in a few moments, and there are also large changes in breathing and GSR (Fisher, Byrne, Edwards, & Kahn, 1970). An observer cannot distinguish an episode of *pavor nocturnis* from a nightmare. However, a nightmare is a true "bad dream," occurring in REM sleep; after awakening, the child shows good orientation, and calming and reassurance are effective. The child can recall the content of the nightmare clearly, and the dream is shorter and less autonomically arousing than *pavor nocturnis*.

The best estimate of incidence of night terrors suggests that 1–3% of the population between the ages of 5 and 12 experience at least one episode (Jacobson *et al.*, 1969). Again, though Stage 4 sleep suppressants have been found to reduce the incidence of night terrors (Fisher, Kahn, Edwards, & Davis, 1972), most authorities recommend no treatment other than reassuring a child's parents that there is nothing wrong and that the child will outgrow the episodes. The adult incubus attack is much rarer. Hypothesized causes range from psychoanalytic concepts stressing the failure of the ego to control anxiety (Fisher *et al.*, 1970) to suggestions of CNS immaturity (Jacobson *et al.*, 1969).

Nocturnal enuresis, or nighttime bed-wetting in children old enough to have acquired bladder control, is the third sleep disturbance that occurs during slow-wave sleep and is found more frequently in the deepest, soundest, hardest-to-wake sleepers (Bakwin & Bakwin, 1972). Incidence ranges from 5 to 15% of all children (Kales & Berger, 1970).

The popular conception that enuresis is due to the child's hostile or dependent feelings may lead the enuretic's parents to feel either guilt or hostility toward the child for deliberate misbehavior. In actuality enuretic children tend to differ from other children in at least three ways: (1) the pressure in the bladder rises higher during the night; (2) neurological control of voluntary muscles lags behind the norm for their age; and (3) their bladder capacities are smaller (Jacobson *et al.*, 1969).

Two treatments for enuresis have been found to be partially effective. The drug Tofranil often reduces bed-wetting, probably because it increases bladder capacity (Kales & Kales, 1970). A conditioning procedure (described in Chapter 10) employs a pad that activates an alarm at the first drops of moisture. This treatment also has been found to produce immediate results, although the subsequent relapse rate is often high (Lovibond, 1963).

Perhaps the worst aspect of enuresis is that parental attitudes toward the child are often quite negative and can contribute additional stresses to the child's life. For this reason, counseling for parents of enuretic children is important. Ordinarily, neither they nor the child are to blame for the condition and the majority of children simply outgrow the problem.

Some researchers believe that all three slow-wave sleep disturbances are due to an unspecified immaturity of the CNS (Broughton, 1968). Supporting evidence derives from genetic data, the decrease in incidence with age, the predominance of the phenomena in males, whose nervous systems mature more slowly, and the fact that sleep EEGs of children with these disturbances display an abundance of slow-wave activity common to earlier ages. We must emphasize again that, at least in children, none of these slow-wave sleep disturbances have been linked to any causative psychopathology, and that education of the child's parents is often the most important form of treatment.

SLEEPTALKING

Sleeptalking (somniloquy) is "the utterance of speech or other psychologically meaningful sound during sleep, without simultaneous subjective awareness of the event [Arkin, 1966, p. 101–102]." Probably everyone talks in his or her sleep periodically. The phenomenon is especially common in childhood and decreases thereafter, although one study found an incidence of 40% among college students (Arkin, 1966). The speech is often mumbled and unclear; in general, the lighter the sleep in which it occurs, the better the articulation. The content tends to be emotional aftersensations of the previous day's experiences. Communication with a sleeptalker is occasionally possible to a degree, but authors disagree on whether secrets are revealed during sleeptalking and whether content can be recalled on awakening.

EEG studies have shown that the majority of sleeptalking incidents occur during Stage 2, with about a third appearing in Stage 4 and 7% in REM sleep (Rechtschaffen, Goodenough, & Shapiro, 1962). They are equally likely to occur throughout the night. Contrary to folklore, no embarrassing or personal secrets were obtained in the experimental situation. In fact, the content of at least half of the incidents was related to the experiment itself. When awakened immediately after sleeptalking, three-fourths of the subjects reported some recall, usually a vague thought rather than a dream image.

The cause of sleeptalking is unknown, but most sources treat it as a completely normal phenomenon. Aarons (1970) was able to increase speech during sleep by two methods: posthypnotic suggestion and an escape–avoidance conditioning procedure involving reinforcement of sleeptalking by reducing light and tone stimuli.

BRUXISM

Bruxism, "the grinding or clenching of the teeth at other times than for the mastication of food [Shepherd & Price, 1971]," usually occurs during sleep. Estimates of childhood bruxism range from 2 to 15% (Kanner, 1972; Reding, Rubright, & Zimmerman, 1966). Incidence decreases with age, but some dental researchers believe that bruxism has been increasing in the general population, to as high as 32%, as modern life becomes more tense and stressful (Shepherd & Price, 1971).

EEG studies have found bruxism to occur mainly during Stage 2 sleep (Reding, 1968). Although a fourth of the incidents are associated with body movements, the grinding activity does not appear to awaken the sleeper.

Bruxism is generally held to be caused by a high level of stress in a person's life, especially if combined with malocclusion of the teeth (Ramfjord, 1961). Research indicates that individuals who are undergoing stressful situations or who tend to be self-punishing are more likely to display the disorder than are matched controls (Thaller, Rosen, & Saltzman, 1967). Other studies show that a predisposition to bruxism may be inherited (Reding *et al.*, 1966), and that low calcium and vitamin intake may also play a contributing role (Cheraskin & Ringsdorf, 1970).

Bruxism should be treated when it causes jaw pain or wears away permanent teeth. Treatment typically involves dental work to correct any malocclusion, counseling to reduce stress, and possibly relaxant drugs and the wearing of a rubber nightguard between the teeth.

NOCTURNAL HEADBANGING

Nocturnal headbanging (*tic de sommeil*) is actually a rhythmic rolling of the head from side to side on the pillow while going to sleep or during Stage 4 sleep. It is quite rare, and occurs mostly in young children. Kanner (1972) regarded many patients with this syndrome to be retarded or to have personality disorders. Instrumental reinforcement for this unusual activity may occur from three sources: (1) attention after waking, (2) the intrinsic comfort of rhythmic activity, and (3) escape behavior in the form of waking from a nightmare or other unpleasant mental content (Ross, Meichenbaum, & Humphrey, 1971). The only treatment for nocturnal headbanging mentioned in the behavioral therapy literature consists of ignoring the behavior and desensitization of repetitive dream content (Ross *et al.*, 1971).

SLEEP-EXACERBATED DISORDERS

Certain medical disorders become worse during sleep, due either to the daily cycles of almost every bodily function, or to certain physiological components of sleep itself. Epileptic discharges and seizures are more frequent during sleep for some individuals (Kales & Berger, 1970), and duodenal ulcer patients secrete many times more gastric acid during sleep than do normals, especially during REM periods (Kales & Kales, 1973). Some heart and breathing disorders and paralyses tend to occur more often during sleep than during waking hours.

Hypnosis

Although procedures like hypnosis have been employed for thousands of years, its modern history began with the theory and practice of Franz Anton Mesmer (1733–1815). Mesmer thought that the body was similar to a magnet and that all diseases were due to an improper balance of magnetic fluid (cf. Moss, 1965). He felt he could restore this balance, and thereby cure patients, through the application of magnets and so he called this procedure animal magnetism. Later, he discovered that the application of his hands alone or just his gaze would suffice. His patients, rather than entering a passive sleeplike trance, would convulse at times for as long as 3 hours. After these violent convulsions, or crises, the patients appeared to be miraculously cured.

One of Mesmer's many followers, the Marquis de Puysegur, later found that he could induce in his subjects a state of somnambulism, so named because the

This illustration, from a 1794 book entitled *A Key to Physic and the Occult Sciences,* shows a mesmerist exerting his animal magnetism on a patient. Despite his ministrations, the lady has not yet fallen into a crisis. (National Library of Medicine)

patient behaved like a sleepwalker. In this state, the subject seemed to be in a peaceful slumber and would converse only with de Puysegur; when awakened, the subject remembered nothing about the experience. This procedure was as effective as Mesmer's, and avoided the violent crises that had seemed indispensable to Mesmer's method. Deep somnambulistic trance therefore replaced convulsive episodes. Following the 1840s theory of James Braid, who suggested that the trance procedures produced a physiological state of nervous sleep, the phenomenon was renamed *hypnotism*.

In the 1880s, an intense debate over the nature of hypnosis raged in France. The Nancy school, represented by Hippolyte Marie Bernheim, maintained that hypnosis was an effective treatment for a wide range of clinical problems but that hypnotism was nothing more than the intensification of normal suggestion. Opposing this view was Jean Martin Charcot, who believed that susceptibility to hypnosis indicated a pathological condition of the hysteric's central nervous system. Charcot's view represented a disguised return to the notions of Mesmer.

In the late 1880s, Sigmund Freud, student of both Charcot and Bernheim, and his colleague, Josef Breuer, developed the "talking cure." Freud and Breuer theorized that hysterical symptoms were caused by pent-up emotions and painful memories. Through the medium of hypnosis, they helped the patient to relive these painful experiences and achieve catharsis, a purging or cleansing of the psyche (Breuer & Freud, 1966). Later, Freud abandoned the use of hypnosis, because it interfered with the emotional aspects of the patient's reexperiencing of past traumas, and thus diminished the curative powers of catharsis.

HYPNOTIC INDUCTION

From these beginnings, a variety of hypnotic procedures, phenomena, and theories have emerged. Although many induction procedures have been developed, eight variables are common to most (Barber & DeMoor, 1972). The first three variables are concerned with preparing the subject for hypnosis. The hypnotist explains to the subject what hypnosis is and tries to remove any misconceptions and fears. Next, the subject's cooperation must be secured; a resisting subject cannot be hypnotized.

Variables 4 and 5 deal with the transition from waking state to hypnosis. In almost all procedures, the hypnotist either asks subjects to close their eyes or suggests that the eyes are becoming heavy and are closing. The hypnotist then suggests that the subject is feeling relaxed and drowsy.

The last three variables involve methods of inducing successful responses to the hypnotist's suggestions. First, simple, straightforward suggestions, such as, "Your arm is getting heavy," are avoided. Instead, the hypnotist gives the subject goal-directed fantasies, such as images of situations that would produce the suggested response. For example, the hypnotist may say, "Imagine you are holding something very heavy in your hand . . . now the hand and arm feel heavy as if the weight were pressing down . . . and as it feels heavier and heavier the hand and arm begin to move down . . . [Weitzenhoffer & Hilgard, 1962]." The hypnotist also tries to match such suggestions with the subject's actual experience. In the previous example, the subject's arm naturally will tire as it remains extended, but this natural feeling is interpreted as resulting from the hypnotist's suggestions. Finally, any failure of the subject to respond is reinterpreted by the hypnotist so that the subject can continue to believe that he or she has done what the hypnotist expected.

Once hypnotized, the subject can engage in many strange behaviors that normal waking subjects presumably cannot perform. The following phenomena are typical of those that can be induced by hypnotic suggestion:

1. Catalepsy—the subject's body or parts of it become completely rigid. A subject exhibiting catalepsy can lie perfectly straight with only his head and feet supported.
2. Amnesia—the subject forgets events, facts, and conversations either during the trance or immediately afterward.
3. Age regression—the subject behaves as he or she did at some earlier time in life.
4. Hallucinations—the subject responds as if he or she sees objects that are

not present (positive hallucinations) or does not see objects that are present (negative hallucinations).

5. Analgesia and anesthesia—the subject reports feeling no pain or no sensations whatsoever.

These phenomena offer compelling evidence that hypnosis is a special state in which people can transcend their normal waking behavior. As we will see, some theories suggest that this is the case, although current research on hypnosis provides little support for this view.

THEORIES OF HYPNOSIS

Despite Freud's abandonment of hypnosis, psychoanalytic theory maintains both a theoretical interest in the phenomenon and an applied interest in its potential therapeutic use. Gill and Brenman (1967) employed the concepts of transference and regression in the service of the ego to explain hypnosis. *Transference,* as you may know, is established in the therapeutic relationship when the patient attributes characteristics of significant others to the therapist. *Regression* occurs when the ego allows a partial return to earlier psychosexual behaviors in an effort to cope with unconscious conflict and thus relinquishes control to id or environmental forces (see Chapter 16 for a more detailed explanation of these concepts). According to psychoanalytic theory, the hypnotic induction procedure breaks down ordinary ego control by forcing the ego to focus on its previous habitual perceptual and motor processes. To accomplish this focus, the ego must redirect its energy, thereby creating conditions conducive to regression. In addition, the induction ritual enables the subject to find a favorable motivational pattern (a suitable transference, usually reflecting the parent–child relationship). Once the favorable motivational pattern is established, a hypnotic state exists. A partial regression occurs in the ego, and an ego subsystem develops that relies upon the hypnotist for control. The major portion of the ego has only moved into the background and can regain control at any time. As is the case with other psychoanalytic hypotheses, the theory is not easily evaluated by experimental testing.

Other contemporary theories of hypnosis fall into one of two categories. The *state* or credulous view suggests that hypnotic trance does involve a phenomenon qualitatively different from other human states. The *nonstate* or skeptical approach maintains that hypnotic behaviors can be explained on the basis of principles already known to govern normal, waking-state behavior.

Exemplifying the credulous position, Hilgard (1965) suggests that hypnosis is more than a state of simple hypersuggestibility; a true trance-state exists, qualitatively different from waking states. All people are presumably born with the ability to develop hypnotic behavior; like all behavior, this ability may be nurtured or stunted. The quality of the child's interactions with his or her parents will influence hypnotic susceptibility, and the child's own developing interests will affect his or her ability to respond to particular suggestions.

Sarbin and Coe (1972), on the other hand, reject the concept of trance state in explaining hypnotic phenomena. Because there are no objective criteria to identify a trance state, the trance can only be identified by the presence of the very hypnotic behaviors it is supposed to explain. Their own interpretation of hypnosis draws heavily from role theory.

As is the case when any role is adopted, subjects bring to the hypnotic situation a set of expectations of how they should behave and they use these expectations to guide their behavior. Orne (1959), in a classic demonstration of this effect, presented a lecture on hypnosis to two undergraduate psychology classes; the lectures were identical, except that one class was told that dominant-hand catalepsy was a characteristic of hypnosis. Volunteers were solicited from both classes to be in a hypnosis experiment. A significantly greater number of students from the class told about dominant-hand catalepsy spontaneously exhibited this phenomenon upon being hypnotized compared to subjects from the other class.

In order to enact a role successfully and fulfill role expectations, the subject needs various role skills. These skills may be motor (e.g., being able to do fine work with one's hands) or cognitive (e.g., being able to think of problems in abstract ways). In hypnosis, the required skill may be acute sensitivity to role demands. That is, the subject must be able to perceive subtle cues from the hypnotist and the audience, so that he can successfully fulfill their expectations. Before a subject is hypnotized, the hypnotist generally helps the subject prepare for the role by telling him or her what experiences and behaviors are expected. The induction procedure then allows the subject to make the transition from waking state to hypnotic "trance." In effect, the subject needs a formal entrance ceremony to provide a justification for adopting such radically different role behavior.

People can become as engrossed in the hypnotic experience as they can while reading a novel and thus feel that the trance is a very special experience. Presumably, roles fall on a continuum of intensity of involvement, from roles performed almost automatically (being a shopper in a grocery store) to roles so involving that death may occur (witchcraft or voodoo). Hypnotic behaviors are hypothesized to fall just above the midpoint of this continuum.

Like Sarbin and Coe, Barber also rejects trance explanations of hypnotic behavior. In his cognitive–behavioral view of hypnosis, "the extent to which subjects respond to test suggestions, depends on their readiness to think and imagine with the themes that are suggested [Barber, Spanos, & Chaves, 1974, p. 49]." The subject's readiness, in turn, depends on his or her motivation, expectancy, and attitude. These three factors exist on a continuum from negative to positive. To be hypnotized, the subject must be on the positive side of all three continua. In other words, the subject must have a desire to be hypnotized, a belief that he or she can be hypnotized, and a view that hypnosis involves an exciting, useful, and worthwhile experience. For Barber, it is not a question of people doing interesting things under hypnosis, but of people being able to do interesting things, whether hypnotized or not. In general, physiological studies have failed to discover any pattern of responses (electroencephalogram, heart rate, blood pressure, galvanic skin responses, etc.) that conclusively distinguishes between the waking state and hypnosis (Barber, 1970). Nor do hypnotized subjects possess any abilities that cannot be elicited during the normal waking state, including the unusual phenomena listed earlier. For example, Barber *et al.* (1974), demonstrated that with appropriate instructions, normal waking controls can tolerate pain as well as hypnotized subjects. Normal waking subjects have similarly been found just as capable as hypnotic subjects of selective amnesia, visual and auditory hallucinations, and control of autonomic response systems.

Currently, theorists from both the skeptical and credulous viewpoints are willing to agree on a number of key issues. The subject's willingness to cooperate with the hypnotist is cited by both as an obvious precondition for being hypnotized. Both agree that there is little the hypnotized subject can do that the waking control subject cannot. Both positions are willing to postulate some shift in cognitive orientation from an objective, pragmatic perspective to one of imagination. The question remains whether this shift constitutes the whole, so-called trance state or simply *accompanies* a separate condition that is the trance state.

HYPNOSIS AND SLEEP

We have already seen that wakefulness and sleep involve very different organismic states, and that the research evidence to date suggests no fundamental difference between waking and hypnotic behavior. Hypnotic phenomena have often been related to sleep, sleepwalking, and dreams, but it appears that their underlying behavioral and physiological processes are quite different. As we saw earlier, sleep can now be diagnosed and defined, both behaviorally and physiologically. On the other hand, no reliable method exists to establish either the presence of hypnosis or its depth (Evans, 1972).

Although a hypnotized subject often looks asleep, observers cannot distinguish a hypnotized subject instructed to act awake from normal waking subjects (Barber, 1972). Furthermore, a sleeplike appearance has not always been associated with hypnosis; recall that hypnosis in Mesmer's time was characterized by violent convulsions.

The EEG patterns of hypnotized subjects can resemble those of nonhypnotized subjects who are in transition from waking state to Stage 1 sleep (Evans, 1972; Tart, 1965). However, the abundance of alpha waves in these two states is also found in many other relaxed waking states, suggesting that such patterns are due to other physiological states, such as relaxation, that accompany hypnosis (Sarbin & Slagle, 1972).

The relationship between hypnosis and sleepwalking also appears to be illusory (Barber *et al.*, 1974). In both phenomena, the individual walks, talks, and responds only to selected environmental stimuli. However, somnambulism occurs in Stage 3 or Stage 4 sleep characterized by slow waves entirely absent from the EEG records of the hypnotic subject. A sleepwalker rarely responds to conversation and is not easily awakened; the hypnotic subject has no trouble responding to commands or being awakened from the trance. Finally, unlike the hypnotic subject who forgets only what he is instructed to forget, the somnambulist appears to have complete amnesia for his or her experience.

Hypnotic dreams have also been suggested as a possible link between sleep and hypnosis (Evans, 1972). Hypnotic imagery can be induced by instructing the subject to fall into a night sleep and to begin dreaming; often a specific dream topic is suggested. Under these conditions, subjects who are successful in having hypnotic dreams often report dream experiences identical to those encountered during a typical night of sleep. As we noted earlier, the most vivid night dreams usually occur in REM sleep. However, physiological studies have not conclusively shown that the EEG or the eye movements of hypnotized subjects instructed to dream are the same as those for subjects who are actually dreaming (Evans, 1972).

Finally, a person who has been deprived of REM sleep over a series of nights will display REM rebound on recovery nights. Halper, Pivik, and Dement (1969) deprived subjects of REM sleep for 2 nights and then gave them two 2½-hour sessions of hypnotically induced dreaming during the third day. They assumed that no REM rebound would occur during normal sleep that night if hypnotic dreams were functionally the same as night dreams. The normal REM-rebound effect did in fact occur, indicating that hypnotic dreams are not functionally the same as night dreams.

Summary

The phenomenon of sleep is not a simple state, but rather involves as many as five stages occurring sequentially throughout the night. Sleep patterns change with age, and sleep deprivation produces small but detectable changes in neurological and behavioral activities. Little is known about the specific ways in which sleep and its distinct stages serve to maintain physical and psychological adjustment.

Disturbances of sleep, however, are of great concern to the afflicted individual and several types of sleep disorders have been defined and studied. Insomnia is by far the most frequent complaint and psychological methods recently have been developed to reduce this problem. Some sleep disturbances (e.g., narcolepsy and hypersomnia) involve the opposite problem of too much sleep; medical treatment has had only limited success in dealing with such disorders. Other sleep disturbances include sleep apnea (respiration ceases briefly), nightmares, night terrors, sleepwalking, enuresis (bed-wetting), sleeptalking, bruxism (teeth-grinding), and nocturnal headbanging. In each case, various forms of medical and psychological treatment have been employed with varying success. There is still much to learn about these disorders before adequate treatment can be routinely prescribed. Research involving monitoring the EEG and autonomic arousal patterns of disturbed subjects is beginning to supply the necessary information.

Hypnosis has a long history of use as a psychological treatment technique and the hypnotized subject often resembles a sleeping person. Research suggests, however, that hypnosis may simply involve an intense role-enactment and therefore be more related to waking than sleeping behavior. The EEG patterns of the hypnotized subject bear little resemblance to sleep records, and hypnotic "dreaming" has not been found to serve as an adequate substitute for the dreaming that occurs when the person is sleeping.

14

Recreational Drug Use and Abuse

ROBERT A. LEVITT
Southern Illinois University at Carbondale

A drug is any chemical substance taken into the body to alter physical or psychological functioning. Since prehistoric times, humans have used various substances to reduce pain and suffering, to alter their feelings, and to achieve euphoria or sedation. Most people in our society consider it one thing to take a psychologically active (*psychoactive*) drug on the medical advice of a physician, but quite something else again to self-administer a drug to achieve some pleasurable effect. We refer to such drug self-administration as *recreational drug use*.

Many people are appalled by any nonmedical drug use whose purpose is the achievement of some pleasurable effect. They consider any such use as drug abuse. Others feel that an individual ought to have a right to use drugs recreationally, and would consider such drug use as abusive only if the individual were to lose control over his or her use of drugs.

Who is right? Can individuals self-administer drugs to produce effects they regard as pleasurable without the drug use being abusive? It is difficult to provide an adequate answer to this question. Psychologists can study and enumerate the psychological effects of particular patterns of drug use; they can determine the side effects and the potential for damage. But then these questions arise: Given this information, should such drug use be considered abusive? Should it be governmentally controlled and regulated? Should there be criminal prosecution for such use? These are ethical and political questions. One's answers to them will be based on religious, philosophical, and political leanings about the nature of human life and culture, about the rights of the individual, and the rights of society. It would appear that this subject transcends psychology and biology, and is a matter of personal beliefs. The psychological and biological consequences of drug use can be presented, but the subject of what patterns of drug use should or should not be allowed is beyond the scope of psychology or biology.

This chapter focuses on the effects of nonmedical use of psychoactive drugs. The first section presents theories used to explain recreational drug use, issues of classification with respect to drug-related psychopathology, the medical classification of drug types, and the legal code concerning recreational drug use. The second section reviews the main classes of recreationally used psychoactive drugs. These are (1) the depressants, (2) the narcotics, (3) the stimulants, and (4) the hallucinogens. Each class is described in terms of the history of its use, the short-term effects of use, toxicity resulting from chronic use, and drug dependence. Finally, some conclusions are offered about the psychoactive drug problem and its solution.

Terminology

Several drug-related terms should be defined before we review the various drug classes. *Tolerance* refers to the decreasing effect most drugs produce as a consequence of repeated administration. Sometimes the initial effect can be reestablished or approximated by increasing the dose. This is usually a progressive phenomenon; continually higher and higher doses are needed as more and more tolerance develops. Tolerance may not develop at all, or it may develop more slowly to some actions of a drug than to others. Eventually, toxic drug effects, or a lethal dose, will be reached.

The many complex processes involved in the development of tolerance can easily be conceptualized. There are several complementary (opposing) functional systems in the body that serve to maintain equilibrium. As an example, consider the autonomic nervous system, which has two divisions. These are the sympathetic division and the parasympathetic division, which oppose each other in the functions they perform. When a drug has a particular action on the autonomic nervous system, the bodily systems that have a similar action slow down to compensate for the presence of the drug, and the bodily systems that have actions opposite to those of the drug speed up, also to compensate for the presence of the drug. The result of these compensatory actions is to return the body to equilibrium.

Cross-tolerance occurs when the development of tolerance to one drug transfers to another drug. When a person who has been taking a particular drug and has become tolerant to its actions now takes a second drug and is also tolerant to its actions, cross-tolerance is taking place. This phenomenon tells us that the two drugs have some commonality in their actions. In fact, this is one way of telling whether drugs should be placed in the same category.

Physical dependence has developed when a person can no longer function normally without the drug. Physical dependence is always preceded by the development of tolerance. We know that physical dependence has developed in a person only when the drug is withdrawn and the person becomes ill. Readminister the drug and the sickness dissipates. The illness produced by drug withdrawal in a physically dependent individual is referred to as the *withdrawal syndrome* (or the *abstinence syndrome*). Although tolerance always precedes physical dependence, tolerance also develops to many drugs for which we do not see physical dependence (such as the amphetamines and LSD, for example). Understanding tolerance, however, is the key to understanding physical dependence. When bodily systems have reacted to compensate for a drug's action and the drug is abruptly withdrawn, the body cannot reverse these changes instantaneously. Therefore, the withdrawal syndrome results because these over- and underactive bodily systems are no longer being compensated for by the drug. This gives you a clue to what a particular withdrawal syndrome will be like. The withdrawal syndrome typically consists of effects opposite to those of the drug. Keep this in mind as you read the descriptions of the withdrawal syndromes for the depressants and the narcotics later in this chapter. *Cross-dependence* has occurred if, after physical dependence has developed to one drug, and it is withdrawn and replaced by a second drug, the second drug prevents the development of the withdrawal syndrome. As with cross-tolerance, the phenomenon of cross-dependence tells us that the two drugs belong to the same class.

Psychological dependence has developed when an individual feels that "the effects produced by a drug, or the conditions associated with its use, are necesssary to maintain an optimal state of well being [Jaffe, 1975, p. 284]." Psychological dependence is found whenever physical dependence has developed. But psychological dependence may also exist in the absence of physical dependence (for example, nicotine in cigarettes, LSD, marijuana, the amphetamines, cocaine). It may be best to consider psychological drug dependence as a learned habit—something like a neurotic attachment.

Another once-popular term, now being used less, is *addiction*. Jaffe defines addiction as "a behavioral pattern of compulsive drug use, characterized by overwhelming involvement with the use of a drug, the securing of its supply, and a high tendency to relapse after withdrawal [1975, p. 285]." According to this definition, addiction can be used to refer to both physical and psychological dependence. Unfortunately, this definition tends to confuse the general public about the comparative dangers of the various drug classes. When *addiction* is used to describe a particular pattern of drug use, remember that a physical dependence may be involved, or only a psychological one. Two other terms that should be mentioned are *craving* and *drug-seeking behavior*. *Craving* refers to the overwhelming desire to take a drug and experience its effects. *Drug-seeking behavior* refers to those behaviors directed toward obtaining a drug. Craving and drug-seeking behavior are found in both psychological and physical dependence. In contrast to *addiction*, these two terms are useful in describing patterns of recreational drug use. *Illicit drug use* is illegal drug use. This term excludes the use of medically prescribed drugs, legal medicinal home remedies, and also the legal recreational use of alcohol, nicotine (in cigarettes), and caffeine (in coffee or tea).

Classification Systems

PSYCHOPATHOLOGICAL SYSTEMS

DSM-II contains a classification scheme for psychopathology associated with drug use. This system is shown in Table 14-1. We might question the classification of an individual who becomes intoxicated as few as four times a year as an alcoholic of the episodic-excessive-drinker variety.

TABLE 14-1

DSM-II Categories of Drug-Associated Psychopathology

Category	Characteristics
II Organic brain syndromes	
Psychotic	Alcoholic psychosis
Nonpsychotic	Acute toxic reactions associated with alcohol (simple drunkenness) and drugs
V Personality disorders and other non-psychotic mental disorders	
Alcoholism	
Episodic excessive drinker	Becomes intoxicated 4 times or more per year
Habitual excessive drinker	Becomes intoxicated 12 times or more per year
Alcohol addict	Is unable to go more than 1 day without drinking, or drinks heavily and continually for at least 3 months
Drug dependence	(Ten separate drug classes listed)

PSYCHOPHARMACOLOGICAL SYSTEMS

Another classification problem is that of categorizing psychoactive drugs. The World Health Organization (WHO) currently recognizes five categories of psychoactive drugs. Dr. Murray Jarvik (1967) recently presented another useful classification system in a *Psychology Today* article. No system is without weakness. However, systems such as these are necessary, otherwise our knowledge cannot be organized. These two classification schemes are summarized in Table 14-2.

LEGAL SYSTEMS

The federal government classifies psychoactive drugs into five groupings called *schedules* (Table 14-3). This system is not based on medical evidence or abuse potential. Rather, it seems to be based on the prevalence of illicit use. The federal legal classification also incorporates a strong dose of politics. For instance,

TABLE 14-2

Two Systems for Classifying Psychoactive Drugs

Drug categories		Medical or recreational use
WHO[a]	Jarvik[b]	
Neuroleptics	Antipsychotics	Have antipsychotic action; effective in the treatment of some psychiatric disorders that are accompanied by neurological signs
Anxiolytic sedatives	Antianxiety drugs	Reduce anxiety without affecting perception or cognition
Antidepressants	Antidepressants	Combat depression
Psychostimulants	Stimulants	Increase level of alertness, elevate mood, increase confidence, prevent fatigue
Psychodysleptics	Psychotogenic drugs	Produce abnormal mental and behavioral phenomena
	Sedatives or hypnotics	Produce general depression (sedation) in low doses, and sleep (hypnotic action) in larger doses, used to treat stress, anxiety, and insomnia
	Anesthetics, analgesics, and paralytics	Produce a total loss of consciousness (general anesthetics), a lack of sensation near the site of application (local anesthetics), relief of pain (analgesics), or paralysis of movement (paralytics)
	Neurotransmitters	Are normally found in the nervous system; act as chemical messengers to carry nerve impulses across the synapses that separate neurons

[a] Categories are from the World Health Organization classification system.
[b] Categories are from the classification system of Dr. Murray Jarvik (1967).

alcohol and tobacco, our two most serious problem drugs, are specifically exempted. One might say that they have been domesticated and are part of "the social system." The most stringent classification is schedule I. It carries the highest penalties for manufacture, distribution, or possession. The drugs in this schedule have one thing in common; they are not in general medical use in this country. This schedule includes heroin, which quickly produces physical dependence, as well as LSD and marijuana, which do not produce physical dependence.

The penalties applied to all five schedules are severe, ranging from up to $5000 fine and 1 year's imprisonment to up to $25,000 fine and 15 years' imprisonment. An unusual feature of the legislation is that the federal government is given power in all illicit drug traffic and use, not just that involving interstate commerce, which is the rule in most federal crime statutes. Many responsible scientists and physicians have been highly critical of the legal criminal code approach to recreational and abusive drug use. An approach to the drug problem

TABLE 14-3

Federal Drug Schedules

Schedule	Abuse potential	Medical use	Examples
I	High	None	Heroin, marijuana, LSD, mescaline, psilocybin
II	High	Yes	Morphine, cocaine, methadone, short-acting barbiturates, amphetamines, methaqualone
III	Moderate	Yes	Nonamphetamine stimulants, intermediate-acting barbiturates, some anti-anxiety tranquilizers
IV	Low	Yes	Long-acting barbiturates, some nonbarbiturate sedatives, meprobamate
V	Lowest	Yes	Compounds containing small amounts of narcotics (paregoric, certain cough syrups)

that reflects agreement with these critics will be presented at the conclusion of this chapter.

In addition to federal legislation, each state also has its own laws regulating licit and illicit drugs. Not surprisingly, there are substantial differences in approach. There has been a recent trend toward enlightenment, especially with respect to decriminalizing the penalties for the private use of marijuana.

Who Uses Drugs?

One question in the psychopathology of drug use is this: What characteristics or experiences are associated with nonmedical drug use? Studies have shown that those who most frequently use legal, medically prescribed drugs also tend to show the highest incidence of nonmedical drug use (Blum, Braunstein, & Stone, 1969; Brehm & Beck, 1968). However, use of a particular drug does not lead directly to other drug use. Rather, it seems to reduce the inhibitions about self-experimentation with drugs, and thus may lead to adopting recreational drug use as a part of a life-style.

There do seem to be some cultural and personal characteristics that are related to drug use. Poor and culturally deprived individuals such as ghetto blacks tend to show a higher incidence of problems with the narcotics (Chein, Gerard, Lee, & Rosenfeld, 1964). Upper-middle-class and educated Caucasians use the major hallucinogens, such as LSD, more frequently. Males of Irish extraction have a higher incidence of alcoholism than males of other ethnic groups (such as Italians and Jews) (McCord, McCord, & Gudeman, 1960). Marijuana use, on the other hand, seems to permeate our society, although it is currently more in vogue among the young, the educated, and the avant-garde (National Commission, 1972).

One interesting and important question is whether any particular psychopathological diagnosis is predictive of a high incidence of recreational or abusive drug use. The answer is no. Groups of drug users, even alcoholics or narcotic addicts, do not show a higher incidence of psychopathology other than their addiction when compared to control groups. If they are at least temporarily drugfree they also do not show any special response patterns on either objective tests of psychological functioning, such as the Minnesota Multiphasic Personality Inventory, or on subjective psychological tests such as the Rorschach Test or the Thematic Apperception Test. They do, of course, show some drug-related responses or answers that differentiate them from nondrug users; for instance, answers to questions about their drug-use history. Not surprisingly, if tests are administered to illicit-drug users while they are under the influence of a drug, the results are similar to those of individuals suffering from some sort of organic brain syndrome. Therefore, although recreational drug users do not function normally while under the influence of the drug, no well-defined psychopathology has been found to lead to such drug use, or to result from the drug use (Greaves, 1971; MacAndrew, 1965; Nathan, 1969; Whitlock, 1970).

ETIOLOGICAL THEORIES

The conditions that induce a person to start self-administering a drug differ from those that are responsible for maintaining the behavior. Chronic drug use may lead to physical dependence on depressants and narcotics or psychological dependence on stimulants and hallucinogens. However, the development of dependence does not explain why an individual starts self-administering a drug in the first place.

PSYCHOANALYTIC VIEWS.   Most analytic views of drug abuse suggest fixation at the oral stage of development as the precipitating cause. Early parent–child interactions are said to frustrate dependency needs during this stage of maturation. Other analysts see drug abuse as a defense mechanism that reduces emotional conflict or guilt. With regard to alcoholism, a common quip defines the superego as the part of the personality that is soluble in alcohol. Evidence to support these theories is difficult to find, and psychoanalysis does not help most alcoholics or drug abusers who seek treatment (DeVito, Flaherty, & Mozdzierz, 1970; Franks, 1970; Sutker, 1971).

BEHAVIORAL THEORIES.   The basic theme of the behavioral approach is that drug use is a learned means of reducing conditioned anxiety. Conger (1951) showed that alcohol can reduce behavior motivated by fear. Rats were trained in a classic approach–avoidance conflict. First they were taught to feed at a particular location, then they were shocked when they approached the food. Animals injected with alcohol were found to approach the food more readily than did controls. In another study, Davis and Miller (1963) allowed rats to self-inject amobarbital (a sedative) by depressing a lever. Those animals that received brief electric shocks to the feet every 60 seconds were found to self-inject the drug, but rats not subjected to the pain/fear stimulus did not do so. A hypothesis derived from this animal research is that drug self-administration is a learned response that is acquired and maintained because it reduces distress.

PHYSIOLOGICAL THEORIES.   Most physiological theories have proposed that individuals who become drug abusers differ from normal individuals in the rate or manner in which they metabolize the drug. Alcoholics and nonalcoholics, however, were not found to differ in their rates of alcohol metabolism (Mendelson, 1968). Studies focusing on genetic factors in alcoholism have been inconclusive. Evidence supporting such a factor comes from human twin studies indicating that monozygotic twins have a higher concordance rate for alcoholism than have dizygotic twins (Kaig, 1960), and from mouse-breeding research that produced a strain of animals preferring alcohol (Rodgers & McClearn, 1962).

Although relatives of alcoholics have a greater incidence of alcoholism than the general population, genetic similarity is confounded with environmental similarity. In one study of children of alcoholic parents, children who were separated from their natural parents and raised in foster homes were no more likely in later life to develop alcoholism than children of nonalcoholic parents (Roe, 1945). Thus, this study suggests that a genetically transmitted physiological defect does *not* trigger alcoholism in alcoholic families.

Depressants

This group of drugs includes alcohol, the barbiturates, the nonbarbiturate sedatives, the antianxiety agents, and even the general anesthetics (Table 14-4).[1] Although not commonly grouped as a single class, they do belong together. In appropriate doses and by the correct route of administration, they all may be used as sedatives and muscle relaxants. Tolerance develops to all these drugs, as does physical dependence. The development of dependence on them, however, occurs more slowly than for the narcotics. The withdrawal syndrome for the depressants is characterized by excitatory and convulsant features, which are opposite to their sedative and muscle relaxant (anticonvulsant) actions. The fact that cross-tolerance and cross-dependence are found between all of these drugs is also convincing evidence of their similarity.

ALCOHOL

Alcohol is the most versatile of the depressants. It is a food, yielding calories in the form of carbohydrates when ingested, as well as a depressant. Prolonged, excessive alcohol intake produces effects that result, somewhat paradoxically,

---

[1] For more detailed treatments of these drugs, see Levitt and Krikstone (1975), and Wilcox and Levitt (1975).

TABLE 14–4

Some Common Depressants

Drug class	Common or generic names	Trade names	Slang names	Usual dose
Alcohol, ethanol, ethyl alcohol	Scotch, bourbon, gin, vodka, wine, beer, etc.	Chivas Regal, Strawberry Hill, Coors, etc.	Booze	20–100 milliliters of pure alcohol
Barbiturates	Secobarbital	Seconal	Redbirds, red devils, reds, seccies	50–200 milligrams
	Pentobarbital	Nembutal	Yellow jackets, yellows, nimbies	100 milligrams
	Amobarbital	Amytal	Blue heavens, blue devils, blue birds	30–200 milligrams
	Phenobarbital	Luminal	Purple hearts	15–100 milligrams
	Secobarbital plus amobarbital	Tuinal	Tooies, rainbows, christmas trees, double trouble	50–200 milligrams
Nonbarbiturate sedatives	Glutethimide	Doriden		125–250 milligrams
	Methaqualone	Quaalude, Sopor, Parest	Quaas, sopers, ludes	75–300 milligrams
	Chloral hydrate	Noctec, Somnos	Knockout drops	.5–2.0 grams
	Bromides	Bromo Seltzer, Miles Nervine		3–5 grams
Antianxiety agents	Meprobamate	Miltown, Equanil		400–800 milligrams
	Chlordiazepoxide	Librium		5–20 milligrams
	Diazepam	Valium		2–10 milligrams

from the beverage's nutritive value (1½ ounces of whiskey contains about 120 calories). An individual ingesting large volumes of alcohol has little appetite for other food, but has not ingested proteins, minerals, or vitamins. Therefore, in chronic alcoholics certain of the toxic symptoms result from these deficiencies, rather than from the effects of the alcohol itself. The suggestion has been made that alcoholic beverages favored by alcoholics be fortified with proteins, vitamins, and minerals. Critics of this idea believe that it is immoral, and might encourage alcoholism.

Alcohol is the natural product of the action of yeast on the sugars present in fruits and vegetables. This process is called *fermentation*. Under certain conditions fermentation occurs naturally, without human intervention. Early in the history of the human race, the pleasant effects of ingesting naturally fermented beverages were discovered, and humanity domesticated the fermentation process for its own use.

Types of alcoholic beverages include the products of fermentation (beer and wine, containing 4–12% alcohol) and distilled spirits (whiskey, vodka, gin, etc., containing 40–50% alcohol). In distillation, the fermented fluid is heated just to the boiling point of alcohol, which is lower than that of water. The alcohol is thus converted into a gas, which is carried by tubes to a vat where it is cooled and converted back into a liquid.

DRUNKENNESS (ACUTE INTOXICATION). Bodily alcohol concentration is mainly determined by the percentage of alcohol in the beverage, the amount of beverage ingested, and the body weight of the imbibing individual. Figure 14-1 shows the effects of consumption in a 150-pound person. Alcohol is more water-soluble than it is fat-soluble, and since women have more fat tissue than men, a woman of equal weight generally has a higher blood alcohol level and more signs of drunkenness than a man who has consumed the same amount of alcohol in the same time period.

Alcohol ingestion produces initial increases in blood pressure, pulse rate, and heart output. These short-lived effects are due to an alcohol-induced release of epinephrine and norepinephrine from the adrenal medulla. The individual also experiences a flushed complexion and feeling of warmth, which result from dilation of peripheral blood vessels. This is an action produced not by the alcohol itself, but by one of its metabolites, acetaldehyde. The increase in urine output following alcohol ingestion results from a blocking action of alcohol on the release of antidiuretic hormone from the posterior lobe of the pituitary gland.

Alcohol acts as a stimulant only by releasing cerebral cortex inhibitions on subcortical systems involved in emotional behavior. At all levels of the nervous system the principal action of alcohol is depression. Alcohol, however, by first depressing the higher brain centers, which have inhibitory effects on behavior, has an initially stimulating effect. Tensions and inhibitions are reduced, and the individual may experience an expansive feeling of sociability and well-being. Larger amounts interfere with thinking, motor coordination, speech, and vision. Pain and other perceptions are also blunted. Finally, the individual lapses into a drunken stupor and falls asleep.

The notion that alcohol has aphrodisiac properties is untrue. According to Masters and Johnson (1966), "The syndrome of overindulgence has particular application to alcohol. While under its influence, many a male of any age has failed for the first time to achieve or maintain an erection. . . . Secondary impotence . . . has a higher incidence of direct association with excessive alcohol consumption than with any other factor [p. 67]." Rubin and Henson (personal communication) have recently provided the first experimental demonstration of alcohol's inhibitory action on sexual responding. They found that the ingestion of moderate to large amounts of alcohol inhibited erection of the penis in males exposed to erotic films. That the effects of alcohol on sexual behavior are due to a

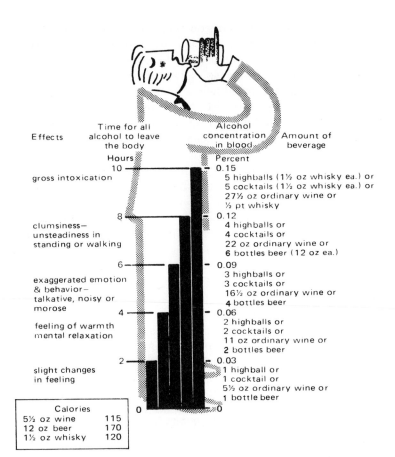

Effects	Time for all alcohol to leave the body	Alcohol concentration in blood	Amount of beverage
	Hours	Percent	

gross intoxication — 10 — 0.15
5 highballs (1½ oz whisky ea.) or
5 cocktails (1½ oz whisky ea.) or
27½ oz ordinary wine or
½ pt whisky

clumsiness—unsteadiness in standing or walking — 8 — 0.12
4 highballs or
4 cocktails or
22 oz ordinary wine or
6 bottles beer (12 oz ea.)

— 6 — 0.09
3 highballs or
3 cocktails or
16½ oz ordinary wine or
4 bottles beer

exaggerated emotion & behavior—talkative, noisy or morose — 4 — 0.06
2 highballs or
2 cocktails or
11 oz ordinary wine or
2 bottles beer

feeling of warmth mental relaxation

slight changes in feeling — 2 — 0.03
1 highball or
1 cocktail or
5½ oz ordinary wine or
1 bottle beer

— 0 — 0

Calories	
5½ oz wine	115
12 oz beer	170
1½ oz whisky	120

Figure 14–1. Alcohol levels in the blood after drinks taken on an empty stomach by a 150-pound person. (Reprinted by permission from *Time, The Weekly Newsmagazine,* April 22, 1974. Copyright Time, Inc.)

loss of inhibition and not to increased coital capacity has been ably phrased by Shakespeare (in *Macbeth,* act 2, scene 3):

> *MacDuff:* What things does drink especially provoke?
> *Porter:* Lechery, sir, it provokes, and unprovokes; it provokes the desire, but takes away the performance.

HANGOVER (ACUTE WITHDRAWAL).   The hangover is a state of drug withdrawal less completely developed than that seen with severe, chronic abuse. The symptoms of hangover include tremors, fatigue, vertigo, throbbing headache, nausea, vomiting, acidosis, and dehydration with persistent thirst. Treatment most logically begins with restraint during the period of ingestion, but additional prophylactic measures may be carried out before retiring. Vomiting may be induced with little difficulty to remove some of the absorbed alcohol. Fluids for dehydration, aspirin for headache, and sodium bicarbonate for the acidosis may also be taken.

TOLERANCE. Two kinds of tolerance are observable following chronic alcohol consumption: lowered blood alcohol levels at equal doses (metabolic tolerance), and decreased behavioral decrement at equal blood alcohol levels (tissue tolerance). Human subjects receiving constant daily doses of alcohol showed a continual decline in blood levels until eventually a near-zero level was reached. Thus, though a constant amount of alcohol was entering the body, each day successively smaller portions of the total dose were found in the blood. This is because the liver became progressively more efficient in metabolizing the alcohol.

Clearly, in these subjects, a process of compensation in the homeostatic mechanisms was occurring. This "return" to equilibrium conditions, however, does not indicate normality. Alcohol ingestion is now as necessary for normal function as are protein, minerals, or vitamins. When the drug is withdrawn, the nervous system rebounds to a new, higher activity level, since the depressing effect of the alcohol is no longer present. The amount of dreaming, for example, shows a rather dramatic increase. Alcoholics, and also barbiturate addicts, may experience intense nightmares and hallucinations during drug withdrawal. These phenomena may drive the patient back to alcohol or barbiturates to relieve either the nightmares or the hallucinations or both (Jaffe, 1975).

PHYSICAL DEPENDENCE. The toxicity that develops following chronic alcohol use is due to two causes. First, many alcoholics suffer a nutritional deficit associated with the "empty calories" (containing no proteins, vitamins, or minerals) provided by alcoholic beverages. Second, no matter what the nutritional status of the individual, chronic ingestion of large amounts of alcohol exerts a direct toxic action on the body. The disease states that occur as a result of alcohol ingestion may loosely be divided into non-CNS and CNS disturbances. The non-CNS disturbances include anemia, resulting from a deficiency of iron and certain B-complex vitamins; pellagra, characterized by extensive dermatitis and inflammation of mucous membranes (due to deficiency of another B-complex vitamin, niacin); cardiac beriberi, or heart failure from prolonged high output due to thiamine (another B vitamin) deficiency; and cirrhosis of the liver. The CNS disturbances include the withdrawal syndrome delirium tremens), Wernicke's syndrome, and Korsakoff's psychosis (Dreyfus, 1971).

Liver cirrhosis is a disease characterized by inflammation and hardening of the liver tissue. There is some controversy as to whether this disorder is due solely to nutritional deficits (protein, minerals, and vitamins) or whether there is some direct effect of alcohol (Dreyfus, 1971; Meyers, Jawetz, & Goldfien, 1972). The weight of the evidence suggests that, though a nutritional deficit may complicate the picture by impairing the actions of a damaged liver, direct toxic action of the alcohol may play a chief part. Chronic alcoholics develop three major types of liver disease: fatty liver, alcoholic hepatitis, and cirrhosis (Gall & Mostof, 1973). Although fatty liver is reversible when the alcohol is discontinued, alcoholic hepatitis appears not to be easily reversed. Inflammation and death of liver tissue are among the characteristic features of the disorder. Both fatty liver and alcoholic hepatitis have been produced in baboons apparently as a direct result of alcohol toxicity. The diets of these animals contained excess proteins, vitamins, and minerals; and pair-fed controls receiving the same diet with isocaloric substitution of sucrose for alcohol showed no degenerative changes upon microscopic examination of liver biopsy specimens. In contrast, the alcohol-fed animals showed marked changes (Rubin & Lieber, 1973).

The various syndromes associated with CNS dysfunction due to alcohol are not separate entities. In an individual classified as having Korsakoff's psychosis, for example, the signs of Wernicke's syndrome will probably be present also. These disturbances all have the same basic etiology: alcohol. Because of its rich vascularization, high degree of irritability, and limited storage capacity for nutrients, CNS tissue is especially vulnerable to chronic alcohol intake. Brain damage and associated mental deterioration have been reported in alcoholic patients with no clinical history of malnutrition (Haug, 1968; Tumarkin, Wilson, & Snyder, 1955). Thus, it is likely that alcohol exerts toxic effects on CNS function and learning despite adequate nutrition.

Cerebral beriberi (which includes both Korsakoff's psychosis and Wernicke's syndrome) is a clinical syndrome associated with shortage of the water-soluble vitamins (especially thiamine). Confusion, disorientation, and amnesia characterize the Korsakoff psychosis. The gradual loss of memory in chronic alcoholics can be permanent if the disease has progressed sufficiently; it appears to involve more recent memories first and then gradually progress further back in time. The Korsakoff psychosis proper is distinguished from simple withdrawal by the duration and intensity of symptoms, which lead to another manifest feature of the psychosis: the tendency to fill in memory gaps by making up answers to questions. This tendency, called *confabulation*, should not be considered a distinct entity. It may be a natural result of the individual's efforts to maintain self-esteem in the face of frightening amounts of confusion and memory loss (Merritt, 1967).

Wernicke's syndrome is manifested by a sudden paralysis of the muscles controlling eye movements, by an inability to maintain balance when walking (ataxia), and by disturbances of consciousness (amnesia, disorientation with respect to time and place). This disorder, like Korsakoff's psychosis, may be produced in complete abstainers who have the appropriate nutritional deficit. *Beriberi* is merely a generic term for a symptom pattern endemic to the Orient, produced by a diet deficient in the B vitamins (for example, consisting primarily of polished rice). However, the direct toxic effects of alcohol almost certainly add further stress to an already damaged nervous system, just as was noted in the case of liver cirrhosis.

Probably the best way to conceptualize the CNS disorders in alcoholics is as a vitamin deficiency disease, complicated by the direct toxicity of alcohol. The term *cerebral beriberi* is used to characterize the entire disorder; *Wernicke's syndrome* refers to the neurological consequences and *Korsakoff's psychosis* to the disorders of behavior and thought processes.

WITHDRAWAL SYNDROME.   In both alcoholic and nonalcoholic individuals, an immediate sequel to about 2 weeks of excessive drinking is delirium tremens (the

Alcoholism is the most destructive form of drug abuse in the United States today—and few alcoholics are loners like this Skid Row derelict. Most alcoholics have jobs, families, responsibilities. As a result, their addiction typically disrupts a wide circle of personal relationships. (Lawrence Fink)

DTs) which occurs when the depressant effects of the alcohol are wearing off. This withdrawal syndrome begins with restlessness, tremor, copious sweating, insomnia, and a headache. The second stage may include nightmares, hallucinations, delirium, and convulsions in any combination. The agitated, muttering, anxious patient is constantly in motion: picking at the bedclothes to remove fancied insects, snakes, or rodents; wandering around; or screaming. People, objects, even the date and time are unknown. All comprehension centers on the illusory, scurrying roaches and rats covering the person's body; around the all-too-real drenching sweat, high fever, and trip-hammering heart. After 3–5 days of this suffering, the patient falls into a sudden sleep, to awaken many hours later, with the DTs gone and no memory of the entire episode.

BARBITURATES

Barbiturates are used clinically in the treatment of insomnia, anxiety, and epilepsy, and in anesthesia. The many drugs in this class differ primarily in the time they take to act and in their length of action. There are long-lasting (phenobarbital), intermediate-acting (amobarbital, pentobarbital, secobarbital) and short-acting (thiopental) barbiturates.

ACUTE TOXICITY.   In contrast to alcohol, barbiturates do not appear to harm the liver, even in physically dependent individuals. In the doses normally used to induce sleep, the sleep is normal and dreams are not suppressed. Further, these doses can be ingested over many months without the development of physical dependence. However, larger doses do suppress dreaming and do lead to physical dependence; withdrawal in a dependent individual, moreover, is followed by dream rebound, nightmares, and hallucinations, as in alcoholics.

HANGOVER.   Even a short-acting barbiturate taken before retiring may result in complaints of dizziness and weakness the following morning. This hangover is very similar to that seen with alcohol, or to that following use of general anesthetics such as ether.

CHRONIC TOXICITY.   Abrupt barbiturate withdrawal following chronic consumption of large quantities results in delirium and convulsions. The delirium may consist of delusions, visual or auditory hallucinations, and disorientation with respect to time and place. The syndrome mirrors that which follows abrupt alcohol withdrawal. Several studies have established the parallel between the barbiturates and alcohol; one small-scale experiment, conducted at the United States Public Health Service Hospital in Lexington, Kentucky, is of special interest because of the many details it provides.

Dr. Harris Isbell and his associates (1950) compared acute and chronic barbiturate intoxication and withdrawal with that due to alcohol. Before the study, five prisoner volunteers serving sentences for narcotics violations were given a battery of neurological and psychological tests. Then, in an isolated hospital research ward, the first phase of the study began. Each volunteer was given a large dose of pentobarbital. Both pentobarbital and alcohol are depressants with a short onset to action and a brief duration of activity within the body. The result was an intoxication that resembled alcohol in "almost all respects." The manifest psychological signs included a lowered performance on the battery of psychological tests. The neurological signs, such as tremors and incoordination, were also indicative of individuals who were "dead drunk." The signs of the intoxication disappeared in about the same time that an equally large dose of alcohol would take to wear off (5 hours). The subjects slept poorly that night, as is common following an evening of alcohol ingestion, and they complained of hangover (nervousness, tremulousness, loss of appetite, and headache) the following day.

The second phase of the experiment consisted of an attempt to reproduce by means of barbiturates all the behavioral signs of chronic alcoholism. For more than 3 months, doses of pentobarbital were given five times a day, from an initial "eye opener" before breakfast to a nightcap at 11 P.M. This method of administration was designed to duplicate the ingestion pattern seen with chronic alcoholics. Generally, the signs of intoxication were minimal early in the morning and increased throughout the day. The subjects' behavior and appearance were indistinguishable from that of skid row alcoholics (Brecher, 1972).

The most impressive demonstration of the barbiturate–alcohol parallel occurred following withdrawal of the pentobarbital. The barbiturate DTs were found to be just as serious as DTs due to alcohol withdrawal; in fact the barbiturate DTs were indistinguishable from those produced by withdrawal from their liquid counterpart. The short-acting barbiturates (such as pentobarbital in this study) may be termed *solid alcohols* with some justification.

The similarity between depressants is highlighted by the phenomenon of cross-tolerance discussed earlier. Alcoholic DTs may be terminated by a dose of alcohol, by administration of a barbiturate (usually phenobarbital), or by administration of any other depressant. It is easier to give a pill than to administer ether but there is no logical reason why an anesthetic could not be used to end DTs. By the same token, an individual feeling the initial signs of withdrawal from secobarbital can stop the incipient full-blown reaction by taking a few drinks.

The parallel among depressants includes the anesthetics, as we have suggested. Ether was used for recreational purposes as early as the eighteenth century (Nagle, 1968). By the mid-1880s it had become the chief substitute for alcohol in Northern Ireland. This massive changeover from one drug to another occurred because the British government placed a high tax on alcoholic beverages while the local constabulary cracked down on the sale and production of home-distilled Irish whiskey. Ether was not subject to a tax and was produced in London. It was no great problem, therefore, to ship huge amounts to Draperstown and other places in Ireland. The drug was preferred in some ways to whiskey: Its effect was almost instantaneous; it was cheap; it could be ingested several times a day without hangover; if arrested for drunkenness, "the offender would be sober by the time the police station was reached [Nagle, 1968, p. 28]." A surgeon visiting Draperstown in 1878 remarked that the main street smelled like his surgery (where ether was used as an anesthetic). Old ether "topers" could (by this surgeon's report) finish off a 3-ounce wineglassful of ether at a single swig without even taking water for a chaser. Under normal circumstances, ether is not used recreationally because of its vile burning taste. We suspect it would eventually damage the gastric system, and that it is likely to share the other dangers of alcohol and the barbiturates.

NONBARBITURATE SEDATIVES

There are a number of nonbarbiturate sedatives. They are very similar to the barbiturates in their clinical usefulness, and in their dangers. In fact, they are chemical relatives of the barbiturates or of alcohol. Tolerance and physical dependence are seen with all these agents. They differ from each other, as do the barbiturates, primarily in their length of action. The following discussion will focus on the most interesting features and peculiarities of some of these agents.

Chloral hydrate has been used as a sedative since the mid-nineteenth century. The combination of several drops of chloral hydrate in an alcoholic beverage produces the infamous "Mickey Finn" or "knockout drops," used to sedate sailors who were then shanghaied aboard ship for the trip from California to the Orient. *Thalidomide* is a member of this class that was used clinically in the early 1960s until it was found to induce fetal abnormalities. The *bromides* were introduced in the mid-nineteenth century for the treatment of epilepsy. They are, in fact, moderately effective in controlling this disorder, even though the rationale for their original use was incorrect. Epilepsy was thought to be a consequence of masturbation or coitus interruptus, and the bromides were thought to inhibit the seizures because they had the anaphrodisiac property of reducing sexual desire. *Methaqualone* has been used clinically in Europe for over a decade. Physicians frequently prescribe it as a sleeping pill or tranquilizer. For some reason, it has become inordinately popular as a street "downer," and rapidly has become one of the most notorious of the abused drugs.

ANTIANXIETY AGENTS

These drugs are also called the minor tranquilizers. They are typical depressants, producing sedation and muscle relaxation. They can also produce tolerance and physical dependence, but not at therapeutic doses. Only high doses over extensive time periods will lead to physical dependence. The main drugs in this category are meprobamate, chlordiazepoxide, and diazepam.

The *antipsychotic agents,* also called the major tranquilizers, are mentioned here only for the sake of completeness. These drugs are not currently abused. They do not produce physical dependence, and even psychological dependence is not well established. The antipsychotic tranquilizers are, in fact, a completely different drug group from the antianxiety tranquilizers. Antipsychotic agents include the phenothiazines (for example, chlorpromazine, trade name Thorazine), the butyrophenones (for example, haloperidol, trade name Haldol), and the thioxanthenes (for example, chlorprothixene, trade name Taractan). They are effective primarily in the treatment of schizophrenia. Chlorpromazine, especially, is also used as an antiemetic (a substance that inhibits vomiting) and as an antidote for the effects of LSD and the other hallucinogens.

Narcotics

The narcotics have brought great benefits to humanity because of their ability to relieve pain and suffering, and they have caused great harm because of their high potential for the development of physical dependence.[2] The narcotics have both sedative and analgesic properties. They include drugs derived from the opium poppy, *Papaver somniferum,* and a number of synthetic drugs that have similar properties to those derived from opium. Opium is the latexlike material that exudes through a cut in the seedpod of the plant. Morphine and codeine are two of the chemicals that may be extracted from opium. Heroin may be produced by chemical treatment of morphine. Methadone (Dolophine) and meperidine (Demerol) are two totally synthetic narcotic analgesic drugs.

Knowledge of the narcotic properties of opium goes back at least to 4000 B.C. It was used by the ancient Egyptians, Greeks, and Romans. In modern times, opium was reintroduced to the Western world by the Arab and Moorish physicians who entered southern Europe from North Africa. The Arab traders also carried opium to the Orient, where the social smoking of dried opium was popularized in the eighteenth century. In Europe the custom was opium eating rather than smoking. Opium came to have a significant effect on English literature. Elizabeth Barrett Browning was addicted to it. Thomas De Quincey wrote of visions seen under the influence of opium, and *Kubla Khan* was written by Coleridge supposedly upon awakening from an opium dream.

The development of the hypodermic syringe by Alexander Wood in 1853 ushered in the more serious problems resulting from the injection of opiates. Wood's wife holds the distinction of being the first person to die from an injected overdose of morphine (Cohen, 1970). Sigmund Freud also died from an overdose of morphine. In the terminal stages of cancer of the jaw, he asked his physician to administer the overdose so that he could be relieved of his misery (Schur, 1972).

In the early United States, opiate use advanced on two fronts. Chinese workers, imported to build the western rail lines, brought with them the social custom of opium smoking. The patent medicines of the time also contained opiates in addition to alcohol, and were responsible for the widespread development of physical dependence. In the late 1800s over 1% of the United States population is estimated to have been dependent on opiates, primarily from the use of patent medicines.

Because of the ease of obtaining opiates and their low price, the problems of the narcotic addict were similar to those of the alcoholic. However, the Harrison Narcotic Act of 1914 changed the situation of the opiate addict in the United States by making the nonprescription sale of opiates a criminal offense, thereby removing narcotic drugs from the open market. Law enforcement officers also interpreted the Act to forbid a physician from prescribing an opiate to maintain the addiction of an addict. The narcotic addict was thus forced to obtain opiates by illegal means. Current estimates of the number of opiate addicts in this country are on the order of 300,000. Several thousand die each year, very few from

---

[2] For more detailed treatments of these drugs see Criswell and Levitt (1975), and Jaffe and Martin (1975).

the drugs themselves, but from hepatitis from unsterile injection equipment, allergic reactions to drug impurities, and other factors associated with the illegal status of these drugs.

ACUTE EFFECTS

MORPHINE. Morphine is the narcotic most frequently used for the relief of severe pain. It is administered by injection; an average dose is about 10 milligrams. It is not taken orally because it is deactivated by the enzymes of the stomach and intestines. Morphine and the other narcotics do *not* act on the pain receptors themselves, but inhibit systems in the brain that mediate the effects of aversive stimuli. Thus, these drugs reduce the neurological and psychological effects of pain.

The narcotics also produce euphoria in some individuals. This sleepy, relaxed "high" feeling is not, however, a universal phenomenon. Of normal individuals not in pain, only about 10% find the effects of an injection of morphine pleasant; 50% find it neutral and fully 40% find it unpleasant. It may be that patients in pain and individuals suffering from psychological distress are more likely to experience euphoric or pleasant effects from the narcotics. One possibility is that the analgesia and euphoria share a common mechanism of action. Both may result from the blocking of a brain mechanism that is responsible for aversion, the emotional reaction to aversion, or both.

A common unpleasant effect of morphine is nausea. Other actions include constriction of the pupils of the eyes and a constipating action on the stomach and intestines. Very little tolerance develops to these effects, and so pupillary constriction and constipation are common in dependent narcotic addicts. Another important effect of morphine, the one responsible for overdose death, is an inhibition of mechanisms in the brain stem that maintain respiration.

CODEINE. The pharmacology of codeine is similar to that of morphine with two notable exceptions: (1) Codeine is only one-twelfth as powerful as morphine on a dose-for-dose basis. (2) The ratio of oral to injected effectiveness for codeine is higher than that for morphine. Codeine retains about two-thirds of its effectiveness when taken orally as compared to injection. Morphine, on the other hand, retains only about one-thirtieth of its potency when taken orally. It has often been stated that codeine is less addicting than morphine, but if equal analgesic doses are used, there is no difference in the addictive properties of the two drugs (Jaffe, 1975). There is, therefore, no reason to use codeine over morphine if the route of administration is injection. The higher oral efficiency of codeine has led to its use in orally administered analgesics and antitussives (cough suppressants). For the relief of minor pain and coughing, relatively small amounts of codeine are effective and present little addictive liability. For this purpose, codeine is often compounded with other, nonnarcotic analgesics such as aspirin. The combination of these drugs (codeine and aspirin) gives greater analgesia than that produced by either drug alone.

HEROIN. This is a semisynthetic narcotic formed from morphine by a slight chemical change of the morphine molecule. Chemically, heroin is diacetyl morphine. Heroin itself has little pharmacological activity but is converted in the brain to morphine. It is morphine rather than the heroin that is responsible for the analgesic and other narcotic properties for which heroin is known (Way, 1968). If the primary active product of heroin is morphine, one might ask how there could be differences in action between the two drugs. In particular, why is heroin known to be more powerful than morphine on a dose-for-dose basis? The answer is that there is a barrier between the blood and the brain that makes it difficult for morphine to enter the brain. This barrier is less effective against heroin, allowing it to enter the brain more rapidly and possibly in greater concentration than morphine. For this reason, heroin is a more potent drug than morphine and its faster onset of action results in a "rush," which is valued by the narcotic addict. Since there is no difference between the action of morphine and heroin on pain perception, but there is an increased addiction risk for heroin, heroin is not used for medical purposes in the United States. In Great Britain, heroin is used in clinical medicine and there are reports that it is more effective than morphine for certain uses (for example, to achieve postoperative analgesia in children). The potency and rapid onset of action with heroin, however, make it the choice for illicit use in both the United States and Great Britain (Jaffe, 1975; Jaffe & Martin, 1975).

The history of heroin use began in 1874 when it was first synthesized from morphine. In 1898, it was placed on the market by the Bayer Company in Germany as a nonaddicting substitute for morphine. Early studies published in the *New York Medical Journal* in 1900 indicated that it was a relatively safe drug with only minor addicting properties. Within a few years, however, the true addicting properties of heroin became known (it is, if anything, more addicting than morphine). This information, together with the Harrison Act of 1914, which made the unauthorized possession and sale of narcotics illegal, removed heroin use from the medical sphere to the underworld (Ray, 1972).

Presently, except for research purposes, heroin is available in the United States only through illegal channels. The pusher prefers heroin to morphine because it is approximately three times as potent (since more of it penetrates the blood–brain barrier in comparison to morphine); for that reason, smaller amounts need to be smuggled into the country. The user prefers heroin to other narcotics because of its more rapid onset of action.

METHADONE. Methadone is a synthetic narcotic analgesic developed in Germany toward the end of World War II. Although it is somewhat similar to morphine in action, methadone has some very important differences. Methadone can be administered by injection or orally and is only about twice as potent by injection as orally. The onset of action is slow, with peak analgesia occurring after 1 or 2 hours. The clinical use of methadone includes its use as an analgesic that, because of its high ratio of oral to injected effectiveness, can be given orally for the control of moderate to severe pain. It is also used in the treatment of heroin addiction, where either of two different procedures may be employed. The first procedure involves transferring dependence from heroin to methadone, which produces milder withdrawal symptoms, and then withdrawing the person from methadone. The second involves transfer of the dependence from heroin to methadone and then maintaining the addict on oral methadone rather than injected heroin.

CHRONIC EFFECTS

OVERDOSE. Recently, detailed studies of deaths that were reported to have resulted from heroin overdose have failed to find evidence of elevated levels of heroin or morphine (the active metabolic product of heroin) in the blood of many of the overdose victims. The commonly observed syndrome of cardiovascular collapse and pulmonary edema, resulting in death, can occur apparently as a result of the injection of relatively small doses of heroin. Syndrome X, as it has been called, may account for a high percentage of the deaths that have been labeled as heroin overdose. The mechanism behind Syndrome X is not known, but it has been suggested that an allergic response to the heroin or to the adulterants commonly mixed with the heroin sold on the street may be responsible. Whatever the causative agent, the response is extremely rapid and victims are often found with the needle still in their arm. The rapidity of the response, its unknown etiology, and apparent occurrence following small doses of narcotic drugs is quite unexpected. The possible causes of this phenomenon are now under study. There is also growing evidence that many apparent heroin suicides may have been the unexpected consequence of a normal dose of heroin (Brecher, 1972).

TOLERANCE. A great deal of tolerance to morphine and heroin may develop rapidly in former addicts. In one study, the effective dose of morphine increased from 18 to 180 milligrams over a 19-day period (Martin & Fraser, 1961). Another experimental addiction study produced a patient with an intake of 1380 milligrams of morphine over a 24-hour period. This is well above the lethal dose for a nontolerant person. A 3-month period was required to produce this high degree of tolerance (Murphree, 1971). Tolerance develops much more rapidly and lasts longer than was once thought; it has been demonstrated as much as 15 months after a single large injection of morphine (Murphree, 1971). Tolerance presents a special problem to the illicit user of narcotic drugs who, as tolerance develops, must increase intake in order to ward off the withdrawal syndrome. If the user then abstains from narcotic intake for a period of time sufficient to decrease tolerance, death can result from the same dose of narcotic that previously was only effective in warding off the withdrawal syndrome for a few hours. Addicts have been known to enter treatment centers and go through withdrawal simply to reduce their tolerance and, therefore, the expense of their habit. These people often return to their drug-taking behavior only to reenter the treatment center again when, because of their increased tolerance, they can no longer afford the large quantities of narcotic drugs needed to sustain them.

TABLE 14–5

Sequence of Appearance of Some of the Abstinence Syndrome Symptoms

Signs	Number of hours after last dose (approximate)		
	Heroin	Morphine	Methadone
Craving for drugs, anxiety	4	6	12
Yawning, perspiration, running nose, tearing eyes	8	14	34–48
Increase in above signs plus pupil dilation, goose bumps (piloerection), tremors (muscle twitches), hot and cold flashes, aching bones and muscles, loss of appetite	12	16	48–72
Increased intensity of above signs, plus insomnia; raised blood pressure; increased temperature, pulse rate, respiratory rate and depth; restlessness; nausea	18–24	24–36	
Increased intensity of above, plus curled-up position, vomiting, diarrhea, weight loss, spontaneous ejaculation or orgasm	26–36	36–48	

PHYSICAL DEPENDENCE.   As tolerance increases, the body gradually develops a physical dependence upon narcotic drugs. This physical dependence is manifested by the appearance of the *withdrawal* or *abstinence syndrome* upon sudden discontinuance of the narcotic drugs. Several of the symptoms comprising the abstinence syndrome are listed in Table 14-5. It can be seen that many of the symptoms of withdrawal from the narcotic drugs represent reversals of the drug's original effects. Thus, the analgesia produced by morphine is replaced during withdrawal by aches and pains and the somnolence by hyperactivity and arousal.

Probably the most serious consequence of the chronic intake of narcotic drugs is the development of a strong desire to continue taking these drugs, even in the face of severe hardship resulting from the drug intake. Drug-taking behavior in the narcotic addict is supported by the rewarding effects of the drug and by the removal of an aversive stimulus (the abstinence syndrome) as a result of drug intake. As both psychological and physical dependence result from the continued use of narcotic drugs, it is not surprising that discontinuing the use of these drugs is extremely difficult.

Stimulants

Although stimulants, like narcotics, can lead to psychological dependence, they do not lead to a true physical dependence and withdrawal syndrome. Some tolerance to their stimulant actions does develop, and with it a tendency to increase dosage. High doses can produce repetitive stereotypical movements and a toxic psychosis sometimes closely resembling paranoid schizophrenia; however, the drug-induced psychosis is only temporary. Stroke and death have occasionally resulted from the increase in blood pressure these agents tend to produce. Although individuals on high stimulant doses are hyperkinetic and confused, these drugs are not nearly as dangerous to life as was once thought (Jaffe, 1975).[3]

AMPHETAMINES

The three main amphetamines, which possess very similar chemical formulas and actions, are amphetamine (Benzedrine, bennies), dextroamphetamine (Dexedrine, dexies, copilots), and methamphetamine (Desoxyn, Methedrine, meth, speed, white cross). Administration of amphetamines to humans tends to promote wakefulness, cause some elevation of mood (euphoria), and decrease feelings of fatigue; it also may improve learning or athletic performance. These effects are more pronounced in sleepy or fatigued individuals. Amphetamines are thus prescribed for a variety of conditions that are not actually medical problems. The effects of amphetamines are quite dose-dependent; high doses cause an intoxication that is incompatible with optimal functioning. Prolonged use is almost invariably followed by mental depression and fatigue (Weiss & Laties, 1962).

The amphetamines are used therapeutically in the treatment of depressive states. They have been administered to children with certain behavioral problems—the so-called *hyperkinetic syndrome*. In these children a paradoxical calming effect is found. The amphetamines are also used to relieve the hangover and depression following alcohol abuse and to counteract the depression from poisoning with depressant drugs such as the barbiturates. Narcolepsy, a disease of unknown etiology characterized by an inability to stay awake, has also been successfully relieved with amphetamines.

When the amphetamines are self-administered, the usual goal is arousal or euphoria. They may also be prescribed for their arousal effect. In occupations such as space flight, naval sonar operation, and military activities, the amphetamines are commonly used to maintain alertness. Since psychotic reactions accompanied by hallucinations and delusions may occur with high doses or prolonged use, this kind of use is not without its risks.

CAFFEINE

Caffeine is a CNS stimulant, which explains much of its use. At a dose of 150 to 250 milligrams (about two cups of brewed coffee or three cups of instant coffee) the cerebral cortex shows an EEG of arousal, and a person reports mood elevation and difficulty in going to sleep. Ritchie (1970b) states that the action of caffeine is to:

> . . . produce a more rapid and clearer flow of thought, and to allay drowsiness and fatigue. After taking caffeine one is capable of a greater sustained intellectual

[3] For more detailed treatment of these drugs see Krikstone and Levitt (1975b) and Levitt and Lonowski (1975).

effort and a more perfect association of ideas. There is also a keener appreciation of sensory stimuli, and reaction time to them is appreciably diminished. . . . In addition, motor activity is increased; typists, for example, work faster and with fewer errors [p. 359].

TOLERANCE AND DEPENDENCE.   A large degree of tolerance may develop to caffeine's diuretic (increased urine flow) and vasodilator actions, but little or no tolerance develops to its CNS stimulation effects. Many people develop considerable dependence on caffeine. This is true in both the habitual user and in the person who just takes a cup or two of coffee in the morning to wake up. The feeling of well-being and alertness and the increased "energy" seem to produce no harm; and the morning cup of coffee has become so ingrained into American life that few would look upon it as a drug habit. Psychological dependence on caffeine, however, is real.

A pathological dependence on caffeine is called *caffeinism* and a typical case history of a patient addicted to caffeine has been described. The patient was a 39-year-old housewife and waitress who had been running a slight fever for 6 months, had lost 20 pounds so that she now weighed 107 pounds, and complained of occasional flushes, chills, insomnia, irritability, and lack of appetite. She was placed in the hospital when antibiotics failed to bring down her temperature, and during her 5-day stay in the hospital, her temperature went down to normal and remained there. The case history of the patient reports that she smoked a pack or more of cigarettes a day and drank between 15 and 18 cups of brewed coffee between 8 A.M. and 4 P.M. When she left the hospital and again resumed her coffee-drinking habit, her temperature began to rise again. Warned that coffee might be producing the symptoms, she stopped drinking the coffee. From then on her sleep improved, her appetite improved, her temperature went back to normal, and she began gaining weight (Reimann, 1967).

COCAINE

Cocaine (coke, snow, candy) is a chemical obtained by extraction from the coca plant (*Erythroxylon coca*) native to Peru. It has a long history of use as a CNS stimulant by the Peruvians living in the Andes (Jaffe, 1975). It is noteworthy that these highlanders characteristically abandon the chewing of coca leaves when they come down from the mountains. After years of continuous use, they do not become physically dependent on the drug. At one time (1885–1906) Coca-Cola contained small amounts of cocaine, but now decocainized coca beans are used in the preparation of this beverage (Kahn, 1960).

The most important chemical action of cocaine is to block nerve conduction upon local application—hence its use as a local anesthetic. However, the most striking systemic effect is that of a general CNS stimulant. The first symptoms seen in humans include talkativeness, restlessness, and excitement. Cognitive abilities do not seem to be debilitated; in fact, they may be heightened. Motor activity is usually well coordinated, at least until higher doses are reached.

After the stimulating effect, however, cocaine produces a pronounced depression. In many cases, the depression then leads the user to another dose of cocaine and hence another stimulation effect, and then another depression, and so on. The contrast between the euphoria produced by the cocaine and the depression following use often leads users to increase the dosage to toxic levels. Toxic dose levels often produce a syndrome resembling schizophrenia, characterized by paranoid ideation, persecutory delusions, and visual, auditory, and tactile hallucinations.

Sigmund Freud, the father of psychoanalysis, was himself a user of cocaine. He described it as "a magical drug" in a letter to his fiancée, Martha, and once wrote that "a small dose lifted me to the heights in a wonderful fashion. I am just now busy collecting the literature for a song of praise to this magical substance [Jones, 1953, p. 84]."

Freud later described a psychosis in his friend (Dr. von Fleichl-Martow) who had been taking 1 gram of cocaine per day; a major symptom was the hallucination of white snakes creeping over his skin. A peculiar characteristic of the hallucinations seen in cocaine toxicity is *formication*—the hallucination that ants, insects, or snakes are crawling along the skin or under it. After this frightening experience with Fleischl, Freud no longer glorified cocaine and became intensely against it (see also Brecher, 1972, pp. 272–277).

Another early user of cocaine is described in the following passage:

[He] took his bottle from the corner of the mantelpiece, and his hypodermic syringe from its neat morocco case. With his long, white nervous fingers he adjusted the delicate needle and rolled back his left shirtcuff. For some little time his eyes rested thoughtfully upon the sinewy forearm and wrist, all dotted and scarred with innumerable puncture-marks. Finally, he thrust the sharp point home, pressed down the tiny piston, and sank back into the velvet-lined armchair with a long sigh of satisfaction.

"Which is it today," I asked, "Morphine or Cocaine?"

The user in this tale is none other than Sherlock Holmes and the questioner is the faithful Dr. Watson (Doyle, 1938, pp. 91–92).

TOLERANCE AND DEPENDENCE.   Cocaine is unusual in several respects. First, it is so rapidly metabolized by the body that little or no tolerance develops to it. Second, it does not show cross-tolerance with the other stimulants. Although psychological dependence may develop to cocaine, physical dependence is not found.

The effects of cocaine were known in medical circles by 1890. In 1914, federal laws classified cocaine as a narcotic and regulated the possession, sale, and use of the drug. This was a misclassification, since cocaine is not at all like the narcotic analgesics. Use of cocaine decreased continually until the 1960s, when its black market sale was relatively small. However, law enforcement cannot be credited for the decrease in cocaine use. Instead, the cocaine user found a new type of drug that would produce similar effects, was cheaper, and was readily available—the amphetamines. Late in the 1960s, when law enforcement officials cracked down on amphetamine sales, the smuggling and black market sale of cocaine increased.

ANTIDEPRESSANTS

These drugs do not produce stimulation when given to a normal healthy human or animal. Curiously, if given to a depressed human or to a sedated animal, they increase affect and arousal. Therefore-they are now widely used in the treatment of depression. There are two groups of such drugs. One group is called the monoamine oxidase inhibitors, and includes isocarboxazid (Marplan), nialamide (Niamid), phenelzine (Nardil), and tranylcypromine (Parnate). The other drug group is called the tricyclic antidepressants, and includes imipramine (Tofranil), amitriptyline (Elavil), desmethylimipramine (Norpramin), and desmethylamitriptyline (Aventyl). Although tolerance does develop to their antidepressant activity, physical dependence has not been found; they have not become a problem with respect to drug abuse.

NICOTINE

Nicotine is a naturally occurring chemical obtained from the tobacco plant. Tobacco was commonly smoked by the American Indians when it was discovered by European explorers in the fifteenth century.

POISONING. Nicotine does not have therapeutic usefulness. It is of great interest because of its widespread use by tobacco smokers and the known dangers associated with smoking. It also can cause toxicological effects as a result of overindulgence in tobacco or accidental contamination from insecticides, many of which contain nicotine. At lethal drug levels there may be little symptomatic warning, as the action of nicotine is extremely rapid. A burning sensation in the mouth and stomach is followed by nausea, salivation, abdominal pain, vomiting, and diarrhea. A cold sweat, headache, dizziness, auditory and visual distortions, confusion, and weakness occur. Respiration is stimulated and blood pressure rises. The pupils are first constricted, because of parasympathetic stimulation, and then dilated, from parasympathetic blockade. The ensuing coma is accompanied by circulatory shock, convulsions, and respiratory paralysis, followed by death (Aviado, 1971).

SMOKING. The average cigarette contains about 2% nicotine (20–30 milligrams) as compared to about 1% in "denicotinized" preparations. A cigar may contain 10 times this amount, or 200–300 milligrams. The acute lethal dose of nicotine for a nonsmoker is between 50 and 75 milligrams, but this level would be difficult to achieve from smoking because nicotine is absorbed very slowly when it is inhaled. A person actually absorbs only 2.5–3.5 milligrams of nicotine from a single cigarette. With this drug dose, the effects observed are comparable to those noted following a 1-milligram dose injected intravenously (Volle & Koelle, 1970). A nonsmoker will usually get sick from smoking only one cigarette. Experienced smokers may smoke many cigarettes or cigars during a day. Fortunately for them, the tolerance they have developed includes tolerance to the lethal effects of tobacco smoke.

Cigarette smoking has generated much interest in the effects of chronic nicotine intake. The heat from the burning tobacco vaporizes the nicotine and about 10% of the available nicotine is inhaled; of this amount, 90% is absorbed into the bloodstream. Smokers also ingest compounds other than nicotine and several of the effects of smoking may result from these other chemicals. In particular, the carcinogenic (cancer-producing) effects of tobacco smoke probably do not directly involve nicotine. Research is currently underway to identify the carcinogenic agents in cigarette smoke and to attempt to produce a "cancerless" cigarette.

ADDICTION.   One important study suggests that, while nicotine has some role in dependence on cigarettes, other substances present in cigarettes and a psychological dependence (or habit) may also be involved. Lucchesi, Schuster, and Emley (1967) had cigarette smokers smoke as much as they wanted while sitting in a laboratory for 6-hour periods and having a chemical solution dripped into a vein. An important feature of this experiment is that the subjects did not know the study had anything to do with smoking. The subjects were permitted to read, smoke, or engage in any other quiet activities. On different days a salt solution or a nicotine solution was administered directly into the vein. When 4 milligrams per hour of nicotine was administered (an amount equal to about two cigarettes) smoking was reduced by 60% compared to saline solution periods. Thus administering nicotine directly into the blood did reduce smoking, suggesting some role for nicotine in addiction to cigarettes. However, the incomplete suppression suggests the operation of other factors; or, perhaps, the amount of nicotine infused (equivalent to two cigarettes per hour) was less than the amount normally smoked.

The buildup of tolerance to nicotine is a part of folklore. Who has not heard of the novice smoker's first cigarette experience? The novice smoker usually cannot tolerate the amount of nicotine present in a single cigarette, but after several years of smoking, the same person may be able to smoke 40 a day without experiencing the toxic symptoms of pallor, sweating, nausea, and vomiting.

Withdrawal from nicotine produces a whole constellation of symptoms in the chronic smoker. These include drowsiness, headache, digestive disorders, sweating, cramps, insomnia, and nervousness (Brecher, 1972). Yet, though narcotic or alcohol addiction often is associated with antisocial behavior, this is seldom seen following chronic nicotine intake. Murder, robbery, mugging, bribery, and extortion are not commonly associated with nicotine addiction. Why? It may be a case of availability rather than pharmacology. Heroin is not generally available and attempts to obtain it lead to socially unacceptable behavior. When heroin or methadone are made readily available to the addict in a maintenance program the incidence of antisocial behavior associated with narcotic addiction declines markedly. In Germany during World War II, tobacco was rationed so that men were allowed only two packs per month and women were allowed only one pack per month. As a result, people stole, bartered, and black-marketed cigarettes—definitely antisocial behavior. American smokers need not face their nicotine addiction or dependence because of the constant availability of the drug.

Hallucinogens

Hallucinogenic drugs have been used for centuries as means of attaining a religious or mystical experience. They are presently used to escape the world in either a religious or a recreational sense. They have been called by a variety of terms. *Psychedelic* emphasizes their "mind-expanding" properties; *psychotomimetic,* the psychoticlike behavior they may produce; and *hallucinogenic,* the hallucinatory sensory experiences they may produce.

It is important to realize that although tolerance (and cross-tolerance) develops to these drugs, there is no physical dependence, and a withdrawal syndrome does not result from their discontinuance. Moreover, deaths directly attributable to their use in the human are rare. As a matter of fact, it is not clear that any cases have been reported in the modern literature of death resulting directly from the toxic effects of a dose. However, accidental or "suicidal" deaths have been reported that may be considered as indirectly caused by these agents.[4]

LSD

LSD (lysergic acid diethylamide) is probably the best known and most researched of the hallucinogens. A synthetic chemical, LSD is the most pharmacologically potent of all of the distorting drugs, with effective doses being calculated in millionths of a gram (micrograms) rather than the more traditional milligram dosage.

THE DISCOVERY OF LSD. On April 16, 1943, Dr. Albert Hofmann, a chemist at the Sandoz Pharmaceutical Laboratories in Basel, Switzerland, became ill and later recorded the following account of his symptoms:

> Later Friday . . . I had to interrupt my laboratory work in the middle of the after-noon and go home, because I was seized with a feeling of great restlessness and mild dizziness. At home, I lay down and sank into a not unpleasant delirium, which was characterized by extremely excited fantasies. In a semiconscious state, with my eyes closed (I felt the daylight to be unpleasantly dazzling), fantastic visions of extraordi-nary realness and with an intense kaleidoscopic play of colors assaulted me. After about two hours this condition disappeared [Hofmann, 1968, pp. 184–185].[5]

---

[4] For a more detailed treatment of these drugs and for a discussion of some of the hallucinogens not included in this chapter, see Krikstone and Levitt (1975a).

[5] This and subsequent quotes cited to Hofmann, 1968 are reprinted from Hofmann, A., Psychotomimetic agents, in A. Burger (Ed.), *Drugs Affecting the Central Nervous System* (Vol. 2), by courtesy of Marcel Dekker, Inc.

At the time of this experience Dr. Hofmann and his colleague, Dr. W. A. Stoll, had been working on derivatives of a fungus called *ergot,* which could not itself have produced these bizarre symptoms. One of these derivatives, nicknamed LSD-25, had been synthesized 5 years earlier. Initial animal testing had indicated that it was not of interest, so it was put on the shelf without human testing. Three days after he wrote his first account in 1943, to find out if this chemical could have produced his bizarre symptoms, Dr. Hofmann ingested what he thought was a small amount and made the following record in his notebook:

April 19, 1943: Preparation of an 0.5% aqueous solution of *d*-lysergic acid diethyl-amide tartrate.

4:20 P.M.: 0.5 cc. (0.25 mg. LSD) ingested orally. The solution is tasteless.

4:50 P.M.: No trace of any effect.

5:00 P.M.: slight dizziness, unrest, difficulty in concentration, visual disturbances, marked desire to laugh [Hofmann, 1968, p. 185].

Dr. Hofmann had begun what now is called an *LSD trip* and he was in for a disturbing, exhausting 6-hour period. After his recovery he noted:

The last words could only be written with great difficulty. I asked my laboratory assistant to accompany me home as I believed that my condition would be a repetition of the disturbance of the previous Friday. While we were still cycling home, however, I had great difficulty in speaking coherently, my field of vision swayed before me, and objects appeared distorted, like images in curved mirrors. I had the impression of being unable to move from the spot, although my assistant told me afterwards that we had cycled at a good pace. . . .

By the time the doctor arrived, the peak of the crisis had already passed. As far as I remember the following were the most outstanding symptoms: vertigo, visual disturbances; the faces of those around me appeared as grotesque, colored masks; marked motor unrest, alternating with paresis; an intermittent heavy feeling in the head, limbs, and the entire body as if they were filled with metal; cramps in the legs, coldness and loss of feeling in the hands; a metallic taste on the tongue; dry, constricted sensation in the throat; feeling of choking; confusion alternating between clear recognition of my condition in which state I sometimes observed, in the manner of an independent, neutral observer, that I shouted half insanely or babbled incoherent words. Occasionally I felt as if I were out of my body.

The doctor found a rather weak pulse but an otherwise normal circulation.

. . . Six hours after ingestion of the LSD-25 my condition had already improved considerably. Only the visual disturbances were still pronounced. Everything seemed to sway and the proportions were distorted like the reflections in the surface of moving water. Moreover, all objects appeared in unpleasant constantly changing colors, the predominant shades being sickly green and blue. When I closed my eyes, an unending series of colorful, very realistic and fantastic images surged in upon me. A remarkable feature was the manner in which all acoustic perceptions (e.g., the noise of a passing car) were transformed into optical effects, every sound causing a corresponding colored hallucination constantly changing in shape and color like pictures in a kaleidoscope. At about 1 o'clock, I fell asleep and awakened next morning somewhat tired but otherwise perfectly well [Hofmann, 1968, pp. 185–186].

The amount of LSD that Hofmann ingested is about five to eight times the normal effective dose. This account of Hofmann's experience is valuable because his experience was uncontaminated with preconceived notions about the drug experience or with specially created stimulating environments (like piercing music, bright posters, and flashing strobe lights). Subsequent to these initial experiments with LSD, scientists in Europe and the United States explored the possibility that LSD was somehow related to the neurophysiological substrates underlying "mental disturbances" like the schizophrenic disorders. Since such a small quantity of LSD (.03–.05 milligrams) is effective in producing bizarre behavior reminiscent of psychotic behavior patterns, it was only reasonable to consider the possible link between the two. The search continues for the neurophysiological link between LSD and the schizophrenic disorders (Byck, 1975).

LSD ART.   There have been many attempts to analyze art drawn under the influence of LSD. Figure 14-2 was drawn by an artist while he was on an LSD trip. Notice the distorted perceptions of the fingers, eyes, nose, and mouth. The entire picture is an example of sensory distortion.

ADVERSE EFFECTS AND HAZARDS OF LSD.   As LSD became more and more popular in the 1960s, the adverse effects and hazards of the drug also became more visible. In a study surveying most of the legal investigations in the United States, Cohen (1960) reported relatively few side effects and complications from LSD. Data were reported from over 25,000 doses in 5000 subjects. In experimental subjects receiving LSD or mescaline, none attempted suicide and .8 out of 1000 reported a psychotic reaction lasting over 48 hours. In patients undergoing psychotherapy, 1.2 out of 1000 attempted suicide, .4 out of 1000 completed suicide, and 1.8 out of 1000 reported a psychotic reaction lasting over 48 hours. In 1963, Cohen and Ditman reflected on these data:

> The actual incidence of serious complications following LSD administration is not known. We believe, however, that they are infrequent. It is surprising that such a profound psychological experience leaves adverse residuals so rarely [p. 479].

The study of adverse reactions to LSD is an emotional area; it is also complex, because of individual differences in those taking it and because of variations in the drug. Brecher (1972) lists 12 reasons for the adverse effects that may be seen. Three of these reasons will be mentioned here.

1. Side effects of law enforcement. In some cases, an individual having a bad trip is imprisoned instead of being helped through the ordeal by a guide. In one example, several people in the San Francisco Haight-Ashbury area had bad trips on LSD distributed at a celebration in a park. Thirty-two users were treated at a local clinic and were returned home or to the care of a friend. Seven others were detained by the police and imprisoned, and later taken to San Francisco General Hospital. A physician

Figure 14–2. This drawing, executed by a well-known Czech artist after recovery from LSD intoxication, illustrates the kind of distorted bodily perception often reported by LSD users. (Courtesy of Panorama Sandoz)

commented that the adverse reactions were due not to the "intensity of the reaction but to its management." A person under the influence of LSD should never be left alone. There is need for supervision, and a guide should always be present. As LSD became more available on the black market, this safeguard was often ignored and people were unable to cope with the drug experience by themselves.

2. Misinterpretation of reaction. In many cases, early tales of side effects came from hospital emergency rooms. Subjects brought in often had their stomachs pumped in order to remove the drug from the system. This is a noxious experience in any case, but probably that much worse under the influence of LSD. In other cases, patients were diagnosed as psychotic and put in psychiatric wards with psychotic patients.

3. Flashbacks. One of the earliest publicized adverse effects was the phenomenon of flashbacks, that is, the sudden recurrence of the LSD experience days, weeks, or months after the drug had been ingested. This led some observers to assume that LSD caused permanent brain damage. Dr. Cohen (1960) in the study quoted earlier, did not report any incidence of flashbacks; as late as 1967 only 11 cases of flashbacks were

reported in the medical literature. One explanation is that all intense emotional experiences may produce flashbacks, whether or not these experiences are LSD-induced. People who have intense emotional experiences—the death of a loved one, the moment of falling in love, the moment of an automobile crash—have reported flashback experiences weeks, months, or years later.

Some investigators have reported that LSD causes chromosomal aberrations. The evidence is contradictory and its significance uncertain. The chromosomal damage from LSD is no greater than that produced by common drugs. In addition, the medical significance of such breakage is uncertain. Breakage has been found in blood or skin cells, but not in the sperm or ova of the male or female reproductive systems. Furthermore, heavy LSD users, in whom chromosomal breakage has been found, tend to use many drugs, have poor nutritional habits, and suffer more from viral and other infections than is normal (Jaffe, 1975; Maugh, 1973).

PSILOCYBIN

The history of the hallucinogenic Mexican mushrooms is closely intertwined with the early Aztec and Mexican cultures. These early cultures used the mushrooms for religious purposes; large stone mushrooms with god figures carved on the stems, dating back to before 9000 B.C., signify the importance of the mushroom to these societies. The Aztecs named the mushrooms *teonanacatl*, which can be translated as "god's flesh" or "sacred mushroom." In the sixteenth century, the use of these mushrooms was banned by the Spanish conquerors of Mexico. Nonetheless, the mushrooms are still being used by Indians in Mexico today.

One of these Mexican mushrooms is *Psilocybe mexicana;* the hallucinogen that has been isolated from it is called *psilocybin*. Albert Hofmann isolated psilocybin in 1958 and later synthesized it. Early users ate the natural mushrooms, but modern experimental usage and "tripping" both rely almost entirely on the synthetic chemical. Before Hofmann synthesized the chemical, he ate 32 of the mushrooms (which is an average dose) and reported the following effects:

Thirty minutes after taking the mushrooms the exterior world began to undergo a strange transformation. Everything assumed a Mexican character. As I was perfectly well aware that my knowledge of the Mexican origin of the mushroom would lead me to imagine only Mexican scenery, I tried deliberately to look on my environment as I knew it normally. But all voluntary efforts to look at things in their customary forms and colors proved ineffective. Whether my eyes were closed or open I saw only Mexican motifs and colors. When the doctor supervising the experiment bent over me to check my blood pressure, he was transformed into an Aztec priest and I would not have been astonished if he had drawn an obsidian knife. In spite of the seriousness of the situation it amused me to see how the Germanic face of my colleague had acquired a purely Indian expression. At the peak of the intoxication, about 1½ hours after ingestion of the mushrooms, the rush of interior pictures, mostly abstract motifs rapidly changing in shape and color, reached such an alarming degree that I feared that I would be torn into this whirlpool of form and color and would dissolve. After about six hours the dream came to an end. Subjectively, I had no idea how long this condition had lasted. I felt my return to everyday reality to be a happy return from a strange, fantastic but quite really experienced world into an old and familiar home [Hofmann, 1968, p. 176].

MESCALINE

Mescaline is one of the alkaloids that may be extracted from the peyote cactus. The drug has a long history of ceremonial religious use by early Mexican Indians (the Mescaleros, hence the derivation of its name) and is used even now by the Native American Church during rituals and ceremonies of prayer. The peyote cactus is a small plant that grows in desert regions. Much of the plant is undergound, and only the part that is above is easily edible. The entire plant contains the psychoactive compound, but it is the top part of the plant that is typically sliced into small disks and dried. These dried slices remain psychoactive indefinitely, and are known as *mescal buttons.* When the buttons are ingested, they are first put into the mouth and soaked until soft. They then are taken into the hand, formed into a small ball, and swallowed. This method of ingestion has been followed for centuries.

THE DISTORTING EFFECTS OF MESCALINE IN HUMANS.   The major effects of mescaline are to induce visual sensory distortions and to diminish one's sense of hunger and thirst. Usually, unpleasant autonomic side effects accompany the psychic effects. These typically include nausea, vomiting, gooseflesh, and dilation of the pupils.

An early experimenter in the area, Havelock Ellis (1902), described his experience with mescaline in these words:

> On the whole, if I had to describe the visions in one word, I should say that they were living arabesques. There was generally a certain incomplete tendency to symmetry, the effect being somewhat as if the underlying mechanism consisted of a large number of polished facets acting as mirrors. It constantiy happened that the same image was repeated over a large part of the field, though this holds good mainly of the forms, for in the colors, there would still remain all sorts of delicious varieties. Thus at a moment when uniformly jewelled flowers seemed to be springing up and extending all over the field of vision, the flowers still showed every variety of delicate tone and tint [p. 59].

MARIJUANA

Marijuana, more than any other psychoactive agent, has typified the drug culture of the 1960s and 1970s. Not only do teenagers, college students, and so-called dropouts use marijuana, but many "straight" adults in business and the professions frequently use the drug (Brecher, 1972; 1975b; Jaffe, 1975). What follows is a summary of the marijuana story.

HISTORICAL CONSIDERATIONS.   *Cannabis,* the plant from which marijuana is made, has a long and varied history. The first description of *Cannabis* as a remedy was recorded in China nearly 4000 years ago by Shen Nung, a Chinese emperor, who recommended it as a sedative and an all-purpose medication. The plant was not used as a hallucinogen in China; however, its medical use spread throughout India and Asia several centuries before Christ.

After India, the next region to discover the psychological effects of this drug was the Middle East. The Arab invasions of the ninth through the twelfth centuries introduced *Cannabis* into North Africa, from Egypt to Tunisia, Algeria, and Morocco. The tales of the *Arabian Nights,* written between A.D. 1000 and 1500, refer often to the marvelous properties of *hashish* (a concentrated form of marijuana).

Hashish and marijuana did not find their way into Europe until the middle of the nineteenth century. The first report of their use was in 1845 by Moreau, who has been called the father of psychopharmacology. After ingesting *Cannabis,* he described the effects of the intoxication. Moreau experimented with the drug and encouraged many of his friends to try it. Before long, a group of French artists was gathering monthly to use drugs. This group, known as The Club of the Hashish Eaters, included such notable writers as Théophile Gautier, Charles Baudelaire, and Alexandre Dumas. Gautier (1846, cited by Nahas, 1973) described his experiences in a magazine article:

> Hallucination, that strange guest, had set up its dwelling place in me. It seemed that my body had dissolved and become transparent. I saw inside me the hashish I had eaten in the form of an emerald which radiated millions of tiny sparks. All around me I heard the shattering and crumbling of multicolored jewels. I still saw my comrades at times but as disfigured half plants half men. I writhed in my corner with laughter. One of the guests addressed me in Italian which hashish in its omnipotence made me hear in Spanish [p. 5].

These recollections are obviously tinted with poetic license, taken by a talented writer enthusiastic about this new drug experience. Charles Baudelaire, another member of the club, was not as enthralled with the drug as Gautier; he wrote of his experiences in *Artificial Paradises* (1858/1971):

> The uninitiated . . . imagine hashish intoxication as a wondrous land, a vast theatre of magic and juggling where everything is miraculous and unexpected. That is a preconceived notion, a total misconception . . . the intoxication will be nothing but one immense dream, thanks to intensity of color and the rapidity of conceptions; but it will always preserve the particular tonality of the individual . . . the dream will certainly reflect its dreamer . . . he is only the same man grown larger . . . sophisticate and ingenu . . . will find nothing miraculous, absolutely nothing but the natural to an extreme. The mind and body upon which hashish operates will yield only their ordinary, personal phenomena increased, it is true, in amount and vitality, but still faithful to the original. Man will not escape the fate of his physical and mental nature: to his impressions and intimate thoughts, hashish will be a magnifying mirror, but a true mirror, nonetheless [pp. 41–43].

Cannabis came to America with the early European settlers, who used its fibers to make hempen ropes. Marijuana, as a pleasure-inducing drug, entered the United States around 1910 from Mexico, when Mexican farmers began smuggling it into Texas. After World War I, marijuana smoking began to spread among poor black and Mexican farm workers in Texas and Louisiana. New Orleans became the major port of entry for illegal marijuana; in 1926 the *New Orleans Morning Tribune* published a series of articles denouncing the "marijuana menace" and linking use of the drug with crime. In 1936, *Scientific American* ("Marijuana Menaces Youth," 1936) stated that marijuana "produces a wide variety of symptoms in the user, including hilarity, swooning, and sexual excitement. Combined with intoxicants, it often makes the smoker vicious, with a desire to fight and kill [p. 151]." The Federal Bureau of Narcotics, led by Harry Anslinger, was concerned about the harmful effects that *Cannabis* might have on the individual and on society. In 1937 the Marijuana Tax Act was passed, which banned cultivation, possession, and distribution of the plants. Only the birdseed industry, which used 2 million tons of *Cannabis* seed every year, escaped the ban; they were permitted to use sterilized seed incapable of germination. The seed was popular because it made the birds sing.

In 1938, the mayor of New York, Fiorello La Guardia, questioned the effects of marijuana and wondered about their seriousness. He recalled two army studies on the use of marijuana by soldiers in the Panama Canal Zone, both of which found the drug to be an innocuous agent. The association with increased crime seemed due to the effect of mixing marijuana and alcohol.

> It was found that marijuana in an effective dose impairs intellectual functioning in general . . . . Marijuana does not change the basic personality structure of the individual. It lessens inhibition and this brings out what is latent in his thoughts and emotions but it does not evoke responses which would otherwise be totally alien to him. It induces a feeling of self-confidence, but this expressed in thought rather than in performance. There is, in fact, evidence of a diminution in physical activity . . . those who have been smoking marijuana for a period of years showed no mental or physical deterioration which may be attributed to the drug [Solomon, 1966, p. 408].

The report was met with challenges left and right. The federal government disapproved, and the American Medical Association labeled it as "unscientific" and "uncritical." The challenges to the La Guardia report were based more on emotional grounds than on intellectual foundations, and to date no evidence has proven the report wrong.

The 1950s, 1960s, and 1970s have marked a turning point in the history of marijuana. The amount of research has been increasing continually as has the amount of everyday, street usage. The use of other hallucinogens has declined, and today marijuana is probably the major hallucinogen used throughout the world.

PHYSIOLOGICAL ACTIONS.   In a report on the effects of marijuana, the U.S. Department of Health, Education, and Welfare (1971) said this:

> Physiological changes accompanying marijuana use at typical levels of American social usage are relatively few. One of the most consistent is an increase in pulse rate.

Another is reddening of the eyes at the time of use. Dryness of the mouth and throat are uniformly reported. Although enlargement of the pupils was an earlier impression, more careful study has indicated that this does not occur. Blood pressure effects have been inconsistent. Some have reported slightly lowered blood pressure, while others have reported small increases. Basal metabolic rate, temperature, respiration rate, lung vital capacity and a wide range of other physiological measures are generally unchanged over a relatively wide dosage range. . . .

There is evidence that the drug in large amounts can slow gastrointestinal passage of an experimental meal and relax an isolated intestine although it is not constipating. The sometimes reported enormous increase in appetite following marijuana smoking may also be related to effects in the gastrointestinal tract. . . .

Because smoking is the typical mode of use of marijuana in America, studies of its effects on lung function are of considerable potential importance . . . even though preliminary experiments have not shown this form of smoking to be as damaging as tobacco smoking [pp. 9–10, 94, 173–174].

TOXICITY, TOLERANCE, AND DEPENDENCE. The lethal dose of *Cannabis* has not been determined for humans, and there have been no reports of death due to an overdose of marijuana. However, experts have estimated the lethal dose to be about 40,000 times the minimal effective dose. *Cannabis* does not produce physical dependence and there do not appear to be any adverse symptoms when the individual stops using the drug. Tolerance, however, is still an issue subject to debate. Tolerance has been shown in animal studies and in some human reports. Yet, the question of whether the tolerance is psychological or physical has not been resolved. Wilson and Linken (1968) reported from England that a few users tend to increase the dosage with continued use. Miras (1969) reports that hashish smokers he has known in Greece for 20 years are able to smoke at least 10 times as much as other people. A beginner smoking the same quantity would collapse. Interestingly, there is no cross-tolerance between marijuana and the other hallucinogens (LSD, mescaline, psilocybin) (Jaffe, 1975; Levine, 1973).

PSYCHOLOGICAL EFFECTS. Tart (1970) has summarized the effects of marijuana, based on subjects' reports:

Sense perception is often improved, both in intensity and in scope. Imagery is usually stronger but well controlled, although people often care less about controlling their actions. Great changes in perception of space and time are common, as are changes in psychological processes such as understanding, memory, emotion, and sense of identity . . . to the extent that the described effects are delusory or inaccurate, the delusions and inaccuracy are widely shared. It is interesting, too, that nearly all the common effects seem either emotionally pleasing or cognitively interesting, and it is easy to see why marijuana users find the effects desirable regardless of what happens to their external behavior [p. 704].

SIDE EFFECTS. A considerable controversy has developed over the question of just how damaging marijuana is to the human organism. Individual studies have reported atrophy of the brain, lowered resistance to infection, increased likelihood of birth defects and hereditary defects, loss of motivation, lung damage, and sterility and impotence in men as results of chronic marijuana use. This is an imposing list of dangers, and, if true, would be enough to convince most people to "keep off the grass." However, each of these studies has been refuted by follow-up experiments. The original studies, carried out with chronic users, did not control for diet, general health, and use of other drugs. When such controls were added to the research protocol, marijuana smokers were *not* found to differ significantly from nonsmokers (Brecher, 1975a).

Treatment of Drug Abuse

The only forms of drug abuse for which there is a substantial literature on treatment are alcoholism, heroin addiction, and smoking. This section will briefly review the various treatment approaches.

DETOXIFICATION

Detoxification is the process by which an individual intoxicated on a drug is withdrawn from it. Withdrawal from alcohol and the other depressants, and from the narcotics, was discussed earlier. Withdrawal is an extremely serious matter, and may be life-threatening. It was once thought that withdrawal, followed by an extended period of abstinence from the drug, would allow the dependence to dissipate and cure the patient of the addiction. Many addicts were held in special hospitals until they were "cured" in this way. There is now ample evidence that better than 90% of alcoholics, heroin addicts, and smokers return to their old habit within a matter of weeks to a couple of years (Brecher, 1972). Therefore, many investigators have been seeking alternative treatment approaches that will work better than withdrawal.

PHYSIOLOGICAL APPROACHES

One alternative is to reduce the stresses of withdrawal by withdrawing the drug gradually, or by substituting another, presumably safer, drug, and then withdrawing it. For instance, alcoholics may receive gradually decreasing doses of a barbiturate (such as phenobarbital) or an antianxiety agent during the withdrawal period. Carbohydrate solutions and B vitamins are also administered to lessen the withdrawal delirium tremens. Heroin addicts are usually transferred to longer-acting methadone, and then withdrawn from the methadone (Table 14-5 on p. 428 shows the difference in withdrawal symptoms).

Once detoxified, the patient may be given a different drug to maintain the drugfree condition. Disulfiram (Antabuse) has been used in this way with alcoholics. The addict is instructed to take the drug orally each morning. As long as disulfiram intake is maintained, alcohol will make the patient sick. Disulfiram interfers with the breakdown of alcohol, causing the accumulation of toxic amounts of acetaldehyde, a metabolite of alcohol. The effects are a hot, flushed face, then throbbing headache, breathing difficulty, blurred vision and dizziness, nausea and vomiting. This reaction may be so severe as to be life-threatening, and an occasional death has resulted. When a person is taking disulfiram, even the small amounts of alcohol in aftershave lotion may cause this reaction when inhaled (Kissin & Beglister, 1971; Ritchie, 1970a).

Recently, drugs have been employed in a similar way to combat narcotics addiction. Drugs called *narcotic antagonists* act to block the actions of the narcotics. These agents have a high affinity for the same tissue as the narcotics themselves, combining readily with the tissue without stimulating it. By occupying the tissue, however, they prevent the narcotics from having their usual actions. These agents include nalorphine (Nalline), levallorphan (Lorfan), and naloxone (Narcan). Their primary use has been in the treatment of acute narcotic intoxication; they rapidly reverse the life-threatening respiratory depression produced by an overdose of narcotics.

Narcotic antagonists have also been used in the diagnosis of narcotic dependence. When a narcotic antagonist is administered to a person who is physically dependent upon narcotic drugs, a withdrawal syndrome is precipitated. This procedure can be dangerous in persons with a high degree of dependence. A severe withdrawal syndrome may develop that cannot be alleviated even by high doses of morphine and death may result. Because of the severity of the withdrawal response, this procedure is seldom used. Withdrawal produced in an addict by a narcotic antagonist is much more severe than that produced by simply withdrawing the person from the narcotic. This is probably caused by the rapidity with which the antagonist reduces the concentration of the narcotic drug at the receptor site. When drugs are withheld, the concentration in the body gradually decreases, allowing some time for adjustment. When an antagonist is administered, its effect is almost immediate (Foldes, 1964; Jaffe, 1970). Narcotic antagonists are used experimentally to control addiction by preventing the addict from returning to narcotics. Some of the antagonists can be administered orally once a day to block the euphoria and other effects that would result from subsequent narcotic intake.

The problem with the use of disulfiram for alcoholism and narcotic antagonists for narcotic addiction is the same. When the mood to take a drug strikes the addict, abstaining from the blocking drug for 1–3 days is all that is required. Therefore, the outpatient must be very well motivated to stay free of alcohol or narcotics. In one recent study, less than 1% of all patients put on disulfiram while in a hospital remained alcoholfree after their release from the hospital (Lubetkin, Rivers, & Rosenberg, 1971).

One method of reducing the craving for narcotics in persons who have become physically dependent on them is to satisfy that craving. This can be accomplished by maintaining the person on a controlled intake of a narcotic. This method has been used for several years in Great Britain, where heroin maintenance is a common form of treatment for narcotic addiction. In this system, the addict is not required to abstain from all intake of narcotic drugs, but is, instead, allowed a controlled dose of heroin. This is sufficient to prevent the onset of the withdrawal syndrome and blocks the strong desire for narcotics. This program has been notably effective. British narcotic addicts number in the hundreds, rather than in the hundreds of thousands as in the United States. Brecher (1972) has suggested that the effectiveness of the British system has stemmed from the lack of publicity surrounding heroin use. Furthermore, the availability of inexpensive heroin eliminates the need for large sums of money, which can drive addicts to criminal activity. At the same time, the British system removes the profit from the black market sale of heroin.

A similar method is used in the United States, where methadone is substituted for the heroin. An advantage of the methadone maintenance plan is that methadone can be taken orally rather than by injection; it is also a longer-lasting narcotic than is heroin, eliminating the need for several doses per day. The desired result of the maintenance program is the stabilization of narcotic drug use by the addict at a low level, which will allow a relatively normal life. There appear to be relatively few serious complications to the chronic intake of a stabilized dose of the narcotic drugs, and once a stable rate of drug intake is reached, tolerance to the effects of the narcotic drugs occurs, and they have little noticeable effect upon the addict.

The primary objection to this type of therapy is that the underlying "illness" (addiction) is not being treated and that the person on a maintenance program is still an addict. The findings that persons on heroin or methadone maintenance can lead normal, productive lives are, however, points in favor of this approach. Supporters of the maintenance approach have noted that diabetics are just as dependent upon insulin as addicts are upon heroin or methadone.

Although both the heroin and methadone maintenance programs have been the subjects of intense criticism and controversy, the abysmal success rate with other treatments suggests they should be continued. It is my opinion that the United States should permit the experimental use of heroin maintenance. Obviously these programs are not without their price; there are some side effects as well as moral objections. However, when the cost of narcotic addiction in terms of crime, money, and human suffering is considered, it seems that maintenance is the lesser evil.

Although there has been little consideration of maintenance with alcohol or cigarette addiction, this is also a possibility. It may be that alcoholics could be maintained on the safer antianxiety agents with some success. Researchers are now focusing on the possibility of delivering nicotine to addicted smokers in a noncarcinogenic form (through some route other than smoking), and on the possibility of substituting another drug such as lobeline for nicotine.

THERAPEUTIC COMMUNITIES

Alcoholics Anonymous (AA) is a therapeutic community of alcoholics that dates back to 1935. At that time a group of alcoholics who wished to remain drugfree organized to help themselves. They began to meet for casual get-togethers and for one formal nightly meeting per week to which all interested people were invited. It was hoped that people with a common problem could help each other, as well as enjoy the fellowship and sociability. The organization has been successful enough that it has expanded to about 25,000 autonomous groups—primarily in the United States, but with groups also in Canada and throughout the world.

The only requirement for AA membership is a desire to stop drinking. The focus of the organization is on a set of rules for living reminiscent of the moral code of religions. The organization also has two other central tenets. The alcoholic must recognize that he or she can never drink again, and must concentrate, not on the long-term problem of alcoholism, but on abstaining for 1 day at a time. Each new member is assigned a sponsor, a recovered alcoholic, who assumes responsibility for helping the new member deal with his or her personal problems and remain free of alcohol. Although objective data on the efficacy of AA are difficult to obtain, most professionals consider it the most effective current treatment for alcoholism. However, the "cure" rate for AA seems to be only about 30–35% at best (Ditman, 1967).

Synanon, Daytop, Phoenix House, Odyssey House, and others, are widely publicized therapeutic communities of heroin ex-addicts. These groups were formed beginning in the late 1950s. They differ from AA in that the AA member continues to live his or her usual life; the narcotic ex-addict must move into the therapeutic community, which usually occupies a large house. The ex-addict must renounce his or her former way of life and addicted friends. The ex-addict lives with the group and is subject to continual group pressure. Intense group therapy sessions are a typical feature, as is the concept that the ex-addict may never leave the safety and influence of the therapeutic community. For instance, the relapse rate among Synanon graduates who have left the community has been found to be near 90%. Furthermore, less than 10% of heroin addicts that approach one of the communities actually join it and remain for any significant period of time. Brecher has described the therapeutic communities as "a major disaster, for they helped persuade the public that heroin addiction is curable, without curing more than a trivial number of addicts [1972, p. 82]."

CONVENTIONAL PSYCHOTHERAPY

Dynamically based individual and group psychotherapy remains a widespread treatment approach to the addictions. Some therapists have claimed success using psychoanalysis or psychoanalytically oriented psychotherapy. However, these claims have not been supported by empirical evidence. Generally, research has failed to demonstrate the value of conventional psychotherapy for drug addiction (Hill & Blanc, 1967; Neuman & Tamerin, 1971).

BEHAVIOR THERAPY

A variety of behavioral control techniques have been employed, primarily with alcoholism, heroin addiction, and smoking. One technique, for example, attempts to pair alcoholic beverages with an aversive event in order to establish a conditioned avoidance response to alcohol. Alcohol use has been paired with drug-induced paralysis (produced by succinylcholine), with painful electric shock, or with drug-induced nausea and vomiting. A pleasant or rewarding event may also be paired with the patient's turning away from alcohol or deciding not to ingest it. The *covert sensitization technique* requires the alcoholic to imagine taking a drink and some highly aversive consequence of that act; or to imagine highly rewarding consequences of choosing not to take a drink (Cautela, 1970). There have been positive reports for the effectiveness of these techniques (Sanderson, Campbell, & Laverty, 1963; Blake, 1965). However, a number of negative or only slightly positive findings have also been reported (Farrer, Powell, & Martin, 1968; Holzinger, Mortimer, & Van Dusen, 1967). Even in the most positive reports, only about 25% of the patients were found to be drugfree at long-term follow-up.

Recent evidence has undermined the widespread assumption that a single drink stimulates in the alcoholic an irresistible impulse to continue drinking. Both alcoholic and social drinkers were recruited for a study, supposedly of taste preferences among different kinds of tonic water. Unknown to the subjects, some of them received tonic spiked with vodka. The subjects were allowed to taste the beverages at will in arriving at their preference judgments. Surprisingly, the alcoholics did *not* consume more of the alcohol-containing beverages than did the social drinkers. However, both groups consumed more of the tonic water when it was spiked with vodka (Marlatt, Demming, & Reid, 1973).

A promising new trend in the treatment of alcoholism is the attempt to retrain alcoholics as social drinkers. In one such study (Lovibond & Caddy, 1970), alcoholics were first given a short period of training to accurately estimate their own blood alcohol level, using their subjective feelings of intoxication. They were then given alcoholic beverages and told to generate the desired moderate level of intoxication and blood alcohol. The experimental group was given painful electric shocks whenever their blood alcohol level rose above the moderate limit; a control group received the same number of randomly delivered electric shocks. The experimental group's subsequent alcohol intake was found to be significantly lower than that of the control group.

In another study of controlled drinking, hospitalized alcoholics were subjected to a series of experimental drinking sessions. They could avoid painful electric shock by employing a social drinking pattern, slowly sipping mixed drinks in small amounts. They received electric shocks whenever they deviated from this pattern by imbibing more concentrated drinks, drinking too much, or drinking too fast. Every one of the 13 subjects acquired the pattern of social drinking. In a subsequent 12-month follow-up, 7 of the 9 experimental subjects who could be located (but only 2 of 8 control group subjects) were found either to be abstinent, or drinking in socially acceptable ways (Mills, Sobell, & Schaefer, 1971; Schaefer, 1972).

Several behavioral approaches have been employed with smoking, with little success. Techniques have included a variety of self-control and aversive procedures. Generally, significant reductions are produced, but when long-term follow-ups are employed a very high relapse rate is found (Bernstein, 1969). Techniques have included the use of a cigarette case that delivers shocks of increasing intensity when opened, and a cigarette case that automatically locks after a cigarette is taken and cannot be reopened for progressively longer intervals. Both techniques temporarily suppressed smoking. But upon follow-up, smoking levels had returned to their pretreatment amounts (Azrin & Powell, 1968; Powell & Azrin, 1968).

One case employed contingency contracting with a female graduate student who was addicted to amphetamines (Boudin, 1972). A 3-month contract was signed by both the patient and the therapist. It required the patient to keep the therapist continuously informed of her whereabouts, to call him three times a day to report on her activities, and also to call him immediately whenever she became involved in situations exposing her to possible drug use. The patient deposited $500 (all the money she had) in a joint bank account which she opened with the therapist. They agreed that in the event of any actual or suspected drug use by the patient, the therapist would draw a $50 check on the joint bank account and send it as a donation to the Ku Klux Klan—a particularly effective aversive contingency for the patient, who was black. The patient slipped only once during the 3-month contract, and the follow-up revealed that she had remained abstinent and was making satisfactory progress toward her Ph.D.

Many theorists consider that the physical dependence and the high relapse rate found for the narcotics is due to a permanent physical change in brain function. Others have suggested that narcotic addiction primarily involves a learned response that must be unlearned. For example, Wikler (1965) has viewed drug addiction as a product of instrumental learning. He suggests that each injection or ingestion of a drug reinforces drug-seeking behavior by providing immediate, powerful reinforcement. According to this view, the extremely high rate of return to drug addiction by detoxified addicts is due simply to incomplete extinction of the reinforced drug-seeking behavior. Extinction procedures are currently being employed as a part of several experimental programs for the treatment of narcotic addiction. However, the effectiveness of these procedures has yet to be established.

Conclusions

There are a number of psychologically active drugs that are used recreationally. Sometimes it is not clear when such recreational drug use becomes drug abuse. The major drugs are alcohol and the other depressants, the narcotics, nicotine in the form of cigarettes, stimulants, and hallucinogens. It seems clear that the most serious and costly drug abuse problems involve alcohol and cigarettes. Although alcohol itself is responsible for the damaging social, psychological, and physiological consequences of its use, the major health hazard in cigarettes may not be the nicotine but other cancer-producing chemicals. Narcotics are a severe problem because they produce a strong physical dependence, but are illegal and expensive to obtain. The stimulants and hallucinogens are not without their faults, yet they do not produce physical dependence, and their toxicity and potential for producing bodily harm is not nearly as great as that of alcohol and the narcotics. The most serious problems may be associated with legal and social consequences rather than specific physical or psychological effects resulting from the use of stimulants and hallucinogens.

A sound public policy toward the recreational and abused drugs would rationally weigh the evidence, match government policy to the relative pharmacological dangers of the various drugs, and provide the public at large with a clear, unbiased statement of the facts, as they are currently known, of the effects, benefits, and dangers of the various drugs. It is virtually impossible to eradicate recreational drug use. An achievable goal would be to convert drug users from the most harmful drugs and patterns of use to other drugs or patterns that are less harmful.

Finally, the reader might want to consider the recommendations of the magazine *Consumer Reports* as provided in Brecher (1972).[6] First are six caveats—things we have been doing and should stop. These are followed by several positive recommendations.

1. Stop emphasizing measures designed to keep drugs away from people. Prohibition does not work. What prohibition does is to raise prices, stimulate a black market, and force addicts to resort to crime to finance their purchases—at a tragic cost in money and in community disruption. Prohibition also converts drug use to more hazardous concentrates and to adulterated and contaminated drugs. Laws and law enforcement should be used to ameliorate the drug abuse problem, not to exacerbate it.
2. Stop publicizing the horrors of the "drug menace." Scare publicity has functioned not as warnings, but to popularize drugs and as a lure to recreational drug use.
3. Stop increasing the damage done by drugs. Efforts should be directed at minimizing damage. The laws making possession and sale of hypodermic paraphernalia illegal drive the addict to nonsterile and shared equipment. The laws forcing addicts to obtain illicit drugs force the use of adulterated, impure, and mislabeled drugs.
4. Stop misclassifying drugs. Our current legal classification system treats alcohol and nicotine—two of the most harmful drugs—essentially as nondrugs, while marijuana is equated with heroin—a shocking and harmful bit of foolishness. A scientifically based legal system must replace the current politically based one.
5. Stop viewing the drug problem as primarily a national problem, to be solved on a national scale. A solution that works in one part of the country may not work in another part.
6. Stop pursuing the goal of stamping out illicit drug use. Attempts to stamp out illicit drug use tend to increase both drug use and drug damage, or to shift the drug user to another, often more dangerous, drug.

[6] Also see the issues of *Consumer Reports* for March and April of 1975 for an update on the health and legal questions with respect to marijuana.

The Consumer's Union also has some positive recommendations: "The heroin black market must be abolished in the only way it can be abolished: by eliminating the demand for black-market heroin. On the central issue of narcotics addiction, accordingly, Consumer's Union recommends (1) that United States drug policies and practices be promptly revised to insure that no narcotics addict need get his drug from the black market; (2) that methadone maintenance be promptly made available under medical auspices to every narcotics addict who applies for it; (3) that other forms of narcotics maintenance, including opium, morphine, and heroin maintenance, be made available along with methadone maintenance under medical auspices on a carefully planned experimental basis (Brecher, 1972, p. 530)."

With respect to marijuana, Consumer's Union makes the following key proposals: "(1) Consumer's Union recommends the immediate repeal of all federal laws governing the growing, processing, transportation, sale, possession, and use of marijuana. (2) Consumer's Union recommends that each of the fifty states similarly repeal its existing marijuana laws and pass new laws legalizing the cultivation, processing, and orderly marketing of marijuana—subject to appropriate regulations [Brecher, 1972, pp. 537, 538]."

Summary

Any chemical taken into the body to alter psychological functioning is a psychoactive drug. Studying the abuse of psychoactive drugs is fraught with difficulty, since moral as well as scientific questions are involved. People are concerned about the moral implications of using drugs to obtain pleasure. and dangerous—of self-administering psychoactive drugs. Most people are also concerned about the moral implications of using drugs to obtain pleasure.

Tolerance develops to most psychoactive drugs; that is, with continued administration, more of the drug must be taken to achieve the same action. The development of tolerance is accompanied by a psychological dependence on the drug, sometimes with both a psychological and a physical dependence. Psychological dependence implies a neurotic attachment to the drug; in physical dependence, withdrawal of the drug makes the person physically sick.

The American Psychiatric Association considers individuals dependent on alcohol or other drugs to be suffering from a personality disorder that is responsible for the drug abuse. However, research has not shown this to be correct; drug abusers do not tend to have any particular psychopathology in common, other than the fact of their drug abuse. When under the influence of drugs, however, they do temporarily show symptoms of brain pathology. The United States federal government and each of the states have also developed politically based systems for classifying the abused psychoactive drugs; these systems regulate the use of these drugs and prescribe criminal penalties for illegal usage. Our medical or psychological classification divides psychoactive drugs into the depressants, the narcotics, the stimulants, and the hallucinogens.

The depressants include alcohol, the barbiturates, the nonbarbiturate sedatives, and the antianxiety agents. These drugs can all be used as sedatives and muscle relaxants. They also have anticonvulsant actions. Tolerance and physical dependence may develop to each of them. Cross-tolerance and cross-dependence are also seen; that is, tolerance and dependence on one of these agents also results in tolerance and dependence on the others. In high doses, they may all produce an acute intoxication like that well known for alcohol. A hangover follows short-term abuse, and something like delirium tremens follows chronic abuse. Especially with alcohol, potentially fatal liver and brain damage can be produced by chronic abuse.

The narcotics include heroin, morphine, codeine, and methadone. They all may be used medically for their analgesic action. They are self-administered for the euphoria they produce. Tolerance and physical dependence are rapidly developed; cross-tolerance and cross-dependence are also seen between them. Dependence on narcotics is an especially important problem because of the criminal activities of addicts and the role of organized crime in narcotics trafficking. Overdose deaths from depression of breathing or from other causes are also a problem.

The stimulants include the amphetamines, caffeine, and cocaine. Nicotine has been included in this section, although it is not related to these other drugs. The amphetamines, caffeine, and cocaine are abused for the feelings of euphoria they produce. In high doses or with chronic use, they can produce a psychosis. Although tolerance develops to the amphetamines and to some of the effects of caffeine, the actions of cocaine are so brief that tolerance is not found. Psychological dependence on these drugs is well established, but physical dependence does not appear to develop. Overdose deaths from these drugs are uncommon. Tolerance and psychological dependence develop to nicotine in the various forms in which it is smoked. The major concern is not nicotine dependence itself, but the serious health hazard from cancer and other diseases that results from smoking. Many of these detrimental effects are produced by other compounds present in the smoke.

The hallucinogens include LSD, mescaline, psilocybin, and marijuana. Tolerance and cross-tolerance develop to the first three drugs, but cross-tolerance between them and marijuana is not found. Psychological dependence may develop to each of these four drugs. They are self-administered for their perceptual and psychological effects. Overdose deaths directly from their use are infrequent, if not nonexistent. However, controversy does surround the possible deleterious effects that may result from their use.

Many techniques have been used to treat drug abuse. Most of these have been employed with alcohol or heroin, or with cigarette smoking. Physiological techniques include detoxification; the administration of a blocking agent to prevent pleasurable sensations from the abused drug, or to make drug use actually unpleasant; and maintaining the patient on a related but safer drug. Psychological approaches include therapeutic communities, conventional psychotherapy, and behavioral training techniques. Although successes have been claimed, such as for methadone maintenance. Alcoholics Anonymous, and Synanon-type programs, controversy surrounds all these approaches. Truly satisfactory approaches for dealing with the bulk of the drug-abuse problem have not yet been developed. Public and governmental attention should be focused on the objective testing of old approaches and the development of new ones, with the goal of minimizing the individual and cultural damage resulting from the recreational self-administration of psychoactive substances.

IV

TREATMENT APPROACHES

15

Behavior Therapy

DAVID C. RIMM[1]

Southern Illinois University at Carbondale

Behavior therapy is relatively new. The present usage of the term *behavior therapy* was introduced independently by Hans Eysenck and Arnold Lazarus in 1958 (see Lazarus, 1971). You may be familiar with the term *behavior modification*, which is sometimes used as a synonym for *behavior therapy*. However, *behavior therapy* is the more inclusive term. That is, behavior modification, which stresses operant conditioning, is only one of several treatment approaches included under the general heading of behavior therapy.

In part, behavior therapy developed as a result of dissatisfaction with some of the more traditional approaches, especially psychoanalysis. This dissatisfaction increased when certain psychologists, including Eysenck (1952) and Levitt (1963), presented data suggesting that traditional methods are no better than no treatment at all. In fact, it is a mistake to talk about traditional psychotherapies as if they constituted a single treatment approach. There are many different psychotherapies, just as there are many behavior therapies. For this reason, it is unwise to make sweeping generalizations concerning the effectiveness of psychotherapy—or, for that matter, of behavior therapy.

---

[1] Present address: Department of Psychology, Old Dominion University, Norfolk, Virginia.

Although the conclusions that traditional approaches were ineffective have drawn criticism (e.g., Bergin, 1966), proponents of the various traditional therapies had, through the late 1950s and early 1960s, offered very little scientific evidence that indeed their methods worked. It was natural, therefore, that many practitioners would begin to seek methods or approaches that had more empirical support. In 1953, the noted psychologist B. F. Skinner published *Science and Human Behavior*. This book, which was widely read, suggested that the principles of operant conditioning could be applied to human behavior. In 1958, Joseph Wolpe, a psychiatrist, published a book called *Psychotherapy by Reciprocal Inhibition*. In this book Wolpe described a variety of techniques for dealing with maladaptive human behavior, especially phobias. Although he discussed some of his earlier experiments with cats that tended to support his position, it was his impressive case history data that had the major impact on practitioners. According to Wolpe, almost all his clients (approximately 90%) showed marked improvement, usually after a relatively brief number of sessions. We shall describe the Skinnerian and Wolpian procedures in subsequent sections of this chapter. The point we wish to make here is that therapists seeking alternative ways of dealing with clients—specifically, procedures having at least some degree of empirical support—can find them in the writings of Skinner and Wolpe. The Skinnerian and Wolpian approaches, taken together, form the foundation of behavior therapy as we know it today.

We have stressed Skinner and Wolpe because their role in the development of behavior therapy has been paramount. However, many others have made major additions to the field. Among them are Bandura and his associates, who have demonstrated the importance of *imitation learning* in the development and modification of maladaptive behavior (see Bandura, 1969, 1971); Stampfl, whose name is associated with *implosive therapy* (see Stampfl & Levis, 1967); Cautela (1967), who developed *covert sensitization;* and Azrin (e.g., Azrin, Naster, & Jones, 1973; Azrin, Sneed, & Foxx, 1973) and his associates, who have made numerous contributions to operant technology. Psychologists such as Goldiamond (1965), Stuart (1967, 1971), Kanfer (see Kanfer & Phillips, 1970), and Mahoney and Thoresen (1974) have made major contributions to the psychology of *self-control*. The approach of Albert Ellis, the founder of *rational emotive therapy* (see Ellis, 1962, 1971), has had a marked influence on the thinking of many behaviorally oriented therapists (for example, Lazarus, 1971; Mahoney, 1974; Meichenbaum, 1971), culminating in a methodology that might best be described as *cognitive-behavior therapy*. Writers such as Lazarus (1971), who has stressed a pragmatic, flexible approach, and Ullmann and Krasner (1969/1975) have made major contributions to the field through their research and writing.

Behavior therapy has grown rapidly. It is now a firmly established part of clinical psychology and, to a somewhat lesser extent, of psychiatry as well. To illustrate, there are presently four scientific journals devoted exclusively to behavior therapy research and practice, and most universities offer graduate (and frequently undergraduate) courses in the area.

Basic Assumptions of Behavior Therapy

As we have suggested, the label *behavior therapy* subsumes a variety of techniques or methods. The use of a single descriptive term such as behavior therapy may be questioned, although in our view there are certain basic assumptions that tend to unite the various techniques. What follows is a brief summary of these assumptions; for a more thorough discussion, see Bandura (1969), Kanfer and Phillips (1970), or Rimm and Masters (1974).

1. Treatment emphasizes overt maladaptive behaviors, or internal activities or processes (such as anxiety or the things people say to themselves) that are related to overt behavior in a relatively straightforward manner.

2. Learning is assumed to play a vital role in the acquisition and modification of maladaptive responding. The principles of learning that give rise to maladaptive behavior are believed to be no different than those that give rise to adaptive or healthy ways of responding. A key concept in the psychology of learning is that of *stimulus control*. In everyday language, this means that the way we behave is largely controlled by environmental events, rather than underlying traits, deep-seated conflicts, or complexes.

3. Treatment is very much oriented to the here and now. It is assumed that the client has, to a considerable extent, learned to behave as he does, but that insight into how he learned the maladaptive ways of responding is not of much value.

4. Treatment goals are very specific. Behavior therapists do not attempt to modify a client's personality; instead, they deal with specific maladaptive or self-defeating ways of behaving in specific situations. In this respect, behavior therapy differs from most of the other treatment approaches presented in this textbook.

5. Behavior therapists place great emphasis on scientific validation of their techniques. Although not every behavior therapy technique originated in the laboratory—most, although not all, appeared first as uncontrolled clinical case histories—controlled research is required in order to legitimize each technique. Except for certain "medical" methods (see Chapter 21), behavior therapy places relatively greater emphasis on the role of experimental validation than most other treatment approaches.

The Applicability of the Behavior Therapies

Given the large number of behavior therapies, it should be no surprise that they may be used in dealing with a large number of psychological disorders. Obviously, the specific behavior therapy method chosen by a therapist will depend on the nature of the problem. For example, the therapist might employ systematic desensitization in connection with a phobia although there are other behavior therapies that might also be effective, including modeling, implosive therapy, and certain cognitive–behavioral techniques. If the client is lacking in interpersonal skills, assertive training might be used. With certain sexual disorders, such as exhibitionism and fetishism, or in the treatment of alcoholism, aversive conditioning may be useful. Behaviorally oriented self-control procedures may be applied to problems such as poor study behavior or overeating. The operant procedures have proven their value in modifying the behavior of severely disturbed hospitalized patients, persons evidencing mental deficiency, and boisterous children in a classroom situation.

The foregoing list by no means exhausts the possible disorders that may be treated by behavior therapies. It is sometimes said that the behavior therapies are applicable to certain *specific* behavior problems but are not effective in dealing with, for example, depression or general unhappiness. There is evidence that depression may indeed be modified by certain behavioral techniques (see Lazarus, 1974; Lewinsohn, 1974), although we are not saying that severe so-called psychotic depression may be cured by such means. As far as general unhappiness is concerned, the behaviorist assumes there are specific reasons why a client describes himself as generally unhappy; therefore, the therapist attempts to help restructure the problem so that very specific treatment goals may be obtained. For example, a male client complaining of general unhappiness may be lonely, and this loneliness may be a direct result of a lack of certain social skills with females. Specific treatment goals would include the development of such skills.

Before getting to the specifics of the different behavior therapies, a comment is in order about the way behavior therapists relate to or interact with their clients. It is easy to get the impression from some of the early behavior therapy literature that the typical behaviorist interacts with his client in a cold, seemingly mechanical fashion. This is far from the truth (see Lazarus, 1971; Rimm & Masters, 1974). Qualities of warmth and concern are important in implementing the behavior therapies just as they are important in implementing the psychotherapies, and any experienced behavior therapist is well aware of this.

Behavior Therapy Techniques

OPERANT PROCEDURES

This technology, most often associated with Skinner (although he is an experimenter and an author, not a practitioner himself), involves the use of reinforcement or reward for certain specific responses to certain specific stimulus situations. The responses or behaviors are referred to as *operants,* which may be thought of as voluntary responses. The fundamental principle in operant conditioning is that reinforcement increases the *probability* or *frequency* of occurrence of the operant responses. This means that once a response has been rewarded in the presence of a particular stimulus (referred to as a *discriminative stimulus*), the response is more likely to occur when the stimulus is presented again. However, if the response does occur and no reinforcement follows, this constitutes an *extinction* trial or experience. Given a sufficient number of extinction trials, the response will no longer occur in the presence of the discriminative stimulus; the response is extinguished.

Another important principle involves using *intermitted* or *partial* reinforcement, as opposed to providing reinforcement for every response the subject makes. This has the effect of retarding the speed with which the response is conditioned, but once it *is* conditioned, the response is much less subject to extinction. When attempting to condition a response, the experimenter or therapist generally begins by reinforcing the desired response each time it occurs, until it reaches a certain optimal level—usually every time the discriminative stimulus is presented. At this point the therapist begins to withhold reinforcement, often at an increasing rate, thus putting the client on a partial reinforcement schedule. The purpose of this, from a practical point of view, is to ensure that the desired response will occur even when no one is around to dispense rewards. After all, in the real world, every time a person makes some desirable response he does not automatically receive some sort of tangible reward such as a smile, money, or a piece of candy.

Another important principle of operant conditioning is *shaping*. Shaping involves initially rewarding even a very poor version or approximation of the desired response, and gradually making the response requirement more stringent, until the response occurs in its desired form.

All these principles are illustrated in the following example: Suppose a mother desires to teach her year-old child to say "Mother." Let us ignore the role of imitation, which is known to be important but which is discussed later in the chapter. Assume that the discriminative stimulus is a smile on the mother's face as she looks directly into her child's eyes. Now, as she smiles at the baby, sooner or later the baby will make some sort of verbal utterance. In order to shape the response, she may begin by providing a reinforcer (for example, a taste of some favorite food) for any verbalization that begins with the sound of the letter *m*. After this has been conditioned, reward may be delivered only for a sound such as "Mo" or "Ma." When this response has been shaped, reward may be *contingent* on a closer approximation to "Mother," for example, "Moth." This general procedure is continued until the child is saying "Mother" every time the mother smiles at the child. Once the verbalization "Mother" has been shaped, the mother may then wish to put the child on a partial reinforcement schedule. Therefore she provides food reward for, let us say, every other response and eventually every fourth or fifth response. Once this is done, the response is not likely to extinguish after the baby utters "Mother" three or four times in the absence of reward.

The procedure we have described involves a mother and a year-old child, but similar procedures have been employed with mute psychotic patients and with mentally retarded children and adolescents. They may be used with non-

Chuck, an autistic child, seemed immune to ordinary human communication; he would spend his days rocking back and forth endlessly. Lovaas and his associates used a variety of operant procedures to draw Chuck and other autistic children into contact with the people around them. Food was the key reinforcer at first, though punishment and approval were also used to shape responses. Billy, another autistic child, grew enraged when asked to pull Chuck around in a wagon—but patient reinforcement with tastes of sherbet eventually lured both Chuck and Billy into a human embrace that neither had tolerated before (facing page). (Allan Grant)

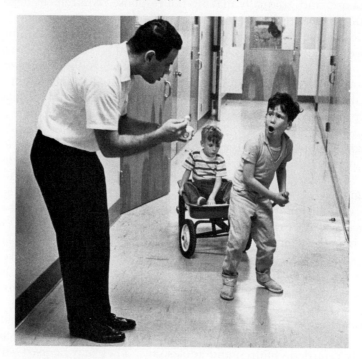

verbal behavior, such as good personal hygiene or appropriate dress, as well as for verbal behavior. In fact, these procedures, in principle, can be used to condition virtually any class of behaviors. There is some evidence that even so-called nonvoluntary or autonomic responses are subject to modification, using procedures that are essentially operant in nature (see Chapter 7).

Biofeedback procedures, which have been receiving a great deal of attention lately, are based on operant conditioning principles. For example, a person with hypertension (high blood pressure) will have a blood pressure measuring device attached to his arm. The therapist monitors the changes in blood pressure, and feeds the information back to the subject, usually employing a visual display or a machine that transforms this information into sound (Blanchard, Young, & Haynes, 1975). Thus, the patient may be able to learn, by keeping the numbers or values low, to maintain his blood pressure at a lower level.

USE OF PUNISHMENT. With some exceptions, operant conditioners have tended to avoid the use of aversive stimuli, or negative reinforcers, in order to modify human behavior. Most decidedly their preference is to "accentuate the positive." We have said that reinforcers increase the probability of responses and this is also true with negative reinforcers. In practical terms, however, negative reinforcers are designed to decrease the likelihood of a particular problem behavior by reinforcing a response that competes with or is antithetical to the problem behavior. Suppose the problem behavior is cigarette smoking. When the client reaches for a cigarette, he receives a painful electric shock, which continues until he puts the cigarette away. The response of putting the cigarette away causes the cessation of shock, which positively reinforces nonsmoking behavior. Thus, negative reinforcers are stimulus events that strengthen those responses associated with the removal of the negative reinforcer.

Presentation of a negative reinforcer (that is, an aversive stimulus) when the client has no control over its cessation is called *punishment*. Shocking a person every time he smokes a cigarette, *without* giving him a chance to escape the shock once it is turned on, illustrates a punishment procedure. As we have noted, most operant conditioners prefer to avoid the use of aversive stimuli. However, one kind of punishment procedure is frequently employed by operant conditioners. By definition (see Skinner, 1953) the removal of positive reinforcers is a type of punishment. The technical term for this is *time out from positive reinforcement* or simply *time out*. For example, suppose a child is misbehaving and the parent wishes to modify this behavior. Time out could be used in two ways. The parent might take away a favorite toy, or turn off the television if there is a program the child enjoys, or the parent might require that the child remove himself physically to some other place, for example, a room in the house that contains no toys or other reinforcers. The child would be required to remain there for a certain period of time.

This brief account is not intended to be a thorough exposition of operant methodology, which has grown rather complex over the years. For a more thorough discussion, see Bandura (1969) or Rimm and Masters (1974).

PRACTICAL APPLICATIONS OF OPERANT METHODS. At this point I would like to discuss, in very practical terms, how operant conditioners may provide a service to their clients. Imagine yourself in each of three roles: First, imagine that you as an adult seek help for some particular personal problem. The operant therapist, with your help, will attempt to determine what you *are* doing that is not in your self-interest—perhaps smoking a great deal or overeating. The two of you will also explore what you *are not* doing that would be in your self-interest—studying more, perhaps, or socializing in a more satisfying manner. The therapist will attempt to analyze your problem in terms of stimuli eliciting problem behaviors and those events that reinforce such behaviors. However, the therapist does not have *control* over the reinforcers in your life or the stimulus events (situations) that typically give rise to problem behaviors. Thus, he can only be an advisor, although he can certainly provide praise for any improvements you report. Praise or social reinforcement from the therapist, whom you might see perhaps once a week, would ordinarily not be sufficient to modify your everyday behavior, however. Thus, the type of advice you receive might be in the form of an operantly based *self-control program*, discussed in more detail later.

Second, imagine yourself in the role of a parent whose child is misbehaving in some manner. In such a situation, the operant conditioner will probably not spend a great deal of time with the child. Instead, the therapist will teach you principles of operant conditioning so that you may function as the therapist with your child. This makes a great deal of sense since, as we have suggested, the practitioner does not have control of the reinforcers, but you as a parent do. There are readable and highly useful manuals devoted specifically to teaching parents how to control their children's behavior using such techniques. Patterson and Gullion's *Living with Children* (1971) is an excellent example. In a school setting, an operant conditioner may similarly train teachers in the use of operant procedures to exert better control of the classroom behavior of their children (see Ayllon, Layman, & Kandel, 1975).

Third, imagine (admittedly, this will be more disturbing) that you are incarcerated in a mental institution. Now, if an operant conditioner happens to be in charge of your particular ward, which is by no means usual, he probably will use his skill in operant technology by setting up a *token economy*. Token economies parallel economic systems in the outside world in that both require certain behaviors of members if the members are to gain material goods. On the outside, you work for dollars, but if you do your job badly or fail to show up for work regularly, you will probably receive fewer dollars. In the token economy, if you behave in a manner considered appropriate to the institution, you will receive a certain number of tokens, which, like dollars, may be exchanged for material goods like cigarettes, candy, and clothes in the institution commissary. Sometimes a certain number of tokens is required for privileges such as watching television or going home on weekend passes. Appropriate behavior in such an institution includes going to work assignments regularly, attending individual and group therapy, maintaining personal hygiene, minimizing "crazy" talk, and avoiding physically aggressive or verbally abusive behavior.

There is ample evidence that mental patients can be shaped into behaving more like so-called "normal" people under a token economy (Ayllon & Azrin, 1968; Schaefer & Martin, 1969). However, two important points should be noted: First, it is not easy to set up a token economy, a fact that often surprises and dismays the novice operant conditioner. A successful token economy requires cooperation from institution staff at *all* levels, from the superintendent to staff psychiatrists and psychologists to aides and kitchen workers (see Atthowe, 1973). Only a small number of uncooperative or even unenthusiastic staff members may undermine the program. Second, the beneficial effects observed when the patient is in such a program do not necessarily generalize to the outside world when he is released. After all, whatever sociopsychological factors contributed to his hospitalization in the first place will probably not have changed a great deal—that is, had he come from a "healthy" environment, he might not have been hospitalized in the first place. Moreover, he now must bear the additional burden of being a former mental patient. Clearly, some sort of follow-up program is needed, which might involve restructuring the person's relationship to his family, friends, and employment.

SELF-CONTROL. In this section, we will describe self-control procedures based primarily on operant principles. As Cautela (1969) has noted, virtually any of the behavior therapy techniques can be used by an individual to control his own behavior. However, when behavior therapists use the term *self-control,* they refer mainly to programs that are essentially operant in nature.

As Kanfer and Phillips (1970) have noted, self-control problems fall into two general categories. One involves behaviors that a person performs that are self-defeating, such as overeating or gambling. The other involves a lack of behaviors that the client considers desirable; for example, failure to study or exercise. A fundamental feature common to both types of problems is that there is *immediate* reinforcement for the undesirable behavior—for instance, the pleasures of eating, or talking with friends rather than studying—whereas the reward for changing such behavior is often very *delayed*. It is well known that more immediate reinforcers are more effective, which is precisely the reason problems in self-control are so common.

The therapist attempting to implement a self-control program begins by explaining certain basic operant principles to the client. Then he has the client establish a baseline over a period of a week or two, during which the client records the frequency of problem behaviors and the circumstances surrounding their occurrence. Finally, the therapist establishes both short-term and long-term treatment goals. For example, in the treatment of obesity, a long-term goal might be the loss of 40 pounds, whereas the short-term goal might be the loss of about 1 pound per week. In any operantly based self-control program it is extremely important that the short-term goals be easily attainable and therefore very modest.

What follows is a brief outline of a self-control program for the treatment of obesity, similar to that described by Ferster, Nurnberger, and Levitt (1962), Stuart (1967, 1971), and Harris (1969).

1. Establish a baseline: Record the frequency, amount, and type of food eaten, and the circumstances surrounding eating behavior.
2. Introduce the various procedures, usually one or two per week:
   a. *Stimulus narrowing.* Eating at the dinner table *only,* and only at certain prescribed times; eating while engaging in other activities such as reading a newspaper or watching television is forbidden.
   b. *Eating slowly,* savoring each mouthful, perhaps putting the eating utensils down for a few minutes until the food is swallowed.
   c. Removing food that requires *no preparation* from the household.
   d. *Providing immediate self-reinforcement* (e.g., praising oneself, watching television), for appropriate eating behavior and also for engaging in activities that make eating impossible, such as going for a walk. The principle of immediate reinforcement for appropriate behavior is of the utmost importance in any self-control program.

Usually the therapist and client meet once a week for a period of a few months. Once the long-term goal has been reached it is recommended that booster sessions be provided, perhaps once a month or once every 2 months, in order to ensure that good eating habits are maintained.

As a second illustration, consider the following brief outline of a self-control program designed to increase study behavior (see Beneke & Harris, 1972; Fox, 1962; Watson & Tharp, 1972).

1. Establish a baseline.
2. Introduce the procedures, usually one or two per week:
   a. *Changing the stimulus environment.* Find a place to study that is free from distraction.
   b. *Cue strengthening.* Once a study area has been selected, the student should perform *no other activity* there such as writing letters or reading novels for pleasure.
   c. *Shaping and self-reinforcement.* The client is instructed to begin by studying for relatively brief periods of time, to stop *before* he begins to experience fatigue or boredom, and to provide some immediate reinforcement (talking to a friend, perhaps eating something, watching some television). Shaping refers to the gradual increasing of study periods from day to day, often increasing the amount only a few minutes per day.
   d. *Improving study efficiency*—for instance, begin by surveying the material, then determine what questions the text is attempting to answer. See Beneke and Harris (1972), for a further discussion of study efficiency.

THE WOLPIAN PROCEDURES: SYSTEMATIC DESENSITIZATION AND ASSERTIVE TRAINING

Although Wolpe (1958, 1969/1973) describes other behavior therapy procedures, these two techniques are generally considered his major contributions. Both are based on the principle of *counterconditioning*. In this context, counterconditioning means substituting a positive emotion for the negative emotion of fear or anxiety (behavior therapists use these terms interchangeably).

SYSTEMATIC DESENSITIZATION. This technique is used for irrational fears or *phobias*. The first task of the therapist is to determine whether the client's fears are indeed irrational. Sometimes people are fearful because they lack the technical or social skills to deal effectively with certain situations. For example, consider a young male client whose complaint is that he gets uptight when contemplating asking a girl for a date. Perhaps the main reason he experiences anxiety is because he knows he is not skillfull in dealing with such situations. For this client, social skill training (assertive training) would probably be most appropriate. Because he lacks social skills, his fear has a rational basis.

If it is established that the fear is irrational, the therapist then determines that the client has relatively few major phobias. This is necessary because there is evidence that desensitization is less effective for clients who have many phobias.

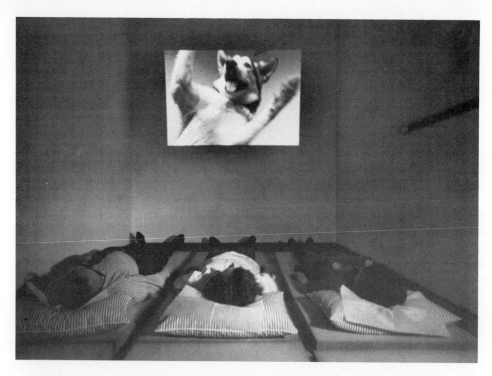

Clients suffering from a phobic fear of dogs are undergoing a program of systematic desensitization. While relaxing on mattresses, they view slides of progressively larger and fiercer dogs. Once their fear is deconditioned, they will complete their course by handling live but friendly dogs. (*The New York Times*)

The cognitive behavior therapy methods are probably more appropriate for such a person. The therapist next determines that the client is able to visualize scenes pertinent to his phobia vividly and is able to experience anxiety while he imagines such scenes. The client is then taught progressive muscle relaxation, which involves tensing and relaxing opposing sets of muscles, until most of the major muscle groups of the body are relaxed. Initially, the therapist "talks" the client through the exercises, which usually requires about 45 minutes. Subsequently, the client relaxes himself. Since there are considerable individual differences (see Malmo, 1962) with respect to where people experience maximal tension, the client learns which muscles are in need of relaxing and which are not. Thus, after the first few sessions, the client may be able to relax effectively in a matter of 10 or 15 minutes. Concurrent with or following relaxation training, the therapist and client develop a *hierarchy* of scenes pertinent to the client's phobias—one hierarchy per phobia. The scenes are ordered in terms of the amount of anxiety they elicit, starting with a minimal level of anxiety. The following are the first 2 items of a 14-item hierarchy set up for a male fearful of heights:

1. You are beginning to climb the ladder leaning against the side of your house. You plan to work on the roof. Your hands are on the ladder and your foot is on the first rung.
2. You are halfway up the ladder, and you happen to look down. You see the lawn below you and a walkway [Rimm & Masters, 1974, p. 58].

The fourteenth and most fear-evoking item required that he imagine himself on a catwalk around a water tank, painting the tank.

The actual desensitization procedure involves having the client imagine the hierarchy scenes in realistic detail while in a state of relaxation. It is assumed that since relaxation is incompatible with anxiety, the fear will be deconditioned. Further, it is assumed that this deconditioning of fear will generalize to actual situations in the real world. The therapist and the client begin with the scene eliciting the least anxiety and work up the hierarchy until the client is able to imagine the most fearful scene without experiencing anxiety. For a more detailed discussion of relaxation and systematic desensitization, see Rimm and Masters (1974).

ASSERTIVE TRAINING.   To be assertive means to express your feelings in an honest, straightforward, but socially appropriate manner. The client may be taught to express affection, disagreement, anger, and other emotions. With respect to anger, it is important to distinguish between *assertiveness* and *aggression*. The assertive response almost always accomplishes the client's goals, without unnecessarily hurting or alienating others. The aggressive response, on the other hand, may also "get the job done," but is often annoying or hurtful to others and is also a good deal riskier.

The main method of assertive training is *behavior rehearsal,* which simply means practicing, with the help of the therapist, to behave more assertively. The therapist begins by explaining that being more assertive will help the client in two important ways. First, he will be interpersonally more effective. Second, he will feel better, especially in relation to situations involving anxiety, since Wolpe assumes that assertion and anxiety are incompatible. (For evidence supporting this, see McFall & Marston, 1970, and Rimm, Hill, Brown, & Stuart, 1974.) The therapist and the client may then proceed with behavior rehearsal, illustrated in the following dialog with a client who has difficulty refusing unreasonable requests. The particular situation involves an acquaintance who often asks to borrow the client's automobile when the client needs it himself.

1. [*Assessment*] *Therapist:* "OK, now pretend I'm this acquaintance of yours, Bill, and I ask to borrow your car. What do you usually say?" *Client:* "Well, I guess I would say, 'Yeah, OK.' "
2. [*Feedback to client*] *Therapist:* "Your eye contact was good, but you gave right in, although you didn't want to."
3. [*Modeling an assertive response by the therapist*] *Therapist:* "Why not try something like this: ' Bill, I would loan you my car, but I need it myself because I've got some errands to run.' "

4. [*Client rehearsal*] *Therapist:* "Let's see you practice something like that. I'll be Bill: 'I'd like to borrow your car today.'" *Client:* "Bill, I wish I could, but I need it myself. I've got some shopping to do."
5. [*Feedback and additional assessment*] *Therapist:* "That was very good. You were direct, but tactful. How anxious did you feel?" *Client:* "Not very anxious at all . . . well, maybe a little bit . . . I'm not used to saying no."
6. [*Additional rehearsal*] *Therapist:* "OK, let's try it again."

The process is continued more or less in this fashion until both client and therapist are satisfied with the client's response, with the client experiencing little or no anxiety.

Most of the literature on assertive training deals with problems associated with timidity. In fact, assertive training has considerable potential in dealing with individuals who get themselves into trouble because they are either verbally or physically abusive. Often such clients keep their anger or resentment bottled up for long periods of time and then "blow up," usually quite inappropriately. The therapist might employ assertive training to aid his client in expressing his anger or resentment in a reasonable manner *before* it reaches a level that is difficult for the client to control. For a detailed discussion of this and other issues pertaining to assertive training, see Rimm and Masters (1974).

MODELING PROCEDURES: LEARNING BY IMITATION

Common experience suggests that a great deal of what human beings learn is acquired through the process of imitation. You may be surprised to learn that widespread investigation of this very important phenomenon is relatively recent. Much of the credit for demonstrating the power of modeling procedures must go to Albert Bandura and his associates. His early studies showing how children can acquire aggressive behavior through imitation (see Bandura, 1969) are classic, and the studies by Bandura and his collaborators (Bandura, Grusec, & Menlove, 1967; Bandura, Jeffery, & Wright, 1974) dealing with modeling procedures in relation to fear reduction have very obvious clinical relevance.

From the discussion of assertive training it should be clear that modeling is a key element in behavior rehearsal.[2] In the illustration of the use of operant procedures in teaching a child to say "Mother," we deliberately ignored modeling procedures. In fact, given what is now known about the potency of modeling procedures, it would be foolish to use a purely operant technique to accomplish such a task. In the example we used, it would have been far more efficient for the mother to provide a verbal model for her baby to imitate. Specifically, the mother would say aloud the word "Mother," which the baby might then imitate, and *then* the mother would provide the reinforcement. Children are able to imitate re-

---

[2] McFall and Twentyman (1973) presented a series of experiments indicating that modeling was not essential to assertive training. However, an examination of the "assertive tasks" required of their subjects suggests that they were of a relatively easy nature. In our view, for more difficult tasks (i.e., tasks involving more complex skills), modeling is probably an essential ingredient in assertive training.

sponses of a relatively simple nature at a very early age. In a classic study, Baer, Peterson, and Sherman (1967) used a combination of modeling and reinforcement in teaching a variety of motor and verbal tasks to mentally retarded children.

As we have implied, the use of modeling procedures to help clients overcome fears is a relatively recent innovation in the psychological literature—though people have been using similar procedures to help others overcome fears for thousands of years. There are two general procedures involving modeling in the reduction of phobic behavior: *vicarious extinction* and *participant modeling*.

VICARIOUS EXTINCTION.   Extinction refers to behavior carried out in the absence of reinforcement. Although we have stressed positive reinforcers, as we pointed out, reinforcers may also be aversive in nature. If a particular behavior is followed by aversive consequences the behavior will be suppressed; in addition, stimuli associated with the aversive consequences will probably give rise to a conditioned fear response. However, if the aversive consequences cease, in most cases the original behavior will return. You could say the suppression has been extinguished, but additionally, the fear response will also dissipate or undergo extinction. *Vicarious extinction* refers to an analogous process. To illustrate, suppose a child is afraid of dogs, a common fear among children. There is some rather convincing experimental evidence that if that child is exposed to other children interacting with dogs in a fearless manner, he will show a marked reduction in fear and avoidance behavior toward dogs (Bandura & Menlove, 1968). The term *vicarious* is used because the child himself is not undergoing direct extinction. Rather, he is observing others interacting with dogs in the absence of aversive consequences. O'Connor (1969) worked with socially withdrawn children, who after observing a film of children interacting with each other, showed a striking increase in their own interaction with other children. The models may be live or presented via film or videotape; it does not appear to make a great deal of difference (see Masters & Driscoll, 1971). It may be significant that the models in such research generally interact with the phobic stimuli in a graduated fashion, just like clients undergoing systematic desensitization. Adults are also capable of undergoing vicarious extinction of fears (see Bandura, Blanchard, & Ritter, 1969), although the effect is not always found (Somervill & Rimm, 1974). It is probably a relatively more effective therapeutic procedure for children than for adults.

PARTICIPANT MODELING.   In the foregoing discussion of vicarious extinction, we have made the tacit assumption that the observer is unlearning behavioral suppression and fear. It is possible that the observer is also learning certain skills that make it easier to cope with the phobic object or situation. This factor of skill learning may be even more important in *participant modeling*. A virtually identical procedure is referred to as *contact desensitization* (Ritter, 1969a). Since most of the research has been done with snake-phobic subjects (Bandura *et al.*, 1969; Rimm & Mahoney, 1969), we shall briefly describe the method when the phobic object is a harmless snake. The therapist first goes through a graduated series of approach behaviors related to the snake; for example, approaching and touching the cage, touching the snake while wearing thick gloves, and so on, until finally the therapist is handling the snake barehanded in a fearless and comfortable manner. The client then goes through the same sequence of behaviors *at his own pace,* until he too is able to handle the snake barehanded while experiencing no particular discomfort. The time required to "cure" even those clients who are very fearful of snakes is remarkably short. Usually, 2–3 hours of treatment is more than sufficient.

The technique has been used successfully with acrophobics, individuals with fears of high places (Ritter, 1969b) and water phobics, e.g., persons who were fearful of immersing themselves in a swimming pool (Hunziker, 1972). A study by Howard (1975) involving rat-phobic subjects is instructive. One of the therapists was extremely confident in his interactions with the harmless laboratory rats, and his subjects showed marked reductions in fear. The second therapist (and this was not by design) was obviously fearful himself, and his subjects did not improve. Clearly, confidence and skill are important components in the model's behavior.[3] As an exercise, you might wish to outline a participant modeling procedure for individuals fearful of riding horses.

FLOODING AND IMPLOSIVE THERAPY

Flooding differs from systematic desensitization in that it is not done in a graduated fashion. Instead, the client is asked to imagine what for him is absolutely the most fear-provoking scene, until his fear response has been extinguished. In flooding, relaxation is not employed. Implosive therapy also requires that the client imagine extremely fear-provoking scenes, again in the absence of relaxation. The important difference between flooding and implosive therapy pertains to the *content* of the scenes the client is required to imagine. In implosive therapy, Stampfl explicitly stresses the importance of psychoanalytic themes (see Stampfl & Levis, 1968). The client is assumed to have unconscious fears relating to infantile rejection sexuality, aggression, and such. The following illustrates a theme pertaining to rejection:

Shut your eyes and imagine that you are a baby in your crib. You are in a dark, shabby, dirty room. You are alone and afraid. You are hungry and wet. You call for your mother, but no one comes. If only someone would change you; if only they would feed you and wrap you in a warm blanket. You look out the window of your room into the house next door, where a mother and father are giving another baby love, warmth and affection. Look how they love the baby. You are crying for your mother now. "Please mother, please come and love me." But no one comes. Finally,

---

[3] Two notes of caution are in order. First, it is imperative that the therapist select a snake, dog, or rat that *is* harmless. There are so-called harmless snakes that do occasionally bite. Though the bite might not be dangerous, the experience would hardly be therapeutic. Second, in dealing with children, it is important that they be taught that there are, for example, very harmful snakes, and that they should be discriminating in their approach to any snake. (Adults almost always know this, but small children rarely do.)

you hear some steps. They come closer, and closer, and closer. You hear someone outside your door. The door slowly opens. Your heart beats with excitement. There is your mother coming to love you. She is unbuttoning her blouse. She takes out her breast to feed you. Then she squirts your warm milk on the floor and steps in it. Look, see her dirty heel mark in your milk. She shouts, "I would rather waste my milk than to give it to you. I wish you were never born; I never wanted you [Hogan, 1969, p. 181].

Actual sessions are presumably long enough for the client to experience very intense anxiety, followed by *extinction* of this anxiety. Although the proponents of implosive therapy have not demonstrated that the psychoanalytic themes are a necessary component of treatment, there is evidence that the technique may be effective. *It is not a technique to be used by amateurs,* however.

AVERSIVE CONDITIONING

In a previous section, we defined *punishment* as the presentation of an aversive stimulus (technically, a negative reinforcer) following a particular response.[4] The punishing stimulus might involve a slap, electric shock, a nausea-inducing drug, or imagined aversive experiences.

At one time, the view that punishment had merely a temporary suppressing effect on behavior was widespread. More recent findings (see Solomon, 1964) have shown that this is most decidedly not the case, especially if the punishing stimulus is of a highly intense, traumatic nature. Needless to say, we are not recommending a procedure that requires inflicting severe pain. We should also point out that punishment, even when not so severe, may lead to undesirable side effects. For example, fear may be conditioned to stimuli quite unrelated to the behavior that the dispenser of punishment is trying to eliminate. Consider, for example, a schoolchild who is disrupting his class with inappropriate verbal behavior. If the teacher administers a painful slap to his wrist, the child may cease his disruptive behavior—but anxiety may be conditioned to other stimuli in the classroom, which may be detrimental to his academic performance. The slap may also have the effect of suppressing appropriate verbal behavior as well.

You may wonder whether punishment procedures, as we are presently defining them, are ever justified. The answer may be affirmative, provided that the problem behavior is of a very serious nature and other procedures have not been effective. This is well illustrated in the research of Lovaas and his associates (Lovaas & Simmons, 1969), who worked with autistic children whose self-mutilating behavior endangered their physical welfare. Intense punishment suppressed this behavior, and in such an extreme context, this punishment can fairly be described as humane.

AVOIDANCE CONDITIONING.   When pyschologists do employ aversive stimuli to control the behavior of their clients, avoidance conditioning is used more often

---

[4] Recall that punishment may also involve removal of a positive reinforcer. As we have indicated, operant conditioners are generally more partial to this form of punishment.

than punishment. The procedure is well illustrated in the treatment of male homosexuals desiring to change their sexual orientation (see Feldman & MacCulloch, 1971). Such clients are shown a slide depicting a nude male, which is accompanied by a painful electric shock. Subsequently, they have the opportunity to terminate the shock by pressing a button that also removes the slide, and later they may avoid shock completely by pressing the button soon after the slide appears (say, within 7 or 8 seconds). The term *avoidance conditioning* is used because in the final stage, the client learns that he can avoid shock by removing stimuli that are symbolically related to homosexual behavior.

Such an avoidance-conditioning procedure is often paired with an anxiety-relief procedure. Thus, when the homosexual presses the button that removes the male slide, a slide of a nude female is presented. The assumption is that the sight of a nude female, because it is correlated with anxiety reduction, will become a more positive stimulus. This assumption is plausible, although as Barlow (1973) has pointed out, the anxiety-relief component has not been researched by itself. Thus, it is not really known whether anxiety-relief conditioning coupled with avoidance conditioning is any more effective than avoidance conditioning alone.

In the treatment of homosexuality, aversive-conditioning procedures by themselves, though they might decrease homosexual desires and increase heterosexual desires, are of limited usefulness. A homosexual who has had no heterosexual contacts probably lacks the social skills necessary to approach and deal with females. For this reason, a more effective treatment program might involve a *combination* of aversive conditioning and assertive training. An analogous argument can be made in the treatment of alcoholism. Aversive conditioning may be helpful, but the chronic alcoholic's existence is so thoroughly centered around alcohol (his "friends" typically are fellow drinkers, and he is inexperienced in finding alternative modes of recreation), that a truly effective treatment procedure must involve a major change in his life-style.

COVERT SENSITIZATION.   One aversive-conditioning procedure that is growing in popularity is covert sensitization. The procedure, developed by Joseph Cautela (1967), requires that the subject imagine both the activity or behavior he desires to eliminate and the aversive consequences—often nausea, but also fear, shame or guilt; hence the term *covert* sensitization.

To illustrate, consider the treatment of an obese subject. First, the therapist establishes types of foods or eating habits that are especially troublesome. He then relaxes the subject, using a method like that described earlier in this chapter. The subject in this example was a student in a workshop conducted in Mexico. She was particularly fond of bananas and cream, obviously high in caloric content. In accordance with the standard procedure, she was presented with three types or categories of trials, one involving escape conditioning, a second involving avoidance conditioning, and a third involving an appropriate eating behavior without aversive consequences. (The third type is presented in order to ensure that the client does not develop a dislike for food in general.)

1. In the *escape trial,* the therapist says, "Imagine that you have just finished lunch, but you really feel like having some bananas and cream. You open the refrigerator and take out the bowl and sit down and put a large spoonful in your mouth. Suddenly you notice you are perspiring, and you begin to feel nausea. Now, you really feel sick . . . like you want to throw up. You feel terrible. Now you throw up . . . that horrible, stinking mixture of vomit . . . bananas and cream . . . all over you. Your mother comes in and says, 'What a disgrace . . . you look like a filthy pig.' You put the bowl back in the refrigerator and begin to feel better. You take a shower and change your clothes and now you feel fine."

2. The *avoidance trial* is similar to the escape trial, but before the client begins eating the bananas and cream, she imagines mild nausea and immediately puts the bowl back in the refrigerator and feels better. The mother reinforces the behavior.

3. In the *neutral trial,* the subject imagines eating something palatable but "allowable"—in this case, lean meat and salad.

Covert sensitization has several obvious advantages. First, the client has control over the aversive stimulation. It is less threatening than electric shock, and does not have a punitive connotation. Second, no apparatus, such as a shock device, is required. Third, the therapist and client have complete freedom with respect to the type of aversive consequences to be employed. Fourth, the client can practice the technique on his own.

COGNITIVE THERAPY

RATIONAL EMOTIVE THERAPY.   Albert Ellis (1962, 1971) has developed a therapy approach that has become very popular in the past decade. To describe this approach in detail is beyond the scope of the present text; the interested reader is referred to any of his books. *The Guide to Rational Living* by Ellis and Harper (1968) is brief and highly readable; Ellis's *Reason and Emotion in Psychotherapy* (1962) is far more definitive, but is also quite readable. The basic assumptions are simple and plausible; they may be illustrated in the following example. Suppose a client is fearful of dogs:

1. He sees a dog, which is actually harmless.
2. He says to himself (although he may not be completely aware that he is saying it): "That dog might bite me and that would be terrible."
3. He experiences fear and takes measures to avoid the dog.
4. The therapist intervenes, leading the client to become aware of his self-defeating and irrational self-verbalizations.
5. The client changes his self-verbalizations and is no longer fearful of harmless dogs.

The self-verbalizations at stage 2 are irrational for two reasons. First, it is most unlikely that the dog will bite the client. Second, even if the client is bitten it is not a catastrophe, as the dog is not likely to be rabid.

Consider as a second example an impotent male. At stage 2 he may say this to himself: "I must perform in order to be a man . . . but I might not be able to, and that would be horrible." This is irrational because sexual performance is not equated with being a man, and it is self-defeating because it gives rise to anxiety sufficient to inhibit penile erection.

We stated earlier that the behavior therapies have specific behavioral goals. Thus, rational emotive therapy (RET) actually does not qualify as a behavior therapy because Ellis attempts to restructure his client's basic belief system. Nevertheless, many behavior therapists employ RET, usually in concert with other methods described earlier in this chapter.

COGNITIVE-BEHAVIOR THERAPY.   The basic idea that self-verbalizations are fundamental to the way we feel and behave has given rise to techniques less pervasive than that of Ellis (and therefore, more consistent with the specific treatment goals associated with behavior therapy). We label these techniques *cognitive-behavior therapy*. Such techniques are illustrated in the work of Meichenbaum (1971), Meichenbaum and Cameron (1973), Rimm (1973), and Rimm, Saunders, and Westel (1975).

Rimm and his associates have provided evidence that a variation of thought stopping, a procedure popularized by Wolpe (1958, 1969) for dealing with obsessional thinking, can be used effectively with clients who ordinarily would be labeled as phobics. In Chapter 4, we discussed the possible role of self-verbalizations in the maintenance of phobic behavior. The procedure employed by Rimm and his colleagues, which is similar in some respects to certain techniques of Meichenbaum's, actually goes beyond thought stopping. After the client has learned to identify his irrational, fear-inducing self-verbalizations and to stop them by saying "stop!" to himself in a convincing and authoritative fashion, he is taught to engage in *covert assertions*—possible self-verbalizations, assertive in content, which presumably inhibit anxiety and also compete with the original, fear-inducing self-verbalization. For a detailed discussion of this method, see Rimm and Masters (1974).

REATTRIBUTION THERAPY.   Another cognitive-behavior therapy method (methodology would be a better term, since a highly structured technique has yet to appear) may be referred to as the *psychology of reattribution*. People attribute the way they feel and behave to factors that they tend to see as either internal or external. An internal factor is something that a person views as very much "part of myself." For example, if a person views himself as very intelligent and does well on an academic examination, he probably will attribute much of his success to his intelligence. An external factor is something that the person views as not part of himself. A person who considers himself lacking in intelligence, for instance, will probably attribute his good test performance to the fact that the examination was easy.

Although the psychology of reattribution has not yet become part of the behavior therapist's stock in trade, certain clinical applications are obvious. Suppose, for example, that a student is far behind in his course work, and examination time is rapidly approaching. He works for 36 solid hours in the solitude of his room, and toward the end of this extremely fatiguing experience, he finds that he is beginning to hear voices. Now, suppose he is concerned and seeks help from a therapist. If the therapist informs him that he *is* schizophrenic, this will be an internal attribution leading to a variety of unfortunate consequences: extreme worry, perhaps hospitalization and the associated stigma. On the other hand, suppose the therapist suggests that, given his client's severe sleep deficit, such an experience is hardly surprising. Such an interpretation implies an external attribution. The student may now say to himself, "I'm not really crazy after all . . . it was just the lack of sleep." The consequences of believing this are not frightening, nor is there any reason for the student to believe he is in need of some help.

The general topic of cognitive-behavior therapy is described in more detail in a highly readable and informative text by Mahoney (1974), entitled *Cognition and Behavior Modification*.

Research Findings

There have been literally thousands of controlled investigations dealing with the various behavior therapies. What follows is merely a sampling of some of the more prominent investigations supporting each of the various techniques. Readers interested in exploring the behavior therapy research in depth are referred to any one of several texts (e.g., Bandura, 1969; Franks, 1969; Franks & Wilson, 1973, 1974, 1975; Kanfer & Phillips, 1970; O'Leary & Wilson, 1975; Rimm & Masters, 1974; Wolpe, 1969/1973; Yates, 1970, 1975) as well as any of the four behavior therapy journals: *Behavior Research and Therapy, Journal of Applied Behavior Analysis* (exclusively operant), *Behavior Therapy,* and *Behavior Therapy and Experimental Psychiatry.*

OPERANT TECHNIQUES

TRAINING NONPROFESSIONALS TO BE OPERANT CONDITIONERS. There is considerable evidence that nonprofessionals, usually parents or teachers, can be trained in the effective use of operant procedures to modify children's behavior. Problems that have been successfully dealt with include depression and hyperdependency (Wahler & Pollio, 1968), social withdrawal (e.g., Allen, Hart, Buell, Harris, & Wolf, 1964; Brawley, Harris, Allen, Fleming, & Peterson, 1969), and hyperactivity and aggression (Allen, Henke, Harris, Baer, & Reynolds, 1967; Hall, Lund, & Jackson, 1968).

SELF-CONTROL. A basic question about any operantly based self-control program is whether people who have free access to reward will perform some desirable behavior prior to reinforcing themselves. Studies by Bandura and Perloff (1967) and Glynn (1970) indicate that even with preadolescent children, self-reward is an effective means of strengthening certain responses. That is, the subjects "worked" for their rewards, rather than rewarding themselves for doing nothing.

To date, most self-control programs have dealt with obesity. In general the results have been positive (see Hall, 1972; Harris, 1969; Mahoney, Moura, & Wade, 1973; Stuart, 1967, 1971; Wollersheim, 1970). Subjects in such programs typically lose on the order of 1 pound per week. Other studies suggest that self-control procedures may be somewhat effective in the reduction of cigarette smoking (e.g., Azrin & Powell, 1968; Sachs, Bean, & Morrow, 1970).

The case histories presented by Fox (1962) and Goldiamond (1965) and experiments by Glynn (1970) and Beneke and Harris (1972) suggest the value of self-control procedures in dealing with study problems. However, as Beneke and Harris point out, the dropout rate was a very high 83%. As in the case of cigarette smoking, considerably more research is needed before any definite conclusions can be drawn regarding the effectiveness of self-control procedures in dealing with study problems.

TOKEN ECONOMIES AND AFTER-CARE PROGRAMS. There is rather clear-cut evidence that institutionalized mental patients may be induced into behaving more appropriately under token economies (Ayllon & Azrin, 1968; Schaefer & Martin, 1969). As I have indicated, there is no assurance that the appropriate behavior shaped by such a system will generalize to the natural environment. One promising approach (see Fairweather, Sanders, Maynard, & Cressler, 1969) involved sending discharged patients to a "lodge," where the ex-patients evidenced considerable independence, including operating a reasonably profitable janitorial service. Patients discharged from the same ward who did not go to the lodge showed a much higher return rate to the hospital than those who remained in the lodge. This particular lodge was not viewed as a half-way house. Rather, it was a community for people whose behavior deficits were such that making an independent adjustment to the demands of society at large would have been difficult.

Token economies have also been shown to be successful in controlling the behavior of delinquent and predelinquent boys (Achievement Place is an excellent example; see Phillips, Phillips, Fixen, & Wolf, 1971).

WOLPIAN PROCEDURES

SYSTEMATIC DESENSITIZATION. Since Lang and Lazovik published the first reasonably well controlled investigation of systematic desensitization in 1963, there have been innumerable investigations exploring the efficacy of this technique. The vast majority of investigations have supported the value of this method. Among the classic studies are those of Paul (1966) dealing with the fear of public speaking; Davison's (1968) investigation dealing with snake phobias (especially valuable because it supported the counterconditioning interpretation that pairing of relaxation and imaginal scenes was crucial to effective treatment); and studies by Emery and Krumboltz (1967) and Suinn (1968) effectively employing desensitization with test-anxious subjects. To illustrate the breadth of problems amenable to treatment, Moore (1965) successfully treated asthmatic patients with desensitization; Rimm, deGroot, Boord, Heiman, and Dillow (1971) obtained results suggesting that anger may be reduced using desensitization; and Curran and Gilbert (1975) found the method effective in reducing dating anxiety.

To be sure, all the data have not been supportive. There is considerable controversy over which components of systematic desensitization are truly essential for fear reduction. For example, some have argued that the subject's expectancies regarding treatment outcome are of fundamental importance (see Lick, 1975; Wilkins, 1971). Although most writers agree that desensitization *is* an effective therapeutic tool, precisely why it works is not yet resolved (see Kazdin & Wilcoxon, 1976).

ASSERTIVE TRAINING.　Wolpe's use of assertive training slightly predates his development of systematic desensitization. However, assertive training has only recently undergone careful experimental examination. Controlled studies demonstrating the efficacy of the technique include those by Hersen, Eisler, and Miller (1974), Lazarus (1966), McFall and Lillesand (1971), McFall and Marston (1970), McFall and Twentyman (1973), and Young, Rimm, and Kennedy (1973). Occasionally, negative results are obtained. For example, Mize (1974) found that subjects undergoing assertive training did not improve significantly more than control subjects, nor did the therapist's exhorting the subject to be more assertive enhance assertive behavior. Young *et al.* (1973) found that reinforcement for improved assertiveness failed to enhance the assertive behavior of their subjects, and as we have noted earlier, McFall and Twentyman (1973) presented evidence that modeling added little to the therapeutic procedure. In view of the power of reinforcement and modeling in the control of human behavior, it is clear that additional research examining these factors in assertive training is needed.

Assertive training lends itself readily to group treatment and indeed there is evidence suggesting that it is effective in such a setting (Hedquist & Weingold, 1970; Rathus, 1972; Rimm *et al.*, 1974). The Rimm *et al.* study is interesting in that the subjects were aggressive rather than timid. As we have stated earlier, aggression, like timidity, exemplifies nonassertive behavior.

MODELING PROCEDURES

VICARIOUS EXTINCTION.　Studies by Bandura *et al.* (1967) and Bandura and Menlove (1968) illustrate the power of vicarious extinction when used with dog-phobic children.

PARTICIPANT MODELING.　The results of participant modeling studies are generally quite impressive, especially for fears of specific animals (Bandura *et al.*, 1969; Howard, 1975; Rimm & Mahoney, 1969). There is also evidence that it may be effective for height phobics (Ritter, 1969b) and water phobics (Hunziker, 1972). When the phobic stimuli are limited and specific, as in these examples, the technique is perhaps the most potent and rapid means of fear reduction.

FLOODING AND IMPLOSIVE THERAPY

Experiments employing flooding procedures have produced equivocal results. Strahley (1965) found it to be superior to systematic desensitization, but Brock (1967) found no significant difference between the two methods. De Moor (1970) also found little difference between flooding and desensitization although there was some indication at a later follow-up test that desensitization was more effective. Rachman (1966b) found flooding to be totally ineffective; Boulougouris, Marks, and Marset (1971) obtained results indicating that flooding was superior to desensitization; Blanchard (1975) obtained positive results with flooding.

The results for implosive therapy are also somewhat mixed. Positive results have been obtained by Hogan and Kirchner (1967), Levis and Carrera (1967), and McCutcheon and Adams (1975), whereas negative results are reported by Fazio (1970) and Hodgson and Rachman (1970). There have been several studies comparing implosive therapy and systematic desensitization (e.g., Barrett, 1969; Borkovec, 1972). Again the results are conflicting, although none showed implosive therapy to be superior to systematic desensitization.

AVERSIVE CONTROL AND PUNISHMENT

The effective use of punishment procedures—that is, the administration of aversive stimulation following a particular behavior, rather than time out from positive reinforcement—is seen in the work of Lovaas and his associates (for example, Bucher & Lovaas, 1968; Lovaas & Simmons, 1969) and in the work of Risley (1968). Sachs and Mayhall (1971) report that punishment procedures reduced spasms and involuntary movements in an individual with cerebral palsy. Lang and Melamed (1969) as well as other experimenters have used punishment to eliminate repeated vomiting. Some degree of success using punishment in the treatment of alcoholics has been reported (Vogler, Lunde, & Martin, 1971; Wilson, Leaf, & Nathan, 1975)—although, as we have suggested, a better program would probably involve other behavioral interventions as well.

Avoidance conditioning, often including anxiety-relief conditioning, has been used with some success in the treatment of homosexuality (Feldman & MacCulloch, 1971) and Blake (1965) reported somewhat positive findings with alcoholics, although the study was poorly controlled. Sexual deviations such as transvestism and fetishism have been treated with some success using related approaches (e.g., see Lavin, Thorpe, Barker, Blakemore, & Conway, 1961). Often the aversive stimulus employed is electric shock; drug-induced nausea has also been used, especially in the treatment of alcoholism (e.g., see Voegtlin, 1940). In one study, Foreyt and Kennedy (1971) successfully employed aversive conditioning based on the inhalation of a noxious odor to treat obese subjects.

We have suggested that covert sensitization holds considerable promise as an aversive-conditioning technique. However, the technique is relatively new and the number of controlled investigations is limited. Janda and Rimm (1972) obtained a moderate weight loss in obese subjects using this technique, and Barlow, Leitenberg and Agras (1969) demonstrated its effectiveness in the treatment of pedophiliac and homosexual behavior. On the other hand Foreyt and Hagen (1973) failed to obtain weight reduction using covert sensitization.

COGNITIVE APPROACHES

Several experimental investigations (for example, Meichenbaum & Goodman, 1969; Rimm & Litvak, 1969; Russell & Brandsma, 1974) have provided evidence that cognitive activities such as self-verbalizations do exert some control over the way in which people feel and behave. Studies by Maes and Heimann (1970), Meichenbaum, Gilmore, and Fedoravicius (1971), and Trexler and Karst (1972) indicate that the specific therapeutic approach advocated by Ellis is effective in reducing a variety of maladaptive response patterns such as anxiety associated with taking examinations and public-speaking phobias.

The work of Meichenbaum and his associates (Meichenbaum, 1971; Meichenbaum & Cameron, 1973) and Rimm and his colleagues (Rimm *et al.*, 1975) demonstrate that procedures aimed at altering highly specific self-verbalizations may be effective in reducing phobic behavior and other patterns of maladaptive responding.

Several studies have pointed to the possible therapeutic value of reattribution therapy. Examples of such investigations include Davison, Tsujimoto, and Glaros (1973) and Davison and Valins (1969). Diverse problems have been dealt with, including insomnia, speech anxiety, and pain tolerance. However, reattribution therapy is still very much in the experimental stage and should not be viewed as an established behavior-therapy technique.

Summary

We have noted that the behavior therapies stress the treatment of behaviors per se, or responses closely related to overt behavior. Learning plays an important role in both the acquisition and the treatment of maladaptive responding. Treatment, which is oriented in the here-and-now, has specific goals; and empirical validation of a particular technique is fundamental.

The behavior therapies comprise a large number of techniques; they would appear to have at least some applicability to a very wide variety of psychological problems. The operant techniques (including the application of these techniques to problems of self-control) have been shown to be effective in eliminating undesirable behaviors and strengthening desirable behaviors. A variety of behavioral techniques have proved useful in reducing or eliminating phobic behavior; among them are systematic desensitization, vicarious extinction and participant modeling, and flooding and implosive therapy. Modeling procedures are demonstrably effective in teaching individuals socially appropriate behaviors. Assertive training is a practical means of imparting interpersonal skills as well as reducing social anxiety. The aversive conditioning techniques, including punishment, avoidance conditioning, and covert sensitization, have proved helpful in reducing a variety of self-defeating behaviors such as self-mutilation, sexual deviations, alcoholism, and overeating, although in general they appear to be most effective in combination with other techniques. The cognitive therapies, including rational emotive therapy and related approaches designed to alter attitudes or self-verbalizations, are useful in dealing with a variety of problems including phobias and impulsivity.

Controlled research supports the effectiveness of all of the aforementioned techniques, and we have cited representative studies in this chapter. However, the amount of scientific support varies considerably, depending on the technique in question. For example, hundreds of studies support the value of the more established techniques such as the operant approaches and systematic desensitization, whereas the newer approaches such as covert sensitization and certain of the cognitive approaches have considerably less empirical support.

16

Psychoanalytic Therapy

GORDON E. RADER

Southern Illinois University at Carbondale

A college student of 20, whom we shall call Ben, sought help shortly after suffering a severe panic attack. During the interview, Ben related that he and his girl friend were driving at night and pulled over to the side of the road to change drivers. Earlier in the day they had decided that they really liked each other and that they would seriously consider a permanent relationship. When they stopped to change drivers, Ben leaned over and kissed his girl friend. She responded very warmly—whereupon he went into a panic and spent the next 3 days in a haze of anxiety, almost out of contact with his surroundings.

How is one to explain his panic? He had kissed his girl friend many times before and it had always been a pleasurable experience. He had never been punished for kissing and could remember no traumatic experiences related to kissing. Completely puzzled by his reaction, Ben searched his mind thoroughly for some understanding of what happened to him. The only thought during his panic that seemed significant or unusual was the thought that he might be homosexual. However, there was little objective reason for such an idea and he could see no connection between that thought and kissing his girl friend. Frightened by his loss of control, Ben was highly motivated to get an intellectual handle on his inexplicable reaction.

It would certainly appear that Ben's reaction was related to some complex of meaning or some threatening fantasy about what could happen, which was somehow associatively connected with and was aroused by that particular kissing situation. Furthermore, we must assume from Ben's puzzlement and inability to offer any explanation for his fear that these ideas or fantasies were not within his awareness, that is, that they were unconscious. We will return to Ben later, but first we will explore the psychoanalytic theories that may lead to an understanding of his frightening experience.

Origins of Psychoanalytic Psychotherapy

Modern personality theory and psychotherapy both began with the work of Sigmund Freud (1856–1939). Most of Freud's observations and many of his ideas, as well as some aspects of his treatment method, were foreshadowed in the isolated comments or in the practices of others. However, it required Freud's combination of keen observation and sweeping vision to perceive the broader significance of the patterns of behavior he observed, and then to develop a comprehensive theory of human behavior and an innovative method of treatment.

Freud began his private practice at a time when most of the medical world perceived all medical phenomena, including those now regarded as psychologically based, solely in physiochemical terms or as physiological–anatomic disorders. As a result, treatment was principally physical in its orientation. Freud's training had been in neurology and he had absorbed the prevailing theories about the causes and treatment of neurotic disorders, which at that time were customarily part of the practice of neurologists. Consequently, when he began his private practice in 1886, Freud began by applying to his neurotic patients the accepted treatment methods of the day: electrical stimulation, hydrotherapy, massage, sedative drugs, and rest.

However, Freud had been impressed when an older colleague, Breuer, used hypnosis successfully in treating a young woman. Freud later collaborated with Breuer in writing the first book that may be regarded as part of the psychoanalytic literature. The case history of Breuer's patient, Anna O., is the first case history described in that book. Freud had also been much impressed by demonstrations of hypnosis by the French neurologist Charcot, who was able to alter or remove the symptoms of patients suffering from hysteria (now called conversion reaction) by means of hypnosis. Although many physicians still disapproved of hypnosis, Freud began to use hypnotic suggestion as a treatment method after 20 months of little success with conventional techniques. Freud continued to experiment. He soon gave up hypnosis in favor of waking suggestion, and then gradually developed the free-association method of classical psychoanalysis. He found that virtually all his neurotic patients presented puzzles—similar to that of Ben's seemingly inexplicable sudden panic.

Freud's approach to his patients had two distinctive features: his assumption that there must be some reason for the timing and choice of his patients' symptoms and his willingness to satisfy his curiosity by spending time listening to his patients at length. He encouraged them to talk freely about their lives, their inner feelings and thoughts, and the circumstances surrounding the outbreak of their symptoms. Freud's approach worked particularly well with patients who had developed hysterical disorders, which were more common at that time. Soon he was specializing in such cases. Freud regularly found that his hysterical patients at first could think of no immediate sufficient cause for the outbreak of their symptoms. However, as he continued to work with them, his patients eventually would recall an upsetting event that closely preceded the appearance of their symptoms. Further work regularly revealed that the upsetting event was itself emotionally disturbing, at least in part, because of its relationship to childhood events. These memories, however, were recovered only with great difficulty.

Initially, Freud was disinclined to believe that there was a sexual factor involved in the disturbances of his patients. In the first 18 cases he analyzed, he was surprised to find a sexual component in the etiology "to hold for every single symptom and, when circumstances permitted, to confirm the fact by therapeutic success [Freud, 1896/1950, p. 193]." Moreover, a close examination of cases manifesting such nonhysterical symptoms as obsessions, compulsions, phobias, and paranoid delusions and hallucinations revealed that these patients, like those with hysterical conversion symptoms, had ideas or wishes arising out of early sexual experiences. These ideas or wishes were intolerable because they affronted the person's moral values or sense of pride. Freud's patients had dealt with these unbearable ideas by simply forcing them out of awareness but later experiences had stimulated the forbidden ideas or wishes. At that point, symptoms developed—expressing, in disguised form, both the original idea or wish and the self-reproach or efforts toward self-control stirred up by the wish. Freud subsequently discovered that many of the "memories" of childhood sexual seduction reported by his patients were mere fantasies. As a result, Freud focused on unconscious wishes and strivings rather than on traumatic external events as prime determinants of psychopathology. As he continued to see more patients, Freud found some for whom aggressive wishes rather than sexual urges seemed to be the primary underlying basis for the psychoneurotic symptoms.

Freud broke with the prevailing physical treatment methods and developed psychological explanations for the disorders he was treating. He also developed psychological explanations of such normal phenomena as dreams, selective memory, thinking, emotion, sexual development, parent–child relationships, and character style. Consequently, Freud can be considered the father of *abnormal psychology* and *personality* as fields of study, and of *psychotherapy* as a treatment method.

Psychoanalytic theory is not a single, coherent, tightly organized theory. Rather, it is a loose collection of theories, subtheories, and empirical propositions. Many of the propositions can be proven false without invalidating others or the basic structure. In fact, this is exactly what occurred, as Freud (and others since) continually modified and revised aspects of the theory to take into account new data. Freud was a very careful observer and a person of great intellectual integrity. He perceived certain connections in the seemingly unrelated associations of his patients, which suggested concerns or conflicts that cropped up again and again in different patients. On the basis of these regularities, he developed psychological explanations of the disordered behaviors he was treating. However, he also wanted to construct a more general and inclusive theory of human behavior. Pursuing this goal, he developed more abstract and general principles by reasoning from his basic observations. In effect, Freud's theories contain propositions of varying degrees of abstractness and distance from his original data base. These can be divided into three parts: (1) the clinical theory of psychoanalysis; (2) the general theory of psychoanalysis (sometimes called psychoanalytic metapsychology); and (3) Freud's anthropological, social, historical, and philosophical speculations. The clinical theory is most clearly tied to the data of observation and involves the least reasoning and abstraction from the data.

Much of Freud's theorizing is open to criticism—as are most other theoretical endeavors of half a century or more ago. Nevertheless, many of his observations, ideas, and points of view have withstood the test of time. The clinical theory of psychoanalysis is more widely accepted and more relevant to an understanding of people's behavior and to clinical work than are his other theoretical conceptions. It derives from the most detailed and prolonged study of people's lives ever undertaken. This clinical theory forms the conceptual base on which the vast majority of psychiatrists, clinical psychologists, and social workers construct their clinical formulations, including many who do not consider themselves psychoanalytically oriented.

Some of the more important assumptions and concepts underlying psychotherapeutic treatment are described in the sections that follow.

Psychological Determinism

Freud was a thoroughgoing determinist in both his theory building and his clinical work. He assumed that no behavior is accidental or random, and that every aspect of behavior has its causal explanation. Determinism was not an unusual position in Freud's day. What was unusual was to assume *psychological* determinism, i.e., to look for explanations in psychological factors. It was fashion of the day to dismiss dreams as random discharges in the nervous system, slips of the tongue as misfirings somewhere in the system, and so on. Thus, by accepting psychological determinism, *all* behavior—normal or abnormal, fundamental or seemingly insignificant—became the subject matter of psychoanalysis. Such an assumption is a necessary precondition for the particular type of attention that psychodynamically oriented therapists pay to their patient's productions. Meaning and pattern are perceived in trains of association, omissions, repetitive accidents, and motor mannerisms—the last illustrated by the patient who tore her styrofoam coffee cup to pieces as she talked of her husband's ambition; only later did she reveal her anger at playing second fiddle to his career. Some patterns may take years to develop—such as the repetitive mistakes in judgment made by the woman who manages to marry three brutal, alcoholic husbands in a row.

Psychoanalytic theory is above all a *motivationally based* theory. The ultimate determiners of all behavior are drives; behavior is motivated. There are minor exceptions, of course, such as reflex behaviors, passive responses such as recoiling from a blow, or responses to somatic conditions such as staggering when drunk. However, within the range of what we normally consider behavior, motivation is regarded as the driving force.

The concept of force is important here. Viewing motivation as a kind of force had its origin in certain observations:

1. Behavior is not always triggered by external stimulation but often occurs without it, spontaneously.
2. Behavior is directional and purposeful—it is directed toward a goal.
3. Subjectively we feel and empirically we observe that the intensity of disposition (or force) impelling the performance of any behavior can vary. Depending on the strength of the motive, there is a greater or lesser degree of internal demand to perform the behaviors toward the indicated goal or purpose.

Physical forces are characterized by intensity, direction, and the capacity to perform work. So, by analogy, is motivation—if we understand work in a psychological, not a neuromuscular, sense. When we focus our attention, think, remember, plan, or emote, we expend psychological energy and this psychological work is guided and energized by whatever motives are active at that moment.

In addition to the motivational drive forces, psychoanalysts note that the defensive tendencies of the individual and his emotions have these same characteristics of forces—intensity, direction, and a psychological energizing effect. When referring to the interplay of these psychological forces and their behavioral resultant, it is common to talk of *psychodynamics*, although the word sometimes has been used in a broader sense. This is consonant with Freud's observation that symptoms usually seem to be a behavioral compromise between the unacceptable wish or motive and the defensive efforts to control and conceal the desire.

The Instinctual Drives: Sex and Aggression

In the psychoanalytic literature, there are many references to instinctual drives or simply to instincts. What do psychoanalysts mean when they refer to instincts? This term is an unfortunate heritage in English of an error in translation from Freud's German term, *Triebe,* which can be translated more accurately as "drive." Freud revised his motivational (instinctual drive) theory several times, finally arriving at a dual drive theory with sex and aggression as the two drives. Although psychoanalysts recognize the existence of motives other than sex and aggression, they consider most psychopathology to be related to conflicts concerning sexual or aggressive drives. However, Freud postulated specific sexual (libidinal) and aggressive energies, which exist in the individual in a relatively fixed quantity and must be accounted for in some way; either they affect behavior or they are neutralized by the individual's defenses. These concepts of Freud's have been much criticized and various proposals for fundamental revision have been put forth (see especially Holt, 1975; Klein, 1967, 1975; Schafer, 1968, 1975; White, 1963).

Sex and aggression figure prominently in psychoanalytic theory because repeated observations and studies in many contexts have pointed to their importance in both normal and pathological behavior and in personality development as well. Such observations, however, provide no explanation. Three characteristics of these drives explain their importance (Loevinger, 1966). Sex and aggression are

1. *Interpersonal:* They normally are directed at other people.
2. Unusually *plastic* in their expression: They can be satisfied by a wide variety of acts as well as a wide variety of goal objects.
3. *Postponable:* Ordinarily (psychosomatic illnesses aside) nothing drastic happens to the physical status of the body if sexual or aggressive urges are not expressed or satisfied quickly.

By contrast, other basic drives, such as thirst, sleep, or the need for oxygen, do not have these three characteristics. What are the implications of sex and aggression being interpersonal, plastic, postponable drives? Very simply, the interpersonal nature of the impulses demands their socialization; their plasticity and capacity to tolerate delay make it possible. Sex and aggression thus are subject to much learning. They become a source of guilt, anxiety, and shame; they are defensively altered and disguised; they may be redirected into fantasy activity in place of immediate, direct expression; and they may be expressed in symbolic ways or bottled up altogether.

Are there other interpersonal drives that are plastic and delayable and should therefore be prominent? Some writers argue that dependency might be in somewhat the same category (Parens & Saul, 1971). But no other drives seem to have the same degree of pervasive importance and psychological urgency as sex and aggression.

Unconscious Processes

Basing his theory on observations of both patients and normal individuals, Freud postulated the existence of mental processes occurring outside of awareness. A concept of unconscious psychological processes is essential to account fully for the descriptions patients give of their problems and for the phenomena that occur in psychotherapy. Freud found such an assumption equally crucial for understanding such normal phenomena as dreams, jokes, memory lapses, and mistakes. In fact, Freud eventually concluded that unconscious factors contributed in greater or lesser degree to virtually every aspect of human behavior, from the choice of career to a person's characteristic habit of punctuality. Most people who have not engaged in intensive psychotherapy find it hard to believe that psychological processes of which they are unaware can wield such a pervasive influence over their lives, yet the observational and experimental data for such an influence seem indisputable. Such a statement does not discount the fact that we exercise a great deal of rational, conscious control over our behavior as well. Most psychotherapy systems acknowledge the existence of unconscious feelings, attitudes, wishes, and fantasies. Psychoanalysis emphasizes the importance of such processes and their relevance to understanding and treating psychopathology.

Conflict and Defense

We have all experienced conflict. Nearly every morning, I experience conflict between my desire to continue sleeping in my nice warm bed and my sense of responsibility, which demands that I get up and get on with my duties. This is a simple, conscious conflict that is easily resolved. However, the kinds of conflicts that Freud began to unearth in each of his patients were largely unconscious, often seriously affecting the behavior or feelings of his patients without their awareness. Further, he found that when his patients did become fully aware of all the dimensions of their conflicts, they generally lost their symptoms and were able to deal more effectively and realistically with those aspects of their lives that had been influenced by their conflicts. Unconscious conflicts, or those that have significant unconscious components, differ from conscious conflicts in that they are generally inappropriate, are not amenable to rational thought and decision making, are not easily resolved, and have their roots in past childhood experience.

As the developing child encounters socializing pressures, he comes to perceive some of his motives and attitudes as dangerous. The child's perception of danger originates in his experiences with those who respond to his behavior, primarily his parents. However, the intensity of the apparent threat in the mind of the child is exaggerated because of his helpless state, and because he cannot understand the educating objectives of his parents or the limitations on what retaliation or punishment he may suffer. Ultimately, the prohibitions and rebukes of his parents are internalized; the child and, later, the adult must answer to his own conscience as he strives to maintain a picture of himself as a moral and worthwhile person. Thus, the basis for conflict is laid between certain drives, wishes, attitudes, or feelings and the demands of the real world and one's own conscience. Yet it is in the nature of all of us to lust after forbidden pleasures and to wish to destroy those who frustrate us. If such wishes were recognized, they would arouse intense anxiety and guilt. *Defense mechanisms* are unconscious avoidance responses, designed to prevent both the recognition and the carrying out of such wishes and thereby to escape the unpleasant emotions and the anticipated punishment or retribution. We must be unaware that we are engaging in defensive activity, of course, for concealment from the self is one immediate

Gesturing and talking, the boy tries to catch his mother's attention—but she is totally absorbed in her new baby. The boy's anger at being displaced and ignored clashes with his need to control his anger in order to maintain his mother's love. Conflicts like this are common in childhood and most are quickly resolved. But if emotions are too frightening or unpleasant for a child to deal with, unconscious avoidance responses such as repression may take over. (Dena)

objective of the defenses. Preventing direct expression of the forbidden drives is the other objective.

Freud and his followers found one conflict that develops regularly during childhood. The way in which this conflict is resolved significantly affects both later personality development and any predisposition to psychological disorder. Children naturally go through a period, usually between the ages of 4 and 6, when they are sexually attracted to their opposite-sexed parent and wish to displace or dispose of their same-sexed parent. The child soon learns that wishes for a sexual relationship with the parent are doomed because of his or her sexual immaturity and inability to compete with the other parent. The child also learns that such wishes are forbidden. Therefore, the child interprets the parents' anxiety and anger over his or her approaches and aggressive rivalry as threatening retaliatory punishment, such as castration if the child is a boy. This pattern of attraction and rivalry is called the *Oedipus complex* and the conflict that results is referred to as *oedipal conflict.* We do not remember going through such a phase, because the very process of defending against such wishes includes driving them from our mind and banishing them from conscious memory, presumably forever.

We often try deliberately to put painful thoughts out of our minds. When we do the same thing automatically and without any awareness of doing so, then we are engaging in *repression,* the original and most basic defense. Forbidden motives and the complex of associated ideas, fantasies, and anxieties are renounced and actively kept out of awareness. However, in so doing a person removes these motives or attitudes and their attendant fears from connection with the rest of the developing personality. As a result, they cannot be corrected by later experience or maturing understanding. The continued necessity to maintain a defense against this inner "danger" does affect behavior, usually to a minor and unnoticed degree as part of one's character style or unique pattern of reacting to certain situations. But sometimes the comfortable balance is upset, often as a result of some triggering event such as Ben's kissing his girl friend. Then the inner conflict becomes more influential and disruptive, requiring more drastic defensive action, causing symptoms, or both. At such a point, people are likely to seek psychotherapeutic assistance.

Resistance

Freud, you will recall, found that his patients had great difficulty in recovering crucial "forgotten" memories. In fact, they acted as if they did not want to remember. As Freud's understanding grew, he recognized resistance as defensive activity brought into the treatment situation. In resisting, the patient is seeking to avoid the pain and anxiety of having to confront aspects of himself that he is striving to keep hidden, to avoid the risk of having to relinquish the security of accustomed patterns of behavior, and to avoid having to give up some of the advantages he receives from having symptoms. These advantages, called secondary gains, include such things as sympathy, relief from responsibilities, and compensation payments. Some resistance is conscious and deliberate but for the most part patients are unaware that they are resisting.

Transference

Stories about patients falling in love with their analysts are quite popular and they contain an element of truth. Patients in psychoanalysis quite regularly develop feelings, sometimes of extraordinary intensity and not always positive, toward the analyst. Occasionally feelings are provoked by the therapist and are quite appropriate to the situation. However, the feelings usually are inappropriate and are derived from past relationships. Greenson (1967) defines transference as "the experiencing of feelings, drives, attitudes, fantasies and defenses toward a person in the present which are inappropriate to that person and are a repetition, a displacement of reactions originating in regard to significant persons of early childhood [p. 33]." Greenson emphasizes that to be transference it must be a repetition of the past and inappropriate to the present.

Psychoanalysis and Psychoanalytic Psychotherapy

There is a distinction between psychoanalysis as a personality theory and psychoanalysis as a method of treatment. Psychoanalysis is only one of a number of forms of psychotherapy based upon psychoanalytic clinical theory, either wholly or in part. A full, formal psychoanalysis is a lengthy and expensive form of treatment, suitable for only a small portion of the population. Critics of psychoanalysis point to the "inefficiency" involved in such a treatment method and often indict psychoanalytic theory along with psychoanalysis as a form of treatment. Yet psychoanalysts have pioneered or figured prominently in the development of many of the briefer forms of therapy while still maintaining the clinical theory of psychoanalysis as the theoretical foundation for their various approaches.

Bion (1961), Burrow (1927), Ezriel (1950), Foulkes (1948), Schilder (1939), Slavson (1943, 1950), Wender (1936), and Wolf (1949) are among the earliest developers of group therapy. Their work has been based largely on psychoanalytic theory. The pioneers of family therapy, such as Ackerman (1958), Bell (1961), and Bowen (1961), were also primarily psychoanalytically oriented. The first 24-hour walk-in crisis centers were developed by psychoanalysts (Bellak & Small, 1965; Jacobson, Wilner, Morley, Schneider, Strickler, & Sommer, 1965). Various approaches to brief or emergency psychotherapies have been developed by analysts (e.g., Alexander & French, 1946; Ferenczi, 1920/1950, 1925/1950; Grinker, 1947; Kardiner, 1941; Lindemann, 1944; Lindemann & Dawes, 1952; Malan, 1963; Mann 1973). Psychoanalytically based psychotherapy can be long or short, individual or group, closely adhering to the classical procedure or greatly divergent in technical approach.

Most psychoanalytically oriented therapists are doing psychoanalytic psychotherapy rather than formal psychoanalysis. I shall describe the classical psychoanalytic method and contrast it with psychoanalytic psychotherapy.

CLASSICAL PSYCHOANALYSIS

As Freud worked with his early patients, he quickly discovered that they were unaware of the experiences, feelings, and motives that were causally connected with their symptoms. He experimented with hypnosis and other direct methods in an attempt to help his patients recover an awareness of what they were repressing. He achieved some degree of success, but these methods were not effective with all patients. Consequently, he developed a more indirect approach, the procedure of free association, which is the core of the classical psychoanalytic method.

After the preliminary assessment interviews are over and the patient is accepted as a suitable candidate for psychoanalysis, he is instructed to lie on a couch with the analyst out of sight behind him. The patient is to say everything that enters his mind, omitting absolutely nothing, no matter how trivial, off the point, nonsensical, embarrassing, or offensive to the analyst. All that is demanded of the patient is that he come regularly three to six times a week for a 45 to 50-minute session and follow this basic rule of free association.

The purpose of these arrangements is to reduce to a minimum those factors that interfere with the expression, even in disguised form, of the ideas, wishes, attitudes, or concerns the patient cannot otherwise communicate because he is not aware of them. By lying on a couch with the analyst seated quietly out of sight, the patient is removed from distracting visual and auditory input. There is little to hold his attention other than his own inner thoughts and experiences. The rule of free association is designed to remove the usual constraints of logic, intentional selection, and purposefulness. Consequently the field is left free for the patient's productions to be influenced by unconscious and irrational ideas and impulses. These influences are highly disguised at first, but are expressed more and more clearly as therapy progresses. In attempting to report the unedited flow of his thoughts, the patient reveals indirectly and without immediate recognition the most salient and pressing aspects of his inner life that he is unable to communicate directly. He also reveals his defenses as he interrupts or resists the task of free associating, often without realizing it. Furthermore, the content and form of his free associations are typically a compromise between his desire to express his wishes and feelings fully and his tendency to control, disguise, and avoid them. The medium of free association provides a stage upon which are enacted all the patient's most pressing conflicts, for the sensitive eyes and ears of the analyst and also for the patient's own observation under the guidance of the analyst.

The analyst's role is to listen and observe, being careful not to interrupt the patient unnecessarily or prematurely, and to comment on or interpret to the patient what he sees and hears. He is an experienced guide in a strange and often frightening world as well as a teacher dealing with a subject matter at once vitally familiar and bewilderingly unknown. The primary tool of the analyst is interpretation and it is by interpretation that he helps the patient to understand what he was not previously aware of. More precisely, interpretation means to make conscious the unconscious meaning, source, history, mode, or cause of a given psychological event (Greenson, 1967). Many interventions may be needed to complete an interpretation. Immense skill is required not only in the choice of what to interpret but also in the timing and in the specific style of interpreting as well.

The process of psychoanalysis is far more complicated than I have just indicated. My analogies to a journey of guided exploration and to instruction omit two vitally important factors, resistance and transference. The patient cannot encounter and accept what he has repressed until he overcomes his resistance. Consequently, a great deal of the analyst's activity is devoted to helping the patient dissolve the inevitable resistances. The analyst does this primarily by confronting the patient with his resistance and then exploring and interpreting its form and its significance. Ultimately this analysis shades into a recognition and exploration of what is being defended against. Thus, the focus is first on the defensive behavior; only later, and as the patient himself is ready, does the focus shift to what is defended against.

As psychoanalysis proceeds, at times very quickly and at other times more slowly, the character of the patient's relationship to the analyst begins to change. The patient starts to hint that the analyst himself is the center of his interest and that he desires much more than understanding from the analyst. These demands take many forms: He may want the analyst's love, forgiveness, or benevolent guidance; he may want to be the analyst's favorite and the center of his life or be helplessly dependent upon him or he may even want sexual union. On the other hand, he may fear that the analyst will abandon, ridicule, exploit, or blame him; compete or be angry with him; force him to comply or take away his autonomy. The patient may develop an intensely angry, critical attitude toward the analyst, especially when the analyst fails to gratify his emerging wishes. These feelings, positive or negative, grow in intensity and may take precedence over all other concerns and topics for analysis during the therapy session. Such emotional reactions to the therapist are characterized by their intensity, infantile character, and utter inappropriateness to the real nature of the analyst–patient relationship. Analysts refer to this reaction as a *transference neurosis*. It is to Freud's credit that he was able to perceive that the transference neurosis is a revival of a past relationship pattern. Furthermore, far from being the disrupting factor it was originally considered to be, transference is the very vehicle for constructive therapeutic change.

In essence, during the analytic hour itself, transference reactions bring past conflict situations vividly to life with an intensity and immediacy that no amount of remembering or rational analysis can provide. The patient, whose maturation or development was left incomplete or distorted, now has an opportunity for a new and better outcome. Freud has called therapy a form of "after-education," whereas Alexander (1946) speaks of "corrective emotional experience." Both imply unlearning of old conflict-generated patterns of response and learning new and more adaptive patterns. The patient discovers that the analyst neither succumbs to his neurotic demands and manipulations nor retaliates when he is hostile or angry. The therapist does not exploit the patient for his own needs. He provides the support of tolerant and compassionate understanding, tactfully offered, primarily in the form of interpretations. He helps the patient to recognize what is happening, that is, to understand his emotional reactions in therapy as a revival of conflicts in past relationships and to see how these same conflicts intrude disruptively upon his current life outside of therapy. Once the patient has accomplished all this, the transference relationship is replaced by a realistic relationship to the analyst. The patient then can apply his mature understanding to developing more adaptive patterns of behavior and more realistic inner responses to situations arising in his life. Such an outcome takes a great deal of time. It is never complete in the ideal sense of removing all influence of past conflicts and thereby achieving maximum adjustment.

To summarize, psychoanalysis is designed specifically to make the unconscious conscious, thereby providing the patient with the opportunity to control and direct his life, to make decisions, and to perceive his feelings and motives consciously and accurately. In a situation with minimal distractions and with uncritical acceptance by the analyst, the basic rule of free association allows the patient's usually concealed inner desires, attitudes, and fantasies to come out of hiding gradually and to be perceived eventually for what they are. Resistances—maneuvers to keep the hidden from being discovered—are countered until there is no place left to hide. Prolonged and frequent contact with an analyst who remains neutral in his attitudes and relatively anonymous with regard to his personal values and preferences provides the patient with unformed clay that he can mold to suit his own inner visions, heavy with unmet desires and fraught with unreasonable conflict. In a repetition based on past experiences, the patient develops an intense emotional relationship to the analyst. As he comes to understand his own transference creation and its historical genesis through the analyst's interpretations, the patient can resolve his transference relationship with a new ending and with insight that frees him from the tyranny of unwittingly living out conflicts from past experience in the present. Thus, insight, acceptance, and awareness of the potential influence of inner conflicts on daily behavior give the patient the handles he needs to take control of his life. The ultimate goal of psychoanalysis is freedom, born of thorough self-knowledge, whereby the successful analysand is free to determine his own fate.

PSYCHOANALYTIC PSYCHOTHERAPY

How does psychoanalytic psychotherapy differ from psychoanalysis? Some psychoanalysts state that there are fundamental differences in the form, in the technique, and in the processes that occur. Others maintain that there are no real differences other than intensity and thoroughness, and that the principles remain the same. The argument is not yet concluded.

Certain differences accrue simply from variations in the form of the therapy. Psychoanalytic psychotherapy is usually carried on once or twice a week, with the patient seated, facing the therapist.[1] In practice, the basic rule of free association may or may not be explicitly stated but the patient is left with the responsibility of talking. Usually the patient is asked not to censor or withhold material. In any case, the therapist's expectation that the patient talk freely and without censorship insofar as he is able soon becomes apparent when the therapist begins to confront the patient's resistances to clear, straightforward, and open communication. Therapists rarely instruct in free association and they do not expect their patients to develop the freedom of association that characterizes the analytic

[1] I shall speak of therapists rather than psychoanalysts or analysts in this section to indicate that I am speaking of the psychotherapist in the role of conducting psychoanalytically oriented psychotherapy rather than psychoanalysis, although many trained and accredited psychoanalysts at times do psychoanalytic psychotherapy.

patient. In essence, the situation in psychotherapy is much more like that of normal human interaction than is the psychoanalytic situation.

What are the consequences of these differences? First of all, the patient's talk is much more reality-oriented and bound by the typical requirement to be logical, organized, and clear. The focus is shifted more toward the patient's present life situation and less toward the patient–therapist relationship. Derivatives of unconscious processes still affect the patient's productions but less obviously, since the patient is exercising greater conscious control over what he is saying.

The goal of psychoanalysis is very broad: basic restructuring of the total personality. The goals of psychotherapy are more limited and more focused on the presenting problems. Thus, both patient and therapist in psychotherapy are inclined to delimit topics and to point more toward specific goals. Whereas psychoanalysis is likely to reach deeper, to work on core conflicts, and to involve feelings, fantasies, and urges that seem very intense and primitive to the average person, psychotherapy focuses more on derivative conflicts and the material discussed generally seems tamer, more civilized, more mature, and more within the experience of the average person.

Not only is the content moderated in psychotherapy but so is the intensity of the transference relationship. The therapist, facing the patient, is much more a real person and consequently less available as a blank screen for transference projection because his expressions and responses are constantly available to the patient. Furthermore, psychotherapy is a more active form of treatment in which the therapist interacts more frequently, sharing his own attitudes and feelings with greater freedom than the analyst. Although transference reactions frequently do occur, the full-blown transference neurosis is not encouraged as a primary vehicle for treatment. The therapist intervenes more rapidly to keep the patient embedded in reality.

Despite these differences in focus, in depth, and in intensity of transference, the basic goals and techniques of psychoanalytic psychotherapy and psychoanalysis are quite similar. Both are primarily nondirective, leaving the selection of topic to the patient and avoiding any giving of advice or direction to the patient. Both seek to elucidate and resolve the unconscious conflicts that complicate the patient's life and interfere with his ability to function effectively. Both focus on resistance and transference manifestations; both use interpretation as a primary technique; and, finally, both strive to provide the patient with mastery and control over himself and his life through understanding. The ultimate goal of each is self-determination through the achievement of insight.

Psychoanalytic Therapy: Process and Technique

People seek psychotherapeutic help when they sense that they are out of control. They know that they are behaving or responding internally in ways that are disagreeable or distressing to them, yet they feel unable to alter their behavior. They may sense that they are responding in an unusual way or they may blame their difficulties on some situation or person other than themselves, but either way they feel helpless. Even an astute outside observer may not see the necessity for the person's helpless posture and may offer advice concerning the "obvious" change in behavior, perspective, or attitude that can solve the person's difficulties. And the advice is ineffective. Such people are unable to deal with their problems because their problems stem from unconscious conflicts; it is hardly possible to exercise control over what one is not even aware of.

The principal aim of psychoanalytic therapy is to help the patient come to know himself, fully and with unrelenting honesty. The patient is led into an understanding of his conflicts and their inappropriate influence on his behavior. He is made aware of the possibilities for responding differently in the future and of his own reluctance to change. The gratifications and secondary pleasures he gains from his neurotic behavior are pointed out to him along with the disadvantages. In the end, he learns enough to be in control. Now fully aware, he can make his own decisions.

So the goal is to create awareness in the patient of what is actively, though unconsciously, influencing his behavior. How do the therapist and the patient arrive at what is unconscious? Unconscious forces—motives, feelings, attitudes, fantasy expectations—influence behavior. The effects of these influences are called *derivatives*. Derivatives in therapy are to be seen in the selection of topics, associative connections, selective memory, emotional reactions, transference feelings, style of response, attitudes toward the therapist, and nonverbal behavior.

Treatment operates by pointing out derivatives of unconscious conflicts, which are brought to the patient's attention within a *tolerant, accepting atmosphere*. A greater and greater tolerance of the derivatives of forbidden impulses and feelings is slowly built up so that the derivatives become less and less distorted. Thus the patient is gradually confronted with what was previously repressed, and he reintegrates these wishes or feelings into the general stream of his conscious, adult life. He is now able to reevaluate the appropriateness of his impulses and feelings—and of the fears that were attached to them—in the light of mature experience, judgment, and adult capacities for control and satisfaction. The individual is thus given conscious control over what formerly influenced his behavior without his awareness or capacity for conscious control.

Let us return to Ben, the college student who panicked when he kissed his girl friend, and observe the gradual clarification of his conflict in the content of his discussions as therapy progressed. The early sessions with Ben were spent developing a trustful relationship and coping with some of the inevitable resistances that arise during any insight-oriented therapy. A good deal of attention was also given to helping Ben deal with some of the more superficial conflicts that were troubling him. During these sessions he also spoke of his relationship with his girl friend, whom we shall call Jill, and of his inexplicable shifts in feeling toward her from love to disdain and disparagement. He was helped to recognize these shifts as indications of his anxiety about getting close to her and his fears of initiating a full sexual relationship, which his negative feelings toward her helped him to avoid. Gradually he began to report various thoughts, memories, and dreams. These reports, when viewed as a series, demonstrate the process of derivatives of his core conflict becoming more and more evident and less and less disguised. He related that these thoughts and long-forgotten memories seemed to be just "popping into his head" with increasing frequency. This was a sign that his repression was beginning to dissolve. The following excerpts are condensed and removed from context, thus losing some of their meaning and much of their richness, but they will illustrate the process of uncovering in insight-oriented therapy.

■ *40th session:* Ben reports the thought that Jill may not like his happiness at being with her. Mother avoids father's kisses. As a child, when he had bad dreams, Ben would try to get in bed with his mother but she would not let him and he felt there was something bad about his being a boy.

45th session: When he thinks about sex or even just a woman's body he feels frightened and guilty. This morning, he suddenly had the feeling that he had seen his mother nude when he was a child. He had a dream in which he saw Jill nude and was very conscious of the hair on her thighs. He immediately thought of seeing his mother nude and the hair on her stomach.

46th session: He remembers 2 months previously catching a glimpse of Jill's pubic hair when she put her feet up on a table while gesturing with her hand. He experienced an intense hatred toward her for her hand gesture. His next thought was of his childhood fear of his father dying even though his father was not ill.

58th session: Any disagreement with his mother has always made Ben feel guilty. He has a feeling of searching for some satisfaction that is never forthcoming but for which he is unwilling to abandon his efforts. He has always had the feeling that he must sacrifice something to be happy—"to have something severed off" that he holds dear.

60th session: Ben has proposed to Jill but is afraid to tell his mother. He feels that there is something he wants that he will not get if he marries Jill and also that he will be deserting and betraying his mother, who expects him to be like her.

63rd session: Racked by doubts about marriage, Ben is also overwhelmed by the desire to eat and eat and sleep and sleep. He feels as though he will lose something if he marries Jill. He feels that eating and sleeping are somehow connected in his mind with wanting his mother.

68th session: Ben remembers feeling as a child that there was something disgusting about being a boy and having a penis. He also recalls his mother catching him playing with himself under the covers and angrily saying, "Stop that!"

72nd session: He suddenly remembers that when he was very young, he thought that he was really a girl who had been made into a boy by plastic surgery. This was a fearful thought; he never wanted to be a girl.

82nd session: Ben is afraid that if he marries Jill he may still want other women. Even if he were to bounce around from woman to woman, he would still feel lonely, as if something were missing.

89th session: Ben feels he is avoiding something and that his avoidance has something to do with sexual activity. His fear seems especially to be focused upon a woman's vagina. He can remember catching sight of his mother without any clothes on and this made her very angry. He now recalls having had the fantasy that she would ask him to have intercourse with her.

90th session: Ben's parents had visited him the previous weekend and during their visit, Ben was aware of wanting to have sexual relations with his mother. He also noted his fear of disagreeing with her or of showing any anger or disapproval toward her. Though he knew it was irrational, Ben nevertheless had the feeling that his mother would die if he did not support her and agree with her.

91st session: During this meeting, Ben skirts around the topic of anger but obviously avoids relating his anger to his mother. When his avoidance is pointed out, Ben associates to an image of himself in a baby carriage with his mother bending over him and his hatred for her for not loving him and then to her anger at his masturbating under the covers. He now remembers feeling that his mother would hate him as long as he had a penis. He used to fantasy "screwing sharp beer cans" so he could get rid of his penis.

92nd session: Since his proposal to Jill, he has been feeling very cold toward her and toward other people in his life whom he aligns against his mother. But he thinks of himself as despicable and has been preoccupied with thoughts of suicide. All his anxiety and distress appears to be centered on Jill's vagina. He remembers having a dream in which his penis was caught in a woman's vagina and he was dragged back into the water to drown. The woman was very vindictive and he knew the water would not hurt her. He also fantasied that his mother's vagina would swallow him up and then he would simply cease to exist.

These excerpts illustrate the increasing explicitness of the oedipal conflict that Ben was experiencing. His initial homosexual thoughts were defensive; if he is homosexual, he cannot be heterosexually attracted to his mother. His love for Jill represented a double threat. On the one hand, as a generalized substitute for his mother, any sexual feelings for her were equivalent to desires for his mother. On the other, marrying her represented giving up once and for all his wishes to finally have his mother all to himself—a combination of an oedipal wish for sexual union and an equally powerful desire for an infantile, dependent, symbiotic relationship with his mother. With the help of therapy, Ben did separate himself psychologically from his mother. When last heard from, he was happily married to Jill, had two children, and appeared to be heading toward a productive career far away from his home town.

Ben had come to recognize and to accept his sexual and aggressive feelings toward his mother. He was able to distinguish his own needs, desires, and values from those of his mother and to see that he had a right to be different from her. He could discriminate between his mother and Jill and with the insight of mature understanding he was able to perceive that he need not feel guilty for his sexual desires toward Jill nor expect Jill to reject him because of these desires. He was free to be himself and to act in accordance with his true needs and feelings. Ben had achieved control over his life.

THE THERAPIST'S ROLE

How does a therapist facilitate the kinds of changes illustrated in Ben's story? First, he must create an atmosphere in which the patient feels free to delve into areas fraught with anxiety, guilt, and shame. The patient must feel adequately understood and must sense the therapist's unwavering acceptance of and respect for him no matter what he may reveal. Such a climate is important for all forms of psychotherapy. Rogers (1957) has written of the necessary and sufficient conditions for therapeutic change: empathic understanding, positive regard, and genuineness. These same qualities are considered essential by psychoanalytic psychotherapists though they do not regard them as sufficient. Psychoanalysts feel that specific interventions by the therapist, typically interpretations, are required in order for the patient to achieve full and genuine insight, which he is able to generalize and apply in his daily life. However, the patient first must learn to trust his therapist and this usually requires some time—more for some, less for others. If the therapist is not truly understanding and respectful, the therapy is doomed from the outset.

Secondly, the therapist must adopt a different way of listening and observing. In a social conversation, our attention is focused on the explicit content of what is being said and on the intended function of behavior. But the therapist must break away from his ingrained habits of social listening and look beyond the manifest meaning and intended function of behavior. In order to understand the influence of unconscious derivatives, it is necessary to unleash oneself from the pull of the obvious. Freud (1912/1950) recommends "making no effort to concentrate the attention on anything in particular, and in maintaining in regard to all that one hears the same measure of calm, quiet attentiveness—of evenly-hovering attention. . . . One has simply to listen and not to trouble to keep in mind anything in particular [p. 324]." The purpose of Freud's recommendation is to prevent some form of deliberate or semideliberate screening of the material. The therapist must maintain his own receptivity to what the patient provides and work with this material at a level where purely rational processing is suspended and unexpected connections or associations may occur. Analysts often speak of allowing their own unconscious to work with the material.

While maintaining an open, receptive attitude to everything the patient is doing and saying, the therapist, of necessity, is doing something with his attention and is responding in some way to the patient's behavior. I find it useful to be receptive in certain ways and I believe most psychoanalytically oriented therapists (and many others) probably operate in a similar manner. I look for *implicit themes* that help me organize and make sense out of the seemingly independent statements and behaviors of the patient. For example, a college man I was seeing was nearing the end of his therapy. The spring semester would soon be over and I had informed him earlier that I had changed jobs and would not be there when he returned in the fall. A few sessions before the last one, with great anxiety and embarrassment, he revealed his fear that his penis was too small and that he could never be attractive to or successful with women because of his inferiority.

We talked of his feelings about his penis and his sexual image in general in the next two sessions, but he was reluctant to explore very deeply and I was equally hesitant to open up areas of the topic that could not be dealt with in the time remaining to us.

During his last hour, he began by reporting a dream in which he had received a letter from the company to which he had sent his trumpet for repair. He was just about to look at the letter and find out what was wrong with his trumpet when the alarm woke him up. I asked him what his next thoughts were after recounting that dream. He then recalled going barefoot in the first grade. It was "sort of a big deal" and he remembered needing his mother's and the teacher's permission. He also remembered that he and another boy made "shoes" by putting gummed tape all over their feet and he was afraid the teacher would be angry about the crackling noise it made. His next association was a memory of joining the band in fifth grade and of having to borrow an old beat-up trumpet because his parents insisted on ordering his trumpet through mail order rather than buying it from the band director as the other children did. The trumpet had no case and he was embarrassed to carry it to school without a case. He couldn't figure out how to look natural carrying it.

What I have just presented represents a summary of the first few minutes of the hour. Manifestly, we have a dream about his trumpet and two memories from childhood. If we interpret the implicit content being expressed it may be something like this: "I told you about my penis and my fears of being sexually inadequate [broken trumpet] and now therapy is ending [dream interrupted] before I even find out what is wrong with me [before the letter is read]. You encourage me to disclose more [teacher's and mother's permission to expose his feet]. Will you be angry if I cover up [gummed tape]? Will you be angry at my anger [disturbing crackling] at your leaving me uncured [trumpet broken]? I am not so well-equipped as other men [beat-up trumpet] and I am afraid others will perceive my inadequacy [embarrassed—how to look natural]." The patient's general concern about therapy being terminated prematurely, while he still has vital concerns about his sexuality, is organizing the flow of content, yet his concern is expressed indirectly rather than directly. My job during the rest of the hour was to make explicit what was implicit and to help him deal with his feelings of abandonment—a theme that had been the focus of a number of previous sessions.

In addition to looking for implicit themes, I look for *purposes* that help "explain" behavior that seems obscure or unwarranted by the immediate, obvious circumstances. I assume behavior to be directed toward some aim. I was astounded to have another male patient tell me during the third session of having fantasies of intercourse with his mother. Such material is not to be expected in the third session from a nonpsychotic patient. Upon exploring further, I found that the patient was fearful that unless he entertained me with fascinating symptoms or exotic content, I would no longer want to see him. Looking beyond the manifest content, I was free to consider the patient's motives in bringing up such material and to explore his transference fear that I might reject him.

Freud's most basic assumption was that all behavior is meaningful. Thus, one would not expect a sequence of seemingly unrelated topics to be simply fortuitous. Therapists can understand a particular event in therapy more fully by focusing attention on its relationship to what immediately precedes or follows it. The young man with the broken trumpet illustrates this. Often, it is possible to detect a basic theme underlying an entire hour in which many different topics are discussed. For example, I was seeing a very religious woman who was very disturbed by her own sexual urges and, at the moment, by the fact that she was having overt sexual fantasies about me. There were three major topics during the hour: (1) a discussion with her minister who advised her to stop psychotherapy, lest it undermine her faith; (2) the Students for a Democratic Society (SDS), who were out to cause trouble, and the Campus Crusade group, which was doing too little to counter their influence; and (3) her overwhelming sexual desire for me, which made her feel sinful and guilty. All three topics, directly or indirectly, reflected her struggle against impulses that frightened her and made her feel guilty. She experienced the forces allied on the side of her sexual impulses (psychotherapy, SDS, the therapist) as being too powerful for her to control and she wished for greater support for the moral, controlling side of her personality (the minister, Campus Crusade, her own conscience).

The content of the patient's talk is not the only source of information. Analytic psychotherapists also pay a great deal of attention to their patients' nonverbal behavior: facial expression, posture, tone of voice, movement of hands and feet. Often, more direct and certainly more valid information is provided by the patient's nonverbal behavior than the patient is able or willing to provide verbally; bringing such behavior into the focus of attention can lead to very productive work. Once, when I was working with a couple, the wife was speaking positively about her husband. I noticed that she had shifted in her chair so that she was leaning as far away from her husband as the chair would permit. I brought this to her attention with a question about the possible significance of her move. After a moment's reflection, she was able to recall being hurt by a remark her husband had made a few minutes earlier—a fleeting reaction which she quickly suppressed. Further exploration, however, showed her reaction to be connected with a very basic attitude that had never been verbalized.

A further clue to what is happening during an interview session is provided by the therapist's own internal reactions. Analysts train themselves to be alert to minute changes in their own level of comfort, mood, attitude, or inclination to respond in a particular way and to use these internal responses as cues to what is going on within the patient or between the patient and therapist. Often, one's own slightly dampened mood is the first clue to a patient's unstated depression, or one's own irritation is a signal that the patient is trying to manipulate the therapist, or one's urge to be helpful is a sign of the patient's willingness to renounce his own ability to help himself.

THE THERAPIST'S TECHNIQUE

The technical procedures of psychoanalytic therapy are difficult to specify since they follow so precisely upon what is happening at the moment in therapy. I have already outlined the basic structure of both psychoanalysis (the couch, free association, frequent sessions, interpretation) and psychoanalytic psychotherapy (sitting face to face, less frequent sessions, modified free association, more frequent intervention). But there is much art to the practice of psychotherapy as well. Even the most structured, technique-oriented forms of psychotherapy, such as behavior therapy, are more or less effective depending upon the personal qualities and style of the therapist. Nevertheless, some comments about technique can be made.

A basic goal in psychoanalytic therapy is insight. Insight is a concept that has been much misunderstood and abused by critics of insight-oriented psychotherapies. Insight means to have understanding, to know. But there are two ways of knowing—to know as a fact accepted on authority and to know through personal experience. I know as a fact that withdrawal from drug dependence is painful; I know from personal experience the pain of feeling utterly alone in an alien and seemingly nonaccepting environment. Knowledge of the first pain has had little influence on my life; experiencing the second pain has had a very considerable impact on my life and the process of self-evaluation and change initiated by that experience is still going on. To have told Ben early in his therapy that he was frightened of an intimate, sexual involvement with Jill because he was still in conflict over sexual and dependent wishes for his mother would have been interesting to him, might well have been accepted, and would probably have had no therapeutic value whatever. It might even have been harmful.

The greater value and impact of the experiential kind of knowing is reflected in technique in such matters as the depth and timing of interpretations. An interpretive intervention should be directed at what is currently on the surface. Such a statement has several corollaries. First, it implies that the patient determines the subject matter of the hour. The subject matter may be not only what the patient chooses to talk about, but also at times what he actively avoids talking about, how he speaks, or what he does. The therapist seeks to work at the point where the patient's feelings and interest are situated at the moment. The therapist responds to what he believes is the patient's actual concern even if the patient seems to be actively avoiding the area of concern. Second, interpretation of resistance precedes interpretation of the content being resisted, since the point of concern is in avoiding and the resistance is more surface than the content. Third, the therapist must avoid too deep an interpretation. The patient must be able to *find* within himself and *experience* the motive, feeling, or defensive attitude when his attention is focused upon it. Fenichel (1941) recommends that one interpret what the patient is barely aware of "and just a little bit more." One must resist the temptation to interpret prematurely or to give more than the patient can assimilate. The time to make an interpretation is while the behavior is occurring or the feeling is aroused. Patience is one prerequisite for doing insight-oriented psychotherapy.

The subject matter for the therapist's interventions is sometimes the patient's resistance, sometimes his transference reactions, and sometimes the content of his associations, fantasies, memories, dreams, current happenings in his daily life, and the like. The end goal is to face the patient with repetitive trouble-some reaction patterns, born of a childhood necessity long since outgrown, but nevertheless persisting both in his relationship with the therapist and in his manner of living his life outside of therapy. The patient is helped to understand why the patterns arose in the first place and how they are used now. Finally, the therapist goes through a process called *working through:* The patient is helped to elucidate all the manifold circumstances in which he reinvokes his customary pattern of responding. At the same time, he is encouraged to take the risk of abandoning the security of his characteristic pattern and to try substituting other responses that may be more appropriate and ultimately more rewarding.

Present Status of Psychoanalysis

At the outset, Freud's ideas and methods stirred up a storm of controversy. Gradually, psychoanalysis became quite popular, not only among psychologists and psychiatrists, but also among sociologists, anthropologists, writers, artists, and the general public. The influence of psychoanalytic ideas on twentieth-century culture has been profound, although most of this influence is no longer identified specifically with psychoanalysis. Now it appears that we have come full circle and psychoanalysis is once again under attack. Each new system of psychotherapy or theory of personality measures itself against psychoanalysis and declares its superiority. Unfortunately, most critics direct their attacks against the Freudian theory of the first quarter of this century—and indeed there is much that can be criticized there, as is true of virtually any theory of 50 to 100 years ago. But the swing away from unquestioning acceptance of Freudian dogma raises the real danger of losing some truly important insights and points of view.

As we noted earlier, Freud developed his ideas at various levels of abstraction. Most closely tied to his observational data were his clinical formulations, spoken of as the clinical theory of psychoanalysis or more loosely as psychodynamics. Another step removed from the basic data of observation were Freud's attempts to construct a general theory of the workings of the mind. He postulated a hypothetical model of the psychic apparatus and outlined the processes occurring within this structure and between its parts—for instance, the relationships between ego, id, and superego. These formulations are referred to as the general theory of psychoanalysis or sometimes as psychoanalytic meta-psychology. They have been the focus of most critical attacks on psychoanalytic theory and also of continuing efforts at revision by modern psychoanalytic theorists. Finally, Freud engaged in some sweeping, highly speculative excursions into philosophical, historical, evolutionary, sociological, and even mystical areas. Few of these writings have much significance for either the clinical or the general theory.

Progress in psychoanalytic theory and practice has been retarded by a tendency toward the doctrinaire acceptance of Freud's ideas and an almost cultist organization of psychoanalysts, with strict rules for membership and an intolerant attitude toward any challenges of theoretical dogma or any deviations in practice under the name of psychoanalysis. Nevertheless, both theory and practice have evolved and many of the early deficiencies have been corrected.

Since the death of Freud in 1939, the rise of *psychoanalytic ego psychology* has corrected the earlier overemphasis on unconscious drive phenomena, called *id psychology,* which had tended to neglect the impact of a person's interactions with his social and material environment. Greater attention and importance is now given to ego functions, that is, to the adaptive and controlling functions of the personality. By emphasizing the normal adaptive functions of the ego, such as perception, memory, learning, thought, motor control, judgment, and self-control (delay of gratification), psychoanalytic ego psychologists have found a way to include the entire subject matter of academic psychology within the context of their theory. The ego psychology framework has encouraged and suggested modifications in the standard psychoanalytic therapy for application to populations previously regarded as unsuitable for psychoanalysis, such as psychotics and those with character disorders. Ego psychology also has served as a framework within which to conceptualize therapeutic efforts in specific situations, such as crisis intervention (Bellak & Small, 1965) or milieu therapy on a psychiatric ward (Edelson, 1964).

During the 1940s and 1950s, psychoanalysis was at its peak in respect and influence. Having given the ego its rightful place of importance, psychoanalysis seemed to be on track and ready to conquer new worlds. During that period, theorists were still reluctant to suggest basic revisions in Freud's metapsychological theory. Instead, they added still more abstract and complex formulations, which seemed to be even more removed from the solid foundation of observational data. In the 1960s, disenchantment set in. Psychoanalysis has since then been increasingly described as antiquated, passé, obsolete, and even defunct (Strupp, 1973). Perhaps responding to the external pressure to reevaluate the scientific basis and worth of psychoanalysis or perhaps for other reasons, a number of psychoanalytic writers recently have been proposing quite fundamental changes in theory (e.g., Gill, 1975; Holt, 1975; Klein, 1967, 1975; Rubinstein, 1975; Schafer, 1968, 1975; Wallerstein, 1975) and a variety of alterations in clinical practice to meet particular problems (e.g., Kernberg, 1976; Nelson, Nelson, Sherman, & Strean, 1968; Szasz, 1965). This process of reexamination may enable psychoanalysis to free itself from its shackles to the past and regain some of the spirit of innovation and dynamic development, if not the revolutionary fervor, of the early days. If not, then psychoanalysis may well wither away.

RESEARCH

Psychoanalytic theory has generated a vast amount of research, stimulating studies in nearly every domain of psychology: perception, cognition, memory, learning, social, developmental, and physiological. Although a few attempts have been made, there is no adequate summary of this research, of its debt to psychoanalysis, or of its implications for the theory. Sears (1943) and Hilgard

(1952) conducted early surveys of the literature; more recently Kline (1972) attempted to summarize the work done in this area, but his compilation is quite incomplete. It is beyond the scope of this chapter to review or evaluate the status of research on psychoanalytic theoretical propositions. I will mention only the status of research on the *outcome* of psychoanalytic psychotherapy. A more complete review of quantitative research on other aspects of psychoanalytic therapy can be found in Luborsky and Spence (1971).

On the face of it, the problem of determining whether a patient who comes for psychotherapy has received some benefit from his treatment would seem to be a simple matter. In fact, the task proved so difficult that for some time psychotherapy researchers shied away from any attempt to evaluate outcome. They devoted their energies to process studies, investigating the relationship of specific events occurring during the course of therapy rather than evaluating the ultimate worth of the total enterprise. The difficulties of outcome research lie primarily in the problem of specifying criteria that are both relevant and unbiased. Because different therapies espouse quite different goals, comparative studies are difficult. What one approach may regard as critical, another may view as secondary—for example, symptom removal versus enhanced capacity for living fully, as a function of character change. Asking the therapist whether the patient improved introduces a bias because, after all, the therapist has a stake in perceiving his efforts as worthwhile. The patient, as the consumer, should be a good judge—but he, too, does not want to regard all his time and effort as wasted. His view also may be influenced by a desire to agree with or please his therapist. Then again, one must be wary of a placebo effect. Perhaps friends, relatives, employers, or independent clinicians interviewing the client before and after therapy can provide an unbiased report of change. However, they are likely to be influenced by what the patient tells them and by his enthusiasm and belief in the efficacy of therapy, so their views are not entirely independent either. The use of various performance measures has been suggested. These are helpful in some cases, but many of the changes sought by clients, such as reduction of anxiety, peace of mind, self-esteem, and a sense of efficacy and control, are internal and subject only to the personal observations and report of the patient. Adding to the complexity of evaluating outcome research is the question of whether the person doing the therapy is truly skillful and the techniques or approach he is employing truly representative of the orientation being evaluated. Finally, there is the question whether certain patients or certain problems are more suitably and beneficially treated by one type of therapy and others by another type of therapy. Bergin (1971) has cogently reviewed these difficulties and agrees with Paul's statement (1967) that outcome research should be directed toward answering "*what* treatment, by *whom,* is most effective for *this* individual with *that* specific problem, and under *which* set of circumstances [p. 111]."

Bergin's (1971) review of past outcome studies in which psychoanalysis or psychoanalytic therapy was employed showed at least moderate improvement in 60–91% of the cases in an earlier group of studies and from 25 to 90% of the patients studied in a dozen more recent investigations, depending on which study was being examined. All these surveys have important deficiencies in design, and it is difficult to draw any solid conclusions from the results. In fact, a summary of a workshop sponsored by the Clinical Projects Research Review Committee, National Institute of Mental Health (Fiske, Hunt, Luborsky, Orne. Parloff, Reiser, & Tuma, 1970) concludes: "There have been few convincing research studies on the effectiveness of the various psychotherapies. . . . We have little systematic experimental knowledge of psychotherapy, of its effectiveness, and of the factors facilitating its effects [p. 727]."

Despite the deficiencies of patients' reports on the success of their own treatment as a criterion of change, they are the consumers of psychotherapeutic services and the degree to which they are satisfied with the service they receive is of considerable importance. Strupp, Fox, and Lessler (1969) report a mail survey follow-up study of patients who had completed therapy at least a year before and had had a minimum of 25 interviews. Obtaining responses from patients who had been out of therapy for at least a year was a deliberate methodological decision, designed to minimize the possible biases associated with patient evaluations of their own therapy. After a year, it might be assumed that patients would have had time to evaluate thoroughly the effects of their treatment on their lives. They would no longer be under the emotional spell of their therapists and would have no need to please them, especially since the questionnaires were anonymous and patients were told that their responses would not be shown to their therapists unless they gave specific permission. The authors believed that the perspective of a year or more would enable patients to give generally valid and objective evaluations of their therapy experience.

Out of 205 questionnaires delivered, returns were obtained from 131 patients. The therapists ranged in experience from those still in training to highly experienced staff members. The orientation of the therapists was almost exclusively psychoanalytic. Several multiple-choice questions were posed regarding the outcome of treatment. A sampling of these questions follows. Results are expressed as percentages of patients endorsing each alternative.

How much have you benefited from your therapy?

A great deal	59%
A fair amount	18%
To some extent	15%
Very little	4%
Not at all	4%

To what extent have your complaints or symptoms that brought you to therapy changed as a result of treatment?

Completely disappeared	6%
Very greatly improved	35%
Considerably improved	24%
Somewhat improved	20%
Not at all improved	9%
Got worse	2%
(No response)	4%

Although it can be seen that psychoanalytic psychotherapy is no panacea, it does seem to satisfy some need for the majority of patients.

Today, the future of full-scale, formal psychoanalysis as a method of treatment remains in doubt. Certainly, no other method has been developed that can compare with psychoanalysis in thoroughness and depth of study into the psychology of an individual human being. As an observational method capable of further extending our knowledge of human behavior, it should be retained. As a form of treatment, it seems best suited to the training of professional psychotherapists and as therapy for those with the time, motivation, and financial resources to undertake such a thoroughgoing search into their own souls. Psychoanalytically derived therapies, on the other hand, seem to have a much brighter future. Despite the plethora of new treatment approaches, many therapists still have a substantial analytic influence in their work. The clinical observations of Freud and his followers and the investigations of normal development and behavior that have followed still provide the richest source yet developed for comprehending the internal experiences and external behavior of human beings.

Summary

Sigmund Freud revolutionized the study of human behavior and the treatment of psychological disorders when he developed psychoanalysis. Psychoanalysis is both a theory of behavior and a method of treatment. The two should be evaluated separately.

Psychoanalysis is a motivationally based theory that emphasizes psychological determinism in all human behavior, the existence and important influence of unconscious mental processes, and the relevance of psychological conflict and defense in both normal personality development and in maladaptive or disordered behavior. The existence of other motives is recognized, but sexual and aggressive drives are believed to be particularly influential in the development of personality and psychopathology, because these drives are interpersonal, plastic, and postponable. These qualities make them critical targets of socialization learning and capable of much distortion or redirection in expression.

Many forms of therapy are based to a greater or lesser degree upon psychoanalytic theory. *Classical psychoanalysis* is a long, intensive treatment approach in which reclining on a couch and the method of free association are designed to encourage the expression of unconscious ideas, attitudes, or concerns. Through the process of interpretation, the analyst helps the patient understand his productions and gain insight into those inner motives, conflicts, and reaction patterns that have governed much of his behavior without his awareness or decision. No matter how cooperative and objective the patient intends to be, he soon brings his customary defensive patterns into therapy in the form of *resistance* and eventually develops intense feelings and responses toward the analyst. These feelings and responses are displaced re-creations of a significant relationship pattern from the past. As such, they are called *transference* reactions. Exploration and interpretation of resistance and transference are the primary activities of the analyst.

Psychoanalytic psychotherapy differs from psychoanalysis primarily in the frequency of sessions and in the depth and intensity of the experience. The patient sits facing the therapist, and a more active interchange takes the place of free association. The focus is more on the patient's present life situation. Attention to resistance, transference, and interpretation are still primary activities of the therapist but he is inclined to be more active and self-revealing, which reduces the intensity of transference. The goals are similar: to expand the patient's knowledge of himself and thereby allow him greater control over the conduct of his own life.

Currently, there are many critics of psychoanalysis as a theory and as a form of therapy. Important changes in both theory and treatment are being proposed by psychoanalysts themselves. Psychoanalysis continues to develop and change; it remains one of the most influential theories of human behavior in the world today, and the basis for most treatment methods as well.

17

The Client-Centered Theory of Personality and Therapy

VINCENT A. HARREN

Southern Illinois University at Carbondale

Carl R. Rogers is the originator of the client-centered approach to psychotherapy. Although there are many client-centered writers today, Rogers continues to be the most prominent proponent of this approach. In looking back over nearly a half-century of professional activity, Rogers spoke of his professional career in an address entitled, "In Retrospect: Forty-Six Years" (Rogers, 1974b). In wonderment over the widespread acceptance of his theory and ideas, he attributes his success to the following:

> To me, as I try to understand the phenomenon, it seems that without knowing it I had expressed an idea whose time had come. . . . It was the gradually formed and tested hypothesis that the individual has within himself vast resources for self-understanding, for altering his self-concept, his attitudes, and his self-directed behavior—and that these resources can be tapped if only a definable climate of facilitative psychological attitudes can be provided [p. 116].

Although Rogers' theories have changed as a result of his counseling experience and research findings, this core idea has remained unchanged throughout. In Rogers and Hart (1970) he dates the discovery of this core idea:

> Between 1937 and 1941, I became infected with Rankian ideas and began to realize the possibilities of the individual being self-directing. This certainly fitted in with earlier ideas I had absorbed from Kilpatrick and John Dewey. I was clearly fasci-

nated by Rankian ideas but didn't quite adopt his emphasis for myself until I left Rochester. But the core idea did develop. I came to believe in the individual's capacity. I value the dignity and rights of the individual sufficiently that I do not want to impose my way upon him. Those two aspects of the core idea haven't changed since that time [p. 517].

From 1940 to 1945, Rogers worked at Ohio State University as professor of clinical psychology. The core idea took shape as a new, distinct approach in *Counseling and Psychotherapy* (1942). Although the book established the core idea of the individual's inherent capacity for self-understanding and self-direction, it too rigidly prescribed the therapeutic technique for releasing this potential: the nondirective, permissive, noninterventive approach.

From 1945 to 1957, Rogers was at the University of Chicago, teaching in the psychology department and doing counseling and research at the counseling center. During this period, he initiated extensive research involving analysis of audiotape recordings of counseling sessions. One of his major works during this period was *Client-Centered Therapy* (1951), which contained an elaboration of the therapeutic approach and the beginnnings of a theory of personality; a second work, "A Theory of Therapy, Personality, and Interpersonal Relationships," published in 1959, formally presented his theory of personality.

From 1957 to 1962, Rogers and some colleagues from the University of Chicago conducted a 5-year study of hospitalized schizophrenic patients at the University of Wisconsin Psychiatric Institute. The challenge to extend the theory to the more severely disturbed inpatient was taken up in earnest. The resultant book, *The Therapeutic Relationship and Its Impact* (Rogers, Gendlin, Kiesler, & Truax), was published in 1967.

Since 1962, Rogers has been living in La Jolla, California; he is a staff member of the Western Behavioral Sciences Institute and resident fellow at the Center for the Studies of the Person. During the sixties, he developed his theory of group counseling, which he labeled the *basic encounter group.* His approach to facilitating groups is contained in *Carl Rogers on Encounter Groups* (1970a) and in a series of audiotape cassette recordings called *How to Use Encounter Groups* (1971). Rogers sees the group movement as the most significant social innovation of our time. In his book, *Freedom to Learn* (1969), he proposes that the group process can become a means of changing existing educational institutions in the direction of making them more self-actualizing environments.

In *Becoming Partners: Marriage and Its Alternatives* (1972), Rogers examines changing views toward marriage, cohabitation, and communal living. His recent works have been devoted to a reconsideration of the nature of empathy (Rogers, 1975), and a restatement of his theory of psychotherapy addressed to the medical profession (1974a). Throughout all Rogers' works, whether about therapy, encounter groups, education, or marriage, the underlying theme of the core idea is present: The individual's capacity for self-direction and self-fulfillment is released in an interpersonal environment of facilitative psychological attitudes.

Carl Rogers, at the right, leads an encounter group at the Western Behavioral Sciences Institute in 1968. Rogers developed his theory and practice of encounter groups during the 1960s with the help of actual group sessions like this one. (Michael Rougier, Time-Life Picture Agency, © Time Inc.)

The Theory of Personality

The individual's capacity for self-understanding and self-direction contained in Rogers' core idea is the starting point for his theory of personality. This capacity Rogers calls the *organismic valuing process,* an inherent wisdom of the body that is present at birth. The infant is capable of evaluating organismically, not consciously or symbolically, what feels good and what does not, at any given moment of his existence. For instance, hunger, pain, cold, wetness, and loud noises are negatively valued, whereas food, warmth, and being held are positively valued. Yet, this is a complex process, changing from moment to moment. Food is positively valued until the infant is full, then he rejects the nipple; the security of being held may be rejected in order to explore his own body or to discover objects in his environment. This behavior is clearly directed from within, based on the input from his own senses and his internal, proprioceptive feedback. At this point, his valuing is not influenced by or dependent upon what others might value.

In the self-actualizing adult, the organismic valuing process operates much like that of the infant, except that the adult trusts the wisdom of his body consciously and knowingly. What is valued depends upon what is experienced in the moment as enhancing or actualizing. Although there is no guarantee that the choices the individual makes will, in fact, be self-actualizing, he can modify his choices because he is open to both experience from within and feedback from others. Nevertheless, since his locus of evaluation is within, other people's opinions or beliefs are not considered to be as significant as his own reactions. Thus, for example, he is less likely to be influenced by the latest fads, or to ignore his own reaction that a movie is dull when others have high praise for it.

When individuals are free to trust their own organismic valuing process, this does not result in social chaos. On the contrary, Rogers' position regarding the individual and society is a synergistic one:

> I find it significant that when individuals are prized as persons the values they select do not run the full gamut of possibilities. I do not find, in such a climate of freedom, that one person comes to value fraud and murder and thievery, while another values a life of self-sacrifice, and another values only money. Instead there seems to be a deep and underlying thread of commonality. I believe that when the human being is inwardly free to choose whatever he deeply values, he tends to value those objects, experiences, and goals which make for his own survival, growth, and development, and for the survival and development of others. I hypothesize that it is *characteristic* of the human organism to prefer such actualizing and socialized goals when he is exposed to a growth promoting climate [Rogers, 1970b, p. 440].

But, what is the motivating principle? The impetus for the behavior in the first place? There exists an *actualizing tendency* or growth force in the organism that is also part of an individual's genetic or constitutional inheritance. It is the force toward development of the organism's potentialities or capacities that are directed toward the maintenance and enhancement of life. Part of this actualizing tendency is common to all living creatures, that is, the force toward the fulfillment of one's biological potentialities. Thus, basic physiological needs are involved, such as the need for food, water, air, and the like. Also included are the development and differentiation of the bodily organs, as in the capacity for reproduction, the development of body coordination, and increased skills in interacting with the environment—for instance, in predatory animals acquiring the skills to stalk and capture the prey, or in man increased mastery in the use of tools, such as eating with a spoon, driving a car, or using a computer. The uniquely human and psychological aspect of the actualizing tendency is the tendency toward *self*-actualization.

The *self* or *self-concept* is formed out of experiences that maintain and enhance the organism and are associated with a sense of *I* or *me*. Included in this sense are the perceptions of one's relationships to others and the values attached to these perceptions. For example, suppose that as a young child I consistently receive affection and approval from my mother whenever I act in a kind, helpful, or cooperative manner in relation to her, to my younger brother, or in response to various housekeeping chores. These experiences are identified as self-experiences and gradually become components of my self-concept. As a result, I see myself as a kind, helpful, and cooperative person; others like me when I am this way, and I like myself for being this way.

Contained in the example is the evaluative aspect of the self-concept. That is, once the self-concept is formed, the individual acquires two additional needs, which are social manifestations of the overall actualizing tendency—the need for *positive regard from others*, and the need for *positive self-regard*. Thus it is important to be liked by others, and then to like oneself, so that one's self-worth does not depend upon consistent and continuous positive regard from others. In this respect, each person needs to become his or her own "significant other," rather than to rely on significant others, such as parents, siblings, or peers.

Inevitably, the child's need for positive regard comes in conflict, at least some of the time, with his organismic needs. In the socialization process, his own organismic needs and desires may come in conflict with his parents' values regarding what is acceptable behavior. The child learns that some of his organismic experiences are not worthy of the positive regard of his parents. For instance, when a boy is frustrated and angry, it feels good to thump his little sister on the head as she walks by, or to tease her and upset her; yet, when he does so, his parents scold him and call him a bad boy. A *condition of worth* thus arises when the child perceives that in some respects he is valued and in other respects he is not. Gradually, he internalizes these conditions of worth into his self-concept. They become introjected values, taken over from others, and provide the basis for valuing an experience positively or negatively, without reference to whether the experience maintains or enhances the organism. The child begins to avoid or deny his organismic experiences and to act in accord with his introjected values in order to continue to regard himself as worthwhile. From this early denial of organismic experiences, the child's gradually formed self-concept is protected and maintained by further denials and distortions of experiences that are contrary to his introjected values.

Thus, as adults, most of us live our lives based on introjected values without awareness of our own organismic responses to these values. For instance, we may believe that sex is bad, obedience without question is good, money and material possessions are good, being intelligent and well-educated is good, and that loving one's neighbor, cooperating, and helping others are good (Rogers, 1970b).

The need to protect one's self-concept from experiences inconsistent with introjected values leads to a state of *incongruence* between one's self-concept and one's experience. Incongruence is the perceived discrepancy between the self-concept and actual experience that generates tension, internal conflict, and confusion, and results in inconsistent and maladaptive behavior. Incongruence, then, is the key concept in the client-centered view of maladjustment, which will be elaborated in the next section.

The major points of the theory of personality can be summarized as follows:

1. The actualizing tendency, which is present at birth, is the source of man's motivation, so that behavior is directed toward maintaining and enhancing the organism, toward self-actualization.

2. The organismic valuing process is also present at birth. Its function is to evaluate experiences as positive or negative in terms of the satisfactions or discomforts organismically experienced, and in terms of the degree of agreement with the actualizing tendency.
3. Those experiences that maintain and enhance the organism are accurately symbolized into an awareness of being and differentiated as self-experiences. These self-experiences become further elaborated, through interactions with significant others, into a self-concept.
4. Once the self-concept is formed, a need for positive regard from others develops, and then a need for positive self-regard develops.
5. Positive regard from others can be provided unconditionally (unconditional positive regard) or conditionally (i.e., conditions of worth are attached to others' positive regarding of the person).
   a. If unconditionally, then the individual will positively regard himself and will continue to evaluate experiences in terms of the organismic valuing process.
   b. If conditionally, the individual will incorporate the conditions of worth into his self-concept such that they become introjected values, and he will evaluate his experiences in terms of these introjected values rather than in terms of the organismic valuing process. The introjected values act as if they were the organismic valuing process and the individual loses touch with, or is cut off from, his organismic valuing process.
6. Thus the individual's need for positive self-regard will be satisfied only when he acts in accordance with his introjected values.
7. In order to maintain the existing self-concept, those experiences that are inconsistent with the introjected values are denied or distorted in their symbolization and the self-concept becomes increasingly inaccurate, unrealistic, and rigid over time. As new events are experienced there is increasing incongruence between these experiences and the self-concept.

The Nature of Psychopathology

In the client-centered view, psychopathological behavior represents only part of a continuum of human behavior, ranging from disorganized behavior at one end to highly self-actualizing behavior at the other end, with defensive and normal behavior falling somewhere between. Thus these behaviors do not differ in kind, but only in degree; that is, the degree of incongruence between a person's self-concept and his or her experiences. At the disorganized pole of the continuum, there is a high degree of incongruence; at the self-actualizing pole, there is a high degree of congruence.

Psychopathology, then, can be described as a state of incongruence between one's self-concept and one's experiences, which results in a vulnerability to threat and anxiety. The self-concept is protected against threat through a defense system of denial or distortion of experiences discrepant with the self-concept, leading to increasingly rigid perceptions and behaviors. Finally, if experiences are extremely inconsistent with the self-concept, the defense system may fail and allow the experiences to be accurately symbolized, resulting in a breakdown of the self-concept and disorganization in behavior (Rogers, 1959).

Two degrees of pathological behavior can be differentiated—*defensive behavior* and *disorganized behavior*—on the basis of whether the self-concept is intact and the defense system successful, or disrupted and broken down and the defense system inoperable. This is not the usual distinction between neurotic and psychotic behavior, since defensive behavior includes paranoid and catatonic states as well as other chronic conditions. Moreover, disorganized behavior includes irrational but not psychotic behavior, as well as some acute psychotic behaviors. In fact, considering the continuum of incongruence, the traditional labels have little useful meaning in this approach (Rogers, 1974a).

Some examples of how defensive behaviors protect the self-concept are as follows: (1) rationalization: "I could have made an A if I had studied" (self-concept includes, "I am intelligent"); (2) fantasy: daydreaming of winning against insurmountable odds (self-concept as competent, strong, successful); (3) projection: "You are seducing me" (self-concept, "I do not have dirty thoughts"). Disorganized behaviors, on the other hand, are evidence that the defenses are unsuccessful. The disorganized behaviors are consistent with the denied aspects of the experience, but inconsistent with the self-concept. For instance, an individual who has characteristically and rigidly denied sexual impulses is likely to act out his sexual impulses indiscriminately during a period of disorganization. After a period of disorganization, the self-concept becomes partially reorganized and some of the defenses are reestablished, but the self-concept has changed to include the experience of disorganization; e.g., "I am sick," "I am losing my mind" (Rogers, 1959).

The Theory of Psychotherapy

Because it views psychopathology as being part of a continuum of incongruence, rather than representing a qualitative distinction, the client-centered approach is little concerned with the traditional clinical concerns of diagnosis, symptomatology, and forms of treatment specifically designed for a particular dysfunction. The client-centered therapeutic approach is thus intended for all persons, regardless of classification (Rogers, 1974a).

CLIENT CHARACTERISTICS

At the beginning of therapy, most clients exhibit the following characteristics, as a result of prolonged and pervasive use of defenses: The client often does not recognize the degree of incongruence between his self-concept and his experiences. He is cut off from his feelings and from whatever personal or subjective meaning is associated with these feelings, so that he lacks self-awareness or access to his inner world of feelings and perceptions. This lack of self-awareness is apparent in his communication, which is usually focused on external events or persons, in which the relationship to self is only implicit or not at all recognized. In his manner of experiencing, the client tends to perceive events in absolute rather than relative terms, to overgeneralize, to be strongly opinionated, to ignore space and time relationships as these modify opinions or feelings, to rely on abstractions rather than to test his perceptions against concrete realities, and, in general, to exemplify a conceptual–perceptual–emotional rigidity. He tends to externalize the responsibility for his problems and to assume that changes in others or in external circumstances are the solution to his problems rather than seeking to change himself or his behavior. Finally, he tends to avoid close interpersonal relationships, which are perceived as threatening or dangerous.

THE GOAL OF THERAPY

In the client-centered approach, the goal of therapy is to intervene in such a way as to remove the incongruence the individual has developed between his experiencing organism and his self-concept. To do this, it is necessary to reunite and reintegrate the organismic and self-concept components of the personality that have become encapsulated as a result of the defense system. In short, the goal is to get the person back in touch with his organismic valuing process, so that the locus of evaluation and control is internal, rather than external.

A number of other changes accrue as a result of accomplishing this goal. The client becomes fully aware of his feelings, accepts ownership for them, and is able to express them appropriately. His experiencing process is more "in the moment" rather than tied to the past or future. His beliefs and opinions are tentatively held, consistently reality-tested against feedback from others, and modified in keeping with new experiences. He recognizes his degree of responsibility for his problems and the degree to which his problems are part of his self-concept rather than an external situation to be solved. Finally, he is capable of, and desirous of, deep personal sharing with others, leading to intimate interpersonal relationships. In fact, he may experience impatience with the superficiality, deceit, and manipulativeness of others. The common thread running throughout these changes is an openness and a flexible response to experience; that is, the ability to modify one's attitudes, values, and self-concept in keeping with new experiences. Of course, the person will continue to experience problems, disappointments, and stress, but his approach to problems will be different, and his capacity for self-resolution and self-direction will be significantly enhanced.

This description of changes in the client's behavior after successful therapy, as well as the description of the client's behavior at the beginning of therapy, are summarized in Table 17–1 (adapted from Walker, Rablen, & Rogers, 1960). The client's behavior is viewed as a process that gradually changes over the course of therapy from a low level of functioning to a high level of functioning. The seven behavioral dimensions are relatively separable at low levels of client functioning, but tend to merge at high levels of client functioning.

TABLE 17-1

Client Levels of Functioning[a]

Behavioral dimensions	Functioning levels		
	Low	Medium	High
Feelings and personal meanings	Unrecognized	Increasing ownership	Living in flow
	Unexpressed	Increasing expression	Fully experienced
Experiencing	Remote from experiencing	Decreasing remoteness	Lives in process of experiencing
	Unaware	Increasing awareness	Uses as major referent
Incongruence	Unrecognized	Increasing recognition	Temporary only
		Increasing direct experiencing	
Communication of self	Lacking	Increasing self-communication	Rich self-awareness communicated when desired
Construing of experience	Rigid constructions	Decreasing rigidity	Tentative constructions
	Constructions seen as fact	Increasing recognition of own contribution	Meaning held loosely to be checked against experiencing
Relationship to problems	Unrecognized	Increasing responsibility assumed	Problem not seen as external object
	No desire to change	Change often feared	Living in some aspect of problem
Manner of relating	Close relationships avoided as dangerous	Decreasing danger felt	Relates openly and freely on basis of immediate experiencing

[a] Adapted from Walker, Rablen, and Rogers, 1960.

THE PROCESS OF THERAPY

The client-centered theory of therapy has gone through many changes since its inception (Gendlin, 1970b; Hart, 1970). Some basic principles, however, have not changed. As early as 1940, in a speech at the University of Minnesota, Rogers made four statements characterizing the approach, and they are still valid:

1. This approach to therapy relies on the individual's drive toward growth, health, and adjustment. Therapy frees the client for normal growth and development.

2. This approach places greater stress upon the feeling aspects of the situation than upon the intellectual aspects.

3. This approach places greater importance on the immediate situation than upon the individual's past.

4. This approach lays stress upon the therapeutic relationship itself as a growth experience—a personal relationship which is a growth-promoting psychological climate [Rogers, 1970c, p. viii].

This last statement of Rogers was elaborated in a 1957 article entitled "The Necessary and Sufficient Conditions for Therapeutic Personality Change." Assuming a motivated and cooperative client, three facilitative or core conditions must be present in the therapist: First, *unconditional positive regard:* a respect, prizing, or valuing of the person or being of the client; second, *empathic understanding:* an emotionally toned, cognitive appreciation of the client's experiencing from the internal frame of reference of the client. This is best defined operationally by the question, "What would I be feeling, based on my own life experiences, if I were saying what the client is saying?" Third is *genuineness:* an honesty or frankness such that the therapist's overt verbal and nonverbal communication is consistent with his covert feelings, reactions, and attitudes.

These essential ingredients or *core conditions* comprise a therapeutic strategy that is entirely consistent with the Rogerian theory of personality. The conditions that create maladjustment—the incorporated conditions of worth (introjected values) and the concomitant need for positive self-regard—determine the behavior of the person. They cause him to act in order to attain the approval of others, rather than in response to his own organismic valuing process. To arrest and reverse this process, it is necessary to provide a climate in which there are no conditions of worth—a climate in which there is unconditional positive regard, or respect, for the client as a worthwhile human being, within the context of empathic understanding. Respect without empathy is of little value, since the client may view this respect as indiscriminate; "If you knew all the horrible secrets about me, you couldn't possibly respect or value me, since I do not value myself" or "You like all people, regardless of their faults, so that's why you like me." Eventually, as the need for positive regard from others is satisfied by the therapist, the need for positive self-regard also is satisfied; "If you still feel I am a worthwhile person in spite of my faults, then maybe I'm not so bad after all." This process assumes that the therapist is honest in his communications, that is, is genuine. Clients frequently test the genuineness of the therapist; "You're pretending that you like me so I won't feel so bad about myself." "You really don't care for me at all, but you have to act as though you do, because that's your job."

These three core conditions Rogers later called *facilitative psychological attitudes* in order to distinguish them from therapist techniques. Regardless of what techniques the therapist uses, the client-centered position states that these attitudes toward the client must be present in the therapist and must be perceived as present by the client for therapeutic change to occur.

The major change in client-centered theory since its beginnings has been with respect to therapist techniques. The early theory stressed reflection of feeling as the primary technique, while forbidding other techniques, such as interpreting, probing, leading, and confronting. Later theory is less concerned with techniques and stresses the three basic attitudes, while encouraging the therapist to be his own person and to communicate these attitudes to the client in a natural way.

Therapists also have come to rely on their own experiencing in the moment and to communicate this more readily to the client. Genuineness has become not merely the absence of phoniness, but an active, self-disclosing sharing with the client, in which the inner experiencing of the therapist is a critical ingredient in the therapeutic relationship. Empathy is not simply restating the client's verbal content, but

> . . . pointing sensitively to his felt meaning to help him focus on it and carry it further. . . . Unconditional positive regard really meant appreciating the client as a person regardless of not liking what he is up against in himself (responding to him in his always positive struggle against whatever he is trapped in). It includes our expressions of dismay and even anger, but always in the context of both of us knowing we are seeking to meet each other warmly and honestly as people, exactly at the point at which we each are and feel [Gendlin, 1970b, p. 549].

An Example of Client-Centered Therapy

Therapist: Can you tell me what brought you to the counseling center today?

Client: Well, I've been having a lot of trouble concentrating on my studies lately.

Therapist: You're worried about getting your homework done, is that it?

Client: Yeah. Well, it's like this. I look over all the assignments I have for tomorrow's classes and I try to decide what needs to be done to get ready for them. I get depressed by all I have to do and I just throw up my hands in frustration. So I end up doing nothing.

Therapist: There's so much to do that it just overwhelms you, and you give up.

Client: Yeah. It's not that I don't care, I really am trying. And I'm not dumb, either. I've always made good grades in high school, but somehow it's different now.

Therapist: Right now you're not able to get the work done, and that's a new experience for you. You're not sure . . .

Client: One thing, around here, nobody seems to care what you do. Most of the profs don't care if you understand the material or not. They've

Therapist:	got to flunk a certain percentage of the class anyway, or else they'll get a reputation for being easy and the dean will be on their case.
Therapist:	It sounds like you feel you're battling the system all alone and there's not much hope.
Client:	Yeah. Anyway, I can't see how anybody can study in our dorm. The guys are always goofing off and raising hell, and my roommate's probably the worst. He's already on probation, and I'm sure he'll flunk out by the end of this semester, he hasn't cracked a book yet, and cuts most of his classes.
Therapist:	If I'm following you, it sounds like you're saying there are good reasons why you are not able to concentrate on your studies.
Client:	Yeah . . . well, I guess I'm using that as an excuse. I don't know. It's like I just don't seem to have it all together, you know?
Therapist:	So, there are a lot of things bothering you, and you're just not handling it all.
Client:	Well, the main thing is my schoolwork, and uh, I'm not getting along too well with my girl. We've been fighting a lot lately.
Therapist:	Could you tell me more about that?

In the initial stages of the counseling relationship, the therapist is primarily concerned with building a good working relationship. That is, he wants to create a climate in which the client will feel that he is being heard and understood, and is respected as a person. In addition, he wants the client to begin to trust him as honest and aboveboard, in no way phony or manipulative. The therapist builds the relationship by taking an attentive, reactive, responsive set, not an active or initiative set. As is apparent in the interview sample, he follows the client's lead, communicating a desire to understand, essentially asking the client, "This is what I get from what you are saying, is this how you see it?"

Let us pick up with the same client about midway in therapy. You will notice that the therapist is much more initiating, that is, coming out of his own immediate experiencing, so that his responses to the client are much more varied than in the initial interview.

Client:	You know, last week, you suggested that maybe I wasn't really leveling with my girl, that I wasn't being honest with her about what I wanted from our relationship. Well, I've been thinking about that, and it's probably true. But she hasn't been honest with me, either. And, besides, if I were to tell her the things she does that bother me, I'd hurt her feelings and we'd probably end up splitting.
Therapist:	Jim, I feel like that's a real cop-out. On the one hand, you've been telling me that you're unhappy with the relationship as it is, but on the other hand you're not willing to risk doing anything to try to change it.

Client:	Dammit! You're not involved in it like I am. Christ! It's easy for you to sit there and say, "You really ought to level with her." Boy, I bet you don't lead your own life that way!
Therapist:	I can see that you're really pissed at me right now. And it's true, I don't always do what I believe to be right. With my wife, for instance, there are lots of times when I don't let her know what I'm feeling, but I've learned that although that may avoid the immediate hassle, I become more and more unhappy with the relationship when I do that.
Client:	Okay. But, for instance, how do I tell her that I wish she'd take a bath more often? Honest-to-God, sometimes the B.O. really turns me off!
Therapist:	I feel like we're arguing right now. I wonder if you're not feeling something toward me that you're not telling me?
Client:	Maybe I am . . . I guess I feel like you don't think I've got enough guts to deal with my girl, and I feel like you're sort of, putting me down. . . . Sometimes I feel like you're getting tired of me, of my coming in, like, maybe you've given up hope that I will get better.
Therapist:	I'm glad you told me, because I don't feel that way at all. I think you've come a long way since we started. I like you a lot, and I don't think less of you because of your problems. I also don't want you to feel that I'm a perfect person either. As far as giving up hope, I'd say just the opposite. I suppose at times I do get impatient, but that's my hang-up.

Research Evidence

The vast number of studies evaluating the client-centered approach cannot be reviewed here. Only a few representative studies and summary findings will be reported.

The early research in the 1940s and 1950s is reviewed in two sources (Cartwright, 1957; Seeman & Raskin, 1953). The first study reported was by Porter (1943). He developed a classification of therapist verbal behavior along a directive–nondirective continuum, and found that judges using the system to rate tape recordings of therapy sessions could reliably differentiate between therapists. The method was then applied by Gump (1944) to client-centered and psychoanalytic recordings and the predicted differences in the therapists' directiveness were demonstrated. These studies set the pattern for many studies to follow. In general, they were directed toward definition of concepts generated by the theory, development of objective measures of these concepts, and the application of these measures to tape-recorded interviews.

An early outcome-study, measuring changes in clients after therapy, was conducted by Cartwright, Kirtner, and Fiske (1963). Several outcome measures were used, including the Thematic Apperception Test, the Minnesota Multiphasic Personality Inventory, sentence completion, Q sort, and therapist's and diagnostician's evaluations of client improvement. Using a factor analysis, they found that although these outcome measures were moderately intercorrelated, no single factor or scale could adequately represent therapy outcome. Rather, the factors tended to represent various instrument–observer combinations. The evaluation of outcome apparently depends upon the vantage point of the evaluator and the particular instrument he uses. This discovery continues to be a problem for all psychotherapy research. That is, who should evaluate outcome—the therapist, the client, expert judges, or even friends, relatives, and co-workers of the client? How should the evaluation be made—test, rating scale, interview? These early studies thus uncovered many measurement and research design problems, and perhaps their chief value has been to increase the sophistication of later researchers.

Two important early studies on the therapist core conditions should be noted. Halkides (1958) related the presence of the core conditions to success in therapy. On the basis of several criteria, 10 cases were identified as successful and 10 cases as unsuccessful. Blind judges (not knowing which cases were successful or unsuccessful) rated the degree to which the core conditions were present in the interview tape recordings of these cases. Halkides found that all three of the conditions were significantly associated with the successful cases. Barrett-Lennard (1959) studied the core conditions from the vantage point of the client rather than judges' interview ratings. He designed the Barrett-Lennard Relationship Inventory, now a widely used client–therapist measure of the quality of the therapeutic relationship. After the fifth interview and at the end of therapy, clients completed the relationship inventory. Barrett-Lennard found that clients' improvement in adjustment was significantly related to their perception of their therapists (after five interviews) as having respect, genuineness, and empathic understanding for them. Thus, these two studies provide initial support for the client-centered theory of psychotherapy.

Perhaps the most definitive studies of the client-centered approach took place at the Wisconsin Psychiatric Institute (Rogers et al., 1967). This large-scale project showed that patients who received therapy, when compared to untreated control patients, showed little difference in average constructive personality change and no difference in average subsequent rehospitalization rates. This finding supports Eysenck's criticism (1952) that psychotherapy produces no greater average client improvement than no therapy at all.

However, the following two findings directly support the client-centered position: (1) Patients whose therapists offered high levels of nonpossessive warmth (unconditional positive regard), genuineness, and empathy showed significant positive personality and behavior change. (2) Patients whose therapists offered low levels of these core conditions exhibited deterioration in personality and behavioral functioning. Since the number of therapists in this study offering high levels of the core conditions approximately equaled the number offering low levels, the finding of no average improvement between the therapy group and the control group is understandable. The finding that clients receiving high levels of the core conditions tend to improve while clients receiving low levels tend to deteriorate has been replicated many times (Carkhuff, 1969; Carkhuff & Berenson. 1967; Truax, Carkhuff, & Kodman, 1965; Truax, Wargo, & Volksdorf, 1970).

More important, a 9-year follow-up of these results (Truax & Mitchell, 1971) indicates that the effects found at the end of treatment tend to persist. Patients whose therapists had offered high levels of the core conditions had a significantly better post-hospitalization history than those patients whose therapists had offered low levels of the conditions. They were also significantly better off than a matched control group of patients who had not received therapy. The measure used was the number of days the patient was able to remain out of the hospital, that is, not having to be rehospitalized, over the 9-year period. Of considerable concern is the persistence of the negative effects on the patients of low-functioning therapists. These patients were less likely to be released from the hospital, and if they were released, they were more likely to have to return. Although the patients of low-functioning therapists were not significantly worse off than the control patients who received no therapy, the data pointed in this direction. The implication is obvious: No therapy at all is as good as therapy provided by a low-functioning therapist, and may be better. This conclusion is further supported by a review of a large body of research in counseling and psychotherapy (Truax & Mitchell, 1971).

Another finding from the Wisconsin studies has significant implications for the theory. Not only is it important that the core conditions be present (as determined by judges' ratings of audiotapes) but also it is important that the client *perceive* them as present in the relationship (as measured by the Barrett-Lennard Relationship Inventory). If both measures indicate the presence of high levels of the core conditions, then there will be considerable client improvement. If only one measure indicates high levels, there will be only slight improvement. If neither measure indicates high levels, the result will be no improvement or actual deterioration.

Finally, the Wisconsin studies indicate that the client's level of involvement in the therapy process at the beginning of therapy is an important predictor of improvement. That is, if the client's level of functioning is too low initially (see Table 17–1), little improvement will result. Contrary to expectation, increases over the course of therapy in client level of self-exploration or level of experiencing were not related to outcome, whereas the client's initial level was related to outcome. This is consistent with the widely held belief that psychotherapy is least effective with those who need it the most. Perhaps other, nonverbal interventions, such as operant procedures, are needed to bring severely disorganized persons to a level of functioning at which verbal forms of psychotherapy can be effective.

One of the best studies comparing different therapeutic orientations was conducted by Raskin (1974). He selected 8-minute audiotape segments from the therapy sessions of six expert therapists, each of whom agreed that the segment selected was representative of the way he worked. The therapists represented the following orientations: rational–emotive, experiential, psychoanalytic, Jungian, client–centered, and direct analytic. Eighty-three therapists then rated the tapes on a four-point scale as to the degree to which the following therapist variables were present in the tape segment: *cognitive, experiential, empathic, therapist directed, equalitarian, warm and giving, unconditional positive regard, congruent, emphasizes unconscious, systematically reinforces, self-confident,* and *inspires confidence* (in the judge). The judges represented a wide range of theoretical orientations, but the bulk of them were about equally represented in three groups: psychoanalytic, client-centered, and eclectic orientations. In addition to rating the audiotape segments, the judges also rated themselves as to the degree to which the therapist variables were present in their own work, and again as to the degree to which the therapist variables should be present in the ideal therapist's work.

Raskin found that the expert therapists were rated as practicing differently from one another; that the orientation and experience level of the judges made little difference in their ratings; and that there was a high degree of agreement in their rating of the ideal therapist. Most important, the judges viewed both their own practice and the ideal as being most like the client-centered expert. Regardless of orientation, the judges tended to agree that the *experiential* aspect of therapy is more important than the *cognitive,* and that *empathy* and *congruence* are to be given greater weight than *therapist direction, emphasizes unconscious,* and *systematically reinforces.* Finally, it was found that the correlation between the client-centered therapist and the ideal was .94; the next highest correlation with the ideal was .57 for the experiential therapist; the remaining four experts all correlated negatively with the ideal, the extreme being −.66 for the Jungian therapist. Thus, this study not only supports the importance of the core conditions but also indicates that the client-centered approach is regarded as quite close to the ideal therapeutic approach by 83 judges, of whom only 23 classified themselves as client-centered.

Thus, the research evidence reported generally supports the major propositions of the client-centered theory of therapy. Yet, some modifications of the theory were made in order to incorporate findings not explicitly predicted. These modifications have led to further research on the therapeutic process and to attempts to extend client-centered principles to nontherapeutic, interpersonal situations.

Summary

Client-centered theory is an integrated system built around two aspects of Rogers' core idea: (1) Individuals have the resources and capacity for self-understanding, self-direction, and self-fulfillment, and (2) this capacity can be discovered and released through a relationship in which the client perceives as present in the therapist the facilitative psychological attitudes of unconditional positive regard, empathic understanding, and genuineness.

In the client-centered view of personality development, man is motivated by an actualizing tendency, or growth force toward self-actualization. Whether or not experiences and behavior are evaluated as self-actualizing is determined by an internal mechanism, called the organismic valuing process. Formed out of experience is the self-concept, a sense of *I* or *me*, following which a need for positive regard from others and a need for positive self-regard arise. If the individual receives unconditional positive regard from others, he will continue to grow toward self-actualization and to evaluate his experiences in terms of the organismic valuing process. However, if others place conditions of worth on their valuing of the individual, he will incorporate these conditions of worth into his self-concept, and they become introjected values, replacing the organismic valuing process as the basis for evaluating experiences. In order to continue to receive positive regard from others, and in order to satisfy his need for positive self-regard, the individual acts in accordance with his introjected values. Experiences that are inconsistent with the introjected values are denied or distorted through the use of defenses, and although the individual's self-concept is defended against threat and anxiety, it becomes increasingly inaccurate, unrealistic, and rigid. This process leads to a state of incongruence between the individual's self-concept and his experiences. Depending on the degree of this incongruence, further defensive or disorganized behavior results.

In client-centered therapy, the therapist helps the client reduce this incongruence between his self-concept and his experience. He helps the client get back in touch with his organismic valuing process and to act in accordance with it, rather than according to his introjected values. As a result, the client increases his positive self-regard, becomes more open to experience, more capable of modifying his self-concept in keeping with new experiences, and more capable of self-direction. These goals are achieved to the extent that the client experiences unconditional positive regard, empathy, and genuineness from the therapist. The therapist uses any therapeutic techniques that are consistent with his personality and that convey or communicate to the client these three facilitative psychological attitudes.

18

Existential–Phenomenological Therapy

ERNEST KEEN

Bucknell University

Neither existentialism nor phenomenology are psychotherapies. They are philosophical traditions, grounded in the work of modern European philosophers. These traditions reflect a distinct theory of man—a theory that leads to a particular understanding of psychotherapy, behavior technology, and psychopathology. This understanding is notably different from the naturalistic, pragmatic, and positivist points of view that underlie most of American psychology. I shall try, in this chapter, to describe the existential–phenomenological point of view and explain its implications for the concrete practices of therapeutic psychology.

Only a few specific techniques may be attributed to existential–phenomenological (EP) therapists. For the most part, psychotherapists who have an EP point of view are distinctive not so much for technique as for strategy. *What* they try to do is more distinctive than *how* they try to do it. Therefore, it is possible to differentiate the actual practices of psychologists with this point of view by a series of general contrasts.

First, the entire range of therapies can be divided into two broad, roughly hewn groups (see Figure 18-1). The first group includes all those therapies that *operate upon* the patient, putting him into the role of passive recipient of treatment and locating control—and responsibility—in the therapist. This group includes such techniques as chemotherapy, shock therapies, and operant

		Power and responsibility concentrated in therapist (medical model)	Power and responsibility distributed between patient and therapist
Explicit goals or targets of therapy	Behavioral change	Electroshock therapy Operant technologies (excluding self-control techniques, but including token economies and individual programs) Psychosurgery	Self-control techniques Desensitization Most family and community psychologies
	Experiential change	Hypnosis and other classical psychiatries Implosive therapies	Psychoanalysis Rogerian therapy Transactional analysis Gestalt therapies Existential–phenomenological therapies

Figure 18-1. The major types of therapy compared, in terms of the goals of therapy and the roles of therapist and patient.

technologies—in short, the medical model.[1] The second group includes all those therapies that operate *in collaboration with* the patient, putting him into the role of active agent of his own change and distributing power and responsibility between therapist and patient. This group includes most face-to-face therapies, psychoanalysis, and many forms of behavior modification. Therapists who operate from an EP point of view are clearly of the second group; their style of therapy grows out of the explicit premise that man is an active agent in his own fate.

A second general contrast can be drawn between those therapies whose goals are primarily behavioral, such as the various technologies of behavior change, and those whose goals are experiential, focusing on the individual's perceptions, feelings, thoughts, and personal orientation to life. Experiential goals, which are almost impossible to measure reliably, are the central concern of an EP therapist because they are understood to be the central facts of human existence. If one understands man as essentially (not accidentally or incidentally) conscious, if consciousness is considered the central fact of human existence, then one must choose between goals that are measurable and goals that are central. EP therapists invariably choose the latter. Obviously, such a choice depends upon one's assumptions about man, and so we see again the importance of the philosophical presuppositions that lie behind a therapist's approach.

These two broad contrasts serve to locate EP therapists within a general

[1] The medical model, so universally under attack in recent years, refers not only to the role structure, as emphasized here, but also to the supposed locus of the problem, as pointed out in Chapter 2. Therapists operating within the medical model locate the problem in a *disease within* the person, rather than in the functional relations *between* persons. This aspect of the medical model often, but not always, varies with the power and responsibility aspect emphasized here.

range of possible orientations to therapy, but they do not yet discriminate EP therapy from psychoanalysis, Gestalt, Rogerian, or even transactional approaches. These more refined distinctions will be developed as we look at (1) the historical roots of EP therapy, (2) its major assumptions, (3) the kinds of persons for whom it is most applicable, (4) what one can expect from a therapist with an EP orientation, and (5) research bearing on therapy approached in this way.

Historical Roots and Recent Developments

In the 1840s, Soren Kierkegaard (1813–1855) published a number of essays satirizing and criticizing conventional religion of the day and the pretentious rationalism of Hegel and naturalist philosophers. His themes were the intensity of the inner experience of the single individual and the irrelevance of conventional rationalist philosophy and institutional religion to this core reality. Friedrich Nietzsche (1844–1900), aiming more broadly at conventional art, morals, and culture, also exalted the heroic possibilities of the individual. The individualist themes of these two philosophers led to the profound innovations of twentieth-century phenomenology and existentialism. They also clashed with the naturalistic and scientific thought of the nineteenth century.

Edmund Husserl (1859–1938), commonly considered the father of modern phenomenology, dealt with the crisis created by the polarization between science and individualism. He sought some common ground underlying both the passionate subjectivity of Kierkegaard and Nietzsche and the rapidly growing naturalistic and scientific modes of thought that are still predominant today. A logician and a man given to scrupulous philosophical discipline, Husserl addressed the problem without the visible passion of Kierkegaard and Nietzsche but also without the self-confident fluency of natural science. His work led to a transcendental philosophy that remains controversial to this day. More important, his task and his approach gave birth to the modern existential phenomenologies of Heidegger, Sartre, and Merleau-Ponty. All these philosophers are working on the task taken up by Husserl—to find and articulate the fundamental ground that underlies all human thought, that common basis from which it derives and to which it refers.

One theme that unites all these thinkers is a radical empiricism—the premise that science, religion, technology, social institutions, art, and culture in general all are rooted in the subtleties of human experience. Experience *as it is experienced,* as opposed to experience theoretically reconstructed in scientific, religious, or conventional thought, is the data base from which all doctrines are abstracted. Experience is the real basis of our understanding, to which abstracted theories ultimately refer in making our lives and the world intelligible to us. Experience as it is experienced gives us access to the most fundamental issues we can take up, the issues of being in general (Why is there something instead of nothing?) and human being in particular (Who am I? What does it mean that I exist?).

These obviously philosophical questions do not occur to people in the usual course of their everyday lives. Yet the sweeping psychologies of Freud, Jung, and

Adler in the first half of the twentieth century clearly took stands on these philosophical issues and dispensed psychiatric treatment on the basis of these stands. Igor Caruso (1964), Ludwig Binswanger (Needleman, 1963), Medard Boss (1963b), and Viktor Frankl (1960) are European psychiatrists who have worked since the 1930s to recast the psychotherapeutic enterprise in existential–phenomenological terms. Their work represents a critique of the naturalism of Freud, the religiosity of Jung, and the sociomoral framework of Adler. It also represents an attempt to find the basis of classical depth psychologies in the exigencies of human being. A similar critique and attempt exists today in the naturalistic and behaviorist psychologies predominant in the United States.

In 1958,[2] Americans were introduced to the possible connections between the existential–phenomenological movement in Europe and modern psychotherapy. The publication of *Existence: A New Dimension in Psychology and Psychiatry*, edited by Rollo May, Ernest Angel, and Henri F. Ellenberger (1958), brought to America the results of several decades of theoretical work by European therapists. This book initiated a burst of literature that attempted to formulate the enterprise of helping people in existential–phenomenological terms (Bugental, 1965; Burton, 1968; Gendlin, 1962; Keen, 1970; Laing, 1960; May, 1969, 1972; Van den Berg, 1972; plus translations of the European pioneers Frankl, Binswanger, Boss, and Caruso). These major statements form the most accessible center of EP psychotherapeutic literature.[3] A few writers have made explicit attempts to compare phenomenology and behaviorism (Correnti, 1965; Corriveau, 1972; Day, 1969; Gatch & Temerlin, 1965; Kvale & Grennes, 1967). Three journals are currently devoted to explorations of the relationship between psychology and existential phenomenology.

EP Therapy: Some Major Assumptions

Anyone who goes to a therapist will be dealing with questions of how to live his or her life. The particular views of the therapist about the necessities and possibilities for human beings are therefore a rightful concern of the patient. Therapists with an EP orientation can be said to hold the following assumptions about human beings, and they base their therapeutic behavior, their personal

---

[2] The year 1958 is also cited by Rimm as an important beginning in behavior therapy, a therapeutic innovation in quite a different direction (See Chapter 15). Clearly, the decades since that time have seen an explosion of new approaches to therapy in the United States, after half a century of nearly total control by psychiatry. Only Carl Rogers, an American humanistic psychologist, had made headway earlier in opening up the field to new ideas from psychology.

[3] Less lengthy but still general statements include Basescu (1962), Beukenkamp (1967), Bugental (1964), Burton (1967), Fisher (1966–1967), Heuscher (1964), Hora (1962b), Kahn (1962), Ledermann (1962), Lefebre (1963), May (1961a), Rinehardt (1960), Stern (1965), Sutherland (1965–1966), Tillich (1961), and Van Dusen (1962). A number of philosophers have been considered in relation to psychotherapy such as Heidegger (Van Kaam, 1961), Sartre (Hopkins, 1970), Marcel (Machado, 1961; Stierlin, 1962), Scheler (Keen, 1966), Tillich (Braaten, 1963), Schütz (Van Zaig, 1965), Socrates (Fireman, 1967), and even the Delphic oracle (May, 1970).

lives, and their expectations for patients on these assumptions. The first two have already been mentioned in the opening paragraphs of this chapter.

1. Human beings are active agents in the determination of their own behavior, their relationships, and their lives. This assumption does not deny that functional relationships can be found between earlier events that "happened to" someone and later choices they make. But many of these earlier causal influences can be overcome, and the general goal of therapy is to liberate the patient from as many of these limitations as possible. This assumption also implies that the course and outcome of therapy are as much the patient's responsibility as the therapist's. No therapist can make someone change who does not, on some level within, want to change.

2. The critical arena of change, indeed of one's life, is one's *experience* of oneself and the world. Although overt behavior is reliably measurable, it is not the center of the action, either in therapy or in one's life. Overt behavior *expresses* our experience of ourselves in the world. Thus the liberation mentioned previously is primarily the liberation of experience, the development of the ability to see and interpret the meanings of events in one's life in new and varied ways.

3. Combining the two premises just listed, it follows that the meanings of the events in our lives are, within certain crucial limits, choices we make, options we take up from an array of possibilities that, although limited, is nevertheless wider than the array of possibilities most clearly and habitually apparent to us.

Both the limits and the possibilities are crucial. One cannot transcend those limits imposed by the existential situation, such as the eventual and usually arbitrary death of oneself and others, the inevitability of disappointments, pain, and physical illness, and of anxiety in the face of an always uncertain future. But one need not be condemned to depression over loss of loved ones, conditioned anxiety from traumas earlier in life, or oppressive guilt over real or imagined transgressions of the past. There are always alternative meanings of both past and future, and we actively choose what they shall mean to us.

4. The therapeutic process is a meeting of two persons in which the basic directions for the life of one of them are at stake for both of them. It is not merely the person's behavior, nor his or her thoughts, feelings, memories, or anticipations that are at stake, but all of these—as they are organized into the complex whole process of being a person. The patient is asked to put his entire being[4] on the line, to bypass attractive but peripheral issues of his thoughts, feelings, or behavior, and to throw into question the most central themes of his life. If the patient is to be challenged at the most basic level of what it means to be a person at all, then the therapist will have to risk these things as well. The therapist will

---

[4] The term *being* becomes, in EP thought, a technical term that may be defined either conceptually or experientially. Conceptually, *being* refers to the whole of which thinking (cognition), feeling (affection), behaving (conation) are parts, which then would include also such processes as perception, learning, imagination, etc., all of which are organized for any person into the coherent whole that he or she "is." Experientially, *being* may be understood as the whole process or activity of being who I am; "I-am-ing."

have to speak and act from the core of his being if he is to reach the patient at the core of his being.

It is clear from the statement of these assumptions that the language used to express them goes considerably beyond the kind of language that is reliably measurable or scientifically amenable. Such phrases as *the core of his being* must have a clear referent in order to be clear to a reader, but the reference cannot be seen through the operational techniques of modern science. It must be grasped intuitively and introspectively in one's own experience. As stated earlier, this sacrifice of scientifically verifiable theory is not made lightly. It is justifiable only if one believes that the most central issues of one's life are in fact like that— embedded in the deepest layers of subjective experience and not immediately available for scientific manipulation. Therapists with an EP orientation certainly share this view.

Indeed, the procedures of scientific measurement and prediction may be analogous to how I know some things, but they are quite irrelevant to how I know other things. I may know what my wife will do in a given situation by making a prediction based on prior observations. This is informal science. But I know *what* she means to me, *whether* I love her and what *that* means to me, *who* she is as an individual to me, who *I* am to her, and why we stay married—I know these things in a very different way. I am not *certain* of any of these things in the sense that scientists are certain when they can predict a dependent variable with a probability of 1.0. But I have *certitude* about them (to borrow Kierkegaard's term) that emerges from a different part of myself than my rational calculations. It emerges from my innermost sense of myself and from my personal response to the entire question of being a person in the world at all. I have access to this part of myself only through my experience as I experience it.

This level of psychological functioning is the stuff of psychotherapy, whether therapists and patients know it or not. Of course patients must be allowed to pretend that these issues are not at stake in their therapy or their lives if they want to. But if patients want to avoid these issues, they are well advised not to choose a therapist with an existential–phenomenological orientation.

The Applicability of EP Therapy

Theoretically, there is no one for whom therapy from an EP point of view is not applicable. The practical situation is much different, of course. Some people want merely to "be fixed," to submit to some procedure that will change this or that feature of their behavior or feelings. They want the greatest efficiency and they do not want to explore what their behavior, feelings, relationships, and life *mean* to them. EP therapists refer these patients to others for treatment. It is the obligation of every therapist to refer clients to that therapist who offers them what they want.

But the decision of referral is not always simple, for prospective patients sometimes *say* they want to explore existential issues when they do not, and others are not sure what they want. The therapy for still others is determined by contingencies irrelevant to what anyone wants. This often happens in public clinics, where therapist and patient are matched by bureaucratic routines, and in legal–penal situations where the judge prescribes therapy on the basis of his convenience, without understanding the patient, the therapist, or what kinds of therapies might be available.

Therefore, though there is always an existential dimension to every therapy, it is not always appropriate for this dimension to come into focus and be the center of the therapy. Certainly those who want merely to be fixed, those who are not willing to share responsibility for therapy and its outcome, are not appropriate candidates for this kind of therapy. There must be a minimum desire to take oneself, one's relationships, and one's life seriously. Certainly those who arrive in therapy by way of the courts, who do not want to change but are coerced into therapy, are not appropriately treated by existential therapy—or perhaps any therapy. A therapist can sometimes evoke in a patient a real concern for the patient's own life, but if a central part of the patient's own initiative is not engaged, existential therapy is not likely to be helpful.

For whom, then, is existential therapy appropriate? The fact seems to be that many patients today, indeed many members of this highly mobile, technological, and bureaucratic culture, do not know what they want, from their therapy or from their lives. Like all cultures, our culture offers a range of definitions of what is valuable, what we should work for, commit ourselves to, and where we can find meaning in our lives. But the standard American dreams have become more than slightly questionable for many Americans. Material wealth and leisure do not make life meaningful or suffering tolerable; political causes cannot deliver a new era of universal happiness; and even our closest personal relationships are threatened by standardization, routine, and the empty clichés of the mass media. Faith in science and technology has been tarnished by a suspicion that our technological solutions are part of our ecological and existential problems. Lurking behind apparently psychological problems is the existential problem of our alienation from a tradition, a cause, a source, a ground of meaning that we can firmly plant our feet in and claim as our own, thereby having some certitude about who we are and why that matters.

In fact, the entire range of psychological symptoms, from phobias to psychoses, can be seen as desperate attempts to fill a void created by a civilization that has come to worship materialistic achievements, only to find that such achievements do not deliver their promised ecstasy. Much of this "problem behind the problem" remains unclear, to therapists as well as to patients. To explore it, by exploring the intricacies of one's most personal experience, is the goal of existential–phenomenological work, in scholarly circles, in everyday life, and in psychological practices.

Therapy with an EP orientation, therefore, is appropriate for all those for whom this modern malaise is a central problem. If a patient is impotent, his potency may be repaired. But is it a problem for him why he wants to be potent? Why successful sexuality matters? Why his marriage, his relationships in general, his life matters? Perhaps he can be happy grasping at one of the straws offered by our culture—leisure, prestige, ecstatic sex—but perhaps he cannot. Perhaps these values fail to mobilize his life in such a way that he can really believe in it, care about it, make sacrifices and endure suffering for it. If this is true, existential–phenomenological therapy is appropriate, not because it gives him answers, for it does not, but because it makes the questions clear, it makes vivid the stakes, and it brings into focus those parts of himself from which his own answers to these existential questions must come.

Impotence, or any symptom, may be seen as a mechanical problem, resolvable by drugs or surgery. Or it may be seen as an expression of psychological tension, resolvable by drugs or desensitization. Or it may be that the tension is an expression of an existential problem. The resolution in this case can come only from the individual's coming into a fuller awareness of who he is and why it is important for him to be who he is.

What to Expect from an EP Therapist

In general, what you can expect from a therapist with an EP orientation are *questions* and not *answers, dilemmas* and not *solutions, paradoxes* and not *logic*. This does not mean that EP therapists talk in riddles, for they talk just like everyone else. It does mean, however, that an EP therapist does not feel he can answer the most important questions in life for you nor can he solve your dilemmas nor reduce life's paradoxes to logic. Indeed, only *your answers* count; their execution in life depends on *your solving and resolving,* not his, and the logic of your life will have to *encompass, not escape,* certain paradoxes.

To be sure, an EP therapist may well agree with you that the answers, resolutions, and paradoxes you are currently living may not be the best possible ones for you. And he will commit himself to trying to put you in a position to answer life's questions better, to solve and resolve more clearly in the face of life's dilemmas, and to face more courageously life's paradoxes. But the critical actions and final result of therapy are yours, not his.

You can also expect an EP therapist to make a distinction between the anxiety, guilt, and shame that are unnecessary, excessive, and destructive, and the anxiety, guilt, and shame that are existential, inevitable, and simply human rather than pathological. The latter, existential contingencies are not to be solved, cured, nor overcome; they are to be faced. They challenge us not to deliver ever more clever technological mastery, but rather to respond with courage, resolve, and self-affirmation.

What are these existential contingencies? What are the paradoxes that are not to be escaped or mastered but can only be faced courageously? We will look at several in the next section, and in the process what can and cannot be expected from an EP therapist will become clear.

In general, however, you can expect him to try to help you see that whatever symptom or problem you have is some version of the existential situation. How could it be anything else, since you are an existing human being? You *cannot* expect him to help you make this existential situation, with its questions, dilemmas, and paradoxes, go away. You cannot expect him to anesthetize you from life, to apply chemotherapy or psychotherapy or behavioral technology in such a way that there is no pain, no suffering, no tragedy, and no anxiety. Indeed, he probably will try to show you how your currently unsatisfactory life evolved from an inability to face these exigencies, or perhaps from an attempt to escape them, or to live the ideal, beautiful life that exists for human beings only in fantasy.

This process cannot happen all at once. I can write these things, and you can read them, and we both can understand them intellectually, but they come to matter only as we can *live* them, only as they connect with and make a difference to the most central, intimate, and urgent parts of ourselves. What I say, think, feel, and even overtly do all have a common core in my sense of being: *that* I am, who I am, and why I am who I am. That core must be approached, touched, and moved if the therapy is to be existential.

Existential Limits

In 1843, in *Fear and Trembling,* Kierkegaard (1843/1954) described three kinds of considerations that might influence a personal decision: aesthetic, ethical, and religious. We see, when we think about it, that all three considerations are ambiguous, and that this ambiguity can lead to confusion, depression, and even disorientation. What is "the good life," considered aesthetically? Ethically? Religiously? Each of these considerations played a part in the consciousness of our nineteenth-century counterparts. Kierkegaard made clear (more for our own century than his, for he was not a popular author in his time) that these issues are not satisfactorily resolved by the conventional wisdom of one's time. All formulas and prescriptions fall short of engaging the core of our being, and hence they fail to enable us to live as our culture seems to promise we can live—happily, confidently, securely. Indeed, each of these ambiguities brings its own kind of melancholy, and so one can rightly speak of *aesthetic melancholy* (confusion and depression over what pleasure is), *ethical melancholy* (over what is right), and *religious melancholy* (over whether and how to have faith).

A century later, more or less independently, Paul Tillich (1952) outlined three approximately parallel kinds or sources of anxiety that are built into the existential situation. These anxieties are *not* neurotic or pathological but are simply human. There is, first, the contingency of *human finitude*. This phrase refers not only to the fact that we shall all die, but also to the inescapable limits of human power to eradicate pain, loss, and the intransigence of all that is not subject to human will. Second, there is built into the life-situation for human beings an absolute necessity to make decisions and to act, without our ever being certain about how we should decide or act. This situation creates the *inevitability of guilt*—the knowledge that we have been responsible for others' suffering, and that we cannot ever know enough about the consequences of our actions to avoid such responsibility in the future. And third, we all suffer the constant *threat of meaninglessness,* the marginal awareness that those commitments, causes, groups, tasks, and values that make our life meaningful are subject to being revealed as groundlessly relative at best, or at worst, sheer shams and frauds.

These problems, which appear regularly in the writings of existential thinkers, are abstract statements of very concrete personal experiences that are universal for human beings but are most especially vivid in technically advanced societies. It is absolutely crucial to have a clear conception of these exigencies as simply human and not neurotic problems. Confusion about this point seems to have led our culture to try to "cure" everything that is unpleasant, even to the extent of curing us of our consciousness and therefore of our humanness. We are capable, with our advancing behavioral, clinical, and psychic technologies, of creating a society of people who cannot feel guilt, recognize tragedy, or face up to the exigencies of the human situation. When the false securities of conventional distractions and technologically created painlessness collapse, the soil is prepared for the flourishing of neurotic symptoms.

Bugental (1965) has added loneliness to this list of three sources of existential anxiety. Fisher (1966–1967) has outlined Tillich's first two sources and Bugental's fourth. Still others (e.g., May, 1969, 1972) have done it yet a little differently. But every psychotherapy reaches a point when what is required is not a fix from outside oneself but rather a mobilization of courage within oneself. Some problems are not to be solved; we can only face them with resolve. Whether or not therapists are explicit about this range of "simply human" (rather than neurotic or pathological) sources of anxiety and distress, each and every therapist operates within some theory of human existence and influences his patients to see it his way. EP therapists are merely explicit on this crucial point.

Existential Choice

Mobilizing my courage is obviously appropriate when my problem is clearly reducible to an existential contingency. Most people, however, refuse to be so simple. Between my current symptom and the existential situation as conceived in its bare-bones contingencies lies the stuff of my whole life, which is neither courageous nor fainthearted in any simple sense. Rather, it is the rich conglomeration of the thousands of little decisions made over the years—some admirable, others foolish, but most just simply obvious to me at the time.

Our most vital decisions are not behavioral (what to *do* in this or that situation) but perceptual (what this situation *means* and *who I am* with respect to it). Of course, what I do behaviorally is the most critical outcome of my personal psychology, but it is the outcome of a rich reservoir of influences—my experience. The crucial arena that must be explored and understood by both patient and therapist—and, I might add, by the theoretician—is the world of experience.

My experience is directly accessible only to me. I can make it partly accessible to you by telling you about it, but my articulations will hardly convey all the nuances, the subtle meanings and shades of feeling that really count in understanding what I do. Of course this elusive quality of experience creates devilish problems for the science of psychology. But in therapy, the chief investigator—the patient—has access to this arena. I already know what it is like to be me and to live in the world as I construe it—*my* world, with its layers of meaning, its tempo, contours, and textures. What I do not know, if I am a patient with a problem, is just which decisions I have made in putting together my world, nor when I made them, nor—most important of all—what my options were and still are. The point of EP psychotherapy is merely to clarify these decisions. That is, of course, difficult work.

EP therapists are not the only psychologists to believe all this. Freud's technique of free association and dream analysis was a systematic methodology for such exploration. A sample of the voluminous commentary on psychoanalysis and existential–phenomenological work is contained in Binswanger (1963), Boss (1963a), Elkin (1965), Keen (1972), May (1969), Ricoeur (1970), and Sartre (1956). Fischer (1971) is particularly clear about the difficult matter of the unconscious. In addition to Freud and the psychoanalysts, there have been others who have understood therapy to be an exploration of experience, or of choice, or of both. Among these are Carl Rogers (1942, 1951, 1961), George Kelly (1955), Harry Stack Sullivan (1947), and Karen Horney (1950). The only advantages EP therapists would claim amidst this distinguished company are the methodical consciousness of presuppositions and the philosophical rigor characteristic of existential–phenomenological work since Husserl.

If we are to take seriously the exploration of experience as a mode of therapy, we shall have to have a theory of experience. For existential phenomenologists, experience is structured around some universal coordinates, without which none of us could be who we are. The theories mentioned previously are all versions of such theory. The list of existential contingencies is also part of this structure, but there is more. I experience myself as a body, in space, as a self, in time, as a role, in a network of interpersonal agreements (Keen, 1975). My most important point, however, is that the world I experience and the self I experience within the world are, within universal limits, choices I make. If I am to explore experience *as choice*, therefore, I shall have to have a theory of that space within which such choices must be made. This has always been the special province of existential phenomenology.

I choose my world. I did not, of course, choose my parents, my age, my culture, or my genetically defined body with its propensities and limits. But I do very definitely choose what all these shall *mean* to me, and I weave them into a coherent self–world relationship that *is* my life and my world. The world I chose and choose is not simply the physical, biological, and sociohistorical givens; it is all these in their meaning to me. I choose my world-as-meaning, or *the* world when I see it as that network of meanings I *live* and *am* in my everyday existence. Unfortunately for psychology, this pattern of choices is immensely complex; unfortunately for patients, exploring it is very hard and seemingly very risky work. But fortunately for both, the task is possible.

Perhaps the most central concept in EP therapy is May's (1961b) notion of the self as *centeredness*. Let us see if we can approach an understanding of this concept through the use of some examples. Holt (1966) has described one of his patients, a priest whom Holt calls Father M, as follows:

■ He presented himself on time, greeted me very forcefully, shook my hand, and admired my furniture. He said that we had an especial affinity because he could see that the pieces came from Italy. He took command of the session and started to speak in great detail about his attitude toward the Church. During much of the subsequent time we spent together—sixty-four sessions in all—he was domineering, cynical, superior, a man who knows it all and feels that humility, though theoretically a Christian virtue, would if practiced, deny to men like himself the leadership role they deserve. He attacked me constantly, questioned my sincerity, ability, capacity, truthfulness to fact, and in one or another form of hostility rejected my interest. At the same time, however, he made excessive demands on me in time, energy, attention, friendliness, and love [p. 370].

Rollo May (1961a) describes one of his patients, Mrs. Hutchens, as follows:

■ Here is a patient, Mrs. Hutchens, who comes into my office for the first time, a suburban woman in her early thirties, who tries to keep her expression poised and sophisticated. But no one could fail to see in her eyes something of the terror of a frightened animal or lost child. I know, from what her neurological specialists have already told me, that her presenting problem is hysterical tenseness of the larynx, as a result of which she can talk only with a perpetual hoarseness. I have been given the hypothesis from her Rorschach that she has felt all her life, "If I say what I really feel, I'll be rejected; under these conditions it is better not to talk at all." During this first hour with her, I also get some hints of the genetic *why* of her problem as she tells me of her authoritarian relation with her mother and grandmother and of *how* she learned to guard firmly against telling any secrets at all [p. 25].

Now these two brief descriptions seem to refer to very different kinds of persons. Father M is too self-confident, intolerant, and arrogant. Mrs. Hutchens is frightened and timid. The crucial concept that ties them together is that they both feel, on the fringe of their awareness, that their center, their self, their sense of their own identity, is under attack. The details of each "attack" from outside must be omitted here, but in each case the feeling goes back many years. However, they have both (as we have all) adopted a certain *posture* with respect to life, acquired a certain *style* of being a self, which is designed to preserve that sense of a center, protect it from encroachments and ensure that, whatever else happens, they will not lose their mind, their grip, their sense of being a self.

Many layers of self-evaluations, self-concepts, and self-affirmations lie between the original threat of attack and the manifest symptoms. These layers are the individual's history of evolving a self that is attuned to safety and danger as these are experienced on the fringe of awareness. These regions of safety and danger are not the physical space of the Newtonian world, but they follow the coordinates of *meaning* as the lived-world of experience evolved over developmental time. Father M could tolerate no weakness and Mrs. Hutchens could risk no disclosure of inner feelings and secrets. Each adopted a style or posture that maximized the safety and minimized the danger. They now identify that style as their *selves*. But each also mapped out the network of regions of life and assigned specific activities, specific other persons, specific physical places and social roles according to the coordinates of meaning of safety and danger. They now identify these regions as *their world*. The sense of self and the sense of world fit together, into a totality of being a person, or as phenomenologists like to put it, a *being-in-the-world*.

This totality, one's being-in-the-world, is at stake in therapy. But the fact that makes therapy possible is that one's self and world are, in terms of the *meanings* I have been speaking of, open to choice. They were chosen originally, under certain identifiable circumstances. That may become quite understandable. But that they may now be *chosen anew*—that is not something one understands intellectually. It is something one *does* existentially. And in doing so, one is changing *who* one is, and *what* the world is. Above all, one is fitting self and world together in such a way that the centeredness of oneself is relatively safe from attack without one's former style, posture, and symptoms.

Finally, the existential situation, with its contingencies as described earlier, is itself an attack on human security. Growing up always involves losses; our decisions are always made in the face of ambiguity; and the gods we worship, whatever they are (and we all have them), are subject to having clay feet. Most of us manage to create a self-world totality that is not so constricted as to be called neurotic or psychotic, but it is only a matter of degree. Many of us avoid problems by being merely conventional from beginning to end—often a safe posture but increasingly less serviceable in times of rapid social change. Often enough, the world we create for ourselves and the selves we create for our world cut us off from genuine desires, inherent tendencies, or even universal human needs. Then we must question who we are, why we are who we are, why it is important, and whether there are further options. Usually, there are.

The Therapeutic Relationship

Contracting for psychotherapy is always an agreement between persons, and the terms of that agreement should be as explicit as possible. Since the patient must share in the responsibility for the outcome of EP therapy, this agreement cannot be of the same type one has with a physician, a dentist, or an automobile mechanic. In some forms of behavior technology, such a contract is not only possible but highly valued. In EP therapy, the patient has a right to expect different kinds of things from the therapist, such as his familiarity with the task at hand, his general goodwill, and his commitment to deal with basic issues of human existence as they are present in the patient's life, in his own, and in the relationship between them. Having made such commitments, however, the therapist assumes the right to expect certain things from the patient, such as a certain seriousness of intent and desire to change. Neither party can make the other totally responsible for his own behavior without distorting the essence of human being as EP therapists see it.

Virtually every major statement of EP psychotherapy mentioned in this chapter describes in detail the therapeutic relationship, but there are specialized articles in the EP literature that deal with this topic (Barron, 1961, 1967; Beets, 1967; Bugental, 1967; Colm, 1965; Jourard, 1967; Mendel, 1970; Moustakas, 1962; Sequin, 1969; Steward, 1965–1966; Whitaker, 1963; Winthrop, 1969).

Twin attitudes of support and confrontation characterize the work of an EP therapist (and most other therapists). There are many words to describe the supportive side of therapy: *empathy, rapport, love, acceptance, encouragement,* and *nurturance.* The atmosphere of support is an atmosphere of warmth and safety. It is what we all need from time to time just in order to live, but is particularly crucial for someone who is risking a journey through a range of options, past, present, and future, about how to be himself or herself. Any therapist must show some understanding of what the patient is going through, or the patient will feel isolated in the crosscurrents of his or her own impulses, demands from others, and existential contingencies.

But love does not cure all. Some hard edge of confrontation is also needed in all psychotherapy—a distanced, interpretive posture in which the therapist does *not* accept what is handed him but rather insists on more rigorous, more searching and honest scrutiny of the layers of meaning embedded in one's experience. The psychotherapeutic process, therefore, is also one of conflict between the two parties. Sometimes in alliance with the patient's own tendency toward growth, but sometimes alone, the therapist must struggle with the patient's tendency to avoid confronting those issues in his own life that he must face squarely if he is to see his options clearly. (See Garner & Jeans, 1962, for a good discussion of confrontation.)

Underlying both sides of this dialectic between support and confrontation should be a fundamental attitude of mutual respect, in which the two parties encounter one another without interference from roles, rules, and pretenses. Such a relationship is as rare in therapy as it is in real life, but it remains a kind of premise for EP therapy—a conviction that we are all struggling with essentially the same human problems.

Bugental (1965) has described those moments when the layers of sham have been chipped away and patient and therapist face a fundamental option about who they have been, are, and shall be, which he calls the *existential crisis.* Many interpretations may be theoretically correct ("Your rage at your wife is really rage at your mother") but existentially in error in that they lead the patient to rationalize away his problem and to avoid finally taking a clear stand about who he is and shall be (e.g., in relation to his wife). At such points, the EP therapist tries to avoid *answering* (e.g., why the patient is enraged at his wife) and to force the *question*—"Who are you with respect to your wife?"—to represent the ambiguity of the human situation as it is, with its inevitable anxiety and uncertainty. For the fact is that this patient must choose who he is in relation to his wife. He cannot drift along, pretending that his being who he is with respect to her is merely up to her, or the effect of childhood traumas or accidental conditioning in his past, or dictated by social norms, traditional values, obligations, or responsibilities. None of these matter unless he chooses to make them matter, unless he chooses to construct the world in this way. What he needs at this point from the therapist is not an answer but the question, and that is all the therapist, or anyone, can rightfully give him after the layers of pretending, feelings about, perceptions of, and reactions to his wife have been explored.

Genuine existential crises must be prepared for by minute explorations of the patient's experience in its many-layered complexity. Meanings abound; they must be seen in their relation to one another, and in how they constitute the relationship between the individual and his world. At the point of existential crisis, new meanings are created, and the patient must create them as a basis for living the rest of his life. Existential crises are also, of course, crises for the therapist, for he must face the limits of his ability to help, to heal, to be the authority or the reservoir of wisdom, even as he has come to care about the patient and his future.

Relevant Research

Research bearing on the kinds of processes we have been discussing is very difficult to do quantitatively. Some (e.g., Van Kaam, 1966) seriously question whether the isolation of variables may not destroy the events we are trying to understand. Others have been more or less successful in translating this highly experiential language into operational terms and have produced some quantitative results. Rogers and Dymond (1954) demonstrate a number of ingenious attempts to grasp operationally the subtleties of self-experience. Self-esteem, as measured by the Q sort, can be shown to improve with Rogerian therapy. Jourard (1964) has explored experimentally the effects of self-disclosure on personality. Self-disclosure can be demonstrated to have a beneficial effect on mental health as measured in a number of ways. More specifically existential are Crumbaugh's (1968) attempt to measure Frankl's notion of purpose in life, and Gendlin's (1968) demonstration that the qualities of experience during psychotherapy change in a patterned direction toward more self-conscious self-affirmation and the creation of new meanings.

Generally, however, the attempts to make numbers and scales appropriate for the experiences dealt with in this chapter have not been impressive. Therefore, an entirely different mode of research is beginning to take shape under the name of *phenomenological psychology.* This nonquantitative research seeks to embody the systematic and rigorous character of science and yet retain a sensitivity to qualities and meanings as they appear in concrete experience (Colaizzi, 1973; Giorgi, 1970; Giorgi, Fischer, & von Eckartsberg, 1971; Keen, 1975; Laing, Phillipson, & Lee, 1972; Van Kaam, 1966). This methodology has not yet been developed enough to attack the difficult subject matter of psychotherapy, but it may hold promise for future research in psychotherapy. Barton (1974) has made a start, as has Esterson (1972). Generally speaking, I believe it is fair to say that phenomenological psychologists are just now beginning to understand how to look and listen systematically and rigorously.

Therefore, the research literature in EP psychotherapy remains largely in case study, anecdotal, and theoretical form. Quite an argument could develop over what constitutes research or good research. I am willing to argue that much of what follows is research, but it is not always very good research, for some of it lacks systematic observation.

SPECIAL TECHNIQUES IN EP THERAPY

Several therapists (Beukenkamp, 1967; Curry, 1966; Hora, 1962a; Meigniez, 1963; Thomas, 1967) have written about the application of existential–phenomenological thinking to group therapy. Hora's description is particularly useful, clarifying how blockages in the group therapy process can usefully be understood existentially. He discusses the dissociation of conceptual thinking from concrete experience—a common problem in most therapies with sophisticated patients; disturbances of the sense of time—also a widely observable phenomenon; encroachments of one self upon another—common in all neurotic problems but particularly vivid in group therapy; and neurotic crutches against existential anxiety.

A number of other special therapeutic techniques have appeared in the literature as a result of understanding psychopathology and psychotherapy in EP terms. Frankl's "logotherapy" is clearly the most technique-conscious of the EP therapies (Crumbaugh, 1965; Frankl, 1961, 1962, 1964; Ungersma, 1961). His best-known technique is called *paradoxical intention,* wherein the patient is told to intentionally exaggerate his symptom. If he is obsessive, he is to concentrate on nothing but his obsession; if he is phobic, he is to generate the fear as dramatically as possible; if he has temper outbursts, anxiety attacks, or fits of depression, he is to indulge his symptom intentionally with concentrated purposefulness. The first result of such a regimen usually is a bringing of the symptom under conscious control. The second, more important, result is a vivid experience of one's self and one's symptom as subject to one's choice, thereby enhancing one's sense of oneself as the active agent in one's own fate.

Stern (1964) reports some success using mirrors with specific types of borderline patients. Both psychodramatic and existential principles underlie this technique. Life is an enactment of who we think we are. The mirrors bring that realization into focus. Frenkel (1964) reports using mirrors in the fashion of a projective technique to overcome the traumatic amnesic period prior to hospitalization in psychotics. This technique reveals to the therapist the repetitive pattern that has led to hospitalization; it also reveals it to the patient who, through his amnesia, was successfully avoiding seeing it as his way of coping (or not coping) with crucial issues in his life.

Heuscher (1965) describes a procedure designed to help a patient to enhance his meaningful identity. This "clinical application of the concept of world design" involves showing patients the structure of meanings of other patients. This procedure makes vivid the way in which each of us constructs his world in its particularity from a general range of human possibilities, and illustrates how some world-designs are more livable than others. This technique enables confrontation to proceed without argument. It facilitates dealing with very "abstract" life-issues without the deadly compartmentalization of overintellectualized abstraction. Heuscher (1967, 1969) explores the same therapeutic technique using myths and fairy tales. Consider, for example, the world-design of Sleeping Beauty. Do we not all live partly in such a fantasy? Does not recognition of that fantasy make it possible to see the world differently? And make it inevitable that we choose our world?

Mendel (1962, 1964) describes psychotherapy as a basis for moving into the future, and therefore he devises techniques for maximizing this orientation in the experience of patients. One aspect of the future is that it will be spent without the therapist, so Mendel juggles the contract of meeting times. These changes orient the patient to an open-ended life in which he must create the world and re-create it with every new circumstance. This technique, unlike Heuscher's, is limited to sophisticated, nonpsychotic patients, but the importance of Mendel's writing is not the technique per se as much as the sensibility it portrays, which is generally applicable to psychotherapy.

Howland (1962) calls our attention to nostalgia and how it permeates the psychotherapeutic enterprise. He distinguishes carefully between longings born of sentimental fantasy and that experience of the past which, though still nostalgic, provides the basis for the present and the future. Of course if our subject matter is experience as it is experienced, kinds of remembering and longing for what is remembered must be described and distinguished. This difficult phenomenological work deals with time in general, with the past and the future as they are experienced—not formulated into a sequence of linear causality as they are in physics. Virtually every major statement in EP therapy attempts to advance this phenomenological understanding of being a self in time, and of qualities of remembering and anticipating.

Van den Berg (1962) explains the use and results of the *guided daydream* in therapy; Shorr (1967–1968) envisions a similar technique, which he calls the *imaginary situation*. Shorr's imaginary-situation technique asks the patient to imagine himself or herself in some situation and tell what happens. The situations can be derived from the patient's answers to a list of "existential questions" such as, "What do you never want to be called?" If the patient says, for example, "sexy," it leads to an imaginary situation in which his or her sexiness is noticed by others. Shorr is interested in this technique as a diagnostic one through which the structure of one's self–world relationship can become vivid. But unlike traditional diagnosis, the patient is the chief diagnostician and the therapist is merely a midwife to his or her clarity about self and world. Such clarity is, of course, an integral goal of therapy.

Like Van den Berg's guided daydream, and other techniques using imagination, the freedom from "reality" that imagination affords is not absolute but always constrained by one's way of constructing self and world. Explicit clarification of these constraints is a necessary precondition to overcoming them, which in turn is a necessary precondition to existential change. Holziger's (1964) use of LSD-25 for certain patients, and working with dreams (Boss, 1957; Dunkell, 1967; Mendel, 1967) follow essentially the same logic.

All one's imaginary psychic products, from hallucinations to art, occur within that margin of freedom beyond mechanistic theories of sense organ and brain but nevertheless within that order of our particular being-in-the-world. To explore and use imaginative techniques is especially appropriate within EP therapy, but techniques by themselves, apart from the context of the relationship, become parlor games. It is well to be suspicious of our modern tendency to hope that a technique can replace the difficulties and anxieties of existential struggle.

SPECIAL CLINICAL PROBLEMS IN EP THERAPY

One of the most difficult and perplexing psychotherapeutic problems is that of suicide. The major theory in psychiatric and psychological thinking has been Freudian, and it would seem that existential thought ought to have a special relevance to understanding someone's decision to cease to exist. But suicides are not all alike, and so a variety of case studies and theoretical efforts appear in the EP literature. Binswanger's (1958) classic study of Ellen West portrays an individual who has reached what appears to be a genuine existential dead end. Ellen West seemed to close off possibilities and create a circle of fate around herself in such a way that suicide became inevitable. Eckhardt (1967–1968) describes a much more typical case of a suicidal patient who was saved by a mobilization of existential freedom. Murphy (1961) describes a successful treatment in a suicide emergency, and Bakan's (1962) paper suggests an interesting method for exploring the experience of suicide.

Theoretical treatments of suicide from an EP perspective include Minkowski (1958), Farber (1962a), Neuringer (1962), Straus (1964), and Keen (1973–1974). Death itself, of course, is a relevant issue in considering suicide. In addition to the classical statements by existential philosophers, there are several interpretations of death from an EP perspective (Feifel, 1961, 1965; Hobart, 1964; Koestenbaum, 1964; Wyschogrod, 1973). A related topic, aging, is given an EP treatment by Korwin (1963). Of course, all the major statements of EP psychotherapy listed earlier treat the topics of suicide, death, and aging.

The other special clinical problem that will be mentioned here is schizophrenia. The diagnostic category itself has come under serious and justifiable attack, as described in Chapter 5. Nonetheless, though within the full range of human possibilities for structuring the experience of self and world, people classified as schizophrenics are at an extreme. Some are so deviant from the norm that they are incomprehensible to others. Attempts to define schizophrenia have combined such criteria as behavioral peculiarities, speech patterns, qualities of relations with others, psychodynamically conceived personality failures, and concrete experience. This mixture reflects and perpetuates a degree of theoretical chaos in psychiatry.

Whether classifying a particular group of deviants into a category like *schizophrenia* makes sense or not is an open question—psychopathologists have not settled on a consistent approach by which to establish a classification scheme. The EP approach is one of a number of theoretical approaches that could produce a coherent answer to questions of classification, but too little is known now to proceed. Acceptance of the EP approach by the profession and its ultimate usefulness depend upon whether experience, self, world, and the question of one's being at all are in fact essential components of being a person. Similarly, other classifications, reclassifications, and nonclassifications in psychopathology, by behaviorists, psychoanalysts, Gestalt psychologists, and others, will be ultimately helpful only to the extent that *their* focus has succeeded in capturing what is essential to being a person.

The pluralism that currently exists in psychology is certainly inevitable and probably healthy. Unification of the science is still impossible to see for the very reason that each of these theories defines truth and usefulness in its own way, and none has the definitive access to truth that each would like to claim.

However, the EP approach does claim to deal with fundamentals, and studies of schizophrenia are perhaps the best argument for such a claim, since phenomenological descriptions of human being attempt to reach those fundamental levels of human existence at which schizophrenics are most different from the rest of us. Moreover, phenomenological studies of the self, world, and the question of being a person at all in schizophrenics have revealed aspects of human being never before brought into focus—such as the inextricable relationship between self and world.

At stake for schizophrenics, as for all human beings, is the self–world relationship as structured in experience. Laing (1960), Farber (1962b), Minkowski (Laing, 1963), Binswanger (1963), and Shulman (1965) offer theoretical statements; Mendel (1963), Gendlin (1964), Basaglia (1965), and Scher (1967) describe therapeutic approaches. However, of all the major statements mentioned at the beginning of the chapter, Burton (1968) gives the most detailed and sensitive account, in my opinion, of both EP theory and EP therapy of schizophrenia.

There are, of course, other special techniques and other special clinical problems, but the techniques described previously and the problems of suicide and schizophrenia are representative of the research literature, as it currently exists in its anecdotal, case study, and theoretical forms.

Conclusion

Some have said that the existential–phenomenological approach does not lead to a distinct therapy, but I believe that is only half true. On the one hand, it may be true that the best psychotherapists have always had an existential–phenomenological sensibility. Therefore, the EP approach offers nothing new. But on the other hand, the explicitness with which the existential and phenomenological aspects of psychotherapy are treated in the EP literature is bound to have a special theoretical value. If one believes that one's very existence is at stake in psychotherapy, and if one believes that experience as it is experienced is the arena in which life must be played out, then the EP approach is bound to be particularly relevant. The burst of EP therapy literature may have peaked in the 1960s or will do so in the 1970s. However, this literature, and the sensibility it makes explicit, has become a permanent part of the psychotherapeutic enterprise. Furthermore, this literature has provoked the birth of an academic counterpart in contemporary phenomenological psychology, which promises to bring continually new perspectives to psychotherapy and to psychology in general.

Summary

Soren Kierkegaard (1813–1855) made the inevitability of human choice clear to us, and Edmund Husserl (1859–1938) made the importance of subjective experience clear to us in this century. The philosophies of these men provide the basic assumptions of the EP approach to therapy—that we must choose our lives, and that difficulties in the choices can only be understood by exploring human experience. Both of these assumptions differ from American behaviorism, and they change the definition of therapy and even of knowledge in psychology. One adopts them only if one believes that they better characterize what it is like to be a person.

An EP approach to therapy, then, explores experience and confronts the client with the choices he must make. The EP approach is appropriate for clients who want to struggle or are struggling with the basic issues of what it means to be a human being, who they are, and why that matters. It is not appropriate for those who simply want an expert to fix them. The struggle with these issues takes place within a structure of limits that characterize human existence, such as the inevitability of uncertainty, death, and suffering. These limits can make us anxious, but this anxiety is not pathological; rather it is simply human. It ought to be faced and lived through rather than cured, and this requires an exploration of who one already is. Who I am is the sum total of the many choices I have made in my life. Most of these choices seemed obvious at the time, but all of them could have been made differently; now they constitute my style of being myself. By understanding these choices, I can see who I have become and how I could have chosen differently. I can also see how the meaning of that past to me is still a matter of choice, as are my future decisions and their meaning to me.

Since EP therapy engages human lives in ways that are very difficult to operationalize, most standing research is in the form of case studies, therapeutic accounts, and theoretical treatises. The phenomenological method, as a research tool, is at a very early stage of development. The chapter concludes by describing some EP therapeutic techniques and the concrete clinical problems of suicide and schizophrenia.

19

Gestalt Therapy

GORDON E. RADER

Southern Illinois University at Carbondale

Gestalt therapy is a modern, humanistically oriented form of treatment. In less than two decades, it has risen from obscurity to become one of the most popular and rapidly expanding forms of psychotherapy today. Its implied philosophy and values fit the tenor of our times. Gestalt therapy has captured the imagination of those who seek to burst from the constraints of a rigid, mechanical existence in a depersonalizing, materialistic society. In this respect, Gestalt therapy is part of the humanistic–human potential movement; it both contributes to and is nourished by the climate that has been established by such figures as Maslow, Rogers, and Jourard, and by the encounter group movement in the United States.

History and Development

Gestalt therapy is primarily the creation of one man, Fritz Perls (1893–1970). Perls' basic training was in psychoanalysis, and he practiced conventional analysis for many years. After attempting to modify the theory and practice of psychoanalysis and receiving a cool reception from other psychoanalysts for his ideas, he eventually broke all formal ties with his psychoanalytic background and accepted his approach as a creation deserving its own title. The name *Gestalt therapy* first appeared in a book published in 1951 (Perls, Hefferline, & Goodman, 1951).

Gestalt is a German word with no exact English equivalent. *Configuration, structure, unique pattern,* or *meaningful organized whole* are approximations of its meaning. The word implies that the whole is something more than, or different from, the sum of its parts. A square is more than four lines; a tree is more than a collection of leaves, limbs, bark, and trunk. The organization of the component parts creates a structure that has its own unique character. In the act of perceiving or experiencing, we add meaning or importance to the incoming stimuli by virtue of the particular patterns or gestalts that are formed. A square is recognized as a square no matter what its size or the nature of the lines or edges defining it. Some trees are immediately perceived as more beautiful or majestic than others.

Gestalt psychology, as distinct from Gestalt therapy, is a theoretical system or orientation founded by Max Wertheimer (1880–1943) and his two colleagues, Wolfgang Köhler (1887–1967) and Kurt Koffka (1886–1961). Gestalt psychology developed as a reaction against the prevailing tendency in psychology to seek an understanding of human consciousness by analyzing it into its components. Gestalt psychologists studied the laws governing the processes of organization and attribution of meaning in human perception.

Gestalt psychologists at first concentrated primarily upon elucidating the principles of gestalt formation in perception. They noted that the perceptual field is organized into a *figure* that stands out as the focus of interest and a background (or *ground,* as it came to be called) that is not attended to. Nevertheless, figure and ground are dynamically related; a change in one affects the other. A gray circle on a black background appears lighter than a circle of the identical shade of gray on a white background (see Figure 19-1). Gestalt figures can be strong or weak and good or poor. A strong form stands out clearly and captures our attention. A good form is one that is experienced as proper and complete in that it cannot be made simpler, more orderly, or more meaningful by a perceptual shift. Perls employed the concepts of gestalt formation, figure–ground relations, and the distinction between strong or weak and good or poor gestalts in his theorizing. These ideas will be discussed more thoroughly when we look at the basic concepts of Gestalt therapy.

Perls was particularly influenced by the early ideas of Wilhelm Reich, who was the last and most significant of the psychoanalysts from whom he received personal therapy and training. Smith (1976) discusses eight aspects of Gestalt therapy that were derived from Reich. Perhaps most significant were Reich's notions about "character armor" and the significance of the body in therapy. Reich taught Perls the importance of rigidified forms of posture and muscular response and automatized behavior patterns, which serve a defensive or avoidant function for the individual. Perls paid close attention from then on to the body and the messages a person conveys through his body. Reich also taught that more is revealed about a person's character in *how* he communicates than in *what* he communicates. Reich de-emphasized delving into past history. Reich also be-

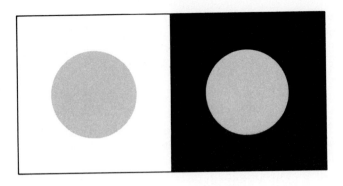

Figure 19-1. Figure and ground are dynamically related; note how the gray circle appears lighter against the black ground than against the white.

lieved that the therapist must be quite active and confrontive. Perls (1969b) credits Reich with teaching him brazenness, which perhaps contributed to his active, often frustrating, confrontive style. Perls believed that psychological growth comes only through frustration and that the therapist must learn to use a balance of frustration and support (1969a).

In 1926, Perls went to Frankfurt, Germany, to work at Kurt Goldstein's Institute for Brain-Injured Soldiers. It was here that he first came into contact with Gestalt psychology. Although Goldstein never regarded himself as a Gestalt psychologist, he applied a number of Gestalt ideas to understanding disturbed behavior and introduced Perls to Gestalt psychology. Perls also had direct contact with Adhemar Gelb, an early Gestalt psychologist who was working with Goldstein. At about the same time, he read the work of some Gestalt laboratory psychologists, notably Wertheimer and Köhler, and was impressed. Later, he read some of Kurt Lewin's writings.

The early Gestalt psychologists had little to say about personality and the process of need satisfaction. Goldstein and Lewin both contributed in this area. Goldstein applied the concepts of figure–ground and the formation and destruction of gestalts to the organism's need-regulated behavior. He postulated a homeostatic model of organismic self-regulation. He proposed self-actualization as the fundamental, master motive, long before Carl Rogers used the concept. All other drives are merely expressions of self-actualization. The satisfaction of any particular need organizes the figure when it becomes the most immediate means of promoting the self-actualization of the total organism. Goldstein expressed a holistic point of view, which stresses the essential unity of the entire organism as the proper object of study. Jan Smuts (1926/1961), the great South African statesman, extended holism beyond the boundaries of the organism to include the organism imbedded in its total environment. Perls was a great admirer of Smuts and much influenced by his ideas. Lewin made many theoretical contributions, but Perls was probably most influenced by his field theory and his tension-reduction model of motivation applied to uncompleted tasks. Perls speaks of *incomplete gestalts,* or *unfinished business* that clamors for attention. The concepts derived from Goldstein and Lewin will become clear in the discussion that follows.

When Perls began to develop his own therapeutic approach, he gave particular attention to his patients' immediate experience, attempting to help them concentrate and focus their attention on what they were doing, sensing, or feeling at the moment. At first he called his approach *concentration therapy* (Perls, 1947/1969). However, when he wrote his second book, in collaboration with Ralph Hefferline and Paul Goodman (Perls *et al.*, 1951), he decided to call his approach Gestalt therapy. He chose that name despite the objections of Hefferline and Goodman and of his own wife, Laura, who in many ways was a co-developer of Gestalt therapy. Laura pointed out that the therapeutic approach bore little relation to academic Gestalt psychology, which she had studied extensively as a graduate psychology student in Europe (Shepard, 1975). But Perls wished to emphasize his shift from an intellectual analysis of unconscious processes revealed in free association, to a focus on conscious awareness, immediate experience, and behavior. Such a focus required a regard for the total gestalt of the behaving human being, acting in the context of his personal psychological, social, physical, and physiological environment. Perls felt that calling his approach Gestalt therapy would best accomplish this purpose. Perls uses a number of concepts and considerable terminology from Gestalt psychology but his work has never been accepted by academic Gestalt psychologists as representing an extension of Gestalt psychology.

In fact, a number of influences were blended in the creation of the theory and approach of Gestalt therapy, and Gestalt psychology was probably not the most important of these influences. Perls' genius is evident in his integration of several unrelated idea systems and in his creativity in developing the technical application of his ideas in a new form of therapy.

The bedrock of his work as a therapist remained his psychoanalytic training and his long clinical experience practicing in the psychoanalytic mode. Though his method of practice changed, his acutely sensitive understanding of clinical phenomena and human behavior in general owed much to his psychoanalytic background. Many of his theoretical formulations were originally published as an effort to revise and extend psychoanalytic theory and practice (Perls, 1947/1969). He continued to use psychoanalysis both as a point of departure and as a reference point for his own ideas (Kogan, 1974).

Although Perls said little about the influence of the existential–phenomenological movement, which was gathering steam in Europe in the 1920s, an existential–phenomenological flavor permeates much of his work. The existentialist's emphasis on the necessity for taking personal responsibility for one's own existence is central to Gestalt therapy. Perls did, however, credit the work of several semanticists, especially I. A. Richards and A. Korzybski, for drawing his attention to the effects of language on thought and behavior. Gestalt therapists still pay very close attention to the language used by their clients.

Perls was always a restless, adventurous soul. Opposed to totalitarianism in any form, he fled Germany shortly after Hitler came to power in 1933. After living for a year in poverty in Holland, he accepted an invitation to go to South Africa as the first teaching psychoanalyst in that country. He lived there during the next dozen years, his most settled period, and developed the seminal ideas

Fritz Perls, at the right, listens intently as an Esalen staff member describes a dream during a Gestalt therapy workshop in 1968. After many restless years, Perls finally found a home at Esalen, and it was there that the explosive growth of Gestalt therapy began. (© Michael Alexander)

and the basic approach that became Gestalt therapy. In 1946, he came to the United States but never really found a home or developed a significant following until he came to Esalen, a West Coast center for humanistic psychology and therapy, in 1963. At Esalen he found a supportive environment and large numbers of people interested in his ideas. Since then, Gestalt therapy has spread its influence among professions as diverse as education, dentistry, nursing, and law. There are now training institutes in Gestalt therapy throughout the United States. Literally thousands of people have been influenced personally and professionally by Gestalt therapy and many therapists trained in other orientations have found ways of integrating some of the technology of Gestalt therapy into their own orientations.

Basic Concepts

HOLISM

It is difficult to discuss any of the basic concepts of Gestalt therapy without immediately bringing in other concepts, not yet introduced, and their interrelationships. The theory is an integrated fabric whose pattern is lost when one starts looking at each concept in turn, much as one must appreciate a medieval tapestry or a piano sonata for its total dynamic form, not thread by thread or note by note. Similarly, one cannot analytically break down a person and his behavior and, for example, comprehend the person's behavior without reference to the state of his feelings, his physiological state, and his relationship to his immediate surroundings. The person in all his aspects and his environment in all its relevant aspects are interdependent, all part of one dynamic field. Furthermore, the entire field is in flux. There is no stop-action in life. No matter how hard we may try to freeze a moment in time, we are never quite the same as we were an instant ago nor is our overall situation quite the same, and we progress toward a further difference an instant from now. Holism is thus a way of regarding living organisms, including people, as part of a unified organism–environment field, ever in process, moving inexorably, like a river toward the sea.

GESTALT

Holism actually is an extension of the fundamental observation about the formation of gestalts. The perceiving organism does not simply mentally register incoming sensory input. Rather, built into the very process of perceiving is an organization and interpretation of the sensory data. Thus, we perceive the figure on the left, not as a collection of dots but as a pattern, an elongated hexagon. Mentally, we fill in the lines, as in the figure on the right.

With a little mental effort, we can restructure our perception and see a different pattern—two triangles and a square:

You may know of other examples, from previous work in psychology.

A gestalt is the meaningful pattern abstracted from the sensory data available to us at the moment. If it fits our expectations—if it "seems right" or "makes sense"—we are comfortable with our perception. At times, however, the pattern seems somehow wrong or incomplete:

 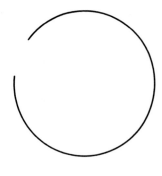

When we have a poor gestalt or an incomplete gestalt, we feel uneasy, tense. We cannot quite let the figure go; we want to do something to fix it up or complete it. When dealing with the gestalts arising out of critical life situations, our discomfort may indeed be intense.

FIGURE AND GROUND

When awake, we experience a steady stream of awareness in which first one pattern of stimuli and then another comes into focus. I sit in my chair writing; my thoughts and my struggle to find the right words to express them are in focus. I tire and withdraw from the struggle for a moment and, looking out the window, I am flooded with sights of the first really warm sunny day of the emerging spring season and with the complex of inner feelings evoked by the sight. My thoughts have receded into the background. Suddenly, my attention is jarred by the sound of the telephone ringing. The spring day disappears for me. What stands out is the telephone and the urgency of my felt need to answer it. At any particular moment, we organize the sensory data available to us into what stands out as *figure*. The rest becomes simply *ground*. Our interests, needs, or intentions of the moment generally determine what is figure for us, unless particularly intense or salient stimuli intrude and capture our attention.

Much of the time our awareness simply flows with our ongoing experience, without specific, deliberate control on our part. However, we can exercise control over our attention. As you read this, direct your attention to what you can hear. Sounds that were merely background become figure for you now as you deliberately attend to available auditory stimuli. Now shift your attention to your body and how you are supporting it. Where do you feel tension? Is there some part of your body that is not receiving adequate support? As I wrote that, I realized that my lower back was not fully supported and was becoming strained. I moved back in my chair to provide myself with better support. Much of Gestalt therapy involves discovery arising from directed awareness. As we learn how to focus our awareness with the help of the therapist, we encounter needs and feelings that we were avoiding or some of the automatic behavior patterns by which we help maintain the avoidance of fully experiencing and living our lives.

ORGANISMIC SELF-REGULATION

We can look to the animal world to provide us with a model of normal functioning uncontaminated with the dos and don'ts that humans learn in growing up. For an animal, a need arises, and when it reaches a certain threshold it becomes the dominant figure in awareness. As the figure develops, the total gestalt also includes awareness of the necessary means to satisfy the need—the goal-seeking and consummatory behaviors required. The animal must engage in some purposeful activity and make contact with the environment in order to meet its need. As the goal is reached and the need consummated, the cycle is finished. The need–consummation gestalt is completed and recedes from awareness, making room for the next emerging figure. The most dominant immediate need organizes perception and behavior. In the natural environment, this whole process works smoothly so that the optimum potentialities of the organism-in-the-situation are realized. A homeostatic balance is maintained in which needs are kept at a comfortable level as long as the environment provides opportunities for their satisfaction. The important point here is that the organism, left alone, regulates itself and naturally sees to its own needs and well-being.

However, humans face an additional complication. Our highly developed intellectual capacities permit a high degree of deliberation, restraint, and modification of our natural responses. Our social environment demands it. Thus a basic conflict is set up between our drive to express ourselves—our needs, our feelings, our aspirations—simply and straightforwardly and the demands of society to meet the expectations of others. To a greater or lesser degree, each of us has responded to this basic conflict by losing our free-flowing awareness and self-regulation. We strive to achieve an ideal, our learned concept of what we feel we ought to be, rather than to actualize ourselves as we really are. In the process we alienate, disown, distort much of ourselves, losing contact with our true wants, feelings, and capacities. We develop rigid patterns of responding (which we call traits of character), engage in phony role-playing, throttle and fail to develop some of our potential, manipulate and seek support from others rather than providing our own support. By losing touch with ourselves, we interfere with our natural homeostatic processes and growth. We take the life out of our lives. You may be thinking, "Not me, I don't do all that." These behaviors are so automatic and so ingrained as part of our particular personality style that we do not recognize how or how much we actually engage in such activities. It is the principal goal of Gestalt therapy to put people back in touch with themselves and thereby help them to live more fully, realizing and utilizing their unused potential.

OPTIMAL AND NONOPTIMAL FUNCTIONING

No one in this world functions perfectly. Each of us has certain physical or mental limitations, some of which we were born with and some of which we developed or allowed to develop. Furthermore, we all have our hang-ups—some more than others. Still, most of us have our moments when we seem to utilize our own capacities fully in expressing our needs and meeting the requirements and possibilities of the situation. Think of Henry Aaron smoothly swinging through the ball and sending it high in the stands with a powerful snap of his wrists, of Martin Luther King inspiring his audience to see new visions for his people, of Groucho delivering the perfect ad-lib crack. Now think of your own high spots, moments when you were fully engrossed in the activity at hand, flowing spontaneously, in full command of the situation. Remember your exhilaration? Remember how there seemed no past, no future, only the moment? Remember that you were simply acting, not simultaneously acting and reflecting upon or observing your actions? At such moments we seem more keenly aware of our relevant surroundings and our purpose (a clear, strong gestalt is formed) and all our faculties needed in meeting the situation seem to operate smoothly and without a sense of control or forcing (organismic self-regulation). If you can recapture the memory of such moments in your own life, then you will have some sense of the Gestalt notion of optimal functioning.

We obviously cannot live our day-to-day lives in the same manner as our peak moments. However, recognizing the characteristics of our functioning in such moments helps us to appreciate the ideal of healthy or supernormal functioning toward which we can aspire and, by contrast, to recognize unhealthy or less than optimal functioning. In the previous section, we noted that in response to socialization pressures we learn to interfere with free, natural expression of our desires and feelings and even to disown them, acting as if we have no such desires or feelings. Unrecognized and unexpressed needs represent incomplete gestalts that compete for attention with other needs. The perceptual field becomes unclear or confused and the smooth, flexible flow of self-regulation of our needs is interrupted. We also learn to become overly dependent on how others evaluate us and thus must constantly seek to impress others, meet their expectations, and make them like us and approve of us so we can feel good about ourselves. Furthermore, we learn how to get other people to meet many of our needs and thus fail to discover our own strengths and capacity for independent functioning. In the process of adapting, most of us lose, to a greater or lesser degree, our spontaneity, creativity, joy and excitement in living, capacity for the full range of emotional expression, sensitive awareness of our own inner states, full empathy for others, sense of freedom and autonomy, and willingness to take risks in our contact with the environment. Table 19-1 summarizes some concepts of positive and negative functioning that are stressed in the Gestalt approach (see, e.g., Carmer & Rouzer, 1974; Latner, 1973; Naranjo, 1970; Ward & Rouzer, 1974).

AWARENESS

Awareness is the most central concept in the Gestalt approach. In fact, the concept of awareness has been at least an implicit theme in almost all the discussion thus far. Organismic self-regulation requires clearly developed figures— good, strong, complete gestalts—which in turn depends on full awareness. Without explaining in detail, it can be said that awareness or its lack figures in each of the items of positive or negative personality functioning listed in Table 19-1. Awareness includes not only thinking, but also feeling and sensing such things as

TABLE 19-1
Concepts of Positive and Negative Personality Functioning

Positive or "healthy"	Negative or "unhealthy"
Integration, wholeness, completeness	Disowning of various aspects of self; lack of integration
Living fully, freshly, spontaneously	Lack of spontaneity; feeling anxious; restraining feelings or behavior; dulling the senses
Actualizing one's potential	Failing to actualize one's potential
Providing self-support	Seeking support from others
Being authentic, fully what one is	Being phony; trying to be what others expect
Being responsible for one's behavior, feelings, thoughts	Disowning responsibility for one's behavior, feelings, thoughts
Living in the here and now	Hanging on to the past or what is absent; overconcern with the future
Taking risks in order to grow	Avoiding risks and the possibility of discomfort
Being fully aware	Restricting or avoiding full awareness

emotions, body sensations, movements, posture, muscular tensions, and facial expression. Awareness also involves an appreciation of the environmental situation and its significance and potentialities in relation to the figure-organizing need. How can we expect to act appropriately if we do not know what is going on, what we want, what we feel, even what we are doing at this moment? We then cannot exercise free, informed choice—so we fall back on moralistic external prescriptions, automatic habit patterns, or various inhibiting or deadening devices.

Seen in this light, awareness becomes the key to healthy, effective personality functioning. Perls (1969a) put the case succinctly: "*Awareness per se—by and of itself—can be curative*. Because with full awareness you become aware of . . . organismic self-regulation, you can let the organism take over without interfering, without interrupting: we can rely on the wisdom of the organism [p. 16]." And elsewhere Perls explains, "If he can become *truly aware* at every instant of himself and his actions on whatever level—fantasy, verbal, or physical—he can see how he is producing his difficulties, he can help himself to solve them in the present, in the here and now [1973, p. 62]." Thus, since awareness is the key to healthy functioning, helping the patient achieve awareness must be the major focus of therapy.

Awareness in the Gestalt system is not the same as insight as that concept is used in psychoanalysis and other insight-oriented psychotherapies. Awareness refers to the ability to be totally in touch with oneself and with the environment and what one is doing in the present moment. Insight is a more cognitive construct, implying an appreciation of the relationship between memories of the past and patterns of feelings, wishes, and behavior in one's current life, including the therapy setting. The emphasis with awareness is on immediate full sensing, total relevant perception. The emphasis with insight is on understanding.

Therapy–Goals and Concepts

The most basic therapeutic task is to help the client (or patient, depending on your semantic preference) learn *how* he loses awareness, *how* he avoids, *how* he interferes with his own natural self-functioning. The emphasis is on process rather than content. By learning how he controls his awareness, the client gains control over his own processes of blocking out awareness. So, most basically, the Gestalt therapist seeks to help the patient learn how to be aware. He learns how to overcome his tendencies to ignore phobically his feelings and needs, and he learns to accept responsibility for being who he is and doing what he does. The successful client is better able to meet his needs and to experience life fully and richly.

A second important aim in Gestalt therapy is to help the individual mature by moving from environmental support to self-support. In the process of growing up, most of us learn how to get many of our needs met through indirect means, by manipulating others or acting phony—manipulating ourselves, in effect. We may try to get others to help us by pretending to be more helpless than we are. We may try to get approval from others with a continual smile or an incessant readiness to be helpful. We may try to get others to do our bidding by playing on their guilt or by threatening them with our scorn or disapproval. We all have learned such methods of getting what we want from others, and engage in such maneuvers automatically without clear awareness of what we are doing. Often we could quite well provide for our own needs rather than resorting to such manipulation. Also, we manipulate ourselves. We may try to live up to some ideal of what we believe we should be rather than accepting ourselves as we are. We may act interested when we are bored, calm when we are excited, brave when we are fearful, polite when we are angry, and stoical when we want sympathy. We may conceal our feminine sides by acting masculine or our masculine sides by acting feminine. We may act sick when we are well and strong when we are weak. As often as not, we fool ourselves with such self-manipulations more than we fool those who watch us. So, an important goal of Gestalt therapy is to help the client discover his own phoniness and manipulation and learn that he can choose to express himself directly and straightforwardly rather than pretending to be helpless, blackmailing, judging, withdrawing, gossiping, whining, flattering, selectively withholding, and so forth.

In essence, Gestalt therapy is an *experience* between *I and thou* in the *here and now*. The client is helped to *discover what and how* he *avoids* by means of *focusing of awareness, directed experimentation, amplification of behavior and feeling,* and *skillful frustration and support,* which allow *fully experienced awareness* of avoidances, projections, and the other processes by which the client interferes with his living fully and satisfyingly. Gradually developed *capacity for awareness* leads to *responsibility,* which in turn permits *choice*. Such a concise statement requires elaboration. In the following pages, each italicized word or phrase in the statement will be discussed separately.

EXPERIENCE.   There is an old saying, "Experience is the best teacher." No amount of talking about or reading about life in a black ghetto can ever replace the experience of actually living in one. We cannot learn how to climb mountains by reading or attending lectures, nor will we ever really be able to experience the agony and the exhilaration of climbing Mount Everest. Memories acquired by rote tend to fade fast; lessons acquired by experience may stay with us for the rest of our lives. All this may seem obvious, but traditional therapies have been built largely around the process of talking about problems, recalling events in the past or outside of the therapy, thinking, speculating, analyzing. Perls returned to the dictum of experience being the best teacher. Though many approaches to therapy recognize the value of learning by experiencing, Perls created a therapy that ensured this form of learning: activities not consistent with direct and immediate experiencing are excluded. The manner in which Perls achieved this will become clear later in this chapter.

I AND THOU.   Gestalt therapy belongs to the so-called humanistically oriented psychotherapies, which include the client-centered and existential approaches (see Chapters 17 and 18). The humanistic therapies stress the importance of the therapist being very much a real person in relation to his client, willing to encounter openly, spontaneously, and with genuine expression of his true feeling. The expression "I and thou, here and now" coined by the existentialist Martin Buber connotes an immediate, human, authentic responsiveness on the part of the therapist in relating to his client. Furthermore, the client is urged to communicate directly to someone. In groups, the client is never allowed to talk *about* someone present but is instructed to direct his comments directly to the person involved. In individual therapy, direct communication to the therapist is encouraged and the various means by which the client avoids or dilutes contact are brought to his attention.

The purpose of such a stance, which contrasts with the traditional psychoanalytic therapist-role (see Chapter 16), is to provide a full-fledged, human experience in relation to a real and genuine human being. The client can learn about human relationships directly by immediate experience within the therapy setting.

HERE AND NOW.   A basic tenet of Gestalt therapy is that one changes by means of discovery through experience. We can only experience in the present. Thus, the basic strategy in Gestalt therapy is to focus the client's attention on what he is actually doing at the moment. Enright (1970) puts it this way:

> We simply tell him, in effect, to sit down and start living, then note where and how he fails. The therapeutic value that we implicitly ask him to accept is that he will probably be more comfortable in his life in the long run if he is more fully aware of what he

is doing from moment to moment, and if he can accept responsibility for this behavior [p. 113].

No specific attempt is made to stay with a topic as presented by the client. The emphasis is on what the client is doing rather than on what he is saying.

At times, however, what the client is doing is trying to deal with and finish some feelings from the past (an unfinished gestalt) or to prepare for or cope with anxiety about some future situation. The past is represented in memory and the future in fantasy, neither are here and now. The Gestalt therapist brings past or future into the here and now in several ways. For example, the client may be asked to tell his memory in the present tense as if it is happening to him right now. Or the client may be asked to role play and interact with the significant figures involved as if they were immediately present. In comparison with the recitation of a memory or an anxiety, the situation comes to life for the individual and often very intense involvement and emotion is mobilized. In place of talking about or intellectually analyzing, an experience that can have significant impact is created.

DISCOVERY.   The Gestalt therapist neither advises nor interprets. He creates conditions whereby the client can discover for himself, then integrate, interpret, or act on the information as he chooses. Allowing the client to make his own discoveries under the guidance of the therapist is an extension of the idea that firsthand experience is the most effective form of learning. The therapist may offer his own observations of what he sees in order to draw the client's attention to it but he omits inference and speculation about the meaning or the causes of what he sees. The basic work of discovering and making use of the discovery is the patient's responsibility (Yontef, 1969).

WHAT AND HOW.   The fundamental questions guiding the client's journey of discovery are *what* and *how*, never *why*. The immediate goal of therapy is to help the patient to an awareness of what he is doing and how he is doing it. According to Perls, when clients start seeking an explanation for their behavior, as they inevitably do, they are avoiding full responsibility for their behavior. Many therapists of other backgrounds do ask why. Perls (1973) states that "the 'why' questions produce only pat answers, defensiveness, rationalizations, excuses, and the delusion that an event can be explained by a single cause [p. 76]." The kinds of questions that are likely to be productive are, What are you aware of now? What are you doing? What do you feel? What do you want? What are you avoiding? What do you expect? (Perls, 1973). Similar questions might be formulated using *how* instead of *what*.

AVOIDANCE.   The central premise of the Gestalt approach is that man creates adjustment problems for himself when he interrupts his natural flow of response to needs and situations and loses awareness of the sense of himself as agent: "It is I who am thinking, feeling, doing this." One cannot control or be responsible for what is out of awareness. In blocking awareness, we avoid responsibility both for our actions and for being as we are. We deny needs and feelings and build a fabricated image of ourselves. We avoid providing for ourselves what we have the capacity to provide. We avoid straightforward, uncomplicated, spontaneous relating to others. We get in our own way in trying to live our lives in a fulfilling way. So the basic task in therapy is to help the client discover how he keeps himself from being aware.

FOCUSING OF AWARENESS.   The Gestalt therapist operates primarily by having the client report what he is aware of and directing his attention to what he is not aware of. The client is asked to attend to as much of what he is doing and experiencing during the therapy as he can. He is asked to become aware not just of his thoughts and fantasies but his posture, his gestures, his inner bodily sensations, the sound of his voice, the words he uses, his emotions, his facial expressions, his breathing, and much more. The skill of the therapist lies in his role as participant–observer and guide, in his ability to discern what is significant in the client's behavior. He draws the client's attention to what he is doing, and helps him to explore his experience as fully as possible.

DIRECTED EXPERIMENTATION.   In a very real sense, Gestalt therapy is a series of experiments. The client is asked to try something out and see what happens. The experimental attitude is frequently made explicit. The aim is for the client to experience himself as he actually lives through an event or series of events under the direction of the therapist without preconceptions as to what will happen.

Consider an example. An adult client spoke of her difficulty in dealing with a real estate agent who was attempting to cheat her. She felt unable to confront him. She imagined he would admit nothing and act as if something was wrong with her in a smoothly condescending way and she would be absolutely helpless. He could be so smug and superior. Besides, she was always polite and considerate and thus could not fight back. I asked her to try out the role of the salesman talking to her and cowing her with his smugness and condescension. She did so, and was quite devastating in her assumed role. I then asked the client what she experienced. She had felt very powerful and to her surprise had really enjoyed putting someone down. She discovered several things from her experiment: that she was more powerful than she had ever supposed, that she was blocking her own power, and that behind her politeness and consideration lay a wish to be inconsiderate, to overwhelm others, and to demonstrate her own superiority. She no longer felt so incapable of dealing with the salesman.

Perls' book *Gestalt Therapy* (Perls *et al.,* 1951) actually consists of a series of 18 experiments that can be carried out at home and are examples of some of the types of experiments that Gestalt therapists might ask their clients to try out in an actual therapy session.

AMPLIFICATION OF BEHAVIOR AND FEELING.   In order to help the client become more fully in touch with himself, the Gestalt therapist may ask him to exaggerate what he is doing or to stay with a feeling and intensify it. The therapist may notice a small shrug and, bringing the client's attention to his movement, ask him to exaggerate it. As he engages in the full-fledged movement, the client is asked what he experiences, how he feels. Perhaps he will discover a characteristic avoidant maneuver such as disclaiming involvement and responsibility with an attitude of, "What does it matter anyway?" Or, he might get more fully in touch with a suppressed sense of helpless despair. Whatever the outcome, the client is better able to have full awareness when he allows himself to convert an implicit act or feeling into a fully developed act or feeling.

SKILLFUL FRUSTRATION AND SUPPORT. When he enters into the therapy situation, the client brings along his customary manipulations and stereotyped patterns of trying to get others to provide what he feels he needs and imagines he cannot provide for himself. The client soon attempts to get the therapist to provide support. Frustration by the therapist is required if the client is to discover first, how he manipulates the environment, and second, that he already has the resources to provide for himself. Skill is required in maintaining a proper balance of frustration and support to provide continual pressure to move toward self-support without overwhelming the client or driving him prematurely out of therapy.

AWARENESS. There is little to add to what has already been said about awareness. I wish only to emphasize that the ultimate goal of therapy is not awareness per se, but rather the means to become aware. When the client has learned how to be aware and to make his own discoveries, then he no longer needs a therapist.

RESPONSIBILITY AND CHOICE. With awareness comes a re-owning of who we are and what we do and, typically, an acceptance of ourselves as we are. Discovering that our makeup includes wishes to annihilate and destroy as well as wishes to love and nurture does not mean that we will commit murder the next time the wish to have someone out of the way becomes strong. Rather, it means that we can accept ourselves as someone capable of such feelings and be responsible for and in control of our behavior toward the person involved. We can choose how we wish to express our feelings and the choice is likely to be far more adaptive and effective than when we conceal our wishes and feelings from ourselves. Awareness does not do away with a conflict or unpleasant experience. However, it is assumed that we are better able to reach creative compromises between our own needs and environmental possibilities and pressures when we are fully aware of them and of our own abilities to deal with them.

Therapy–Framework and Technique

Gestalt therapy operates within a specified framework that distinguishes it from other forms of therapy. One might conceive of this framework as a statement of fundamental policies or guidelines. Perls was remarkably inventive in developing techniques for promoting the therapeutic process within his basic framework. Levitsky and Perls (1970) speak of the "rules and the games" of Gestalt therapy that partially correspond with the distinction between framework and technique.

The fundamental framework of Gestalt therapy was spelled out in the previous section and consists of the following:

1. Staying with here-and-now events
2. Promoting direct experiencing as opposed to other activities (talking about, analyzing, speculating, etc.)
3. The experimental model, which emphasizes self-discovery by the client
4. Focus on the client's awareness
5. Skillful frustration
6. Emphasis on responsibility and choice

Not all these "policies" are exclusive to the Gestalt approach, but they do define the limits within which all Gestalt therapists work when they are doing Gestalt therapy.

Given this framework as a guide to technique, the possible number of techniques is limited only by the creativity of the individual therapist. In fact, the more experienced and more skillful Gestalt therapists tend to create their own experiments or situations for the client to experience on an individual basis rather than falling back on past collections of techniques. A few sample techniques follow, to illustrate the great variety of possibilities.

THE AWARENESS CONTINUUM. The basic instruction is to report whatever becomes figure in one's awareness from moment to moment. One can begin by continually repeating the sentence, "Now I am aware of . . ." and completing it. Those who do this experiment and try to stay with it soon discover that they tend to lapse from being aware of what they can immediately sense into thinking, remembering, or some other activity, without being aware of the transition. This exercise allows us to experience how much more we can be aware of than we customarily attend to. It also allows us to experience some of the ways we avoid staying with here-and-now awareness. Developing the ability to attend here and now to what is happening, what one is doing, feeling, and sensing is part of the work of Gestalt therapy and is critically involved in later experiments. Attention to the simple awareness continuum is a first step.

THE EMPTY CHAIR. The empty chair is one of the most widely used techniques. The empty chair has almost the same degree of association with Gestalt therapy as the couch does with psychoanalysis. The empty-chair technique involves the client's switching back and forth between two chairs or positions that represent himself and another person or two contrasting aspects of himself and carrying on both sides of a dialog between the two positions. The therapist directs the encounter as necessary, sometimes indicating when to change seats, suggesting sentences to use, encouraging the client to express himself with affect and vocal expression appropriate to what is being said, calling attention to gestures or other nonverbal behavior, or having the client repeat with greater emphasis a particularly important communication.

For example, a young woman began therapy because of feelings of anxiety, dizziness, and weakness, which seemed to arise without cause. She was also characteristically unusually pleasant, nonassertive, and easily hurt by criticism. One day she reported that she had felt anxious while visiting her mother and could not understand it because her mother was very supportive, loving, and kind and she loved her mother very much. I suggested to the client that she put her mother in the empty chair and try completing the sentence, "What I resent about you, Mom, is . . ." The client began and soon, caught up in the task, began to pour out her anger at her mother's smothering overprotectiveness and her many subtly expressed suggestions that the client was no good and not to be trusted out of her sight. She expressed the wish that her mother would disappear, would literally die. The client was startled by the vehemence of these suddenly released feelings, which were in such contrast to her typical loving, concerned, dependent attitude toward her mother. Further work using the empty chair was done with these two aspects of herself—the angry, resentful, rebellious, destructive aspect and the loving, appreciative, obedient, gentle aspect. The resolution lay in the client's accepting both sides as being part of her, seeing something positive in both and something negative in both, and working toward a more effective merger.

SEMANTIC CLARIFICATIONS. Perls was much impressed with the work of early semanticists and became very aware of the relationship between the way we use language and our experience. He emphasized the importance of personalizing pronouns as a way of reinforcing the sense of personal responsibility for one's feelings and actions:

Client: One can never please one's parents.

Therapist: Try saying, "I can never please my parents." [*Client repeats*] What is the difference?

Client: Yes, it's me who can't please my parents.

Perls also paid serious attention to the distinction between *can't* and *won't*:

Client: I just can't study.

Therapist: Try saying these two sentences: "I can't study" and "I won't study." [*Client repeats them*] Again. [*Client repeats again*] What is your experience with those two sentences? Which feels more genuine?

Client: "I won't study" is correct.

USING BODY LANGUAGE.   The Gestalt orientation, with its holistic emphasis, regards mind and body as part of a total system. What the mind hides, the body is likely to reveal. Gestalt therapists take bodily movements and reports of internal sensations or symptoms as important clues to what the individual may be avoiding.

Client: I wish I had more intimate relationships. I would like to feel really intimate with someone. [*Client moves hands away from body, palms out*]

Therapist: Did you notice what you just did with your hands?

Client: I don't know. I guess I moved them like this.

Therapist: Try repeating that but exaggerate the motion. [*Client complies*] Again. Do it more. [*Client complies*] What does that feel like?

Client: Well, it's like pushing—pushing something away. I guess what I really do is push people away so they can't get too close.

Research and Evaluation

Gestalt therapy as a system with more than a handful of adherents actually became established only in the mid-1960s. Perls and his followers have been more concerned with developing the clinical features of their approach than with formal evaluation of therapeutic efficacy or research on the theoretical assumptions. There has been very little research involving Gestalt therapy or its principles.

I have alluded to the series of 18 graded experiments developed by Perls *et al.* (1951) that can be done without a therapist. These experiments—actually homework exercises—were given to undergraduate students in psychology at three universities to assess the potential of the exercises for aiding personal growth. Although Perls gave no specific quantitative data, he indicated that the results supported the value of the experiments. Written reports were obtained at intervals over the 4-month school term, and excerpts from many of these reports are quoted throughout the book. Some indicate rather dramatic, positive experiences in carrying out the exercises. A follow-up of a number of cases indicated continuing development "at an accelerated rate even when the material is no longer a part of their 'homework.'"

Perls rests his case with the following statement:

"Where is your proof?" Our standard answer is that we present nothing that you cannot *verify for yourself in terms of your own behavior,* but, if your psychological make-up is that of the experimentalist . . . , this will not satisfy you and you will clamor for "objective evidence" of a verbal sort, *prior to* trying out a single nonverbal step in the procedure [Perls *et al.,* 1951, p. 7].

Thus Perls asks each reader to validate the value of his procedures for himself in terms of his own experience.

Gannon (1972) completed a more systematic evaluation of the effectiveness of a Gestalt-oriented group approach. His subjects were high school students who had exhibited negative school behaviors such as absences, tardiness, discipline problems, and appearances on police reports. He divided his subjects into three groups:

1. A *Gestalt group* in which Gestalt therapy was conducted 9 hours a week for one semester in both a large total group and smaller subgroups.
2. An *alternate treatment group,* consisting of a special team-teaching program, large and small group discussions, and field trips away from the school. This group controlled for the personalized attention, opportunity for interpersonal discussion, and excitement of a special program as offered by the Gestalt group but without the Gestalt orientation.
3. A *control group,* attending classes as usual.

As predicted, the Gestalt group showed greater openness and improved interpersonal contact as a result of their experience, in comparison with the other two groups.

Lieberman, Yalom, and Miles (1973) conducted a carefully designed, intensive study of 17 growth-oriented groups, representing nine different theoretical approaches. One of the groups was leaderless, conducted with the aid of taped instructions. Two Gestalt groups were involved in the study. A variety of outcome measures was used, expert observers watched each group, and an assessment was made of negative outcomes, or casualties, among individual clients. One of the two Gestalt groups seems to have been very successful. Its group-member ratings placed it first among all groups in being a pleasant experience and in "turning them on." The group tied for first as being considered a constructive experience and was second in terms of the members feeling they had learned a great deal. An overall summary of objective measures of benefit at time of final follow-up showed this group to be second best of the 17 groups.

However, the second Gestalt group fared poorly; it had the highest rate of casualties of any of the groups and the lowest benefit to its members. The difference seemed to be in the contrasting personality characteristics of the two leaders and the type of group atmosphere that resulted. Observers described the leader of the first group as highly supportive though still challenging and confrontive. He offered friendship as well as protection to group members. He openly revealed his here-and-now feelings and his values, and in many ways participated as a member of the group. Observers rated him as expressing considerable warmth, acceptance, genuineness, and caring for other human beings. By contrast, the leader of the second group was seen as highly unpredictable, frequently taunting or ridiculing, and sometimes markedly obtrusive. On one occasion he jumped up to one of the male members, saying "You turn me on," lunged on top of him, hugged him on the ground for a few minutes, and kissed him on the cheek. He gave support fairly frequently as well as offers of his love or friendship, but the overall atmosphere of the group seemed to remain tense and threatening. The observers did not admire this leader as a person and regarded him as ineffective and not understanding of the group.

On the basis of these results, it can be said that the Gestalt approach is a powerful one. In the hands of a good and sensitive therapist, it can offer significant possibilities for beneficial change. In the wrong hands, it can be a destructive influence. Like atomic energy, it has impact that can be used for good or ill. In general, it is being recognized increasingly that the personality, sensitivity, and skill of the therapist may actually be a more important factor in the outcome of therapy than the particular approach being used.

Summary

Gestalt therapy is a humanistically oriented psychotherapy developed by Fritz Perls. It has grown rapidly in popularity and now holds a prominent position among the various approaches for treating psychological disorders and enhancing human functioning.

Perls drew from several sources in developing his new approach. From his psychoanalytic training, especially that with Wilhelm Reich, Perls obtained his basic clinical understanding, his appreciation of nonverbal communication, and his focus upon clients' patterns of avoidance. Gestalt psychology, especially as it was extended into a holistic–organismic theory by Kurt Goldstein, provided a conceptual framework for Perls' ideas. An existential flavor pervades Perls' work and is perceptible especially in his emphasis on personal responsibility and an I–thou, here-and-now relationship between client and therapist. His extensive reading in general semantics, stimulated by Kurt Goldstein's interest in language, sensitized Perls to the importance of language in psychotherapy.

The central thesis of Gestalt therapy is that psychological difficulties arise when the individual loses touch or avoids full awareness of himself, his relevant environment, and what he is doing at the present moment. The goal of therapy is to restore awareness, or, more precisely, to restore the *capacity* to be aware. The basic therapeutic task is to help the client learn *how* he loses awareness, *how* he avoids, *how* he interferes with his own natural self-functioning, so that he may gain control over these processes and exercise informed choice in conducting his life. A second aim of Gestalt therapy is to help the client learn to use and depend on his own resources. The client is confronted with the ways he manipulates others or himself in an effort to satisfy his needs by indirect means rather than trusting his ability to obtain satisfaction by direct, undisguised means.

The fundamental framework of Gestalt therapy consists of

1. Staying with here-and-now events
2. Promoting direct experiencing
3. An experimental model that promotes self-discovery by the client
4. Focus on the client's awareness

5. Skillful frustration
6. Emphasis on responsibility and choice

Within this framework, specific technique flows from the creativity of the individual therapist in creating situations or experiments that will promote experiential learning suited to the client's needs at that moment in therapy.

20

Community Mental Health

PATRICK E. COOK

Psychiatry Associates

Community mental health includes a broad area of mental health theory and practice. In this chapter, we will explore the more important modes of community mental health intervention. These interventions represent both extensions of and radical departures from traditional psychotherapeutic treatment techniques and orientations. Because of the newness of community mental health, there are divergent and sometimes contradictory views about the important elements of community mental health within the field.

This is especially true of views on the role of psychotherapeutic treatment as opposed to alternative human service strategies. Many workers in the field view the usual forms of psychotherapy—psychoanalytic treatment, behavior modification, client-centered counseling, group therapy—as virtually worthless or even actively harmful. Others view psychotherapy as a desirable service that should be made readily available to all individuals in the community who need it, including the poor and minority group members. These workers generally emphasize the desirable effects of community-based treatment as compared to institutional treatment. However, most workers in community mental health stress the need for new kinds of treatment, such as crisis intervention, and more efficient, community-oriented strategies of intervention, such as providing consultation to community care-givers and instituting early detection and preventive programs. Some go further, suggesting interventions aimed toward organizational and social reform and ecological change.

To gain some perspective on these contradictory approaches, we will review briefly some historical highlights in the development of the community mental health movement. We will explore the strategies of intervention that have come to be identified with community mental health. And finally, we will consider some criticisms of the field.

First, let us look at several definitions of community mental health.

What Is Community Mental Health?

Community mental health can be defined from a theoretical perspective, an applied perspective, or both. The theoretical perspective identifies the key ideas that guide community mental health activities. The practical perspective defines the field in terms of the activities that actually take place in community mental health programs. We will look at each of these perspectives in turn.

COMMUNITY MENTAL HEALTH AS IDEOLOGY

Several writers have pointed out that community mental health is an *ideology*. Golann and Eisdorfer (1972) discuss community mental health as the "most recent of several phases of mental health ideology" and trace its origin to dissatisfaction with earlier orientations and to recent political changes. As an ideology, community mental health is based on the assertion that there must be ways to improve the level of social and emotional functioning of the residents of the community, thereby reducing the number or severity of social and emotional problems loosely referred to as *mental illness*—in other words, to foster mental health. The traditional ways of helping people have been unsuccessful, or, at best, inefficient. Consequently, new ways of better meeting human needs must be developed. It will make the most sense if these new ways are (1) applicable to groups of people, such as populations that are "at risk"; (2) available in or near the target group's natural habitat, i.e., in the community; (3) designed to use community resources efficiently, and in a way that will ensure that there is a residual effect—an increase in the community's ability to solve similar problems in the future; and (4) undertaken with a strong commitment to preventing problems before they occur, rather than treating problems after they occur (Cook, 1970). Deibert (1971) has characterized the effects of community mental health programs in terms of *accessibility* (mental health *in* the community), involvement (mental health *for* the community), and, ultimately, *self-implementation* (mental health *by* the community).

COMMUNITY MENTAL HEALTH AS ACTIVITY

Others have defined community mental health in terms of the activities that are carried out in community mental health programs. Definitions range from those including all activities that are carried out in the community in the name of mental health (Bloom, 1973; Newbrough, 1964/1969) to detailed descriptions of the innovative programs and techniques that are unique to the movement. From

When North Dakota ran short of psychiatrists recently, the state's mental health association sought help from the informal care-givers that people often tell their troubles to—hairdressers and bartenders. The hairdressers in this state-sponsored class are learning how to give sympathetic advice along with permanents. They will also learn how to guide their more troubled customers to professional help. (Ben Ross)

this perspective a crisis intervention "hotline," or telephone counseling service, would be considered a community mental health activity. Psychoanalysis and behavior modification would not, except insofar as a community mental health program might make them more readily available to the residents of the community.

The domain of community mental health includes such activities as screening programs for the early detection of emotional maladjustment; programs designed to prevent problems and foster emotional development and competence; coordination of community services; development of new helping techniques; consultation with traditional community care-givers, such as teachers, clergy, and police, and with informal care-givers, such as bartenders and community leaders; training of new types of manpower for delivering mental health services, such as volunteers and paraprofessionals; social systems change activities, such as consultation, advocacy on behalf of system clients, and political activism; program evaluation research to assess the cost and effectiveness of mental health programs; research on factors basic to the well-being of the inhabitants of the community; and many other activities (Cook, 1970).

THE COMMUNITY MENTAL HEALTH CENTERS PROGRAM

In 1963, Congress established an ambitious program to provide community-based mental health services for the entire nation. In order to qualify for federal funding under this legislation, the Community Mental Health Centers Act, centers are required to provide five services: (1) inpatient care, (2) outpatient care, (3) partial hospitalization, (4) emergency care on a round-the-clock basis, and (5) community consultation and education. Five additional services are suggested to make a center's program comprehensive: (6) diagnostic service, (7) rehabilitative service, (8) pre-care and after-care, (9) training, and (10) research and evaluation. Critics have pointed out the traditional "clinical" emphasis of most of these requirements: They are directed toward diagnosing and treating individuals rather than trying to prevent problems on a community-wide scale. How well the Community Mental Health Centers Program has met community needs will be discussed in the last section of this chapter.

In response to the program outlined by the Community Mental Health Centers Act, the American Psychological Association published a position paper, which included the following guidelines or principles:

1. For the comprehensive community mental health center to be an effective agency of the community, community control of center policy is essential.
2. The community mental health center is "comprehensive" in the sense that it offers, probably not under one roof, a wide range of services, including both direct care to troubled people and consultative, educational, and preventive services to the community.
3. Effective community action for mental health requires continuity of concern for the troubled individual in his involvements with society regardless of awkward jurisdictional boundaries of agencies, institutions, and professions.
4. Programs must be designed to reach the people who are hardly touched by our best current efforts, for it is actually those who present the major problems of mental health in America.
5. Since current patterns of mental health service are intrinsically and logistically inadequate to the task, responsible programming for the comprehensive community mental health center must emphasize and reward innovation [Smith & Hobbs, 1966, pp. 499–509].

In other words, the center should involve the community in its administration, provide a wide range of helping and preventive services, be concerned with the whole client, reach out to poor people and minority group members who do not generally make use of mental health resources, and encourage new approaches.

The Historical Perspective

The concepts and innovative services that characterize community mental health had their origins in earlier social thought and social reform and technical developments in psychiatry, psychology, public health, and allied fields. In a general way, the antecedents of contemporary community mental health can be found in the history of conceptions of mental illness dating to the ancient Greeks. More specifically, they can be traced to the beginning of reforms in the treatment of the mentally ill. This is what Hobbs (1964) has referred to as mental health's *first* revolution, which was "based on the heretical notion that the insane are people and should be treated with kindness and dignity [p. 822]." Some of the treatment techniques associated with the period of the "rise and fall of moral treatment," such as home treatment and preventive education, were developed during the nineteenth century only to be discarded and then rediscovered in the middle of the twentieth century. A number of community mental health concepts, including prevention, also were proposed during the mental hygiene movement that emerged in the United States during the period 1900–1930. According to Hobbs (1964), many of these developments were given lower priority during the period of emphasis on individual psychopathology and treatment that developed from mental health's *second* revolution—the "Freudian revolution."

Mental health's *third* revolution began when concepts of public health, such as prevention and population-at-risk, were brought to bear on mental health problems (Hobbs, 1964). This third revolution has been marked by increased federal attention to mental illness and mental health. Beginning with the National Mental Health Act of 1946 and the establishment of the National Institute of Mental Health, which has supported extensive mental health training and research activities, the federal role in mental health has increased steadily. The Mental Health Study Act of 1955 resulted in the 1961 report of the Joint Commission on Mental Illness and Health, which recommended a number of changes in the treatment of the mentally ill. Of particular importance was the suggestion of community-based treatment as an alternative to the dehumanizing, alienation-producing institutional treatment in large, geographically isolated state hospitals. This was followed by President John F. Kennedy's message to Congress in 1963, calling for a "bold new approach" and proposing the establishment of comprehensive community mental health centers (Bloom, 1973). President Kennedy's message resulted in the Community Mental Health Centers Act of 1963.

A number of other factors contributed to the growing interest in community mental health that emerged in the 1950s and 1960s. One important factor was the epidemiologic studies done during this period. These studies highlighted the extent of the problem of emotional disorder and suggested relationships between the incidence and prevalence of various kinds of emotional disorders (and other kinds of social problems) and various demographic and socioeconomic factors. Studies like *The Midtown Manhattan Study* (Srole, Langner, Michael, Opler, & Rennie, 1962) and the New Haven Study (Hollingshead & Redlich, 1958) demonstrated that the mental health status of individuals within the community was related to other kinds of variables, such as socioeconomic status or family composition. These findings suggested that there might be some underlying causative factors that would be amenable to modification, particularly community change.

A broader approach was especially appealing; the mental health professions realized that there would never be enough manpower to meet the need if only traditional forms of manpower and clinical interventions were used.

By this time the work of Caplan (1961) and others had demonstrated that preventive psychiatry was a feasible alternative to individually oriented clinical approaches. The notion of preventing rather than treating problems had a great appeal to those who were overwhelmed by the magnitude of the problem of emotional disturbances, as suggested by the epidemiologic research.

Interest in community mental health was intensified by political and social developments in the 1960s. New attention was given to the problems of the poor and minority ethnic groups, and to problems of undereducation, underemployment, and discrimination. Mental health professionals and social scientists were involved in the Peace Corps, Project Headstart, the Job Corps, the Community Action Program, VISTA, and many other new programs. New concepts, theories, and techniques were required. Emergent consumerism and requirements for citizen participation made a tremendous impact on the kinds of services provided. In 1968, Harris Peck wrote,

> The community mental health center movement, in its orientation toward enlisting full community participation in its operations, makes its appearance on the national scene alongside of the new anti-poverty programs, in which this orientation has essentially become the central principle. Community action programs in particular are insistent that the "target population" play a central role in the planning and development of anti-poverty programs. . . . this similarity in emphasis to be discerned within these two movements is hardly a coincidence, since both are developing in a national atmosphere so significantly colored by the civil rights movement. Whatever else these developments represent they reflect the increasing demand from those who most need a variety of human services that they be consulted and enlisted in the planning, development and operation of programs that are vital to their interests. This demand carries with it a great potential for important mental health effect [pp. 195–196].

These new social action programs gave rise to the hope that massive social change of the scope that could bring about *prevention* of social problems was now feasible.

Prevention in Community Mental Health

The concept of prevention is probably the single most important element of the community mental health ideology. The application of public health prevention principles to mental health problems had been suggested by several forward-looking writers (Bower, 1963; Caplan, 1961, 1964). Gerald Caplan's work in preventive psychiatry has had an immeasurable impact on the community mental health field. The discussion of prevention in this section will draw heavily from his work.

The public health concept of prevention refers to interventions designed to reduce rates of disorder in a given population—in a community, or in a particular *catchment area*. A catchment area is a specified, geographically bounded area, all the inhabitants of which are entitled to receive services from or benefit from a particular program or agency. For example, a mental health center may have a seven-county catchment area and thus be responsible for developing programs to meet the needs of all the people who live in those counties.

There are three types of prevention. Only one type, primary prevention, is what the general public would think of as prevention. The distinctions between the three types are important:

1. *Primary prevention* is directed at reducing the *incidence*—the rate of occurrence of new cases of social and emotional problems—in a population.
2. *Secondary prevention* is directed at reducing the *prevalence*—the number of cases of social and emotional problems that exist at any one time in a population—by shortening the duration of disorders.
3. *Tertiary prevention* has as a goal the reduction of the rate of residual defects in a population.

PRIMARY PREVENTION

An emphasis on primary prevention is one feature that distinguishes community mental health from other mental health approaches. Primary prevention can be accomplished by modifying the environment or by strengthening individual resistance to stress and individual capacities to cope with situations (Caplan & Grunebaum, 1967). In the public health field, for example, an environmental modification would be mosquito control to prevent mosquito-borne disease, while a public immunization program would strengthen the resistance of individuals in the population. In the mental health field, environmental manipulations could ensure that all individuals within the population have adequate food and housing, which are important for cognitive growth and development. A program designed to prepare all the children for the stresses of school entry would increase the ability of individuals within the population to cope with a stressful situation. In this example, attention is focused on a *population at risk*. A population at risk is an identifiable subpopulation whose members will probably face a situation that is frequently disruptive, or whose members, as a group, show higher susceptibility to disorder.

In one primary prevention program, psychologists and social workers from a mental health center developed a parent-education program for the mothers of children enrolled in Project Headstart classes. In a series of 10 weekly meetings, the mental health workers gave a course on child development, stimulated group discussion, and answered the mothers' questions. The goal was to benefit all the children in the target families by increasing the mothers' understanding of child development, their knowledge of community resources, and their feelings of self-worth. These families were considered high-risk families.

Directing preventive efforts toward children has been encouraged by many writers. Among the goals for prevention outlined by Bower (1963) are efforts to increase "the biological robustness of human beings by strengthening those institutions and agencies involved in prenatal, pregnancy and early infant care [p. 840]." Another of Bower's goals is to help primary institutions, such as schools, to promote immunity to stress and greater coping ability in the children served and their families.

Hunt (1968) points out that many forms of human incompetence (which would include, but not be limited to, mental illness) might be prevented and many forms of competence might be fostered. He states,

> If the behavioral sciences have discovered anything that approaches in significance for human welfare, the antibiotics and the contraceptive pills of biochemical science and the atomic energy of the physical sciences, it may well be this new evidence of great plasticity in infantile and early childhood development. In the light of this new evidence, it no longer is sensible to consider the incompetence of lower-class adults and children, be they black or white, as an inevitable consequence of their biological inheritance and nature. This new evidence is the basis for a justified hope that both this incompetence and the fearful impersonality of our megalopoli can be changed. . . . perhaps we have a start and some guidelines for the immediate implementation of innovations in early childhood education that correspond to the traditions of public health [pp. 40–41].

SECONDARY AND TERTIARY PREVENTION

Secondary prevention is accomplished by early detection of problems as well as by diagnostic, treatment, and remedial interventions. Most of the activities of community mental health programs fall within this category, including most crisis-intervention efforts. An example of secondary prevention is an arrangement whereby 24-hour emergency temporary hospitalization is available to any resident of the catchment·area who becomes acutely disturbed. The problem is dealt with quickly and long-term hospitalization may be avoided as a result.

Tertiary prevention "seeks to ensure that people who have recovered from mental disorder will be hampered as little as possible by their past difficulties in returning to full participation in the occupational and social life of the community [Caplan & Grunebaum, 1967, p. 332]." Programs providing vocational rehabilitation or a social club for ex-patients exemplify tertiary prevention. The population or community emphasis of these preventive programs distinguishes them from individual-oriented treatment and rehabilitation programs.

Some programs fall within more than one category of prevention. The program of early detection, intervention, and prevention with young schoolchildren, operated by Cowen and his colleagues at Rochester (Zax & Cowen, 1969) is probably the best example to date of a program that screens for problems and also develops both preventive and remedial interventions. It has both primary and secondary prevention aspects.

CONCEPTUAL MODELS FOR PREVENTION

A number of conceptual models have been proposed for community mental health interventions in general and preventive programs in particular. Caplan

In the slums of New York's South Bronx, many children have no warm and lasting family relationships. To counteract the damage that such deprivation can cause, Dr. Edward Eismann of the Lincoln Community Mental Health Center created a street family called Unitas. Each day, the Unitas family meets in their street to discuss the problems of life together. Teenage volunteers from the neighborhood are trained to give loving care to children who are troubled. Everything is designed to create what Dr. Eismann calls "a natural system within which the community can heal itself." (Charles Biasiny)

(1974) has proposed four etiological models, which provide distinct vantage points for understanding the causes of disorder in the community and developing preventive programs. Obviously, they are not mutually exclusive.

1. The *nutritional* model. Certain supplies and opportunities are necessary if members of a population are to achieve optimum development. Caplan categorizes supplies as physical, such as a balanced diet and the absence of toxic substances; psychosocial, such as opportunities for satisfying social relationships and intellectual stimulation; and sociocultural, such as educational and vocational opportunities. Primary prevention is directed at improving the provision of such long-term resources as these (Caplan & Grunebaum, 1967).

2. The *developmental adjustment or crisis* model "offers a guide to primary prevention by enhancing healthy personality development, to secondary prevention by showing how to use therapeutic workers most efficiently, and to tertiary prevention by identifying the crucial intervention points in preventing and counteracting alienation [Caplan, 1974, pp. 247–248]."

3. The *community organization and development* model. This view holds that the mental health of a community is dynamically imbedded in the overall fabric of the community. Factors such as geography, power, and communication networks influence and are influenced by the mental health of community members. Klein's book *Community Dynamics and Mental Health* (1968) presents an excellent discussion of the relationship of community variables to mental health. Preventive programs cannot hope to change the mental health status of the community without taking these factors into account.

4. The *socialization* or *effective role performance* model. This is essentially a sociological model. It looks at the complementary role functioning of community members, the ways people are recruited and trained for societal roles, and the forces that operate to maintain certain roles. Emotional and social problems are viewed as deviations from prescribed role functions. The preventive implications involve producing more efficient or appropriate role socialization (primary prevention) and resocialization and reeducation (secondary and tertiary prevention).

The belief that social and emotional disorders can be prevented may be overly optimistic. Sometimes simple preventive techniques have proven effective; chlorination of public drinking water is one public health example. In other instances, the development of preventive techniques has proven much more complicated and tedious, as was the case with vaccines for poliomyelitis. If prevention can be demonstrated to be effective in the mental health field, we can then mount the necessary social action programs. Given the magnitude of the problem, and the ineffectiveness of traditional approaches, the effort necessary to develop preventive programs is easily justified.

Crisis Theory and Intervention

Caplan has proposed another conceptual model for prevention in community mental health—one that focuses on short-term or *crisis* factors. Current thinking about crisis factors dates from Lindemann's classic study of bereavement in the families of victims of a Boston nightclub fire (Lindemann, 1944). Lindemann's study describes the survivors' grief reactions and outlines the basic concept of crisis theory and crisis intervention. It is considered to be one of the most important articles in the history of the community mental health field (Bloom, 1973).

DEFINITION OF CRISIS

Crises are time-limited periods of emotional disequilibrium precipitated by a life situation that the individual is temporarily unable to handle. According to Caplan and Grunebaum:

> Crisis may be due to either internal or external changes necessitating adaptation. The internal changes may be developmental or due to illness or trauma, while the external changes involve (a) the loss of a significant person or source of need satisfaction, (b) the threat of a loss, or (c) a challenge which threatens to overtax adaptive capacities. This list strikingly resembles the causes of neurosis delineated by Freud, who in 1912 mentioned (1) frustration due to loss of an object, (2) inability to adapt to a challenge such as marriage, (3) inhibition in development, and (4) biologic maturation [1967, p. 337].

A crisis reaction is time-limited, and most people resolve the crisis situation within a short period of time, usually 4 to 6 weeks. An individual in crisis may postpone his reaction, make a maladaptive adjustment, develop symptoms of emotional disorder, or make an adaptive response (Caplan, 1974). Thus he may emerge from a crisis reaction worse off than before, or better off because he has mastered a life challenge and, in doing so, has learned new coping skills. It is possible to identify situations that are crises for large segments of the community or subpopulations. Crises typically result from death of a loved one, divorce, illness, retirement, birth of a sibling, and school entry. Obviously, what may be a crisis for one individual may not be a crisis for another. Some characteristics of crises that make them of particular interest to community mental health practitioners and justify crisis intervention programs are these:

1. The effects of an emotionally disruptive situation can be reduced.
2. The end results of many untreated crises, e.g., hospitalization and institutionalization, can often be avoided.
3. The growth aspects of most crises can be promoted, and the debilitating aspects minimized.
4. Crisis intervention can frequently save time and effort on the part of mental health professionals.
5. A period of emotional crisis is the only time a large segment of a population will seek mental health assistance and be amenable to it [McGee, 1968, p. 321].

CRISIS INTERVENTION

Based on his own research, the research of his colleagues at Harvard, and the work of others, Caplan (Caplan, 1974; Caplan & Grunebaum, 1967) has suggested a number of preventive approaches based on crisis theory:

1. It is possible to reduce crises in the community by reducing community stresses.
2. It is possible to provide to those in crisis services that will encourage adaptive methods of coping with the crisis. These services include
   a. Ensuring that professional help is available during crisis. Community

mental health examples of this are suicide prevention and 24-hour telephone counseling programs (Cook, Kalafat, & Tyler, 1975; Helig, Farberow, Litman, & Shneidman, 1968) which have proliferated around the country. There may be 500 or more crisis phone services in the United States (Slem & Cotter, 1973). The 24-hour walk-in clinics are another example of the principle of providing help to individuals when they need it most.

b. Educating community care-givers who are most likely to confront individuals in crisis. This includes both formal care-givers such as doctors and police and informal care-givers such as bartenders. Training police to deal with family crises is an example of this type of program (Bard, 1971).

c. Mental health consultation, which will be discussed in the next section, can be provided to assist care-givers in understanding the problems of their clients so that crises can be prevented or appropriate crisis help can be given.

d. Individuals can be prepared to cope with crises through education and anticipatory guidance. There have been numerous efforts to "humanize" the public school curriculum. Does the typical curriculum prepare our children to deal with such life crises as the death of a loved one or divorce in the family? *Anticipatory guidance* is a technique in which individuals are prepared emotionally for crises by anticipating the upsets that can occur in a crisis. Peace Corps efforts to prepare volunteers for "culture shock" in their foreign assignments is a good example of anticipatory guidance.

How do these preventive approaches work in practice? As the following examples show, they can work well if the channels of communication are kept open.

A 20-year-old student discovers she is pregnant. She broods about her situation and becomes increasingly depressed and despondent. At 2 A.M., when most help resources are unavailable, she decides to commit suicide. At the last moment she decides to reach out for help. Fortunately, she lives in a community where there is a 24-hour telephone counseling service. She dials the number and reaches a student volunteer telephone counselor who has received extensive training in crisis counseling—more training, in fact, than many professionals receive. This counselor is prepared to give information, make referrals, listen and counsel, and, if necessary, dispatch emergency help such as the police or an ambulance. In this case, the counselor listens to the caller, helps her explore her alternatives, and gives her support in deciding on an adaptive solution. She decides to go to a local clergyman who is experienced in counseling women with "problem" pregnancies. The telephone service is available to anyone in the community, with any problem, who dials the number. Thus, competent help is always available.

In addition to suggesting preventive community programming, crisis theory demands that human service agencies look closer to home to see whether they are responding adequately to individuals in crisis. If an agency is geographically inaccessible to clients, if there is a waiting list, if it operates on a 9 to 5 basis, if there are complicated intake procedures and no walk-ins, and if the *"gatekeeper"* (e.g., receptionist) is untrained—then the agency is probably set up to meet the needs of the professionals, not the community members in crisis.

In one mental health center, a secretary was engaged in an animated phone conversation. She was repeatedly telling the caller, "Dr. B is not in. He only sees people by appointment. Do you wish to talk to someone else?" A staff member, overhearing this, finally took the phone from the secretary and talked with the caller. He quickly learned that the woman calling felt she needed to talk to Dr. B., a psychologist she had met at a discussion meeting at a public housing project. When the staff member finally succeeded in gaining the caller's trust, he discovered that she had just attempted to kill her 4-year-old son and wanted someone to keep her from trying it again. A crisis team was dispatched to help her—and the center immediately launched a training program for secretaries who answer incoming calls. Such "gatekeepers" are too important to be unsophisticated in crisis-intervention techniques.

Mental Health Consultation

With the possible exception of crisis intervention, mental health consultation probably has received more attention than any other type of community mental health intervention. One reason for this is the fact that consultation, as an indirect effort, is consistent with a preventive philosophy. Another reason is that too many professionals feel qualified to be consultants, failing to recognize that consultation is a very specialized area of community mental health practice. To be a consultant requires training and skills beyond those usually derived from a professional education.

Consultation and education were among the five "essential" services called for by the Community Mental Health Centers legislation. The original rationale for mental health consultation was based on both theoretical and practical considerations. Realizing that there would never be enough manpower to meet the need, Caplan and others looked to mental health consultation as a way in which mental health principles and skills could benefit larger numbers of people in the community. A natural pathway exists—via the front-line people in human services, the care-givers. Through mental health consultation to general practitioners, public health nurses, schoolteachers, and others, it might be possible to have a preventive impact on the lives of the many individuals served by these care-givers. Thus, for example, consultation with a teacher could have a preventive effect on 30 or more children each year. This has been termed the *multiplier effect*. Kelly (1970) suggests that mental health consultation also may be a "radiating process." It may, in fact, affect significant others in the environment, including the colleagues of the care-giver who receives consultation.

A DEFINITION OF CONSULTATION

Mental health consultation focuses on the relationship between the *consultant* and the *consultee(s)*. The consultant and the consultee work together to help the consultee solve a problem or better understand the problem of the consultee's *client*. For example, a psychologist from a community mental health center (the consultant) might work collaboratively with a fourth grade teacher (the consultee) about the best ways to motivate an underachieving child (the client). In most types of consultation, a consultant is brought in as an expert to solve problems and hopes to prove his expertise so he will be hired again. The mental health consultant, in contrast, works to help the consultee solve the problem so that the consultee will be more competent to deal with similar situations on his own in the future. Working together so that the problem is solved *and* the consultee becomes more competent is an example of the community mental health principle of *mileage*—doing something in such a way that multiple and maximum benefits will occur (Cook *et al.*, 1975). These aspects of mental health consultation are reflected in Altrocchi, Spielberger, and Eisdorfer's statement that "the goals are to assist key professional workers of a community to carry out their professional responsibilities by becoming more sensitive to the needs of their clients and associates and more comfortable and adept in their relationships with them [1965, p. 127]."

TYPES OF CONSULTATION

Various types of mental health consultation have been identified. The most widely quoted typology was suggested by Caplan (1963). He differentiates between consultation that is focused on the consultee's client and that focused on the problems a consultee has with a program. He also differentiates between consultation directed at solving the problem at hand and consultation directed at increasing the objectivity and competence of the consultee. These four types of consultation he identifies as

1. Client-centered case consultation
2. Consultee-centered case consultation
3. Program-centered administrative consultation
4. Consultee-centered administrative consultation

Consultee-centered case consultation may be appropriate when the consultant evaluates the consultee as contributing, however unknowingly, to the client's problem. The consultant then tries to bring about change in the consultee. The consultee may be unable to deal with his client's problem because he doesn't understand it, because he lacks the necessary skill, because he lacks confidence and self-esteem, or because he lacks objectivity (Caplan, 1963). According to Caplan, the consultee may lack objectivity because of *theme interference*. This concept obviously grows out of Caplan's psychoanalytic background. It refers to the "symbolic inhibition of free perception and communication between a consultee and a client and a concomitant disorder of objectivity [1964, p. 223]." In other words, something about the client triggers an irrational belief or mistaken perception—a *theme* interferes with the consultee's work. The consultant is trained to recognize themes when they occur and to give *messages* to the consultee that are designed to reduce the interference caused by the theme. For example, a teacher might be having difficulty with a child because she believes that all minority-group children are below average in intelligence, and she is treating the child accordingly. Recognizing this, the consultant might respond with messages designed to help the teacher come to see that all minority-group children are *not* below average in intelligence. Theme interference is a special instance of what has been called *consultee-linkage*. A large number of problems for which consultees seek consultation involve factors external to the client—factors that originate, at least in part, from the consultee or the social systems that impinge upon the client or consultee. The problems are linked to these other factors. Thus, we can identify *consultee-linkage* and *system-linkage* (Cook, 1971).

In an instance of consultee-centered administrative consultation for a consultee-linkage, two psychologists from a mental health center worked with the director of a community action program. The director was having a number of problems with his program, including serious public-relations problems with agencies and people in the power structure of the community. The consultants practiced *aggressive availability* with the consultee, going out of their way to work with the director in his own bailiwick when he needed help. The consultants talked with the staff, attended community meetings, and functioned as *participant conceptualizers* (Bennett, Anderson, Cooper, Hassol, Klein, & Rosenblum, 1966; Cook, 1970) by being actively engaged in the program, at the same time bringing their social science knowledge to bear on the problems they observed. They persuaded the director to subcontract some services to other agencies. In marked contrast to his earlier approach, which was to challenge agencies with "What are *you* doing for the poor?", the director was now able to win friends for his programs. This change was probably best exemplified when the consultants planted the idea that the director might hire off-duty policemen to work in a recreation program in the public housing project. By doing so, the director won new municipal support for his program, and gave the police and young people the opportunity to learn about each other as people rather than as stereotypes.

The observation that problems can be system-linked leads to the view that consultation and other preventive interventions need to be directed toward changing the social system and institutions. In the conclusion of an outstanding article on the preventive aspects of consultation, Hassol and Cooper make this statement:

> Consultation focuses its efforts on the modification of environments—social, emotional, and organizational—often in conscious preference to intervention at the level of the individual case. The favored techniques of consultation are educational rather than remedial. The commitment is toward assisting both individuals and social systems to gain knowledge concerning organizational and community dynamics as they impinge not only on troubled individuals but on entire populations [1970, pp. 731–732].

Levels of Intervention in the Community

As Caplan and Nelson point out,

> The way a problem is defined determines not only what is done about it, but also what is *not* done—or what apparently need not be done. . . . whether the social problem to be attacked is delinquency, mental health, drug abuse, unemployment, ghetto riots. . . . the action (or inaction) taken will depend largely on whether causes are seen as residing within the individuals or in the environment [1973, p. 201].

If problems are defined in *person-centered* terms, then *person-change* treatment techniques are called for. This has been the major psychological and psychiatric approach to virtually all human problems, sometimes to the extent that people caught in difficult situations are blamed for their predicaments. If problems are defined in *situation-centered* terms, however, then *system-change* treatments are appropriate (Caplan & Nelson, 1973). The exceptionalistic–universalistic dimension proposed by Ryan (1971b) represents a similar distinction between person-centered and situation-centered viewpoints.

Programs adhering to the person-centered or exceptionalistic viewpoint emphasize individually oriented diagnostic, psychotherapeutic, and rehabilitative services offered to individuals, families, and groups by the community mental health agency.

Programs adhering to the situation-centered or universalistic viewpoint emphasize population-oriented social change interventions, which are most likely to take place outside of the community mental health agency.

Nagler and Cooper (1969) suggest that mental health interventions can be described in terms of the *target* of the service, the *goal* of the service, the *means* of intervention, and the *locus* of operation. As shown in Table 20-1, these parameters encompass three levels of social and community intervention, ranging from concern for an individual patient to concern for the community as a whole.

Expanding upon Nagler and Cooper's application of their model to the problem of school dropouts, we see that at Level I, the in-agency approach would be to use individual, family, or group treatment to get the young person to stay in school. At Level II, the agency might invite guidance counselors to attend case conferences at the agency in the hope that the counselors would become more effective in preventing students from dropping out. At Level III, the agency might agree to operate a program for potential dropouts, if the school system would revise its curriculum to make it more relevant for all students.

The experiences of one consultant illustrate community interventions at all three levels. The consultant was called upon to consult with high school teachers and guidance counselors about the cases of several high school seniors who had dropped out of school and run away. This consultation was client-centered; it was directed toward better understanding of the clients involved. It quickly became apparent that an epidemic was occurring—there were far too many similar cases. The consultant broached the subject with the school system's director of guidance, only to discover a linkage—the director of guidance, the

TABLE 20-1

Levels of Community Intervention[a]

			Locus of intervention	
Level	Target	Goal	In-agency intervention	Community intervention
I	Client or patient (family; group)	Behavior change	Client-focused clinical services—psychotherapy, marriage counseling, drug therapy, crisis counseling, etc.	Case-centered interventions—case-centered mental health consultation, telephone counseling
II	Community care-giver	Enhanced effectiveness	Case conferences with involved community workers	Care-giver–centered interventions—consultee-centered consultation; in-service training programs
III	Social system (agency, community)	Social or institutional change	Program delivery management	Program, organization, and system interventions—administrative consultation, social systems analysis, social activism, political protest

[a] Adapted from Nagler and Cooper, 1969.

school system, and indeed, the town were highly oriented toward college careers for young people. Students who could not stand the pressure or were rejected by colleges left town. Therefore, the consultant tried a consultee-centered approach with the director of guidance. The director was not receptive either to learning about the problem or developing a program to prevent it. At Level III, however, some success occurred. The superintendent of schools was interested in learning about the problem and wanted to develop programs to combat it. The programs planned with his cooperation included increasing vocational alternatives to college and PTA meetings to discuss alternatives to college, to reduce the community pressure for college admission.

SOCIAL ACTION

Hersch argues that the mental health profession's concern with prevention has drawn it into the "arenas of social change and political action [1972, p. 750]." Transcending the traditional problems and methods of mental health, the clinical and public health communities have added a third frame of reference: social action.

Social action calls for new techniques such as advocacy, e.g., siding with a client in a dispute with an agency (National Association of Social Workers, 1969), protest, and professional involvement in social movements and social action

(Scribner, 1968). Mental health workers' professional and political involvement in civil rights, antipoverty, and ecology activities are important examples.

Evaluation of Community Mental Health

Since the beginning, the community mental health movement has had perhaps as many critics as proponents. Basic conceptions such as prevention have been challenged (Dunham, 1965). Whether or not prevention is possible, or economical, is an empirical question and the definitive studies have yet to be done. Other criticisms have been directed at community mental health practice, challenging its goals, philosophy, and intervention techniques, its use of the medical model, and its lack of citizen participation. Albee (1968) states that "we hear about the 'psychiatric revolution' and about emerging new patterns of patient care [p. 172]." He goes on to quote the comments of one official of the National Institute of Mental Health about 173 functioning community mental health centers, which Albee says make "the bold new approach sound like the timid old approach." Regarding plans of some of these centers to establish new outpatient clinics and others to expand and improve outpatient treatment including individual, group, family, and chemotherapy, Albee asks, "What is new about these? [p. 172]" Unfortunately, not much. Far too many centers have emphasized traditional "psychiatric" services, paying little or no attention to crisis intervention, primary prevention, and community change within their catchment areas.

COMMUNITY MENTAL HEALTH RESEARCH

One of the most cogent criticisms of the community mental health field is the relative lack of significant research. Although some excellent studies do exist (e.g., many examples reported in Golann & Eisdorfer, 1972), they are relatively rare in the literature compared to program descriptions and articles discussing general concepts. Among the types of research needed to increase our understanding of community mental health are epidemiologic community studies, including studies of the demographic, social, and cultural characteristics of the community; studies of the mental health status and role functioning of community residents; and studies of community perceptions of and attitudes toward social and emotional problems. Studies of patient populations and systems-analysis studies of what happens to clients as they are processed through the human services system are also needed (Bahn, 1965; Halpert, 1970).

Of particular importance is outcome research and program evaluation. If community mental health interventions are not doing what they are supposed to do, or if they are too costly, or too inefficient, then they should be discarded. There are a number of possible approaches to program evaluation. Bloom (1972) has suggested four types of evaluation studies: (1) program description, (2) recipient judgment, (3) expert judgment, and (4) measurement of community variables. Unfortunately, few community mental health programs have engaged in *any* systematic efforts in any of these categories, even to the point of keeping systematic records on what it is they do and what it costs.

Rossi (1969) has identified some of the difficulties in accomplishing evaluation research, not the least of which is the fact that some people and agencies may not want to know whether they are truly accomplishing their stated program objectives! Admittedly, community variables might be difficult to study. Because social action programs might have only small effects, new types of experimental study designs are required (Campbell, 1969) and new measuring instruments are necessary (Cook, Looney, & Pine, 1973).

Another problem is that most workers in mental health programs are doers rather than researchers. Service-press—that is, the pressure to provide direct client service—requires attention to clinical duties before evaluative research. Also, few practitioners have had enough training to do quality research.

THE COMMUNITY MENTAL HEALTH CENTERS PROGRAM

By July, 1973 there were approximately 400 community mental health centers in actual operation (Chu & Trotter, 1974)—far fewer than the proposed federal goal of 2000 (Bloom, 1973). It is doubtful that the program will ever reach the magnitude once predicted. The program is not the panacea for human suffering it was originally claimed to be. When any social action program is oversold—when it does not produce the expected benefits—there will eventually be a backlash. Such a backlash has struck the community mental health program, and the funding for community mental health centers has been sharply curtailed.

Although some of the basic assumptions of community mental health may be quite valid, the actual implementation of these assumptions in meaningful community programs has been less than impressive. One reason for this is that most people working in community mental health programs have not been trained in community mental health theory or practice. Consequently we have "old wine in new bottles"—the same old kinds of clinical interventions in new buildings and with new names. Even well-trained community specialists may be more comfortable dealing with clinical issues rather than tackling social and system issues (Nagler & Cook, 1973).

There have been some very successful examples of community mental health programs. There is no question that the Community Mental Health Centers Program has brought some types of clinical service (especially diagnosis and psychotherapy) to more people than received professional attention previously—as many as 1 million patients in 1972 (Chu & Trotter, 1974). There has been some degree of innovation, particularly in the use of volunteers (Siegel, 1973) and nonprofessional manpower. Some programs, such as storefront neighborhood centers and telephone counseling services, are staffed almost exclusively with specially trained nonprofessionals or paraprofessionals, many of whom are volunteers. Neighborhood people and others who have been specially trained may now comprise 40% of all community mental health workers.

Chu and Trotter's 1974 book, *The Madness Establishment,* reports the findings of Ralph Nader's study group on the National Institute of Mental Health and presents a number of cogent criticisms of the Community Mental Health Centers Program. All these criticisms had been raised previously by professionals in the community mental health field. The study group found that the program has not been appropriately accountable, either to the National Institute of Mental Health or to community consumers. The program has not achieved its goal of reducing the number of admissions to state mental hospitals; in fact, it probably has increased admissions. As it has developed, the program has been primarily an extension of the psychiatric treatment establishment and has functioned under the medical model. There has been very little community participation in center operation and policy formation, and especially little client input. Emphasis on primary and tertiary prevention has been minimal. Many centers are inaccessible, do not provide continuity of care, or do not offer comprehensive services for children. Many do not collect or report basic information about their operations. The class system of care, wherein more advantaged clients receive better care, has been perpetuated (Chu & Trotter, 1974).

These are damaging criticisms, but they are criticisms of the Community Mental Health Centers Program. That program has not provided a valid test of programs developed from the basic ideology and technology of community mental health.

We can only hope that the basic concepts of community mental health—community as client, prevention, crisis intervention, social system change—will not be discarded before they have been adequately tested. If properly employed, they may well help to reduce the incidence and prevalence of social and emotional disorder and increase the quality of life in our communities.

Summary

Community mental health interventions have been proposed as alternatives to traditional *person-centered* approaches to emotional and social problems. In this chapter, we have seen that community mental health can be defined as an ideology that emphasizes population-oriented preventive programs, or as activities that are carried out in various mental health programs. Some of the historical factors that have contributed to the field were reviewed. Various models for prevention, crisis theory and crisis intervention, and types of mental health consultation, all based on the work of Gerald Caplan, were discussed. Caplan has probably been the single most influential person in community mental health. Nagler and Cooper's model for different levels of intervention—from individual psychotherapy to social action—was applied to the problem of school dropouts.

The chapter closed with an evaluation of community mental health. The field can be criticized for its lack of program evaluation research to test programs based on community mental health concepts. The Community Mental Health Centers Program has also been a disappointment, but it has not provided a true test of the basic concepts.

21

Medical Treatments

DAVID L. DUNNER
New York State Psychiatric
Institute and Columbia University
College of Physicians and Surgeons

JOHN W. SOMERVILL[1]
Southern Illinois University at Carbondale

Various forms of medical treatment are used for different psychological disorders. Despite their general effectiveness, some forms of treatment, such as electroconvulsive therapy for depression and stimulants for hyperactive children, have been the subject of considerable controversy. In fact, there is some skepticism regarding the value of *any* form of medical treatment. Such skepticism often reflects a misunderstanding of both the medical approach and the nature of certain kinds of psychological disorders.

A popular but poorly documented view is that most if not all psychological problems are caused by environmental forces. Because of this belief, many patients entering treatment think that their problems are a result of their interactions with their environment. Initially, they seek to understand what they have done to cause their problems and frequently express a desire for psychotherapy rather than medication. Often, such patients believe that psychotherapy will lead to a clearer understanding of their role in the development of the illness and ultimately will aid in the prevention of future problems.

By contrast, the physician who uses medication usually perceives the patient's problems as a constellation of symptoms defining a syndrome typical of many patients, rather than a set of problems uniquely related to a particular

[1] Present address: Psychology Department, University of Northern Iowa, Cedar Falls, Iowa.

patient's interaction with his environment. This view represents the medical approach to physical illnesses. Thus, the physician who uses medication tends to approach treatment with what is termed the *medical model*—that is, treating the patient with mental problems according to the same principles used in treating physical illnesses.

The medical approach to treatment should not imply that psychological problems necessarily have a physical origin. The etiology of most mental disorders is unknown. But whether one assumes an environmental or an organic etiology, medical treatments are often more effective than psychotherapy in the treatment of relatively severe disorders. A good example of research supporting the value of medical treatment is provided by May (1968, 1975). May (1968) assessed the effects of psychotherapy, antipsychotic drugs, and electroconvulsive therapy (ECT) in the treatment of schizophrenic patients during their initial psychiatric admission. The subjects were patients whose severity of illness warranted hospitalization but who were able to be discharged and maintained by continued outpatient treatment after less than 2 years of hospitalization. Patients with a good prognosis or acute onsets were excluded, as were patients with organic brain damage or alcoholism. A total of 228 subjects were randomly assigned to one of five treatments: (1) individual psychotherapy alone, (2) antipsychotic drugs alone, (3) individual psychotherapy plus antipsychotic drugs, (4) ECT, and (5) milieu therapy. (The milieu therapy group was considered a control group; milieu therapy refers to the social and physical benefits believed to result from the environmental surroundings in the hospital setting.)

All patients were evaluated by trained raters before, during, and after treatment on several scales designed to assess psychiatric and social symptoms. Other dependent variables were (1) the length of hospital stay, (2) the cost of treatment, (3) ratings by the patients themselves, and (4) ratings by therapists. General findings were that antipsychotic drugs (with or without psychotherapy) and ECT were both more effective than psychotherapy or milieu therapy. Antipsychotic drugs resulted in fewer psychiatric symptoms and a shorter hospital stay than psychotherapy. The cost of treatment was lowest for the group treated with antipsychotic drugs and highest for the group treated with psychotherapy.

May (1975), in a 5-year follow-up study, reported that patients whose initial treatment consisted of antipsychotic drugs (with or without psychotherapy) or ECT spent less time in the hospital during the follow-up period than patients who received psychotherapy or milieu therapy.

May's findings indicate that medical treatment—particularly treatment with antipsychotic drugs—is more effective than psychotherapy for patients with moderately severe schizophrenia. Since schizophrenia is the most frequent of all psychotic disorders, these findings are of obvious importance. Other research indicating the effectiveness of medical treatments will be cited when specific forms of treatment are considered.

In presenting the various forms of medical treatment, we are differentiating between the older treatments, which were physical, and the newer treatments, which are chemical. Physical treatments such as insulin coma, electroconvulsive therapy (ECT), and frontal lobotomy were in use for several years prior to the introduction of the currently popular chemical agents, known as psychotropic (mind-affecting) drugs. The first part of this chapter will be devoted to the treatment of psychological problems with psychotropic drugs; the second part will deal with physical treatments.

The Psychotropic Drugs

Since their introduction in the 1950s, the psychotropic drugs have become the most widely used medical treatment of psychological disorders. Psychotropic drugs, like most medications, have at least three names: the chemical formula, the generic name, and the brand name used to market the drug by pharmaceutical companies. The generic names will be used almost exclusively in this chapter. However, because public familiarity with medication usually involves brand names, the brand names of some of the more commonly used psychotropic drugs are listed in Tables 21-1 through 21-5.

The psychotropic drugs are grouped into the following categories: (1) antipsychotic drugs, (2) lithium carbonate, (3) antidepressant drugs, (4) antianxiety drugs, (5) sedatives and hypnotics, (6) stimulants, (7) narcotics, and (8) other drugs. For the most part, the classifications denote the major effect of the drugs. For example, drugs used to treat psychotic disorders are included with antipsychotic agents.

ANTIPSYCHOTIC DRUGS: THE MAJOR TRANQUILIZERS

The use of antipsychotic drugs, particularly phenothiazines, in the treatment of psychosis represents one of the most important advances in psychiatry. According to Gellhorn and Kiely (1973), "The therapeutic use of phenothiazines has revolutionized the treatment of millions of seriously disturbed mental patients during the past fifteen years [p. 252]."

Generally, the antipsychotic drugs presented in this section are useful in the treatment of schizophrenia, manic states, and psychoses associated with organic mental syndromes. They are also used at times to treat depression and anxiety, although other medications may be more effective in the treatment of these conditions.

Table 21-1 presents three classes of antipsychotic agents: (1) phenothiazines, (2) butyrophenones, and (3) thioxanthines.

Because of their extensive use, much attention will be devoted to phenothiazines. However, some recently developed synthetic antipsychotic drugs of the butyrophenone and the thioxanthine group appear to be just as effective as phenothiazines in the treatment of psychosis (Gellhorn & Kiely, 1973).

PHENOTHIAZINES.   Phenothiazines are major tranquilizing drugs that have been used in the United States since the 1950s. They are still the most important class of drugs used in the treatment of schizophrenia. Phenothiazines are effective in reducing psychomotor excitement (*psychomotor* refers to both psychological and physical activity), agitation, aggressive behavior, delusions, and hallucina-

TABLE 21-1

Antipsychotic Agents

Chemical basis	Generic name	Brand name
Phenothiazines		
Dimethylamine	Chlorpromazine	Thorazine
Piperazine	Trifluoperazine	Stelazine
	Perphenazine	Trilafon
	Fluphenazine	Prolixin, Permitil
Piperadine	Thioridazine	Mellaril
	Mesoridázine	Serentil
Butyrophenones	Haloperidol	Haldol, Serenace
Thioxanthines	Chlorprothixine	Taractan, Solatran
	Thiothixene	Navane

tions. The thought disorders and the progressive social deterioration seen in schizophrenia, however, do not usually respond to these drugs.

The different classes of phenothiazines are based on chemical differences that result in differences in potency (ratio of antipsychotic effect per milligram of drug) and side effects.

Probably the best known and most frequently prescribed phenothiazine in psychiatry is chlorpromazine, for which the common brand name is Thorazine. The use of chlorpromazine in the treatment of chronic schizophrenia has permitted the discharge of thousands of patients who formerly would have spent most of their lives in institutions (Brill & Patton, 1959). In chronic schizophrenia, the antipsychotic effects of chlorpromazine are not generally seen at doses below 600 milligrams daily and in less than 4 to 6 weeks. Lack of improvement may indicate that (1) the patient is not taking his medication, (2) sufficient doses have not been given for a long enough time, or (3) the patient has been misdiagnosed.

The phenothiazines with the highest potency are the piperazines, which include trifluoperazine, perphenazine, fluphenazine, and prochlorperazine. Of this group, the most frequently used drug is probably trifluoperazine; the common brand name is Stelazine. The piperazines are prescribed in comparatively low doses because of their high potency. Extrapyramidal side effects are common with drugs of the piperazine class. (Extrapyramidal side effects involve the extrapyramidal system, a part of the nervous system that coordinates motor behavior.) Three types of extrapyramidal syndromes occur: (1) Parkinson's syndrome, characterized by a "pill-rolling" tremor of the fingers, muscular rigidity, drooling, and a general stiffness in posture, (2) dystonia and dyskinesia, which refer to a rolling upward of the eyes and turning of the neck and head, and (3) akasthesia, the inability to sit still, which may be manifested by pacing, chewing, and lip movements.

BUTYROPHENONES AND THIOXANTHINES. As indicated earlier, butyrophenones and thioxanthines represent two new groups of synthetic antipsychotic drugs that appear to be as effective as phenothiazines. Butyrophenones, which are used in the treatment of schizophrenia and mania, have relatively high potency and extrapyramidal side effects are common. Thioxanthines are used as antipsychotic drugs and may also have antidepressant effects. Extrapyramidal side effects also occur with the thioxanthines, which are not as frequently prescribed as the phenothiazines.

Side effects frequently are seen for all the antipsychotic drugs. In addition to extrapyramidal side effects, orthostatic hypotension is a common and important side effect. In orthostatic hypotension, the blood pressure falls when patients rise from a prone position, resulting in dizziness and possible fainting. A recently described side effect of the antipsychotic drugs is tardive dyskinesia. The syndrome, often seen in chronic users of antipsychotic agents, is characterized by movements of the lips, tongue, and jaw. Jerky movements of the extremities can occur, and swallowing may be impaired. The syndrome may be worsened by withdrawal of antipsychotic agents. There is no known treatment for tardive dyskinesia.

Despite the frequency of side effects, antipsychotic drugs successfully alleviate the major symptoms of psychotic disorders. The physiological changes underlying improvement resulting from these drugs are not fully understood. One recent physiological theory of schizophrenia is that the illness may be due to an excess of the neurotransmitter dopamine (Snyder, Banerjee, Yamamura, & Greenberg, 1974). Neurotransmitters are amines such as serotonin, dopamine, norepinephrine, and histamine—small-molecule chemicals that relay messages from one nerve cell to the next. Chlorpromazine and other antipsychotic drugs are believed to function by blockading nerve cell receptors. In this way, they have the effect of reducing the excess of the neurotransmitter dopamine. The more potent antipsychotic drugs may actually produce a relative deficiency of dopamine. Thus, extrapyramidal side effects, which are more common with the relatively potent antipsychotic drugs, may be the result of the relative deficiency of dopamine.

Another hypothesis about antipsychotic drugs reflects neurophysiological studies of the effects of antipsychotic agents on the functioning of the hypothalamus, a subcortical brain system that plays a major role in regulating activity of the autonomic nervous system. Psychotic behavior is thought to be related to a state of excitability in the posterior hypothalamus, characterized by upward and downward hypothalamic discharges. The primary effect of antipsychotic drugs is believed to be a reduction in these upward and downward discharges, or a dampening of hyperarousal patterns associated with a state of excitability. According to Gellhorn and Kiely (1973), drug research with animals and EEG studies with humans support the hypothesis that the reactivity of the hypothalamic system is fundamentally altered by antipsychotic drugs.

Although no definite conclusions can be drawn as to exactly *how* the antipsychotic drugs are effective in the treatment of psychosis, recent physiological and pharmacological research has yielded promising and testable hypotheses. It is possible that eventual understanding of the mechanism of drug action may lead to new insights regarding the psychobiology of mental disorders.

CLINICAL APPLICATIONS. The following case history illustrates the use of antipsychotic drugs in the treatment of schizophrenia.

■ A 37-year-old man was brought to the hospital by the police because he threatened to kill his mother. His mother indicated he had begun to become less social in his mid-twenties, and at about age 27 he told her that his thoughts were being broadcast on television. In the ensuing years, he had written to several communications agencies complaining that people on television were talking about him and revealing details of his personal life. The hospital admission was precipitated by his accusing his mother, with whom he lived, of plotting with the local radio station to produce radio waves that were controlling his thoughts.

On admission, the patient was somewhat agitated. Within a few days, however, he became seclusive and withdrawn. He stated he sometimes heard voices commenting on his behavior. He was treated with a phenothiazine (chlorpromazine) at doses of 1000 milligrams daily. No change in his behavior was noted until the beginning of his tenth week of hospitalization, at which time he said he no longer heard voices and that the feelings of mind control had gone. He also became more sociable with other patients. After a 3-month hospitalization, he was discharged to live at home and was checked once a week in the aftercare clinic. He succeeded in getting a part-time job and continued his medication for 18 months. However, at that time he decided not to take medication and also ceased coming to the clinic. During the next 4 months he again became withdrawn and seclusive and complained that people at work had arranged furniture in special ways so as to indicate to other people that he was mentally ill. He began writing letters to a local radio station, complaining that radio waves were being used to control his thoughts. His mother brought him back to the hospital, and he was treated with injections of fluphenazine enanthate every week. The psychotic symptoms diminished and he was able to return to work, with continued follow-up treatment in the aftercare clinic.

COMMENT. The insidious onset, presence of hallucinations and delusions, and social isolation suggest a diagnosis of schizophrenia. Response to phenothiazines was not prompt but the psychotic symptoms abated over several weeks of treatment. Chronic phenothiazine treatment is indicated for this type of illness. The psychotic symptoms usually return if treatment is discontinued.

LITHIUM CARBONATE

Lithium carbonate was only recently approved by the Food and Drug Administration (FDA) for the treatment of manic states. It was also approved as a preventive medicine for manic-depressive disorders. Lithium carbonate is a naturally occurring salt, used in medicine in the 1940s as a sodium substitute for patients with cardiac disease. Severe toxicity was noted, and the drug was taken off the market. The effectiveness of lithium salts in manic states was serendipitously discovered by Cade (1949). Double-blind studies using placebo control groups provided stronger evidence for their effectiveness (Schou, Juel-Nielson, Stromgren, & Voldby, 1954).[2] A later report by Danish investigators (Baastrup & Schou, 1967) indicated that lithium carbonate, used chronically, prevented manic and depressive episodes. The results sparked worldwide controversy over what statistical approaches were most appropriate for assessing the effectiveness of drugs in the prevention of recurrent disorders. The controversy led to several double-blind, placebo-controlled studies on the effectiveness of lithium carbonate as a preventive drug.

Two well-controlled studies were conducted by Prien, Caffey, and Klett (1973) and Stallone, Shelley, Mendlewicz, and Fieve (1973). In both studies, the patients selected met diagnostic criteria for manic-depressive illness; they had had at least two affective episodes in the 2 years prior to the research. Such patients would be likely to have future episodes. Patients were randomly assigned to lithium carbonate or identical-appearing placebo capsules during their normal phase and were followed in research outpatient clinics. Evaluations of mental state were made at regular intervals by raters who did not know whether the patient was receiving lithium carbonate or a placebo. A unique feature of lithium treatment is that the dose of medication is determined by the lithium ion concentration in the blood. Thus, all patients had blood samples taken at each visit, and fictitious lithium blood levels were created for those patients who received a placebo in order to maintain the double-blind.

Both studies were conducted over a 2-year period, and the results were strikingly similar. First of all, patients who received lithium carbonate tended to continue their participation until the research was complete, whereas placebo-treated patients tended to drop out of the study. A major reason for the dropouts in the placebo group was the development of manic episodes with subsequent hospitalization. There was a statistically significant reduction of manic episodes in the group treated with lithium carbonate. Another finding was that more of the patients who received lithium carbonate had no episodes during the research period, as compared to the placebo group. For those lithium carbonate-treated patients who did have affective episodes, the initial episodes came later in the research period than did episodes among subjects in the placebo group. Finally, the lithium carbonate-treated patients also had a reduction in the rate of depressive episodes as compared to the placebo group. Thus, both studies showed lithium carbonate to be superior to a placebo control.

As a result of these findings and similar findings by other investigators, the chronic administration of lithium carbonate to bipolar manic-depressive patients is now an accepted form of treatment. Approximately 80% of patients with acute

---

[2] Double-blind studies are employed in order to control for bias by the patient or the investigator. In a double-blind drug trial, the patient is given identical-appearing capsules that may contain an active drug, a placebo, or a second active drug. Neither the patient nor the evaluator knows what drug the patient is receiving. A placebo (nonactive medication) is often used as the comparison drug to control for the "placebo effect." The placebo effect is illustrated by instant relief of a symptom, such as a headache, immediately after taking the medication—that is, before the medication has been absorbed and could be effective.

mania will respond to lithium carbonate treatment (Schou *et al.,* 1954). It should be pointed out that the prophylactic effect is not complete; most patients continue to have some affective episodes in spite of chronic treatment (Dunner & Fieve, 1974). These periods, however, are usually milder in severity, duration, and frequency compared to episodes during placebo treatment. Lithium carbonate, although one of our newest drugs, has been thoroughly researched. The introduction of lithium carbonate treatment has tremendously increased our awareness of the diagnosis, the genetics, and the biology of affective disorders.

Side effects of lithium carbonate may include nausea, vomiting, diarrhea, and mild tremor. The dose of the drug must be carefully determined by the blood level. At higher blood levels, lithium carbonate can have very serious side effects, such as ataxia (loss of balance), confusion, coma, and even death. At therapeutic blood levels, however, the drug is well tolerated and has sufficiently few side effects that patients do not feel drugged.

CLINICAL APPLICATIONS. The following case illustrates the use of chemotherapy in the management of manic-depressive illness. In this particular case, lithium carbonate was used in combination with an antipsychotic agent (chlorpromazine) while the patient was hospitalized. After she was discharged, lithium carbonate was continued and an antidepressant agent (amitriptyline) was added to control a subsequent episode of depression. The use of more than one drug to control manic depressive illness is common.

■   A 30-year-old housewife was brought to the hospital by her husband for evaluation. Over a 2-week period she had begun staying up late at night writing a book about world peace. Although of modest means, she had bought an expensive new car and several hundred dollars' worth of clothes, and had scheduled a world tour to publicize her book. Her mood was euphoric and she spoke rapidly. She had a history of being hospitalized for depression beginning at age 22 while in college and again at the age of 27 following a suicide attempt. Her father had been an alcoholic and his sister had committed suicide during a depressive episode.

She was admitted to the hospital and treated with lithium carbonate and chlorpromazine. Over a 1-week period she began to sleep normally, had a reduction in her speed of speech, and was able to restore her relationship with her husband. She returned to her normal mood state after 3 weeks of treatment and was discharged. Lithium carbonate was continued; the chlorpromazine had been discontinued a week prior to discharge. A month later she again became depressed and amitriptyline was added to the lithium carbonate treatment. Her depressive symptoms improved with continued outpatient treatment over a 3-month period. During the ensuing 5 years she was maintained with lithium carbonate and had no recurrence of symptoms.

COMMENT.   Sudden onset of euphoria, hyperactivity, decreased sleep, and impulsive behavior with a history of depressive illness is a classic example of manic-depressive illness. In over half of all patients with manic-depressive illness, the family history is positive (that is, one or more blood relatives of the patient also suffered from the illness). The response of acute mania to lithium carbonate treatment is usually good. The drug is continued in manic-depressive patients in order to reduce the frequency and severity of future attacks. Current therapeutic practice holds that lithium carbonate treatment should be maintained indefinitely.

ANTIDEPRESSANT DRUGS

Antidepressant drugs are effective in treating depression in a great majority of patients. Many cases that formerly were treated with electroconvulsive therapy are now managed by medication. Most depressed patients are treated as outpatients with tricyclic antidepressants, the compounds of which will be described here.

Two classes of antidepressant drugs (tricyclic and monoamine oxidase inhibitors) are presented in Table 21-2. The two classes are based on the chemical structure of the drugs and their side effects. The first class, the tricyclic compounds, is used more frequently than the second class, the compounds of monoamine oxidase inhibitors.

TRICYCLIC COMPOUNDS. These drugs are called tricyclic because they are chemically structured in three rings. The most frequently prescribed tricyclic compounds are *amitriptyline* and *imipramine*. Amitriptyline is sedating and is frequently prescribed for depressed patients who have insomnia. Imipramine is activating and is often used in depressed patients with psychomotor retardation, which is characterized by a very low level of both psychological and physical activity. Side effects of tricyclic antidepressants include dry mouth, increased sweating, constipation, and orthostatic hypotension.

MONOAMINE OXIDASE INHIBITORS. The use of monoamine oxidase inhibitors was stopped temporarily a few years ago by the FDA because severe side

TABLE 21-2

Antidepressant Agents

Chemical basis	Generic name	Brand name
Tricyclic	Amitriptyline	Elavil
	Nortriptyline	Aventyl
	Protriptyline	Vivactil
	Imipramine	Tofranil, Presamine
	Desipramine	Norpramin, Pertofrane
	Amitriptyline + perphenazine	Triavil, Etrafon
Monoamine oxidase inhibitors	Isocarboxazid	Marplan
	Phenelzine	Nardil
	Tranylcypromine	Parnate

effects were associated with ingestion of certain foods during administration of monoamine oxidase inhibitors. Monoamine oxidase is an enzyme that normally metabolizes certain agents that raise blood pressure. The inhibition of the enzyme results in sudden and severe increases in blood pressure if foods containing the chemical tyramine are eaten. The sudden increase in blood pressure may lead to a headache and even to a stroke. The use of these drugs is now permitted so long as patients avoid tyramine-containing foods and other medications.

In general, the effects of antidepressant drugs on depression are not evident until after 2–4 weeks of treatment. Since depressions are often episodic disorders, the dose of the antidepressant drugs is usually tapered off and eventually discontinued after the symptoms begin to disappear. It should be emphasized that although antidepressant drugs are generally effective in outpatient treatment, the risk of suicide among depressed patients should always be evaluated. For their own safety, patients who are considered serious suicidal risks should be hospitalized.

ANTIANXIETY DRUGS

Whereas solid research support exists for the clinical effectiveness of antipsychotic drugs, antidepressants, and lithium carbonate, there is a lack of convincing evidence that the antianxiety drugs are very effective, despite the fact that they are widely used. The patients for whom antianxiety drugs are prescribed often have syndromes that are defined less adequately than schizophrenia or depression. In addition, the placebo effect in anxious patients is generally quite large. These two factors—poorly defined syndromes and the magnitude of the placebo effect—have hampered research efforts to establish the clinical effectiveness of the antianxiety drugs.

A list of antianxiety drugs is presented in Table 21-3. Of all the drugs listed in this table, chlordiazepoxide (Librium) and diazepam (Valium) are currently the most widely used. Meprobamate (Miltown, Equanil), which was the first popular antianxiety drug, is infrequently prescribed today.

In general, antianxiety drugs are used in the treatment of anxiety attacks or nervousness. Clinical experience indicates that they should be prescribed as needed rather than on a regular daily basis. Their effectiveness seems to diminish

TABLE 21-3

Examples of Antianxiety Agents

Generic name	Trade name
Chlordiazepoxide	Librium
Diazepam	Valium
Oxazepam	Serax
Clorazepate dipotassium	Tranxene
Tybamate	Solacen
Hydroxyzine	Vistaril, Atarax
Meprobamate	Miltown, Equanil

if taken daily over several weeks. These drugs have few side effects but may be addicting at higher doses. They cost much more than barbiturates, which are equally effective in treating anxiety states. Barbiturates, however, have a higher addiction potential than the antianxiety drugs. As will be discussed in the next section, barbiturates are frequently prescribed to produce a hypnotic or sedative action. The major side effects of antianxiety drugs are sedation, slurred speech, and lowering of blood pressure.

SEDATIVES AND HYPNOTICS

The value of sedatives and hypnotics in psychiatric treatment is often offset by undesirable consequences. Patients can become easily addicted to these drugs and their use often appears to be unnecessary. Drugs in this group are CNS depressants; they are frequently prescribed in general medicine for patients who complain of anxiety or insomnia.

The only difference between the hypnotic action and sedative action of the drugs in this group is the degree of CNS depression. Moderately high doses are used to induce sleep (hypnotic action) whereas minimal doses, given several times a day, are intended to reduce excitement or calm anxious patients (sedative action). The two major classes of sedatives and hypnotics are the barbiturates and the nonbarbiturate hypnotics.

The barbiturates are the most widely used hypnotic–sedative drugs. They were first developed in 1864 by combining urea from the urine of animals with malonic acid derived from the acid of apples. The new compound was named *barbituric acid*. The barbiturates have become the second leading method of suicide in the United States, carbon monoxide poisoning being the first (Jones, Shainberg, & Byer, 1973). Addiction to barbiturates occurs easily. If taken with alcohol, barbiturates can have a synergistic effect that results in profound CNS depression. Fatalities resulting from this combination of drugs are not uncommon.

It has been estimated by Jones *et al.* (1973) that each year persons in the United States take 3–4 billion doses of barbiturates prescribed by their physicians. Some of the more frequently prescribed barbiturates are presented in Table 21-4. Regardless of their drawbacks, barbiturates such as phenobarbital and amobarbital are effective in the treatment of anxiety states.

TABLE 21-4

Examples of Barbiturates Used as Sedatives or Hypnotics

Generic name	Brand name
Amobarbital	Amytal
Secobarbital	Seconal
Amobarbital plus secobarbital	Tuinal
Pentobarbital	Nembutal
Phenobarbital	Luminal

TABLE 21-5

Examples of Nonbarbiturate Hypnotics

Generic name	Brand name
Methyprylon	Noludar
Glutethimide	Doriden
Ethchlorvynol	Placidyl
Methaqualone	Quaalude

Nonbarbiturate hypnotic–sedative drugs produce reactions very similar to those of the barbiturates. A list of some of the most popular nonbarbiturate hypnotics is presented in Table 21-5. Like the barbiturates, the nonbarbiturate hypnotics are highly addictive. An additional drawback of the nonbarbiturates is that less is known about their pharmacology and toxicology than is known about the barbiturates (Sharpless, 1970).

In psychiatric practice, alternatives to the sedatives and hypnotics may be preferred. For example, in treating depressed patients who complain of insomnia, an antidepressant such as amitriptyline is often used because it has a known sedative effect. Psychotic patients who have insomnia may be treated by giving most of the daily total dose of antipsychotic drugs at bedtime, since the larger dosage facilitates sleep. Barbiturates, however, remain as important therapeutic agents in the treatment of anxiety states.

OTHER DRUG CATEGORIES

The remaining categories include *stimulants, narcotics,* and an *other* category for drugs used in special circumstances. Because these drugs are seldom used in the practice of psychiatry, they will be mentioned only briefly.

Stimulants, such as amphetamines and methylphenidate, are rarely used in current psychiatric practice. These drugs were formerly used to counteract the sedation produced by phenothiazines. However, since amphetamine use itself can be associated with a paranoid psychosis, their use has diminished.

Amphetamines and methylphenidate (Ritalin) are useful in the treatment of hyperactive children. Methylphenidate is preferred because it has fewer side effects. The drug is usually administered on school days, with improvement in mental concentration and academic performance being the treatment goals.[3] The use of drugs to treat young children is understandably controversial. Articles in newspapers and magazines occasionally have depicted the use of stimulants as an early introduction to the drug scene. Drug treatment of hyperactive children, however, usually is discontinued after the early elementary grades and there is no evidence of a relationship between drug therapy in early childhood and sub-

---

[3] It is an interesting phenomenon that hyperactive children become more active when treated with sedatives but less active when treated with stimulants.

sequent drug abuse. Carefully conducted studies using placebo controls have indicated that methylphenidate improves both cognitive functioning (Campbell, Douglas, & Morgenstern, 1971) and classroom behavior (Sprague, Barnes, & Werry, 1970). It is possible, however, that stimulant drugs may be used too frequently in general medical practice to treat children with relatively minor learning or behavioral problems. Stimulants, along with barbiturates, hypnotics, and narcotics, are now under stricter federal control regarding their prescription.

Narcotics are separately listed although most psychiatrists never prescribe them. Methadone threatment of heroin addiction is the most familiar use of narcotics in psychiatry.

The *other* category includes anti-Parkinson agents, which are used to treat the extrapyramidal syndromes of antipsychotic drugs; hormones, such as thyroid hormone, which have been used with tricyclic antidepressants in the treatment of depression; disulfiram, which is used in the treatment of chronic alcoholism; and megavitamin therapy, which has been evaluated as a treatment for schizophrenia (Wittenborn, Weber, & Brown, 1973).

In summary, the psychotropic drugs have become the most important form of medical treatment for psychiatric disorders. Extensive reliance on chemotherapy has lead to a decline in the use of physical treatments. Because of the effectiveness of chemotherapy, some treatments presented in the next section, such as prefrontal lobotomies, have only historical significance.

Physical Treatments

Physical treatments are not used as frequently as chemotherapy. The popularity of the physical treatments rapidly declined with the introduction of antipsychotic agents. The use of prefrontal lobotomies, a form of psychosurgery, to treat severe psychotic disorders was virtually discontinued when the effectiveness of the phenothiazines became recognized. Although prefrontal lobotomies are no longer done in the United States, newer psychosurgical procedures involving lesions in subcortical areas of the brain are still occasionally performed for certain kinds of disorders. In 1973, for example, it was estimated that about 500 such operations were performed annually in the United States by no more than a dozen neurosurgeons (Holden, 1973). The use of psychosurgery has resulted in considerable controversy. The major issues involved in this controversy will be discussed later in this section.

The physical treatment most frequently used today is electroconvulsive therapy (ECT). ECT is often used to treat depression and is preferred in some situations to the use of antidepressant drugs. An older form of shock therapy (insulin shock therapy) is rarely if ever currently employed.

ELECTROCONVULSIVE THERAPY

ECT was first used as a medical treatment in 1938 by two Italian physicians, Cerletti and Bini. In 1940, Lothar Kalinowsky introduced ECT in the United

States. The use of convulsive therapies was based on the erroneous belief that epilepsy and schizophrenia did not coexist and therefore seizures should reduce schizophrenic symptoms.[4] Thus, the initial use of ECT was as a treatment for schizophrenia. However, it was soon found that ECT was effective in the treatment of depression. In fact, certain patients who are depressed, almost mute, and have profound psychomotor retardation can be returned to a normal state within a few days following the use of two or three treatments with ECT. Few other treatments in psychiatry result in such rapid and dramatic improvement.

Studies of the efficacy of ECT in hospitalized depressed patients demonstrated the superiority of ECT over no treatment or treatment with a variety of antidepressant drugs. With ECT, patients spent less time in the hospital, had fewer complications, and had a shorter duration of depressive symptoms as compared with other treatments (Huston & Locher, 1948; Hutchinson & Smedberg, 1963; Norris & Clancy, 1961).

ECT is effective in treating depression, mania, and certain schizophrenic states involving immobility or very aggressive behavior (Klein & Davis, 1969). ECT treatments are usually given in the hospital but are occasionally administered on an outpatient basis. Treatment of depression typically consists of a total of 7 to 10 treatments administered three times a week. For acute states, such as mania, treatments may be given more frequently.

The usual procedure is to administer a sedative and a neuromuscular depolarizer (succinylcholine). A small, measured electrical current is then given through two electrodes placed on the patient's temples, over the temporal lobes. The current induces a modified convulsion; the succinylcholine acts on the muscles and prevents the usual clonic movements seen in grand mal epileptic seizures. The patient is usually awake within 10 to 15 minutes, although he may be temporarily confused. This confusion gradually disappears; it lasts longer after a series of treatments than after a single treatment. *Bilateral ECT* refers to treatments given by placing an electrode over each temple. In unilateral ECT, the electrodes are placed on one temple over the nondominant side of the brain. In both instances a bilateral convulsion results. Proponents of unilateral ECT claim that the effectiveness of treatment is not reduced and that less confusion results. Outpatients usually receive unilateral ECT.

Confusion is the most common side effect of ECT. An interesting phenomenon is that patients who have an organic deficit, but who are misdiagnosed as depressed, often have an inordinate degree of confusion after a single ECT. For example, many cases of Huntington's chorea are diagnosed only after the patient is given ECT for "depression," develops a severe confused state, and is then observed to have the spontaneous, involuntary movements characteristic of Huntington's chorea.

---

[4] Insulin shock therapy—the induction of convulsions with large doses of insulin—was actually the first method used. ECT replaced insulin shock therapy when it was found that the insulin method was associated with serious medical complications and side effects.

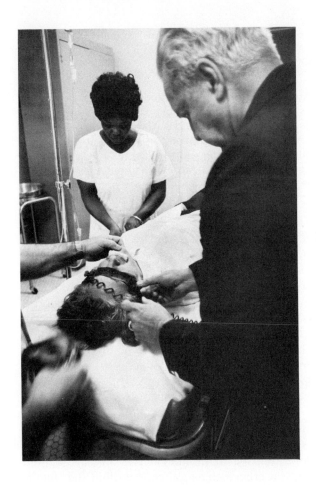

Electrodes are strapped over a patient's temples in preparation for electroconvulsive therapy in a hospital. Though ECT relieves depression more quickly than other treatments and has fewer complications, it has been the subject of considerable controversy. (Paul Fusco, Magnum)

The only absolute contraindication to ECT is increased intracranial pressure. In patients who are depressed and who have recently had a myocardial infarction (heart attack), ECT is often considered a safer treatment than psychotropic drugs. Similarly, ECT is preferred to drug therapy during the first trimester of pregnancy. ECT has often been viewed negatively by both professionals and the general public. Despite evidence to the contrary, fears of permanent side effects, beliefs that the procedure is extremely painful, and anecdotal reports of patients "getting worse" have served to perpetuate controversy regarding the desirability of ECT as a form of treatment.

Although ECT is effective in treating depression, a series of treatments has no effect in preventing future episodes. After treatment, there are no apparent adverse side effects and the patient typically returns to his usual level of social functioning. Since ECT is the fastest and surest method of treating depression, it is often used in situations where quick return to social functioning is important (Mendels, 1973).

CLINICAL APPLICATIONS. An example of the use of ECT in an inpatient psychiatric setting follows:

■   A 40-year-old man was hospitalized because of a 3-month history of worsening depression. His symptoms included low moods, crying spells, inability to concentrate, suicidal thoughts, loss of appetite, and a 15-pound weight loss. Within 2 days after admission he became mute, tended to sit in one position for most of the day, and hesitantly spoke of being unfit to live. ECT was begun because of concern over the patient's refusal to eat and his continued weight loss. After two treatments he became more cheerful, spoke spontaneously, moved normally, and ate full meals. He recovered completely after eight treatments and was discharged.

PSYCHOSURGERY

Psychosurgery is brain surgery for the purpose of alleviating psychiatric symptoms or modifying certain behaviors. The use of brain surgery to control behavior was first reported in 1891 by Gottlieb Burckhardt, a Swiss physician who removed parts of the cerebral cortex in order to calm six hallucinating patients. Five patients, although still psychotic, appeared to be calmer; one patient died. The surgery performed by Burckhardt was not accepted as a medical treatment and was generally opposed by his colleagues.

Psychosurgery did not become popular until after a series of frontal lobe operations were performed by a Portuguese neurologist named Antonio Egas Moniz. At the Second International Neurology Congress in 1935, Moniz heard two American brain researchers, Carlyle Jacobsen and John Fulton, describe the behavioral effects of frontal lobe damage in monkeys. The animals showed deficits in learning and memory and other behavioral changes, but the change that most interested Moniz was the animals' marked indifference to stimuli that had previously elicited intense agitation. Moniz shocked Fulton by asking whether it might be possible to alleviate anxiety in man by surgical means. Despite the unfavorable reaction to his question, when Moniz returned to Portugal he performed 20 operations in a 10-week period, with the assistance of his colleague Almeida Lima. Initially, he attempted to use alcohol injections to coagulate or destroy fiber tracts in the frontal lobe. This procedure, however, was abandoned in favor of cutting the fibers with a small device called a *leucotome*. The leucotome consisted of cutting wire inside a thin hollow tube. By pushing in a small handle attached to the wire on one end of the tube, a portion of the wire on the other end could be forced out so as to form a small semicircle. Thus, after inserting the tube in the brain through a burr hole drilled through the skull, the handle could be pushed in, extending the cutting wire. By rotating the tube, a small circle or core could be cut in the brain tissue. Moniz and Lima inserted this device at different angles through two holes drilled in the top frontal portion of the skull. Six circular lesions were made on each side of the frontal cortex (Valenstein, 1973). Moniz claimed that the surgery "cured" seven patients and calmed eight additional patients who were violent and agitated (Chorover, 1974).

This operation became known as a prefrontal leucotomy or prefrontal lobotomy. Moniz performed or supervised only about 100 of these operations. Ironically, he was later paralyzed on one side of his body after being shot by a patient whom he had lobotomized for the purpose of controlling agitated behavior.

In 1936, Walter Freeman and James Watts, who had been in correspondence with Moniz, introduced psychosurgery in the United States. Their surgical procedure, which they called the *precision method,* utilized skull landmarks and X rays in order to gain more precise control over which areas of the frontal lobe were severed. By 1950, Freeman and Watts had performed psychosurgery on over 1000 patients. As psychosurgery became increasingly popular, other techniques for performing surgery on the frontal lobes were developed. In general, however, two types of lobotomy were used: prefrontal and transorbital. Prefrontal techniques involved drilling two burr holes in either the top, side, or front of the skull, through which an instrument could be inserted to sever sections of the frontal lobes. The transorbital lobotomy, first described in Italy in 1937 by Fiamberti, became the technique preferred by Freeman in the United States during the late 1940s. Basically, the leucotome was pushed underneath the eyelid and over the eyeball. It was then tapped through the bony cavity over the eye with a mallet so that it could be inserted in the brain. Fibers at the base of the frontal lobe were severed by swinging the leucotome toward the middle then toward the side. Freeman had practiced the technique on cadavers with an ice pick. The surgical procedure was so simple that it was sometimes performed in the doctor's office rather than in a hospital (Valenstein, 1973).

The effectiveness of frontal lobe surgery was difficult to evaluate, partly because it was hard to recognize side effects that could clearly be attributed to the surgery among severely psychotic, chronically hospitalized patients.

As psychosurgery increased in frequency, not only severely psychotic patients were operated on; psychoneurotics and individuals with psychosomatic complaints were sometimes lobotomized. In fact, Watts eventually ceased to collaborate with Freeman because Freeman seemed to regard transorbital lobotomies as minor surgery appropriate for patients who did not have severe psychological disturbances (Valenstein, 1973). Among these less disabled patients, the side effects of frontal lobe surgery became more and more obvious. Patients were not only calmed, but, in some cases, rendered apathetic, irresponsible, and asocial. Other negative effects included a blunting of intellectual functions, impaired judgment, and reduced creativity (Chorover, 1974). In addition to these undesirable behavioral changes, epileptic seizures were a significant complication, occurring in about 22% of prefrontal lobotomy patients and about 1% of transorbital lobotomy patients. In multiple prefrontal lobotomy cases, the incidence of seizures following surgery increased to 50% (Greenblatt, 1967).

Why was psychosurgery continued despite these serious and permanent side effects? Prior to the introduction of physical treatments and psychotropic medication, hospitalization of psychiatric patients usually meant years of confinement in an institutional setting. Against this background, over 70% of patients who were lobotomized were able to be discharged and about half of this number were either employed or functioning as housewives on follow-up (Freeman, 1957). Although lobotomies did reduce the populations of mental hospitals, Holden (1973) maintains that "they also left an indeterminate number of semi-vegetables in their wake [p. 1109]."

The use of psychosurgery reached a peak during the late 1940s and continued at a high rate until the mid-1950s. Freeman later stated that he had performed or supervised over 3500 prefrontal lobotomies. By the late 1950s, it was estimated that in the United States alone, 40,000 prefrontal lobotomies had been performed. A major reason for the dramatic increase in psychosurgery was that World War II had left many psychiatrically disabled veterans in urgent need of treatment. There was a limited number of trained psychiatrists; effective psychoactive drugs were not yet available; and authorities of the Veterans Administration believed that psychosurgery was effective and encouraged its use (Valenstein, 1973). When psychoactive drugs became available in the late 1950s, prefrontal lobotomies and transorbital leucotomies were discontinued in the United States. Many of the patients lobotomized between the 1940s and mid-1950s are alive today. It would be of interest to have long-range, follow-up information on the psychological adjustment of these individuals.

NEWER FORMS OF PSYCHOSURGERY. Although prefrontal lobotomies are no longer performed, various forms of neurosurgery are, on rare occasions, still used in the treatment of psychiatric disorders. The new procedures involve the use of stereotaxic instrumentation, which allows for much greater surgical precision. The development of stereotaxic brain surgery permits neurosurgeons to make lesions in areas of the brain that were previously inaccessible to surgery. By utilizing three coordinates, with anatomical features of the head as reference points, the surgeon can locate a precise area within the brain. An incision is then made in the scalp and a small burr is drilled through the skull. With the aid of the stereotaxic instrument, an electrode, insulated except for the tip, can be guided into a particular area of the brain. To verify the exact location of the electrode, X rays are used.

After the tip of the electrode is in the desired location, it can serve three functions: (1) recordings of electrical activity of the brain area, (2) electrical stimulation of the area with a weak current, (3) coagulation or destruction of the brain tissue surrounding the tip of the electrode. Recordings of electrical activity might reveal spiking or abnormal activity indicative of a localized disturbance in brain functioning. Electrical stimulations permit the surgeon to observe behavioral responses that presumably are mediated by the particular brain area being stimulated. Both recordings and electrical stimulations may be used as aids in determining whether or not to make a lesion in the area. A lesion can be made by destroying tissue around the tip of the electrode with stronger currents.

Unlike the prefrontal lobotomies performed over two decades ago, the newer forms of psychosurgery involve restricted lesions in various areas of the *limbic system*. The limbic system includes the hippocampus, the hippocampal gyrus, the cingulate gyrus, and deeper connecting structures such as the amygdala, septal nuclei, anterior thalamic nuclei, and hypothalamus (Chorover, 1974). The surgical procedures performed most often include (1) cingulotomy—lesions in the cingulate gyrus, (2) thalamotomy—lesions in the thalamus, and (3) amygdalatomy—lesions in the amygdala (Snodgrass, 1973a).

Cingulotomy. Cingulotomies represent psychosurgery in its purest form because they may be performed for behavioral disorders in persons without any apparent brain pathology (Holden, 1973). A leading proponent of this operation in the United States has been H. T. Ballantine, professor of neurosurgery at Harvard Medical School. Ballantine considered cingulotomies as a safe and effective treatment for disorders of affect that have not responded to any other acceptable forms of treatment. Examples of such disorders are manic-depressive psychosis, obsessive compulsive neurosis, anorexia nervosa, and severe disabling anxiety and tension.

Between 1962 and 1973, Ballantine performed 295 cingulotomies on 207 patients (some were operated on more than once). Thirty-three of these operations were done to relieve intractable pain and 174 were performed for psychiatric reasons. In a follow-up report on 68 of the psychiatric patients, Ballantine stated that 14 were well, 38 were markedly improved, 5 were improved, and 9 showed no change (Snodgrass, 1973b). Although Ballantine, Cassidy, Flanagan, and Marino (1967) report that there are no measurable physical or psychological complications associated with cingulotomies, it is conceivable that less obvious capabilities may be altered. Assessment of potential changes is complicated by the absence of acceptable measures of subtle intellectual or cognitive capacities. The profound losses that eventually were recognized as resulting from prefrontal lobotomies were not initially detected by psychological testing. Various reports, for example, indicated no losses on intelligence test scores, even after extensive prefrontal damage (Valenstein, 1973).

Thalamotomies. Thalamotomies used to be a fairly common surgical procedure for severe, intractable cases of Parkinson's disease. On rare occasions, thalamotomies have been performed to modify aggressiveness and overactivity among hyperactive children.

Unlike cingulotomies, which may be performed for behavioral reasons alone, thalamotomies are usually performed only when a structural defect of the CNS is the suspected cause of the disturbed behavior. A neurosurgeon who has defended the use of thalamotomies for children with "hyperresponsive syndromes" marked by violence and unmanageability is Orlando J. Andy at the University of Mississippi Medical School. Andy has performed 13 or 14 thalamotomies on hyperactive children 6–19 years of age (Chorover, 1974). Most of Andy's patients were children who were wards of the state and institutionalized. According to Andy, all these patients suffered from structural pathology of the brain. Although Andy's motives have not been impugned, his methods of diagnosis, patient selection, and follow-up have been described as too "casual" (Holden, 1973).

A case report by Andy presented before a Senate subcommittee investigating psychosurgery was quoted in full by Chorover (1974):

> A seven-year-old, mentally retarded child had sudden attacks of screaming, yelling, running, and beating the head against the wall. The walls were actually indented by the blows. Following thalamotomy three years ago, the patient did not display the wild, aggressive and screaming behavior. The improved behavior was an enjoyment for both child and the parents [p. 69].

As is true of other psychosurgery procedures, evaluation of the effects of thalamotomies may be hampered by the lack of measures sensitive enough to detect subtle changes. The fact that the surgery usually has been performed on brain-damaged or retarded children further complicates efforts to assess behavioral changes attributable to the surgery.

Amygdalatomy. Amygdalatomies have been performed to control violent behavior, which is presumably associated with abnormalities of the amygdala, a limbic system structure located near the base of the temporal lobe. Like thalamotomies, amygdalatomies are usually performed only when a pathological condition of the brain appears to be indicated by signs of abnormal neurological activity. Signs of abnormality may include a history of temporal lobe epilepsy, abnormal spiking activity recorded from electrodes implanted in the amygdala, and behavior patterns such as hyperexcitability, violent aggressiveness, or assaultive behavior. Although epilepsy and abnormal spiking activity are clearly signs of neurological dysfunction, violence and aggressiveness may result from a number of diverse causes. For this reason, behavioral signs alone are not sufficient evidence for the existence of neurological dysfunction. Vernon Mark, a neurosurgeon who has frequently defended amygdalatomies, has stated that all his patients had brain abnormalities. Over a 10-year period he performed psychosurgical operations on 13 patients who had been diagnosed as epileptics and had a history of violent behavior (Snodgrass, 1973a). However, Peter Breggin, a psychiatrist and outspoken critic of psychosurgery, has maintained that in many cases no real evidence of brain abnormalities exists. In particular cases, he has argued that relatively successful individuals have been essentially destroyed by psychosurgery. He has alluded to the possibility of psychosurgery being performed for political reasons or to repress and "vegetabilize" helpless individuals such as prisoners and minority groups (Holden, 1973).

A well-publicized example of a case that illustrates the controversy over psychosurgery is that of Thomas R. (not the real name or initial). Vernon Mark and Frank Ervin introduced the case in their book called *Violence and the Brain* (1970). In 1967, Vernon Mark performed a bilateral amygdalatomy on Thomas

R. According to Mark (1974), the procedure was successful in stopping violent rage attacks even though seizures and thought disorders continued.

Breggin, who read the records of Thomas R. and interviewed him, his family, and relevant professionals, maintains that nearly all Thomas R.'s serious problems are a direct result of psychosurgery. According to Breggin (1973), prior to surgery Thomas R. "had worked as an engineer, had never required psychiatric hospitalization or restraint, and never had a diagnosis more serious than 'personality pattern disturbance.' All the hospital records clearly relate his personal disaster to surgery [p. 1121]." Since surgery, says Breggin (1973), Thomas R. "has been almost continuously hospitalized, carries a diagnosis of brain damage and schizophrenia with a poor prognosis, is chronically deluded and hallucinated, lives in constant terror that the surgeons will again control his mind, and is frequently so violent that he requires sedation, a locked ward, and even restraints [p. 1121]."

Mark's account, however, is quite different from Breggin's. Mark (1974) states that Thomas R. was a temporal lobe epileptic with localized cerebral atrophy, rage attacks, and occasional thought disorders. Prior to surgery, says Mark, the patient's records showed 15 years of episodic hallucinations and on at least one occasion he had been committed to a locked ward. In addition, he had had 3 years of psychotherapy and 2 years of anticonvulsant medication. According to Mark, there were no further rage attacks or epileptic seizures for 4 years after the patient's surgery.

The case of Thomas R. is not the only case that has resulted in conflicting accounts by Breggin and Mark. Another patient discussed in *Violence and the Brain* is Julia. Mark reports that an amygdalatomy ended her violent episodes and sometimes dangerous assaultive behavior. Julia, the daughter of a physician, suffered seizures following encephalitis at the age of 18 months. She dropped out of high school in her junior year at age 20. Her records include a long history of periodic violent episodes and 12 major attacks on other persons. The most serious attack occurred when Julia was 18. While waiting for her parents in the lounge of a movie theater, she looked at a mirror and perceived the left side of her face and part of her body as shriveled, disfigured, and evil—a delusion that may have signaled the onset of a psychomotor seizure. Another girl entered the room and accidently bumped Julia's left arm. Julia panicked, drew a knife and stabbed the girl with sufficient force to penetrate her heart. Fortunately, the girl survived. In another assault, also possibly occurring during a psychomotor seizure, she stabbed a nurse in the chest with a pair of scissors. The nurse also recovered.

When Julia was 21, EEG records obtained from electrodes implanted in the amygdala revealed abnormal activity in the posterior amygdala in the right temporal lobe. On one occasion, a burst of abnormal spike-like epileptic activity and violent aggressive behavior followed electrical stimulation of the area.

When surgery was performed, a lesion was made in the right amygdala. Following surgery, the epileptic seizures and psychotic episodes continued. During the first year, there were two mild rage episodes (Valenstein, 1973). More recent reports were that Julia was living at home with her parents, had attended adult education classes, passed her high school equivalency test, and was singing in a choir (Mark, 1974; Snodgrass, 1973a).

In contrast to this account, Breggin states that Julia was "completely destroyed" by surgery. Prior to surgery, he says, Julia was a beautiful 19-year-old honors student whose father was upset by her occasional temper tantrums. He offers as partial evidence a letter from a nurse who stated she was "sick" about what happend to Julia. The nurse lamented that Julia's interest in music and fondness for playing the guitar were no longer evident after surgery.

It is difficult to evaluate such conflicting accounts as those presented by Mark and Breggin. As Valenstein (1973) suggests, it is hard for most professionals to be objective about psychosurgery—either they are flatly opposed to all psychosurgery or they are very defensive about its use, particularly if they are neurosurgeons who have performed such procedures. Neurosurgeons generally focus on the effectiveness of amygdalatomies in controlling violent or aggressive episodes. Although violent episodes may be reduced in some patients, there are also undesirable changes associated with amygdalatomies. Valenstein (1973) quotes the following observations of 15 amygdalatomized patients by Ruth Anderson, a psychologist:

> Typically the patient tends to become more inert, and shows less zest and intensity of emotions. His spontaneous activity tends to be reduced and he becomes less capable of creative productivity, which is independent of the intelligence level. . . .
>
> With these changes in initiative and control of behavior, our patients resemble those with frontal lesions. It must be pointed out, however, that the changes are very discrete and there is no evidence of serious disturbances in the establishment and execution of their major plans of action [p. 231].

Although only a few amygdalatomies have been performed each year in the United States, the procedure, widely publicized by the book *Violence and the Brain,* has resulted in professional controversy, attention in national media, and congressional investigations regarding all forms of psychosurgery (Snodgrass, 1973b). What has emerged is a strong opposition to any type of psychosurgery in the United States. According to Breggin (1973), this opposition has produced the following consequences:

> . . . all federal funding of psychosurgery has been stopped; state funded projects in California, Missouri, Oregon, Michigan, and Virginia have been called off; a number of professional groups, including the American Orthopsychiatric Association and the Medical Committee on Human Rights, have criticized psychosurgery; neurologist Robert Grimm has written a brief against psychosurgery for the American Civil Liberties Union; and a three-judge panel in Michigan has declared psychosurgery unconstitutional in the state hospitals [p. 1121].

In summary, the newer forms of psychosurgery involving stereotaxic instrumentation have generated considerable controversy. Major procedures include cingulotomies, which have been performed for behavioral reasons alone, and thalamotomies and amygdalatomies, which have been used to modify behavior that presumably is a result of a pathological condition of the brain. Despite the attention devoted to psychosurgery, very few operations are performed each year. Still, psychosurgery is permanent and irreversible. It is always possible that a new drug may be developed that may be more beneficial and have less potentially disastrous side effects. Such was the case when the antipsychotic drugs terminated a decade of over 40,000 irreversible prefrontal lobotomies.

Summary

Medical treatments were presented in two parts, the first on psychotropic drugs and the second on physical treatments. The major form of medical treatment currently used for psychiatric disorders is psychotropic drugs. Psychotropic drugs were categorized as (1) antipsychotic agents, (2) lithium carbonate, (3) antidepressant agents, (4) antianxiety agents, (5) sedatives and hypnotics, (6) stimulants, (7) narcotics, and (8) other drugs.

The introduction of the antipsychotic drugs in the late 1950s revolutionized the treatment of mental patients and led to a marked decline in the use of physical treatments such as psychosurgery. The major class of antipsychotic drugs is the phenothiazines, the use of which has led to a substantial reduction in the number of chronically hospitalized mental patients.

Lithium carbonate represents one of the most recent advances in the treatment of manic states and manic-depressive disorders. Regular use of lithium carbonate also serves to prevent recurrence of manic and depressive episodes.

Antidepressant drugs have been shown to be effective in the treatment of depression and have resulted in a decline of the use of electroconvulsive therapy (ECT).

The two most commonly used antianxiety drugs are chlordiazepoxide (Librium) and diazepam (Valium). Despite widespread use of these drugs in medical practice, there is a lack of sound research that could provide convincing evidence that they are effective.

Sedatives and hypnotics are frequently prescribed for patients who complain of anxiety and insomnia. The value of this class of drugs is offset by the risk of addiction. The barbiturates are the most widely used of the hypnotic–sedative drugs; they are also the second leading method of suicide in the United States.

The remaining categories (stimulants, narcotics, and other drugs) are seldom used in the practice of psychiatry.

The use of physical treatments in psychiatry has shown a notable decline. The most frequent form of physical treatment in use today is ECT. The primary use of ECT is in the treatment of depression. In some situations, such as the first trimester of pregnancy or where quick return to social functioning is important, ECT is preferred to antidepressant drugs.

Prefrontal lobotomies were performed on as many as 40,000 patients between the early 1940s and late 1950s. The introduction of the phenothiazines led to their discontinuation. However, newer forms of psychosurgery, involving stereotaxic instrumentation, are still used on rare occasions to modify behavior. Various areas of the limbic system are the primary targets of the few neurosurgeons who perform these operations. Despite the rarity of their use, the newer forms of psychosurgery have been the object of much controversy, among both professionals and the general public.

References

Aarons, L. Evoked sleep-talking. *Perceptual and Motor Skills,* 1970, *31,* 27–40.

Abe, K., & Shimakawa, M. Genetic–constitutional factors and childhood insomnia. *Psychiatria et Neurologia,* 1966, *152,* 363–369.

Abel, G., Barlow, D., Blanchard, E., & Guild, D. *The components of rapist's sexual arousal.* Paper presented at the 128th annual meeting of the American Psychiatric Association, Anaheim, California, May 5, 1975.

Abraham, S., & Nordsieck, M. Relationship of excess weight in children and adults. *Public Health Report,* 1960, *75,* 263.

Absee, D. W. *Hysteria and related mental disorders.* Bristol, England: Wright, 1966.

Achenbach, T. M. The classification of children's psychiatric symptoms: A factor-analytic study. *Psychological Monographs,* 1966, *80,* 6.

Ackerman, N. *The psychodynamics of family life.* New York: Basic Books, 1958.

Ackerson, L. *Children's behavior problems.* Chicago: University of Chicago Press, 1931.

Ackner, B. Depersonalization, I. Aetiology and phenomenology. *Journal of Mental Science,* 1954, *100,* 838–853.

Agate, J. *The practice of geriatrics.* Springfield, Ill.: Charles C Thomas, 1970.

Agnew, H. W., Jr., Webb, W. B., & Williams, R. L. Comparison of stage four and 1-REM sleep deprivation. *Perceptual and Motor Skills,* 1967, *24,* 851–858.

Ainsworth, M. D. *Deprivation of maternal care: A reassessment of its effects* (Public Health Paper No. 14). Geneva: World Health Organization, 1962.

Akiskal, H. S., & McKinney, W. T., Jr. Depressive disorders: Toward a unified hypothesis. *Science,* 1973, *182,* 20–29.

Albee, G. W. The relation of conceptual models to manpower needs. In E. L. Cowen, E. A. Gardner, & M. Zax (Eds.), *Emergent approaches to mental health problems.* New York: Appleton-Century-Crofts, 1967.

Albee, G. W. Models, myths, and manpower. *Mental Hygiene,* 1968, *52,* 168–180.

Alexander, F. *Psychosomatic medicine.* New York: Norton, 1950.

Alexander, F., & French, T. M. *Psychoanalytic therapy.* New York: Ronald Press, 1946.

Alexander, F., & French, T. M. *Studies in psychosomatic medicine.* New York: Ronald Press, 1948.

Alexander, F., French, T. M., & Pollock, G. H. *Psychosomatic specificity.* Chicago: University of Chicago Press, 1968.

Alexander, F. G., & Selesnick, S. T. *The history of psychiatry: An evaluation of psychiatric thought and practice from prehistoric times to the present.* New York: Harper & Row, 1966.

Allen, K. E., Hart, B. M., Buell, J. S., Harris, F. R., & Wolf, M. M. Effects of social reinforcement on isolate behavior of a nursery school child. *Child Development,* 1964, *35,* 511–518.

Allen, K. E., Henke, L. B., Harris, F. R., Baer, D. M., & Reynolds, N. J. Control of hyperactivity by social reinforcement of attending behavior. *Journal of Educational Psychology,* 1967, *58,* 231–237.

Allen, R. C. Abolition of the insanity defense. In R. C. Allen, E. Z. Ferster, & J. G. Rubin (Eds.), *Readings in law and psychiatry* (rev. ed.). Baltimore: Johns Hopkins, 1975.

Allen, R. C., Ferster, E. Z., & Rubin, J. G. (Eds.), *Readings in law and psychiatry* (rev. ed.). Baltimore: Johns Hopkins, 1975.

Alsted, G. *The changing incidence of peptic ulcer.* London: Oxford University Press, 1934.

Altrocchi, J., Spielberger, C. D., & Eisdorfer, C. Mental health consultation with groups. *Community Mental Health Journal,* 1965, *1,* 127–134.

American Law Institute. Model penal code, 1962, proposed official draft. In R. C. Allen, E. Z. Ferster, & J. G. Rubin (Eds.), *Readings in law and psychiatry* (rev. ed.). Baltimore: Johns Hopkins, 1975.

American Medical Association. Mental retardation: A handbook for the primary physician. (Report of the American Medical Association Conference on Mental Retardation, Chicago, April 9 to 11, 1964). *Journal of the American Medical Association,* 1965, *191,* (3), 183–231.

American Psychiatric Association. *The diagnostic and statistical manual of mental disorders* (2nd ed.). Washington, D.C.: American Psychiatric Association, 1968.

Ames, L. B. Sleep and dreams in children. In E. Horms (Ed.), *Problems of sleep and dreams in children.* New York: Macmillan, 1964.

Anderson, W. F. *Practical management of the elderly.* Philadelphia: Davis, 1967.

Anthony, J. E. An experimental approach to the psychopathology of childhood encopresis. In S. I. Harrison & J. F. McDermott, *Childhood psychopathology.* New York: International Universities Press, 1972.

Anthony, W. A., Buell, G. J., Sharratt, S., & Althoff, M. E. Efficacy of psychiatric rehabilitation. *Psychological Bulletin,* 1972, *78,* 447–456.

Arena, J. M. *Poisoning: Chemistry, symptoms, treatments.* Springfield, Ill.: Charles C Thomas, 1963.

Aring, J., & Trufant, S. A. Effects of heavy metals on the central nervous system. In H. H. Merritt & C. C. Hare (Eds.), *Metabolic and toxic diseases of the nervous system: Proceedings of the association.* Baltimore: Williams & Wilkins, 1953.

Arkin, A. M. Sleep-talking: A review. *Journal of Nervous and Mental Disorders,* 1966, *143,* 101–122.

Aronson, J. *Psychopathological disorders in childhood.* New York: Group for the Advancement of Psychiatry, 1974.

Aserinsky, E., & Kleitman, N. Regularly occurring periods of eye motility and concomitant phenomena during sleep. *Science,* 1953, *118,* 273–274.

Aserinsky, E., & Kleitman, N. Two types of ocular motility occurring in sleep. *Journal of Applied Physiology,* 1955, *8,* 1–10.

Atkinson, R. C., Bower, G. H., & Crothers, E. J. *An introduction to mathematical learning theory.* New York: Wiley, 1965.

Atthowe, J. J. Token economies come of age. *Behavior Therapy,* 1973, *4,* 646–654.

Averill, J. R. Personal control over aversive stimuli and its relationship to stress. *Psychological Bulletin,* 1973, *80,* 286–303.

Aviado, D. M. Ganglionic stimulant and blocking drugs. In J. R. DiPalma (Ed.), *Drill's pharmacology in medicine* (4th ed.). New York: McGraw-Hill, 1971.

Ax, A. F. The physiological differentiation between fear and anger in humans. *Psychosomatic Medicine,* 1953, *15,* 433–442.

Ayllon, T., & Azrin, N. H. The measurement of reinforcement of behavior of psychotics. *Journal of the Experimental Analysis of Behavior,* 1965, *8,* 357–383.

Ayllon, T., & Azrin, N. H. The token economy: *A motivational system for therapy and rehabilitation.* New York: Appleton-Century-Crofts, 1968.

Ayllon, T., Haughton, E., & Hughes, H. B. Interpretation of symptoms: Fact or fiction. *Behaviour Research and Therapy,* 1965, *3,* 1–7.

Ayllon, T., Layman, D., & Kandel, H. A behavioral–educational alternative to drug control of hyperactive children. *Journal of Applied Behavior Analysis*, 1975, *8*, 137–146.

Azrin, N. H., Naster, B. J., & Jones, R. Reciprocity counseling: A rapid learning-based procedure for marital counseling. *Behaviour Research and Therapy*, 1973, *11*, 365–382.

Azrin, N. H., & Powell, J. Behavioral engineering: The reduction of smoking behavior by a conditioning apparatus and procedure. *Journal of Applied Behavior Analysis*, 1968, *1*, 193–200.

Azrin, N. H., Sneed, T. J., & Foxx, R. M. Dry bed: A rapid method of eliminating bedwetting (enuresis) of the retarded. *Behaviour Research and Therapy*, 1973, *11*, 435–442.

Azrin, N. H., Sneed, T. J., & Foxx, R. M. Dry-bed training: Rapid elimination of childhood enuresis. *Behaviour Research and Therapy*, 1974, *12*, 147–156.

Baastrup, P. C., & Schou, M. Lithium as a prophylactic agent: Its effects against recurrent depression and manic-depressive psychosis. *Archives of General Psychiatry*, 1967, *16*, 167–172.

Baba Ram Dass. *Remember Be Here Now*. San Cristobel, N.M.: Lama Foundation, 1971.

Bacon, H. E. *Ulcerative colitis*. Philadelphia: Lippincott, 1958.

Baekeland, F., & Lasky, R. Exercise and sleep patterns in college athletes. *Perceptual and Motor Skills*, 1966, *23*, 1203–1207.

Baer, D. M., Peterson, R. F., & Sherman, J. A. The development of imitation by reinforcing behavioral similarity to a model. *Journal of the Experimental Analysis of Behavior*, 1967, *10*, 405–416.

Bahn, A. K. An outline for community mental health research. *Community Mental Health Journal*, 1965, *1*, 23–28.

Bakan, D. Suicide and the method of introspection. *Journal of Existential Psychiatry*, 1962, *2*, 313–322.

Bakwin, H. Sleep walking in twins. *Lancet, 1970, 2*, 446.

Bakwin, H., & Bakwin, R. M. *Clinical management of behavior disorders in children*. Philadelphia and London: Saunders, 1966.

Bakwin, H., & Bakwin, R. M. *Behavior disorders in children* (4th ed.). Philadelphia: Saunders, 1972.

Ballantine, H. T., Cassidy, W. L., Flanagan, N. B., & Marino, R. Stereotaxic anterior cingulotomy for neuropsychiatric illness and intractable pain. *Journal of Neurosurgery*, 1967, *26*, 488–495.

Bancroft, J. A comparative study of aversion and desensitization in the treatment of homosexuality. In L. E. Burns & J. L. Worsley (Eds.), *Behavior therapy in the 1970's*. Bristol: Wright, 1970.

Bancroft, J. The application of psychophysiological measures to the assessment and modification of sexual behavior. *Behaviour Research and Therapy*, 1971, *9*, 119–130.

Bandura, A. Vicarious processes: A case of no-trial learning. In L. Berkowitz (Ed.), *Advances in experimental social psychology* (Vol. 2). New York: Academic Press, 1965.

Bandura, A. *Principles of behavior modification*. New York: Holt, Rinehart and Winston, 1969.

Bandura, A. Psychotherapy based on modeling principles. In A. E. Bergin & S. L. Garfield (Eds.), *Handbook of psychotherapy and behavior change*. New York: Wiley, 1971.

Bandura, A., Blanchard, E. B., & Ritter, R. The relative efficacy of desensitization and modeling approaches for inducing behavioral, affective, and attitudinal changes. *Journal of Personality and Social Psychology*, 1969, *13*, 173–199.

Bandura, A., Grusec, J. E., & Menlove, F. L. Vicarious extinction of avoidance behavior. *Journal of Personality and Social Psychology*, 1967, *5*, 16–23.

Bandura, A., Jeffery, R. W., & Wright, C. L. Efficacy of participant modeling as a function of response induction aids. *Journal of Abnormal Psychology*, 1974, *83*, 56–64.

Bandura, A., & Menlove, F. L. Factors determining vicarious extinction of avoidance behavior through symbolic modeling. *Journal of Personality and Social Psychology*, 1968, *8*, 99–108.

Bandura, A., & Perloff, B. Relative efficacy of self-monitored and externally imposed reinforcement systems. *Journal of Personality and Social Psychology*, 1967, *7*, 111–116.

Bandura, A., & Rosenthal, T. L. Vicarious classical conditioning as a function of arousal level. *Journal of Personality and Social Psychology*, 1966, *3*, 54–62.

Bandura, A., & Walters, R. H. *Adolescent aggression*. New York: Ronald Press, 1959.

Barber, T. X. *LSD, marihuana, yoga, and hypnosis*. Chicago: Aldine, 1970.

Barber, T. X. Suggested ("hypnotic") behavior: The trance paradigm versus an alternative paradigm.

In E. Fromm & R. E. Shor (Eds.), *Hypnosis: Research and perspectives.* Chicago: Aldine–Atherton, 1972.

Barber, T. X., & DeMoor, W. A theory of hypnotic induction procedures. *American Journal of Clinical Hypnosis,* 1972, *15,* 112–135.

Barber, T. X., Spanos, N. P., & Chaves, J. F. *Hypnosis, imagination, and human potential.* New York: Pergamon, 1974.

Bard, M. The role of law enforcement in the helping system. *Community Mental Health Journal,* 1971, *7,* 151–160.

Barker, W., & Perlman, D. Volunteer bias and personality traits in sexual standards research. *Archives of Sexual Behavior,* 1975, *4,* 161–170.

Barlow, D. Increasing heterosexual responsiveness in the treatment of sexual deviation: A review of the clinical and experimental evidence. *Behavior Therapy,* 1973, *4,* 655–671.

Barlow, D., & Agras, W. S. Fading to increase heterosexual responsiveness in homosexuals. *Journal of Applied Behavior Analysis,* 1973, *6,* 355–366.

Barlow, D., Becker, R., Leitenberg, H., & Agras, W. S. A mechanical strain gauge for recording penile circumference change. *Journal of Applied Behavior Analysis,* 1970, *3,* 73–76.

Barlow, D., Leitenberg, H., & Agras, W. S. Experimental control of sexual deviation through manipulation of the noxious scene in covert sensitization. *Journal of Abnormal Psychology,* 1969, *74,* 596–601.

Barlow, D., Reynolds, J., & Agras, W. S. Gender identity change in a transsexual. *Archives of General Psychiatry,* 1973, *28,* 569–576.

Baron, J. H. Aetiology. In C. Wastell (Ed.), *Chronic duodenal ulcer.* New York: Appleton-Century-Crofts, 1972.

Baron, J. H., & Wastell, C. Medical treatment. In C. Wastell (Ed.), *Chronic duodenal ulcer.* New York: Appleton-Century-Crofts, 1972.

Barraclough, B. M., Nelson, B., Bunch, J., & Sainsbury, P. The diagnostic classification and psychiatric treatment of 100 suicides. *Proceedings of the Fifth International Conference for Suicide Prevention,* London, 1969.

Barrett, C. L. Systematic desensitization versus implosive therapy. *Journal of Abnormal Psychology,* 1969, *74,* 587–592.

Barrett-Lennard, G. T. *Dimensions of the client's experience of his therapist associated with personality change.* Unpublished doctoral dissertation, University of Chicago, 1959.

Barron, D. Intuition as a response to patient potential. *Journal of Existential Psychiatry,* 1961, *5,* 237–242.

Barron, D. Fundamental aspects of Kaiserian-oriented psychotherapy. *International Forum for Existential Psychiatry,* 1967, *6,* 58–73.

Barrow, L., & Fabing, D. *Epilepsy and the law* (rev. 2nd ed.). New York: Harper & Row, 1966. (Originally published, 1956.)

Barton, A. *Three worlds of therapy.* Palo Alto: National Press Books, 1974.

Basaglia, F. Silence in the dialogue with the psychotic. *Journal of Existentialism,* 1965, *6,* 99–102.

Basescu, S. Human nature and psychotherapy: An existential view. *Review of Existential Psychology and Psychiatry,* 1962, *2,* 149–158.

Batchelor, I. R. C. *Henderson and Gillespie's textbook of psychiatry.* London: Oxford University Press, 1969.

Bates, H. D. Factorial structure and MMPI correlates of a fear survey schedule in a clinical population. *Behaviour Research and Therapy,* 1971, *9,* 355–360.

Bateson, G. Minimal requirements for a theory of schizophrenia. *Archives of General Psychiatry,* 1960, *2,* 477–491.

Baudelaire, C. *Artificial paradises, on hashish and wine as means of expanding individuality.* New York: Herder & Herder, 1971. (Originally published, 1858.)

Bauman, E., & Murray, D. J. Recognition versus recall in schizophrenia. *Canadian Journal of Psychology,* 1968, *22,* 18–25.

Beam, J. C. Serial learning and conditioning under real life stress. *Journal of Abnormal and Social Psychology,* 1955, *51,* 543–551.

Beck, A. T. A systematic investigation of depression. *Comprehensive Psychiatry,* 1961, *2,* 162–170.

Beck, A. T. Reliability of psychiatric diagnosis: A critique of systematic studies. *American Journal of Psychiatry*, 1962, *119*, 210–216.

Beck, A. T. *Depression: Causes and treatment*. Philadelphia: University of Pennsylvania Press, 1967. (a)

Beck, A. T. *Depression: Clinical, experimental, and theoretical aspects*. New York: Harper & Row, 1967. (b)

Beck, A. T., & Hurvich, M. S. Psychological correlates of depression. 1. Frequency of "masochistic" dream content in a private practice sample. *Psychosomatic Medicine*, 1959, *21*, 50–55.

Beck, A. T., & Lester, D. Components of depression in attempted suicides. *Journal of Psychology*, 1973, *85*, 257–260.

Beck, A. T., & Ward, C. H. Dreams of depressed patients: Characteristic themes in manifest content. *Archives of General Psychiatry*, 1961, *5*, 462–467.

Beck, A. T., Ward, C. H., Mendelson, M., Mock, J. E., & Erbaugh, J. K. Reliability of psychiatric diagnoses: 2. A study of consistency of clinical judgements and ratings. *American Journal of Psychiatry*, 1962, *119*, 351–357.

Becker, J. *Depression: Research and theory*. New York: Halstead, 1974. (a)

Becker, J. *Depression: Theory and research*. New York: Wiley, 1974. (b)

Beers, C. W. *A mind that found itself*. New York: Doubleday, 1953.

Beets, N. Ego-psychology and the meeting face-to-face in psychotherapy. *Review of Existential Psychology and Psychiatry*, 1967, *7*, 72–94.

Begab, M. J., Foreword in J. Grossman (Ed.), *Manual on terminology and classification in mental retardation*. Baltimore: Garamond/Pridemark Press, 1973.

Bell, J. E. *Family group therapy* (U.S. Public Health Service Monograph No. 64). Washington, D.C.: U.S. Government Printing Office, 1961.

Bellak, L., & Small, L. *Emergency psychotherapy and brief psychotherapy*. New York: Grune & Stratton, 1965.

Benda, C. E. *Developmental disorders of mentation and cerebral palsies*. New York: Gruen & Stratton, 1952.

Benedict, R. *Patterns of culture*. Boston: Houghton Mifflin, 1934.

Beneke, W. M., & Harris, M. B. Teaching self-control of study behavior. *Behavior Research and Therapy*, 1972, *10*, 35–41.

Bennett, C. C., Anderson, L. S. Cooper, S., Hassol, L., Klein, D. C., & Rosenblum, G. *Community psychology: A report of the Boston Conference on the Education of Psychologists for Community Mental Health*. Boston: Boston University, 1966.

Benson, H., Shapiro, D., Tursky, B., & Schwartz, G. E. Decreased systolic blood pressure through operant conditioning techniques in patients with essential hypertension. *Science*, 1971, *173*, 740–742.

Berde, B. New studies on the circulatory effects of ergot compounds with implications to migraine. In J. N. Cumings (Ed.), *Background to migraine*, Fourth Migraine Symposium Sept. 11, 1970. New York: Springer-Verlag, 1971.

Berger, R. J., Olley, P., & Oswald, I. The EEG eye movements and dreams of the blind. *Quarterly Journal of Experimental Psychology*, 1962, *14*, 183–186.

Berger, R. J., & Oswald, I. Effects of sleep deprivation on behavior, subsequent sleep, and dreaming. *Journal of Mental Science*, 1962, *108*, 457–465.

Bergin, A. E. Some implications of psychotherapy research for therapeutic practice. *Journal of Abnormal Psychology*, 1966, *71*, 235–246.

Bergin, A. E. The evaluation of therapeutic outcomes. In A. E. Bergin & S. L. Garfield (Eds.), *Handbook of psychotherapy and behavior change*. New York: Wiley, 1971.

Bernstein, A. S. Electrodermal base level, tonic arousal and adaptation in chronic schizophrenics. *Journal of Abnormal Psychology*, 1967, *73*, 221–232.

Bernstein, A. S. Phasic electrodermal orienting response in chronic schizophrenics: II. Response to auditory signals of varying intensity. *Journal of Abnormal Psychology*, 1970, *75*, 146–156.

Bernstein, D. A. Modification of smoking behavior: An evaluative review. *Psychological Bulletin*, 1969, *71*, 418–440.

Bettelheim, B. *The empty fortress*. New York: Free Press, 1967.

Beukenkamp, C. Meaning as structure in psychotherapy. *International Forum for Existential Psychiatry*, 1967, *1*, 473–479.

Bijou, S. W. Theory and research in mental (developmental) retardation. *Psychological Record,* 1963, *13,* 95–110.

Bijou, S. W. The mentally retarded child. *Psychology Today,* June 1968, pp. 46–51.

Binswanger, L. The case of Ellen West. In R. May, E. Angel, & H. F. Ellenberger (Eds.), *Existence: A new dimension in psychology and psychiatry.* New York: Basic Books, 1958.

Binswanger, L. Introduction to schizophrenia. In J. Needleman (Ed.), *Being-in-the-world: Selected papers of Ludwig Binswanger.* New York: Basic Books, 1963.

Bion, W. R. *Experiences in groups and other papers.* London and New York: Tavistock and Basic Books, 1961.

Bishop, M. P., Elder, S. T., & Heath, R. G. Attempted control of operant behavior in man with intracranial self-stimulation. In R. G. Heath (Ed.), *The role of pleasure in behavior.* New York: Harper & Row, 1964.

Bitterman, M., & Holtzman, W. Conditioning and extinction of the galvanic skin response as a function of anxiety. *Journal of Abnormal and Social Psychology,* 1952, *47,* 615–623.

Blake, B. G. The application of behavior therapy to the treatment of alcoholism. *Behaviour Research and Therapy,* 1965, *3,* 75–85.

Blanchard, E. B. Brief flooding treatment for a debilitating revulsion. *Behaviour Research and Therapy,* 1975, *13,* 193–195.

Blanchard, E. B., & Young, L. D. Self-control of cardiac functioning: A promise as yet unfulfilled. *Psychological Bulletin,* 1973, *79,* 145–163.

Blanchard, E. B., Young, L. D., & Haynes, M. R. A simple feedback system for the treatment of elevated blood pressure. *Behavior Therapy,* 1975, *6,* 241–245.

Blashfield, R. An evaluation of the DSM-II Classification of Schizophrenia as a nomenclature. *Journal of Abnormal Psychology,* 1973, *82,* 382–389.

Bleuler, E. *Dementia praecox oder die Gruppe der Schizophrenien.* Leipzig: Deuticke, 1911.

Bliss, E. L., & Branch, C. H. *Anorexia nervosa,* New York: Paul B. Hoeber, 1960.

Bloom, B. L. Mental health program evaluation. In S. E. Golann & C. Eisdorfer (Eds.), *Handbook of community mental health.* New York: Appleton-Century-Crofts, 1972.

Bloom, B. L. *Community mental health: A historical and critical analysis.* Morristown, N.J.: General Learning Press, 1973.

Blum, R., Braunstein, L., & Stone, A. Normal drug use: An exploratory study of patterns and correlates. In J. Cole & J. Wittenborn (Eds.), *Drug abuse.* Springfield, Ill.: Charles C Thomas, 1969.

Blumberg, S., & Giller, D. W. Some verbal aspects of primary-process thought: A partial replication. *Journal of Personality and Social Psychology,* 1965, *1,* 517–520.

Bockoven, J. S. *Moral treatment in American psychiatry.* New York: Springer, 1963.

Bockoven, J. S. *Moral treatment in community mental health.* New York: Springer, 1972.

Bolles, R. C. *Theory of motivation* (2nd ed.). New York: Harper & Row, 1975.

Bond, I., & Hutchison, H. Application of reciprocal inhibition therapy to exhibitionism. *The Canadian Medical Association Journal,* 1960, *83,* 23–25.

Bond, P. A., Jenner, F. A., & Sampson, G. A. Daily variations of the urine content of 3-methoxy-4-hydroxyphenylglycol in two manic-depressive patients. *Psychological Medicine.* 1972, *2,* 81–85.

Bootzin, R. *Stimulus control of insomnia.* Paper presented at the meeting of the American Psychological Association, Montreal, August 1973.

Borkovec, T. D. Effects of expectancy on the outcome of systematic desensitization and implosive treatments for analogue anxiety. *Behavior Therapy,* 1972, *3,* 29–40.

Borkovec, T. D., Kaloupek, D. G., & Slama, K. M. The facilitative effect of muscle tension-release in the relaxation treatment of sleep disturbance. *Behavior Therapy,* 1975, *6,* 301–309.

Boshes, L. D., & Gibbs, A. *Epilepsy handbook* (2nd ed.). Springfield, Ill.: Charles C Thomas, 1972.

Boss, M. *The analysis of dreams.* London: Ryder, 1957.

Boss, M. The impact of daseinsanalysis on traditional psychoanalytic techniques. In M. Boss *Psychoanalysis and daseinsanalysis.* New York: Basic Books, 1963. (a)

Boss, M. *Psychoanalysis and daseinsanalysis.* New York: Basic Books, 1963. (b)

Boudin, H. M. Contingency contracting as a therapeutic tool in the deceleration of amphetamine use. *Behavior Therapy*, 1972, *3*, 604–608.

Boulougouris, J., Marks, I. M., & Marset, P. Superiority of flooding (implosion) to desensitization for reducing pathological fear. *Behaviour Research and Therapy*, 1971, *9*, 7–16.

Bourjaily, V. *Confessions of a spent youth.* New York: The Dial Press, 1960.

Bowen, M. Family psychotherapy. *American Journal of Orthopsychiatry*, 1961, *31*, 42–60.

Bower, E. M. Primary prevention of mental and emotional disorders: A conceptual framework and action possibilities. *American Journal of Orthopsychiatry*, 1963, *33*, 832–848.

Bower, G. H. *Mental imagery and memory.* Colloquium, Arizona State University, Tempe, Arizona, May 1967.

Bower, G. H., Clark, M. C., Lesgold, A. M., & Winenz, D. Hierarchical retrieval schemes in recall of categorized word lists. *Journal of Verbal Learning and Verbal Behavior*, 1969, *8*, 323–343.

Bowlby, J. Grief and mourning in infancy and early childhood. *Psychoanalytic Study of the Child*, 1960, *15*, 9–52.

Braaten, L. J. Tillich and the art of healing. *Journal of Existential Psychiatry*, 1963, *4*, 3–14.

Brady, J. P., & Lind, D. L. Experimental analysis of hysterical blindness. *Archives of General Psychiatry*, 1961, *4*, 331–339.

Braginsky, B. M., & Braginsky, D. D. Schizophrenic patients in the psychiatric interview: An experimental study of their effectiveness at manipulation. *Journal of Consulting Psychology*, 1967, *31*, 543–547.

Braginsky, B. M., Braginsky, D. D., & Ring, K. *Methods of madness: The mental hospital as a last resort.* New York: Holt, 1969.

Braginsky, B. M., Grosse, M., & Ring, K. Controlling outcomes through impression management: An experimental study of the manipulative tactics of mental patients. *Journal of Consulting Psychology*, 1966, *30*, 295–300.

Brandon, S. *An epidemiological study of maladjustment in childhood.* Unpublished M.D. thesis, University of Durham, England, 1960.

Brawley, E. R., Harris, F. R., Allen, K. E., Fleming, R. S., & Peterson, R. F. Behavior modification of an autistic child. *Behavioral Science*, 1969, *14*, 87–97.

Brecher, E. M., & the Editors of *Consumer Reports*. *Licit and illicit drugs.* Boston: Little, Brown, 1972.

Brecher, E. M., & the Editors of *Consumer Reports*. Marijuana: The health questions. *Consumer Reports*, 1975, *40*, 143–150. (a)

Brecher, E. M., & the Editors of *Consumer Reports*. Marijuana: The legal question. *Consumer Reports*, 1975, *40*, 265–266. (b)

Brecher, R., & Brecher, E. (Eds.). *An analysis of human sexual response.* New York: New American Library, 1966.

Breggin, P. R. Psychosurgery (letter to the editor). *Journal of the American Medical Association*, 1973, *226* (9), 1121.

Brehm, M., & Beck, K. Self image and attitudes toward drugs. *Journal of Personality*, 1968, *36*, 299–314.

Breuer, J., & Freud, S. *Studies in hysteria.* New York: Avon Books, 1966.

Brill, H., & Patton, R. E. Analysis of population reduction in New York State mental hospitals during the first four years of large scale therapy with psychotropic drugs. *American Journal of Psychiatry*, 1959, *116*, 495–508.

Brock, L. D. *The efficacy of various extinction procedures on a conditioned avoidance response in humans: An experimental analogue.* Unpublished doctoral dissertation, Southern Illinois University, 1967.

Brodsky, C. M. Rape at work. In M. J. Walker & S. L. Brodsky (Eds.), *Sexual assault: The victim and the rapist.* Lexington, Mass.: Lexington Books (D. C. Heath), 1976.

Brodsky, S. L. *Psychologists in the criminal justice system.* Urbana: University of Illinois Press, 1973.

Brodsky, S. L. Sexual assault: Perspectives on prevention and assailants. In M. J. Walker & S. L. Brodsky (Eds.), *Sexual assault: The victim and the rapist.* Lexington, Mass.: Lexington Books (D. C. Heath), 1976.

Brodsky, S. L., & Eggleston, N. E. (Eds.). *The military prison: Theory, research and practice.* Carbondale: Southern Illinois University Press, 1970.

Broen, W. E., Jr. *Schizophrenia research and theory.* New York: Academic Press, 1968.

Broughton, R. Sleep disorders—disorders of arousal? *Science,* 1968, *159,* 1070–1078.

Brownmiller, S. *Against our will: Men, women and rape.* New York: Strauss and Schuster, 1975.

Bruch, H. Obesity in childhood and personality development. *American Journal of Orthopsychiatry,* 1941, *11,* 467–474.

Brune, G. G., & Himwich, H. E. Effects of methionine loading on behavior of schizophrenic patients. *The Journal of Nervous and Mental Disease,* 1962, *134,* 447–450.

Brussel, J. *Casebook of a crime psychiatrist.* New York: Dell, 1968.

Brutten, G., & Shoemaker, D. A. A two-factor learning theory of stuttering. In L. Travis (Ed.), *The handbook of speech pathology and audiology.* New York: Appleton-Century-Crofts, 1971.

Bucher, B., & Lovaas, O. I. Use of aversive stimulation in behavior modification. In M. R. Jones (Ed.), *Miami symposium on the prediction of behavior, 1967: Aversive stimulation.* Coral Gables, Florida: University of Miami Press, 1968.

Budzynski, T. H., Stoyva, J. M., Adler, C. S., & Mullaney, D. M. EMG biofeedback and tension headache: A controlled outcome study. *Psychosomatic Medicine,* 1973, *35,* 484–496.

Bugental, J. F. T. The nature of the therapeutic task in intensive psychotherapy. *Journal of Existentialism,* 1964, *5,* 199–205.

Bugental, J. F. T. *The search for authenticity.* New York: Holt, Rinehart and Winston, 1965.

Bugental, J. F. T. Commitment and the psychotherapist. *International Forum for Existential Psychiatry,* 1967, *6,* 285–292.

Bunney, W. E., Jr. & Davis, J. M. Norepinephrine in depressive reactions. A review. *Archives of General Psychiatry.* 1965, *13,* 483–494.

Bunney, W. E., Jr., Goodwin, F. K., & Murphy, D. L. The "switch process" in manic-depressive illness: III. Theoretical implications. *Archives of General Psychiatry,* 1972, *27,* 312–317.

Bunney, W. E., & Hartmann, E. L. A study of a patient with 48-hour manic-depressive cycles: I. An analysis of behavioral factors. *Archives of General Psychiatry,* 1956, *12,* 611.

Bureau of Prisons. *Differential treatment . . . a way to begin.* Washington, D.C.: U.S. Department of Justice, Bureau of Prisons, 1970.

Burgess, A. W., & Holmstrom, L. L. *Rape: Victim of crisis.* Bowie, Md.: Robert J. Brady, 1974. (a)

Burgess, A. W., & Holmstrom, L. L. Rape trauma syndrome. *American Journal of Psychiatry,* 1974, *9,* 981–986. (b)

Burgess, A. W., & Holmstrom, L. L. Rape: Its effect on task performance at varying stages in the life cycle. In M. J. Walker & S. L. Brodsky (Eds.), *Sexual assault: The victim and the rapist.* Lexington, Mass.: Lexington Books (D. C. Heath), 1976.

Buros, O. K. *Mental measurements yearbook.* Princeton: Gryphon, 1965.

Burrow, T. The group method of analysis. *Psychoanalytic Review,* 1927, *14,* 268–280.

Burstein, A. G. Primary process in children as a function of age. *Journal of Abnormal and Social Psychology,* 1959, *59,* 284–286.

Burstein, A. G. Some verbal aspects of primary process thought in schizophrenia. *Journal of Abnormal and Social Psychology,* 1961, *62,* 155–157.

Burton, A. The meaning of psychotherapy. *Journal of Existentialism,* 1967, *8,* 49–64.

Burton, A. *Modern humanistic psychotherapy.* San Francisco: Jossey-Bass, 1968.

Buss, A. H. *The psychology of aggression.* New York: Wiley, 1961.

Buss, A. H. *Psychopathology.* New York: Wiley, 1966.

Buss, A. H., Wiener, M., Durkee, A., & Baer, M. The measurement of anxiety in clinical situations. *Journal of Consulting Psychology,* 1955, *19,* 125–129.

Byck, R. Drugs and the treatment of psychiatric disorders. In L. S. Goodman & A. Gilman (Eds.), *The pharmacological basis of therapeutics* (5th ed.). New York: Macmillan, 1975.

Cade, J. F. J. Lithium salts in the treatment of psychotic excitement. *Medical Journal of Australia,* 1949, *2,* 349–352.

Caird, W. K., & Wincze, J. P. *The treatment of sexual dysfunctions: A behavioral approach.* Hagerstown, Md.: Harper & Row, in press.

Cameron, N. Schizophrenic thinking in a problem-solving situation. *Journal of Mental Science,* 1939, *85,* 1012–1035.

Cameron, N. & Magaret, A. *Behavior pathology*, Cambridge, Mass.: Riverside Press, 1951.

Campbell, D. T. Reforms as experiments. *American Psychologist,* 1969, *24,* 409–429.

Campbell, D. T., Sanderson, R. E., & Laverty, S. G. Characteristics of a conditioned response in human subjects during extinction trials following a single traumatic conditioning trial. *Journal of Abnormal and Social Psychology,* 1964, *68,* 627–639.

Campbell, S. B., Douglas, V. I., & Morgenstern, G. Cognitive styles in hyperactive children and the effect of methylphenidate. *Journal of Child Psychiatry and Psychology,* 1971, *12,* 55–67.

Caplan, G. *An approach to community mental health.* New York: Grune & Stratton, 1961.

Caplan, G. Types of mental health consultation. *American Journal of Orthopsychiatry,* 1963, *33,* 470–481.

Caplan, G. *Principles of preventive psychiatry.* New York: Basic Books, 1964.

Caplan, G. *Support systems and community mental health.* New York: Behavioral Publications, 1974.

Caplan, G., & Grunebaum, H. Perspectives on primary prevention. *Archives of General Psychiatry,* 1967, *17,* 331–346.

Caplan, N., & Nelson, S. D. On being useful: The nature and consequences of psychological research on social problems. *American Psychologist,* 1973, *28,* 199–211.

Carkhuff, R. R. *Helping and human relations.* New York: Holt, Rinehart and Winston, 1969.

Carkhuff, R. R., & Berenson, B. G. *Beyond counseling and psychotherapy.* New York: Holt, Rinehart and Winston, 1967.

Carlsson, A. Summation of the conference and conclusions. In A. Barbeau & F. H. McDowell (Eds.), L-*Dopa and parkinsonism.* Philadelphia: F. A. Davis, 1970.

Carmer, J. C., & Rouzer, D. L. Healthy functioning from the Gestalt perspective. *The Counseling Psychologist,* 1974, *4,* 20–23.

Carter, C. H. Handbook of mental retardation syndromes. Springfield, Ill.: Charles C Thomas, 1966.

Cartwright, D. S. Annotated bibliography of research and theory construction in client-centered therapy. *Journal of Counseling Psychology,* 1957, *4,* 82–100.

Cartwright, D. S., Kirtner, W. L., & Fiske, D. W. Method factors in changes associated with psychotherapy. *Journal of Abnormal and Social Psychology,* 1963, *66,* 164–175.

Caruso, I. A. *Existential psychology.* New York: Herder & Herder, 1964.

Cattell, R. B., & Scheier, I. H. *The meaning and measurement of neuroticism and anxiety.* New York: Ronald Press, 1961.

Cautela, J. R. Covert sensitization. *Psychological Reports,* 1967, *74,* 459–468.

Cautela, J. R. Behavior therapy and self-control: Techniques and implications. In C. M. Franks (Ed.), *Behavior therapy: Appraisal and status.* New York: McGraw-Hill, 1969.

Cautela, J. R. The use of covert sensitization in the treatment of alcoholism. *Psychotherapy: Theory, Research and Practice,* 1970, *7,* 86–90.

Chapman, L. J., & Chapman, J. P. *Disordered thought in schizophrenia.* New York: Appleton-Century-Crofts, 1973.

Chapman, L. J., Chapman, J. P., & Miller, G. A. A theory of verbal behavior in schizophrenia. In B. A. Maher (Ed.), *Progress in experimental personality research* (Vol. I). New York: Academic Press, 1964.

Chein, L., Gerard, D., Lee, R., & Rosenfeld, E. *The road to H.* New York: Basic Books, 1964.

Cheraskin, E., & Ringsdorf, W. M. Bruxism: A nutritional problem? *Dental Survey,* 1970, *46,* 38–40.

Chodoff, P., & Lyons, H. Hysteria, the hysterical personality and hysterical conversion. *American Journal of Psychiatry,* 1958, *114,* 734–740.

Chorover, S. L. The pacification of the brain. *Psychology Today,* May 1974, pp. 59–60; 63–64; 66; and 69.

Chronback, L. J. Essentials of psychological testing. New York: Harper, 1960.

Chu, F. D., & Trotter, S. *The madness establishment: Ralph Nader's study group report on the National Institute of Mental Health.* New York: Grossman, 1974.

Clark, K. B. *Dark ghetto: Dilemmas of social power.* New York: Harper & Row, 1965.

Clarke, A. M., & Clarke, A. D. B. (Eds.). *Mental deficiency: The changing outlook* (rev. ed.). New York: Free Press, 1965.

Clayton, P. J., Pitts, F. N., & Winokur, G. Affective disorder IV. Mania. *Comprehensive Psychiatry,* 1965, *6,* 313.

Cleckley, H. *The mask of sanity* (4th ed.). St. Louis: C. V. Mosby, 1964.

Cochrane, R. High blood pressure as a psychosomatic disorder: A selective review. *British Journal of Social and Clinical Psychology,* 1971, *10,* 61–72.

Cohen, B. R., Nachmani, G., & Rosenberg, S. Referent communication disturbances in acute schizophrenia. *Journal of Abnormal Psychology,* 1974, *83,* 1–13.

Cohen, J. *Secondary motivation I: Personal motives.* Chicago: Rand McNally, 1970.

Cohen, M., Seghorn, T., & Calmas, W. Sociometric study of the sex offender. *Journal of Abnormal Psychology,* 1969, *74,* 249–255.

Cohen, S. Lysergic acid diethylamide side effects and complications. *Journal of Nervous and Mental Disease,* 1960, *130,* 30–40.

Cohen, S., & Ditman, K. S. Prolonged adverse reactions to lysergic acid diethylamide. *AMA Archives of General Psychiatry,* 1963, *8,* 475–480.

Colaizzi, P. R. *Reflection and research in psychology.* Dubuque, Iowa: Kendall/Hunt, 1973.

Coleman, J. C. *Abnormal psychology and modern life* (4th ed.). Glenview, Ill.: Scott, Foresman, 1972.

Collmann, R. D., & Stoller, A. *American Journal of Public Health and the Nation's Health,* 1962, *52,* 813.

Colm, H. The therapeutic encounter. *Review of Existential Psychology and Psychiatry,* 1965, *5,* 137–159.

Comfort, A. *The joy of sex.* New York: Crown, 1972.

Compton, R. D. Changes in enuretics accompanying treatment by the conditioned response technique. *Dissertation Abstracts,* 1968, *28* (7-A), 2549.

Conger, J. J. The effects of alcohol on conflict behavior in the albino rat. *Quarterly Journal of Studies on Alcohol,* 1951, *12,* 1–29.

Conners, C. K. Symptom patterns in hyperkinetic, neurotic, and normal children. *Child Development,* 1970, *41,* 667–682.

Conrad, S., & Wincze, J. P. Orgasmic reconditioning: A controlled study of its effects upon the sexual arousal and behavior of adult male homosexuals. *Behavior Therapy,* 1976, *7,* 155–166.

Cook, P. E. (Ed.). *Community psychology and community mental health: Introductory readings.* San Francisco: Holden-Day, 1970.

Cook, P. E. Case analysis: Consultation and counseling. *Elementary School Guidance and Counseling,* 1971, *5,* 302–306.

Cook, P. E., Kalafat, J., & Tyler, M. Development of a campus telephone counseling service. In B. Bloom (Ed.), *Psychological stress in the campus community: Theory, research, and action.* New York: Behavioral Publications, 1975.

Cook, P. E., Looney, M. A., & Pine, L. The community adaptation schedule: A validational study with psychiatric inpatients and outpatients. *Community Mental Health Journal,* 1973, *9,* 11–17.

Correnti, S. A comparison of behaviorism and psychoanalysis with existentialism. *Journal of Existentialism,* 1965, *20,* 379–388.

Corriveau, M. Phenomenology, psychology, and radical behaviorism: Skinner and Merleau-Ponty on behavior. *Journal of Phenomenological Psychology,* 1972, *3,* 7–34.

Costello, C. G. Classification and psychopathology. In C. G. Costello (Ed.), *Symptoms of psychopathology: A handbook.* New York: Wiley, 1970.

Court, J. H., & Garwoli, E. Schizophrenic performance on a reaction time task with increasing levels of complexity. *British Journal of Social and Clinical Psychology,* 1968, *7,* 216–223.

Coville, W. J., Costello, T. W., & Rouke, F. L. *Abnormal psychology.* New York: Barnes & Noble, 1960.

Craig, R. J. Interpersonal competition, overinclusive thinking and schizophrenia. *Journal of Consulting and Clinical Psychology,* 1973, *40,* 9–14.

Cramer, B. Delusion of pregnancy in a girl with drug-induced lactation. *American Journal of Psychiatry,* 1971, *27* (7), 960–963.

Criswell, H. E., & Levitt, R. A. The narcotic analgesics. In R. A. Levitt, *Psychopharmacology: A biological approach.* Washington, D.C.: Hemisphere/Wiley, 1975.

CRM Publishing. *Abnormal psychology: Current perspectives.* Del Mar, Calif.: CRM Publishing, 1972.

Crocetti, G. M., Spiro, H. R., Lemkau, P. V., & Siassi, I. Multiple models and mental illnesses: A rejoinder to "Failure of a moral enterprise: Attitudes of the public toward mental illness" by T. R. Sarbin and J. C. Mancuso. *Journal of Consulting and Clinical Psychology,* 1972, *39,* 1–5.

Crumbaugh, J. C. The application of logotherapy. *Journal of Existentialism,* 1965, *5,* 403–412.

Crumbaugh, J. C. Cross validation of the purpose-in-life test based on Frankl's concepts. *Journal of Individual Psychology,* 1968, *18,* 230–238.

Crumpton, E., Weinstein, A. D., Acker, C. W. & Annis, A. P. How patients and normals see mental patients. *Journal of Clinical Psychology,* 1967, *23,* 46–49.

Cumings, J. N. (Ed.). *Background to migraine,* Fourth Migraine Symposium Sept. 11, 1970. New York: Springer-Verlag, 1971.

Cumming, E., & Cumming, J. *Closed ranks.* Cambridge, Mass.: Commonwealth Fund, Harvard University Press, 1957.

Curran, J. P., & Gilbert, F. S. A test of the relative effectiveness of a systematic desensitization program and interpersonal skills training program with date anxious subjects. *Behavior Therapy,* 1975, *6,* 510–521.

Curry, F. A. Group psychotherapy: Phenomenological considerations. *Review of Existential Psychology and Psychiatry,* 1966, *6,* 63–70.

Da Fonseca, A. F. Analise heredo-clinica des perturbacoes affectivas. Doctoral dissertation, Universidade do Porto, Portugal, 1959.

Dahlstrom, W. G., & Welsh, G. S. *An MMPI handbook: A guide to use in clinical practice and research.* Minneapolis: Univeristy of Minnesota Press, 1960.

Darnton, R. *Mesmerism and the end of the enlightenment in France.* Cambridge, Mass.: Harvard University Press, 1968.

Davis, J., & Miller, N. Fear and pain: Their effect on self-injection of amobarbital sodium in rats. *Science,* 1963, *141,* 1286–1287.

Davis, K. Extreme social isolation of a child. *American Journal of Sociology,* 1940, *45,* 554–565.

Davis, K. Final note on a case of extreme isolation. *American Journal of Sociology,* 1947, *52,* 432–437.

Davison, G. C. Systematic desensitization as a counterconditioning process. *Journal of Abnormal Psychology,* 1968, *73,* 91–99.

Davison, G. C. *Homosexuality: The ethical challenge.* Paper presented at the annual convention of the Association for Advancement of Behavior Therapy, Chicago, November 2, 1974.

Davison, G. C., & Neale, J. M. *Abnormal psychology: An experimental clinical approach.* New York: Wiley, 1974.

Davison, G. C., Tsujimoto, R. N., & Glaros, A. G. Atribution and the maintenance of behavior change in falling asleep. *Journal of Abnormal Psychology,* 1973, *82,* 124–133.

Davison, G. C., & Valins, S. Maintenance of self-attributed and drug-attributed behavior change. *Journal of Personality and Social Psychology,* 1969, *11,* 25–33.

Day, W. F. Radical behaviorism in reconciliation with phenomenology. *Journal of the Experimental Analysis of Behavior,* 1969, *12,* 315–328.

Deibert, A. N. Community mental health: In? By? For? *Professional Psychology,* 1971, *2,* 394–400.

Deichmann, W. B., & Gerarde, H. W. *Symptomatology and therapy of toxicological emergencies.* New York: Academic Press, 1964.

Dement, W. C. *Some must watch while some must sleep.* Stanford, Calif.: Stanford Alumni Association, 1972.

Dement, W. C., & Kleitman, N. The relation of eye movements during sleep to dream activity: An objective method for the study of dreaming. *Journal of Experimental Psychology,* 1957, *53,* 339–346.

De Moor, W. Systematic desensitization versus prolonged high intensity stimulation (flooding). *Journal of Behavior Therapy and Experimental Psychiatry,* 1970, *1,* 45–52.

Dennis, W. Causes of retardation among institutional children. *Journal of Genetic Psychology,* 1960, *96,* 47–59.

Dennis, W., & Najarian, P. Infant development under environmental handicap. *Psychological Monographs,* 1957, *71* (7).

Depue, R. A., & Evans, R. The psychobiology of depressive disorders. In B. H. Maher (Ed.), *Progress in experimental personality research* (Vol. 8). New York: Academic Press, 1976.

Derman, H. Lead poisoning. In F. W. Sunderman & F. W. Sunderman, Jr. (Eds.), *Laboratory diagnosis of diseases caused by toxic agent.* St. Louis: Warren H. Green, 1970.

DesLauriers, A. M., & Carlson, C. F. *Your child is asleep: Early infantile autism, etiology, treatment, parental influences.* Homewood, Ill.: Dorsey, 1969.

DeVito, R. A., Flaherty, L. A., & Mozdzierz, G. J. Toward a psychodynamic theory of alcoholism. *Diseases of the Nervous System,* 1970, *31,* 43–49.

Dexter, L. A. Research on problems of subnormality. *American Journal of Mental Deficiency,* 1960, *64,* 835–838.

Dexter, L. A. *The tyranny of schooling.* New York: Basic Books, 1964.

Ditman, K. S. A controlled experiment on the use of court probation for drunk arrests. *American Journal of Psychiatry,* 1967, *124,* 160–163.

Dix, D. L. *On behalf of the insane poor: Selected reports.* New York: Arno Press, 1971.

Dixon, J. C. Depersonalization phenomena in a sample of population of college students. *British Journal of Psychiatry,* 1963, *109,* 371–375.

Dohrenwend, B. P., & Dohrenwend, B. S. The problem of validity in field studies of psychological disorder. *Journal of Abnormal Psychology,* 1965, *70,* 52–69.

Doll, A. The essentials of an inclusive concept of mental deficiency. *American Journal of Mental Deficiency,* 1941, *46,* 214–219.

Dorwith, T. R. The effect of electroconvulsive shock on "helplessness" in dogs. *Dissertation Abstracts International,* 1971, *32,* (6-B), 3662.

Doyle, A. C. *The complete Sherlock Holmes.* New York: Garden City, 1938.

Drachman, D. B., & Gumnit, R. J. Periodic alteration of consciousness in the "Pickwickian" syndrome. *Archives of Neurology,* 1962, *6,* 471–477.

Dreyfus, P. M. Nutritional disorders of the nervous system. In P. B. Beeson & W. McDermott (Eds.), *Cecil-Loeb textbook of medicine* (13th ed.). Philadelphia: Saunders, 1971.

DSM-II [*The diagnostic and statistical manual of mental disorders* (2nd ed.)]. Washington, D.C.: American Psychiatric Association, 1968.

Dublin, L. I. *Suicide: A sociological and statistical study.* New York: Ronald Press, 1963.

Dunham, H. W. Community psychiatry: The newest therapeutic bandwagon. *Archives of General Psychiatry,* 1965, *12,* 303–313.

Dunkell, S. The daseinsanalytic method of dream interpretation. *International Forum for Existential Psychiatry,* 1967, *1,* 517–523.

Dunn, L. M. (Ed.). *Exceptional children in the schools: Special education in transition* (2nd ed.). New York: Holt, Rinehart and Winston, 1973.

Dunner, D. L., & Fieve, R. R. Clinical factors in lithium carbonate prophylaxis failure. *Archives of General Psychiatry,* 1974, *30,* 229–233.

Duster, T. Mental illness and criminal intent. In S. C. Plog & R. B. Edgerton (Eds.), *Changing perspectives in mental illness.* New York: Holt, Rinehart and Winston, 1969.

Eberhard, G. The personality of peptic ulcer. Preliminary report of a twin study. In N. Retterstol & F. Magnussen (Eds.), *Report on the Fifteenth Congress of Scandanavian Psychiatrists, Geilo Norway, 1965. Acta Psychiatrica Scandinavica, Supplementum 203,* 1968, 131–133.

Eckhardt, W. Psychotic depression: Phenomenological presentation and existential interpretation. *International Forum for Existential Psychiatry,* 1967–1968, *6,* 491–497.

Edelson, M. *Ego psychology, group dynamics, and the therapeutic community.* New York: Grune & Stratton, 1964.

Edwards, A. J. *Individual mental testing. Part I. History and theories.* Scranton, Pa.: Intext, 1971.

Elder, S. T., Ruiz, Z. R., Deabler, H. L., & Dillenkoffer, R. L. Instrumental conditioning of diastolic blood pressure in essential hypertensive patients. *Journal of Applied Behavior Analysis,* 1973, *6,* 377–382.

Eliseo, T. S. Overinclusive thinking in process and reactive schizophrenics. *Journal of Consulting Psychology,* 1963, *27,* 447–449.

Elkin, H. The unconscious and the integration of personality. *Review of Existential Psychology and Psychiatry,* 1965, *5,* 176–189.

Ellenberger, H. F. *The discovery of the unconscious.* New York: Basic Books, 1970.

Ellis, A. *Reason and emotion in psychotherapy.* New York: Lyle Stuart, 1962.

Ellis, A. *Growth through reason.* Palo Alto, Calif.: Science and Behavior Books, 1971.

Ellis, A., & Harper, R. A. *Guide to rational living.* New York: Lyle Stuart, 1968.

Ellis, H. Mescal: A study of a divine plant. *Popular Science Monthly,* 1902, *61,* 59.

Emery, J. R., & Krumboltz, J. D. Standard versus individual hierarchies in desensitization to reduce test anxiety. *Journal of Counseling Psychology,* 1967, *14,* 204–209.

Enright, J. B. An introduction to Gestalt techniques. In J. Fagan & I. Shepherd (Eds.), *Gestalt therapy now.* Palo Alto, Calif.: Science and Behavior Books, 1970.

Epstein, S. Overinclusive thinking in a schizophrenic and a control group. *Journal of Consulting Psychology,* 1953, *17,* 384–388.

Epstein, S. The measurement of drive and conflict in humans: Theory and experiment. In M. R. Jones (Ed.), *Nebraska Symposium on Motivation.* Lincoln: University of Nebraska Press, 1962.

Erikson, K. T. Notes on the sociology of deviance. *Social Problems,* 1962, *9,* 307–314.

Essen-Moller, E. *Psychiatrische Untersuchungen an einer Serie von Zvillingen.* Copenhagen: Munksgaard, 1941.

Esterson, A. *The leaves of spring.* Harmondsworth, Middlesex, England: Penguin, 1972.

Evans, F. J. Hypnosis and sleep: Techniques for exploring cognitive activity during sleep. In E. Fromm & R. E. Shor (Eds.), *Hypnosis: Research developments and perspectives.* Chicago: Aldine–Atherton, 1972.

Everitt, B. S., Gourlay, A. J., & Kendell, R. E. An attempt at validation of traditional psychiatric syndromes by cluster analysis. *British Journal of Psychiatry,* 1971, *119,* 399–412.

Eysenck, H. J. The effects of psychotherapy: An evaluation. *Journal of Consulting Psychology,* 1952, *16,* 319–324.

Eysenck, H. J. *Handbook of abnormal psychology.* New York: Basic Books, 1961.

Eysenck, H. J. *Crime and personality.* London: Routledge & Kegan Paul, 1964.

Eysenck, H. J. The classification of depressive illness. *British Journal of Psychiatry,* 1970, *117,* 241–271.

Eysenck, H. J., & Eysenck, S. B. G. *Personality, structure and measurement.* London: Routledge & Kegan Paul, 1968.

Ezriel, H. A psychoanalytic approach to group treatment. *British Journal of Medical Psychology,* 1950, *23,* 59–74.

Fairweather, G. W., Sanders, D. H., Maynard, H., & Cressler, D. L. *Community life for the mentally ill: An alternative to institutional care.* Chicago: Aldine, 1969.

Farber, I. E. Response fixation under anxiety and non-anxiety conditions. *Journal of Experimental Psychology,* 1948, *38,* 111–131.

Farber, L. Despair and the life of suicide. *Review of Existential Psychology and Psychiatry,* 1962, *2,* 125–140. (a)

Farber, L. Schizophrenia and the mad psychiatrist. *Review of Existential Psychology and Psychiatry,* 1962, *2,* 209–240. (b)

Farberow, N. L., & McEvoy, T. L. Suicide among patients with anxiety or depressive reactions. In E. S. Shneidman, N. L. Farberow, & R. E. Litman (Eds.), *The psychology of suicide.* New York: Science House, 1970.

Farina, A., Gliha, D., Boudreau, L. A., Allen, J. G., & Sherman, J. Mental illness and the impact of believing others know about it. *Journal of Abnormal Psychology,* 1971, *77,* 1–5.

Farina, A., Holland, C. H., & Ring, K. The role of stigma and set in interpersonal interaction. *Journal of Abnormal Psychology,* 1966, *71,* 421–428.

Farrer, C. H., Powell, B. J., & Martin, K. L. Punishment of alcohol consumption by apneic paralyses. *Behaviour Research and Therapy,* 1968, *6,* 13–16.

Fazio, A. F. Treatment components in implosive therapy. *Journal of Abnormal Psychology,* 1970, *76,* 211–219.

Feifel, H. Death: A relevant variable in psychology. In R. May (Ed.), *Existential psychology.* New York: Random House, 1961.

Feifel, H. *The meaning of death.* New York: McGraw-Hill, 1965.

Feighner, J. P., Robins, E., Guze, S. B., Woodruff, R. A., Winokur, G., & Munoz, R. Diagnostic criteria for use in psychiatric research. *Archives of General Psychiatry,* 1972, *26,* 57–63.

Feinberg, I. Effects of age on human sleep patterns. In A. Kales (Ed.), *Sleep: Physiology and pathology.* Philadelphia: Lippincott, 1969.

Feinberg, I., Braun, M., Koresko, R. L., & Gottlieb, F. Stage 4 sleep in schizophrenia. *Archives of General Psychiatry*, 1969, *21*, 262–266.

Feinberg, I., & Carlson, V. R. Sleep variables as a function of age in man. *Archives of General Psychiatry*, 1968, *18*, 239–250.

Feinberg, I., Koresko, R. L., & Heller, N. EEG sleep patterns as a function of normal and pathological aging in man. *Journal of Psychiatric Research*, 1967, *5*, 107–144.

Feldman, M., & MacCulloch, M. *Homosexual behavior: Theory and assessment.* Oxford: Pergamon, 1971.

Fenichel, O. *Problems of psychoanalytic technique.* Albany, N.Y.: Psychoanalytic Quarterly Press, 1941.

Fenichel, O. *The psychoanalytic theory of neurosis.* New York: Norton, 1945.

Ferdinand, T. N. *Typologies of delinquency: A critical analysis.* New York: Random House, 1966.

Ferenczi, S. The further development of an active therapy in psychoanalysis. In *Further contributions to the theory and technique of psychoanalysis.* London: Hogarth, 1950. (Article originally published, 1920.)

Ferenczi, S. Contraindications to the "active" psychoanalytic technique. In *Further contributions to the theory and technique of psychoanalysis.* London: Hogarth, 1950. (Article originally published, 1925.)

Ferguson, J., Henricksen, S., McGare, K., Belensky, G., Mitchell, G., Gonda, W., Cohen, H., & Dement, W. Phasic event deprivation in the cat. *Psychophysiology*, 1968, *5*, 238–239.

Ferster, C. B. Positive reinforcement and behavioral deficits of autistic children. *Child Development*, 1961, *32*, 437–456.

Ferster, C. B., Nurnberger, J. I., & Levitt, E. B. The control of eating. *Journal of Mathematics*, 1962, *1*, 87–109.

Ferster, C. B., & Skinner, B. F. Schedules of reinforcement. New York: Appleton, 1957.

Fields, W. S., & Blattner, R. J. *Viral encephalitis.* Springfield, Ill.: Charles C Thomas, 1958.

Finch, J. R., Smith, J. P., & Pokorny, A. D. *Vehicular studies.* Paper presented at the meeting of the American Psychiatric Association, May 1970.

Fireman, A. E. Socrates and psychotherapy. *International Forum for Existential Psychiatry*, 1967, *6*, 74–83.

Fischer, J. Negroes and whites and rates of mental illness: Reconsideration of a myth. *Psychiatry*, 1969, *32*, 428–446.

Fischer, M. *Preliminary report of a Danish twin study on schizophrenia.* Prepublication copy, 1968.

Fischer, W. The problem of unconscious motivation. In A. Giorgi, W. Fischer, & R. Von Eckartsberg (Eds.), *Duquesne studies in phenomenological psychology* (Vol. 1). Pittsburgh, Pa.: Duquesne University Press, 1971.

Fisher, C., Byrne, J., Edwards, A., & Kahn, E. A psychophysiological study of nightmares. *Journal of the American Psychoanalytic Association*, 1970, *18*, 747–782.

Fisher, C., Kahn, E., Edwards, A., & Davis, D. Effects of Valium on NREM night terrors. *Psychophysiology*, 1972, *9*, 91.

Fisher, K. A. Ultimate goals in therapy. *Journal of Existentialism*, 1966–1967, *7*, 215–232.

Fiske, D., Hunt, H., Luborsky, L., Orne, M., Parloff, M., Reiser, M., & Tuma, A. Planning of research on effectiveness of psychotherapy. *American Psychologist*, 1970, *25*, 727–737.

Foldes, F. F. Treatment of acute narcotic intoxication. In F. F. Foldes, M. Swerdlow, & E. Spiker (Eds.), *Narcotics and narcotic antagonists.* Springfield, Ill.: Charles C Thomas, 1964.

Foreyt, J. P., & Hagen, R. L. Covert sensitization: Conditioning or suggestion? *Journal of Abnormal Psychology*, 1973, *82*, 17–23.

Foreyt, J. P., & Kennedy, W. A. Treatment of overweight by aversion therapy. *Behaviour Research and Therapy*, 1971, *9*, 29–34.

Foulkes, S. H. *Introduction to group-analytic psychotherapy.* New York: Grune & Stratton, 1948.

Fox, L. Effecting the use of efficient study habits. *Journal of Mathematics*, 1962, *1*, 75–86.

Foxx, R. M., & Azrin, N. H. Dry pants: A rapid method of toilet training children. *Behaviour Research and Therapy*, 1973, *11*, 435–442.

Frankl, V. E. *The doctor and the soul.* New York: Knopf, 1960.

Frankl, V. E. Logotherapy and the challenge of suffering. *Review of Existential Psychology and Psychiatry*, 1961, *1*, 3–7.

Frankl, V. E. Basic concepts of logotherapy. *Journal of Existential Psychiatry*, 1962, *3*, 111–118.

Frankl, V. E. Philosophical foundations of logotherapy. In E. W. Straus (Ed.), *Phenomenology: Pure and applied.* Pittsburgh, Pa.: Duquesne University Press, 1964.

Franks, C. M. (Ed.). *Behavior therapy: Appraisal and status.* New York: McGraw-Hill, 1969.

Franks, C. M. Alcoholism. In C. G. Costello (Ed.), *Symptoms of psychopathology.* New York: Wiley, 1970.

Franks, C. M., & Wilson, G. T. (Eds.). *Behavior therapy: Theory and practice* (Vol. 1). New York: Brunner/Mazel, 1973.

Franks, C. M., & Wilson, G. T. (Eds.). *Behavior therapy: Theory and practice* (Vol. 2). New York: Brunner/Mazel, 1974.

Franks, C. M., & Wilson, G. T. (Eds.). *Behavior therapy: Theory and practice* (Vol. 3). New York: Brunner/Mazel, 1975.

Frazer, A., & Stinnett, J. L. Distribution and metabolism of norepinephrine and serotonin in the central nervous system. In J. Mendels (Ed.), *Biological Psychiatry.* New York: Wiley, 1973.

Freedman, B., & Chapman, L. J. Early subjective experience in schizophrenic episodes. *Journal of Abnormal Psychology,* 1973, *82,* 46–54.

Freeman, W. Frontal lobotomy 1936–1956: A follow-up study of 3000 patients from one to twenty years. *American Journal of Psychiatry,* 1957, *113,* 877–886.

Frenkel, R. E. Psychotherapeutic reconstruction of the traumatic amnesic period by the mirror image projective technique. *Journal of Existential Psychiatry,* 1964, *5,* 77–96.

Fresco, R. Le syndrome de Kleine–Levin: Hypersomnie recurrente des adolescents males. *Annales Medico-Psychologiques,* 1971, *1,* 625–668.

Freud, S. The aetiology of hysteria. In *Collected papers* (Vol. 1). London: Hogarth, 1950. (Article originally published, 1896.)

Freud, S. Recommendations for physicians on the psycho-analytic method of treatment. *Collected papers* (Vol. 2). London: Hogarth, 1950. (Article originally published, 1912.)

Freud, S. On the history of the psycho-analytic movement. In *Collected papers of Sigmund Freud* (Vol. 1). London: Hogarth, 1953. (Article originally published, 1914.)

Freud, S. *The interpretation of dreams.* New York: Basic, 1955. (Originally published, 1915.)

Freud, S. Mourning and melancholia. In *Collected papers* (Vol. 4). London: Hogarth Press and the Institute of Psychoanalysis, 1950. (Article originally published, 1917.)

Freud, S. Trauer und melancholie. In *Standard edition of the complete psychological works of Sigmund Freud.* (Vol. 14). London: Hogarth, 1957. (Article originally published, 1917.)

Freund, K. A laboratory method for diagnosing predominance of homo- or hetero-erotic interests in the male. *Behaviour Research and Therapy,* 1963, *1,* 85–93.

Freund, K., Langevin, R., & Barlow, D. Comparison of two penile measures of erotic arousal. *Behaviour Research and Therapy,* 1974, *12,* 355–359.

Friedhoff, A. J., & Van Winkle, E. Isolation and characterization of a compound from the urine of schizophrenics. *Nature,* 1962, *194,* 897–898.

Friedman, A. S. Minimal effects of severe depression on cognitive functioning. *Journal of Abnormal and Social Psychology,* 1964, *69,* 237–243.

Furth, H. G., & Youniss, J. Schizophrenic thinking on nonverbal conceptual, discovery and transfer tasks. *Journal of Nervous and Mental Disease,* 1968, *146,* 376–383.

Galdston, I. (Ed.). *Historic derivations of modern psychiatry.* New York: McGraw-Hill, 1967.

Gall, E. A., & Mostof, F. K. *The liver.* Baltimore: Williams & Wilkins, 1973.

Gallinek, A. The Kleine–Levin syndrome. *Diseases of the Nervous System,* 1967, *28,* 448–451.

Gannon, W. *The effects of the Gestalt oriented group approach on the interpersonal contact attitudes of selected high school students.* (Doctoral dissertation, Case Western Reserve University). Ann Arbor, Michigan: University Microfilms, 1972, No. 72–26, 155.

Garner, H. H., & Jeans, R. F. Confrontation technique in psychotherapy: Some existential implications. *Journal of Existential Psychiatry,* 1962, *2,* 393–408.

Gatch, V. M., & Temerlin, M. K. The belief in psychic determinism and the behavior of the psychotherapist. *Review of Existential Psychology and Psychiatry,* 1965, *5,* 16–33.

Geer, J. H. Fear and autonomic arousal. *Journal of Abnormal and Social Psychology,* 1966, *71,* 253–255.

Geer, J. H., Morokoff, P., & Greenwood, P. Sexual arousal in women: The development of a measurement device for vaginal blood volume. *Archives of Sexual Behavior,* 1974, *3,* 559–564.

Geer, J. H., & Silverman, I. Treatment of a recurrent nightmare by behavior modification procedures: A case study. *Journal of Abnormal Psychology,* 1967, *72,* 188–190.

Gellhorn, E., & Kiely, W. F. Autonomic nervous system in psychiatric disorder. In J. Mendels, *Biological psychiatry.* New York: Wiley, 1973.

Gendlin, E. T. *Experiencing and the creation of meaning.* Glencoe, Ill.: Free Press, 1962.

Gendlin, E. T. Schizophrenia: Problems and methods of psychotherapy. *Review of Existential Psychology and Psychiatry,* 1964, *4,* 168–179.

Gendlin, E. T. The experiential response. In E. Hammer (Ed.), *Use of interpretation in treatment.* New York: Grune & Stratton, 1968.

Gendlin, E. T. Research in psychotherapy with schizophrenic patients and the nature of that illness. In J. T. Hart & T. M. Tomlinson (Eds.), *New directions in client-centered therapy.* Boston: Houghton Mifflin, 1970. (a)

Gendlin, E. T. A short summary and some long predictions. In J. T. Hart & T. M. Tomlinson (Eds.), *New directions in client-centered therapy.* Boston: Houghton Mifflin, 1970. (b)

Gerard, D. L., & Siegel, J. The family background of schizophrenia. *Psychiatric Quarterly,* 1950, *24,* 47–73.

Gill, M. M. Metapsychology is not psychology. In M. M. Gill & P. S. Holzman, (Eds.), *Psychology versus metapsychology.* New York: International Universities Press, 1975. [Also *Psychological Issues,* 1975, *9* (Monograph 36)].

Gill, M. M., & Brenman, M. The metapsychology of regression in hypnosis. In J. E. Gordon (Ed.), *The handbook of clinical and experimental hypnosis.* New York: Macmillan, 1967.

Giorgi, A. *Psychology as a human science: A phenomenologically based approach.* New York: Harper & Row, 1970.

Giorgi, A., Fischer, W., & Von Eckartsberg, R. (Eds.). *Duquesne studies in phenomenological psychology* (Vol. 1). Pittsburgh, Pa.: Duquesne University Press, 1971.

Glynn, E. L. Classroom applications of self-determined reinforcement. *Journal of Applied Behavior Analysis,* 1970, *3,* 123–132.

Goffman, E. *Asylums.* Garden City, N.Y.: Anchor Books, 1961.

Golann, S. E., & Eisdorfer, C. Mental health and the community: The development of issues. In S. E. Golann & C. Eisdorfer (Eds.), *Handbook of community mental health.* New York: Appleton-Century-Crofts, 1972.

Goldberg, S. C., Schooler, N. R., & Mattsson, N. Paranoid and withdrawal symptoms in schizophrenia: Relationship to reaction time. *British Journal of Psychiatry,* 1968, *114,* 1161–1165.

Goldfarb, W. The effects of early institutional care on adolescent personality. *Journal of Experimental Education,* 1943, *12,* 106–129.

Goldfarb, W. Psychological privation in infancy and subsequent adjustment. *American Journal of Orthopsychiatry,* 1945, *15,* 247–255.

Goldfarb, W. Variations in adolescent adjustment of institutionally reared children. *American Journal of Orthopsychiatry,* 1947, *17,* 449–457.

Goldfarb, W. Emotional and intellectual consequences of psychologic deprivation in infancy: A reevaluation. In P. H. Hoch & J. Zubin (Eds.), *Psychopathology of childhood.* New York: Grune & Stratton, 1955.

Goldfarb, W. Childhood psychosis. In P. H. Mussen (Ed.), *Carmichael's manual of child psychology* (3rd ed.), Vol. II. New York: Wiley, 1970. Pp. 765–830.

Goldiamond, I. Self-control procedures in personal behavior problems. *Psychological Reports,* 1965, *17,* 851–868.

Goldstein, K. The significance of special mental tests for diagnosis and prognosis in schizophrenia. *American Journal of Psychiatry,* 1939, *96,* 575–587.

Goldstein, K. Methodological approach to the study of schizophrenic thought disorders. In J. S. Kasanin (Ed.), *Language and thought in schizophrenia.* New York: Norton, 1964, (Originally published, 1944.)

Goldstein, K., & Scheerer, M. Abstract and concrete behavior: An experimental study with special tests. *Psychological Monographs,* 1941, *53* (2, Whole No. 239).

Goldstein, M. J., & Acker, C. W. Psychophysiological reactions to films by chronic schizophrenics: II.

Individual differences in resting levels and reactivity. *Journal of Abnormal Psychology,* 1967, *72,* 23–29.

Goldstein, M. J., Judd, L. K., Rodnick, E. H., & La Polla, A. Psychophysiological and behavioral effects of phenothiazine administration in acute schizophrenics as a function of premorbid states. *Journal of Psychiatric Research,* 1969, *6,* 271–287.

Goodell, H., Lewontin, R., & Wolff, H. G. The familial occurrence of migraine headache: A study of heredity, genetics and the inheritance of integrated neurological and psychiatric patterns. *Association for Research in Nervous and Mental Disease Processes, 33,* 346. Baltimore: Williams & Wilkins, 1954.

Gottesman, I. I., & Shields, J. Schizophrenia in twins: 16 years, consecutive admissions to a psychiatric clinic. *British Journal of Psychiatry,* 1966, *112,* 809–818.

Gottesman, L. Forced-choice word associations in schizophrenia. *Journals of Abnormal and Social Psychology,* 1964, *69,* 673–675.

Gottfredson, D. M. Five challenges. In S. L. Brodsky, *Psychologists in the criminal justice system.* Urbana: University of Illinois Press, 1973.

Grace, W. J., & Graham, D. T. Relationship of specific attitudes and emotions to certain bodily diseases. *Psychosomatic Medicine,* 1952, *14,* 243–251.

Grace, W. J., Wolf, S., & Wolff, H. G. *The human colon.* New York: Paul Hoeber, 1951.

Graham, D. T., Kabler, J. D., & Graham, F. K. Physiological response to the suggestion of attitudes specific for hives and hypertension. *Psychosomatic Medicine,* 1962, *24,* 159–169.

Graham, D. T., & Wolf, S. Pathogenesis of urticaria. Experimental study life situations, emotions and cutaneous vascular reactions. *Journal of American Medical Association,* 1950, *143,* 1936. *Executive Medicine,* 1951, XIII, 5, 123, Abstract 576.

Graham, F. K., & Clifton, R. K. Heart-rate change as a component of the orienting response. *Psychological Bulletin,* 1966, *65,* 305–320.

Grant, M. Juvenile obesity— Chronic, progressive, and transient. *Medical Officer,* 1966, *115,* 331–335.

Greaves, G. MMPI correlates of chronic drug abuse in hospitalized adolescents. *Psychological Reports,* 1971, *29,* 12–22.

Green, R. *Sexual identity conflict in children and adults.* New York: Basic Books, 1974.

Greenblatt, M. Psychosurgery. In A. M. Freedman & H. I. Kaplan (Eds.), *Comprehensive textbook of psychiatry.* Baltimore: Williams & Wilkins, 1967.

Greenhill, J. P. Frigidity in women. *Postgraduate Medicine,* 1952, *12,* 145–151.

Greenson, R. R. *The technique and practice of psychoanalysis.* New York: International Universities Press, 1967.

Greenspan, K., Schildkraut, J. J., Gordon, E. K., Baer, L., Aronoff, M. S., & Durrell, J. Catecholamine metabolism in affective disorders. 3 MHPG and other catecholamine metabolites in patients treated with lithium carbonate. *Journal of Psychiatric Research,* 1970, *7,* 171–183.

Grinker, R. R. Brief psychotherapy in psychosomatic problems. *Psychosomatic Medicine,* 1947, *9,* 78–103.

Gross, M. M., & Goodenough, D. R. Sleep disturbances in the acute alcoholic psychoses. *Psychiatric Research and Reports of the American Psychiatric Association,* 1968, *24,* 132–147.

Grossman, J. (Ed.). *Manual on terminology and classification in mental retardation.* Baltimore: Garamond/Pridemark Press, 1973.

Group for the Advancement of Psychiatry. *Misuse of psychiatry in the criminal courts: Competency to stand trial.* New York: Group for the Advancement of Psychiatry, 1974.

Gruba, G. H., & Rohrbaugh, M. MMPI correlates of menstrual distress. *Psychosomatic Medicine,* 1975, *37* (3), 265–273.

Grummon, D. L., & Barclay, A. M. (Eds.). *Sexuality: A search for perspective.* New York: Van Nostrand Reinhold, 1971.

Guerrant, J., Anderson, W. W., Fischer, A., Weinstein, M. R., Jaros, R. M., & Deskins, A. *Personality in epilepsy.* Springfield, Ill.: Charles C Thomas, 1962.

Gulevich, G. D. & Bourne, P. G. Mental illness and violence. In D. N. Daniels, M. G. Gilula, and F. M. Ochberg (Eds.), *Violence and the Struggle for Existence.* Boston: Little, Brown, 1970.

Gull, W. Anorexia nervosa, *Transactions of the Clinical Society of London,* 1874, *7,* 22.

Gump, P. V. *A statistical investigation of one psychoanalytic approach and a comparison of it with non-directive therapy.* Unpublished master's thesis, Ohio State University, 1944.

Gustavson, K. H. *Down's syndrome: A clinical and cytogenetical investigation.* Sweden: Institute for Medical Genetics of University of Uppsala, 1964.

Guze, S. B., & Perley, M. J. Observations on the natural history of hysteria. *American Journal of Psychiatry,* 1963, *119,* 960–965.

Hadfield, J. The cure of homosexuality. *British Medical Journal,* 1958, *1,* 1323–1326.

Halkides, G. *An experimental study of four conditions necessary for therapeutic change.* Unpublished doctoral dissertation, University of Chicago, 1958.

Hall, R., Lund, D., & Jackson, D. Effects of teacher attention on study behavior. *Journal of Applied Behavior Analysis,* 1968, *1,* 1–12.

Hall, S. M. Self-control and therapist control in the behavioral treatment of overweight women. *Behaviour Research and Therapy,* 1972, *10,* 59–68.

Hallahan, D. P., Cruickshank, W. M. *Psycho-educational foundations of learning disabilities.* Englewood Cliffs, N.J.: Prentice-Hall, 1973.

Halper, C., Pivik, T., & Dement, W. *An attempt to reduce REM rebound effect following REM deprivation by the use of induced waking mentation.* Paper presented at the meeting of the Association for the Psychophysiological Study of Sleep, Boston, March 1969.

Halpert, H. P. Models for the application of systems analysis to the delivery of mental health services. In P. E. Cook (Ed.), *Community psychology and community mental health: Introductory readings.* San Francisco: Holden-Day, 1970.

Haney, C., Banks, C., & Zimbardo, P. Interpersonal dynamics in a simulated prison. *International Journal of Criminology and Penology,* 1973, *1,* 69–97.

Hare, R. D. *Psychopathy: Theory and research.* New York: Wiley, 1970.

Harkins, P. W. *Galen on the passions and errors of the soul.* Columbus: Ohio State University Press, 1963.

Harlow, H., & Harlow, M. In J. Money (Ed.), *Sex research: New developments.* New York: Holt Rinehart and Winston, 1965.

Harris, M. B. Self-directed program for weight control: A pilot study. *Journal of Abnormal Psychology,* 1969, *74,* 263–270.

Harrison, S. I., & McDermott, J. F. *Childhood psychopathology.* New York: International Universities Press, 1972.

Hart, J. T., The development of client-centered therapy. In J. T. Hart & T. M. Tomlinson (Eds.), *New directions in client-centered therapy.* Boston: Houghton Mifflin, 1970.

Hartmann, E. L. *The functions of sleep.* New Haven: Yale University Press, 1973.

Harvald, B., & Hauge, M. Hereditary factors elucidated by twin studies. In J. V. Neel, M. W. Shaw, & W. J. Schull (Eds.), *Genetics and the epidemiology of chronic diseases.* Washington, D.C.: U.S. Department of Health, Education, and Welfare, 1965.

Hassol, L., & Cooper, S. Mental Health consultation in a preventive context. In H. Grunebaum (Ed.), *The practice of community mental health.* Boston: Little, Brown, 1970.

Haug, J. Pneumoencephalographic evidence of brain damage in chronic alcoholics. *Acta Psychiatry and Neurology Scandinavia,* 1968, *203,* 135–143.

Heath, R. G. Pleasure responses of human subjects to direct stimulation of the brain: Physiological and psychodynamic considerations. In R. G. Heath (Ed.), *The role of pleasure in behavior.* New York: Harper & Row, 1964.

Heath, R. G., Cohen, S. B., Silva, F., Leach, B. E., & Cohen, M. Administration of taraxein in humans. *Diseases of the Nervous System,* 1959, *20,* 206–208.

Heath, R. G., & the Department of Psychiatry and Neurology, Tulane University. *Studies in schizophrenia.* Cambridge, Mass.: Harvard University Press, 1954.

Heath, R. G., Guschwan, A. F., & Coffey, J. W. Relation of taraxein to schizophrenia. *Diseases of the Nervous System,* 1970, *31,* 391–395.

Heber, R. F. A manual on terminology and classification in mental retardation. Monograph Supplement to *American Journal of Mental Deficiency* (2nd ed.), 1961.

Heber, R. F. U.S. President's Panel on Mental Retardation. Washington: U.S. Department of Health, Education and Welfare, Public Health Service. Government Printing Office, 1963.

Heber, R. F. *Epidemiology of mental retardation.* Springfield, Ill.: Charles C Thomas, 1970.

Hedquist, F. J., & Weingold, B. K. Behavioral group counseling with socially anxious and unassertive college students. *Journal of Counseling Psychology, 1970, 17,* 237–242.

Helig, S. M., Farberow, N. L., Litman, R. E., & Shneidman, E. S. The role of nonprofessional volunteers in a suicide prevention center. *Community Mental Health Journal, 1968, 4,* 287–295.

Henderson, D., & Gillespie, R. D. *Textbook of psychiatry* (9th ed.). London: Oxford University Press, 1963.

Herrnstein, R. J. Method and theory in the study of avoidance. *Psychological Review, 1969, 76,* 49–69.

Hersch, C. Social history, mental health, and community control. *American Psychologist, 1972, 27,* 749–754.

Hersen, M., Eisler, R. M., & Miller, P. M. An experimental analysis of generalization in assertive training. *Behaviour Research and Therapy, 1974, 12,* 295–310.

Heuscher, J. E. What is existential psychotherapy? *Review of Existential Psychology and Psychiatry, 1964, 4,* 158–167.

Heuscher, J. E. Clinical application of the concept, "world-design": A procedure. *Journal of Existentialism, 1965, 5,* 371–378.

Heuscher, J. E. Mythologic and fairy-tale themes in psychotherapy. *American Journal of Psychotherapy, 1967, 21,* 655–665.

Heuscher, J. E. The use of fairy-tale and mythological themes in psychotherapy (Part II). *International Journal for Existential Psychiatry, 1969, 7,* 34–42.

Hicks, S. P. Effects of ionizing radiation on the adult and embryonic nervous system. In H. H. Merritt & C. C. Hare (Eds.), *Metabolic and toxic diseases of the nervous system: Proceedings of the association.* Baltimore: Williams & Wilkins, 1953.

Higgins, J. Process–reactive schizophrenia: Recent developments. *Journal of Nervous and Mental Disease, 1969, 149,* 450–472.

Hilgard, E. R. Experimental approaches to psychoanalysis. In E. Pumpian-Mindlin (Ed.), *Psychoanalysis as science.* Stanford: Stanford University Press, 1952.

Hilgard, E. R. *Hypnotic susceptibility.* New York: Harcourt, Brace & World, 1965.

Hilgard, E. R., & Bower, G., *Theories of learning.* New York: Appleton-Century-Crofts, 1966.

Hill, M. J., & Blanc, H. T. Evaluation of psychotherapy with alcoholics: A critical review. *Quarterly Journal of Studies on Alcohol, 1967, 28,* 76–104.

Hilliard, L. T., & Kirman, B. H. *Mental deficiency* (2nd ed.). Boston: Little, Brown, 1965.

Hirschi, T. *Causes of delinquency.* Berkeley: University of California Press, 1970.

Hobart, C. W. The meaning of death. *Journal of Existential Psychiatry, 1964, 4,* 219–224.

Hobbs, N. Mental health's third revolution. *American Journal of Orthopsychiatry, 1964, 34,* 822–833.

Hoch, P. H., & Knight, R. P. (Eds.). *Epilepsy: Psychiatric aspects of convulsive disorders.* New York: Hafner, 1965.

Hodgson, R. J., & Rachman, S. An experimental investigation of the implosion technique. *Behaviour Research and Therapy, 1970, 8,* 21–27.

Hodgson, R. J., & Rachman, S. The effects of contamination and washing in obsessional patients. *Behaviour Research and Therapy, 1972, 10,* 111–117.

Hodgson, R. J., Rachman, S., & Marks, I. M. The treatment of chronic obsessive–compulsive neurosis: Follow-up and further findings. *Behaviour Research and Therapy, 1972, 10,* 181–189.

Hoffer, A., & Osmond, H. Some schizophrenic recoveries. *Diseases of the Nervous System, 1962, 4,* 204–210.

Hoffer, A., & Osmond, H. Treatment of schizophrenia with nicotinic acid: A 10 year followup. *Acta Psychiatrica Scandinavica, 1964, 40,* 171–189.

Hoffer, A., & Osmond, H. Nicotinamide adenine dinucleotide in the treatment of chronic schizophrenic patients. *British Journal of Psychiatry, 1968, 114,* 915–917.

Hoffer, A., Pollin, W., Stabenau, J. R., Allen, M., & Hrubeck, Z. Schizophrenia in the National Research Council's register of 15,909 veteran twin pairs (in preparation).

Hofmann, A. Psychotomimetic agents. In A. Burger (Ed.), *Drugs affecting the central nervous system* (Vol. 2). New York: Marcel Dekker, 1968.

Hogan, R. A. Implosively oriented behavior modification: Therapy considerations. *Behaviour research and therapy,* 1969, *7,* 177–184.

Hogan, R. A., & Kirchner, J. H. A preliminary report of extinction of learned fears via short term implosive therapy. *Journal of Abnormal Psychology,* 1967, *72,* 106–111.

Holden, C. Psychosurgery: Legitimate therapy or laundered lobotomy? *Science,* 1973, *179,* 1109–1112.

Hollingshead, A. B., & Redlich, F. C. *Social class and mental illness.* New York: Wiley, 1958.

Holt, H. The case of Father M: A segment of an existential analysis. *Journal of Existentialism,* 1966, *6,* 369–396.

Holt, R. R. Drive or wish? A reconsideration of the psychoanalytic theory of motivation. In M. M. Gill & P. S. Holzman (Eds.), *Psychology versus metapsychology.* New York: International Universities Press, 1975. [Also *Psychological Issues,* 1975, *9* (Monograph 36)].

Holziger, R. Analytic and integrative therapy with the help of LSD-25. *Journal of Existential Psychiatry,* 1964, *4,* 225–236.

Holzinger, R., Mortimer, R., & Van Dusen, W. Aversion conditioning treatment of alcoholism. *American Journal of Psychiatry,* 1967, *124,* 246–247.

Hooker, E. An empirical study of some relations between sexual patterns and gender identity in male homosexuals. In R. Brecher & E. Brecher (Eds.), *An analysis of human sexual response.* New York: New American Library, 1966.

Hoon, P., Wincze, J. P., & Hoon, E. Physiological assessment of sexual arousal in women. *Psychophysiology,* 1976, *13,* 196–204.

Hoover, C. F., & Franz, J. D. Siblings in the families of schizophrenics. *Archives of General Psychiatry,* 1972, *26,* 334–342.

Hopkins, J. Sartrean philosophy and existential psychotherapy. *Review of Existential Psychology and Psychiatry,* 1970, *10,* 51–62.

Hora, T. Existential psychiatry and group psychotherapy. In H. Ruitenbeek (Ed.), *Psychoanalysis and existential philosophy.* New York: Dutton, 1962. (a)

Hora, T. Psychotherapy, existence, and religion. In H. Ruitenbeek (Ed.), *Psychoanalysis and existential philosophy.* New York: Dutton, 1962. (b)

Horney, K. *Neurosis and human growth.* New York: Norton, 1950.

Horowitz, M. J. *Psychosocial function in epilepsy.* Springfield, Ill.: Charles C Thomas, 1970.

Horst, P. Psychological measurement and prediction. Belmont, Calif.: Wadsworth, 1966.

Howard, G. *Participant modeling in the treatment of rat phobics.* Unpublished doctoral dissertation, Southern Illinois University, 1975.

Howland, E. S. Nostalgia. *Journal of Existential Psychiatry,* 1962, *3,* 197–204.

Hsu, E. H. On the application of Viennese infant scale to Peiping babies. *Journal of Genetic Psychology,* 1946, *69,* 217–220.

Humes, J. J. Toxicity from exposure to mercury. In F. W. Sunderman & F. W. Sunderman, Jr. (Eds.), *Laboratory diagnosis of diseases caused by toxic agents.* St. Louis: Warren H. Green, 1970.

Hunt, J. McV. Toward the prevention of incompetence. In J. W. Carter, Jr. (Ed.), *Research contributions from psychology to community mental health.* New York: Behavioral Publications, 1968.

Hunt, W. A., Wittson, C. L., & Hunt, E. B. A theoretical and practical analysis of the diagnostic process. In P. H. Hoch & J. Zubin (Eds.), *Current problems in psychiatric diagnosis.* New York: Grune & Stratton, 1953.

Hunziker, J. C. *The use of participant modeling in the treatment of water phobias.* Unpublished master's thesis, Arizona State University, 1972.

Huston, P. E., & Locher, L. M. Manic-depressive psychosis—course when treated and untreated with electric shock. *Archives of Neurology and Psychiatry,* 1948, *60,* 37–48.

Hutchinson, J. J., & Smedberg, D. Treatment of depressions: A comparative study of ECT and six drugs. *British Journal of Psychiatry,* 1963, *110,* 641–647.

Imura, T., Kawakubo, Y., Mochizuki, A., Misu, S., & Makihara, H. The families of schizophrenic patients. In R. Cancro (Ed.), *Annual review of the schizophrenic syndrome, 1973,* New York: Brunner/Mazel, 1974.

Ingelfinger, F. J. Let the ulcer patient enjoy his food. In F. J. Ingelfinger, A. S. Relman, & M. Finland (Eds.), *Controversy in internal medicine.* Philadelphia: Saunders, 1966.

Ingram, I. M. Obsessional illness in mental hospital patients. *Journal of Mental Science,* 1961, *107,* 382–402.

Inouye, E. Similarity and dissimilarity of schizophrenia in twins. *Proceedings of the Third World Congress on Psychiatry,* Montreal, 1961, *1,* 524–530. (Published in book form by University of Toronto Press, Toronto.)

Ironside, R., & Batchelor, I. R. C. The ocular manifestations of hysteria in relation to flying. *British Journal of Ophthalmology,* 1945, *29,* 88–98.

Irvin, R. E., Bagnall, M. K., & Smith, B. J. *The older patient: An introduction to geriatrics.* London: English Universities Press, 1970.

Isbell, H., Altschule, S., Kornetsky, C. H., Eisenman, A. J., Flanary, H. G., & Fraser, H. F. Chronic barbiturate intoxication. *AMA Archives of Neurology and Psychiatry,* 1950, *64,* 1–28.

Israel, S. L. *Menstrual disorders and sterility* (5th ed.). New York: Harper & Row, 1967.

Jacobson, A., Kales, J. D., & Kales, A. Clinical and electrophysiological correlates of sleep disorders in children. In A. Kales (Ed.), *Sleep: Physiology and pathology.* Philadelphia: Lippincott, 1969.

Jacobson, G. F., Wilner, D. M., Morley, W. E., Schneider, S., Strickler, M., & Sommer, G. J. The scope and practice of an early-access brief treatment psychiatric center. *American Journal of Psychiatry,* 1965, *121,* 1176–1182.

Jaffe, J. H. Narcotic analgesics. In L. S. Goodman & A. Gilman (Eds.), *The pharmacological basis of therapeutics* (4th ed.). New York: Macmillan, 1970.

Jaffe, J. H. Drug addiction and drug abuse. In L. S. Goodman & A. Gilman (Eds.), *The pharmacological basis of therapeutics* (5th ed.). New York: Macmillan, 1975.

Jaffe, J. H., & Martin, W. R. Narcotic analgesics and antagonists. In L. S. Goodman & A. Gilman (Eds.), *The pharmacological basis of therapeutics* (5th ed.). New York: Macmillan, 1975.

Jahoda, M. *Current concepts of positive mental health.* New York: Basic Books, 1958.

James, B. Case of homosexuality treated by aversion therapy. *British Medical Journal,* 1962, *1,* 768–770.

Janda, L. H., & Rimm, D. C. Covert sensitization in the treatment of obesity. *Journal of Abnormal Psychology,* 1972, *80,* 37–42.

Jarvik, M. The psychopharmacological revolution. *Psychology Today,* 1967, *1,* 51–59.

Johnson, L. C. Physiological and psychological changes following total sleep deprivation. In A. Kales (Ed.), *Sleep: Physiology and pathology.* Philadelphia: Lippincott, 1969.

Johnson, L. C. Are stages of sleep related to waking behavior? *American Scientist,* 1973, *61,* 326–338.

Jones, E. *The life and work of Sigmund Freud* (Vol. 1). New York: Basic Books, 1953.

Jones, H. S., & Oswald, I. Two cases of healthy insomnia. *Electroencephalography and Clinical Neurophysiology,* 1968, *24,* 378.

Jones, K. L., Shainberg, L. W., & Byer, C. O. *Drugs and alcohol* (2nd ed.). New York: Harper & Row, 1973.

Jones, M. C. The elimination of children's fears. *Journal of Experimental Psychology,* 1924, *7,* 382–390.

Jourard, S. *The transparent self: Self-disclosure and well-being.* Princeton, N.J.: D. Van Nostrand, 1964.

Jourard, S. Psychotherapy as invitation. *International Forum for Existential Psychiatry,* 1967, *6,* 19–34.

Jouvet, M. Neurophysiological and biochemical mechanisms of sleep. In A. Kales (Ed.), *Sleep: Physiology and pathology.* Philadelphia: Lippincott, 1969.

Kaelbling, R. & Volpe, P. A. II. Constancy of psychiatric diagnoses in readmissions. *Comprehensive Psychiatry,* 1963, *4,* 29–39.

Kahn, E. An appraisal of existential analysis. In H. Ruitenbeek (Ed.), *Psychoanalysis and existential philosophy.* New York: Dutton, 1962.

Kahn, E. J. *The big drink: The story of Coca-Cola.* New York: Random House, 1960.

Kaig, L. *Alcoholism in twins: Studies on the etiology and sequels of abuse of alcohol.* Stockholm: Alcaquist & Wiksell, 1960.

Kales, A. The evaluation and treatment of sleep disorders: Pharmacological and psychological studies. In M. H. Chase (Ed.), *The sleeping brain.* Los Angeles: Brain Information Service, UCLA, 1972.

Kales, A., & Berger, R. J. Psychopathology of sleep. In C. G. Costello (Ed.), *Symptoms of psychopathology.* New York: Wiley, 1970.

Kales, A., Jacobson, A., Paulson, M. J., Kales, J. D., & Walter, R. D. Somnambulism: Psychophysiological correlates. I. All-night EEG studies. *Archives of General Psychiatry,* 1966, *14,* 586–594.

Kales, A., & Kales, J. Evaluation, diagnosis, and treatment of clinical conditions related to sleep. *Journal of the American Medical Association,* 1970, *213,* 2229–2235.

Kales, A., & Kales, J. Recent advances in the diagnosis and treatment of sleep disorders. In G. Usdin (Ed.), *Sleep research and clinical practice.* New York: Brunner/Mazel, 1973.

Kales, A., Paulson, M. J., Jacobson, A., & Kales, J. D. Somnambulism: Psychophysiological correlates. II. Psychiatric interviews, psychological testing, and discussion. *Archives of General Psychiatry,* 1966, *14,* 595–604.

Kallmann, F. J. The genetic theory of schizophrenia. *American Journal of Psychiatry,* 1946, *103,* 309–322.

Kallmann, F. J. Genetic principles in manic-depressive psychoses: Depression, *Proceedings of the 42nd Annual Meeting of the American Psychopathological Association,* 1952.

Kallmann, F. J. *Heredity in health and mental disorder.* New York: Norton, 1953.

Kane, F., Lipton, M., & Ewing, J. Hormonal influences in female sexual response. *Archives of General Psychiatry,* 1969, *20,* 202–203.

Kanfer, F. H., & Phillips, J. S. *Learning foundations of behavior therapy.* New York: Wiley, 1970.

Kanner, L. Autistic disturbances of affective contact. *Nervous Child,* 1943, *2,* 217–240.

Kanner, L. *Child psychiatry* (4th ed.). Springfield, Ill.: Charles C Thomas, 1972.

Kanner, L. *Childhood psychosis: Initial studies and new insights.* Washington, D.C.: Winston, 1973.

Kaplan, H. S. *The new sexual therapy.* New York: Brunner/Mazel, 1974.

Kardiner, A. *The traumatic neuroses of war.* New York: Hoeber, 1941.

Karush, A., Daniels, G. E., O'Connor, J. F., & Stern, L. O. The response to psychotherapy in chronic ulcerative colitis. *Psychosomatic Medicine,* 1969, *31* (3), 201–226.

Kasl, S. V., & Cobb, S. Blood pressure changes in men undergoing job loss: A preliminary report. *Psychosomatic Medicine,* 1970, *32* (1), 19–38.

Kasl, S. V., & Mahl, G. F. The relationship of disturbances and hesitations in spontaneous speech to anxiety. *Journal of Personality and Social Psychology,* 1965, *1,* 425–433.

Katz, M. M., Cole, J. O., & Lowery, H. A. Studies of the diagnostic process: The influence of symptom perception, past experience, and ethnic background on diagnostic decisions. *American Journal of Psychiatry,* 1969, *125,* 937–947.

Kay, D. W. K. Epidemiological aspects of organic brain disease in the aged. In C. M. Gaitz (Ed.), *Aging and the brain: The proceedings of the fifth annual symposium held at the Texas Research Institute of Mental Sciences in Houston, October 1971.* Houston, 1972.

Kaye, D., Kirschner, P., & Mandler, G. The effect of test anxiety on memory span in a group test situation. *Journal of Consulting Psychology,* 1953, *17,* 265–266.

Kazdin, A. E., & Wilcoxon, L. A. Systematic desensitization and nonspecific treatment effects: A methodological evaluation. *Psychological Bulletin,* 1976, *83,* 729–758.

Kear-Colwell, J. J. The taxonomy of depressive phenomena and its relationships to the reactive-endogenous dichotomy. *British Journal of Psychiatry,* 1972, *121,* 665–671.

Keen, E. Scheler's view of repentance and rebirth and its relevance to psychotherapy. *Review of Existential Psychology and Psychiatry,* 1966, *6,* 84–88.

Keen, E. *Three faces of being: Toward an existential clinical psychology.* New York: Appleton-Century-Crofts, 1970.

Keen, E. *Psychology and the new consciousness.* Monterey, Calif.: Brooks/Cole, 1972.

Keen, E. Suicide and self-deception. *Psychoanalytic Review,* 1973–1974, *60,* 575–585.

Keen, E. *A primer in phenomenological psychology.* New York: Holt, Rinehart and Winston, 1975.

Kelly, G. *The psychology of personal constructs.* New York: Norton, 1955.

Kelly, J. G. The quest for valid preventive interventions. In C. D. Spielberger (Ed.), *Current topics in clinical and community psychology* (Vol. 2). New York: Academic Press, 1970.

Kendall, E., Cooper, E., Gourlay, J., & Copeland, R. M. Diagnostic criteria of American and British psychiatrists. *Archives of General Psychiatry,* 1971, *25,* 123–130.

Kendell, R. E. *The classification of depressive illness.* London: Oxford University Press, 1968.

Kendig, I., & Richmond, W. V. *Psychological studies in dementia praecox.* Ann Arbor, Mich.: Edwards, 1940.

Kennedy, T. D. Verbal conditioning without awareness. The use of programmed reinforcement and recurring assessment of awareness. *Journal of Experimental Psychology,* 1970, *84,* 487–494.

Kennedy, T. D. Reinforcement frequency, task characteristics, and interval of awareness assessment as factors in verbal conditioning without awareness. *Journal of Experimental Psychology,* 1971, *88,* 103–112.

Kent, H., & Rosanoff, A. J. A study of association in insanity. *American Journal of Insanity,* 1910, *67,* 326.

Kenyon, F. E. Hypochondriasis: A survey of some historical, clinical, and social aspects. *International Journal of Psychiatry,* 1966, *2,* 308–325.

Kernberg, O. *Object relations theory and its applications.* New York: Jason Aronson, 1976.

Kessler, J. W. *Psychopathology of childhood.* Englewood Cliffs, N.J.: Prentice-Hall, 1966.

Kessler, J. W. Nosology in child psychopathology. In H. E. Rie (Ed.), *Perspectives in child psychopathology.* Chicago: Aldine, 1971.

Kessler, P., & Neale, J. M. Hippocampal damage and schizophrenia: A critique of Mednick's theory. *Journal of Abnormal Psychology,* 1974, *83,* 91–96.

Kety, S. S. Toward hypotheses for a biochemical component in the vulnerability to schizophrenia. *Seminars in Psychiatry,* 1972, *4,* 233–238.

Kierkegaard, S. [*Fear and trembling*] (W. Lowrie, trans.). Princeton, N.J.: Princeton University Press, 1954. (Originally published, 1843.)

Kiesler, D. J. Some myths of psychotherapy research and the search for a paradigm. *Psychological Bulletin,* 1966, *65,* 110–136.

Kilburg, R. R., & Siegel, A. W. Formal operations in reactive and process schizophrenics. *Journal of Consulting and Clinical Psychology,* 1973, *40,* 371–376.

King, A., & Nicol, C. *Venereal diseases.* Philadelphia: F. A. Davis, 1969.

Kingsley, L., & Struening, E. L. Changes in intellectual performance of acute and chronic schizophrenics. *Psychological Reports,* 1966, *18,* 791–800.

Kinsey, A., Pomeroy, W., & Martin, C. *Sexual behavior in the human male.* Philadelphia: Saunders, 1948.

Kinsey, A., Pomeroy, W., Martin, C., & Gebhard, P. *Sexual behavior in the human female.* Philadelphia: Saunders, 1953.

Kissin, B., & Beglister, H. (Eds.). *The biology of alcoholism:* Vol. 1, *Biochemistry.* New York: Plenum Press, 1971.

Klebanoff, L. B. Parents of schizophrenic children: I. Parental attitudes of mothers of schizophrenic, brain-injured and retarded, and normal children. *American Journal of Orthopsychiatry,* 1959, *29,* 445–454.

Klein, D. C. *Community dynamics and mental health.* New York: Wiley, 1968.

Klein, D. F., & Davis, J. M. *Diagnosis and drug treatment of psychiatric disorders.* Baltimore: Williams & Wilkins, 1969.

Klein, G. S. Peremptory ideation: Structure and force in motivated ideas. In R. R. Holt (Ed.), Motives and thought: Psychoanalytic essays in honor of David Rapaport. *Psychological Issues,* 1967, *5* (Monograph 18/19).

Klein, G. S. *Psychoanalytic theory: An exploration of essentials.* New York: International Universities Press, 1975.

Kleinmuntz, B. *Essentials of abnormal psychology.* New York: Harper & Row, 1974.

Kleitman, N. *Sleep and wakefulness* (2nd ed.). Chicago: University of Chicago Press, 1963.

Kline, P. *Fact and fantasy in Freudian theory.* London: Methuen, 1972.

Knoff, W. A history of the concept of neurosis, with a memoir of William Cullen. *American Journal of Psychiatry,* 1970, *127,* 80–84.

Koestenbaum, P. The vitality of death. *Journal of Existentialism,* 1964, *5,* 139–166.

Kogan, G. The history, philosophy and practice of Gestalt therapy: Theory of human nature and conduct in Frederick Perls' psychology. Doctoral dissertation, University of California, Berkeley, 1974. (University Microfilms No. 74-1329).

Kohlenberg, R. J. Behavioristic approach to multiple personality: A case study. *Behavior Therapy*, 1973, *4*, 137–140.

Kohlenberg, R. Directed masturbation and the treatment of primary orgasmic dysfunction. *Archives of Sexual Behavior*, 1974, *3*, 349–356.

Kolb, L. C. *Modern clinical psychiatry* (8th ed.). Philadelphia: Saunders, 1973.

Kolodny, R. C., Masters, W. H., Hendryx, J., & Toro, G. Plasma testosterone and semen analysis in male homosexuals. *New England Journal of Medicine*, 1971, *285*, 1170–1174.

Korwin, M. Aged humanity in cocoons. *Journal of Existential Psychiatry*, 1963, *4*, 69–88.

Kraepelin, E. *Lehrbuch der Psychiatrie*. Leipzig: Barth, 1883.

Kraepelin, E. [*Dementia praecox and paraphrenia*] (R. M. Barclay, trans.). Edinburgh: E. and S. Livingstone, 1919. (Originally published, 1913.)

Kramer, M. Cross-national study of diagnosis of the mental disorders: Origin of the problem. *American Journal of Psychiatry*, 1965, *125*, 1–11. (Supplement)

Kramer, M. Introduction: The historical background of ICD-8. In *The diagnostic and statistical manual of mental disorders* (2nd ed.). Washington, D.C.: American Psychiatric Association, 1968.

Kraus, S. J. Stress, acne and skin surface free fatty acids. *Psychomatic Medicine*, 1970, *32* (5), 503–508.

Kreitman, N. The reliability of psychiatric diagnosis. *Journal of Mental Science*, 1961, *107*, 876–886.

Kremer, M. M. Psychological impact of acne in adolescence. In J. E. Jeffress (Ed.), *Psychosomatic medicine current journal articles*. New York: Medical Examination Publishing Co., 1971. (Reprinted from *Journal of the American Women's Association*, 1969, *4*, 24.)

Krikstone, B. J., & Levitt, R. A. Distorting drugs. In R. A. Levitt, *Psychopharmacology: A biological approach*. Washington, D.C.: Hemisphere/Wiley, 1975. (a)

Krikstone, B. J., & Levitt, R. A. Stimulant and antidepressant drugs. In R. A. Levitt, *Psychopharmacology: A biological approach*. Washington, D.C.: Hemisphere/Wiley, 1975. (b)

Kringlen, E. Hereditary and social factors in schizophrenic twins: An epidemiological–clinical study. In J. Romano (Ed.), *The origins of schizophrenia*. New York: Excerpta Medica Foundation, 1967.

Kroger, W. S., & Freed, S. C. *Psychosomatic gynecology*. Glencoe, Ill.: Free Press, 1956.

Krugman, S., & Ward, R. *Infectious diseases of children and adults*. St. Louis: C. V. Mosby, 1973.

Kubie, S. The fundamental nature of the distinction between normality and neurosis. *Psychoanalytical Quarterly*, 1954, *23*, 167–204.

Kutner, L. The illusion of due process in commitment proceedings. *Northwestern University Law Review*, 1962, *57*, 383–399.

Kvale, S., & Grennes, C. E. Skinner and Sartre: Toward a radical phenomenology of behavior. *Review of Existential Psychology and Psychiatry*, 1967, *7*, 128–150.

L'Abate, L. Early infantile autism: A reply to Ward. *Psychological Bulletin*, 1972, *77*, 49–51.

Lacey, J. I. Psychophysiological approaches to the evaluation of psychotherapeutic process and outcome. In E. A. Rubinstein & M. B. Parloff (Eds.), *Research in psychotherapy*. Washington, D.C.: National Publishing Co., 1959.

Lader, M. H. Palmer skin conductance measures in anxiety and phobic states. *Journal of Psychosomatic Research*, 1967, *11*, 271–281.

Lader, M. H., & Wing, L. Habituation of the psycho-galvanic reflex in patients with anxiety states and in normal subjects. *Journal of Neurology, Neurosurgery and Psychiatry*, 1964, *27*, 210–218.

Laing, R. D. *The divided self: A study in sanity and madness*. Chicago: Quadrangle Books, 1960.

Laing, R. D. Minkowski and schizophrenia. *Review of Existential Psychology and Psychiatry*, 1963, *3*, 195–208.

Laing, R. D., Phillipson, H., & Lee, A. R. *Interpersonal perception: A theory and a method of research*. New York: Harper & Row, 1972.

Lamy, R. E. Social consequences of mental illness. *Journal of Consulting Psychology*, 1966, *30*, 450–455.

Landau, S. Future time perspective of delinquents and non-delinquents: The effects of institutionalization. *Criminal Justice and Behavior*, 1975, *2*, 22–36.

Landis, C., & Page, J. D. *Modern society and mental disease*. New York: Farrar and Rinehart, 1938.

Landy, F. J., & Gaupp, L. A. A factor analysis of the fear survey schedule—III. *Behaviour Research and Therapy,* 1971, *9,* 89–93.

Lang, P. J., & Melamed, B. G. Avoidance conditioning therapy of an infant with chronic ruminative vomiting. *Journal of Abnormal Psychology,* 1969, *74,* 1–8.

LaPointe, K. *A comparison of cognitive therapy and assertive training in the treatment of depression.* Unpublished doctoral dissertation, Southern Illinois University, 1975.

Lapouse, R., & Monk, M. A. Fears and worries in a representative sample of children. *American Journal of Orthopsychiatry,* 1959, *29,* 803–818.

Latner, J. *The Gestalt therapy book.* New York: Julian Press, 1973.

Lavin, N. I., Thorpe, J. G., Barker, J. C., Blakemore, C. B., & Conway, C. G. Behavior therapy in a case of transvestism. *Journal of Nervous and Mental Disease,* 1961, *133,* 346–353.

Lazarus, A. A. Behavior rehearsal vs. nondirective therapy vs. advice in effecting behavior change. *Behaviour Research and Therapy,* 1966, *4,* 209–212.

Lazarus, A. A. *Behavior therapy and beyond.* New York: McGraw-Hill, 1971.

Lazarus, A. A. Multimodal behavioral treatment of depression. *Behavior Therapy,* 1974, *5,* 549–554.

Ledermann, E. K. Clinical applications of existential psychotherapy. *Journal of Existential Psychiatry,* 1962, *3,* 45–68.

Lefebre, L. B. Existentialism and psychotherapy. *Review of Existential Psychology and Psychiatry,* 1963, *3,* 271–286.

Lehrer, P. M. Physiological effects of relaxation in a double-blind analog of desensitization. *Behavior Therapy,* 1972, *3,* 193–208.

Leitenberg, H., Agras, W. S., & Thomson, L. E. A sequential analysis of the effect of selective positive reinforcement in modifying anorexia nervosa. *Behaviour Research and Therapy,* 1968, *6,* 211–218.

Lejeune, J., Gautier, M., & Turpin, R. Etude des chromosomes somatique de neuf enfants mongoliens. *Comptes Rendus Academie demie Sciences,* 1959, *248,* 1721–1722.

LeJeune, R., & Alex, N. On being mugged: The event and its aftermath. *Urban Life and Culture,* 1973, *2,* 259–287.

Lester, D. The evaluation of suicide prevention centers. *International Behavioral Scientist,* 1971, *3,* 40–47.

Levine, G., & Burke, C. J. *Mathematical model techniques for learning theories.* New York: Academic Press, 1972.

Levine, R. R. *Pharmacology: Drug actions and reactions.* Boston: Little, Brown, 1973.

Levis, D. J., & Carrera, R. N. Effects of 10 hours of implosive therapy in the treatment of outpatients: A preliminary report. *Journal of Abnormal Psychology,* 1967, *72,* 504–508.

Levitsky, A., & Perls, F. S. The rules and games of Gestalt therapy. In J. Fagan & I. Shepherd (Eds.), *Gestalt therapy now.* Palo Alto, Calif.: Science and Behavior Books, 1970.

Levitt, E. E. Psychotherapy with children: A further evaluation. *Behaviour Research and Therapy,* 1963, *1,* 45–51.

Levitt, E. E. *The psychology of anxiety.* Indianapolis, Ind.: Bobbs-Merrill, 1967.

Levitt, R. A. *Psychopharmacology: A biological approach.* Washington, D.C.: Hemisphere/Wiley, 1975.

Levitt, R. A., & Krikstone, B. J. The tranquilizers. In R. A. Levitt, *Psychopharmacology: A biological approach.* Washington, D.C.: Hemisphere/Wiley, 1975.

Levitt, R. A., & Lonowski, D. J. Adrenergic drugs. In R. A. Levitt (Ed.), *Psychopharmacology: A biological approach.* Washington, D.C.: Hemisphere/Wiley, 1975.

Levy, R. J. Effects of institutional vs. boarding home care on a group of infants. *Journal of Personality,* 1941, *15,* 233–241.

Lewinsohn, P. M. Clinical and theoretical aspects of depression. In K. S. Calhoun, H. E. Adams, & K. M. Mitchell (Eds.), *Innovative treatment methods in psychopathology.* New York: Wiley, 1974.

Lewinsohn, P. M., & Graf, M. Pleasant activities and depression. *Journal of Consulting and Clinical Psychology,* 1973, *41,* 261–268.

Lewinsohn, P. M., & Libet, J. Pleasant events, activity schedules, and depressions. *Journal of Abnormal Psychology,* 1972, *79,* 291–296.

Lewinsohn, P. M., & Shaffer, M. Use of home observations as an integral part of the treatment of depression: Preliminary report and case studies. *Journal of Consulting and Clinical Psychology,* 1971, *37,* 87–95.

Lewis, A. Melancholia: A clinical survey of depressive states. *Journal of Mental Science,* 1934, *80,* 277.

Ley, P. Quantitative aspects of psychological assessment. London: Duckworth, 1972.

Liberman, R. P., and Raskin, D. C. Depression: A behavioral formulation. *Archives of General Psychiatry,* 1971, *24,* 515–523.

Libet, J. M., & Lewinsohn, P. M. Concept of social skill with special reference to the behavior of depressed persons. *Journal of Consulting and Clinical Psychology,* 1973, *40,* 304–312.

Lick, J. Expectancy, false galvanic skin response feedback, and systematic desensitization in the modification of phobic behavior. *Journal of Consulting and Clinical Psychology,* 1975, *4,* 557–567.

Lidz, T. Family studies and a theory of schizophrenia. Stanley R. Dean Award lecture to the American College of Psychiatrists, New Orleans, February 1973.

Lidz, T., Cornelison, A. R., Fleck, S., & Terry, D. Intrafamilial environment of the schizophrenic patient. I. The father. *Psychiatry,* 1957, *20,* 329–342.

Lidz, T., Cornelison, A. R., Terry, D., & Fleck, S. Irrationality as a family tradition. *Archives of Neurological Psychiatry,* 1958, *79,* 305–316.

Lieberman, M., Yalom, I., & Miles, M. *Encounter groups: First facts.* New York: Basic Books, 1973.

Lilienfeld, A. M., & Benesch, C. H. *Epidemiology of mongolism.* Baltimore: Johns Hopkins, 1969.

Lindemann, E. Symptomatology and management of acute grief. *American Journal of Psychiatry,* 1944, *101,* 141–148.

Lindemann, E., & Dawes, L. G. The use of psychoanalytic constructs in preventive psychiatry. In *The psychoanalytic study of the child* (Vol. 7). New York: International Universities Press, 1952.

Litman, R. E. Medical–legal aspects of suicide. In E. S. Shneidman, N. L. Farberow, & R. E. Litman (Eds.), *The psychology of suicide.* New York: Science House, 1970. (a)

Litman, R. E. Suicide as acting out. In E. S. Shneidman, N. L. Farberow, & R. E. Litman (Eds.), *The psychology of suicide.* New York: Science House, 1970. (b)

Livingston, S. *Living with epileptic seizures.* Springfield, Ill.: Charles C Thomas, 1963.

Loeb, A., Beck, A. T., & Diggory, J. Differential effects of success and failure on depressed and nondepressed patients. *Journal of Nervous and Mental Disease,* 1971, *152,* 106–114.

Loeb, A., Beck, A. T., Diggory, J., & Tuthill, R. *The effects of success and failure on mood, motivation, and performance as a function of predetermined level of depression.* Unpublished study, 1966.

Loeb, A., Feschbach, S., Beck, A. T., & Wolf, A. Some effects of reward upon the social perception and motivation of psychiatric patients varying in depression. *Journal of Abnormal and Social Psychology,* 1964, *68,* 609–616.

Loevinger, J. Three principles for a psychoanalytic psychology. *Journal of Abnormal Psychology,* 1966, *71,* 432–443.

London, P. Morals and mental health. In S. C. Plog & R. B. Edgerton (Eds.), *Changing perspectives in mental illness.* New York: Holt, Rinehart and Winston, 1969.

Longerich, M. C., & Bordeaux, J. *Aphasia therapeutics.* New York: Macmillan, 1954.

Lopiccolo, J., & Lobitz, C. The role of masturbation in the treatment of orgasmic dysfunction. *Archives of Sexual Behavior,* 1972, *2,* 163–171.

Lore, R. K. Palmar sweating and transitory anxiety in children. *Child Development,* 1966, *37,* 115–124.

Lorei, T. W., & Gurel, L. Demographic characteristics as predictors of post-hospital employment and readmission. *Journal of Consulting and Clinical Psychology,* 1973, *40,* 426–430.

Lorenz, T. H., Graham, D. T., & Wolf, S. Relation of life stress and emotions to human sebum secretion and to the mechanism of acne vulgaris. In *Yearbook of dermatology and syphilis,* 1953–1954. (Reprinted from *Journal of Laboratory and Clinical Medicine,* 1953, *41,* 11.)

Lorr, M. *Explorations in typing psychotics* (1st ed.). Oxford: Pergamon, 1966.

Lorr, M. A typology for functional psychotics. In M. M. Katz, J. O. Cole, & W. E. Barton (Eds.), *The role and methodology of classification in psychiatry and psychopathology.* Chevy Chase, Md.: National Institute of Mental Health, 1968.

Lorr, M., Klett, C. J., & McNair, D. M. *Syndromes of psychosis.* New York: Macmillan, 1963.

Lovaas, O. I. A program for the establishment of speech in psychotic children. In J. K. Wing (Ed.), *Early childhood autism.* New York: Pergamon, 1966.

Lovaas, O. I., Freitag, G., Kinder, M. I., Rubenstein, B. D., Schaeffer, B., & Simmons, J. Q. Establishment of social reinforcers in two schizophrenic children on the basis of food. *Journal of Experimental Child Psychology*, 1966, *4*, 109–125.

Lovaas, O. I., Schreibman, L., Koegel, R., & Rehm, R. Selective responding by autistic children to multiple sensory input. *Journal of Abnormal Psychology*, 1971, *77*, 211–222.

Lovaas, O. I., & Simmons, J. Q. Manipulation of self-destruction in three retarded children. *Journal of Applied Behavior Analysis*, 1969, *2*, 143–157.

Lovibond, S. H. The mechanism of conditioning treatment of enuresis. *Behaviour Research and Therapy*, 1963, *1*, 17–21.

Lovibond, S. H., & Caddy, G. Discriminated aversive control in the moderation of alcoholic drinking behavior. *Behavior Therapy*, 1970, *1*, 437–444.

Lubetkin, B. S., Rivers, P. C., & Rosenberg, C. M. Difficulties of disulfiram therapy with alcoholics. *Quarterly Journal of Studies on Alcohol*, 1971, *32*, 168–171.

Luborsky, L., & Spence. D. P. Quantitative research on psychoanalytic therapy. In A. E. Bergin & S. L. Garfield (Eds.), *Handbook of psychotherapy and behavior change*. New York: Wiley, 1971.

Lucchesi, B. R., Schuster, C. R., & Emley, G. S. The role of nicotine as a determinant of cigarette smoking frequency in man with observations of certain cardiovascular effects associated with the tobacco alkaloid. *Clinical Pharmacology and Therapeutics*, 1967, *8*, 789–796.

Lundquist, G. Prognosis and course in manic-depressive psychoses. *Acta Psychiatrica Neurologica Scandanavia Supplementum 35*, 1945.

Luxenburger, H. Vorläufiger Bericht über psychiatrische Sereinuntersuchungen an Zwillingen. *Z. Ges. Neurol. Psychiat*, 1928, *116*, 297–347.

Luxenburger, H. Psychiatrisch-neurologische Zwillingspathologie. *Z. Ges. Neurol. Psychiat.*, 1930, *56*, 145–180.

Luxenburger, H. Die Manifestations wahrscheinlichkeit der Schizophrenie im Lichte der Zwillingsforschung. *Z. Psychol. Hyg.*, 1934, *7*, 174–184.

Lykken, D. T. A study of anxiety in the sociopathic personality. *Journal of Abnormal and Social Psychology*, 1957, *55*, 6–10.

Maas, J. W., Dekirmenjian, H., & Fawcett, J. Catecholamine metabolism, depression and stress. *Nature*, 1971, *230*, 330–331.

MacAndrew, C. The differentiation of male alcoholic outpatients from nonalcoholic psychiatric outpatients by means of the MMPI. *Quarterly Journal of Studies on Alcohol*, 1965, *26*, 238–246.

Machado, M. A. Existential encounter in Gabriel Marcel: Its value in psychotherapy. *Review of Existential Psychology and Psychiatry*, 1961, *1*, 53–62.

Maes, W. R., & Heimann, R. A. *The comparison of three approaches to the reduction of test anxiety in high school students.* Unpublished manuscript, Arizona State University, 1970.

Magaro, P. A. Skin conductance basal level and reactivity in schizophrenia as a function of chronicity, premorbid adjustment, diagnosis, and medication. *Journal of Abnormal Psychology*, 1973, *81*, 270–281.

Maher, B. *Principles of psychopathology.* New York: McGraw-Hill, 1966.

Mahoney, M. J. *Cognition and behavior modification.* Cambridge, Mass.: Ballinger, 1974.

Mahoney, M. J., Moura, N., & Wade, T. The relative efficacy of self-reward, self-punishment, and self-monitoring techniques for weight loss. *Journal of Consulting and Clinical Psychology*, 1973, *40*, 404–407.

Mahoney, M. J., & Thoresen, C. E. (Eds.). *Self-control: Power to the person.* Monterey, Calif.: Brooks/Cole, 1974.

Maier, N. R. F. *Frustration: The study of behavior without a goal.* New York: McGraw-Hill, 1949.

Maier, N. R. F., Glaser, N. M., & Klee, J. B. Studies of abnormal behavior in the rat. II. The development of behavior fixations through frustration. *Journal of Experimental Psychology*, 1940, *26*, 521–546.

Malamud, N. Neuropathology of organic brain syndromes. In C. M. Gaitz (Ed.), *Aging and the brain: The proceedings of the fifth annual symposium held at the Texas Research Institute of Mental Sciences in Houston, October 1971.* Houston, 1972.

Malan, D. H. *A study of brief psychotherapy.* London: Tavistock, 1963.

Malmo, R. B. Activation. In A. J. Bachrach (Ed.), *Experimental foundations of clinical psychology.* New York: Basic Books, 1962.

Malmo, R. B. Studies of anxiety: Some clinical origins of the activation concept. In C. D. Spielberger (Ed)., *Anxiety and behavior.* New York: Academic Press, 1966.

Malmo, R. B., & Shagass, C. Physiological studies of reaction to stress in anxiety and early schizophrenia. *Psychosomatic Medicine,* 1949, *11,* 9–24.

Malmo, R. B., & Shagass, C. Studies of blood pressure in psychiatric patients under stress. *Psychosomatic Medicine,* 1952, *14,* 82–93.

Mandler, G., & Sarason, S. B. A study of anxiety and learning. *Journal of Abnormal and Social Psychology,* 1952, *47,* 166–173.

Mann, J. *Time-limited psychotherapy.* Cambridge, Mass.: Harvard University Press, 1973.

(*Scientific American* Editors.) Marihuana menaces youth. *Scientific American,* 1936, *154,* 151.

Mark, V. H. The continuing polemic of psychosurgery (letter to the editor). *Journal of the American Medical Association,* 1974, *227* (8), 943.

Mark, V. H., & Ervin, E. P. *Violence and the brain.* New York: Harper & Row, 1970.

Marks, I., & Gelder, M. Transvestism and fetishism: Clinical and psychological changes during faradic aversion. *British Journal of Psychiatry,* 1967, *113,* 711–729.

Marlatt, G. A., Demming, B., & Reid, J. B. Loss-of-control drinking in alcoholics: An experimental analogue. *Journal of Abnormal Psychology,* 1973, *81,* 233–241.

Marquart, D. I. The pattern of punishment and its relation to abnormal fixation in adult human subjects. *Journal of General Psychology,* 1948, *39,* 107–144.

Marquart, D. I., & Arnold, L. P. A study in the frustration of human adults. *Journal of General Psychology,* 1952, *47,* 43–63.

Martin, B., & Sroufe, L. A. Anxiety. In C. G. Costello (Ed.), *Symptoms of psychopathology: A handbook.* New York: Wiley, 1970.

Martin, W. R., & Fraser, H. F. A comparative study of physiological and subjective effects of heroin and morphine administered intravenously in postaddicts. *Journal of Pharmacology and Experimental Therapeutics,* 1961, *133,* 388–399.

Masserman, J. H., & Jacques, M. G. Experimental masochism. *Archives of Neurological Psychiatry,* 1948, *60,* 402–404.

Masters, J. C., & Driscoll, S. A. Children's "imitation" as a function of the presence or absence of a model and the description of his instrumental behaviors. *Child Developmental,* 1971, *42,* 161–170.

Masters, W. H., & Johnson, V. E. *Human sexual response.* Boston: Little, Brown, 1966.

Masters, W. H., & Johnson, V. E. *Human sexual inadequacy.* Boston: Little, Brown, 1970.

Matarazzo, J. D., & Phillips, J. S. Digit symbol performance as a function of increasing levels of anxiety. *Journal of Consulting Psychology,* 1955, *19,* 131–134.

Mather, M. D. Obsessions and compulsions. In C. G. Costello (Ed.), *Symptoms of psychopathology: A handbook.* New York: Wiley, 1970.

Maugh, T. H., II. LSD and the drug culture: New evidence of hazard. *Science,* 1973, *179,* 1221–1222.

Maxwell, H. *Migraine background and treatment.* Bristol: John Wright, 1966.

May, P. R. A. *Treatment of schizophrenia.* New York: Science House, 1968.

May, P. R. A. A follow-up study of treatment of schizophrenia. In R. L. Spitzer & D. F. Klein (Eds.), *Evaluation of psychological therapies.* Baltimore: Johns Hopkins, 1975.

May, R. The emergence of existential psychotherapy. In R. May (Ed.), *Existential psychology.* New York: Random House, 1961. (a)

May, R. Existential bases of psychotherapy. In R. May (Ed.), *Existential psychology.* New York: Random House, 1961. (b)

May, R. *Love and will.* New York: Norton, 1969.

May, R. The Delphic oracle as therapist. *Review of Existential Psychology and Psychiatry,* 1970, *10,* 201–217.

May, R. *Power and innocence.* New York: Norton, 1972.

May, R., Angel, E., & Ellenberger, H. F. (Eds.). *Existence: A new dimension in psychology and psychiatry.* New York: Basic Books, 1958.

Mayer, J. Some aspects of the problem of regulation of food intake and obesity. *New England Journal of Medicine*, 1966, *274*, 610–616, 662–673, 722–731.

Mayer-Gross, W. On depersonalization. *British Journal of Medical Psychiatry*, 1935, *15*, 103–121.

Mayer-Gross, W., Slater, E., & Roth, M. *Clinical psychiatry*. London: Cassell, 1954.

Mayerson, P., & Lief, H. Psychotherapy of homosexuals: A follow-up of nineteen cases. In J. Marmor (Ed.), *Sexual inversion*. New York: Basic Books, 1965.

McCord, W., & McCord, J. *The psychopath: An essay on the criminal mind*. Princeton, N.J.: D. Van Nostrand, 1964.

McCord, W., McCord, J., & Gudeman, J. *Origins of alcoholism*. Stanford, Calif.: Stanford University Press, 1960.

McCreary, C. P. Comparison of measures of social competency in schizophrenics and the relation of social competency to socioeconomic factors. *Journal of Abnormal Psychology*, 1974, *83*, 124–129.

McCutcheon, B. A., & Adams, H. E. The physiological basis of implosive therapy. *Behaviour Research and Therapy*, 1975, *13*, 93–100.

McFall, R. M., & Lillesand, D. B. Behavior rehearsal with modeling and coaching in assertion training. *Journal of Abnormal Psychology*, 1971, *77*, 313–323.

McFall, R. M., & Marston, A. R. An experimental investigation of behavior rehearsal in assertive training. *Journal of Abnormal Psychology*, 1970, *76*, 295–303.

McFall, R. M., & Twentyman, C. T. Four experiments on the relative contributions of rehearsal, modeling, and coaching to assertion training. *Journal of Abnormal Psychology*, 1973, *81*, 199–218.

McGee, T. F. Some basic considerations in crisis intervention. *Community Mental Health Journal*, 1968, *4*, 319–325.

McGhie, A., Chapman, J., & Lawson, J. S. The effect of distraction on schizophrenic performance. (I) Perception and immediate memory. *British Journal of Psychiatry*, 1965, *111*, 383–390.

McGlynn, F. D., Puhr, J. J., Gaynor, R., & Perry, J. W. Skin conductance responses to real and imagined snakes among avoidant and non-avoidant college students. *Behaviour Research and Therapy*, 1973, *11*, 417–426.

McGuire, R. J., Carlisle, J. M., & Young, B. G. Sexual deviations as conditioned behavior. *Behaviour Research and Therapy*, 1965, *2*, 185–190.

McInnis, T. L., & Ullmann, L. P. Positive and negative reinforcement with short- and long-term hospitalized schizophrenics in a probability learning situation. *Journal of Abnormal Psychology*, 1967, *72*, 157–162.

McKegney, F. P., Gordon, R. O., & Levine, S. M. A psychosomatic comparison of patients with ulcerative colitis and Crohn's disease. *Psychosomatic Medicine*, 1970, *32* (2), 153–166.

McKinney, W. T., Jr., Suomi, S. J., & Harlow, H. F. Depression in primates. *American Journal of Psychiatry*, 1971, *127*, 1313–1320.

McKown, R. *Pioneers in mental health*. New York: Dodd, Mead, 1961.

McNichol, R. W. *The treatment of delirium tremens and related states*. Springfield, Ill.: Charles C Thomas, 1970.

Mechanic, D. Some factors in identifying and defining mental illness. *Mental Hygiene*, 1962, *46*, 66–74.

Medea, A., & Thompson, K. *Against rape*. New York: Farrar, Straus and Giroux, 1974.

Mednick, B. R. Breakdown in high-risk subjects: Familial and early environmental factors. *Journal of Abnormal Psychology*, 1973, *82*, 469–475.

Mednick, S. A. A learning theory approach to research in schizophrenia. *Psychological Bulletin*, 1958, *55*, 316–327.

Mednick, S. A. Breakdown in individuals at a high risk for schizophrenia: Possible predispositional perinatal factors. *Mental Hygiene*, 1970, *54*, 50–63.

Mednick, S. A. Birth defects and schizophrenia. *Psychology Today*, 1971, *4*, 48–50, 80–81.

Mednick, S. A. & Schulsinger, F. Some premorbid characteristics related to breakdown in children with schizophrenic mothers. In D. Rosenthal & S. S. Kety (Eds.), *The transmission of schizophrenia*. Oxford: Pergamon, 1968.

Meehl, P. E. Schizotaxia, schizotypy, schizophrenia. *American Psychologist*, 1962, *17*, 827–838.

Megargee, E. I. The role of inhibition in the understanding and control of violence. In J. L. Singer

(Ed.), *The control of aggression and violence: Cognitive and physiological factors.* New York: Academic Press, 1971.

Megargee, E. I. The prediction of dangerous behavior. *Criminal Justice and Behavior,* 1976, *3,* 1–22.

Meichenbaum, D. H. The effects of instructions and reinforcement on thinking and language behavior of schizophrenics. *Behaviour Research and Therapy,* 1969, *7,* 101–114.

Meichenbaum, D. H. *Cognitive factors in behavior modification.* (Research Report No. 25). Ontario, Canada: University of Waterloo, Dept. of Psychology, 1971.

Meichenbaum, D. H., & Cameron, R. Training schizophrenics to talk to themselves: A means of developing attentional controls. *Behavior Therapy,* 1973, *4,* 515–534.

Meichenbaum, D. H., Gilmore, J., & Fedoravicius, A. Group insight vs. group desensitization in treating speech anxiety. *Journal of Consulting and Clinical Psychology,* 1971, *36,* 410–421.

Meichenbaum, D. H., & Goodman, J. Reflection–impulsivity and verbal control of motor behavior. *Child Development,* 1969, *40,* 785–797.

Meigniez, R. Group therapy from the existential point of view. *Review of Existential Psychology and Psychiatry,* 1963, *3,* 91–98.

Meikle, S. Frigidity and impotence. *Medical Aspects of Human Sexuality,* 1972, *2,* 28–33.

Meiselman, K. C. Broadening dual modality cue utilization in chronic nonparanoid schizophrenics. *Journal of Consulting and Clinical Psychology,* 1973, *41,* 447–453.

Melges, F., & Bowlby, J. Types of hopelessness in psychopathological process. *Archives of General Psychiatry,* 1969, *20,* 690–699.

Mendel, W. M. The future in the model of psychotherapy. *Journal of Existential Psychiatry,* 1962, *2,* 363–370.

Mendel, W. M. Hospital treatment for chronic schizophrenics. *Journal of Existential Psychiatry,* 1963, *4,* 49–58.

Mendel, W. M. Structure as process in psychotherapy. *Journal of Existential Psychiatry,* 1964, *4,* 301–308.

Mendel, W. M. The tactical use of dreams in psychotherapy. *International Forum for Existential Psychiatry,* 1967, *6,* 332–346.

Mendel, W. M. The seduction of the therapist: An editorial. *International Forum for Existential Psychiatry,* 1970, *7,* 3–6.

Mendels, J. (Ed.). *Biological psychiatry.* New York: Wiley, 1973.

Mendels, J., & Cochrane, C. The nosology of depression: The endogenous–reactive concept. *American Journal of Psychiatry,* 1968, *124* (May supplement), 1–11.

Mendels, J., & Hawkins, D. R. Sleep and depression. A controlled EEG study. *Archives of General Psychiatry,* 1967, *16,* 334–354.

Mendelson, J. H. Ethanol-1-C14 metabolism in alcoholics and non-alcoholics. *Science,* 1968, *159,* 319–320.

Mercer, J. R. *Labeling the mentally retarded: Clinical and social system perspectives on mental retardation.* Berkeley: University of California Press, 1973.

Merritt, H. H. *Textbook of neurology* (4th ed.). Philadelphia: Lea & Febiger, 1967.

Meyers, F. H. Jawetz, E., & Goldfien, A. *Review of medical pharmacology* (3rd ed.). Los Altos, Calif.: Lange, 1972.

Miller, L. C., Barrett, C. L., Hampe, E., & Noble, H. Comparison of reciprocal inhibition, psychotherapy, and waiting list control for phobic children. *Journal of Abnormal Psychology,* 1972, *79,* 269–279.

Miller, L. C., Hampe, R., Barrett, C. L., & Noble, H. Children's deviant behavior within the general population. *Journal of Consulting and Clinical Psychology,* 1971, *37,* 16–22.

Miller, N. E. Learning of visceral and glandular responses. *Science,* 1969, *163,* 434–445.

Miller, R. E., Banks, J. H., Jr., & Ogawa, N. Communication of affect in "cooperative conditioning" of rhesus monkeys. *Journal of Abnormal and Social Psychology,* 1962, *64,* 343–348.

Miller, R. E., Banks, J. H., Jr., & Ogawa, N. Role of facial expression in "cooperative avoidance conditioning" in monkeys. *Journal of Abnormal and Social Psychology,* 1963, *67,* 24–30.

Mills, K. L., Sobell, M. B., & Schaefer, H. H. Training social drinking as an alternative to abstinence for alcoholics. *Behavior Therapy,* 1971, *2,* 18–27.

Minkoff, K., Bergman, E., Beck, A. T., & Beck, R. Hopelessness, depression, and attempted suicide. *American Journal of Psychiatry*, 1973, *130*, 455–459.

Minkowski, E. Findings in a case of schizophrenic depression. In R. May, E. Angel, & H. F. Ellenberger (Eds.), *Existence: A new dimension in psychology and psychiatry*. New York: Basic Books, 1958.

Miras, C. J. Experience with chronic hashish smokers. In J. R. Wittenborn, H. Brill, J. P. Smith, & S. A. Wittenborn (Eds.), *Drugs and youth*. Springfield, Ill.: Charles C Thomas, 1969.

Mitamura, T. *Chinese eunuchs* (Charles A. Pomeroy, trans.). Rutland, Vt.: Charles E. Tuttle, 1970.

Mize, S. *The role of therapists exhortation in assertive training*. Unpublished doctoral dissertation, Southern Illinois University, 1974.

Moldawsky, S., & Moldawsky, P. C. Digit span as an anxiety indicator. *Journal of Consulting Psychology*, 1952, *16*, 115–118.

Molnar, G. E., & Taft, L. T. Cerebral palsy. In J. Wortis (Ed.), *Mental retardation and developmental disabilities: An annual review*. New York: Brunner/Mazel, 1973.

Monahan, J. The prediction of violence. In D. Chappell & J. Monahan (Eds.), *Violence and criminal justice*. Lexington, Mass.: Lexington Books (D. C. Heath), 1975.

Money, J. *Sex research: New developments*. New York: Holt, Rinehart and Winston, 1965.

Money, J., & Alexander, D. Psychosexual development and absence of homosexuality in males with precocious puberty. *Journal of Nervous and Mental Disease*, 1969, *148*, 111–123.

Money, J., & Ehrhardt, A. A. *Man and woman, boy and girl*. Baltimore: Johns Hopkins, 1972.

Money, J., Hampson, J. G., & Hampson, J. L. Imprinting and the establishment of gender role. *Archives of Neurological Psychiatry*, 1957, *77*, 333–336.

Monroe, L. J. Psychological and physiological differences between good and poor sleepers. *Journal of Abnormal Psychology*, 1967, *72*, 255–264.

Moore, D. J. A response to R. A. Webb's comments. *Psychological Review*, 1972, *79*, 280.

Moore, D. J., & Shiek, D. A. Toward a theory of early infantile autism. *Psychological Review*, 1971, *78*, 451–456.

Moore, N. Behavior therapy in bronchial asthma: A controlled study. *Journal of Psychosomatic Research*, 1965, *9*, 257–276.

Moran, L. J., Mefferd, R. B., Jr., & Kimble, J. P., Jr. Idiodynamic sets in word association. *Psychological Monographs*, 1964, *78* (2, Whole No. 579).

Morris, H. H., Jr., Escoll, P. J., & Wexler, R. Aggressive behavior disorders of childhood: A follow-up study. *American Journal of Psycholoyy*, 1956, *112*, 991–997.

Morrison, J. R. Changes in subtype diagnosis of schizophrenia: 1920–1966. *American Journal of Psychiatry*, 1974, *131*, 674–677.

Moss, C. S. *Hypnosis in perspective*. New York: Macmillan, 1965.

Mourer, S. A. A prediction of patterns of schizophrenic error resulting from semantic generalization. *Journal of Abnormal Psychology*, 1973, *81*, 250–254.

Moustakas, C. E. Confrontation and encounter. *Journal of Existential Psychiatry*, 1962, *2*, 263–290.

Mowrer, O. H. On the dual nature of learning—A re-interpretation of "conditioning" and "problem-solving." *Harvard Educational Review*, 1947, *17*, 102–148.

Mowrer, O. H. *Learning theory and behavior*. New York: Wiley, 1960.

Mucha, T. F., & Reinhardt, R. F. Conversion reactions in student aviators. *American Journal of Psychiatry*, 1970, *127*, 493–497.

Murphree, H. B. Narcotic analgesics I: Opium alkaloids. In J. R. DiPalma (Ed.), *Drill's pharmacology in medicine* (4th ed.). New York: McGraw-Hill, 1971.

Murphy, G. Types of word-association in dementia praecox, manic-depressives, and normal persons. *American Journal of Psychiatry*, 1923, *2*, 539–571.

Murphy, H. B. Cultural factors in the genesis of schizophrenia. In D. Rosenthal & S. S. Kety (Eds.), *The transmission of schizophrenia*. Oxford: Pergamon, 1968.

Murphy, R. C., Jr. A suicidal emergency. *Journal of Existential Psychiatry*, 1961, *2*, 133–146.

Murray, M. A. *The god of the witches*. New York: Oxford University Press, 1970.

Myrianthopoulos, N. C. Huntington's chorea. *Journal of Medical Genetics*, 1966, *3*, 298–314.

Myrianthopoulos, N. C. Huntington's chorea: The genetic problem five years later. In A. Barbeau,

T. N. Chase, & G. W. Paulson (Eds.), *Advances in neurology, Volume I: Huntington's chorea, 1872–1972*. New York: Raven Press, 1973.

Nagle, D. R. Anesthetic addiction and drunkenness. *International Journal of the Addictions,* 1968, *3,* 23–36.

Nagler, S., & Cook, P. E. Some ideological considerations underlying a mental health consultation program to the public schools. *Community Mental Health Journal,* 1973, *9,* 244–252.

Nagler, S., & Cooper, S. Influencing social change in community mental health. *Canada's Mental Health,* 1969, *17,* 6–12.

Nahas, G. G. *Marihuana—Deceptive weed.* New York: Raven, 1973.

Naranjo, C. I. Present-centeredness: Technique, prescription, and ideal. In J. Fagan & I. Shepherd (Eds.), *Gestalt therapy now.* Palo Alto, Calif.: Science and Behavior Books, 1970.

Nathan, P. E. A systems analytic model of diagnostic validity of disordered consciousness. *Journal of Clinical Psychology,* 1969, *25,* 243–246.

National Association of Social Workers. The social worker as advocate: Champion of social victims. *Social Work,* April 1969, 16–22.

National Commission on Marihuana and Drug Abuse. *Marihuana: A signal of misunderstanding.* New York: New American Library, 1972.

Neale, J. M., & Cromwell, R. L. Attention and schizophrenia. In B. A. Maher (Ed.), *Progress in experimental personality research* (Vol. 5). New York: Academic Press, 1970.

Neale, J. M., & Kessler, P. Hippocampal damage and schizophrenia: A critique of Mednick's theory. *Journal of Abnormal Psychology,* 1974, *83,* 91–96.

Neale, J. M., & Liebert, R. M. *Science and behavior.* Englewood Cliffs, N.J.: Prentice-Hall, 1973.

Needleman, J. *Being-in-the-world: Selected papers of Ludwig Binswanger.* New York: Basic Books, 1963.

Nelson, M. C., Nelson, B., Sherman, M. H., & Strean, H. S. *Roles and paradigms in psychotherapy.* New York: Grune & Stratton, 1968.

Neuman, C. P., & Tamerin, J. S. The treatment of adult alcoholics and teenage drug addicts in one hospital: A comparison and critical appraisal of factors related to outcome. *Quarterly Journal of Studies on Alcohol,* 1971, *32,* 82–93.

Neuringer, C. The problem of suicide. *Journal of Existential Psychiatry,* 1962, *3,* 69–74.

Newbrough, J. R. Community mental health: A movement in search of a theory. In A. J. Bindman & A. D. Spiegel (Eds.), *Perspectives in community mental health.* Chicago: Aldine, 1969. (Reprinted from J. R. Newbrough, *Community mental health: Individual adjustment or social planning?* Bethesda, Md.: National Institute of Mental Health, 1964.)

Nicassio, P., & Bootzin, R. A comparison of progressive relaxation and autogenic training as treatments for insomnia. *Journal of Abnormal Psychology,* 1974, *83,* 253–260.

Nielsen, J., & Videbech, T. Suicide frequency before and after introduction of community psychiatry in a Danish island. *British Journal of Psychiatry,* 1973, *123,* 35–39.

Norris, A. S., & Clancy, J. Hospitalized depressions: Drugs or electrotherapy. *Archives of General Psychiatry,* 1961, *5,* 276–279.

Nunnally, J. C., Jr. *Popular conceptions of mental health.* New York: Holt, Rinehart and Winston, 1961.

Obermayer, M. E. *Psychocutaneous medicine.* Springfield, Ill.: Charles C Thomas, 1955.

O'Connor, R. D. Modification of social withdrawal through symbolic modeling. *Journal of Applied Behavior Analysis,* 1969, *2,* 15–22.

O'Keefe, G. S., & DeWolfe, A. S. Reversal shift preferences in process and reactive schizophrenic, brain-damaged and control group patients. *Journal of Abnormal Psychology,* 1973, *82,* 390–398.

Olds, J. Pleasure centers in the brain. *Scientific American,* 1956, *195,* 105–117.

O'Leary, K. D., & Wilson, G. T. *Behavior therapy: Application and outcome.* Englewood Cliffs, N.J.: Prentice-Hall, 1975.

Oliver, J. F. *Clinical sexuality.* New York: Lippincott, 1974.

Oppelt, W. Toxicity from exposure to solvents. In F. W. Sunderman & F. W. Sunderman, Jr. (Eds.), *Laboratory diagnosis of diseases caused by toxic agents.* St. Louis: Warren H. Green, 1970.

Orne, M. T. The nature of hypnosis: Fact or artifact. *Journal of Abnormal and Social Psychology,* 1959, *58,* 277–299.

Osborne, E. D., & Murray, P. F. Atopic dermatitis: A study of its natural course, and wool as a dominant allergenic factor. *American Medical Association Archives of Dermatology and Syphilis,* 1953, *68,* 619.

Osgood, C. E., & Miron, M. S. *Approaches to the study of aphasia.* Urbana: University of Illinois Press, 1963.

Osmond, H., & Smythies, J. Schizophrenia: A new approach. *The Journal of Mental Science,* 1952, *98,* 309–315.

Ostfeld, A. M. *The common headache syndromes: Biochemistry, pathophysiology, therapy.* Springfield, Ill.: Charles C Thomas, 1962.

Overmier, J. B., & Seligman, M. E. P. Effects of inescapable shock upon subsequent escape and avoidance responding. *Journal of Comparative and Physiological Psychology,* 1967, *63,* 28–33.

Pacht, A. R. The rapist in treatment: Professional myths and psychological realities. In M. J. Walker & S. L. Brodsky (Eds.), *Sexual assault: The victim and the rapist.* Lexington, Mass.: Lexington Books (D. C. Heath), 1976.

Paivio, A., & Yuille, J. C. Mediation instructions and word attributes in paired-associate learning. *Psychonomic Science,* 1967, *8,* 65–66.

Palmer, E. D. *Functional gastrointestinal disease.* Baltimore: Williams & Wilkins, 1967.

Panek, D. M. *Word association learning by chronic schizophrenics under conditions of reward and punishment.* Paper presented at the Western Psychological Association convention, 1967.

Parens, H., & Saul, L. J. *Dependence in man.* New York: International Universities Press, 1971.

Park, L. C., Baldessarini, R. J., & Kety, S. S. Methionine effects on chronic schizophrenics: Patients treated with monoamine oxidase inhibitors. *Archives of General Psychiatry,* 1965, *12,* 346–351.

Parrinder, G. *Witchcraft: European and African.* New York: Barnes & Noble, 1963.

Parry-Jones, W. W., Santer-Weststrate, H. C., & Crawley, R. C. Behaviour therapy in a case of hysterical blindness. *Behaviour Research and Therapy,* 1970, *8,* 79–85.

Parsonage, M. Chairman's summing-up. In G. F. B. Birdwood, S. S. B. Gilder, & C. A. S. Wink (Eds.), *Parkinson's disease: A new approach to treatment.* New York: Academic Press, 1971.

Pasamanick, B. A comparative study of the behavioral development of Negro infants. *Journal of Genetic Psychology,* 1946, *69,* 3–44.

Paskind, H. A. Brief attacks of manic-depressive depression. *Archives of Neurological Psychiatry,* 1929, *22,* 123–134.

Patterson, G. R., & Gullion, M. E. *Living with children.* Champaign, Ill.: Research Press, 1971.

Paul, G. L. *Insight vs. desensitization in psychotherapy: An experiment in anxiety reduction.* Stanford, Calif.: Stanford University Press, 1966.

Paul, G. L. Strategy of outcome research in psychotherapy. *Journal of Consulting Psychology,* 1967, *31,* 109–118.

Pavlov, I. P. [*Conditioned reflexes: An investigation of the physiological activity of the cerebral cortex*] (G. V. Anrep, trans.). London and New York: Oxford University Press, 1927.

Paykel, E. S., Prusoff, B., & Klerman, G. L. The endogenous-neurotic continuum in depression: Rater independence and factor distributions. *Journal of Psychiatric Research,* 1971, *8,* 73–90.

Payne, R. W. Cognitive abnormalities. In H. J. Eysenck (Ed.), *Handbook of abnormal psychology.* New York: Basic Books, 1961.

Payne, R. W. Disorders of thinking. In C. G. Costello (Ed.), *Symptoms of psychopathology: A handbook.* New York: Wiley, 1970.

Payne, R. W. Cognitive defects in schizophrenia: Overinclusive thinking. In J. Hellmuth (Ed.), *Cognitive Studies,* Vol. 2 *Deficits in Cognition.* New York: Brunner/Mazel, 1971.

Payne, R. W., Matussek, P., & George, E. I. An experimental study of schizophrenic thought disorder. *Journal of Mental Science,* 1959, *105,* 627–652.

Pearce, J. Discussion (arteriosclerotic parkinsonism, early diagnosis). In G. F. B. Birdwood, S. S. B. Gilder, and C. A. S. Wink (Eds.), *Parkinson's disease: A new approach to treatment.* New York: Academic Press, 1971.

Pearce, J. M. S. General review of migraine. In J. N. Cumings (Ed.), *Background to migraine,* Fourth Migraine Symposium Sept. 11, 1970. New York: Springer-Verlag, 1971.

Pearson, J. S. Behavioral aspects of Huntington's chorea. In A. Barbeau, T. N. Chase, & G. W.

Paulson (Eds.), *Advances in neurology,* Vol. 1 . *Huntington's chorea, 1872–1972.* New York: Raven Press, 1973.

Peck, H. The small group: Core of the community mental center. *Community Mental Health Journal,* 1968, *4,* 191–200.

Perls, F. S. *Ego, hunger, and aggression.* New York: Random House, 1969. (Originally published, 1947.)

Perls, F. S. *Gestalt therapy verbatim.* Lafayette, Calif.: Real People Press, 1969. (a)

Perls, F. S. *In and out of the garbage pail.* Lafayette, Calif.: Real People Press, 1969. (b)

Perls, F. S. *The Gestalt approach and eyewitness to therapy.* Ben Lomond, Calif.: Science and Behavior Books, 1973.

Perls, F. S., Hefferline, R. F., & Goodman, P. *Gestalt therapy: Excitement and growth in the human personality.* New York: Julian Press, 1951; Dell, 1951.

Pesikoff, R. B., & Davis, P. O. Treatment of *pavor nocturnis* and somnambulism in children. *American Journal of Psychiatry,* 1971, *128,* 778–781.

Peterson, D. R. Behavior problems of middle childhood. *Journal of Consulting Psychology,* 1961, *25,* 205–209.

Pettigrew, T. F. *A profile of the Negro American.* Princeton, N.J.: Van Nostrand Reinhold, 1964.

Petzel, T. P., & Johnson, J. E. Formation of concepts of varying degrees of dominance by process and reactive schizophrenics. *Journal of Consulting and Clinical Psychology,* 1973, *41,* 235–241.

Phillips, E. L., Phillips, E. S., Fixen, D. L., & Wolf, M. M. Achievement Place: Modification of the behaviors of pre-delinquent boys within a token economy. *Journal of Applied Behavior Analysis,* 1971, *4,* 45–59.

Phillips, L. Case history data and prognosis in schizophrenia. *Journal of Nervous and Mental Disease,* 1953, *117,* 515–525.

Pokorny, A. D. Human violence: A comparison of homicide, aggravated assault, suicide and attempted suicide. *Journal of Criminal Law, Criminology and Police Science,* 1965, *56,* 488–498.

Pomeroy, W. The Masters-Johnson report and the Kinsey tradition. In R. Brecher & E. Brecher (Eds.), *An analysis of human sexual response.* New York: New American Library, 1966.

Porter, E. H. The development and evaluation of a measure of counseling interview procedures. *Educational and Psychological Measurement,* 1943, *3,* 105–126, 215–238.

Powell, J., & Azrin, N. The effects of shock as a punisher for cigarette smoking. *Journal of Applied Behavior Analysis,* 1968, *1,* 63–71.

Powell, N. B. Urinary incontinence in children. *Archives of Pediatrics,* 1951, *68,* 151–157.

Prange, A. J., Wilson, I. C., Lynn, C. W., Alltop, L. B., & Stikeleather, R. A. L-tryptophan in mania. *Archives of General Psychiatry,* 1974, *30,* 56–62.

Pratt, R. T. C. *The genetics of neurological disorders.* New York: Oxford University Press, 1967.

Prien, R. F., Caffey, E. M., Jr., & Klett, C. J. Prophylactic efficacy of lithium carbonate in manic-depressive illness. *Archives of General Psychiatry,* 1973, *28,* 337–341.

Prien, R. F., Klett, C. J., & Caffey, E. M. Lithium prophylaxis in recurrent affective illness. *American Journal of Psychiatry,* 1974, 131, 198–203.

Proctor, J. T. Hysteria in childhood. *American Journal of Orthopsychiatry,* 1958, *28,* 394–407.

Provence, S., & Lipton, R. C. *Infants in institutions: A comparison of their development with family-reared infants during the first year of life.* New York: International Universities Press, 1962.

Purcell, K., Brady, K., Chai, H., Muser, J., Molk, L., Gordon, N., & Means, J. The effect on asthma in children of experimental separation from the family. *Psychosomatic Medicine,* 1969, *31,* 144–164.

Purcell, K., & Weiss, J. H. Asthma. In C. G. Costello (Ed.), *Symptoms of psychopathology.* New York: Wiley, 1970.

Quay, H. C. Dimensions of personality in delinquent boys as inferred from the factor analysis of case history data. *Child Development,* 1964, *35,* 479–484. (a)

Quay, H. C. Personality dimensions in delinquent males as inferred from the factor analysis of behavior ratings. *Journal of Research in Crime and Delinquency,* 1964, *1,* 33–37. (b)

Quay, H. C., & Parsons, L. B. *The differential behavioral classification of the juvenile offender.* Morgantown, W.Va.: Robert F. Kennedy Youth Center, 1970.

Rachman, S. Sexual fetishism: An experimental analogue. *Psychological Record,* 1966, *16,* 293–296. (a)

Rachman, S. Studies in desensitization—II: Flooding. *Behaviour Research and Therapy,* 1966, *4,* 1–6. (b)

Rachman, S. The passing of the two-stage theory of fear and avoidance—fresh possibilities. *Behaviour Research and Therapy*, 1976, *14*, 125–131.

Rachman, S., Hodgson, R., & Marks, I. M. Treatment of chronic obsessive–compulsive neurosis. *Behaviour Research and Therapy*, 1971, *9*, 237–247.

Rachman, S., Hodgson, R., & Marzillier, J. Treatment of an obsessional–compulsive disorder by modelling. *Behaviour Research and Therapy*, 1970, *8*, 385–392.

Rachman, S., Marks, I. M., & Hodgson, R. The treatment of obsessive–compulsive neurotics by modelling and flooding in vivo. *Behaviour Research and Therapy*, 1973, *11*, 463–471.

Ramfjord, S. P. Bruxism, a clinical and electromyographic study. *Journal of the American Dental Association*, 1961, *62*, 21–44.

Ramond, C. K. Anxiety and task as determiners of verbal performance. *Journal of Experimental Psychology*, 1953, *46*, 120–124.

Randrup, A., & Munkvad, I. Evidence indicating an association between schizophrenia and dopaminergic hyperactivity in the brain. *Orthomolecular Psychiatry*, 1972, *1*, 2–7.

Raskin, N. J. *Studies of psychotherapeutic orientation: Ideology and practice.* Orlando, Fla.: American Academy of Psychotherapists, 1974.

Rathus, S. A. An experimental investigation of assertive training in a group setting. *Journal of Behavior Therapy and Experimental Psychiatry*, 1972, *3*, 81–86.

Ray, D. S. *Drugs, society, and human behavior.* St. Louis: C. V. Mosby, 1972.

Razani, J. Ejaculatory incompetence treated by deconditioning anxiety. *Journal of Behavior Therapy and Experimental Psychiatry*, 1972, *3*, 65–67.

Rechtschaffen, A., & Dement, W. C. Narcolepsy and hypersomnia. In A. Kales (Ed.), *Sleep: Physiology and pathology.* Philadelphia: Lippincott, 1969.

Rechtschaffen, A., Goodenough, D. R., & Shapiro, A. Patterns of sleeptalking. *Archives of General Psychiatry*, 1962, *7*, 418–426.

Rechtschaffen, A., & Maron, L. The effect of amphetamine on the sleep cycle. *Electroencephalography and Clinical Neurophysiology*, 1964, *16*, 438–445.

Rechtschaffen, A., & Monroe, L. J. Laboratory studies of insomnia. In A. Kales (Ed.), *Sleep: Physiology and pathology.* Philadelphia: Lippincott, 1969.

Rechtschaffen, A., Wolpert, E. A., Dement, W. C., Mitchell, S. A., & Fisher, C. Nocturnal sleep of narcoleptics. *Electroencephalographica Clinica Neurophysiologica*, 1963, *15*, 599–609.

Rechy, J. *City of night.* New York: Grove Press, 1963.

Reding, G. R. Sleep pattern of bruxism: A revision. *Psychophysiology*, 1968, *4*, 396.

Reding, G. R., Rubright, W. C., & Zimmerman, S. O. Incidence of bruxism. *Journal of Dental Research*, 1966, *45*, 1198–1204.

Redmond, D. P., Gaylor, M. S., McDonald, R. H., & Shapiro, A. P. Blood pressure and heart-rate response to verbal instruction and relaxation in hypertension. *Psychosomatic Medicine*, 1974, *36* (4), 285–297.

Rees, W. L. Psychiatric and psychological factors in migraine. In J. N. Cumings, (Ed.), *Background to migraine*, Fourth Migraine Symposium Sept. 11, 1970. New York: Springer-Verlag, 1971.

Refsum, S. Some genetic aspects of neurological diseases. In W. S. Fields & M. M. Desmond (Eds.), *Disorders of the developing nervous system.* Springfield, Ill.: Charles C Thomas, 1961.

Reimann, H. A. Caffeinism. *Journal of the American Medical Association*, 1967, *202*, 1105–1106.

Rennie, T. A. C. Prognosis in manic-depressive psychoses. *American Journal of Psychiatry*, 1942, *98*, 801–814.

Rheingold, H. L. The modification of social responsiveness in institutional babies. *Monographs of Social Research on Child Development*, 1956, *21*, 3–48.

Rheingold, H. L. The measurement of maternal care. *Child Development*, 1960, *31*, 565–575.

Rheingold, H. L. The effect of environmental stimulation upon social and exploratory behaviour in the human infant. In B. M. Foss (Ed.), *Determinants of infant behaviour.* New York: Wiley, 1961.

Ribble, M. A. *The rights of infants.* New York: Columbia, 1943.

Richards, B. W. (Ed.). *Mental subnormality: Modern trends in research.* London: Pitman, 1970.

Richter, P. R. *Biological clocks in medicine and psychiatry.* Springfield, Ill.: Charles C Thomas, 1965.

Ricoeur, P. *Freud and philosophy.* New Haven: Yale University Press, 1970.

Rie, H. E. *Perspectives in child psychopathology.* Chicago: Aldine, 1971.

Riklan, M. L-*Dopa and parkinsonism.* Springfield, Ill.: Charles C Thomas, 1973.

Rimland, B. *Infantile autism.* New York: Meredith, 1964.

Rimm, D. C. Thought–stopping and covert assertion in the treatment of phobias *Journal of Consulting and Clinical Psychology,* 1973, *41,* 466–467.

Rimm, D. C., deGroot, J. C., Boord, P., Heiman, J., & Dillow, P. V. Systematic desensitization of an anger response. *Behaviour Research and Therapy,* 1971, *9,* 273–280.

Rimm, D. C., Hill, G. A., Brown, N. N., & Stuart, J. E. Group assertive training in the treatment of expression of inappropriate anger. *Psychological Reports,* 1974, *34,* 791–798.

Rimm, D. C., Kennedy, T. D., Miller, H. L., & Tchida, G. R. Experimentally manipulated drive level and avoidance behavior. *Journal of Abnormal Psychology,* 1971, *78,* 43–48.

Rimm, D. C., & Litvak, S. B. Self-verbalization and emotional arousal. *Journal of Abnormal Psychology,* 1969, *74,* 181–187.

Rimm, D. C., & Mahoney, M. J. The application of reinforcement and participant modeling procedures in the treatment of snake-phobic behavior. *Behaviour Research and Therapy,* 1969, *7,* 369–376.

Rimm, D. C., & Masters, J. C. *Behavior Therapy: Techniques and empirical findings.* New York: Academic Press, 1974.

Rimm, D. C., Saunders, W., & Westel, W. Thought–stopping and covert assertion in the treatment of snake phobics. *Journal of Consulting and Clinical Psychology,* 1975, *43,* 92–93.

Rinehardt, K. F. Existential psychotherapy and the synthesis of existence. In K. F. Rinehardt, *The existentialist revolt.* New York: Ungar, 1960.

Ringel, S. P., Guthrie, M., & Klawans, H. L., Jr. Current treatment of Huntington's chorea. In A. Barbeau, T. N. Chase, & G. W. Paulson (Eds.), *Advances in neurology, Volume I: Huntington's chorea, 1872–1972.* New York: Raven Press, 1973.

Ripley, H. S., Shorr, E., & Papanicolaou, G. N. The effect of treatment of depression in the menopause with estrogenic hormone. *American Journal of Psychiatry,* 1940, *96,* 905–914.

Risley, T. R. The effects and side effects of punishing the autistic behaviors of a deviant child. *Journal of Applied Behavior Analysis,* 1968, *1,* 21–34.

Ritchie, J. M. The aliphatic alcohols. In L. S. Goodman & A. Gilman (Eds.), *The pharmacological basis of therapeutics* (4th ed.). New York: Macmillan, 1970. (a)

Ritchie, J. M. Central nervous system stimulants: II. The xanthines. In L. S. Goodman & A. Gilman (Eds.), *The pharmacological basis of therapeutics* (4th ed.). New York: Macmillan, 1970. (b)

Ritter, B. Eliminating excessive fears of the environment through contact desensitization. In J. D. Krumboltz & C. E. Thoreson (Eds.), *Behavioral counseling: Cases and techniques.* New York: Holt, Rinehart and Winston, 1969. (a)

Ritter, B. Treatment of acrophobia with contact desensitization. *Behaviour Research and Therapy,* 1969, *7,* 41–45. (b)

Roback, A. A. *History of psychology and psychiatry.* New York: Philosophical Library, 1961.

Roberts, A. H. *Brain damage in boxers.* London: Pitman, 1969.

Roberts, W. W. Normal and abnormal depersonalization. *Journal of Mental Science,* 1960, *106,* 478–493.

Robins, E., Gassner, J., Kayes, J., Wilkinson, R. H., & Murphy, G. E. The communication of suicidal intent: A study of 134 consecutive cases of successful (completed) suicides. *American Journal of Psychiatry,* 1959, *115,* 724–733.

Robins, L. N. Follow-up studies of behavior disorders in children. In H. C. Quay & J. S. Werry, *Psychopathological disorders of childhood.* New York: Wiley, 1972.

Robinson, H. B., & Robinson, N. M. *The mentally retarded child: A psychological approach.* New York: McGraw-Hill, 1965.

Rodgers, D. A., & McClearn, G. E. Mouse strain differences in preference for various concentrations of alcohol. *Quarterly Journal of Studies on Alcohol,* 1962, *23,* 26–33.

Roe, A. Children of alcoholic parentage raised in foster homes. In *Alcoholism, science and society.* New Haven: Yale Sumner School of Alcohol Studies, 1945.

Roebuck, J. *Criminal typologies.* Springfield, IU.: Thomas, 1966.

Rogers, C. R. *Counseling and psychotherapy.* Boston: Houghton Mifflin, 1942.

Rogers, C. R. *Client-centered therapy.* Boston: Houghton Mifflin, 1951.

Rogers, C. R. The necessary and sufficient conditions of therapeutic personality change. *Journal of Consulting Psychology,* 1957, *21,* 95–103.

Rogers, C. R. A theory of therapy, personality, and interpersonal relationships. In S. Koch (Ed.), *Psychology: A study of a science* (Vol. 3). New York: McGraw-Hill, 1959.

Rogers, C. R. *On becoming a person.* Boston: Houghton Mifflin, 1961.

Rogers, C. R. *Freedom to learn: A view of what education might become.* Columbus, Ohio: Charles E. Merrill, 1969.

Rogers, C. R. *Carl Rogers on encounter groups.* New York: Harper & Row, 1970. (a)

Rogers, C. R. Toward a modern approach to values: The valuing process in the mature person. In J. T. Hart & T. M. Tomlinson (Eds.), *New directions in client-centered therapy.* Boston: Houghton-Mifflin, 1970. (b)

Rogers, C. R. Foreword. In J. T. Hart & T. M. Tomlinson (Eds.), *New directions in client-centered therapy.* Boston: Houghton-Mifflin, 1970. (c)

Rogers, C. R. *How to use encounter groups.* Chicago: Human Development Institute, 1971.

Rogers, C. R. *Becoming partners: Marriage and its alternatives.* New York: Dell, 1972.

Rogers, C. R. Client-centered psychotherapy. In A. M. Freedman, H. I. Kaplan, & B. J. Sadock (Eds.), *Comprehensive textbook of psychiatry.* Baltimore: Williams & Wilkins, 1974. (a)

Rogers, C. R. In retrospect: Forty-six years. *American Psychologist,* 1974, *29,* 115–123. (b)

Rogers, C. R. Empathic: An unappreciated way of being. *The Counseling Psychologist,* 1975, *5,* 2–9.

Rogers, C. R. & Dymond, R. F. (Eds.), *Psychotherapy and personality change.* Chicago: University of Chicago Press, 1954.

Rogers, C. R., Gendlin, E. T., Kiesler, D. V., & Truax, C. B. *The therapeutic relationship and its impact: A study of psychotherapy with schizophrenics.* Madison: University of Wisconsin Press, 1967.

Rogers, C. R., & Hart, J. T. Looking back and ahead: A conversation with Carl Rogers. In J. T. Hart & T. M. Tomlinson (Eds.), *New directions in client-centered therapy.* Boston: Houghton-Mifflin, 1970.

Roper, G., Rachman, S., & Hodgson, R. An experiment on obsessional checking. *Behaviour Research and Therapy,* 1973, *11,* 271–277.

Rosanoff, A. J., Handy, L. M., & Plesset, I. R. The etiology of manic-depressive syndromes with special reference to their occurrence in twins. *American Journal of Psychiatry,* 1934, *91,* 247–286.

Rosanoff, A. J., Handy, L. M., Plesset, I. R., & Brush, S. The etiology of so-called schizophrenic psychoses. *American Journal of Psychiatry,* 1934–1935, *91,* 247–286.

Rosen, E., Fox, R. E., & Gregory, I. *Abnormal psychology* (2nd ed.). Philadelphia: Saunders, 1972.

Rosenbaum, C. P. Patient–family similarities in schizophrenia. *Archives of General Psychiatry,* 1961, *5,* 120–126.

Rosenberg, B., & Sutton-Smith, B. *Sex and identity.* New York: Holt, Rinehart and Winston, 1972.

Rosenberg, C. E. *The trial of the assassin Giteau.* Chicago: University of Chicago Press, 1968.

Rosenhan, D. L. On being sane in insane places. *Science,* 1973, *179,* 250–258.

Rosenthal, D. *Genetic theory and abnormal behavior.* New York: McGraw-Hill, 1970.

Rosenthal, S., & Gudeman, J. The endogenous depressive pattern: An empirical investigation. *Archives of General Psychiatry,* 1967, *16,* 241–249.

Ross, A. O. *Psychological disorders of children (A behavioral approach to theory, research, and therapy).* New York: McGraw-Hill, 1974.

Ross, R. R., Meichenbaum, D. H., & Humphrey, C. Treatment of nocturnal headbanging by behavior modification techniques: A case report. *Behaviour Research and Therapy,* 1971, *9,* 151–154.

Rossi, P. H. Practice, method and theory in evaluating social action programs. In J. L. Sundquist (Ed.), *On fighting poverty.* New York: Basic Books, 1969.

Roth, M. The phobic anxiety–depersonalization syndrome. *Proceedings of the Royal Society of Medicine,* 1959, *52,* 587–595.

Rothschild, D. Senile psychoses and psychoses with cerebral arteriosclerosis. In O. J. Kaplan (Ed.), *Mental disorders in later life.* Stanford, Calif.: Stanford University Press, 1945.

Rubin, E., & Lieber, C. S. Experimental alcoholic hepatitis: A new primate model. *Science,* 1973, *182,* 712–713.

Rubin, S. E., Lawlis, G. F., Tasto, D. L., & Namenek, T. Factor analysis of the 122-item Fear Survey Schedule. *Behaviour Research and Therapy,* 1969, *7,* 381–386.

Rubinstein, B. B. On the possibility of a strictly clinical psychoanalytic theory: An essay in the philosophy of psychoanalysis. In M. M. Gill & P. S. Holzman (Eds.), *Psychology versus metapsychology.* New York: International Universities Press, 1975. [Also *Psychological Issues,* 1975, *9* (Monograph 36).]

Ruskin, A., & Beard, O. W. The Texas City disaster: Cardiovascular studies, with follow-up results. *Texas Report of Biology and Medicine,* 1948, *6,* 234.

Russell, J. B. *Witchcraft in the Middle Ages.* Ithaca, N.Y.: Cornell University Press, 1972.

Russell, P. L., & Brandsma, J. M. A theoretical and empirical integration of rational–emotive and classical conditioning theories. *Journal of Consulting and Clinical Psychology,* 1974, *42,* 389–397.

Rutter, M., Greenfeld, D., & Lockyer, L. A five- to fifteen-year follow-up study of infantile psychosis: II. Social and behavioural outcome. *British Journal of Psychiatry,* 1967, *113,* 1183–1199.

Rutter, M., & Lockyer, L. A five- to fifteen-year follow-up study of infantile psychosis: I. Description of sample. *British Journal of Psychiatry,* 1967, *113,* 1169–1182.

Ryan, D. V., & Neale, J. M. Test-taking sets and the performance of schizophrenics on laboratory tests. *Journal of Abnormal Psychology,* 1973, *82,* 207–211.

Ryan, W. *Blaming the victim.* New York: Vintage, 1971. (a)

Ryan, W. Emotional disorder as a social problem: Implications for mental health programs. *American Journal of Orthopsychiatry,* 1971, *41,* 638–645. (b)

Sachs, D. A., & Mayhall, B. Behavioral control of spasms using aversive conditioning with a cerebral palsied adult. *Journal of Nervous and Mental Disorders,* 1971, *152,* 362–363.

Sachs, L. B., Bean, H., & Morrow, J. E. Comparison of smoking treatments. *Behavior Therapy,* 1970, *1,* 465–472.

Saghir, M. T., & Robins, E. *Male and female homosexuality: A comprehensive investigation.* Baltimore: Williams & Wilkins, 1973.

Saghir, M. T., Robins, E., & Walbran, B. Homosexuality. I. Sexual behavior of the female homosexual. *Archives of General Psychiatry,* 1969, *20,* 192–201. (a)

Saghir, M. T., Robins, E., & Walbran, B. Homosexuality. II. Sexual behavior of the male homosexual. *Archives of General Psychiatry,* 1969, *21,* 219–229. (b)

Sainsbury, P. Muscle responses: Muscle tension and expressive movements. *Journal of Psychosomatic Research,* 1964, *8,* 179–186.

Sanderson, R. E., Campbell, D., & Laverty, J. G. An investigation of a new aversive conditioning treatment for alcoholism. *Quarterly Journal of Studies on Alcoholism,* 1963, *24,* 261–275.

Sandifer, M. G., Jr., Pettus, C., & Quade, D. A study of psychiatric diagnosis. *Journal of Nervous and Mental Disease,* 1964, *139,* 350–356.

Sapira, J. D., Scheib, E. T., Moriarty, R., & Shapiro, A. P. Differences in perception between hypertensive and normotensive populations. *Psychosomatic Medicine,* 1971, *33* (3), 239–250.

SAR guide for a better sex life. San Francisco: National Sex Forum, 1975.

Sarbin, T. R. Anxiety: The reification of a metaphor. *Archives of General Psychiatry,* 1964, *10,* 630–638.

Sarbin, T. R. The dangerous individual: An outcome of social identity transformations. *British Journal of Criminology,* 1967, *23,* 285–295.

Sarbin, T. R. The scientific status of the mental illness metaphor. In S. C. Plog & R. B. Edgerton (Eds.), *Changing perspectives in mental illness.* New York: Holt, Rinehart and Winston, 1969.

Sarbin, T. R., & Coe, W. C. *Hypnosis: A social psychological analysis of influence communication.* New York: Holt, Rinehart and Winston, 1972.

Sarbin, T. R., & Mancuso, J. C. Failure of a moral enterprise: Attitudes of the public toward mental illness. *Journal of Consulting and Clinical Psychology,* 1970, *35,* 159–173.

Sarbin, T. R., & Mancuso, J. C. Paradigms and moral judgments: Improper conduct is not disease. *Journal of Consulting and Clinical Psychology,* 1972, *39,* 6–8.

Sarbin, T. R., & Slagle, R. W. Hypnosis and psychophysiological outcomes. In E. Fromm & R. E. Shor (Eds.), *Hypnosis: Research developments and perspectives.* Chicago: Aldine–Atherton, 1972.

Sargent, J. D., Green, E. E., & Walters, E. D. Preliminary report on the use of autogenic feedback training in the treatment of migraine and tension headaches. *Psychosomatic Medicine*, 1973, *35*, 129–135.

Sartre, J. P. *Being and nothingness*. New York: Philosophical Library, 1956.

Schachter, J., Kerr, J. L., Wimberly, F. C., & Lachin, J. M. Heart rate levels of black and white newborns. *Psychosomatic Medicine*, 1974, *36* (6), 513–524.

Schacter, S., & Singer, J. E. Cognitive, social, and physiological determinants of emotional state. *Psychological Review*, 1962, *69*, 379–399.

Schacter, S., & Wheeler, L. Epinephrine, chlorpromazine, and amusement. *Journal of Abnormal and Social Psychology*, 1962, *65*, 121–128.

Schaefer, H. H. Self-injurious behavior: Shaping "head banging" in monkeys. *Journal of Applied Behavior Analysis*, 1970, *3*, 111–116.

Schaefer, H. H. Twelve-month follow-up of behaviorally trained ex-alcoholic social drinkers. *Behavior Therapy*, 1973, *3*, 286–289.

Schaefer, H. H., & Martin, P. L. *Behavioral therapy*. New York: McGraw-Hill, 1969.

Schafer, R. *Aspects of internalization*. New York: International Universities Press, 1968.

Schafer, R. Psychoanalysis without psychodynamics. *International Journal of Psychoanalysis*, 1975, *56*, 41–55.

Scheff, T. J. Social conditions for rationality: How urban and rural courts deal with the mentally ill. *American Behavioral Scientist*, 1964, *7*, 21–27.

Scheff, T. J. *Being mentally ill*. Chicago: Aldine, 1966.

Scher, J. The transitional juncture: A study in the discontinuous nature of therapeutic process in schizophrenia. *International Forum for Existential Psychiatry*, 1967, *6*, 175–189.

Schilder, P. *Selbstbewusstsein und Persönlichkeitsbewusstsein*. Berlin: Julius Springer, 1914.

Schilder, P. Results and problems of group psychotherapy in severe neurosis. *Mental Hygiene*, 1939, *23*, 87–98.

Schmidt, H. O., & Fonda, C. P. The reliability of psychiatric diagnosis: A new look. *Journal of Abnormal and Social Psychology*, 1956, *52*, 262–267.

Schneck, J. M. *A history of psychiatry*. Springfield, Ill.: Charles C Thomas, 1960.

Schneider, K. *Psychopathic personalities*. London: Cassell, 1958.

Schou, M. Lithium in psychiatric therapy and prophylaxis. *Journal of Psychiatric Research*, 1968, *6*, 67–95.

Schou, M., Juel-Nielson, N., Stromgren, E., & Voldby, H. The treatment of manic psychoses by administration of lithium salts. *Journal of Neurology, Neurosurgery, and Psychiatry*, 1954, *17*, 250–260.

Schuham, A. I. The double-bind hypothesis a decade later. *Psychological Bulletin*, 1967, *68*, 409–416.

Schur, M. *Freud living and dying*. New York: International Universities Press, 1972.

Schwartz, B., Guilbaud, G., & Fishgood, H. Etudes electroencephalographiques sue le sommeil de nuit. I. L'insomnie chronique. *Presse Medicale*, 1963, *71*, 1474–1476.

Schwartz, G. E. Biofeedback as therapy: Some theoretical and practical issues. *American Psychologist*, 1973, *28*, 666–673.

Schwartz, G. E., & Shapiro, D. Biofeedback and essential hypertension: Current findings and theoretical concerns. *Seminars in Psychiatry*, 1973, *5*, 493–503.

Schwartz, G. E., Shapiro, D., & Tursky, B. Learned control of cardiovascular integration in man through operant conditioning. *Psychosomatic Medicine*, 1971, *33*, 57–62.

Scribner, S. What is community psychology made of? American Psychological Association Division of Community Psychology *Newsletter*, 1968, *2*, 4–6.

Sears, R. R. *Survey of objective studies of psychoanalytic concepts* (Bulletin 51). New York: Social Science Research Council, 1943.

Seay, B. E., Hansen, E., & Harlow, H. F. Mother–infant separation in monkeys. *Journal of Child Psychology and Psychiatry*, 1963, *3*, 123–132.

Seeman, J., & Raskin, N. J. Research perspectives in client-centered therapy. In O. H. Mowrer (Ed.), *Psychotherapy theory and research*. New York: Ronald Press, 1953.

Selesnick, S. Psychotherapy in chronic peptic ulcer. *Gastroenterology*, 1950, *14*, 364.

Seligman, M. E. P. Fall into helplessness. *Psychology Today*, 1973, 7, 43–48.

Seligman, M. E. P. *Helplessness: On depression, development, and death.* San Francisco: W. H. Freeman, 1975.

Seligman, M. E. P., Maier, S., & Geer, J. H. Alleviation of learned helplessness in the dog. *Journal of Abnormal Psychology*, 1968, 73, 256–262.

Selling, L. S. *Men against madness.* New York: Greenberg, 1940.

Semans, J. H. Premature ejaculation: A new approach. *Southern Medical Journal*, 1956, 49, 353–358.

Sequin, C. A. Opening, love, and permissiveness in psychotherapy. *International Forum for Existential Psychiatry*, 1969, 7, 27–32.

Shakow, D., & McCormick, M. Y. Mental set in schizophrenia studied in a discrimination reaction setting. *Journal of Personality and Social Psychology*, 1965, 1, 88–95.

Shapiro, D., Schwartz, G. E., & Tursky, B. Control of diastolic blood pressure in man by feedback and reinforcement. *Psychophysiology*, 1972, 9, 296–304.

Shapiro, D., Tursky, B., Gershon, E., & Stern, M. Effects of feedback and reinforcement on the control of human systolic blood pressure. *Science*, 1969, 163, 588–589.

Shapiro, D., Tursky, B., & Schwartz, G. E. Control of blood pressure in and by operant conditioning. *Circulation Research*, 1970, 26 (Supplement 1), I-27 to I-32.

Sharan, S. Family interaction with schizophrenics and their siblings. In E. G. Mishler & N. E. Waxler (Eds.), *Family processes and schizophrenia.* New York: Science House, 1968.

Sharpless, S. K. Hypnotics and sedatives. In L. S. Goodman & A. Gilman, (Eds.), *The pharmacological basis of therapeutics* (4th ed.). New York: Macmillan, 1970.

Sheed, F. J. (trans.). *Confessions of St. Augustine.* New York: Sheed and Ward, 1942.

Shepard, M. *Fritz.* New York: Bantam Books, 1975.

Shepherd, R. W., & Price, A. S. Bruxism: The changing situation. *Australian Dental Journal*, 1971, 16, 243–248.

Shimkunas, A. M., Gynther, M. D., & Smith, K. Schizophrenic responses to the proverbs test: Abstract, concrete, or autistic? *Journal of Abnormal Psychology*, 1967, 72, 128–133.

Shneidman, E. S., & Farberow, N. L. The logic of suicide. In E. S. Shneidman, N. L. Farberow, & R. E. Litman (Eds.), *The psychology of suicide.* New York: Science House, 1970.

Shneidman, E. S., & Mandelkorn, P. How to prevent suicide. In E. S. Shneidman, N. L. Farberow, & R. E. Litman (Eds.), *The psychology of suicide.* New York: Science House, 1970.

Shorr, J. E. The existential question and the imaginary situation in therapy. *International Forum for Existential Psychiatry*, 1967–1968, 6, 443–465.

Shorvon, J. J. The depersonalization syndrome. *Proceedings of the Royal Society of Medicine*, 1946, 39, 779–792.

Shrag, C. *Crime and justice: American style.* Washington, D.C.: U.S. Government Printing Office, 1971.

Shulman, B. H. On the theory of schizophrenic ontology: A phenomenological holistic synthesis. *Journal of Existentialism*, 1965, 5, 353–358.

Shusterman, L. R. The treatment of impotence by behavior modification techniques: A review. *Journal of Sex Research*, 1973, 9, 226–240.

Siegel, J. M. Mental health volunteers as change agents. *American Journal of Community Psychology*, 1973, 1, 138–158.

Silver, M. A., Bohnert, A. M., Beck, A. T., & Marcus. Relation of depression to attempted suicide and seriousness of intent. *Archives of general psychiatry*, in press.

Silverman, J. The problem of attention in research and theory in schizophrenia. *Psychological Review*, 1964, 71, 352–379. (a)

Silverman, J. Scanning-control mechanism and "cognitive filtering" in paranoid and nonparanoid schizophrenia. *Journal of Consulting Psychology*, 1964, 28, 385–393. (b)

Singer, N. S. *Family interaction with schizophrenic and nonschizophrenic siblings.* New York: Yeshiva University, 1965.

Sintchak, G., & Geer, J. A vaginal plethysmograph system. *Psychophysiology*, 1975, 12, 113–115.

Skeels, H. M., & Dye, H. B. A study of the effects of differential stimulation on mentally retarded children. *Proceedings and Addresses of the American Association on Mental Deficiency*, 1939, 44, 114–136.

Skinner, B. F. Are theories of learning necessary? *Psychological Review,* 1950, *57,* 193–216.

Skinner, B. F. *Science and human behavior.* New York: Macmillan, 1953.

Skinner, B. F. *Beyond freedom and dignity.* New York: Knopf, 1971.

Skipper, J. & McCaghy, C. Stripteasers: The anatomy and career contingencies of a deviant occupation. *Social Problems,* 1969, *17,* 391–405.

Slater, E. *Psychotic and neurotic illnesses in twins.* London: Her Majesty's Stationery Office, 1953.

Slater, E. A review of earlier evidence on genetic factors in schizophrenia. In D. Rosenthal and S. S. Kety (Eds.), *The transmission of schizophrenia.* London: Pergamon, 1968.

Slavson, S. R. *An introduction to group therapy.* New York: Commonwealth Fund, 1943.

Slavson, S. R. *Analytic group psychotherapy with children, adolescents and adults.* New York: Columbia University Press, 1950.

Slem, C. M., & Cotter, S. Crisis phone services: Evaluation of a hotline program. *American Journal of Community Psychology,* 1973, *1,* 219–227.

Smith, A. Mental deterioration in chronic schizophrenia. *Journal of Nervous and Mental Disorders,* 1964, *139,* 479–487.

Smith, E. W. L. *The growing edge of Gestalt therapy.* New York: Brunner/Mazel, 1976.

Smith, J. L. *Spirochetes in late seronegative syphilis, penicillin notwithstanding.* Springfield, Ill.: Charles C Thomas, 1969.

Smith, M. B., & Hobbs, N. The community and the community mental health center. *American Psychologist,* 1966, *21,* 499–509.

Smuts, J. C. *Holism and evolution.* New York: Viking Compass, 1961. (Originally published, 1926.)

Smythies, J. R. *Brain mechanisms and behavior.* New York: Academic Press, 1970.

Smythies, J. R., & Antun, F. The biochemistry of psychosis. *Scottish Medical Journal,* 1970, *15,* 34–40.

Snodgrass, V. Medical news. *Journal of the American Medical Association,* 1973, *225* (8), 913–920. (a)

Snodgrass, V. Medical news. *Journal of the American Medical Association,* 1973, *225* (9), 1035–1046. (b)

Snyder, S. H. Catecholamines in the brain as mediators of amphetamine psychosis. *Archives of General Psychiatry,* 1972, *27,* 169–179.

Snyder, S. H., Banerjee, S. P., Yamamura, H. I., & Greenberg, D. Drugs, neurotransmitters and schizophrenia. *Science,* 1974, *184,* 1243–1253.

Sokolov, E. M. Higher nervous functions: The orienting reflex. *Annual Review of Physiology,* 1963, *25,* 545–580.

Solomon, D. (Ed.). *The marihuana papers.* New York: New American Library, 1966.

Solomon, R. L. Punishment. *American Psychologist,* 1964, *19,* 239–253.

Solomon, R. L., & Wynne, L. C. Traumatic avoidance learning: Acquisition in normal dogs. *Psychological Monographs,* 1953, *67,* 354.

Somervill, J. W., & Brophy, P. D. *Teacher perceptions of distractibility: A two year follow-up.* Paper presented at the meeting of the Midwestern Psychological Association, Chicago, May 1975.

Somervill, J. W., & Rimm, D. C. Effects of sex of subject and sex of experimenter on acquisition of a modeled response. Unpublished manuscript. Southern Illinois University, Carbondale, 1974.

Somervill, J. W., Warnberg, L. S., & Bost, D. E. Effects of cubicles versus increased stimulation on task performance by first-grade males perceived as distractible and nondistractible. *Journal of Special Education,* 1973, *7* (2), 169–185.

Sours, J. A. Narcolepsy and other disturbances in the sleep–waking rhythm: A study of 115 cases with review of the literature. *Journal of Nervous and Mental Disease,* 1963, *137,* 525–542.

Spence, K. W. Anxiety (drive) level and performance in eyelid conditioning. *Psychological Bulletin,* 1964, *61,* 129–139.

Spence, K. W., Farber, I. E., & McFann H. H. The relation of anxiety (drive) level to performance in competitional and non-competitional paired-associates learning. *Journal of Experimental Psychology,* 1956, *52,* 296–305.

Spence, K. W., Taylor, J. A., & Ketchel, R. Anxiety (drive) level and degree of competition in paired-associates learning. *Journal of Experimental Psychology,* 1956, *52,* 306–310.

Spielberger, C. D. (Ed.). *Anxiety and behavior.* New York: Academic Press, 1966.

Spielberger, C. D., Auerbach, S., Wadsworth, M., Dunn, M., & Taulbee, E. Emotional reactions to surgery. *Journal of Consulting and Clinical Psychology,* 1973, *40,* 33–38.

Spitz, R. A. Hospitalism: An inquiry into the genesis of psychiatric conditions in early childhood. In O. Fenichel *et al.* (Eds.), *The psychoanalytic study of the child.* New York: International Universities Press, 1945.

Spitz, R. A. Anaclitic depression. In O. Fenichel *et al.* (Eds.), *The psychoanalytic study of the child.* New York: International Universities Press, 1946. (a)

Spitz, R. A. Hospitalism: A follow-up report on investigation described in Vol. I, 1945. In O. Fenichel *et al.* (Eds.), *The psychoanalytic study of the child.* New York: International Universities Press, 1946. (b)

Sprague, R. L., Barnes, K. R., & Werry, J. S. Methylphenidate and thioridazine: Learning, reaction time, activity, and classroom behavior in disturbed children. *American Journal of Orthopsychiatry,* 1970, *40,* 615–628.

Srole, L., Langner, T. S., Michael, S. T., Opler, M. K., & Rennie, T. A. C. *Mental health in the metropolis: The Midtown Manhattan Study* (Vol. 1). New York: McGraw-Hill, 1962. (a)

Srole, L., Langner, T. S., Michael, S. T., Opler, M. K., & Rennie, T. A. C. *Mental health in the metropolis: Midtown Manhattan Study* (Vol. 2). New York: McGraw-Hill, 1962. (b)

Stallone, F., Shelley, E., Mendlewicz, J., & Fieve, R. R. The use of lithium in affective disorders, III: A double-blind study of prophylaxis in bipolar illness. *American Journal of Psychiatry,* 1973, *130,* 1006–1010.

Stampfl, T. G., & Levis, D. J. Essentials of implosive therapy: A learning-theory-based psychodynamic behavioral therapy. *Journal of Abnormal Psychology,* 1967, *72,* 496–503.

Stampfl, T. G., & Levis, D. J. Implosive therapy—A behavioral therapy? *Behaviour Research and Therapy,* 1968, *6,* 31–36.

Steadman, H. J., & Cocozza, J. J. *Careers of the criminally insane.* Lexington, Mass.: Lexington Books (D. C. Heath), 1974.

Stein, L., & Wise, C. D. Possible etiology of schizophrenia: Progressive damage to the noradrenergic reward system by 6-hydroxydopamine. *Science,* 1971, *171,* 1032–1036.

Steinmark, S. W., & Borkovec, T. D. Active and placebo treatment effects on moderate insomnia under counterdemand and positive demand instructions. *Journal of Abnormal Psychology,* 1974, *83,* 157–163.

Stephens, J. H., & Kamp, M. On some aspects of hysteria: A clinical study. *Journal of Nervous and Mental Disease,* 1962, *134,* 305–315.

Stern, E. M. The mirror-dialogue approach to the treatment of borderline psychosis. *Journal of Existential Psychiatry,* 1964, *4,* 207–218.

Stern, E. M. Direction for psychotherapy. *Journal of Existentialism,* 1965, *5,* 287–296.

Stevens, H. A., & Heber, R. (Eds.). *Mental retardation.* Chicago: University of Chicago Press, 1964.

Steward, D. A. Empathy—A revised concept. *Journal of Existentialism,* 1965–1966, *6,* 215–222.

Stewart, W. A. *Psychoanalysis: The first ten years (1888–1898).* New York: Macmillan, 1967.

Stierlin, H. Some comments on the relevance for psychotherapy of the work of Gabriel Marcel. *Review of Existential Psychology and Psychiatry,* 1962, *2,* 145–148.

Stoller, R. J. Transvestites' women. *American Journal of Psychiatry,* 1967, *124,* 333–339.

Stone, L. J. A critique of studies of infant isolation. *Child Development,* 1954, *25,* 9–20.

Strahley, R. F. *Systematic desensitization and counterphobic treatment of an irrational fear of snakes.* Unpublished doctoral dissertation, University of Tennessee, 1965.

Straus, E. W. Chronognosy and chronopathy. In E. W. Straus (Ed.), *Phenomenology: Pure and applied.* Pittsburgh, Pa.: Duquesne University Press, 1964.

Strauss, M. E. Behavioral differences between acute and chronic schizophrenics: Course of psychosis, effects of institutionalization, or sampling biases. *Psychological Bulletin,* 1973, *79,* 271–279.

Strauss, M. E., Foureman, W. C., & Parwatikar, S. D. Schizophrenics' size estimations of thematic stimuli. *Journal of Abnormal Psychology,* 1974, *84,* 117–123.

Strauss, M. E., Sirotkin, R. A., & Grisell, J. Length of hospitalization and rate of readmission of paranoid and nonparanoid schizophrenics. *Journal of Consulting and Clinical Psychology,* 1974, *42,* 105–110.

Strupp, H. H. The future of psychoanalysis. In *Psychotherapy: Clinical, research, and theoretical issues.* New York: Jason Aronson, 1973.

Strupp, H. H., Fox, R. E. & Lessler, K. *Patients view their psychotherapy*. Baltimore: Johns Hopkins, 1969.

Stuart, R. B. Behavioral control over eating. *Behaviour Research and Therapy*, 1967, *5*, 357–365.

Stuart, R. B. A three-dimensional program in the treatment of obesity. *Behaviour Research and Therapy*, 1971, *9*, 177–186.

Sturm, I. E. Overinclusion and concreteness among pathological groups. *Journal of Consulting Psychology*, 1965, *29*, 9–18.

Suinn, R. M. The desensitization of test anxiety by group and individual treatment. *Behaviour Research and Therapy*, 1968, *6*, 385–387.

Suinn, R. M. *Fundamentals of behavior pathology*. New York: Wiley, 1970.

Sullivan, A. J., & McKell, T. E. *Personality in peptic ulcer*. Springfield, Ill.: Charles C Thomas, 1950.

Sullivan, H. S. *Conceptions of modern psychiatry*. Washington, D.C.: William Allison White Institute, 1947.

Summers, M. *Malleus Maleficarum*. London: Hogarth, 1969.

Sutherland, R. Structure, experience, and psychotherapy. *Journal of Existentialism*, 1965–1966, *6*, 197–202.

Sutherland, S., & Scherl, D. Patterns of response among victims of rape. *American Journal of Orthopsychiatry*, 1970, *3*, 503–511.

Sutker, R. B. Personality differences and sociopathy in heroin addicts and non-addict prisoners. *Journal of Abnormal Psychology*, 1971, *78*, 247–251.

Szasz, T. S. *The ethics of psychoanalysis: The theory and method of autonomous psychotherapy* New York: Dell, 1965.

Szasz, T. S. *The manufacture of madness*. New York: Harper & Row, 1970.

Tart, C. T. The hypnotic dream: Methodological problems and a review of the literature. *Psychological Bulletin*, 1965, *63*, 87–99.

Tart, C. T. Marijuana intoxication: Common experiences. *Nature*, 1970, *226*, 701–704.

Taylor, A. A. A personality scale of manifest anxiety. *Journal of Abnormal and Social Psychology*, 1953, *48*, 285–290.

Thaller, J. L., Rosen, G., & Saltzman, S. Study of the relationship of frustration and anxiety to bruxism. *Journal of Periodontology*, 1967, *38*, 193–197.

Thigpen, C. H., & Cleckley, H. A case of multiple personality. *Journal of Abnormal and Social Psychology*, 1954, *49*, 135–151.

Thigpen, C. H., & Cleckley, H. M. *Three faces of Eve*. New York: McGraw-Hill, 1957.

Thomas, A., Chess, S., & Birch, H. G. *Temperament and behavior disorders in children*. New York: New York University Press, 1968.

Thomas, H. F. An existential attitude in working with individuals and groups. In J. F. T. Bugental (Ed.), *Challenges of humanistic psychology*. New York: McGraw-Hill, 1967.

Thorne, F. C. A factorial study of sexuality in adult males. *Journal of Clinical Psychology*, 1966, *22*, 378–386.

Tienari, P. Psychiatric illness in identical twins, *Acta Psychiatrica Neurologica Scandanavia*, Supplementum, 171, 1963.

Tienari, P. Schizophrenia in monozygotic male twins. In D. Rosenthal and S. S. Kety (Eds.), *The transmission of schizophrenia*. London: Pergamon, 1968.

Tillich, P. *The courage to be*. New Haven: Yale University Press, 1952.

Tillich, P. Existentialism and psychotherapy. *Review of Existential Psychology and Psychiatry*, 1961, *1*, 8–16.

Tokarz, T., & Lawrence, P. S. *An analysis of temporal and stimulus factors in the treatment of insomnia*. Paper presented at the meeting of the Association for the Advancement of Behavior Therapy, Chicago, November 1974.

Tonks, C. M., Rack, P. H., & Rose, M. J. Attempted suicide and the menstrual cycle. In J. E. Jeffress (Ed.), *Psychosomatic medicine current journal articles*. New York: Medical Examination Publishing Co., 1971. (Reprinted from *Journal of Psychosomatic Research*, 1968, *11*.)

Trexler, L. D., & Karst, T. O. Rational–emotive therapy, placebo, and no-treatment effects on public-speaking anxiety. *Journal of Abnormal Psychology*, 1972, *79*, 60–69.

Truax, C. B., Carkhuff, R. R., & Kodman, R. Relationships between therapist offered conditions and patient change in group psychotherapy. *Journal of Clinical Psychology,* 1965, *21,* 327–329.

Truax, C. B., & Mitchell, K. M. Research on certain therapist interpersonal skills in relation to process and outcome. In A. E. Bergin & S. L. Garfield (Eds.), *Handbook of psychotherapy and behavior change,* New York: Wiley, 1971.

Truax, C. B., Wargo, D. G., & Volksdorf, N. R. Antecedents to outcome in group counseling with institutionalized juvenile delinquents: Effects of therapeutic conditions, patient self-exploration, alternate sessions, and vicarious therapy pre-training. *Journal of Abnormal Psychology,* 1970, *76,* 235–242.

True, J. E. Learning of abstract responses by process and reactive schizophrenic patients. *Psychological Reports,* 1966, *18,* 51–55.

Tumarkin, B., Wilson, J., & Snyder, G. Cerebral atrophy due to alcoholism in young adults. *U.S. Armed Forces Medical Journal,* 1955, *6,* 64–74.

Udry, J. R., & Morris, N. M. A method for validation of reported sexual data. *Journal of Marriage and the Family,* 1967, *5,* 442–446.

Ullmann, L. P., & Giovannoni, J. M. The development of a self-report measure of the process–reactive continuum. *Journal of Nervous and Mental Disease,* 1964, *138,* 38–42.

Ullmann, L. P., & Krasner, L. *A psychological approach to abnormal behavior* (2nd ed.). Englewood Cliffs, N.J.: Prentice-Hall, 1975. (Originally published, 1969.)

Ullmann, L. P., Krasner, L., & Edinger, R. L. Verbal conditioning of common associations in long-term schizophrenic patients. *Behaviour Research and Therapy,* 1964, *2,* 15–18.

Ungersma, A. J. *The search for meaning.* Philadelphia: Westminster, 1961.

U.S. Department of Health, Education, and Welfare. *Marihuana and health.* Washington, D.C.: U.S. Government Printing Office, 1971.

Valenstein, E. S. *Brain control.* New York: Wiley, 1973.

Van den Berg, J. H. An existential explanation of the guided daydream in psychotherapy. *Review of Existential Psychology and Psychiatry,* 1962, *2,* 5–35.

Van den Berg, J. H. *A different existence.* Pittsburgh, Pa.: Duquesne University Press, 1972.

Van Dusen, W. The theory and practice of existential psychotherapy. In H. Ruitenbeek (Ed.), *Psychoanalysis and existential philosophy.* New York: Dutton, 1962.

Van Kaam, A. Clinical implications of Heidegger's concept of will, decision, and responsibility. *Review of Existential Psychology and Psychiatry,* 1961, *1,* 205–216.

Van Kaam, A. *Existential foundations of psychology.* Pittsburgh, Pa.: Duquesne University Press, 1966.

Van Zaig, J. Verstehen claim and the tuning-in relationship. *Review of Existential Psychology and Psychiatry,* 1965, *5,* 190–193.

Veith, I. *Hysteria: The history of a disease.* Chicago: University of Chicago Press, 1965.

Verville, E. *Behavior problems of children.* Philadelphia and London: Saunders, 1967.

Victor, M., & Adams, R. D. The effect of alcohol on the nervous system. In H. H. Merritt & C. C. Hare (Eds.), *Metabolic and toxic diseases of the nervous system: Proceedings of the association.* Baltimore: Williams & Wilkins, 1953.

Vitols, M. M. The significance of the higher incidence of schizophrenia in the Negro race in North Carolina. *North Carolina Medical Journal,* 1961, *22,* 147–158.

Voegtlin, W. L. The treatment of alcoholism by establishing a conditioned reflex. *American Journal of Medical Science,* 1940, *199,* 802–810.

Vogler, R. E., Lunde, S. E., & Martin, P. L. Electrical aversion conditioning with chronic alcoholics: Follow-up and suggestions for research. *Journal of Consulting and Clinical Psychology,* 1971, *36,* 450.

Volle, R. L., & Koelle, G. B. Ganglionic stimulating and blocking agents. In L. S. Goodman & A. Gilman (Eds.), *The pharmacological basis of therapeutics* (4th ed.). New York: Macmillan, 1970.

Wahl, C. W. Some antecedent factors in the family histories of 568 male schizophrenics of the U.S. Navy. *American Journal of Psychiatry,* 1956, *113,* 201–210.

Wahler, R. G., & Pollio, H. R. Behavior and insight: A case study in behavior therapy. *Journal of Experimental Research in Personality,* 1968, *3,* 45–56.

Walker, A. M., Rablen, R. A., and Rogers, C. R. Development of a scale to measure process changes in psychotherapy. *Journal of Clinical Psychology*, 1960, *16*, 79–85.

Walker, K. *The story of medicine*. Essex, England: Anchor Press, 1959.

Wallerstein, R. S. Psychoanalysis as a science: Its present status and its future tasks. In M. M. Gill & P. S. Holzman (Eds.), *Psychology versus metapsychology*. New York: International Universities Press, 1975. [Also in *Psychological Issues*, 1975, *9* (Monograph 36).]

Ward, A. J. Early infantile autism. *Psychological Bulletin*, 1970, *73*, 350–362.

Ward, C. H., Beck, A. T., Mendelson, M., Mock, J. E., & Erbaugh, J. K. The psychiatric nomenclature: Reasons for diagnostic disagreement. *Archives of General Psychiatry*, 1962, *7*, 198–205.

Ward, P., & Rouzer, D. L. The nature of pathological functioning from a Gestalt perspective. *The Counseling Psychologist*, 1974, *4*, 24–27.

Warkeny, J., & Dignan, P. St. J. Congenital malformations: Microcephaly. In J. Wortis (Ed.), *Mental retardation and developmental disabilities: An annual review*. New York: Brunner/Mazel, 1973.

Warren, J. No rave reviews for community care. *APA Monitor*, 1976, *7* (5), 1, 10.

Warren, M. Q. Classification on offenders as an aid to efficient management and effective treatment. *Journal of Criminal Law, Criminology and Police Science*, 1971, *62*, 239–258.

Wastell, C. *Chronic duodenal ulcer*. New York: Appleton-Century-Crofts, 1972.

Watson, C. G. Abstract thinking deficit and autism in process and reactive schizophrenics. *Journal of Abnormal Psychology*, 1973, *82*, 399–403.

Watson, C. G., & Baugh, V. S. Patterns of psychiatric patients on the revised beta examination. *Journal of Clinical Psychology*, 1966, *22*, 188–190.

Watson, D. L., & Tharp, R. G. *Self-directed behavior: Self-modification for personal adjustment*. Monterey, Calif.: Brooks/Cole, 1972.

Watson, J. B. *The ways of behaviorism*. New York and London: Harper, 1928.

Watson, J. B., & Rayner, R. Conditioned emotional reactions. *Journal of Experimental Psychology*, 1920, *3*, 1–14.

Watson, R. I. *The great psychologists from Aristotle to Freud*. Philadelphia and New York: Lippincott, 1963.

Waxler, N. E., & Mishler, E. G. Parental interaction with schizophrenic children and well siblings. *Archives of General Psychiatry*, 1971, *25*, 223–231.

Way, E. L. Distribution and metabolism of morphine and its surrogates. In A. Winkler (Ed.), *The addictive states*. Baltimore: Williams & Wilkins, 1968.

Webb, R. A. A comment on D. J. Moore and D. A. Shiek's "Toward a theory of early infantile autism." *Psychological Review*, 1972, *79*, 278–279.

Webb, W. B. Twenty-four hour sleep cycling. In A. Kales (Ed.), *Sleep: Physiology and pathology*. Philadelphia: Lippincott, 1969.

Webster, L. M., & Brutten, G. An audiovisual behavioral analysis of the stuttering moment. *Behavior Therapy*, 1972, *3*, 555–560.

Wechsler, D. *The measurement and appraisal of adult intelligence*. Baltimore: Williams & Wilkins, 1958.

Weckowicz, T. Depersonalization. In C. G. Costello (Ed.), *Symptoms of psychopathology: A handbook*. New York: Wiley, 1970.

Weinar, H. Some psychological factors related to cardiovascular responses: A logical and empirical analysis. In R. Roessler & N. X. Greenfield (Eds.), *Physiological correlates of psychological disorders*. Madison: University of Wisconsin Press, 1962.

Weiss, B., & Laties, V. G. Enhancement of human performance by caffeine and the amphetamines. *Pharmacological Reviews*, 1962, *14*, 1–36.

Weiss, J. M., Glazer, H. I., & Pohorecky, L. A. Neurotransmitters and helplessness: A chemical bridge to depression? *Psychology Today*, 1974, *8*, 58.

Weitzenhoffer, A. M., & Hilgard, E. R. *Stanford susceptibility scale: Form c*. Palo Alto, Calif.: Consulting Psychologists Press, 1962.

Welgan, P. R. Learned control of gastric acid secretion in ulcer patients. *Psychosomatic Medicine*, 1974, *36* (5), 411–419.

Welsh, G. S. An anxiety index and an internalization ratio for the MMPI. *Journal of Consulting Psychology*, 1952, *16*, 65–72.

Wender, L. The dynamics of group psychotherapy and its application. *Journal of Nervous and Mental Diseases,* 1936, *84,* 54–60.

Wender, P. H. *Minimal brain dysfunction in children.* New York: Wiley, 1971.

Werry, J. S. Childhood psychosis. In H. C. Quay & J. S. Werry, *Psychopathological disorders of childhood.* New York: Wiley, 1972. (a)

Werry, J. S. Organic factors in childhood psychopathology. In H. C. Quay & J. S. Werry, *Psychopathological disorders of childhood.* New York: Wiley, 1972. (b)

Werry, J. S. Psychosomatic disorders (with a note on anesthesia, surgery and hospitalization). In H. C. Quay & J. S. Werry, *Psychopathological disorders of childhood.* New York: Wiley, 1972. (c)

Werry, J. S., & Quay, H. C. The prevalence of behavior symptoms in younger elementary school children. *American Journal of Orthopsychiatry,* 1971, *41,* 136–143.

Whitaker, C. A. Experiential psychotherapy: Evaluation of relatedness. *Journal of Existential Psychiatry,* 1963, *3,* 247–254.

White, R. Ego and reality in psychoanalytic theory. *Psychological Issues,* 1963, *3,* (Monograph 11).

Whitlock, F. A. The syndrome of barbiturate dependence. *Medical Journal of Australia,* 1970, *2,* 391–396.

Whittier, J. E. Management of Huntington's chorea: The disease, those affected, and those otherwise involved. In A. Barbeau, T. N. Chase, & G. W. Paulson (Eds.), *Advances in neurology, Volume I: Huntington's chorea, 1872–1972.* New York: Raven Press, 1973.

Wikler, A. Conditioning factors in opiate addiction and relapse. In D. M. Wilner & G. G. Kassebaum (Eds.), *Narcotics.* New York: McGraw-Hill, 1965.

Wilcox, R. E., & Levitt, R. A. The depressants. In R. A. Levitt, *Psychopharmacology: A biological approach.* Washington, D.C.: Hemisphere/Wiley, 1975.

Wilcoxon, H. C. "Abnormal fixation" and learning. *Journal of Experimental Psychology,* 1952, *44,* 324–333.

Wilkins, W. Desensitization: Social and cognitive factors underlying the effectiveness of Wolpe's procedures. *Psychological Bulletin,* 1971, *76,* 311–317.

Williams, R. L., & Karacan, I. Clinical disorders of sleep. In G. Usdin (Ed.), *Sleep research and clinical practice.* New York: Brunner/Mazel, 1973.

Wilson, C., & Linken, A. *The use of cannabis in adolescent drug dependents.* New York: Pergamon, 1968.

Wilson, G. T., Leaf, R. C., & Nathan, P. E. The aversive control of excessive alcohol consumption by chronic alcoholics in the laboratory setting. *Journal of Applied Behavior Analysis,* 1975, *8,* 13–26.

Wincze, J. P., & Caird, W. K. The effects of systematic desensitization and video desensitization in the treatment of essential sexual dysfunction in women. *Behavior Therapy,* 1976, *7,* 335–342.

Wing, J. K. (Ed.) *Early childhood autism.* New York: Pergamon, 1966.

Winokur, G., Guze, S. G., & Pfeiffer, E. Developmental and sexual factors in women: A comparison between control, neurotic, and psychotic groups. *American Journal of Psychiatry,* 1959, *115,* 1097–1100.

Winthrop, H. Authentic dialogue and the presentation of self. *International Forum for Existential Psychiatry,* 1969, *7,* 72–90.

Wishner, J. Neurosis and tension: An exploratory study of the relation of physiological and Rorschach measures. *Journal of Abnormal and Social Psychology,* 1953, *2,* 253–260.

Withington, E. T. *Medical history: From the earliest times. A popular history of the healing art.* London: Holland Press, 1964.

Wittenborn, J. R., Weber, E. S. P., & Brown, M. Niacin in the long-term treatment of schizophrenia. *Archives of General Psychiatry,* 1973, *28,* 308–315.

Wittkower, E. D., & Dubreuil, G. Cultural factors in mental illness. In E. Norbeck, D. Price-Williams, & W. M. McCord (Eds.), *The study of personality: An interdisciplinary appraisal.* New York: Holt, 1968.

Wittman, M. P. A scale for measuring prognosis in schizophrenic patients. *Elgin State Hospital Papers,* 1941, *4,* 20–23.

Wolf, A. The psychoanalysis of groups. *American Journal of Psychotherapy,* 1949, *3,* 525–558.

Wolf, S., Cardon, P. V., Shepard, E. M., & Wolff, H. G. *Life stress and essential hypertension.* Baltimore: Williams & Wilkins, 1955.

Wolf, S., & Wolff, H. G. Psychosomatic aspects of peptic ulcers. *Scope,* 1946, *11,* 4–9.

Wolff, W. M., & Morris, L. A. Intellectual and personality characteristics of parents of autistic children. *Journal of Abnormal Psychology,* 1971, *77,* 155–161.

Wolfgang, M., & Ferracuti, F. *The subculture of violence.* London: Social Science Paperbacks, 1967.

Wollersheim, J. P. Effectiveness of group therapy based upon learning principles in the treatment of overweight women. *Journal of Abnormal Psychology,* 1970, *76,* 462–474.

Wolpe, J. *Psychotherapy by reciprocal inhibition.* Stanford, Calif.: Stanford Univ. Press, 1958.

Wolpe, J. *The practice of behavior therapy* (2nd ed.). New York: Pergamon, 1973. (Originally published, 1969.)

Wolpe, J., & Lang, P. J. A fear survey schedule for use in behavior therapy. *Behaviour Research and Therapy,* 1964, *2,* 27–30.

Woodburne, L. S. *The neural basis of behavior.* Columbus, Ohio: Charles E. Merrill, 1967.

Woolley, D. W. *The biochemical bases of psychoses.* New York: Wiley, 1962.

Woolley, D. W., & Shaw, E. A biochemical and pharmacological suggestion about certain mental disorders. *Science,* 1954, *119,* 587–588.

Wright, M. W. A study of anxiety in a general hospital setting. *Canadian Journal of Psychology,* 1954, *8,* 195–203.

Wyatt, R. J., Termini, B. A., & Davis, J. Biochemical and sleep studies of schizophrenia: A review of the literature— 1960–1970. *Schizophrenia Bulletin,* 1971, *4,* 10–66.

Wynne, L. C., Ryckoff, I. M., Day, J., & Hirsch, S. I. Pseudo-mutuality in the family relations of schizophrenics. *Psychiatry,* 1959, *21,* 205.

Wynne, L. C., & Solomon, R. L. Traumatic avoidance learning: Acquisition and extinction in dogs deprived of normal peripheral autonomic function. *Genetic Psychology Monographs,* 1955, *52,* 241–284.

Wyschogrod, E. (Ed.). *The phenomenon of death: Faces of mortality.* New York: Harper & Row, 1973.

Yates, A. J. *Behavior therapy.* New York: Wiley, 1970.

Yates, A. J. *Theory and practice in behavior therapy.* New York: Wiley, 1975.

Yontef, G. A. *A review of the practice of Gestalt therapy.* Doctoral dissertation, University of Arizona, 1969. (Copies published privately and available from The Trident Shop, California State College, Los Angeles, 5153 State College Drive, Los Angeles, California 09932.)

Yoss, R. E., & Daly, D. D. Narcolepsy. *Archives of Internal Medicine,* 1960, *106,* 168–171.

Young, E. R., Rimm, D. C., & Kennedy, T. D. An experimental investigation of modeling and verbal reinforcement in the modification of assertive behavior. *Behaviour Research and Therapy,* 1973, *11,* 317–319.

Yuille, J. C., & Paivio, A. Imagery and verbal mediation instructions in paired-associated learning. *Journal of Experimental Psychology,* 1968, *78,* 436–441.

Yusin, A., Nihira, K., & Mortashed, C. Major and minor criteria in schizophrenia. *American Journal of Psychiatry,* 1974, *131,* 688–692.

Zacks, S. I. *Atlas of neuropathology.* New York: Harper & Row, 1971.

Zaslow, R. W., & Breger, L. A theory and treatment of autism. In L. Breger (Ed.), *Clinical-cognitive psychology: Models and integrations.* Englewood Cliffs, N.J.: Prentice-Hall, 1969.

Zax, M., & Cowen, E. L. Research on early detection and prevention of emotional dysfunction in young school children. In C. D. Spielberger (Ed.), *Current topics in clinical and community psychology* (Vol. 1). New York: Academic Press, 1969.

Zax, M., & Cowen, E. L. *Abnormal psychology: Changing conceptions.* New York: Holt, Rinehart and Winston, 1972.

Ziegler, F. J., Imboden, J. B., & Meyer, E. Contemporary conversion reactions: A clinical study. *American Journal of Psychiatry,* 1960, *116,* 901–909.

Zilboorg, G., & Henry, G. W. *A history of medical psychology.* New York: Norton, 1941.

Ziskin, J. *Coping with psychiatric and psychological testimony* (2nd ed.). Beverly Hills, Calif.: Law and Psychology Press, 1975.

Zubin, J. Classification of the behavior disorders. *Annual Review of Psychology,* 1967, *18,* 373–401.

Zuckerman, M. The development of an affect adjective check list for the measurement of anxiety. *Journal of Consulting Psychology,* 1960, *24,* 457–462.

Zuckerman, M. Physiological measures of sexual arousal in the human. *Psychological Bulletin*, 1971, *75*, 347–356.

Zulch, K. J. *Brain tumors: Their biology and pathology* (2nd ed.). New York: Springer, 1965.

Zussman, S. Treatment of the victim of rape. In *Clinical uses of the female sex hormones and early diagnosis and treatment of mammary cancer*. New York: Lippincott, 1972.

Zweig, S. *Mental healers: Mesmer, Eddy, Freud* (Eden Paul & Cedar Paul, trans.). Garden City, N.Y.: Garden City Publishing Company, 1931.

Author Index

Numbers in italics refer to the pages on which the complete references are listed.

Subject Index

Because complex concepts seldom can be defined in a sentence or two, this book has no glossary. Instead, a boldface page number indicates the place in the text where a concept is discussed and defined.

Allergens, in neurodermatitis, 185
Alpha activity, 382
Alzheimer's disease, **243**
Amantadine, in parkinsonism, 245
Ambivalence, in schizophrenia, 104
Amenorrhea, **197–200**
  in anorexia nervosa, 199–200, 295
  emotional, 197
  galactorrhea and, 197–199
  primary, 197
  secondary, 197
Amino acids, metabolic disorders affecting, 280
Amitriptyline, 599
Amnesia, hysterical, 83
Amnesic aphasia, **223–224**
Amniocentesis, 272
Amphetamines, **429**, 602
  in schizophrenia, 135–136
Amygdalatomy, **610–612**
Anaclitic depression, 168
Androgen, acne and, 187
Angioneurotic edema, 186
Angry aggression, 329
Angst, 66
Anorexia nervosa, **295–296**
  amenorrhea with, 199–200
Anoxia
  in cerebral palsy, 277
  in schizophrenia, 132n
Antabuse, 443–444
Antianxiety agents, **423, 600–601**
Antidepressants, **432, 599–600**
Antipsychotics, 423, **593–596**
  side effects of, 594, 595
Antisocial behavior, of psychopaths, 334
Anxiety, 58, **65–76**
  compulsive behavior and, 96
  effects on learning, 72–74
  effects on memory, 72
  effects on performance, 74–75
  existential, 535–536
  fear compared with, 66
  free-floating, 61–62
  measurement of, 65–66
    behavioral, 71–72
    physiological, 66–69
    questionnaires in, 69–71
  in schizophrenia, 124, 133
Anxiety neurosis, **61–65**
  defense mechanisms in, 63
  definition of, 59
Anxiety reaction, associated with sex, treatment of, 374–375
Anxiety-relief conditioning, 472

Anxiety state, diagnosis of, 58
Apathy, in schizophrenia, 124
Aphasia, **222–224**
  amnesic, 223–224
  developmental, 222
  expressive, 222–223
  receptive, 223
Apnea, in sleep, 393
Apraxia, **223**
Arousal dysfunction, treatment of, 374
Arteriosclerotic dementia, **241–242**
Asocial behavior, of psychopaths, 334
Aspirin poisoning, **225**
Assertiveness, in depression, 172
Assertive training, **467–468**
  research findings in, 477
Associations, in schizophrenia, 103, 127, 129–130
Asthma, in children, 301–304
Atheroma, 241
Atherosclerosis, 241
Atopic dermatitis, **183–185**
Attention
  aggression to obtain, 289–290
  in schizophrenia, 138–139
Attic children, 262–264
Attitude(s)
  toward epilepsy, 230–231
  toward mental illness, 41–44
  toward sexual behavior, 343
  specificity of, in urticaria, 186–187
Atypical children, **310**
Auras, in epilepsy, 233
Autism, 104
  early infantile, **314–318**
  etiology of, 315–318
  treatment of, 317–318
Autonomic nervous system (ANS), 68, **214–215**
Aversion therapy, **471**
  avoidance, 471–472
  covert sensitization in, 472–473
  for drug abuse, 446–447, 448
  for fetishism and transvestism, 363
  for homosexuality, 357–358
  research findings in, 478–479
Avoidance
  as anxiety measure, 71–72
  Gestalt concept of, 561–562
  personality problems as, 290–291
  two-factor theory of, 90
Avoidance conditioning, **471–472**
  research findings in, 478
  under traumatic conditions, 91

Awareness, in Gestalt psychology, 557–559, 562, 563, 564

B

Barbiturates, 421, 601
  toxicity and withdrawal from, 421–422
Basal ganglia, in parkinsonism, 245
Beck Depression Inventory, 149–150, 151
Behavioral measures of anxiety, 71–72
Behavioral theory
  development of, 28–29
  of drug abuse, 413–414
Behavior Classification System, 331, 332
Behavior modification, **455**
  experimental approach to, 49
Behavior rehearsal, 467–468
Behavior therapy, **455–456**
  applicability of, 457–458
  assertive training in, 467–468
  aversive conditioning, 471–473
  basic assumptions of, 457
  cognitive, 473–475
  in drug abuse, 446–448
  flooding and implosive therapy, 470–471
  in homosexuality, 357–359
  operant procedures in, 458–465
  research findings in, 475–479
  modeling in, 468–470
  systematic desensitization in, 465–467
Being, in EP theory, 531n
Beriberi, cerebral, 419
Bielschowsky-Jansky disease, 279
Biochemical factors
  in depression, 165–167
  in schizophrenia, 133–137
Biofeedback, 461
  autonomic responses and, 181–183
  duodenal ulcers and, 195
  in hypertension, 207–209
  in migraine headache, 210–211
Bizarre behavior, 35
Blame, of victims of crimes, 336–338
Blood pressure, 68, see also Hypertension; Hypotension
Body language, in Gestalt therapy, 566
Brachycephaly, 266
Brain, see also specific structures
  arousal mechanisms in, in autism, 317
  microcephalic, 275
  psychosurgery to, 606–613
Brain injury, traumatic, 216–218
Brain stem, 214
  in etiology of autism, 317
  tumors near, 219
Brain tumors, **218–219**
  benign, 219
  malignant, 219
Bromides, 423
  poisoning by, 225
Bruxism, **397–398**
Butyrophenones, 423, **594–595**
  dopamine action and, 136

C

Caffeine, 429–430
Caffeinism, 430
Cannabis, see Marijuana
Carbohydrates, metabolic disorders affecting, 280–281
Case history approach, 47
Castration anxiety, 87
Cataplexy, in narcolepsy, 392
Catatonic schizophrenia, **115–117**
Catecholamine hypothesis of depression, 165–166
Centeredness, 538
Central nervous system (CNS), **213–214**
  effects of caffeine on, 429, 430
  menstrual cycle and, 196–197
Central nervous system (CNS) disorders, **215–216**
  alcohol-induced, 419
  associated with aging, 240–247
  associated with injury, tumors, and infections, 216–224
  associated with toxic conditions, 224–230
  epilepsy, 230–240
Cerebellum, 213
Cerebral beriberi, 419
Cerebral cortex, **213**
  sleep and, 389
Cerebral lipoidosis, 279–280
Cerebral palsy, mental retardation and, 277–278
Cerebrospinal fluid, 272–273
  in hydrocephaly, 273
Chiari-Frommel syndrome, 197–198
Childhood schizophrenia, **310**
Children
  anorexia nervosa in, 295–296
  asthma in, 301–304
  atypical, **310**
  autism in, **314–318**

behavior in clinic and nonclinic populations, 284–285
conduct problems in, 287–290
encopresis in, 299–301
enuresis in, 296–299
fears of, 87
food refusal in, 294–295
learning difficulties in, 304–309
treatment of, 309
obesity in, 293–294
personality problems in, 290–293
primary preventive program for, 577
psychosis in, 310–318
selection for treatment, 285–287
sleep disturbances in, 394–396
thinking in, schizophrenic thought compared with, 128–129
vicarious extinction with, 469
Chloral hydrate, 423
Chlordiazepoxide, 423
Chlorpromazine, 423, 594
amenorrhea and galactorrhea with, 198–199
Chlorthalidone, in hypertension, 207
Choice, existential, 536–539
Chorea, 245
Choreiform movements, 307
Choroid plexuses, 273
Chronic brain syndromes, associated with aging, 240–244
Cingulotomy, 609
Cirrhosis, of liver, 418–419
Classical conditioning, 88
of autonomic responses, 181
in etiology of schizophrenia, 137
Classification systems, diagnostic reliability and, 59–60
Client-centered therapy, **509–510**
client characteristics and, 515–516
goal of, 516
personality theory and, 511–514
process of, 517–521
psychopathology and, 514–515
research findings in, 521–524
Clonic phase, 234
CNS, *see* Central nervous system
Cocaine, 430–432
Codeine, 424
acute effects of, 425
Cognitive-behavior therapy, **474**
Cognitive factors, in depression, 171–172
Cognitive therapy, **473–475**
research findings in, 479

Colitis, **189–191**
Commitment
civil, 44
criminal, 44
process of, 40–41
Community mental health, **571–572**
as activity, 572–573
community intervention in, 586–588
consultation in, 583–585
crisis intervention in, 580–583
development of, 574–576
evaluation of, 588–590
as ideology, 572
prevention in, 576–577
conceptual models for, 578–580
primary, 577–578
secondary and tertiary, 578
services provided by, 574
Competence, legal, 338–339
Comprehensive retardation, 256
Compulsion(s), 93, **95–97**
Compulsion neurosis, 93
Concentration, in schizophrenia, 125–126
Conceptual disorganization, in schizophrenia, 124
Concordance rate, **130, 164n**
in depression, 164–165
in schizophrenia, 130–133
Concurrent validity, of diagnosis, 52
Concussions, **216–217**
Conditioned response, 88
Conditioned stimulus, 88
Conduct problems
in children, 287–290
learning disabilities and, 308
Confabulation, in Korsakoff's psychosis, 419
Conflict, **487–489**
Confrontation, therapeutic, 540
Confusion, following electroconvulsive therapy, 604
Construct validity, of diagnosis, 52
Contact desensitization, 469
Content validity, of diagnosis, 52
Control, in murderers, 329
Control groups, 48
Contusions, of brain, 217–218
Conversion hysteria, **78–83**
compared with other disorders, 78–83
Correlation, **47n**
Correlation study approach, 47–48
Cortical immaturity, in psychopaths, 336
Cortisol, in depression, 166–167
Counterconditioning, 465

Covert sensitization, **472–473**
  for drug abuse, 447
  research findings in, 478–479
Craving, for drugs, 409
Cretinism, 266
Criminal(s), typologies of, 331–333
Criminal behavior, **323–327**
  psychopathic, 333–336
  psychopathology of, 328–331
  rape, 366–368
  victim of, 336–338
Crisis, **581**
  existential, 540–541
Crisis intervention, **580–583**
Crohn's disease, 190–191
Cross-dependence, 409
Cross-tolerance, 408, 422
Cultural factors, in mental retardation, 258–
  265

D

Dangerous behavior, **327–328**
  prediction of, 327–328
Death, depression following, 168
Defense mechanisms, **487–490**
  in anxiety neurosis, 63
  client-centered therapy and, 515
Delinquents, typologies of, 332–333
Delirium tremens
  alcohol-induced, 419–420
  barbiturate-induced, 422
Delusion(s), 110
  in depression, 153–154
  of grandeur, 110
  in hebephrenic schizophrenia, 113
  of reference, 110
Dementia praecox, 103, *see also* Schizophrenia
Demerol, 424
Dependence
  physical, 409
    on alcohol, 418–419
    on caffeine, 430
    on narcotics, 428
    on nicotine, 433
  psychological, 409
Depersonalization neurosis, **100–101**
  etiology of, 101
Depressants, 414–423
Depression, **146–148, 150–155**
  anaclitic, 168
  electroconvulsive therapy in, 604, 605–606

etiology of
  biological considerations in, 163–167
  psychological considerations in, 167–172
exogenous versus endogenous, 162–163
incidence of, 150
neurotic versus psychotic, 160–161
onset of, 155
prognosis for, 155
reliability of diagnosis, 148–150
suicide and, 173
symptomatology of, 150–154
Depressive reactions, **147–148**
Derealization, *see* Depersonalization neurosis
Derivatives, 495
Dermographism, 186
Determinism, psychological, **484–485**
Detoxification, **443**
Deviance, direction of, 31–32
Dextroamphetamine, 135, 429
Diagnosis
  primary, 60–61
  reliability of, 51–52
    in depression, 148–150
    in neuroses, 58–61
    in phobias, 87
  of schizophrenia, 105–108
  validity of, 52–53
Diagnosticians, diagnostic reliability and,
  60–61
Diathesis-stress theory, 133
Diazepam, 423
Diet
  in control of epilepsy, 235
  in control of galactosemia, 281
  in control of phenylketonuria, 280
  in control of ulcers, 193–195
Discomfort, personal, abnormality as, 35–36
Disorganization, client-centered therapy and,
  515
Disorientation, in schizophrenia, 124
Displacement, in phobia, 85–86
Dissociative hysterical reactions, 83–85
Distractibility, learning difficulties and, 308
Disulfiram, 443–444
DMPEA (3,4-Dimethoxyphenethylamine), in
  schizophrenia, 135
Dolophine, *see* Methadone
Dominant response, 74
L-Dopa, in parkinsonism, 245
Dopamine
  antipsychotics and, 595
  in etiology of depression, 166
  in schizophrenia, 134, 135, 136

Performance, anxiety and, 74–75
Peripheral nervous system, 214, *see also* Autonomic nervous system
Persecution, 110
Personality
  antisocial, *see* Psychopathy
  client-centered theory and, 511–514
  criminal, 331–333
  duodenal ulcers and, 193
  migraine headaches and, 210
  multiple, 84–85
  neurodermatitis and, 185
  paranoid, 112
  of psychopaths, 336
  psychophysiological disorders and, 181
  split, 85
  three-dimensional view of, 64n
Personality problems, in children, 290–293
Perspiration, anxiety and, 68
Petit mal epilepsy, **234–235**
pH, 195n
  of gastric acid, biofeedback and, 195
Phenomenology, *see* Existential–phenomenological therapy
Phenothiazines, 423, **593–594**
  dopamine action and, 136
Phenylketonuria (PKU), 280
Phobias, **85–92**
  clustering of fears in, 87
  diagnosis of, 59
  displacement in, 85–86
  incidence of, 86
  origin of, 87–89
  participant modeling and, 469–470
  reliability of diagnosis of, 87
  systematic desensitization for, 465–467
  two-factor theory and, 89–92
Physiological theory, of drug abuse, 414
Pica, 226
Pick's disease, **244**
Piperazines, 594
Pituitary gland, menstrual cycle and, 196
Placebo control group, 48
Positive regard, 513, 514
  unconditional, 518
Posture, in depression, 152
Predictability
  constructs and, 50–51
  lack of, 34–35
Predictive validity, of diagnosis, 52
Prefrontal lobotomy, 606–607
Pregnancy
  complications of, schizophrenia and, 132
  false, 198

syphilis during, 221
Premenstrual tension, **201–203**
Premorbid adjustment, 121n
  in schizophrenia, 120–121
Presenile dementias, **243–244**
Primary diagnosis, 60–61
Process schizophrenia
  familial patterns in, 141
  reactive schizophrenia distinguished from, 120–122
Projection, in schizophrenia, 110, 124
Pseudocyesis, **198–199**
Psilocybin, **438–439**
Psychedelic drugs, *see* Hallucinogens
Psychiatric classification, 53
Psychoanalysis, **490**
  classical, 490–493
Psychoanalytic theory
  of depression, 167–168
  development of, 25–28
  of drug abuse, 413
  of hypnosis, 401
  of neurodermatitis, 184–185
Psychoanalytic therapy, **502**
  drives in, 485–486
  origin of, 482–484
  process and technique in, 494–497
  psychoanalysis and, 490–494
  psychological determinism in, 484–485
  research in, 503–506
  theory in, 503
  therapist's role in, 498–500
  unconscious processes in, 486–490
Psychodynamic therapy
  for homosexuality, 357
Psychomotor epilepsy, **235–236**
  psychological problems and, 236–240
Psychoneurosis(es), 57
Psychopathology, *see also specific disorders*
  drug-associated, 410
Psychopathy, 333–335
  time perspective in, 335–336
Psychophysiological disorders
  cardiovascular, 203–211
  in children, 293–304
  conversion hysteria versus, 78
  gastrointestinal, 189–196
  genitourinary, 196–203
  nature of, 179–183
  of skin, 183–188
Psychosis(es)
  amphetamine-induced, 135–136
  antipsychotics in, 593–596
  in childhood, 283–284, 310–318

Korsakoff's, 419
LSD and, 436, 437
manic-depressive, 146–147
presenile, *see* Presenile dementias
sleep deprivation and, 387
symbiotic, **310**
Psychosomatic disorders, 179
Psychosurgery, **606–613**
Psychotherapy, *see also specific therapies*
in drug abuse, 446
duodenal ulcers and, 195
for ulcerative colitis, 191
Psychotic depression, 147
neurotic depression compared with, 160–161
Psychotomimetics, *see* Hallucinogens
Puberty, acne during, 187–188
Pulse, in anorexia nervosa, 295
Punch-drunk syndrome, 218
Punishment
in aversive conditioning, 471
in operant conditioning, 461–462
Pupil reactivity, anxiety and, 68

Q

Quasi-retardation, 256
Questionnaires
in anxiety measurement, 69–71
in study of sexual behavior, 348

R

Race
Down's syndrome and, 268–269
rape and, 330
suicide and, 175
Radiation damage, 229
Random sampling, 48
Rape, **366–368**
victims of, 337–338
Rapists, **329–331**
types of, 367
Rational emotive therapy, **473–474**
Reactive depression, 58, *see also* Exogenous depression
Reactive schizophrenia
familial patterns in, 141
process schizophrenia distinguished from, 120–122
Reality, misperception of, abnormality as, 35
Reality contact, 58

Reattribution therapy, **474–475**
Receptive aphasia, **223**
Regression
depression as, 167
in hebephrenic schizophrenia, 113
Regression hypothesis, of schizophrenic thought, 128–129
Reinforcement
compulsive thought as, 94–95
in depression, deficiency of, 168, 169–170
partial, 95–96, 459
compulsive behavior and, 95–96
time out from, 290, 462
Relaxation training, in insomnia, 391
Reliability
of diagnoses, 51–52
in depression, 148–150
in neuroses, 58–61
Religion, suicide and, 175
Remission, spontaneous, 89n
REM sleep, **384–385**
age changes in amount of, 385, 387
deprivation of, 388
functions of, 389
hypnotic drugs and, 391
in narcolepsy, 392
nightmares during, 394
following sleep deprivation, 387–388
Repression, 63, 489
Resentment, urticaria and, 186–187
Reserpine, in hypertension, 207
Resistance, **489**
Respiration, anxiety and, 68
Respondent conditioning, *see* Classical conditioning
Response, dominant, 74
Responsibility, in Gestalt therapy, 563
Retardation, *see also* Mental retardation
in depression, 154
in schizophrenia, 124
Reticular formation, in autism, 317
Reward(s), in instrumental conditioning, 90
Reward center, in schizophrenia, 136
Rules
residual, 34
violation of, as abnormality, 34

S

Sadism, **365–366**
Schizo-affective schizophrenia, **117–118**
Schizophrenia, **103–108**
acute versus chronic, 118–120

childhood, **310**
classifications of
    behavioral comparisons in, 125–126
    statistical approaches to, 123–125
diagnosis of, 105–107
drugs used in, 423, 593–594, 596
etiology of, 130
    biological considerations in, 130–137
    environmental considerations in, 137–142
    existential–phenomenological therapy and,
      544–545
paranoid versus nonparanoid, 122–123
process versus reactive, 120–222
simple, diagnosis of, 106
split personality and, 85
subcategories of, 108–118
theories of, 126–127
    thought in, 127–130
usage of label, 106–107
Schizophrenogenic parents, 140, 313
Schizotaxia, 133
Schizotypy, 133
Scientific approach
    role of theory in, 49–51
    value of, 45–46
Sebum, 187
    acne and, 188
Secondary gain, in conversion hysteria, 81–82
Sedatives, **601–602**
Seizures, *see also* Epilepsy
    clinical and subclinical, 232
    following encephalitis, 220
Self-actualization, in Gestalt psychology, 551
Self-concept
    client-centered theory and, 512–513, 514
    enuresis and, 297–298
Self-control
    operant procedures and, 464–465
    research findings in, 475–476
Self-regulation, in Gestalt psychology, 556
Self-verbalization, 473–474
    in phobias, 89
Semantics, in Gestalt therapy, 565
Senile dementia, **242–243**
Sensate focus, 374–375
Serotonin, 134
    in etiology of depression, 166
    in etiology of schizophrenia, 134
Sex
    anorexia nervosa and, 295–296
    childhood psychosis and, 313
    of conversion hysterics, 79
    duodenal ulcers and, 192
    exhibitionism and, 330–331

migraine headaches and, 209–210
    personality problems and, 291–292
    suicide and, 175
Sex-change operations, 361–362
Sex drive, 486
Sex offenders, **329–331**
Sexual behavior
    alcohol and, 416–417
    development of, 344–347
    normal, 344
    scientific study of, 347–350
Sexual deviance, **350–351**
    exhibitionism, 365
    fetishism, 362–363
    homosexuality, 351–359
    pedophilia, 363–365
    rape, 366–368
    sadism and masochism, 365–366
    transsexualism, 361–362
    transvestism, 359–361
    voyeurism, 368
Sexual dysfunction, **369–378**
    description and etiology of, 369–372
    misconceptions and, 372–373
    primary and secondary, 372
    treatment of
      in female, 373–376
      in male, 376–378
Shaking palsy, *see* Parkinsonism
Shaping, 459
Side effects, extrapyramidal, 594
Significance, 48n
Simple schizophrenia, **108–109**
    diagnosis of, 106
Situational retardation, 256
Skeletal responses, 181
Skin conductance, in chronic schizophrenia,
    119
Sleep, **382**
    age and patterns of, 385–386
    cycles of, 385
    disorders exacerbated during, 398
    enuresis and, 298
    hypnosis compared with, 403–404
    need for and functions of, 388–389
    NREM, 382–384
      functions of, 389
    REM, 384–385
      functions of, 389
      in narcolepsy, 392
Sleep deprivation, 386–388
Sleep disturbances, **388–398**
    apnea, 393
    bruxism, 397–398

in depression, 153
headbanging, 398
insomnia, 390–392
narcolepsy and hypersomnia, 392–393
nightmares, 393–394
sleeptalking, 397
slow-wave, 394–396
Sleeptalking, **397**
Sleepwalking, 85, **394–395**
  hypnosis compared with, 403–404
Slow-wave sleep, 382
  disturbances of, 394–396
Smoking
  behavior therapy for, 447–448
  nicotine and, 432–433
Social action, **587–588**
Socialization, prevention and, 580
Social skills, in depression, 170
Sociocultural factors, in etiology of schizo-
    phrenia, 141–142
Socioeconomic status, of obsessive-compulsive
    neurotics, 96–97
Sociopath, *see* Psychopathy
Sodium, in depression, 167
Soft signs, 307
Somnambulism, *see* Sleepwalking
Somniloquy, **397**
Speech
  anxiety and, 72
  in schizophrenia, 126
Speed, 135
Spielmeyer-Vogt disease, 279–280
Spontaneous remission, 89n
State theory, of hypnosis, 401
State–Trait Anxiety Inventory, 70–71
Stelazine, 594
Stimulants, **428–434, 602–603**
Stimulus(i), overselectivity among in autism,
    317
Stimulus control, 457
  in insomnia, 391
Stomach activity, anxiety and, 68
Strabismus, 307
Stress
  acne and, 188
  amenorrhea and, 197
  bruxism and, 397–398
  duodenal ulcers and, 192–193
  hypertension and, 205–207
Stuttering, as anxiety measure, 72
Subcortical areas, 213
Subdural hematoma, 218
Suicide
  causes of, 177

depression and, 173
existential–phenomenological therapy and,
    544
incidence of, 173–174
predictors of, 152–153, 174–177
prevention of, 177–178
Surgery
  to brain, 606–613
  for sex change, 361–362
Surplus meaning, 51
Sweaty palms, anxiety and, 68
Symbiotic psychosis, **310**
Sympathetic nervous system, 214–215
  anxiety and, 68–69
Symptomatology, of depression, 150–154
Symptom substitution, 86
Syndrome, concept of, 53–54
Syndrome X, 427
Syphilis, paresis associated with, 220–222
Systematic desensitization, 66, **465–467**
  flooding and implosive therapy compared
    with, 478
  research findings in, 476–477
Systolic pressure, anxiety and, 68

T

Taraxein, in schizophrenia, 134
Tardive dyskinesia, 595
Taylor Manifest Anxiety Scale (TMAS), 69–70
Tay-Sachs disease, 279
Temperament, in children, 289
Temporal lobe epilepsy, *see* Psychomotor
    epilepsy
Tension, *see also* Stress
  premenstrual, 201–203
Thalamotomies, **609–610**
Thalidomide, 423
Theme interference, 584–585
Theory, role of, 49–51
Therapeutic communities, **445–446**
Therapeutic relationship, existential–
    phenomenological, 539–541
Therapist
  client-centered, 521–524
  existential–phenomenological, 534–535
  in psychoanalytic therapy, 498–502
Thioxanthenes, 423, **594–595**
Thorazine, *see* Chlorpromazine
Thought, *see also* Obsession
  in depression, 171–172
  schizophrenic, 104, 125, 127–130
    operant modification of, 138–139

Thrombosis, 241
Tic de sommeil, **398**
Time out, 290, **462**
Time perspective, in psychopathy, 335–336
Tofranil, in enuresis, 396
Token economy, **463**
  research findings in, 476
  schizophrenic behavior and, 137–138
Tolerance, **408**
  to alcohol, 418
  to caffeine, 430
  to cocaine, 431
  to narcotics, 427
  to nicotine, 432–433
Tonic phase, 234
Toxicity
  of barbiturates, 421–422
  of nicotine, 432
Tranquilizers
  major, *see* Antipsychotics
  minor, 423
Transference, **489–490**
Transmethylation hypothesis, of schizo-
    phrenia, 134–135
Transsexualism, **361–362**
Transvestism, **359–361**
Trauma
  in etiology of schizophrenia, 139–140
  sexual dysfunction and, 370
Tremor, as anxiety measure, 72
Tricyclic compounds, **599**
Trifluoperazine, 594
Trisomy 21, *see* Down's syndrome
Tumors, of brain, 218–219
Twin studies
  of depression, 164–165
  of homosexuality, 355
  of schizophrenia, 130–133
  in sleepwalking, 395
Two-factor theory, **89–92**

U

Ulcer
  duodenal, 191–196
  gastric, 192
  peptic, 192
Ulcerative colitis, **189–191**
Unconditional positive regard, 518
Unconditioned stimulus, 88
Undifferentiated schizophrenia, 125
Urticaria, **185–187**

V

Vaginismus, 369, 376
  treatment of, 376
Validity, of diagnosis, 52–53
Vicarious conditioning, 88
Vicarious extinction, **469**
  research findings in, 477
Victim(s), **336–338**
Vineland Social Maturity Scale, 255
Voyeurism, **368**

W

Waxy flexibility, 116 154
Wernicke's syndrome, 419
Witchcraft, mental illness as, 14–17, 38–39
Withdrawal syndrome, 409
  alcoholic, 419–420
    acute, 417
  barbiturate, 421
  in children, 292
  narcotic, 428
    narcotic antagonists and, 444

A 7
B 8
C 9
D 0
E 1
F 2
G 3
H 4
I   5
J